FileMaker® 12
DEVELOPER REFERENCE
FUNCTIONS, SCRIPTS, COMMANDS, AND GRAMMARS

Bob Bowers

Dawn Heady

Steve Lane

Scott Love

800 East 96th Street, Indianapolis, Indiana 46240 USA

FileMaker 12 Developer Reference

ISBN-13: 978-0-7897-4847-8
ISBN-10: 0-7897-4847-9

Library of Congress Cataloging-in-Publication data is on file.

First Printing August 2012

Trademarks
All terms mentioned in this book that are known to be trademarks or service marks have been appropriately capitalized. Que Publishing cannot attest to the accuracy of this information. Use of a term in this book should not be regarded as affecting the validity of any trademark or service mark.

Warning and Disclaimer
Every effort has been made to make this book as complete and as accurate as possible, but no warranty or fitness is implied. The information provided is on an "as is" basis. The author(s) and the publisher shall have neither liability nor responsibility to any person or entity with respect to any loss or damages arising from the information contained in this book or from the use of the CD or programs accompanying it.

Bulk Sales
Que Publishing offers excellent discounts on this book when ordered in quantity for bulk purchases or special sales. For more information, please contact

U.S. Corporate and Government Sales
1-800-382-3419
corpsales@pearsontechgroup.com

For sales outside of the U.S., please contact

International Sales
international@pearsoned.com

Editor-in-Chief
Greg Wiegand

Executive Editor
Loretta Yates

Development Editor
Charlotte Kughen

Managing Editor
Sandra Schroeder

Project Editor
Seth Kerney

Copy Editor
Chuck Hutchinson

Indexer
Brad Herriman

Proofreader
Kathy Ruiz

Technical Editor
Micah Woods

Editorial Assistant
Cindy Teeters

Book Designer
Anne Jones

Compositor
Trina Wurst

Contents at a Glance

Table of Contents

About the Authors

Bob Bowers is CEO of Soliant Consulting, a 50-person firm that specializes in custom database and web application development. He is a recipient of the FileMaker Excellence Award and has co-authored seven books on FileMaker Pro development. In 2008 he was inducted into the Chicago Area Entrepreneurship Hall of Fame. After graduating *summa cum laude* in Music and English from Wabash College, Bob earned a master's degree in Musicology from the University of Chicago. Bob is also a proud dad of two young children, an avid banjo player, and an accomplished woodworker.

Dawn Heady, a Senior Technical Project Lead for Soliant Consulting, has 20-plus years of FileMaker solution architecting experience during which time she's also been a successful business owner, served as a CIO in the credit restoration industry, and as Vice President of a company specializing in FileMaker plug-ins. She is an authorized FileMaker Training Series instructor, a regular speaker at the annual FileMaker Developer Conference and FileMaker webinars, and a contributor to the *FileMaker Newsletter.* In 2004 FileMaker selected Dawn as a FileMaker 7 Idol finalist for her Interface-RAD solution. Dawn is an avid fan of the Indianapolis Colts and Indiana Fever, loves to dote on her grandchildren, and is learning to sail her small wooden boat, *Boxy Lady*, which was handcrafted by her loving husband.

Steve Lane, Chief Technology Officer of Soliant Consulting, served as Special Projects Developer at Scott Foreman, a leading K–6 Educational publisher. He has written for *FileMaker Advisor* magazine, and co-authored six books on FileMaker Pro. He has led training classes in FileMaker technologies all over the country and is authorized to teach the FileMaker Training Series. He regularly speaks at the annual FileMaker Developer Conference where in 2003 he was awarded the FileMaker Excellence Award for "pushing the boundaries of FileMaker Pro." When not writing about technology, Steve is likely to be found being chased about by his children or grumbling over the fingerings of J. S. Bach. Or just grumbling.

Scott Love, Chief Operating Officer of Soliant Consulting, served at Ziff-Davis Interactive as an online managing editor, served at Apple Computer as its web publishing technology evangelist, and led the technical marketing team at Macromedia. He has written dozens of feature and review articles on database and Internet/web topics for a wide range of computer publications including *MacWorld* magazine and *FileMaker Advisor.* He has co-authored four books: *Special Edition Using FileMaker 7*, *Special Edition Using FileMaker 8*, *FileMaker 8 Functions and Scripts Desk Reference*, and *FileMaker 9 Developer Reference*. He is also the producer for Grem Legends, an arcade game on the iOS App Store, and has written a technical brief on FileMaker Go. He is an authorized FileMaker Training Series instructor and a regular speaker at the FileMaker Developer Conference. In 2006 he was awarded the FileMaker Excellence Award "for developing outstanding technical and training resources for FileMaker." Scott lives in the California Bay Area, where his penchant for gardening can be indulged year round.

Dedications

To my wife, Rebecca, and children, Nate and Eleanor, for your unconditional love and support through extracurricular projects like this.

—Bob Bowers

For my husband, David, who introduced me to FileMaker so many years ago. Thank you for all your love and encouragement; I would be nothing without you, my darling.

—Dawn Heady

To my fellow authors and the entire Soliant team—this book continues to be a labor of "many hands."

—Steve Lane

Dedicated to my fellow authors. We're a team; alone none of this would be possible. I genuinely thank you.

—Scott Love

Acknowledgments

First, we extend our deepest gratitude to our spouses, children, and other family members. It takes a great deal of time locked away in our various writing nooks to craft a book, and much of that time is at the expense of our loved ones. Thank you for your unwavering support, unconditional love, and occasional kicks in the pants.

Thanks to all our friends and colleagues at Soliant Consulting. Your encouragement, suggestions, and inspiration have been invaluable. Special thanks for occasionally covering other responsibilities so we could complete this book. The people you work with can make a huge difference in how much you enjoy your work, and the people we work with are truly amazing.

We extend a big thanks to Micah Woods, the technical editor of this book. Micah's careful reading and insightful suggestions have improved this book immeasurably.

We would be remiss if we did not thank all the good folks at FileMaker, Inc. Your fine products are our life's work and passion. We want to especially acknowledge Rick Kalman, Heather Winkle, Vin Addala, Terry Barwegen, Andy LeCates, Eric Jacobsen, Bill Heizer, and all the other talented engineers and technicians at FileMaker. Thank you for continuing to refine and improve what is the most accessible and feature-rich database on the market.

Finally, we want to thank Loretta Yates, our acquisitions editor, and her entire team at Que. Loretta's patience and quiet prodding helped us see this book through to completion. We want to especially thank Charlotte Kughen, the development editor of this book. Charlotte's editorial suggestions and comments greatly influenced our content and improved the readability of this book.

We Want to Hear from You!

As the reader of this book, *you* are our most important critic and commentator. We value your opinion and want to know what we're doing right, what we could do better, what areas you'd like to see us publish in, and any other words of wisdom you're willing to pass our way.

We welcome your comments. You can email or write to let us know what you did or didn't like about this book—as well as what we can do to make our books better.

Please note that we cannot help you with technical problems related to the topic of this book.

When you write, please be sure to include this book's title and author as well as your name and email address. We will carefully review your comments and share them with the author and editors who worked on the book.

Email: feedback@quepublishing.com

Mail: Que Publishing
ATTN: Reader Feedback
800 East 96th Street
Indianapolis, IN 46240 USA

Reader Services

Visit our website and register this book at quepublishing.com/register for convenient access to any updates, downloads, or errata that might be available for this book.

INTRODUCTION

Welcome to FileMaker 12 Developer Reference

In the five years that have passed since the publication of our last developer reference, the FileMaker product line has matured and evolved in many exciting ways. Back then, things we now use on a daily basis, such as FileMaker Go, script triggers, charting, and layout themes, were merely ideas on a whiteboard at FileMaker, Inc. Despite the huge effort that goes into preparing a book like this, it felt like it was time for a new version. Developers around the world have told us that the previous developer reference was the most useful (and most used) book that they had in their collection; with each new release of FileMaker they have asked us if we would be publishing a new version. We greatly appreciate your feedback and prodding, and we are proud to offer this new and completely updated developer reference for FileMaker 12.

Our intent, as before, has been to write the book that we, as developers, want within arm's reach on our desks. Just as a writer always needs a dictionary nearby, we've found over years of developing FileMaker solutions that it's great to have a quick set of reminders handy. It's impossible to recall each function's syntax or every script step's attributes. We find FileMaker's built-in help system, online resources, and other documentation, while generally being quite excellent, often lacks practical examples, real-world syntax, and good old-fashioned advice; it tells you *what* something is, not *why* you would want to use it. We have therefore attempted here to assemble into one single resource all the most useful and interesting information, and wherever possible, to provide the sort of examples and advice that will enable you to make the best use of that information.

As before, the largest sections of this book are the calculation and script step references. Moreover, you'll still find a wealth of other handy reference material, such as product specs, version history, error codes, ports, and keyboard shortcuts. Beyond this, however, we've added completely new material on topics including charting, layout mode, script triggers, and FileMaker Go.

Finally, we intend this desk reference to be just that—a reference. It should serve beginners and experts alike and isn't intended to be read from cover to cover. Rather, the intent is that you'll look up functions you've forgotten, dog-ear useful pages, take notes, and find it a handy tool for building solutions quickly in FileMaker.

How This Book Is Organized

FileMaker 12 Developer Reference is divided into eight parts, each of which can stand on its own.

Part I: FileMaker Specifications

Part I covers the nuts and bolts of FileMaker's product family:

- Chapter 1, "FileMaker 12 Product Line," provides an overview of all FileMaker products and what purposes and audiences they serve.
- Chapter 2, "FileMaker 12 New Features," provides an overview of the main features added to FileMaker Pro and FileMaker Pro Advanced in version 12.
- Chapter 3, "Specifications and Storage Limits," details the various hardware and software specifications for each product and other pertinent load statistics.
- Chapter 4, "Field Types and Import/Export Formats," reviews FileMaker's field data types and the details of supported import/export formats.

Part II: Layout Tools & Objects

Part II details all FileMaker Pro calculation functions, syntax, and usage:

- Chapter 5, "Layout Tools," covers all the major tools and dialogs for creating and managing layouts, including the Inspector and the Layout Setup dialog.
- Chapter 6, "Charting," discusses Quick Charts, chart types, styles, and data series.
- Chapter 7, "Other Layout Objects," provides in-depth information on Tab Controls, Portals, and Web Viewers.

Part III: Functions

Part III details all FileMaker Pro calculation functions, syntax, and usage:

- Chapter 8, "Calculation Primer," reviews the layout and functionality of the calculation dialog.
- Chapter 9, "Calculation Signatures," lists by category the syntax and the output type for each calculation function.
- Chapter 10, "Calculation Functions," provides a complete description of every calculation function, lists examples, and, in many cases, offers additional comments on usage.
- Chapter 11, "Custom Function Primer," introduces the mechanics of creating custom functions, including how to build functions that use recursive logic.

Part IV: Script Steps & Triggers

Part IV reviews FileMaker's script steps and script triggers in detail:

- Chapter 12, "Scripting Primer," provides an overview of the mechanics of the Manage Scripts dialog, and of working with script parameters, script results, and script variables.

- Chapter 13, "Script Triggers," provides general information on working with script triggers, plus detailed information and examples for every script trigger.
- Chapter 14, "Script Step Reference," lists in alphabetical order all script steps in FileMaker Pro, their options, and notes on usage.

Part V: FileMaker Go

Part V provides everything you need to know to develop and deploy solutions for FileMaker Go:

- Chapter 15, "FileMaker Go Specifications," provides detailed information on the differences between FileMaker Pro and Go including a concise listing of script step differences, the devices and iOS versions supported, and the security features.
- Chapter 16, "Designing for FileMaker Go," delves into the architectural models, workflow optimizations, deployment methods, synchronization strategies, and security recommendations for delivering great FileMaker Go solutions.

Part VI: FileMaker Connectivity

Part VI provides reference materials covering some of the major ways to connect to a FileMaker solution:

- Chapter 17, "FileMaker XML Reference," details FileMaker's XML grammars and provides a Custom Web Publishing command reference.
- Chapter 18, "FileMaker API for PHP," documents FileMaker's external API for PHP connectivity.
- Chapter 19, "JDBC/ODBC and External SQL Connectivity," reviews how to prepare a FileMaker solution for access from external applications via ODBC or JDBC, and how to configure a DSN for connecting a FileMaker solution to an ODBC data source.
- Chapter 20, "AppleScript Integration," provides an overview of the AppleScript object model for FileMaker.

Part VII: Quick Reference

Part VII provides quick reference to commonly needed FileMaker facts:

- Chapter 21, "FileMaker Error Codes," provides a complete list of all error codes.
- Chapter 22, "FileMaker Version and Feature History," provides a matrix of features and versions.
- Chapter 23, "FileMaker Keyboard Shortcuts," lists shortcuts for both Mac and Windows.
- Chapter 24, "FileMaker Network Ports," lists information useful for IT/infrastructure support.
- Chapter 25, "FileMaker Server Command-Line Reference," provides syntax and examples for administering FileMaker Server from a command line.

Part VIII: Other Resources

Part VIII helps you discover other ways to learn about FileMaker:

- Appendix A, "Additional Resources," presents a list of additional resources we have found helpful in FileMaker development.

Special Features

This book includes the following special features:

- Notes, Tips, and Cautions can be found in various spots throughout the book.

Note

A Note contains information that offers additional details about the topic being discussed. These notes give you added insight into the discussion, but aren't absolutely essential to understanding the given topic.

Tip

A Tip provides you with additional information that goes beyond what you might ordinarily know about a certain topic. Often, these tips contain helpful hints from our personal experience working with FileMaker over the years.

Caution

Pay special attention to Cautions. They are provided to help you avoid certain pitfalls, or to reiterate a specific point that could trip you up if you aren't careful.

Typographic Conventions Used in This Book

This book uses a few different typesetting styles, primarily to distinguish among explanatory text, code, and special terms.

Key Combinations and Menu Choices

Key (and possibly mouse) combinations that you use to perform FileMaker operations are indicated by presenting the Mac command first followed by the Windows command: Cmd-click for Mac and Ctrl+click for Windows, for example.

Submenu choices are separated from the main menu name by a comma: File, Manage, Value Lists.

Typographic Conventions Used for FileMaker Scripts

Monospace type is used for all examples of FileMaker scripting. FileMaker scripts are not edited as text but are instead edited through FileMaker's graphical script design tool. As a result, scripting options presented visually in the Edit Script dialog need to be turned into text when written out. We follow FileMaker's own conventions for printing scripts as text: The name of the script step comes first, and any options to the step are placed after the step name, in square brackets, with semicolons delimiting multiple script step options, as in the following example:

```
Show All Records
Go to Record/Request/Page [ First ]
Show Custom Dialog [Title: "Message window"; Message; "Hello, world!"; Buttons: "OK"]
```

Who Should Use This Book

We hope that anyone who develops FileMaker systems will find many aspects of this book useful. It's a book we, the authors, use in our day-to-day work, but that doesn't mean its use is limited to experts. This reference material is meant to be convenient and accessible to everyone.

CHAPTER 1

FileMaker 12 Product Line

The FileMaker product line is composed of a number of distinct pieces. Understanding their different strengths, capabilities, and requirements is an important part of your FileMaker knowledge base. This chapter provides a quick overview of the purpose and profile of each piece of the FileMaker software suite, along with relevant operating system requirements.

FileMaker Pro 12

FileMaker Pro is the original, all-in-one database design, development, deployment, and access tool. Users of FileMaker Pro have access to a full suite of database design tools and can create their own databases from scratch, with full authoring privileges. FileMaker Pro can host databases, sharing them across small groups of users, via FileMaker network sharing or Instant Web Publishing (IWP). A copy of FileMaker Pro is required to open and use FileMaker databases created by others, unless you are using IWP.

If you are an advanced developer or working to build a complex system, we recommend FileMaker Pro Advanced. If you want to share your databases with more than a few FileMaker users at a time, you need FileMaker Server. If you need to share your databases with similar numbers of users via the Web or ODBC/JDBC, you need FileMaker Server Advanced.

The following are the FileMaker Pro 12 operating system requirements:

Mac: OS X 10.6 or greater (Intel Mac only), OS X 10.7 or greater (Intel Mac only)

Windows: Windows XP (Service Pack 3), Windows Vista (Service Pack 2), Windows 7

FileMaker Pro 12 Advanced

FileMaker Pro 12 Advanced includes all the features and functionality present in the regular FileMaker Pro software but has a series of additional features aimed at application developers. They include tools for debugging scripts, the capability to define custom functions and custom menus, the capability to perform file maintenance, a Database Design Report that can help document a system, and a set of tools that enables you to create a variety of "runtime" executable solutions. FileMaker Pro 12 Advanced also includes many features that speed development, such as the capability to copy and paste fields, custom functions, scripts, and tables.

We strongly recommend FileMaker Pro Advanced for any FileMaker developers who are serious about designing high-quality database systems. The extra tools are well worth the additional cost and, by using Advanced, developers can extend the functionality of their systems to end users by utilizing custom menus.

The following are the operating system requirements for FileMaker Pro Advanced 12:

Mac: OS X 10.6 or greater (Intel Mac only), OS X 10.7 or greater (Intel Mac only)

Windows: Windows XP (Service Pack 3), Windows Vista (Service Pack 2), Windows 7

FileMaker Server 12

FileMaker Server is the tool of choice for sharing FileMaker files with more than a handful of concurrent FileMaker users. Whereas the peer-to-peer file hosting available in FileMaker Pro and Pro Advanced can host no more than 10 files for no more than 9 users, FileMaker Server can host as many as 125 files for as many as 250 concurrent FileMaker users. FileMaker Server can also perform regular, automated backups of database files; log various usage statistics; and execute server-side scripts including FileMaker scripts as well as system-level scripts such as Windows batch, Perl, VBScript, and AppleScript.

If you want to share your databases with more than a few users, you should invest in FileMaker Server.

FileMaker Server 12 also includes the FileMaker API for PHP and XML custom web publishing. Note that the PHP Site Assistant has been discontinued.

The following are the operating system requirements for FileMaker Server 12:

Mac: OS X 10.6.7 or greater (Intel Mac only), OS X 10.7 or greater (Intel Mac only), OS X Server 10.6.7 or greater (Intel Mac only), OS X Server 10.7 or greater (Intel Mac only)

Windows: Windows 2003 Server Standard Edition SP2 (32-bit only), Windows 2008 Server SP2, Windows 2008 Server R2, Windows 7 Professional Edition

FileMaker Server 12 Advanced

FileMaker Server Advanced is required to host databases via Instant Web Publishing or to connect via ODBC/JDBC to external SQL sources. FileMaker Pro and Pro Advanced can perform hosting for IWP or ODBC/JDBC for a small number of clients. For more than nine connections, organizations need to install FileMaker Server 12 Advanced. It can host up to 50 ODBC/JDBC connections, 200 Custom Web Publishing sessions, 100 IWP sessions, and an unrestricted number of FileMaker Pro and FileMaker Go clients.

Note that the installation for both Server and Server Advanced is identical. Advanced features are unlocked via serial keys and do not require additional installation.

The following are the operating system requirements for FileMaker Server 12 Advanced:

Mac: OS X 10.6.8 or greater (Intel Mac only), OS X 10.7 or greater (Intel Mac only), OS X Server 10.6.8 or greater (Intel Mac only), OS X Server 10.7 or greater (Intel Mac only)

Windows: Windows 2003 Server Standard Edition SP2 (32-bit only), Windows 2008 Server SP2, Windows 2008 Server R2, or Windows 7 Professional Edition

FileMaker Go 12

FileMaker Go is a full FileMaker client developed exclusively for the Apple iPhone and iPod touch. Its purpose is to consume and generate FileMaker data. With it, you can create, edit, and delete records; execute scripts; import and export data; view richly formatted layouts; and print wirelessly to an AirPrint-enabled printer. Because FileMaker Go is a thin client, you cannot use it to create a database or modify its structure (that is, you cannot modify or create tables, fields, layouts, or scripts).

FileMaker Go can access databases hosted by FileMaker Server 12 and FileMaker Pro 12 over the network (including the advanced versions of each) as well as interact with a database stored locally on the iPhone or iPod touch.

Although FileMaker Go works with layouts developed for the desktop, you often get a better user experience by developing screens especially built for the device's smaller size. It is also important to keep in mind that FileMaker Go does not support all script steps, so be sure to test thoroughly. You can use the "Show Compatibility" feature set to "iOS" to quickly see incompatible script steps.

→ *For more information, see Chapter 15, "FileMaker Go Specifications," and Chapter 16, "Designing for FileMaker Go."*

The following are the requirements for FileMaker Go 12:

iOS: iPod touch or iPhone running iOS 4.3 or greater, iPad running iOS 4.3 or greater

Hosts: FileMaker Server 12, FileMaker Server 12 Advanced, FileMaker Pro 12, FileMaker Pro 12 Advanced

FileMaker Go 12 for iPad

FileMaker Go for iPad provides the same features as FileMaker Go while taking full advantage of the iPad's big, beautiful screen. Although the iPad can also run FileMaker Go, the app either displays the database small in the center of the screen or blown up via the 2x option.

FileMaker Go for iPad can often work well with your existing database layouts because the native resolution of the iPad more closely resembles that of a desktop or laptop computer. However, because the iPad is a touch device and fingers are a bit chunky, it is still advisable to develop layouts optimized for the device. Be sure to test thoroughly because FileMaker Go does not support all script steps.

➔ *For more information, see Chapter 15, "FileMaker Go Specifications," and Chapter 16, "Designing for FileMaker Go."*

The following are the requirements for FileMaker Go 12 for iPad:

iOS: iPad running iOS 4.3 or greater

Hosts: FileMaker Server 12, FileMaker Server 12 Advanced, FileMaker Pro 12, FileMaker Pro 12 Advanced

CHAPTER 2

FileMaker 12 New Features

This chapter presents a broad overview of the many new features and benefits of the FileMaker 12 product line. If you're thinking of upgrading from a previous version, this chapter will give you an idea of the benefits that await you; if you're already using FileMaker 12, use this overview to ensure you're taking full advantage of everything the newest version has to offer.

→ *For a full listing of the features introduced with each version of FileMaker, see Chapter 22, "FileMaker Version and Feature History."*

New File Format

FileMaker 12 introduces a new file format: fmp12. You need to convert files created using the older fp7 file format before you can use them with any product in the FileMaker 12 family. FileMaker Pro 12, FileMaker Pro 12 Advanced, FileMaker Server 12, FileMaker Server 12 Advanced, FileMaker Go 12, and FileMaker Go 12 for iPad support only the new fmp12 format.

The new file format is long overdue and more than justified by the powerful new features FileMaker 12 delivers. The great news is the conversion process is relatively painless. Some layout formatting might change during the conversion because FileMaker 12 does not support fill patterns or effects such as embossing and engraving. Of course, as with any conversion, we highly recommend you perform a trial conversion to thoroughly test all your layouts and scripts.

FileMaker Pro 12 can directly convert existing FileMaker Pro 11, 10, 9, 8, and 7 files, all of which have the .fp7 format. However, you must convert existing FileMaker Pro 6, 5, 4, and 3 files to the .fp7 format before you can convert them to FileMaker Pro 12.

For the best results, convert multifile solutions at one time by selecting a folder or group of files and then dropping them on the FileMaker Pro 12 application icon. Alternatively, you can select File, Open and then select multiple files in the same directory before clicking the Open button. FileMaker Pro 12 displays the Open Multiple Files dialog, shown in Figure 2.1, which enables you to specify conversion and location to save the converted files. Note that this dialog is displayed whenever you open multiple files, even when they are all fmp12 files.

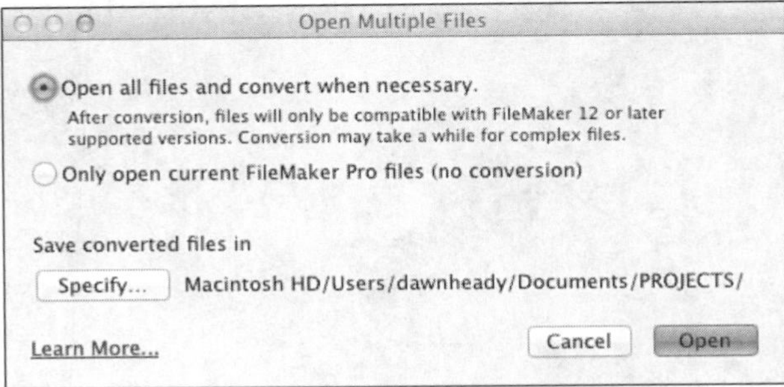

Figure 2.1
FileMaker displays the Open Multiple Files dialog when you specify to open more than one file. It provides the option to convert the files when necessary.

Multiple Application Versions

A computer can run only one version of FileMaker Server or Server Advanced. However, you can install the 11 and 12 versions of a FileMaker client (Pro, Pro Advanced, Go, and Go for iPad) on the same desktop or iOS device and run them at the same time. Just keep in mind that by default FileMaker plug-ins are installed at the system level and are accessed by all versions of Pro and Pro Advanced. If you need to install different versions of a plug-in for each FileMaker application, you can still manually install them in the application's Extensions folder.

FileMaker Pro/Advanced 12

FileMaker Pro 12 contains a redesigned architecture for developing layouts. It has added many new features that make it faster and easier to create beautiful layouts that are consistent and professional across your entire solution. These tools include screen stencils, dynamic alignment guides, guidelines that drag out from rulers, grid control, and multiple undo.

FileMaker Pro also includes new features for applying gradient fills, image fills, and rounded corners to objects. Each FileMaker object can have a different look, depending on the layout's state: Normal State, Hover, In Focus, and Pressed. You can use object states to create rollover buttons, indicate the currently active field or row in list view, and provide a host of other usability improvements to your solutions.

Themes

FileMaker 12 includes modernized themes. A layout's theme controls the default appearance of new field, text, tab, and other objects you add to a layout.

At the time you create a layout, you assign one of 40 themes, including several themes optimized for the touch device. You can also use the Layout, Change Theme menu item to apply a new theme to a layout.

Tip

When the new theme is applied, all your style customizations are initially lost. However, if you perform an undo (⌘-Z for Mac, Ctrl+Z for Windows), FileMaker restores your customizations to the applied theme. Another undo reverts the theme entirely.

When a file is converted, FileMaker assigns the "Classic Theme" to all layouts. We recommend that you *do not* change existing layouts to a different theme; instead, you should develop new layouts from scratch.

FileMaker provides no built-in mechanism for developing your own themes. Although it is possible to "hack" an existing theme, FileMaker does not support this capability; in fact, you might put your solution at risk of being incompatible with future FileMaker releases. Of course, you can customize the look of individual objects of a layout using the standard formatting tools.

➔ *See Chapter 5, "Layout Tools," for more information on building layouts.*

Enhanced Container Fields

Container fields have been greatly enhanced with FileMaker Pro 12. You can now interact with audio, video, and PDF files in container fields and even stream video. You can drag and drop files into container fields

In addition to the options to store container data inside the database or to reference an externally stored field, FileMaker 12 includes the capability to store the file outside the database in managed storage. You configure managed storage as part of the field's definition. FileMaker can even encrypt the data when it is stored. When users insert data into the container field, FileMaker automatically creates a copy of the file in a directory structure local to the file, even for a file hosted by FileMaker Server 12.

Caution

The container field data stored by FileMaker 12 via managed storage is exclusively for FileMaker's use. You should never access it using any other application, nor move, delete, or alter files in the managed storage directory.

You can further enhance the performance when working with container data over the network by directing FileMaker 12 to generate thumbnails. You have the option to have FileMaker permanently store the thumbnails or keep them in temporary storage that it empties when the file is closed.

Note that FileMaker generates a thumbnail optimized for each size the container field appears across your layouts. You can increase performance by standardizing your layouts so a given container field is displayed in only a couple of sizes across all the layouts of your solution.

➔ *See Chapter 4, "Field Types and Import/Export Formats," to learn more about container fields.*

Enhanced Charting Features

FileMaker reworked the charting interface and doubled the number of chart types available with the addition of the Stacked Column, Positive Negative Column, Stacked Bar, Scatter, and Bubble chart styles. In addition, FileMaker 12 provides controls for the chart's text formatting, including font, type size, and number formatting. Table view includes a Chart option in the contextual menu displayed for a field that quickly builds a chart based on the current context and renders it in its own window.

➔ *To learn more about charting, see Chapter 6, "Charting."*

Advanced Window Styles

FileMaker Pro 12 makes available advanced window styles that enable you to control the look and behavior of the window you create using a script. Using the `New Window` script step or as part of the `Go to Related Record` script step, you can specify one of three styles for the window: Document window, Floating document window, and Dialog window.

- **Document window**: The standard window that has always been available
- **Floating document window:** A window displayed on top of all other windows, even when it is not the active window
- **Dialog window:** A modal window that must be closed before the user can select a menu item, another window, and so on

Figure 2.2 shows the style options available when creating a new window via a script.

The New Window menu item creates a document window; it does not provide a way to specify a different style. After you create a window, you cannot change its style, even by script. Your only option is to close the window and open a new one.

Figure 2.2
Use the "Specify Advanced Style" Options when creating a new window via script to control the type of window and the window controls it will make available for the user.

Plug-in Updating

FileMaker Pro 12 has eliminated the Auto-Update plug-in and transformed plug-in updating into a much simpler process. Rather than storing the plug-in on FileMaker Server, you simply use Insert File to store the plug-in in a container field. Then you create a deployment script that uses the new function Get (InstalledFMPlugins) to test what version, if any, of the plug-in is currently installed, and perform the new script step Install Plug-In File to instruct FileMaker to install the plug-in stored in the specified container field.

→ *See Chapter 14, "Script Step Reference," to learn more about the* Install Plug-in File *script step, and for more information on the* Get (InstalledFMPlugins) *function, see Chapter 10, "Calculation Functions."*

ExecuteSQL

FileMaker Pro 12 includes the new function ExecuteSQL, which performs SQL select queries against FileMaker data. It also has optional parameters for you to specify the field and record delimiter of the returned result. This function works independently of the user's current context and enables you to join data from unrelated tables.

→ *To learn more about the* ExecuteSQL *function, see Chapter 10.*

And More...

In addition to the qualities already described, FileMaker Pro 12 introduces a number of other features and enhancements. Here's a quick overview:

- **Improved accessibility**—FileMaker supports assistive technology. You can use the new Accessibility Inspector to include labels on layout objects, which the user's screen reader can read aloud.
- **Enhanced tab controls**—You can assign conditional formatting to the individual tab panels and the tab labels of a tab control. In addition, there is a new script trigger OnTabSwitch that fires when the tab control changes panels.
- **Layout variable symbols**—You can display the result of any Get function directly on a layout using one of the new layout variable symbols. The symbol is enclosed in double curly brackets; for example, {{UserName}} displays the current user's name. Note that FileMaker converts the older symbols for date, time, and page number to the new style.
- **Improved ESS**—FileMaker has improved the linking to external SQL sources (ESS) so that when a table name is changed in the ODBC data source, you can update the links to the source.
- **Insert File script step enhanced**—In the Insert File script step, you can now control the accepted file formats, specify whether the content can be inserted as a reference, and indicate whether the file can be compressed.
- **Import data ignores new fields**—When you add a new field to a FileMaker Pro 12 database, the new field is no longer automatically added to the import mapping.
- **Auto-Complete Value List performance**—To enhance performance, FileMaker now displays only the first 100 entries that match followed by an ellipsis (...) to indicate there are more values. The user can click the ellipsis to cause FileMaker to display the remainder of the list.
- **Other new script steps**—There are seven new script steps: Find Matching Records, Insert Audio/Video, Insert from URL, Insert PDF, Install Plug-In File, Open Managed Containers, and Sort Records by Field.
- **Record sorting**—You can now control whether a layout's record sorting is persistent using the Keep Records in Sorted Order layout setting.
- **Table view refinements**—The column headers of Table view include more options for grouping, sorting, and summarizing the data.
- **Custom menus**—Custom menus and menu items include the Install When option with a calculated Boolean value. With this feature, a menu set can dynamically update based on the current user, privilege set, or other condition.
- **Unified URL scheme**—FileMaker 12 has a new URL protocol (FMP://), recognized by FileMaker Pro and FileMaker Go alike, that enables you to execute a script in a remote file.

→ *For more information on the FileMaker URL scheme, see Chapter 16, "Designing for FileMaker Go."*

FileMaker Server/Advanced 12

The FileMaker Server 12 architecture is more stable because the engineers have moved additional functions out of the database core into their own process spaces. FileMaker Server 12 includes separate processes for scheduled tasks, such as backups and scripts, and ODBC/JDBC access. Now if a server-side script crashes or an issue occurs with an ODBC connection, the database core continues to run. The result is better stability and less opportunity for file corruption.

Improved WAN Performance

FileMaker Server 12 and FileMaker Server 12 Advanced deliver improved WAN performance. They achieve this increase with overhauled network protocols, which they use to communicate with the client. Less data is sent across the network, so fewer roundtrips are required. FileMaker also optimized the Find feature, so it performs up to 40% faster.

In previous versions of FileMaker, the server would send to the client all the data specified by the relationship and leave it to the client to perform the portal filtering. FileMaker Server 12 now performs the filtering on the server and sends only the smaller set of records to the client. Because of this improvement, we now consider it best practice to utilize portal filtering, rather than creating additional relationships, whenever possible.

Value lists are also performed server side in FileMaker Server 12, so only the subset of data is sent to the client. The Auto-Complete feature is much faster because FileMaker Server sends only the first 100 values to the client by default.

64-bit Application

FileMaker Server 12 is available in 32-bit and 64-bit versions. When it is deployed on a 64-bit system, the Database Server and Web Publishing Engine are now 64-bit capable and can take advantage of a great deal more RAM. A 32-bit process can address no more than 4GB of RAM, so FileMaker Server 11 can address a maximum of an 800MB cache because it was limited to 25% of the system's total RAM. By comparison, a 64-bit system can address up to 1TB of RAM. Because FileMaker Server 12 can use up to 50% of the RAM for its cache, it is quite possible to have a cache large enough to store your entire database. FileMaker has also improved the cache-flushing algorithm, which makes file corruption much less likely when working with a large cache.

Rewritten Web Engine

FileMaker has completely rewritten the Web Publishing Engine (WPE) for FileMaker Server 12, a change necessary to support 64-bit systems. FileMaker's engineers took the opportunity to optimize the architecture so that the WPE is now composed of two cores: the Java Web Publishing Core (JWPC), which communicates with web clients, and the C++ Web Publishing Core (SWPC), which communicates with the database engine. WPE also includes more efficient memory management for handling concurrent requests. WPE provides improved stability and increased performance, especially when handling multiple requests, so much so that FileMaker Server 12 Advanced now supports up to 200 Custom Web Publishing (CWP) sessions, which is twice the capacity of FileMaker Server 11.

Backup Improvements

FileMaker Server 12 potentially performs scheduled backups much faster because it takes advantage of hard links when no changes have been made to the database file since its last backup. The operating system utilizes hard links to point to another file instead of creating a duplicate file. It is as if the system has made a shortcut to the most recent backup. Although it gives all the outward appearance of being a file, it is actually just a reference. When you need to use a backup, always make a system copy of the file instead of moving it.

Caution

When you need to use a backup, make a copy of the file. Do NOT move or delete scheduled backup files; otherwise, you risk deleting the most recent backup that is being referenced by a hard link.

FileMaker Server 12 includes an additional backup option: progressive backups. A progressive backup is an incremental block level backup of the file and executes more quickly because FileMaker Server writes only the changes made since the last backup instead of overwriting the entire file. You can choose a backup frequency of 1 to 60 minutes, with 5 minutes as the default. Technically, FileMaker Server creates two incremental backups and alternates updating one file and then the other so the files take turns as to which is the most current. Even if you were to experience a failure while FileMaker Server was updating one copy, the other file would still be intact.

Caution

When your server is a Macintosh computer that uses Time Machine, be sure to exclude FileMaker Server folder items from the Time Machine backup.

By default, FileMaker does not enable the progressive backup feature when you deploy the server. Figure 2.3 shows the Admin Console screen where you configure progressive backups. When this feature is enabled, FileMaker Server performs a full backup of all the files to create a baseline. This process can take some time and can affect the user's performance, so we recommend you enable this setting after hours. The progressive backup is a server-level setting and applies to all the files hosted by the server; you cannot specify different frequencies for individual files or group folders.

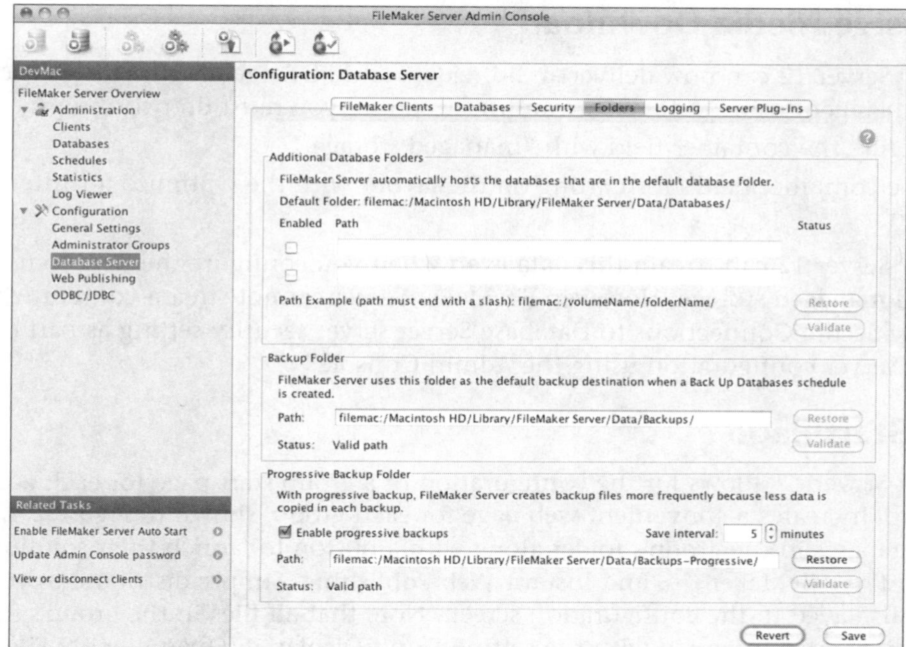

Figure 2.3
Use the FileMaker Server Admin Console to enable progressive backup. You can access the setting on the Database Server configuration screen, on the Folders tab.

Both backup types, progressive and scheduled, are critical to a comprehensive backup strategy. Use progressive backup to ensure you have as recent a backup as possible while having the least effect on performance. To have an archival history, use scheduled backups slated at longer intervals and save multiple copies. Scheduled backups are particularly useful for recovering data accidentally deleted by users, an action that might go unnoticed for days, weeks, or even months.

Managed Container Fields

FileMaker Server 12 fully supports the manage container field settings configured in each file, including encrypting the data. The contents are stored in the same directory as the hosted database. When you upload or download a database using the Admin Console (yes, Admin Console can now download a file!), the entire folder of managed container field content is also included.

> *Caution*
>
> The container field data stored by FileMaker Server 12 via managed storage is exclusively for FileMaker's use. You should never access it using any other application, nor move, delete, or alter files in the managed storage directory.

Progressive Media Download

FileMaker Server 12 can now deliver audio, video, and PDF documents stored in container fields to the client using buffered streaming. To do so, you must do two things:

1. Configure the container field with "managed storage."
2. Set the container field's formatting on the layout with the Optimize for Interactivity option.

FileMaker Server 12 can stream this data even when you configure the field to use encrypted managed storage. However, FileMaker Server cannot stream content when you enable the Secure Connections to Database Server server security setting as part of the Database Server configuration using the Admin Console.

Group Start Page

FileMaker Server 12 allows for the configuration of a group start page for each administration group. It creates a convenient web page for each group, shown in Figure 2.4, listing all the databases in the group's folder along with a button to launch their solution using FileMaker Pro, FileMaker Go, and Instant Web Publishing. Simply distribute to your team the URL displayed in the configuration screen. Note that all files in the group's folder are listed, even those configured with the setting Don't Display in Open Remote File Dialog.

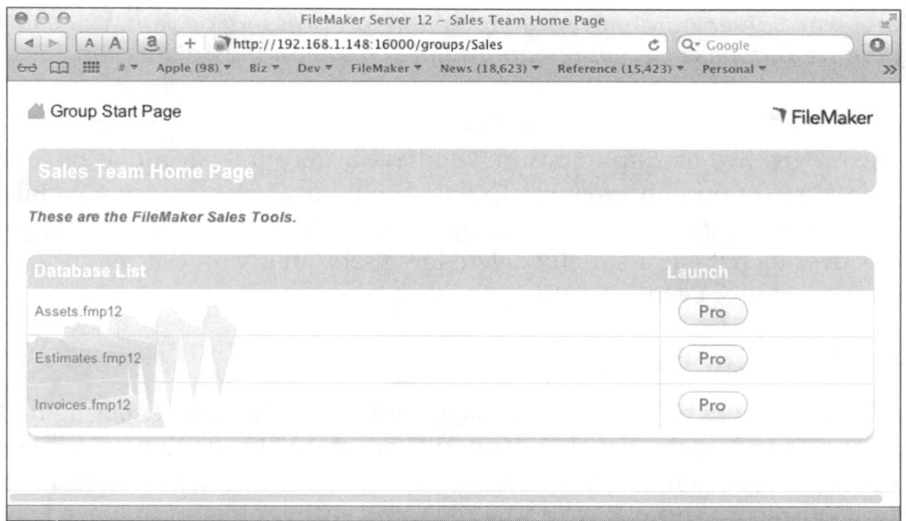

Figure 2.4
Each admin group, configured in the Admin Console, can have its own group start page.

FileMaker Go/Go for iPad

FileMaker Go 12 and FileMaker Go 12 for iPad are now free. This makes it much easier to deploy solutions for the touch device in business, education, and not-for-profit organizations because there is no longer the obstacle of making payment to the App Store.

Many of the improvements to FileMaker Pro and FileMaker Server that we've already mentioned are there to improve the user experience on the touch device. FileMaker Go benefits handsomely from the new touch themes, enhanced container fields, thumbnails, streaming media from FileMaker Server, and increased WAN performance.

Multitasking Support

FileMaker Go now takes advantage of the multitasking features first made available in iOS 4. The result is you can switch between applications much more quickly, and when you return to FileMaker Go, it generally picks up right where you left off.

→ *For more information on FileMaker Go multitasking, see "Background Behavior" in Chapter 15, "FileMaker Go Specifications," and "Implications of the Background Behavior" in Chapter 16.*

Improved Media Integration

Using FileMaker Go 12, you can record video or audio directly within your database and store the resulting file in a container field, even a container field that utilizes managed storage as long as the database is hosted. (Note that FileMaker Go does not support managed storage for a local file.) You can also play back media directly in FileMaker Go 12. Figure 2.5 shows the media options available in FileMaker Go, and Figure 2.6 shows the integrated audio capture dialog.

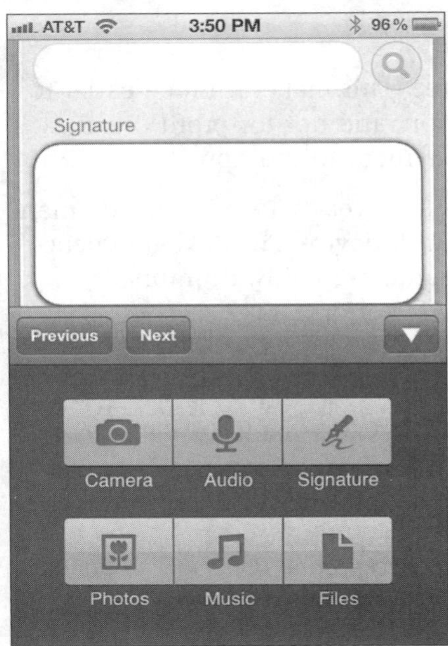

Figure 2.5
FileMaker Go includes new media capture options to create and store content in a container field, even one configured to use managed storage by the host.

Figure 2.6
Use FileMaker go to record audio directly within your database.

Export Data

With FileMaker Go 12, you can export data in several formats: TAB, CSV MER, DBF, HTML, and XLSX files. You can save the resulting file to the FileMaker Go documents space or to the temporary folder when the export is scripted.

→ *For more information on export data, see "Export Records" in Chapter 15.*

Location Functions

FileMaker Go returns the user's current location using the new FileMaker Pro functions Location and LocationValues.

→ *For more information on location functions, see Chapter 10.*

CHAPTER 3

Specifications and Storage Limits

Whenever you work with a piece of software, it's a good idea to be aware of the software's limits, both practical and theoretical. Important design considerations can hinge on a correct appraisal of the capabilities of your tools. For example, if you need to build a system that can correctly work with dates prior to those in the AD era (anno Domini: from the year 1 forward), it's a good idea to be aware of the storage capabilities of the date field type in FileMaker Pro.

Knowing Your Limits

Some of these limits are more theoretical than practical, and you're better off observing the practical limits. We don't recommend you build systems with a million tables, for example, or write calculations containing 30K of text characters. If you feel you need to push these upper limits, you might want to recheck your assumptions and, if necessary, rethink your approach.

Table 3.1 provides the limits of some of the most important measurable capacities of the FileMaker product line.

Table 3.1 FileMaker Specifications

Characteristic	Capacity
File size	8 terabytes
Files per disk	Limited only by disk space
Files/windows open simultaneously in FileMaker Pro client	Limited only by the memory available; recommended not to exceed 125
Files/windows open simultaneously in FileMaker Go	Limited only by the memory available; recommended not to exceed 20
Tables per file	1 million
Fields per table	256 million over the life of the file
Records per file	64 quadrillion over the life of the file
Record size	Limited by disk space or maximum file size
Relationships per file	Limited by disk space or maximum file size
Field name length	100 characters

Table 3.1 Continued

Characteristic	Capacity
Table name length	100 characters
Field comment length	30,000 characters
Text field data limit for FileMaker Pro client	2 gigabytes (about a billion Unicode characters)*
Text field data limit for FileMaker Go	Can display/edit only approximately the first 64,000 characters
Text field index	First 100 characters of each word or value
Number field value range	10^{-400} to 10^{400}
Number field index	First 400 significant digits
Serial number options	Next value can hold up to 255 characters; increment in the range 1 to 32767
Date field value range	1/1/0001 to 12/31/4000
Time field value range	1 to 999999; may be preceded by a negative sign
Timestamp field value range	1/1/0001 0:00:00 to 12/31/4000 23:59:59.999999
Container field data	4 gigabytes
Calculation result length	Depends on the result type
Calculation formula size	30,000 characters, including text and numbers, any referenced fields, operators, functions, and parentheses
Custom function text length	30,000 characters
Custom function nested recursions	10,000 function calls
Custom function tail recursions	50,000 function calls
Layout dimensions in FileMaker Pro client	444 inches wide by 444 inches long
Table view width limit	444.125 inches
Layout object name length	100 characters
Layout objects per layout	32,768
Columns across a page	99
Labels across a page	99
Web Viewer objects per file	No hard limit
Web Viewer objects per layout in FileMaker Pro client	No hard limit but may affect performance
Web Viewer objects per layout in FileMaker Go	Renders only the first 6 Web Viewers
Scripts per file	Limited by disk space
Scripts displayed in the Scripts menu	Windows: 512 Mac OS: 32,767
Variable repetitions in an iterative loop	10^{400} when defined as numbers
Sort levels	No limit

Table 3.1 Continued

Characteristic	Capacity
Database files hosted by FileMaker Pro client, peer-to-peer	10
Connected FileMaker Pro clients, peer-to-peer	9 concurrent clients
Files hosted by FileMaker Server	125
FileMaker Pro client connections, using FileMaker Server	250
FileMaker Pro client connections, using FileMaker Server Advanced	Connections are limited only by your hardware and operating system
Custom Web Publishing sessions, using FileMaker Server	100
Custom Web Publishing sessions, using FileMaker Server Advanced	200
Instant Web Publishing (IWP) clients, using FileMaker Server Advanced	100
ODBC/JDBC clients, using FileMaker Server Advanced	50
RAM addressable by FileMaker Server	4 gigabytes on 32-bit systems; 64-bit systems can make use of much greater system RAM size
Cache setting for FileMaker Server	800 megabytes for 32-bit systems; 64-bit systems can use up to 50% of the physical RAM
IWP records in table view	50
IWP records in list view	25
IWP clients, peer-to-peer	10

Notes to Table 3.1:

* Unicode characters take up a variable number of bits, dependent on the character, so it's not possible to define a precise upper limit to the size of a text field.

External SQL Sources (ESS) Specifications

The FileMaker 12 product line has the capability to integrate data tables from external SQL sources (ESS). At present, FileMaker can integrate data tables from the following external SQL sources:

- Oracle 10g or 11g
- Microsoft SQL Server 2005 or 2008
- MySQL 5.1 Community Edition (free)

Each of these data sources has its own set of field sizes and limitations. If you're integrating one or more of these external sources into a FileMaker solution, you also need to be aware of the different limits and features of the data types in the other data sources you use. Date and number fields in external sources might have different ranges from their FileMaker counterparts, for example.

→ *For more discussion of the differences between FileMaker and SQL field types, and some links to reference material on the supported SQL data types,* **see** *Chapter 4, "Field Types and Import/Export Formats."*

CHAPTER 4

Field Types and Import/Export Formats

Besides just knowing the raw statistics and capacities of your software tools ("speeds and feeds," as the machinists like to say), it's wise to understand the basic data formats with which your database software can work. This chapter gives a brief overview of each of the underlying FileMaker field data types and also discusses the various data formats available for import and export.

First, a word about data types in FileMaker. Unlike certain other database engines, FileMaker is somewhat forgiving about data types. You can add text characters to a number field, for example, without FileMaker stopping you. The price you pay for this flexibility is the possibility that you'll make a mistake or permit something undesirable to happen. So you need to have a firm grasp of FileMaker's data types and how each of them works and relates to the others.

FileMaker can also integrate tables from External SQL Sources (ESS), so you might also need to come to grips with the vagaries of field types in various SQL systems. You need to understand two things if you're working with SQL data:

- How SQL field types map to FileMaker field types. (FileMaker treats an Oracle `nvarchar2` field as a text field, for example.)
- How SQL field types might behave differently from their FileMaker counterparts. (For example, `date` fields in MySQL 5.0 can handle dates between 1/1/1000 and 12/31/9999, whereas FileMaker can handle dates between 1/1/0001 and 12/31/4000.)

We cover each of those topics as we discuss the individual FileMaker field types in the "ESS Notes" subsections within each of the "FileMaker Field Types" sections. A complete discussion of the behaviors of SQL field types is beyond the scope of this book, but near the end of this chapter we offer links to detailed reference material on field types in each of the supported SQL sources.

Most field types have the same behaviors and limitations in FileMaker Go as they do for FileMaker Pro. The few differences are called out in the "FileMaker Go Notes" section for the appropriate data type.

FileMaker Field Types

Chapter 3, "Specifications and Storage Limits," called out a number of the raw capacities of FileMaker's field types, in the briefest possible format. Here we dwell on each data type and its characteristics in a bit more detail.

> *Caution*
>
> Because FileMaker 12 can interact directly with certain SQL data sources, you need to take special care if you're building a solution that integrates with a SQL source. SQL data types are similar to, but not identical to, those found in FileMaker. Data that "fits" in a FileMaker field might get changed, truncated, or misinterpreted when inserted into a SQL field and vice versa. If you're working with SQL sources, take special note of the subsections labeled "ESS Notes" within each of the sections that follow.

Text

FileMaker's text field type holds up to 2 gigabytes of character data per text field. FileMaker stores text internally as Unicode, which requires about 2 bytes per character (the exact number varies by the specific character and encoding). A single FileMaker text field can hold about one billion characters of data (nearly half a million regular pages of text).

You don't need to specify the "size" of the text field in advance; FileMaker automatically accommodates any text you enter, up to the field size maximum.

FileMaker's text field can be indexed on a word-by-word basis, so it's possible to search quickly for one or more words anywhere within a text field.

ESS Notes

The following ESS data types are represented in FileMaker as text fields:

- **Oracle**—char, clob, long, nchar, nclob, nvarchar2, varchar2
- **Microsoft SQL Server**—char, nchar, ntext, nvarchar, text, varchar
- **MySQL**—char, enum, longtext, mediumtext, set, text, tinytext, varchar, year

Many of the ESS text types listed cannot hold as much text data as FileMaker text fields. If you need to move data from a FileMaker text field into an ESS text field, be aware of potential sizing conflicts. In such cases you might need to consider imposing validation limits on the amount of text the FileMaker field can store.

FileMaker Go Notes

FileMaker Go can read and display up to 2 gigabytes of character data in a text field. However, it can edit only approximately the first 64,000 characters. FileMaker Go displays an error if you attempt to edit or even just select text beyond the first 64,000 characters.

Number

The number field type is FileMaker's only numeric data type. Unlike many SQL sources, FileMaker does not have separate data types for integers and floating-point numbers. All numbers are capable of being treated as floating point.

FileMaker's numeric data type can store numbers in the range 10^{-400} through 10^{400}, and -10^{400} through -10^{-400}, as well as the value 0. The data type can account for 400 digits of precision. By default, though, functions involving numbers account for only 16 digits of precision. To achieve higher precision, you need to use the SetPrecision() function.

Numeric fields can accept character data entry, though the character data is ignored. If the field's validation is also set to Strict Data Type: Numeric Only, the entry of character data is disallowed.

ESS Notes

In other database systems, such as those based on SQL, integers and floating-point numbers are generally treated as two different data types, and you often need to choose in advance between lower-precision and higher-precision floating-point numbers, although SQL does also offer arbitrary precision numbers.

The following ESS data types are represented in FileMaker as number fields:

- **Oracle**—float, number, raw
- **Microsoft SQL Server**—bigint, decimal, float, int, money, numeric, real, smallint, smallmoney, tinyint
- **MySQL**—decimal, double, float, int, integer, mediumint, numeric, real, smallint, tinyint

If you're working with ESS data, be aware of the distinction between integer and floating-point types. If you try to move data from a FileMaker field containing floating-point data into an ESS field that supports only integer data, you may get a validation error or suffer some data loss.

Date

FileMaker's date type can store dates from 1/1/0001 to 12/31/4000. Internally, these dates are stored as integer values between 1 and 1460970, indicating the number of days elapsed between 1/1/0001 and the date in question. This capability is significant in that it means that integer math can be performed on dates: 12/31/2001 + 1 = 1/1/2002, and 12/21/2001 – 365 = 12/21/2000.

FileMaker's date type is stricter than the text and number types and rejects any date outside the range just mentioned, including those containing textual data. Field validation options can also be configured to force entry of a full four-digit year.

Although the date type is stored as an integer, it can be entered and displayed in a variety of well-known or local date display formats. By default, it uses settings it inherits from the current user's operating system, but the date display format can be overridden on a field-by-field basis on each individual layout.

ESS Notes

SQL sources vary widely in how they store and manage date and time information. Oracle and MySQL are similar to FileMaker in that they manage such data with three different field types, representing date information, time information, and timestamp information. Microsoft SQL Server differs in providing only timestamp-style fields.

The following ESS data types are represented in FileMaker as date fields:

- **Oracle**—date, interval year.
- **Microsoft SQL Server**—SQL Server has no direct equivalent to a date-only field. SQL Server's datetime and smalldatetime fields map to FileMaker timestamp fields, whereas SQL Server's timestamp field type is currently not supported.
- **MySQL**—date.

Be especially aware of the limits of ESS date, time, and timestamp fields: Their supported ranges may be different from the ranges supported in corresponding FileMaker field types.

Time

Like the date type, FileMaker's time data type stores its information in an underlying integer representation. In the case of the time field type, what's being stored is the number of seconds since midnight of the previous day, yielding a range of possible values from 1 to 86400. As with the date type, it's possible to perform integer math with time values: So Get(CurrentTime) + 3600 returns a time an hour ahead of the current time. And 15:30:00 - 11:00:00 returns 4:30:00 or 16200, depending on whether the calculation is set to have a time or number result, so "time math" can be used to compute time intervals correctly as well.

Also like the date data type, the time data type can accept entry and display of time data in a variety of formats. "Overlapping" times work in the same way as overlapping dates: FileMaker interprets the value 25:15:00 as representing 1:15 a.m. on the following day. (This is exactly what happens when you store a value greater than 86,400 in a time field, which FileMaker certainly allows.)

ESS Notes

SQL sources vary widely in how they store and manage date and time information. Oracle and MySQL are similar to FileMaker in that they manage such data with three different field types, representing date information, time information, and timestamp information. Microsoft SQL Server differs in providing only timestamp-style fields.

The following ESS data types are represented in FileMaker as time fields:

- **Oracle**—interval_day.
- **Microsoft SQL Server**—SQL Server has no direct equivalent to a time-only field. SQL Server's datetime and smalldatetime fields map to FileMaker timestamp fields, whereas SQL Server's timestamp field type is currently not supported.
- **MySQL**—time.

Be especially aware of the limits of ESS date, time, and timestamp fields: Their supported ranges may be different from the ranges supported in corresponding FileMaker field types.

Timestamp

FileMaker's timestamp data type is like a combination of the date and time types. A timestamp is displayed as something like 11/20/2005 12:30:00. Internally, like both dates and times, it is stored as an integer. In this case the internally stored number represents the number of seconds since midnight on 1/1/0001. The timestamp can represent date/time combinations ranging from 1/1/0001 00:00:00 to 12/31/4000 23:59:59.999999 (a range of more than a hundred billion seconds).

As with the related date and time field types, timestamps can be displayed and entered in a variety of formats. It's also possible to perform math with timestamps as with dates and times, but the math can get a bit unwieldy because most timestamps are numbers in the billions.

ESS Notes

SQL sources vary widely in how they store and manage date and time information. Oracle and MySQL are similar to FileMaker in that they manage such data with three different field types, representing date information, time information, and timestamp information. Microsoft SQL Server differs in providing only timestamp-style fields.

The following ESS data types are represented in FileMaker as timestamp fields:

- **Oracle**—timestamp.
- **Microsoft SQL Server**—datetime, smalldatetime. SQL Server's timestamp field type is a binary data type and so is not currently supported.
- **MySQL**—timestamp, datetime.

Be especially aware of the limits of ESS date, time, and timestamp fields: Their supported ranges might be different from the ranges supported in corresponding FileMaker field types.

Container

The container data type is FileMaker's field type for binary data (meaning data that, unlike text and numbers, does not have an accepted plain-text representation). Binary data generally represents an electronic file of some sort, such as a picture, movie, sound file, or file produced by some other software application, such as a word processor or page layout program.

A single container field can store a single binary object up to 4 gigabytes in size. Although any type of electronic file can be stored in a container field (one file per field), FileMaker has specialized knowledge of a few types of binary data and can play or display such objects directly, by calling on operating system services. Specifically, FileMaker can play or display pictures, sounds, and movies with the following formats:

Picture Formats

- Encapsulated Postscript (.eps)
- FlashPix (.fpx)
- GIF (.gif)
- JPEG/JIFF (.jpg)
- JPEG 2000 (.JP2) *(Macintosh only)*
- MacPaint (.mac) *(Macintosh only)*
- PDF (.pdf) *(Macintosh only)*
- Photoshop (.psd)
- PICT (.pct)
- PNG (.png)
- QuickTime Image File (.qt)
- SGI (.sgi)
- Targa (.tga)
- TIFF (.tif)
- Windows bitmap (.bmp)
- Windows Metafile (.wmf)
- Windows Enhanced Metafile (.emf) *(Windows only)*

Audio/Video Formats

- AIFF Audio File (.aif, .aiff)
- AVI Movie (.avi)
- MP3 Audio File (.m4a)
- MPEG-4 Audio File (.m4a)
- MPEG-4 Movie (.mp4)
- MPEG Movie (.mpg, .mpeg)
- MPEG-4 Video File (.m4v)
- QuickTime movie (.mov, .qt) *(Windows requires QuickTime be installed; QTVR and other formats are not supported.)*
- Sun Audio File (.au)
- WAVE Audio File (.wav)
- Windows Media Audio (.wma)
- Windows Media Videos (.wmv) (*Mac OS requires Flip4Mac be installed.*)

QuickTime Formats

- AVI (.avi)
- Cubic VR
- DV (.dv)
- FLC

- Karaoke (.kar)
- Flash 5 (.fiv)
- MPEG (Playback)
- QuickTime Movie (.qtm)
- Virtual Reality (VR)

Sound Format

- AIFF (.aif)
- AU
- Audio CD Data *(Mac OS)*
- MP3 (.mp3)
- Sound (.snd)
- WAV (.wav)

FileMaker Pro 12 can also interact with PDF files.

Note that FileMaker 12 can no longer insert or display object linking and embedding (OLE) objects, but can save OLE objects to their original formats and activate them.

FileMaker provides several options for storing the container field data. The data can be stored directly (embedding the entire file in the FileMaker database and increasing its file size by tens or hundreds of kilobytes or indeed by megabytes). The file can be stored by a reference (storing just the path to the specified file).

FileMaker Pro 12 now offers managed storage as an option for stored-by-reference data. Because managed storage is enabled within a field's storage options, FileMaker stores a copy of the file on the host computer at a given path in a relative directory. The additional option Secure Storage encrypts the externally stored file. Figure 4.1 shows the Container field storage options dialog.

When FileMaker Server 12 hosts the database, remote container field data is stored within the server's Database folder, making the file available to all users. FileMaker Server 12 delivers PDF, movie, and audio files kept within managed storage as a buffered stream, which greatly improves the performance.

ESS Notes

All of FileMaker's supported external SQL sources support a field type similar to FileMaker's container fields. In most SQL sources, these are often referred to as binary large object (BLOB) types.

Unfortunately, the present implementation of ESS in FileMaker does not support any of the various BLOB types offered in supported SQL sources. The BLOB types are not supported, and database columns based on those types are not available when the table is accessed via FileMaker.

Figure 4.1
FileMaker Pro 12 can manage externally stored content within the new Container settings on the field options Storage tab.

Calculation

From the point of view of data types, calculations are not a data type at all. They are instead a field type and can be constructed to return their results as any of the six fundamental data types: text, number, date, time, timestamp, or container.

ESS Notes

SQL sources vary in how they represent this field concept. From a strict point of view, calculation is not a data type (unlike, for example, text or date). Some SQL sources do have means for creating additional columns that automatically calculate based on values in other columns.

In any case, no field from a SQL source is ever represented in FileMaker as a Calculation field.

Summary

Summary fields are another example of a field type rather than a data type. Summary fields perform summary operations on sets of grouped records and always return a numeric result.

ESS Notes

SQL sources have no concept, at the level of field/column definition, that maps to the FileMaker concept of a summary field.

No field from a SQL source is ever represented in FileMaker as a summary field.

Additional ESS References

It's well worth your while to become aware of the differences and distinctions among the various data types used by the supported external SQL sources. Although a full discussion is beyond the scope of this book, the following links should provide a starting point for delving more deeply into the specifics of data typing in each supported data source:

- **Oracle**—http://docs.oracle.com/cd/B28359_01/server.111/b28318/datatype.htm
- **Microsoft SQL Server**—http://msdn.microsoft.com/en-us/library/ms187752.aspx
- **MySQL**—http://dev.mysql.com/doc/refman/5.0/en/data-types.html

Importing Data

FileMaker Pro can import data from one or more files on the hard drive of a FileMaker client machine or on a shared network volume. FileMaker can also import data from remote data sources. The following sections outline the various sources for importing data and the specific requirements and limitations of each.

File-Based Data Formats

FileMaker can import data from individual files, available on a local hard drive or networked volume, in any of the following formats:

- Tab-separated text (.tab or .txt)
- Comma-separated text (.csv or .txt)
- Merge files (.mer)
- dBASE III and IV DBF files (.dbf)
- Bento 2, 3, or 4 files (.bentodb—Macintosh only)

In addition to importing from these common text file formats, FileMaker can also perform more specialized imports from files created in Excel, or in FileMaker itself, as well as from ODBC-based and XML-based data sources.

Importing from Excel

When you are importing data from an Excel file, FileMaker can detect multiple worksheets within the source Excel file. FileMaker can also detect the existence of any named ranges in the source document. When you are importing, if named ranges or multiple worksheets are detected, FileMaker gives you a choice as to whether to import from a worksheet or named range and enables you to select the specific worksheet or range from which to import.

When you are importing from Excel, as with all imports, FileMaker brings in only the raw data it finds in the source file. Formulas, macros, and other programming logic are not imported.

FileMaker Pro assigns an appropriate field type (text, number, date, or time) if all rows in the column hold the same Excel data type. Otherwise, a column becomes a text field when imported into FileMaker.

Mac OS 10.7 users cannot export data to the older .xls file format because it requires Rosetta, which is not available on Lion.

Importing from FileMaker

You also can import data from other FileMaker Pro files or even between tables in the same file. The only restriction is that you can import data only from versions of FileMaker that share the same file format as the file you're importing into. You can import data from FileMaker Pro 12 into a FileMaker Pro 12 solution. These may be files present on the local client machine or files hosted on another machine. To import data from a FileMaker Pro file with the .fp7 file extension, you must first convert the file to FileMaker Pro 12.

Much as an Excel file can contain multiple worksheets, a FileMaker database can contain multiple tables. You need to choose a single table as your data source when importing from a FileMaker file.

Importing from FileMaker can be particularly convenient if the source file has a structure that matches that of the target file. In this case, rather than manually configuring the import mapping on a field-by-field basis, you can choose the Arrange by Matching Field Names option. When you do so, fields of the same name in the source and target tables are paired in the import mapping.

Importing Multiple Files at Once

You also are able to import data from multiple files at a time by selecting File, Input Records, Folder. You can import data in this fashion from either text or image files. You can import both the raw data in the file and also extra data about each source file's name and location.

In each case, the files being imported must reside within a single folder. You can specify whether to look simply inside the one folder or also to include files stored within subfolders.

Importing from Multiple Text Files

When importing from a batch of text files, you may import up to three pieces of data from each text file:

- Filename
- Full path to file
- Text contents

You may choose to import any or all of these.

Unlike a regular import from a text file, when you import from multiple text files, the internal structure of the text file is disregarded. The entire contents, whether containing tabs, carriage returns, commas, or other potential delimiters, are imported into a single target field.

Importing from Multiple Image Files

Importing from multiple image files is similar to importing from multiple text files. When importing a batch of images, you may import any or all of the following data fields:

- Filename
- Full path to file
- Image
- Image thumbnail

In addition to filename, file path, and file contents (an image, in this case), FileMaker enables you to import an image thumbnail, either in addition to or instead of the full image. You might want to do this to save file space or screen space. FileMaker creates these thumbnails via its own algorithms, so you have no control over the exact details of thumbnail size or quality.

When importing images, you have the choice (as you always do when working with data in container fields) of importing the full image into the database or merely storing a reference. Importing full images takes up more space in the database (probably much more), whereas importing only the references means that you need to make the original files continuously available from a hard drive or network volume that all users of the database can access.

Importing Digital Photos (Mac OS)

Support for importing directly from a digital camera has been discontinued with FileMaker 12. The menu commands and script steps for this feature have been removed from FileMaker.

Importing from an ODBC Data Source

FileMaker can import data from a data source accessed via ODBC. Many types of data can be accessed via ODBC, but it's most commonly used to retrieve data from a remote database, often one running some flavor of the SQL language.

Working with OBDC data sources requires three things:

- **A data source capable of providing data via ODBC**—Again, this is most often a remote database server of some kind. The administrators of the data source might need to perform specific configuration of the data source before it can accept ODBC connections.

- **An ODBC driver, installed on the local computer that's running FileMaker Pro, that can talk to the specific ODBC data source in question**—ODBC drivers need to be installed on each computer that can access a data source. So, much like a FileMaker plug-in, ODBC drivers generally need to be installed on the computer of each FileMaker user who will be using ODBC access. ODBC drivers are specific to a particular data source (the PostgreSQL or Sybase databases, for example) and also specific to a particular platform (Mac or PC). To connect to an ODBC data source, you must have a driver specific to both your data source and platform (Sybase 12 driver for Mac OS, for example).
- **A DSN (Data Source Name) that specifies the details of how to connect to a specific data source**—DSNs are configured differently on each platform and generally contain information about a specific data source (server name, username, password, database name, and the like).

After you have successfully configured and connected to an ODBC data source, the process for selecting data to import is a bit different than it is for regular imports. Before proceeding to the field mapping dialog, you need to build a SQL query that selects the specific fields and specific records you want. (For example, your SQL query might read `SELECT name_last, name_first, city, state, zip FROM customer`). After you've built this query, you can map the resulting fields to those in your FileMaker database.

ESS Notes

With the introduction, in FileMaker 9, of the capability to integrate tables from external SQL sources (ESS) directly into the structure of your FileMaker database, it's now possible to access data from certain SQL sources much more fluidly, without an explicit import step. Those data sources are Oracle 10g and 11g, Microsoft SQL Server 2005 and 2008, and MySQL 5.1 Community Edition (free).

If you need to work with data from supported sources, using the new ESS feature may be a better choice. If you need to work with data from a SQL data source that's not currently supported by ESS, the ability to import from an ODBC data source is important to consider.

➔ *For more information on configuring FileMaker to work with external SQL sources, see Chapter 19, "JDBC/ODBC and External SQL Connectivity."*

Importing from an XML-Based Data Source

FileMaker Pro has the convenient capability to import from an XML-based data source. This could be something as simple as an XML-based disk file, but can be something as complex as an XML-based web service. The capability of importing from remote XML-based data sources is potentially very powerful. Just keep in mind that, before XML can be imported into FileMaker, it must follow the rules of the FMPXMLRESULT grammar. If the XML you're working with isn't in that format, you need to apply an XSLT style sheet to the incoming XML to transform into data that follows the FMPXMLRESULT grammar.

→ *For further discussion of FileMaker XML grammars, see Chapter 17, "FileMaker XML Reference."*

Creating New Tables on Import

When importing data, you can specify that the inbound data should be placed in a new table instead of adding to or updating an existing table. The new table takes its field names from those present in the data source.

Exporting Data

FileMaker can export its data to a variety of data types, as follows:

- Tab-separated text (.tab or .txt)
- Comma-separated text (.csv or .txt)
- Merge files (.mer)
- FileMaker Pro files (.fmp12)
- Microsoft Excel files (.xlsx)
- XML files (.xml)
- dBASE III and IV DBF files (.dbf)
- HTML Table format (.htm)

Most of these are straightforward: The records in the found set are exported to a file of the specified format. You may export data only from a single FileMaker table at a time, along with its related data.

A few of these formats deserve special mention and are detailed in the sections that follow.

Exporting to HTML

When you are exporting to an HTML table, the resulting file is a complete HTML document consisting of an HTML table that displays the chosen data, somewhat like FileMaker's Table view.

Exporting to FileMaker Pro

The result of the FileMaker Pro export choice is a new FileMaker Pro file, with fields and field types that generally match those of exported fields. But note that the logic underlying calculation and summary fields is not preserved. Those fields are re-created based on their underlying data type. A calculation field returning a text result is inserted into a text field, whereas summary field data, if exported, is inserted into a number field. Only the raw data from the original file is exported; none of the calculation or scripting logic carries over. Container fields can only be exported to FileMaker files.

Exporting to Excel

When exporting records to Excel, you have the option to create a header row where the database field names appear as column names. You can also specify a worksheet name, document title, document subject, and document author.

Exporting records to Excel is similar to, but a bit more flexible than, the Save Records as Excel feature. Save Records as Excel exports fields only from the current layout and does not export fields on Tab panels other than the active one.

Exporting to XML

FileMaker can create an export text file in XML format. Without any transformation, the resulting file is organized according to the FMPXMLRESULT grammar. It's also possible to transform the XML as it is being exported by specifying an XSLT style sheet. The style sheet needs to be able to process data in the FMPXMLRESULT grammar. The output format can be any text format capable of being generated by an XSLT style sheet, including HTML, or more complex formats such as RTF or WordML.

➔ *For further discussion of FileMaker XML grammars, see Chapter 17, "FileMaker XML Reference."*

Automatically Opening or Emailing Exported Files

FileMaker Pro has the capability to automatically open and/or email an exported file. You can select these choices via two check boxes in the Export dialog.

Automatically opening a file is a convenience for the user. Newly created Excel files open right away in Excel. Automatic email is an even more powerful tool. When this choice is selected, a new email message is created in the user's default email client with the exported file as an attachment. (The user still needs to specify the email recipients manually.)

CHAPTER 5

Layout Tools

FileMaker Pro developers spend much of their time in Layout mode, crafting user interfaces and reports with the help of dozens of tools for creating, styling, and arranging objects. The better you know these tools of the trade, the better your databases will be. Of course, creativity and an eye for effective interfaces help too, but they are well beyond the scope of what can be taught here.

Unless otherwise noted, assume that you need to be in Layout mode to access all tools and menus referenced in this chapter. You can access Layout using the File, Layout Mode menu item.

About Layouts

Layout is the FileMaker term for a screen or interface that a user interacts with, whether it is a data entry screen, formatted report, or simple table view. A database may have only a single layout, or it could contain hundreds; there is no limit to the number of layouts you can have within a database solution. Generally, a developer creates and maintains layouts, but anyone with sufficient access privileges can create and modify layouts, even while other users continue to use the system.

A layout is composed of objects. Many different types of objects are available to you—fields, lines, buttons, portals, web viewers, charts, to name a few—and all have properties and attributes that you can configure. There is no practical limit to the number of objects that you can place on a layout.

Layouts in FileMaker Pro 12 have a maximum size of 32,000 points (width and height), which is approximately 444 inches. That's significantly larger than previous versions, which had a maximum width and height of approximately 121 inches.

The Layout Setup Dialog

Within Layout mode, you create new layouts using the Layout, New Layout/Report menu item. Selecting this item takes you through a multiscreen wizard that enables you to begin to set up and customize the layout. Even after you have created a layout, though, you can still modify all its properties. The main tool to do this is the Layout Setup dialog (Layouts, Layout Setup), which is shown in Figure 5.1.

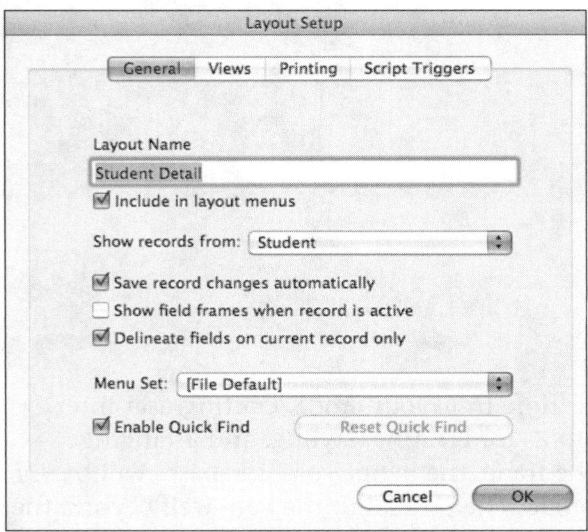

Figure 5.1
Using the Layout Setup dialog, you can alter many of the core attributes of a layout, including its name and the table occurrence with which it is associated.

The layout properties specified by the Layout Setup dialog include the following:

- **Layout Name**—The layout name cannot exceed 100 characters. Layouts do not need to be uniquely named, although it is a good practice to do so.
- **Include in Layout Menus**—This setting determines whether users can see and select the layout from the list of layouts presented in the formatting bar. You might, for instance, have developer layouts that you want to hide from users.
- **Show Records From**—Every layout must be associated with one, and only one, table occurrence from the Relationships Graph. Because a table occurrence is associated with a source table, this setting determines what type of data is shown on the layout (that is, invoice records, student records, and so on), as well as what related data can be shown via relationships. Generally, you should not change this setting after the layout has been created.
- **Save Record Changes Automatically**—When this option is checked, data changes are automatically committed when a user clicks out of a field or navigates to another record or layout. Uncheck this option if you would like users to be presented with a dialog that explicitly asks them whether they would like to save their changes.
- **Show Field Frames When Record Is Active**—When this option is enabled, fields are framed with a dotted line to make them easier to see. Generally, adding frames is not necessary because you can set borders or fill colors to achieve this effect.
- **Delineate Fields on Current Record Only**—This setting is pertinent only to list views. If it is enabled, style attributes (such as border and fill color, for all object states) show for only the current record.

- **Menu Set**—By default, a layout uses the file's default menu set. However, you can override the default by specifying a custom menu set that is installed anytime a user navigates to this layout. Creating custom menu sets requires FileMaker Pro Advanced.
- **Enable Quick Find**—This option enables or disables Quick Find when the current layout is active. You might disable it, for instance, on layouts that contain a lot of summary fields or related fields to avoid performance issues. Individual fields can be enabled or disabled for Quick Find as well, using the Data tab of the Inspector.
- **Views**—A user can normally control whether a layout is set to View as Form, View as List, or View as Table. Using the Views tab, however, you can prevent a user from switching to certain modes. At least one mode must be available. Table view has many properties that you can customize, including the presence of a header and/or footer, and the capabilities to resize and/or reorder columns.
- **Printing**—On the Printing tab, you can specify fixed page margins for a layout, although generally this is neither necessary nor advised. You can also set up a layout to print in multiple columns. Be aware that you see data in multiple columns only in Preview mode.
- **Script Triggers**—A layout can be configured with up to nine script triggers. For instance, you can configure the layout so that a particular script is activated anytime a user navigates to the layout.

➔ *To learn more about script triggers, see Chapter 13, "Script Triggers."*

Layout Themes

A *theme* is a collection of coordinated styles that determine the appearance of new objects placed on a layout. Background color, text attributes, and borders are examples of attributes controlled by the layout's theme. Every layout must be based on a particular theme, which you originally choose in the New Layout/Report assistant. You can change the layout's theme at any point, though, using the Layouts, Change Theme menu item.

You should, of course, choose a theme that best suits the purpose of your layout. Generally, you should use the same theme for all or most of the layouts in a given database to provide a consistent look and feel for users. If your layout will be used on an iOS device, consider using one of the themes developed specifically for this purpose.

You can specify custom appearance attributes for any object, overriding those provided by the theme. If you subsequently change the layout's theme, all objects are given the new theme's appearance settings. However, if you undo the change, custom styles reappear. If you undo a second time, the theme change itself is reverted. This is important to remember so that you can retain custom settings as you change themes.

Using FileMaker Pro 12, you cannot create new themes or edit the default properties of existing themes.

Organizing Layouts

You can keep your layouts organized using the Manage Layouts dialog (File, Manage, Layouts). Here, you can reorder layouts simply by clicking and dragging them to a new location. You can also create folders and place layouts within them. This capability is particularly useful when a solution contains dozens or hundreds of layouts.

Another helpful feature of the Manage Layouts dialog is the ability to pull up the Layout Setup dialog for any layout without navigating to the layout itself by using the Edit button at the bottom of the dialog.

Several other tools, notably screen stencils and guides, are helpful in keeping your layouts well organized.

Screen stencils, new in FileMaker Pro 12, help you design layouts for a particular size screen resolution. This feature is particularly useful when you are designing for FileMaker Go. As you can see in Figure 5.2, you can turn stencils on or off using a tool in the layout bar. If desired, you can have multiple stencils visible at the same time.

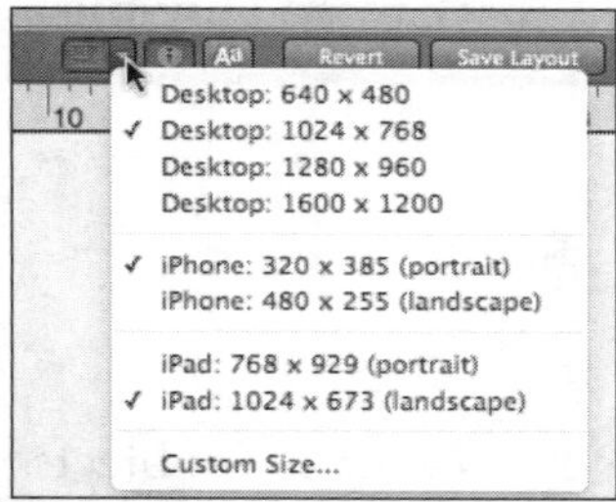

Figure 5.2
Screen stencils help you design layouts for a particular screen resolution.

Two types of guides can help you position layout objects precisely:

- **Manual guides**—You can set up any number of vertical or horizontal guides on a layout by clicking on either the horizontal or vertical ruler (rulers must be active for you to be able to create guides) and dragging the guide on to the layout. Once there, you can right-click the guide to lock it or to share it across all layouts. You can show or hide guides using the View, Guides, Show Guides menu item.
- **Dynamic guides**—When dynamic guides have been enabled (View, Dynamic Guides), as you move or resize an object, you see small blue guides appear when an object becomes aligned with other layout objects. Dynamic guides also appear when the new width or height of an object matches the size of another object on the layout.

With dynamic guides enabled, objects automatically snap as they approach alignment with another object. You can enable similar behavior for manual guides by enabling the View, Guides, Snap to Guides option.

The Inspector

The Inspector is a floating palette available in Layout mode that contains most of the tools available for configuring layout objects. You can activate it (in Layout mode) using the View, Inspector menu item. You can also toggle it on and off using the Ctrl-I (Windows)/Cmd-I (Mac OS) keyboard shortcut.

The tools of the Inspector are organized into three tabs: Position, Appearance, and Data. Each tab is organized into a handful of sections, which are illustrated and described in detail next.

Position Tab

The Position tab of the Inspector not only contains controls for specifying the position of objects, but also for determining how an object's position is affected by things like resizing the window and empty space above it.

Position

You can use the Position section of the Inspector (see Figure 5.3) to see and/or set an object's position, as well as to name an object and set a tooltip.

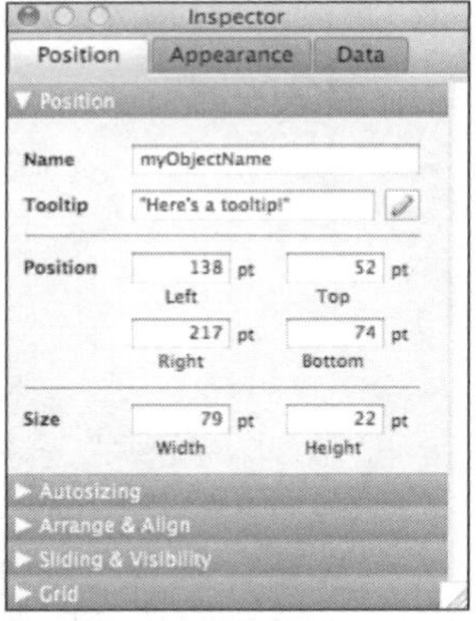

Figure 5.3
The Position section of the Inspector.

- **Name**—You can assign a name to any object on a layout using the Inspector. Object names must be unique to the layout. Generally, you give an object a name only if you need to be able to reference it using a script step such as Go To Object or Set Web Viewer, or to be able to investigate it using the GetLayoutObjectAttribute function, all of which require an object name as a parameter.
- **Tooltip**—Any object on a layout can be configured with a ToolTip that is displayed when a user mouses over the object in Browse or Find mode. ToolTips are often used to provide information or instructions to the user, but you can also configure them to display the result of a calculation formula. The calculation formula is evaluated when the ToolTip is activated, not when the layout is first loaded.

- **Position**—The Position fields display the location of the left, top, right, and bottom edges of the object. The location is relative to the inside top-left corner of the current layout. You can toggle the unit of measure between points, inches, and centimeters by clicking on any of the unit labels in the Inspector. (It is generally easiest to work in points.) In addition to displaying the position of an object, you can use this section of the Inspector to set the position of an object, which makes it quick and easy to precisely align objects even across layouts.
- **Size**—The Size fields display the width and height of the selected object. As with the Position fields, you can resize an object by manually entering a number into either field.

Autosizing

An object's autosizing settings (see Figure 5.4) determine how the object behaves if a user expands the window. By default, every object is anchored to the top and left edges of the layout, which means that its position is fixed relative to the top left of the layout; it does not move or resize as the window is enlarged.

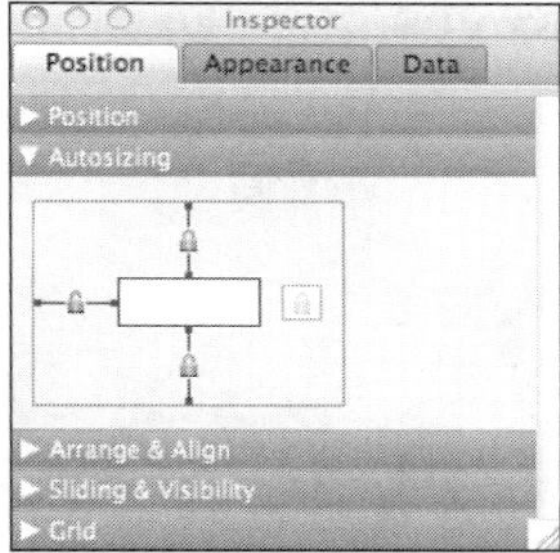

Figure 5.4
The Autosizing section of the Inspector.

Other possible behaviors are as follows:

- When you set a right anchor and no left anchor, the object's position remains fixed relative to the right side of the window. It appears to move right as the window is expanded horizontally.
- When you set a bottom anchor and no top anchor, the object's position remains fixed relative to the bottom of the window. It appears to move down as the window is expanded vertically.
- When you set both a right and left anchor, the object stretches horizontally as the window is expanded so that both its right and left edges remain a fixed distance from the edges of the window.
- When you set both a top and bottom anchor, the object stretches vertically as the window is expanded so that both its top and bottom edges remain a fixed distance from the edges of the window.

- If neither a left nor right anchor is set, the object remains a constant distance from the center of the layout as it is expanded horizontally. Similarly, if neither a top nor bottom anchor is set, it remains a constant distance from the center of the layout as it expanded vertically.

→ *Some further anchoring behaviors that are specific to tab control and portal objects are discussed in Chapter 7, "Other Layout Objects."*

Arrange & Align

The Arrange & Align section (see Figure 5.5) of the Inspector contains tools for grouping and aligning objects, for example. Menu commands are available for all these operations, and many also have keyboard shortcuts.

→ *For a comprehensive list of keyboard shortcuts, see Chapter 23, "FileMaker Keyboard Shortcuts."*

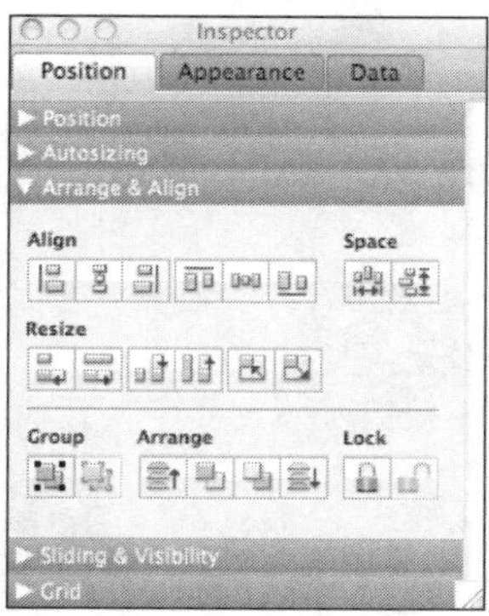

Figure 5.5
The Arrange & Align section of the Inspector.

- **Align**—When multiple objects are selected, you can align them left, center, right, top, middle, or bottom. For example, when you select multiple objects and align left, they are all repositioned to align to the left edge of the leftmost object you have selected. When you align center, the centers of the objects are aligned to the midpoint between the left edge of the leftmost object and the right edge of the rightmost object.
- **Space**—You can select multiple objects and then choose to distribute them horizontally or vertically. Objects are repositioned so that the space separating the two objects furthest apart is evenly divided among all the selected objects.
- **Resize**—When multiple objects are selected, you can use these tools to resize them to a uniform height and/or width. From left to right, the buttons resize the objects to the smallest width, the largest width, the smallest height, the largest height, the smallest height and width, and the largest height and width.

- **Group/Ungroup**—You can group multiple objects together so that they appear and act like a single object. This capability can be helpful to ensure that a set of objects is all positioned consistently even if they are moved. Be aware that when you apply attributes such as script triggers, conditional formatting, or ToolTips to a grouped object, if you ever ungroup the object, each of the objects of the group retains all the group's attributes.
- **Arrange**—Even though a layout displays in two dimensions and can be thought of as an x,y grid, there is an implied third dimension, which is often referred to as the z-axis or the stacking order. The stacking order determines which object appears on top when two objects overlap; it can be changed using the four Arrange buttons. An object can be moved forward (toward the top) or backward (toward the bottom) in the stacking order, or it can be moved to the front or back. When FileMaker displays a layout, it renders objects from back to front.
- **Lock/Unlock**—When you lock an object, its handles display as an X instead of an open square. A locked object cannot be moved, resized, deleted, or otherwise altered in any way. This capability can very useful when you have layered objects (such as a colored rectangle behind a set of fields) so that you don't inadvertently move or select the background object when working with foreground objects.

Sliding & Visibility

The behaviors controlled by the Sliding & Visibility options (see Figure 5.6) are evident only in Preview mode or when printing.

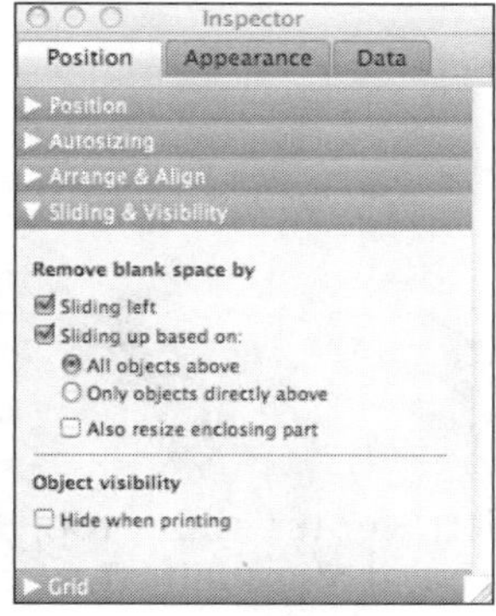

Figure 5.6
The Sliding & Visibility section of the Inspector.

- **Remove Blank Space By**—In Browse mode, if a field is not large enough to display all the text that has been entered into it, the user can simply scroll to see the rest of the text. You cannot do that, however, with a printed report; the text is simply clipped. As a result, on a layout that will be printed, you often must size fields much larger than you would for screen display; typically, you would size it to comfortably fit the longest field entry, which means that many records will have extra blank space in fields. By using the Remove blank space settings, you can have FileMaker close up the blank space in Preview mode and when printing; these settings have no effect in Browse or Find mode.

- **Sliding Left**—If two fields are placed side by side and you want the field on the right to slide left to close the gap between the fields, place this option on both fields. The distance between the fields does not actually change; if you specify a 5-point gap between the fields in Layout mode, that 5-point gap is always respected. However, the right edge of the first field is adjusted based on the length of the field entry. As an example, if you have First Name and Last Name fields next to each other on a layout, you would likely set the First Name to slide left so that there is not a large gap between the fields for people with short first names.
- **Sliding Up Based On**—A common use for this setting is to eliminate blank space at the bottom of a comment or note field. You place this option both on the comment field as well as on all objects below it that should move upward to fill the vacated space. As a further option, you can choose whether an object slides up based on all objects above it or only those directly above it. Generally, the latter is necessary only when you have a printout with multiple columns that need to slide independently of each other.
- **Also Resize Enclosing Part**—This option enables you to have a list view in which the height of the body part (and/or subsummary parts) varies depending on the amount of data in a field. For example, imagine you have a status report that needs to include a comments field that might or might not have multiple lines of text. You would begin by setting up the layout so that the body part and the comments field were both long enough to display the longest record. Then you would turn on sliding for the comments field and also resize the enclosing part (the body part) so that each row on a printout is just as long as it needs to be to display the comment.
- **Object Visibility**—When you set the Hide When Printing option for an object, that object becomes invisible in Preview mode and when the layout is printed. Choosing this setting enables you to place buttons and instructions on a layout but have them disappear when printing.

Grid

Unlike the other settings of the Inspector, the Grid settings (see Figure 5.7) are not applied to an individual object. Rather, they govern some basic properties of Layout mode itself.

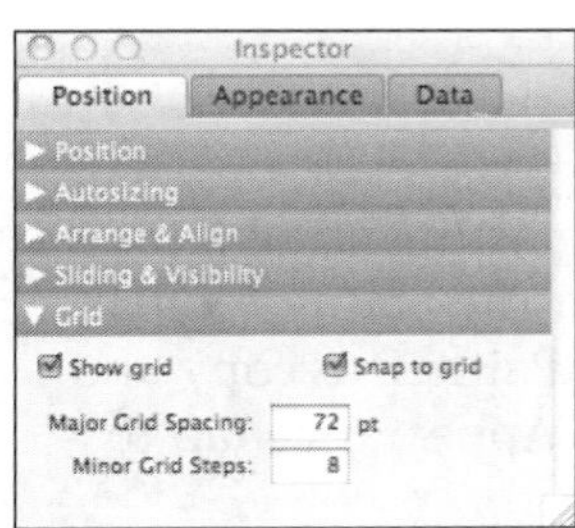

Figure 5.7
The Grid section of the Inspector.

- **Show Grid**—When you turn on this option, both major and minor gridlines display on your layout. This feature can be helpful for aligning objects and creating forms that need precise measurements.
- **Snap to Grid**—Regardless of whether or not the grid is visible, when the Snap to Grid option is enabled, objects snap to the nearest minor gridline when they are moved or resized. Depending on the grid spacing specified, this likely results in chunky movement; objects move and resize from gridline to gridline rather than in 1-point increments. You can temporarily override this option by holding the Alt key (Windows) or Command key (Mac OS) as you move or resize an object.
- **Major Grid Spacing**—The default major grid spacing is 72 points (1 inch). You can toggle the unit of measure between points, inches, and centimeters by clicking on the unit label.
- **Minor Grid Steps**—This setting controls the number of subdivisions within the major grid spacing. For instance, if the major grid spacing is set to 100 points and you specify 20 for the minor grid steps, the minor grid spacing is 5 points.

Note

If you have multiple snapping effects enabled, grid snapping takes precedence, followed by dynamic guides, and then guides.

Appearance

The Appearance tab of the Inspector governs most physical aspects of an object's appearance, including its color, text formatting, line spacing, and indents. The layout's theme determines an object's initial appearance, so any changes you make result in a custom style. As a result, you see either Theme Default or Custom as the Style at the top of the Appearance tab (shown in Figure 5.8).

The four buttons to the right perform the following actions:

- Copy Object Style
- Paste Object Style
- Apply Theme Style
- Remove Styles

You also can access these actions using the Edit menu. Copying and pasting an object's style does the exact same thing as using the Format Painter tool from the Status Toolbar; the only difference between them is that you cannot use the Format Painter to copy and paste styles to a layout part, whereas you can use the buttons on the Appearance tab to do so.

Applying the theme's style reverts the object to the theme defaults. Removing styles clears all styles—custom and theme defaults—from the object.

Be aware that all four of these actions affect the appearance of all the object's states.

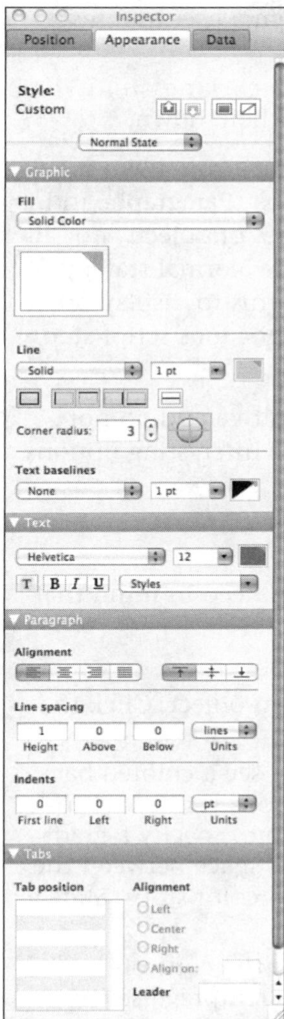

Figure 5.8
The Appearance tab of the Inspector.

Object States

In FileMaker Pro 12, you can configure objects to have a different physical appearance in different "states." Doing so can add a high level of visual polish to a database. The following four states can be configured:

- **Normal**—This is the state of an object when it is not in focus, pressed, or being hovered over.
- **In Focus**—An object is in focus when a user tabs or clicks into it. In other words, it is in focus when it is the active object.

- **Hover**—The hover state controls the appearance of an object when a user mouses over it.
- **Pressed**—This state controls how an object appears while a user is clicking on it. The pressed state appears only when a mouse button is actually being held down.

You can see and set the attributes for each state by selecting it from the drop-down menu at the top of the Appearance tab. All the attributes in the Graphic, Text, Paragraph, and Tabs sections can be configured for each state, although for some types of objects, not all object states are pertinent. For instance, a text object displays only the Normal state; it cannot be made active or pressed. If you ever need an object such as this to display other states, you can do so by setting it up as a button that performs an innocuous script step such as Set Variable.

The Text, Paragraph, and Tabs sections of the Appearance tab are intuitive and do not require detailed explanation. The Graphic section, however, has some interesting options for specifying background fill and line properties.

Fill

Four options are available for the background fill of an object or part. Keep in mind that each state can use a different fill, if you so desire.

- **None**—If no background fill is specified, the object is transparent.
- **Solid Color**—You can set a solid color as the background fill for an object. Click the color swatch to bring up a color picker and select a color.
- **Gradient**—When you specify gradient as the background fill, you see a colored bar with two color stops below it. The space between the two color stops is filled with a smooth transition from one color to the other. You can click a tab to specify a gradient color, and you can slide it to change the amount of transition space between the colors. By clicking the bar itself, you can add up to five additional color stops. Slide a color stop off the end of the bar to remove it.

  In addition to setting the colors that will be blended, you can use the controls beneath the color bar to switch between a linear and circular gradient, reverse the order of the color stops, and change the angle at which the gradient will appear on the object.
- **Image**—The final background fill option is to use an image; supported formats include .png, .bmp, .tif, .gif, or .jpg. After choosing an image to use, you can specify whether the image should display at its original size or whether it should scale to fill or fit. You can also tile the image, which means it displays in a repeated pattern to fill the space.

  The final option, shown in Figure 5.9, is to slice the image. With this option, you can slide two horizontal and two vertical lines on the image to specify where it should be sliced. The four corners that result are displayed as the corners for the background fill; the space between the lines are repeated to fill the space. Effectively, this allows the image to be stretched without losing any resolution.

  If you use the same image to fill multiple objects, FileMaker stores only one copy of the image. Additionally, FileMaker reduces any image that is larger than 20MB down to 20MB.

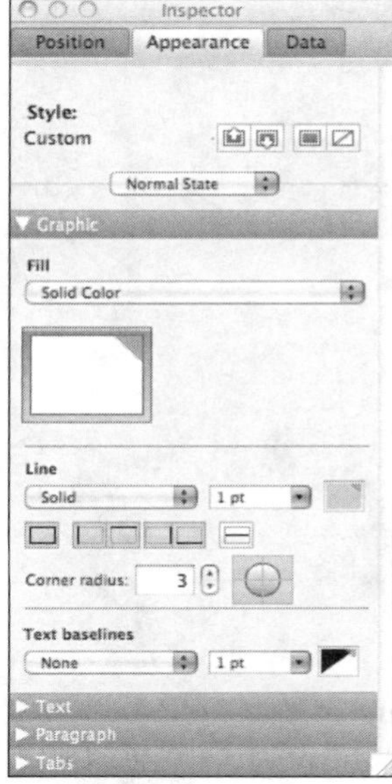

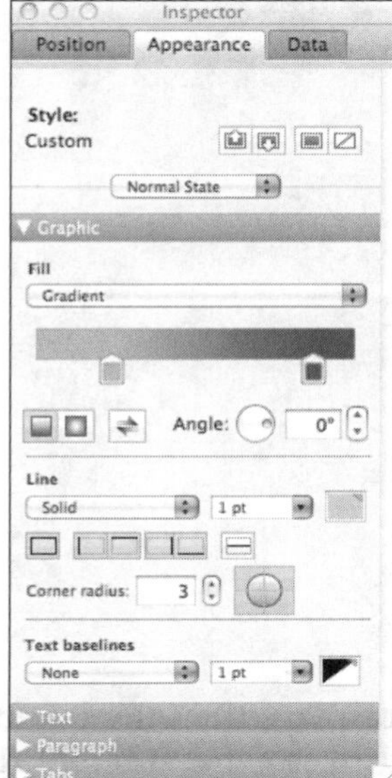

Figure 5.9
The background fill can be set to display a solid color, a gradient, or an image.

Line

In addition to the background fill, several options are available for customizing an object's border. You can specify the style of the border (None, Solid, Dashed, Dotted), its thickness, and its color. You can also specify on which edges of the object the border should appear.

Finally, you can customize the corner radius by specifying a number from 0 to 100, which represents the distance (in points) from each corner that the curve will begin. You can also specify which of the four corners of the object should have a radius by clicking on the pieces of the circle to the right of the radius setting.

Data

The Data tab of the Inspector contains useful tools for formatting field objects and controlling various aspects of their behavior.

Field

The Field section of the Data tab (see Figure 5.10) enables you to format a field as a drop-down menu, for example, or auto-complete as you type. These tools can be applied only to field objects; they are grayed out for other types of objects.

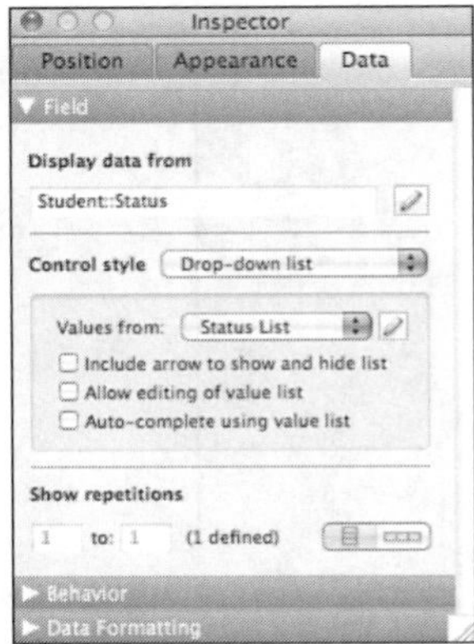

Figure 5.10
The Field section of the Data tab.

- **Display Data From**—This setting displays the fully qualified name of the field attached to the layout object. You can select a different field by double-clicking on the field itself or by clicking on the pencil icon next to the field name in the Inspector.
- **Control Style**—The control styles available are Edit Box, Drop-Down List, Pop-Up Menu, Checkbox Set, Radio Button Set, and Drop-Down Calendar. Depending on your selection, further options are available for configuring. For instance, with an Edit box, if the field is an indexed text field, you also can specify an option to auto-complete using existing values. With a calendar, you can choose to have the field display an icon to show and hide the calendar.

  With all the other four control styles, you need to specify a value list to use. You can access the Manage Value List dialog directly from the Inspector by clicking the pencil icon next to the value list drop-down list.
- **Show Repetitions**—If the selected field object has been defined to use repetitions, you can specify which repetitions to display as well as their orientation (vertical or horizontal).

Behavior

You can configure several behavior settings for fields (see Figure 5.11). Keep in mind that these settings need to be applied to fields on a layout-by-layout basis; they cannot be specified as part of the field definition.

- **Field Entry, Browse Mode**—If users should be able to see fields but not click into them, you can disable field entry for Browse mode. Typically, you might do this for a primary key field so that users do not inadvertently change its value. If users cannot enter the field, they are not able to scroll or see data that goes beyond the field's boundaries.

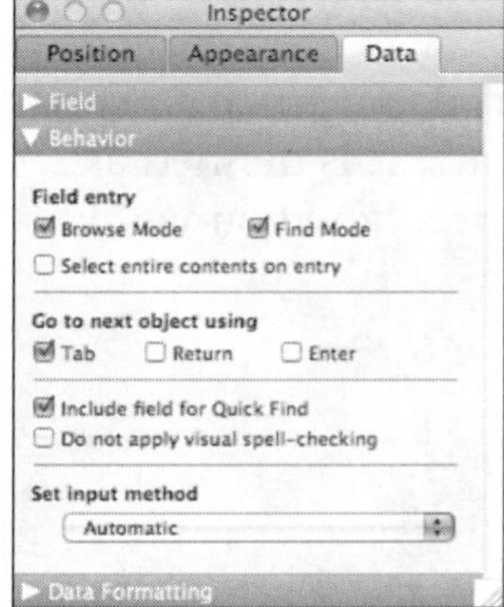

Figure 5.11
The Behavior section of the Data tab.

- **Field Entry, Find Mode**—Similar to the Browse mode option, you can allow or prevent users from entering a field in Find mode using this tool. You might use it, for instance, to prevent users from searching on unindexed fields.
- **Select Entire Contents on Entry**—When this option is enabled, the entire contents of a field are selected when users tab to or click into a field. This capability is useful if users generally replace the entire contents of the field (as opposed to appending additional data).
- **Go to Next Object Using**—By default, the Tab key is configured for moving from object to object in the tab order. However, sometimes you might want the Return/Enter key to perform this way as well. For instance, to prevent users from entering stray return characters at the end of a FirstName field, you could configure the field so that the Return key moves the users to the next object. If you disable the Tab key from moving to the next object, you can then use the Tab key to place a tab within a field. (You must use Option+Tab [Mac OS] or Control+Tab [Windows] to insert a tab into a field if the Tab key is configured to move to the next object.)
- **Include Field for Quick Find**—If you want fields on a layout omitted from a Quick Find, you can uncheck this option for those field objects. Typically, to avoid performance issues, you should disable Quick Find for related fields and unstored calculation fields. You can disable Quick Find for the entire layout in the Layout Setup dialog.
- **Do Not Apply Visual Spell-checking**—A setting on the Spelling tab of the File Options dialog, when enabled, causes words with questionable spelling to be indicated with a red underline. However, there might be specific fields, such as names or email addresses, for which you want to suppress this behavior. You can do so by checking the option not to apply visual spell-checking.
- **Set Input Method**—This option is pertinent only for entering Japanese text into a FileMaker field. Input methods are utilities that convert keystrokes into another language.

Data Formatting

Number, date, time, timestamp, and container fields can have various data formatting settings applied to them. The formatting is not stored with the record data; it is defined as an attribute of a particular layout object. For instance, Figure 5.12 shows how you would typically set up a field to display currency.

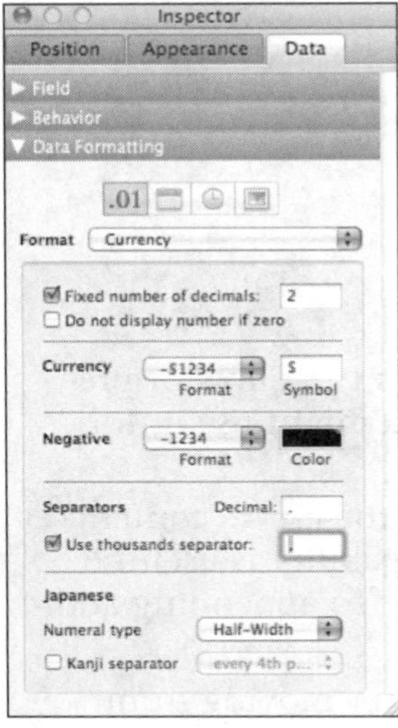

Figure 5.12
Using the Data Formatting section of the Inspector, you can configure a number field to display as currency.

There are similar options for configuring numbers as percents, decimals, and Boolean values.

For date and time fields, you can choose among various predefined formatting options (for example, 5/21/2012 could be displayed as "May 21, 2012", "5/21/12," or even as "Wed, May 21, 2012"). You can also specify a custom format, which can be useful if you want to display only a portion of the date, such as "May, 2012" or "05/21."

With container fields, the data formatting options include resizing to fit and alignment within the container. You can also choose to optimize a container field either for images (for example, .jpg or .bmp) or for interactive content (such as PDF or QuickTime). By optimizing for interactive content, you can work directly with certain types of files. For example, you are able to scroll through the pages of a PDF and to play audio or movies. Note that a container field in a portal cannot be optimized for interactive content.

Additional Object Formatting

Although you can use the Inspector to configure most object properties, three important properties are controlled by other means: button setup, conditional formatting, and script triggers. You access all three using either the Format menu or the contextual menu that appears when you right-click (Windows) or Control-click (Mac OS) an object in Layout mode.

Button Setup

You can create buttons using the Button tool from the Status Toolbar, but in fact, you can turn any object on a layout into a button simply by selecting it and then accessing the Button Setup menu. Generally, buttons should be configured to perform a script rather than execute single script steps. This centralizes all script logic in one place, and it gives you more flexibility should you ever need to alter or expand the button's capability down the road.

➔ *For more information on setting up buttons, see Chapter 12, "Script Primer."*

Conditional Formatting

You can use conditional formatting to alter an object's appearance under specified conditions. For instance, you might want a due date field to appear with a red background color when it is empty or a customer's name to appear in italic when she has past due invoices. Using the Conditional Formatting dialog, shown in Figure 5.13, you can specify whatever conditions you want, along with formatting to apply when that condition is true.

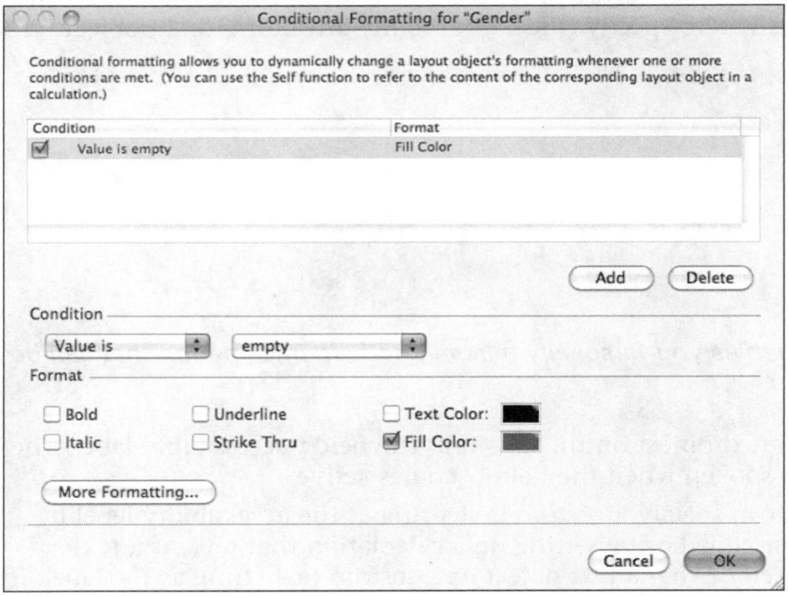

Figure 5.13
You can use the Conditional Formatting dialog to specify object formatting that is applied only under certain circumstances you define.

If you specify multiple conditions, the formatting for all true conditions is applied cumulatively. In the event of a conflict, the formatting of the last true condition is used. You can drag the conditions to reorder them to ensure proper evaluation order.

You can specify a conditional test in two ways. The first is to use the Value Is option and choose from one of the predefined conditions (such as empty, greater than, or equal to). The other is to specify Formula Is and supply an equation that returns True or False (1 or 0).

Script Triggers

Most types of objects can be configured to activate script triggers. Simply select the object and then choose Script Triggers from the object's contextual menu. Examples of actions that you can configure to trigger an object-level script trigger are OnObjectEnter, OnObjectKeystroke, and OnTabSwitch.

➔ *For more details about script triggers, see Chapter 13, "Script Triggers."*

Accessibility Inspector

A new feature in FileMaker Pro 12 is the ability to make layout objects accessible to screen readers, such as JAWS for Windows and VoiceOver for Mac OS X. To add accessibility labels to a layout object, choose View, Accessibility Inspector. The Accessibility Inspector, shown in Figure 5.14, enables you to specify three accessibility attributes for an object.

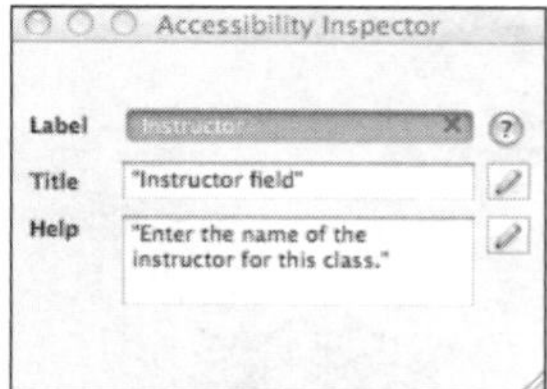

Figure 5.14
The Accessibility Inspector enables you to specify a label and help information that can be read via a screen reader.

- **Label**—You can specify a text object on the layout as the field's accessibility label. The text of the label object is spoken when the field becomes active.
- **Title**—Alternatively, you can specify a custom text string as the accessibility label by typing it into the space provided or by setting up a calculation that returns a text string. Generally, you specify either a text object or a custom text string as the label. If you specify both, the screen reader first speaks the text of the label field and then the custom text string.
- **Help**—When a user first clicks into a field, the contents of the field are read, along with the label and/or title. If the user takes no other action for several seconds, the screen reader speaks the text from the Help section of the Accessibility Inspector.

CHAPTER 6

Charting

The ability to create charts of data is one of the most practical and useful features of FileMaker Pro. Although lists and subsummary reports are important in their own right, a chart can be much more effective at identifying and communicating trends and correlations in data. Charting was first introduced in FileMaker Pro 11, and it was substantially revised and improved in FileMaker Pro 12.

Having general experience with charting in spreadsheets and other applications is irrefutably helpful, but in many ways charting in FileMaker is unique and requires a reasonable understanding of database principles. Foremost are the three options for specifying the chart's data series, which you learn about in detail in this chapter. This chapter also introduces the various chart types available in FileMaker and general style and formatting options available to you. In the end, charting in FileMaker is a skill that requires hands-on practice, so we recommend that you have a database at hand as you read through this chapter.

Creating Charts

The first thing to understand about charts in FileMaker Pro 12 is that they are implemented as layout objects, and as such, they are inexorably tied to the context of the layout on which they appear. Context, in this sense, means such things as the current record, the current found set, the current sort order, and the table occurrence upon which the layout is based. Because of this, where you place the chart affects how you build it, and you might need to use scripts to find and sort the data you intend to chart. A chart is a creature of its context.

There are two ways to create charts in FileMaker Pro 12. The first is to use the Quick Chart feature, which is discussed in the next section. The second is to use the Chart tool from the Status toolbar, shown in Figure 6.1. Although there is no difference in what can be created using either method, Quick Charts are generally more appropriate for creating charts based on the current found set, whereas the Chart tool provides more flexibility for working with delimited or related data sets.

Figure 6.1
You can create charts in Layout mode using the Chart tool from the Status toolbar.

Quick Charts

Quick Charts are ad hoc charts that you create directly in Browse mode. If you right-click (Windows)/Control-click (Mac OS) on any field, you see a Chart By option in the field's contextual menu. Choosing this option creates a Quick Chart that, by default, shows a column chart of data from the field you specified across the found set. Figure 6.2 shows the initial Chart Setup dialog of a Quick Chart created by right-clicking on a number field called Score1 when the found set consists of 20 records. The default color scheme (here, Sea Glass) depends on the theme of the current layout (here, Wave).

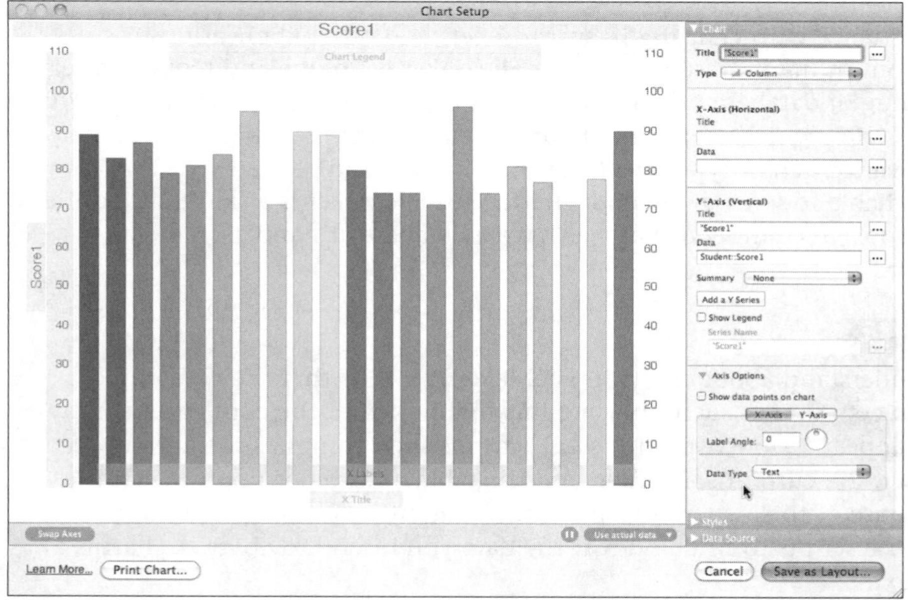

Figure 6.2
When you create a Quick Chart, FileMaker uses data from the current found set to automatically create a chart that you can then refine and edit as necessary.

You can edit the style and format of the chart as you would for any chart. What makes a Quick Chart unique are the options at the bottom of the Chart Setup dialog: Print Chart, Cancel, and Save as Layout. If you click Cancel, all formatting work done on the Quick Chart is lost. Print Chart, as expected, enables you to print the current chart and then keep working with it.

Save as Layout is the interesting option. It creates a new layout in the current file (you have the opportunity to name it as part of the save process), which is placed in a Charts folder (one is created if necessary). The layout is based on the same table occurrence of the current layout, but it always uses the Cool Gray theme by default. It also creates a new script, which is attached to the layout using an OnLayoutEnter trigger; the purpose of the script is to capture the sort order necessary for the chart. You can then go into Layout mode and continue to make edits to the chart as you would any chart created using the Chart tool in the first place.

The Save as Layout option is available only to users who have privileges to create new layouts and scripts. Additionally, if a Quick Chart summarizes data (that is, Count, Total, Average) and no appropriate summary field already exists in the table, Save as Layout requires [Full Access] privileges. Saving the chart as a layout creates whatever summary fields are necessary for rendering the chart.

If the found set you are working with is sorted, or if you are in Table view, you have even more flexibility when creating a Quick Chart. When the found set is sorted, the contextual menu still has the option to Chart by *<Active Field>*, but it also has an option to Chart *<Active Field>* by *<Sort Field>*. Choosing the latter results in a summary chart (one data point per subsummary group) rather than a chart of individual record data. And, in Table view, by selecting multiple columns, you can create Quick Charts that contain multiple data series by default.

The Chart Tool

To create a chart using the Chart tool, simply activate the tool in the Status toolbar and then draw a rectangle on the layout where you want the chart to appear. The Chart Setup dialog displays so you can specify data series and other chart settings manually. You can place chart objects in any layout part, but you may not place them in portal rows.

Specifying a Chart's Data Source

Data series is a term used to represent a set of data points (or their labels) that will be rendered on a chart. In FileMaker, it is best to visualize a data series as a list of numbers. How that series is assembled is the most important (and potentially confusing) concept to understand for creating charts in FileMaker Pro.

As shown in Figure 6.3, there are three options for specifying the data source. This part of the Chart Inspector should be your first stop whenever you create a new chart; all other decisions flow from this setting.

The first option, Current Found Set, has two distinctly different options—summarized or individual record data—so it's more appropriate to think of four options for the data source, as described in the following sections.

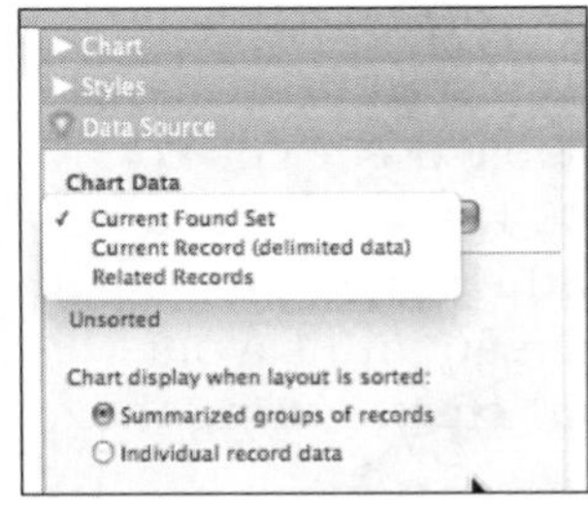

Figure 6.3
In the Chart Setup dialog, you can choose for FileMaker to assemble all of a chart's data and label series using the Current Found Set, Current Record, or Related Records.

Current Found Set – Summarized Groups of Records

With Current Found Set - Summarized Groups of Records specified for the data source, FileMaker expects that each data series contains one value per subsummary group. The found set needs to be sorted appropriately for a subsummary chart to render properly. If it is not sorted, the chart contains one data point per record rather than one data point per subsummary group.

This data source option is useful for synthesizing and aggregating data. For instance, imagine you have a found set of 3,000 orders but that all orders fall into just three calendar years. After sorting the data by year, you could easily create a line or column chart that contains just three data points representing the order totals by year. To do so, you would specify a summary field as the Y-Axis data series and the year field as the X-Axis data series.

Figure 6.4 shows the Chart Setup dialog of another example. In this instance, imagine that the user has sorted a found set of 20 students by instructor; the two data series present the students' average scores for two tests.

As a general rule, when charting summarized groups of records, select the break field (the field the found set is sorted by) as the label series, and a summary field that counts, averages, or sums as each data series.

Current Found Set – Individual Record Data

If a chart uses individual record data from the current found set as the data source, each data series contains one value *per record*. The sort order of the current found set determines the order of the values in each data series.

Generally, you should select a number field as the data series and a text field as the label series. In the example shown in Figure 6.5, the found set consists of a set of nine student records. The label series consists of the students' first names; the individual student scores on Test 1 and Test 2 comprise the two data series.

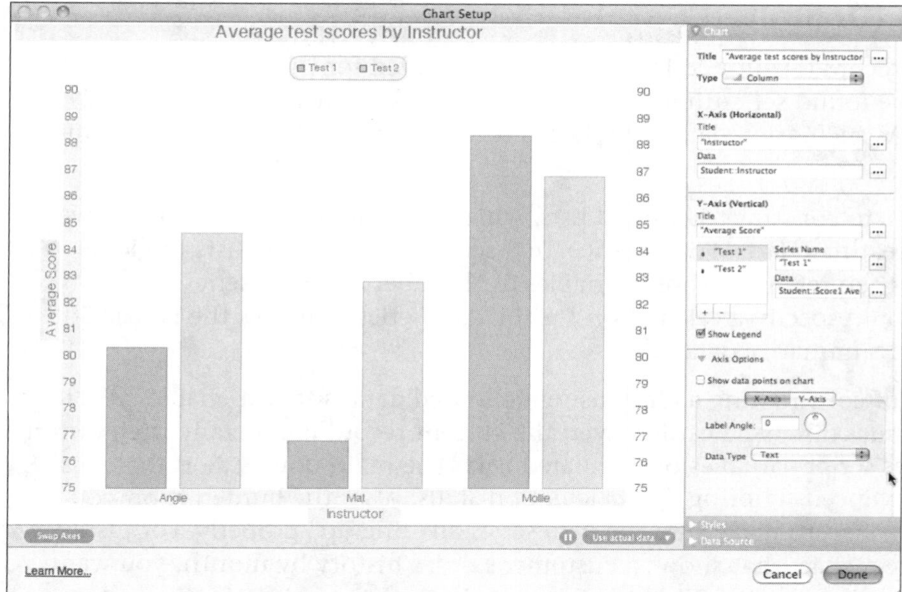

Figure 6.4
When the data source is set to Summarized Current Found Set, each data series contains one value per subsummary group. Here, the 20 students in the found set are grouped by their instructor.

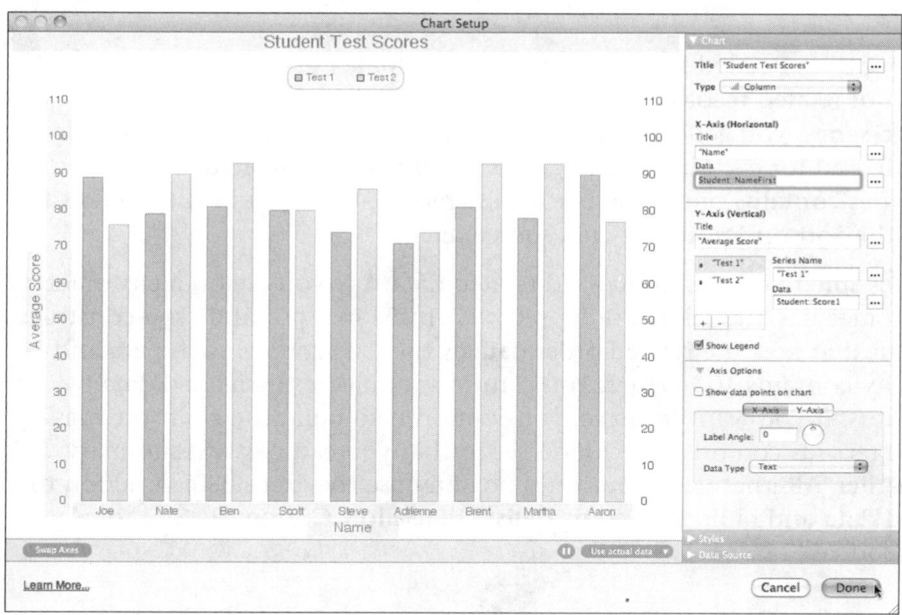

Figure 6.5
Because the data source for this chart has been set to use individual record data from the current found set, each of the nine records in the found set contributes one value per data series.

Current Record (Delimited Data)

When the Current Record (Delimited Data) option is specified for the data source, FileMaker ignores the found set entirely, focusing instead, as the name suggests, only on the current record. As such, each data series needs to be constructed as a return-delimited list of values.

There are many ways to construct delimited lists, which provides for tremendous power and flexibility for creating charts. For instance, in a script you can store lists in global script variables and then reference those variables as the label and data series. Alternatively, you could specify a calculation for the data series that uses the `ExecuteSQL` function to find and summarize data.

The biggest benefit of constructing a chart using delimited data is that it enables you to avoid the context issues discussed earlier. Even the current record is generally irrelevant if your chart references script variables or calculated lists. The main downside is that this can require fairly advanced scripting and calculation skills. Also, the burden is on you when assembling the lists to make sure the data series all "line up" properly. For instance, if you want to create a chart that shows a customer's order history by month, you want the label series to be a list like "Jan¶Feb¶Mar¶Apr…". In the data series, the first value represents January sales; the second value, February; and so on. But if a customer didn't have any sales in February, you need to leave a blank value (or zero) in the appropriate place in the list so that the series lines up properly: "432.54¶¶67.34¶883.34…".

Related Records

The final data series option, Related Records, is to have FileMaker assemble the label and data series from a set of related records. In practice, this is the least used data source option. For each data series, you generally specify a number field from the related table (*not* a summary field), and for each label series, a text field from the related table. The result is that each series contains one value per related record; the order of the values can be controlled using the Sort option in the data source dialog.

Note that it is not possible to chart summarized related data. Say you are on a customer record and that customer has 100 related order records visible in a portal. If you construct a chart on that layout that uses the related order data as the data source, each data and label series you specify contains 100 values. You cannot summarize the related data by month or year or status. If you want to do so, your option is to build the chart on a layout where those 100 records comprise the found set so that you can create a summary chart as described earlier. Alternatively, you could possibly use the `ExecuteSQL` function to aggregate the related data and build the requisite lists that allow Current Record to be selected as the data source.

Chart Types

You can create 10 types of charts using FileMaker Pro 12. See Table 6.1 to learn about typical uses for each type, as well as special requirements for specifying data series.

Table 6.1 Chart Type Options

Chart Type	Description	Data Requirements
Column or Bar	Column and bar charts are excellent for comparing data across categories, such as sales by product type or test scores by grade.	Minimally requires one data series and a corresponding label series; can have up to 12 data series represented.
Stacked Column or Bar	Similar to a regular column or bar chart, except data points for each series are stacked rather than presented next to one another. Use this type of chart to show the relationship of part to the whole for a given category of information; it should be used only if the sum of the data points is meaningful. For instance, sales by region broken out by quarter would be meaningful to show both the relationship of total sales across regions as well as the quarterly breakdown within each. Average high and low temperature across multiple cities would not be appropriate for a stacked bar or column because the sum of the temperatures is meaningless.	Minimally requires two data series and a corresponding label series. If only one data series is present, it looks exactly like a regular column or bar chart. Can have up to 12 data series.
Line or Area	Line and area charts are appropriate for showing changes in values across time. The x-axis for a line or area chart should be a periodic time unit, such as days, hours, months, or years. Be careful creating a line or area chart using summarized data from the found set because all time periods may not be represented in the data. For instance, if you intend to chart a customer's sales by month and the customer had sales for May and July, but not June, June would be absent and the line chart would directly connect May to July.	Minimally requires one data series on the y-axis and a label series for the x-axis. Can have up to 12 data series; each series is represented by a separate line on the chart.
Positive/ Negative Column	A positive/negative column chart is useful for comparing positive and negative values relative to a defined midpoint. The midpoint is zero by default, but you can change it to whatever you need it to be. For instance, you might create a positive/negative chart that compares employees' average weekly hours to a midpoint of 40. Those employees over 40 hours would appear as upward columns; those under 40 hours would be downward columns.	Must have exactly one data series and one label series.

Table 6.1 Continued

Chart Type	Description	Data Requirements
Pie	A pie chart shows the comparison of parts to the whole. Be careful to use a pie chart only when the sum of the values being represented is meaningful. For instance, a pie chart would be appropriate to show the breakdown of monthly sales by salesperson (and this would be easy to accomplish using a summarized found set as the data source), but a pie chart would not work for comparing students' scores on a test because each student's contribution to the total score is nonsensical (that is, Steve received 8% of the total class score).	Must have exactly one data series (slice data) and one label series (category labels).
Scatter	A scatter chart is generally used to show the correlation between two data series. A pattern that *rises* from left to right indicates a positive correlation, whereas a pattern that *falls* from left to right indicates a negative correlation. As an example, you might use a scatter chart to plot a set of students' scores on two tests. One test would be represented on the x-axis and the other on the y-axis; each data point would represent a single student's scores on the two tests.	The data series required for a scatter chart are different from those for other chart types. For each series specified, you need to specify an x-axis data series, a y-axis series, and a label series. The x-axis and y-axis series cannot contain text; they must be numbers, dates, times, or timestamps.
Bubble	A bubble chart is similar to a scatter chart in that it plots the x,y intersection of two values, but instead of marking the intersection with a single point, a bubble chart adds another dimension by marking the intersection with a variable-sized bubble. Be aware that if a data point has a bubble radius of zero, no bubble is visible (though its label still displays). If a radius is negative, its absolute value is used to plot the bubble. An example of a bubble chart would be comparing students' scores on two tests, with a radius showing the number of school days absent.	For each series specified (typically there is only one), you need to specify an x-axis data series, a y-axis series, a radius series, and a label series. The x-axis, y-axis, and radius series cannot contain text; they must be numbers, dates, times, or timestamps.

Chart Styles

You can change the appearance of a chart using the Styles section of the Chart Inspector. Be aware that some appearance settings are specific for certain types of charts (such as Bubble Opacity) and that not all settings are available for all chart types.

- **Chart Style**—For most chart types, you can choose between Solid – Flat, Solid – 3D, Shaded – Flat, or Shaded – 3D.
- **Color Scheme**—FileMaker provides you with 20 coordinated color themes to choose from (for example, Pastels, Earth, Muted Rainbow). The default theme assigned

depends on the theme of the layout on which you place the chart. FileMaker automatically assigns colors to the values and/or data series; you cannot manually set the color of a particular series or data point. However, you can choose the Single Color option from the top of the Color Scheme pop-up list and assign a single color to the entire chart. For positive/negative charts, you can use the single color option to manually assign both a positive color and negative color.

- **Chart Background**—Choose between transparent, solid fill, or many types of gradients.
- **Gridlines**—You can enable or disable major or minor gridlines and specify their color (but not their weight or style). You can change the major and minor spacing in the Axis Options section of the Chart section of the Chart Inspector.
- **Legend Attributes**—The option to include the legend is in the Chart section of the Chart Inspector. If it is enabled, you can use the Styles section to specify a location of top, bottom, left, or right. You can also specify appearance settings for the legend background and border.
- **Chart Text**—By default, the appearance of all text on a chart (such as labels, legend, title) is controlled automatically by FileMaker. When the chart text setting is Automatic, you can still specify a global font, color, and relative text size. If you want more control over individual text elements, set the Chart Text setting to Custom; you are then able to independently set the font, color, and size for various text elements.

Settings for the axes themselves, including the data type, format, angle, and min/max, are configured at the bottom of the Chart section of the Chart Inspector. The choices available are appropriate for the chart type you have specified.

Tips for Effective Charting

Charting in FileMaker is a feature that lends itself to learning through trial, error, and experimentation. Here are some tips to help you get started:

- If you are working with a large data set or with multiple summary fields, the live chart preview might take time to render. You can pause or refresh the preview using the controls beneath the preview pane.
- In the chart preview, you can click on any chart element with a gray bar behind it (for example, the title, legend, axis, and axis labels) to activate the section of the Chart Inspector that controls that element.
- Be careful when creating charts that subsummarize the found set. If the found set is not sorted, it renders as if you had specified individual record data. Worse still, if the data is sorted by the wrong break field, the chart might appear to contain logical data, but the label series is incorrect.
- Generally, you place summary charts in a body part or a leading or trailing grand summary. However, they behave differently if you place them in a subsummary part. Instead of charting one data point per subsummary group, the chart then renders one data point per secondary subsummary group (if a second sort field is specified), or individual records in the subsummary group (if no second sort is specified).
- You can copy chart objects to the Clipboard by right-clicking on them in Browse mode. You can then paste them into other applications or even container fields in

FileMaker Pro. Chart objects are rendered at 72 dpi, so if you intend to copy and paste into another application, it is usually a good idea to make the chart large enough in FileMaker that you do not have to stretch it in the target application. Another helpful trick to avoid pixilation is to zoom in FileMaker to 400% before copying the object. When you paste it, it is 16 times as large, but then you can compress it to the proper size and have much better resolution. This trick can, of course, be scripted.

- If you set an object name for a chart object, you can use the function `GetLayoutObjectAttribute ("myObjectName"; "source")` to return an XML description of a chart object. Using `"content"` as the attribute name returns a bitmap representation of the chart object.

CHAPTER 7

Other Layout Objects

Chapter 5, "Layout Tools," discussed layout objects in general, and Chapter 6, "Charting," discussed one particular object, the chart object, in detail. This chapter focuses on three additional layout objects—namely portals, tab controls, and Web Viewers—each of which has specialized uses and attributes. These tools are among the most useful in a FileMaker developer's toolbox.

As you can see in Figure 7.1, you can find all three tools in the Status Toolbar (in Layout mode, of course). You also have access to them via the Insert menu, but you should avoid accessing them this way because you cannot control their location or size.

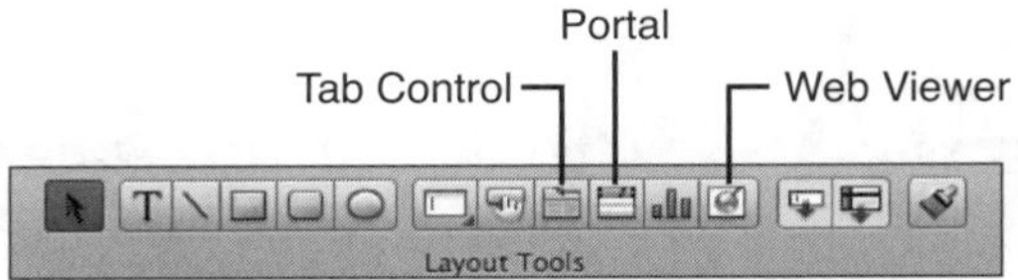

Figure 7.1
The three tools discussed in this chapter—the tab control, portal, and Web Viewer—are all accessed via the Status Toolbar.

Tab Controls

A tab control is useful for organizing information on a layout. Users immediately grasp the tab metaphor; by clicking a tab, you activate a tab panel that contains a particular set of content. It creates the illusion of a third dimension and enables you to use screen real estate very effectively. As an example, Figure 7.2 shows two versions of the same layout. In the first, Contact Info is the active tab panel, and in the second, Notes is active.

To add a tab control object to a layout, click on the tool in the Status Toolbar, and then click and drag to form the object. The Tab Control Setup dialog is displayed (see Figure 7.3), and you can specify the number and names of the tab panels, as well as several appearance options. You can access this dialog anytime by double-clicking on the object.

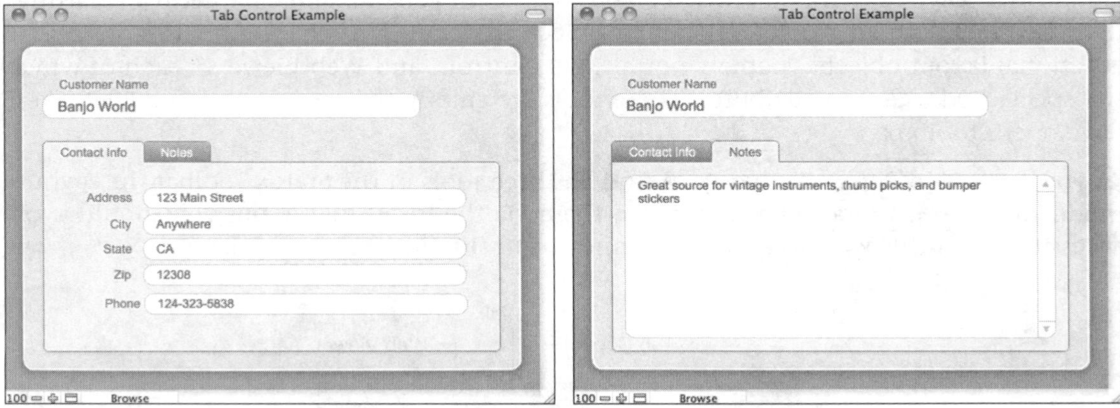

Figure 7.2
A tab control is composed of any number of tab panels, each of which can contain unique content.

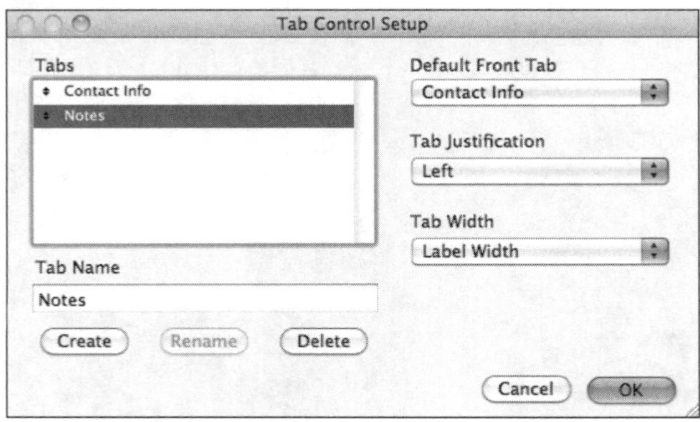

Figure 7.3
Use the Tab Control Setup dialog to create, delete, and rename tab panels, as well as to specify several appearance options.

The appearance options controlled by the Tab Control Setup dialog are the following:

- **Default Front Tab**—This option controls which tab is active when a user first navigates to the layout. If a user activates a different tab and then switches layouts, when he returns to the layout, the default front tab is active again; FileMaker does not remember the active tab.
- **Tab Justification**—This control specifies the position of the tabs relative to the top edge of the tab panel: Left, Center, Right, or Full.
- **Tab Width**—By default, tabs have a variable size based on their label width, but you can also give them some extra padding by choosing Label Width + Margin Of. Other options include sizing all tabs to the width of the widest label, setting a fixed width for all tabs, and setting a minimum tab width. If you a set a fixed width of zero, the tab names effectively disappear; you can use your own buttons and scripts to control tab navigation.

Here are a few points to keep in mind when you are specifying names for tabs in the Tab Control Setup dialog:

- You can reorder tab panels by clicking the tab name and dragging it to a different position.
- If you delete a tab, all objects that were on that panel are also removed.
- Tab names do not need to be unique.
- You can create tab panels without entering a tab name.
- Although there is no practical limit to the number of tabs you can have, the tabs are truncated at the point they exceed the width of the tab control itself.
- A tab name can be up to 255 characters long.

Formatting a Tab Control

The layout's theme controls the default appearance of the tab control, but you can customize many attributes. Text formatting attributes of the tab labels are set for the entire object; you cannot specify a different text size, font, or color for an individual tab label.

Even though the tab control as a whole is considered a single object, you can configure many things for individual tab panels. To do so, select the tab panel by clicking on it twice (not double-clicking). (You can tell that it's selected if the name of the tab has a black border.)

At the tab panel level, you can set attributes such as the background fill, border, and corner radius. You can set these attributes for three states: Normal, Hover, and In Focus. A tab control does not display a pressed state. The Hover and In Focus states appear only when a tab is inactive and the user mouses over it (Hover) or activates it via the tab order (In Focus).

Using the Inspector, you can also specify an object name for an individual tab panel, which allows for scripted navigation to a particular panel.

Individual tab panels can also have conditional formatting configured for them. Conditional formatting affects the display of the tab label.

Finally, several script triggers can be set for tab controls. OnObjectEnter and OnObjectExit activate when you tab to and from a tab control. OnTabSwitch and OnObjectModify activate when you switch from one tab to another.

Autosizing of Tab Controls

There are a few special behaviors to be aware of when configuring autosizing settings for the objects contained on a tab control. The tab control object itself can move or stretch just like any other object. However, objects contained on a tab control are limited by the tab control's settings. This is necessary so that the objects do not exceed the boundaries of the tab control.

The rule to keep in mind is that objects on a tab control can only resize in the same way as the tab control itself. If the tab control has only left and top anchors set (no moving or stretching), regardless of how you anchor objects contained on it, those objects do not move or stretch. If the control has both left and right anchors (horizontal stretch), objects within it can have left, right, or left/right anchors set. Another way to think about this is to imagine that you anchor objects on a tab control to the edges of the tab control rather than the edges of the layout.

Other Tab Control Notes

Here are few other issues to keep in mind when working with tab control objects:

- You can include a tab control object in the tab order. After tabbing to a tab control, you can use the arrow keys to navigate to other tabs, and use the spacebar or Return key to switch to the tab.
- Objects on inactive tabs are omitted from the tab order.
- You can nest tab controls within each other.
- When you move a tab control, all objects it contains move with it.
- The blank space to the left or right of the tab labels is considered part of the current tab panel. This means that you can place objects such as buttons outside the apparent boundary of the panel, yet have them be visible only when that given panel is active.
- You cannot place a tab control within a portal.
- If you print a layout that contains a tab control, only the active tab panel is printed.
- If you spellcheck a record, only the active tab is checked.
- If you choose Save Records As Excel, only the fields on the active tab are included in the export.
- If you change the view to View As Table, all fields on any tab panel are displayed.

Portals

Portals are among the most powerful and useful tools available to a FileMaker developer. A portal enables you to view a set of related records; each row in a portal represents a record from a related table. For instance, Figure 7.4 shows a layout that presents data about a customer, and the portal displays three related order records.

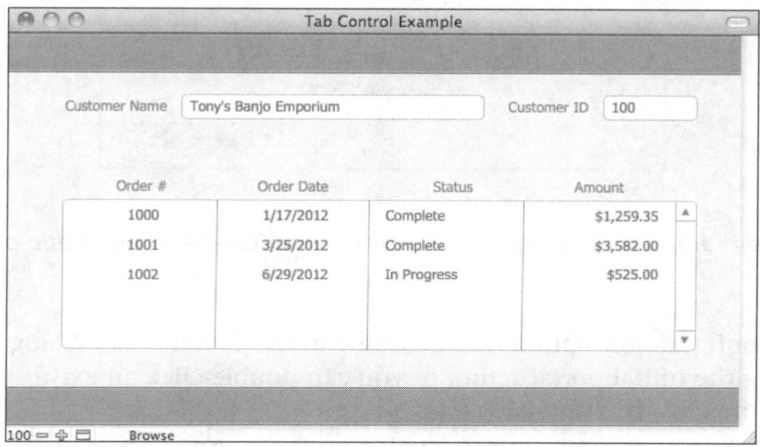

Figure 7.4
A portal is used to display a set of related records. Here, the layout is based on a Customer table occurrence, and the portal shows Orders related to the current customer.

Portal Setup

To add a portal to a layout, click the Portal tool in the Status Toolbar; then click and drag a rectangle on the layout where you want the portal to appear. You are then taken to the Portal Setup dialog, which is shown in Figure 7.5.

The most important setting in the Portal Setup dialog is the choice of where to show related records from. Layouts are linked to table occurrences; this situates them on a particular node in the Relationships Graph. A portal placed on a layout must show records from a table occurrence that is related (however distantly) to the table occurrence of the layout. From the current record, if you were to traverse the relationship path that linked these two table occurrences, the resulting set of records is what appears in the portal. In a sense, then, a portal shows the results of performing a relational query.

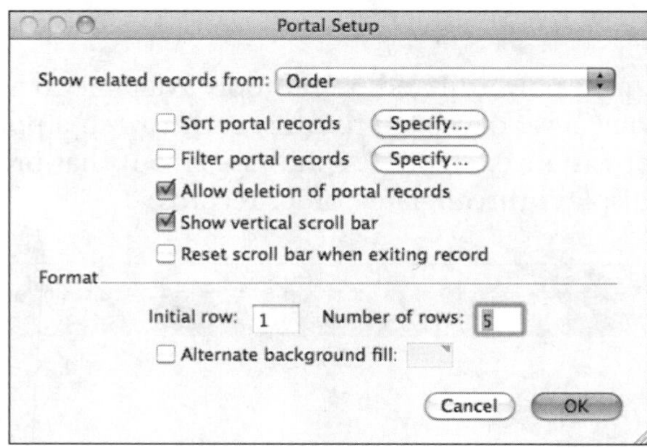

Figure 7.5
The Portal Setup dialog enables you to configure functional and aesthetic properties of a portal.

Several other configuration options are available in the Portal Setup dialog. You can specify them during the initial portal setup, or you can double-click an existing portal at any time to access the Portal Setup dialog.

- **Sort Portal Records**—By default, related records are sorted according to the relationship's settings; if no sort has been set at the relationship level, they are displayed in creation order. You can override this setting, if desired, in the Portal Setup dialog. Keep in mind that if a portal displays hundreds or thousands of records, there might be some performance penalty to sort the related set. Operations such as Go to Related Records and the GetNthRecord function return results based on the relationship's sort order; they are not affected by the portal's sort order.
- **Filter Portal Records**—In some situations you might not want to see all the related records in a portal. Rather than altering the relationship, you can filter the results by specifying a condition by which records should be displayed. For instance, imagine you have a Project database that includes a portal into a related Task table. If you want the portal to display only records with a status of In Progress, you simply base the portal on a relationship from Project to Task, but you can specify a filter such as Status = In Progress to filter out completed or canceled tasks.

  Unlike previous versions, in FileMaker Pro 12 portal filters are evaluated on the server (rather than the client), which means that performance for a filtered portal should be similar to what you would experience with a filtered relationship.
- **Allow Deletion of Portal Records**—This setting controls whether a user can delete related records via the portal. Assuming it is allowed, there are a few ways the user could initiate the deletion of a related record. If a user clicks into a field in the portal and she selects Records, Delete Records, she sees a dialog asking whether she wants to delete the entire master record or just the one related record. If the user activates a portal row without clicking into any field in the portal (that is, if she clicks on a portal row but clicks outside an enterable field), she can initiate deletion either by pressing

the Delete or Backspace key or by selecting Records, Delete Records. The dialog in this case, however, simply confirms whether the user wants to delete the related record; she does not have the option to delete the master record.

- **Show Vertical Scroll Bar**—This setting governs whether the portal has a vertical scrollbar. Generally, it is a good idea to select this option. Without it, there is no way to see more related records than could be displayed in the allotted rows. The exception is a situation in which you know there will never be more than a certain number of related records.
- **Reset Scroll Bar When Exiting Record**—If a user scrolls down within a portal and then exits the record (typically by clicking somewhere on the layout background), should the portal jump back up to display the top rows, or should it stay scrolled? You can control that behavior with this setting. When it is selected, the portal pops back to the top when the user exits the record.
- **Initial Row and Number of Rows**—The number of rows setting determines how many rows are displayed in the portal. Resizing the portal object itself determines only the size of the top row of the portal, not the number of rows. That must be set in the Portal Setup dialog. Generally, you leave the initial row setting as 1, indicating that the portal should begin with the first related record. The setting is useful, however, if you ever need to put multiple portals next to each other. For instance, you might display the first four related records in one portal (Initial row: 1, Number of rows: 4, no scrollbar) and then place the identical portal next to it to display the remaining rows (Initial row: 5, Number of rows: 4, show scrollbar).
- **Alternate Background Fill**—The color you specify is used for every other portal row. An alternating background fill can make a large portal easier to read.

Working with Records in a Portal

It is important to remember that each portal row is actually a record in a related table. As such, you can use portals to create, edit, and delete related records.

You can use a portal to create related records if the relationship it is based on is the Allow Creation of Records in This Table via This Relationship option. When it is, the portal displays a blank row beneath any existing related records. By entering data into the blank row, the user initiates creation of a new record in the related table. The foreign key of the related record is set automatically. This means that the match field in the relationship (in the target table) cannot be a calculation field and that the relationship has to be based on an equality operator.

Deletion of related records can be controlled via script (the `Delete Portal Row` script step) or by the setting in the Portal Setup dialog to allow deletion of portal records.

A user can edit records in a portal as he would any other record data, but there is a crucial distinction when it comes to committing records. If the user edits data in one portal row and then clicks into another portal row, the prior data is not committed. Similarly, if data is edited in a portal and then the user clicks into a field in the master record, the portal row data is not committed. When a user finally exits the record (by clicking outside any field, by navigating to another record, or by pressing the Enter key), the master record and all related records are committed at once as a single transaction. This has a few practical implications. The first is that a given user might have locks on many records simultaneously. The second is that all data changes made within a portal—including record creation and deletion!—can be reverted using the Records, Revert Record menu item. As a developer, you can use this feature to your advantage to ensure that multiple records that make up a single "transaction" are fully committed together or reverted together.

> ➔ *This transactional approach is particularly useful for databases that will be accessed via FileMaker Go. For more details on this topic, see Chapter 16, "Designing for FileMaker Go."*

Autosizing of Portals

Portals, like tab controls, are designed to contain other objects, and, as such, they have special behaviors when it comes to autosizing. Similarly to a tab control, the objects in a portal are constrained by the settings of the portal itself. That is, autosizing settings on objects in a portal are irrelevant if the portal itself does not resize. Just imagine that the objects within a portal are anchored to the edges of the portal row, rather than to the edges of the window.

If a portal object has both a top and bottom anchor set, the portal stretches as the window is enlarged vertically, just as it would for any object with opposing top and bottom anchors. But how that stretch affects the individual portal rows themselves is another matter. There are two options, which are controlled by the anchoring settings of the objects within the portal:

- If none of the objects in the portal have a bottom anchor set, as the portal stretches vertically, additional rows appear.
- If any object contained in the portal has a bottom anchor set, and regardless of any other anchoring, each portal row expands proportionally—like an accordion—as the window is enlarged.

Other Notes About Portals

Here are a few miscellaneous details about portals that you should know:

- Objects placed in a portal row don't display unless there is a related record present.
- When you move a portal, all objects contained within the portal move with it (this was not the case in previous versions of FileMaker Pro). Similarly, if you delete a portal object, all objects it contains are also deleted.
- You cannot place a tab control, chart, or Web Viewer in a portal.
- You cannot nest portals within each other.

- You can place the Record Number Symbol ({{RecordNumber}}) in a portal to display the portal row number.
- You cannot work interractively with container fields that are in portals.
- The OnObjectEnter and OnObjectExit script triggers can be applied to a portal object. They activate anytime a different row in the portal is entered or exited.
- You can apply the OnObjectKeystroke script trigger to a portal object. It activates if a portal row is active and the user is not clicked into a field within the portal row. So, for instance, if you have a portal in which the fields are set not to allow entry in Browse mode, you can configure a keystroke trigger so that the up- and down-arrow keys navigate up and down the portal, perhaps triggering the display of additional detail about the portal row somewhere else on the layout.
- You can specify different fill and line settings for a portal for its Normal, Hover, and In Focus states. The state settings are applied to the entire portal, not just a single portal row. The Hover state does not appear when the user mouses over a field in the portal that can be entered in Browse mode. Similarly, the In Focus state appears only when the user activates a portal row, but not when he clicks into a field within the portal. In other words, the state settings of objects within the portal have priority over the state settings of the portal itself.
- When displayed using FileMaker Go, the scrollbar on a portal is a little small and can be difficult to use. Rendering a portal that contains many records can be quite slow when it is accessed over the WAN, particularly over 3G. You might consider creating a fixed row portal that relies on relationship filtering and then provide Next and Previous buttons to control the subset of records displayed.

Web Viewer

A Web Viewer, essentially, is a web browser that you can embed into a FileMaker Pro layout. Web Viewers use the operating system's web browser technology—Safari on Mac, Internet Explorer on Windows—and render most content just as a browser would. Their real power, though, derives from your ability to control the Web Viewer's URL via calculation or script.

There is a plethora of practical uses for Web Viewers. For instance, if you have a customer's website URL stored in a field, you can display it in a Web Viewer. You might have another that uses data stored in address fields to show a map of the customer's location or perhaps directions from your office. JavaScript widgets also make great Web Viewer content and can provide user interface devices not possible through FileMaker alone. Imagine, for instance, placing a news crawl or a clock at the top of a layout. Using something known as a data URL, you can even use Web Viewers to produce highly stylized and dynamic reports.

To create a Web Viewer, select the Web Viewer tool from the Status Toolbar and then click and drag a rectangle on the layout where you want it to appear. The Web Viewer Setup dialog is displayed as shown in Figure 7.6.

The Web Address field in the middle of the dialog contains a calculation expression that determines the URL that is initially displayed in the Web Viewer. You can specify this calculation yourself—perhaps something as simple as "http://" & Customer::URL—or you can use one of the templates provided in the top half of the dialog. For instance, you can see in Figure 7.6 that the Google Web Search (US) template is selected, and this requires one Query value, which has been populated with the name of a field. The calculation shown in the Web Address field is automatically built based on the template and the query values specified.

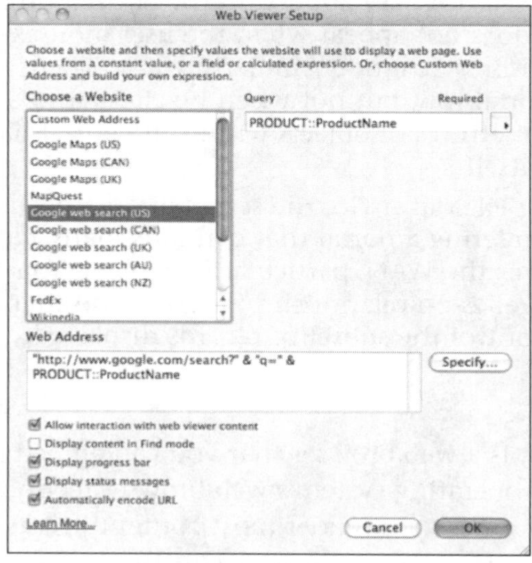

Figure 7.6
A Web Viewer can display web pages or other web-based content directly in a FileMaker Pro layout.

> *Note*
>
> When entering your own formula for a web address, be sure that it begins with the correct schema, such as http://, https://, ftp://, or file://. If you omit the schema, the Web Viewer might not display properly.

Several check boxes are available at the bottom of the Web Viewer Setup dialog:

- **Allow Interaction with Web Viewer Content**—If this option is unchecked, the Web Viewer becomes a read-only object. The user cannot click on hyperlinks or enter values into forms. Typically, you leave this option checked.

- **Display Content in Find Mode**—If the URL for a Web Viewer is based on dynamic content, it might not function properly in Find mode. Check or uncheck this option depending on whether it makes sense for the Web Viewer to render content in Find mode. If this option is unchecked, the Web Viewer is simply blank in Find mode.
- **Display Progress Bar**—When this option is selected, the bottom of the Web Viewer displays a progress bar as the page loads.
- **Display Status Messages**—Enable this option if you want status messages to display at the bottom of the Web Viewer. They include, for example, loading messages, error messages, and security status (including a lock icon when secure web pages are loaded).
- **Automatically Encode URL**—If this option is selected, FileMaker applies URL encoding rules as necessary. For instance, if a field used to construct a URL contains characters such as spaces, ampersands, percents, and backslashes, these generally need to be encoded for the URL to function properly. You can prevent automatic encoding by deselecting this option; deselecting might be appropriate if you have query parameters in a field and need special characters to remain as entered.

Setting a Web Viewer via Script

You can specify the initial URL for a Web Viewer object in the Web Viewer Setup dialog. Subsequently, you can control it using the `Set Web Viewer` script step. This script step requires two parameters. The first is the object name of the Web Viewer to set. This is required because a layout could conceivably contain multiple Web Viewers and the script step needs a way to distinguish which one to act upon. You can use the Position tab of the Inspector to set an object name for a Web Viewer, just as you would any other layout object.

For the second parameter, you select from the following possible actions:

- **Reset**—Resets the Web Viewer to the web address specified in the Web Viewer Setup dialog. This also clears the object's Back and Forward history.
- **Reload**—Reloads whatever page the Web Viewer is currently displaying.
- **Go Forward**—Goes forward one page in the Web Viewer's history.
- **Go Back**—Goes back one page in the Web Viewer's history.
- **Go to URL**—Allows you to specify an entirely new URL for the Web Viewer. The interface for specifying the URL is similar to the Web Viewer Setup dialog.

Other Web Viewer Notes

Just as with portals and tab controls, there are many other interesting and useful details to learn about Web Viewers:

- You cannot place a Web Viewer in a portal.
- A Web Viewer works with a layout set to View as Form or View as Table. If the layout is set to View as Table, the Web Viewer needs to be in the header or footer part to be displayed.
- You cannot rotate a Web Viewer object.

- You can configure a Web Viewer's fill and line attributes for all states (Normal, Hover, In Focus, and Pressed). However, if the Web Viewer does not allow a user to interact with it, the Hover and In Focus states are not available.
- You can render a string of HTML content directly in a Web Viewer using a data URL. For instance, if you specify the string "data:text/html,<html><body>Testing 123</body></html>" as the web address for a Web Viewer, you set the words Testing 123 in the Web Viewer. This is very powerful in that it enables you to build and display entire web pages dynamically. Images that are BASE64 encoded can also be displayed using data URLs.
- Although there is no hard limit as to the number of Web Viewer objects you may display on a layout, having multiple Web Viewers on a layout might affect performance, especially when viewed on an iOS device.

CHAPTER 8

Calculation Primer

The Calculation dialog in FileMaker serves as a fundamental element in nearly all development activities. Beyond simply defining calculation fields, you also work with the dialog within scripts, for setting some auto-enter field options, for field validation, for tooltips, for conditional field formatting, for charting, and even within a file's security settings. We encourage all developers to become deeply familiar with calculation functions. To that end, this chapter provides a concise reference of how the dialog works.

The Calculation Function Interface

The Specify Calculation dialog gives developers easy access to the data fields in their solutions and to a complete function list (see Figure 8.1).

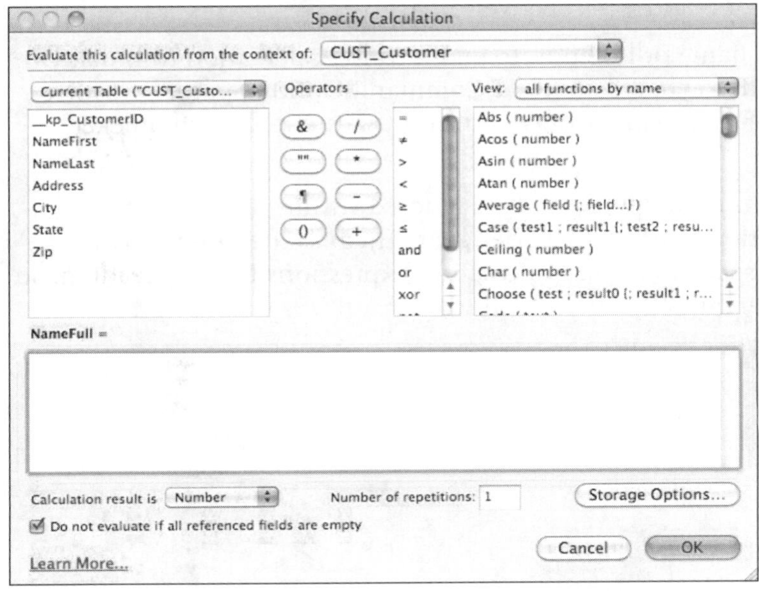

Figure 8.1
Both field names and calculation functions can be double-clicked to insert them into the expression editing area.

→ *If you would like more detail on specific functions, including complete examples of how they work,* ***see*** *Chapter 10, "Calculation Functions."*

Calculations: Things to Remember

When you are working with calculation functions, there are some common issues to keep in mind.

The four special operators in FileMaker are

- & Concatenates the result of two expressions. "Joe" & "Smith" results in "JoeSmith"; 1 & 2 results in "12".
- "" Designates literal text. You don't need quotation marks around numbers, field names, or functions.
- ¶ Carriage return.
- () Designates a function's parameter list and controls the order of operations for math expressions.

Entering a less-than character followed by a greater-than character (<>) equates to the "not equal to" operator (≠) within an expression. The following expressions are functionally identical:

```
1 <> 2
1 ≠ 2
```

This is also true for >= and <= for ≥ and ≤, respectively.

You can double-click on a field name or function to add it to the calculation formula. On the Mac OS, you can also use the keyboard shortcut Command-Option-Space. Of course, manually typing the formula or field name works, too, and that's often much quicker than scrolling through lists.

Spaces, tabs, and carriage returns (¶ or "pilcrows") are ignored within the calculation syntax, except when within quotation marks (which designate them as literal text). This allows developers to use white space to format calculation expressions for easy reading. So the following two expressions are functionally identical:

```
If (fieldOne < 10;"less than 10";"not less than 10")

If (
   fieldOne < 10 ;
   "less than 10" ;
   "not less than 10"
)
```

You may insert comments into calculation expressions in two forms:

```
// this is a one-line comment, designated by two forward-slash characters

/* this is a multi-line comment designated in a block
by a beginning forward-slash-asterisk and
closed by an ending asterisk-forward-slash.
*/
```

To enter a tab character into an expression (either as literal text or simply to help with formatting), use Ctrl+Tab on Windows and Option+Tab on Mac OS.

Because a quotation mark character (") designates the beginning or ending of a literal text string, if you need to include a quotation mark within a text string, it must be "escaped" by preceding it with a backslash (\). For example:

```
Length ( "The boy exclaimed, \"Gee willikers!\"" )
```

FileMaker allows for a shorthand approach to entering conditional Boolean tests for non-null, non-zero field contents. The following two expressions are functionally identical:

```
Case ( fieldOne; "true"; "false" )

Case ( IsEmpty (text) or text = 0; "false"; "true" )
```

Note

We do not recommend this shortcut as a best practice. We tend to believe you should write explicit (and, yes, at times more verbose) code, leaving no room for ambiguity.

FileMaker allows for optional negative or default values in both the Case and If conditional functions. The following are all syntactically valid:

```
Case ( fieldOne = 1; "true" )

Case (
  fieldOne = 1; "one";
  fieldOne = 2; "two"
)


Case (
  fieldOne = 1; "one";
  fieldOne = 2; "two";
  "default"
)
```

We strongly recommend you always provide a default condition at the end of your Case statements, even if that condition should "never" occur. The next time your field shows a value of "never happens," you'll be glad you did. At the very least, use a null string ("") as the default so that you have explicitly defined how the function should resolve if none of the tests are true.

The Case function features a short-circuiting functionality whereby it evaluates conditional tests only until it reaches the first true test. In the following example, the third test will never be evaluated, thus improving system performance:

```
Case (
   1 = 2; "one is false";
   1 = 1; "one is true";
   2 = 2; "two is true"
)
```

Similarly, logical functions involving and and or also have short-circuiting behavior such that FileMaker stops evaluating an expression after it can determine whether the condition will be satisfied. For example, consider this statement:

```
If ( color = "blue" or color = "white", "something", "something else")
```

If the color is indeed blue, FileMaker does not need to evaluate whether the color is white. In a series of or tests, after one test has been determined to be true, that is enough for FileMaker to evaluate the entire expression as true.

Functions inserted from the function list in the upper right of the Specify Calculation dialog use curly braces ({}) to denote either optional or repeating elements.

Fields with repeating values can either be accessed using the GetRepetition( ) function or via a shorthand of placing an integer value between two brackets ([]). The following are functionally identical:

```
Quantity[2]

GetRepetition ( Quantity; 2 )
```

Although the default menu in the function list says All Functions by Name, it does not actually display all FileMaker functions (to the general bemusement of all). The Get and External functions are excluded from those listed. To view these functions, you need to choose to view the desired function group specifically by choosing Get or External from the menu of function groups.

When defining calculation fields, make careful note of the context option at the top of the Specify Calculation dialog. If the calculation's source table is represented by more than one table occurrence on the Relationships Graph, this menu becomes active. Calculation expressions involving related fields can vary depending on the context from which a calculation is evaluated.

Also when defining calculation fields, note the Calculation Result Is menu at the lower-left portion of the dialog. It is a common source of bugs for developers to forget to choose the correct data type for calculation results. (Returning a result as a number instead of a text type is a common and bewildering bug, at least the first time you see it.)

Turning off the Do Not Evaluate If All Referenced Fields Are Empty option ensures that no matter the condition of referenced fields, at least some value is returned. This capability is useful for cases involving, for example, financial data where it is often desirable to see an explicit zero listed in a field rather than for the field to be empty.

Calculation fields that reference related data, summary fields, other unindexed calculation fields, or globally stored fields cannot be indexed; otherwise, even though, by definition, a calculation field returns different results based on different input values, a calculation field can be indexed.

In a multiuser setting, most find operations on unstored calculations are performed on the host. The exceptions to this include unstored calcs that reference most Get functions, any Design function, or a related field from a table in a different file. In these situations, a find operation is performed on the client.

For several Get functions, values are sent from the client to the host when a client first connects and do not change on the host while the connection is active. In the event the item that the Get function references changes, the host returns the cached result instead of what is currently active. These functions are the following:

- Get(ApplicationLanguage)
- Get(DesktopPath)
- Get(DocumentsPath)
- Get(FileMakerPath)
- Get(PreferencesPath)
- Get(PrinterName)
- Get(SystemDrive)
- Get(SystemIPAddress)
- Get(SystemNICAddress)
- Get(TemporaryPath)
- Get(UserName)

CHAPTER 9

Calculation Signatures

Calculation functions in FileMaker Pro are organized into categories, which makes it easier to find and remember how to use them. This chapter not only presents the calculation signatures, which are readily available through the calculation dialog as well, but also the data type returned, which is also useful to know.

Aggregate Functions

Aggregate functions apply to a group of fields, a set of related records, or repeating fields (see Table 9.1).

Table 9.1 Aggregate Functions

Syntax	Data Type Returned
Average (field { ; field...})	Number
Count (field { ; field...})	Number
List (field { ; field...})	Text
Max (field { ; field...})	Text, number, date, time, timestamp
Min (field { ; field...})	Text, number, date, time, timestamp
StDev (field { ; field...})	Number
StDevP (field { ; field...})	Number
Sum (field { ; field...})	Number
Variance (field { ; field...})	Number
VarianceP (field { ; field...})	Number

Container Functions

You can use the Container functions to get information about a container's contents, as well as to create thumbnails of images in a container (see Table 9.2).

Table 9.2 Container Functions

Syntax	Data Type Returned
GetHeight (sourceField)	Number
GetThumbnail (sourceField ; fitToWidth ; fitToHeight)	Container
GetWidth (sourceField)	Number
VerifyContainer (sourceField)	Number

Date Functions

FileMaker Pro offers a range of date manipulation functions, including those for the Japanese calendar (see Table 9.3).

Table 9.3 Date Functions

Syntax	Data Type Returned
Date (month; day; year)	Date
Day (date)	Number
DayName (date)	Text
DayNameJ (date)	Text (Japanese)
DayOfWeek (date)	Number
DayOfYear (date)	Number
Month (date)	Number
MonthName (date)	Text
MonthNameJ (date)	Text (Japanese)
WeekOfYear (date)	Number
WeekOfYearFiscal (date; startingDay)	Number
Year (date)	Number
YearName (date; format)	Text (Japanese)

Design Functions

Design functions generally extract information about a database and are helpful in debugging or for advanced scripting (see Table 9.4).

Table 9.4 Design Functions

Syntax	Data Type Returned
DatabaseNames	Text
FieldBounds (fileName; layoutName; fieldName)	Text
FieldComment (fileName; fieldName)	Text
FieldIDs (fileName; layoutName)	Text

Table 9.4 Continued

Syntax	Data Type Returned
FieldNames (fileName; layout/tableName)	Text
FieldRepetitions (fileName; layoutName; fieldName)	Text
FieldStyle (fileName; layoutName; fieldName)	Text
FieldType (fileName; fieldName)	Text
GetNextSerialValue (fileName; fieldName)	Text
LayoutIDs (fileName)	Text
LayoutNames (fileName)	Text
LayoutObjectNames (filename ; layoutName)	Text
RelationInfo (fileName; tableOccurrence)	Text
ScriptIDs (fileName)	Text
ScriptNames (fileName)	Text
TableIDs (fileName)	Text
TableNames (fileName)	Text
ValueListIDs (fileName)	Text
ValueListItems (fileName; valueListName)	Text
ValueListNames (fileName)	Text
WindowNames { (fileName)}	Text

External Functions

External functions originate from installed plug-ins and vary widely based on the plug-ins used. When you access the External category of functions, you see a list of all the functions available from the currently installed plug-ins. There is also a function named External, which was used in previous versions of FileMaker to access plug-in functions, but it is not necessary with modern plug-ins.

Financial Functions

Financial functions assist with various specialized mortgage and interest calculations (see Table 9.5).

Table 9.5 Financial Functions

Syntax	Data Type Returned
FV (payment; interestRate; periods)	Number
NPV (payment; interestRate)	Number
PMT (principal; interestRate; term)	Number
PV (payment; interestRate; periods)	Number

Get Functions

Get functions generally provide information about a given user's current state, whether from within FileMaker Pro, from a computer, or from a given network (see Table 9.6).

Table 9.6 Get **Functions**

Syntax	Data Type Returned
Get (AccountExtendedPrivileges)	Text
Get (AccountName)	Text
Get (AccountPrivilegeSetName)	Text
Get (ActiveFieldContents)	Text, number, date, time, timestamp, container
Get (ActiveFieldName)	Text
Get (ActiveFieldTableName)	Text
Get (ActiveLayoutObjectName)	Text
Get (ActiveModifierKeys)	Number
Get (ActivePortalRowNumber)	Number
Get (ActiveRepetitionNumber)	Number
Get (ActiveSelectionSize)	Number
Get (ActiveSelectionStart)	Number
Get (AllowAbortState)	Number
Get (AllowFormattingBarState)	Number
Get (ApplicationLanguage)	Text
Get (ApplicationVersion)	Text
Get (CalculationRepetitionNumber)	Number
Get (ConnectionState)	Number
Get (CurrentDate)	Date
Get (CurrentExtendedPrivileges)	Text
Get (CurrentHostTimestamp)	Timestamp
Get (CurrentPrivilegeSetName)	Text
Get (CurrentTime)	Time
Get (CurrentTimestamp)	Timestamp
Get (CustomMenuSetName)	Text
Get (DesktopPath)	Text
Get (DocumentsPath)	Text
Get (DocumentsPathListing)	Text
Get (ErrorCaptureState)	Number
Get (FileMakerPath)	Text
Get (FileName)	Text
Get (FilePath)	Text
Get (FileSize)	Number

Table 9.6 Continued

Syntax	Data Type Returned
Get (FoundCount)	Number
Get (HighContrastColor)	Text
Get (HighContrastState)	Number
Get (HostApplicationVersion)	Text
Get (HostIPAddress)	Text
Get (HostName)	Text
Get (InstalledFMPlugins)	Text
Get (LastError)	Number
Get (LastMessageChoice)	Number
Get (LastODBCError)	Text
Get (LayoutAccess)	Number
Get (LayoutCount)	Number
Get (LayoutName)	Text
Get (LayoutNumber)	Number
Get (LayoutTableName)	Text
Get (LayoutViewState)	Number
Get (MultiUserState)	Number
Get (NetworkProtocol)	Text
Get (PageNumber)	Number
Get (PersistentID)	Text
Get (PreferencesPath)	Text
Get (PrinterName)	Text
Get (QuickFindText)	Text
Get (RecordAccess)	Number
Get (RecordID)	Number
Get (RecordModificationCount)	Number
Get (RecordNumber)	Number
Get (RecordOpenCount)	Number
Get (RecordOpenState)	Number
Get (RequestCount)	Number
Get (RequestOmitState)	Number
Get (ScreenDepth)	Number
Get (ScreenHeight)	Number
Get (ScreenWidth)	Number
Get (ScriptName)	Text
Get (ScriptParameter)	Text
Get (ScriptResult)	Text, number, date, time, timestamp, container
Get (SortState)	Number

Table 9.6 Continued

Syntax	Data Type Returned
Get (StatusAreaState)	Number
Get (SystemDrive)	Text
Get (SystemIPAddress)	Text
Get (SystemLanguage)	Text
Get (SystemNICAddress)	Text
Get (SystemPlatform)	Number
Get (SystemVersion)	Text
Get (TemporaryPath)	Text
Get (TextRulerVisible)	Number
Get (TotalRecordCount)	Number
Get (TriggerCurrentTabPanel)	Text
Get (TriggerKeystroke)	Text
Get (TriggerModifierKeys)	Number
Get (TriggerTargetTabPanel)	Text
Get (UserCount)	Number
Get (UserName)	Text
Get (UseSystemFormatsState)	Number
Get (UUID)	Text
Get (WindowContentHeight)	Number
Get (WindowContentWidth)	Number
Get (WindowDesktopHeight)	Number
Get (WindowDesktopWidth)	Number
Get (WindowHeight)	Number
Get (WindowLeft)	Number
Get (WindowMode)	Number
Get (WindowName)	Text
Get (WindowStyle)	Text
Get (WindowTop)	Number
Get (WindowVisible)	Number
Get (WindowWidth)	Number
Get (WindowZoomLevel)	Text

Logical Functions

The logical functions are a disparate collection of tools for performing conditional tests and evaluating expressions (see Table 9.7).

Table 9.7 Logical Functions

Syntax	Data Type Returned
Case (test1; result1 { ; test2; result2; defaultResult...})	Text, number, date, time, timestamp, container
Choose (test; result0 { ; result1; result2...})	Text, number, date, time, timestamp, container
Evaluate (expression { ; [field1; field2; ...]})	Text, number, date, time, timestamp, container
EvaluationError (expression)	Number
ExecuteSQL (sqlQuery ; fieldSeparator ; rowSeparator { ; arguments... }))	Text
GetAsBoolean (data)	Number
GetField (fieldName)	Text, number, date, time, timestamp, container
GetFieldName (field)	Text
GetLayoutObjectAttribute (objectName ; attributeName { ; repetitionNumber ; portalRowNumber})	Text
GetNthRecord (fieldName; recordNumber)	Text, number, date, time, timestamp, container
If (test; result1; result2)	Text, number, date, time, timestamp, container
IsEmpty (expression)	Number
IsValid (expression)	Number
IsValidExpression (expression)	Number
Let ({ [} var1=expression1 { ; var2=expression2 ...] } ; calculation)	Text, number, date, time, timestamp, container
Lookup (sourceField { ; failExpression })	Text, number, date, time, timestamp, container
LookupNext (sourceField; lower/higher Flag)	Text, number, date, time, timestamp, container
Self	Text, number, date, time, timestamp, container

Mobile Functions

New in FileMaker 12, the Mobile functions provide location services for FileMaker Go (see Table 9.8).

Table 9.8 Mobile Functions

Syntax	Data Type Returned
Location (accuracy {; timeout})	Text
LocationValues (accuracy {; timeout})	Text

Number Functions

Number functions perform various mathematical operations within FileMaker Pro (see Table 9.9).

Table 9.9 Number Functions

Syntax	Data Type Returned
Abs (number)	Number, time
Ceiling (number)	Number
Combination (setSize; numberOfChoices)	Number
Div (number; divisor)	Number
Exp (number)	Number
Factorial (number { ; numberOfFactors })	Number
Floor (number)	Number
Int (number)	Number
Lg (number)	Number
Ln (number)	Number
Log (number)	Number
Mod (number; divisor)	Number
Random	Number
Round (number; precision)	Number
SetPrecision (expression; precision)	Number
Sign (number)	Number
Sqrt (number)	Number
Truncate (number; precision)	Number

Repeating Functions

Repeating functions facilitate working with repeating fields within other calculations (see Table 9.10).

Table 9.10 Repeating Functions

Syntax	Data Type Returned
Extend (non-repeatingField)	Text, number, date, time, timestamp, container
GetRepetition (repeatingField; repetitionNumber)	Text, number, date, time, timestamp, container
Last (repeatingField)	Text, number, date, time, timestamp, container

Summary Function

There is only one function in the Summary category: GetSummary. It returns the value of a summary field when records are sorted by the specified break field. The function's signature is

GetSummary (summaryField; breakField)

Depending on the definition of the summary field, this function can return text, number, date, time, or timestamp data.

Text Functions

Text functions provide a means for investigating and manipulating text strings within FileMaker Pro (see Table 9.11).

Table 9.11 Text Functions

Syntax	Data Type Returned
Char (number)	Text
Code (text)	Number
Exact (originalText; comparisonText)	Number
Filter (textToFilter; filterText)	Text
FilterValues (textToFilter; filterValues)	Text
GetAsCSS (text)	Text
GetAsDate (text)	Date
GetAsNumber (text)	Number
GetAsSVG (text)	Text
GetAsText (data)	Text
GetAsTime (text)	Time
GetAsTimestamp (text)	Timestamp
GetAsURLEncoded (text)	Text
GetValue (listOfValues; valueNumber)	Text
Hiragana (text)	Text (Japanese)
KanaHankaku (text)	Text (Japanese)
KanaZenkaku (text)	Text (Japanese)
KanjiNumeral (text)	Text (Japanese)

Table 9.11 Continued

Syntax	Data Type Returned
Katakana (text)	Text (Japanese)
Left (text; numberOfCharacters)	Text
LeftValues (text; numberOfValues)	Text
LeftWords (text; numberOfWords)	Text
Length (text)	Number
Lower (text)	Text
Middle (text; startCharacter; numberOfCharacters)	Text
MiddleValues (text; startingValue; numberOfValues)	Text
MiddleWords (text; startingWord; numberOfWords)	Text
NumToJText (number; separator; characterType)	Text (Japanese)
PatternCount (text; searchString)	Number
Position (text; searchString; start; occurrence)	Number
Proper (text)	Text
Quote (text)	Text
Replace (text; start; numberOfCharacters; replacementText)	Text
Right (text; numberOfCharacters)	Text
RightValues (text; numberOfValues)	Text
RightWords (text; numberOfWords)	Text
RomanHankaku (text)	Text (Japanese)
RomanZenkaku (text)	Text (Japanese)
SerialIncrement (text; incrementBy)	Text
Substitute (text; searchString; replaceString)	Text
Trim (text)	Text
TrimAll (text; trimSpaces; trimType)	Text
Upper (text)	Text
ValueCount (text)	Number
WordCount (text)	Number

Text Formatting Functions

Text formatting functions provide a means to manipulate the actual formatting of data within text and number fields in FileMaker Pro (see Table 9.12).

Table 9.12 Text Formatting Functions

Syntax	Data Type Returned
RGB (red; green; blue)	Number
TextColor (text; RGB (red; green; blue))	Text, number
TextColorRemove (text { ; RGB (red; green; blue)})	Text, number
TextFont (text; fontName { ; fontScript })	Text, number
TextFontRemove (text { ; fontName; fontScript })	Text, number
TextFormatRemove (text)	Text, number
TextSize (text; fontSize)	Text, number
TextSizeRemove (text { ; sizeToRemove })	Text, number
TextStyleAdd (text; styles)	Text, number
TextStyleRemove (text; styles)	Text, number

Time Functions

Time functions provide a means of manipulating time data within FileMaker Pro (see Table 9.13).

Table 9.13 Time Functions

Syntax	Data Type Returned
Hour (time)	Number
Minute (time)	Number
Seconds (time)	Number
Time (hours; minutes; seconds)	Time

Timestamp Function

The Timestamp function generates a timestamp from a date and a time. Its signature is

```
Timestamp ( date ; time )
```

It returns a timestamp.

Trigonometric Functions

Trigonometric functions extend math and number functions within FileMaker Pro to trigonometry (see Table 9.14).

Table 9.14 Trigonometric Functions

Syntax	Data Type Returned
Acos (number)	Number
Asin (number)	Number
Atan (number)	Number
Cos (number)	Number
Degrees (number)	Number
Pi	Number
Radians (angleInDegrees)	Number
Sin (angleInRadians)	Number
Tan (angleInRadians)	Number

CHAPTER 10

Calculation Functions

Abs (number)

Data type returned: **Number, Time**

Category: **Number**

Parameters:

- **number**—Any expression that resolves to a numeric value.

Description:

Returns the absolute value of number; absolute value is always a positive number.

Examples:

Function	Results
Abs (-92)	Returns 92.
Abs (Get (SystemPlatform))	Returns 1 for Mac OS, 2 for Windows, and 3 for iOS.
Abs (RetailPrice - WholeSalePrice)	Returns the difference between the two prices, regardless of which one is larger.

Acos (number)

Data type returned: **Number**

Category: **Trigonometric**

Parameters:

- **number**—Any expression that resolves to a numeric value from –1 to 1.

Description:

The arc cosine of a number is the angle (measured in radians) whose cosine is the specified number. The range of values returned by the Acos function is 0 to Pi.

If Acos (x) = y, then Cos (y) = x.

Examples:

Function	Results
Acos (1)	Returns 0.
Acos (-1)	Returns 3.1415926535897931, which is Pi radians, or 180 degrees.
Acos (0)	Returns 1.5707963267948966, which is Pi/2 radians, or 90 degrees.

Asin (number)

Data type returned: **Number**

Category: **Trigonometric**

Parameters:

- **number**—Any expression that resolves to a numeric value from –1 to 1.

Description:

The arc sine of a number is the angle (measured in radians) whose sine is the specified number. The range of values returned by the Asin function is –(Pi/2) to Pi/2.

If Asin (x) = y, then Sin (y) = x.

Asin (x) = Asin (-x).

Examples:

Function	Results
Asin (0)	Returns 0.
Asin (1)	Returns 1.5707963267948966, which is Pi/2 radians, or 90 degrees.
Asin (Sqrt (2) / 2)	Returns .7853981633974485, which is Pi/4 radians, or 45 degrees.

Atan (Number)

Data type returned: **Number**

Category: **Trigonometric**

Parameters:

- **number**—Any expression that resolves to a numeric value.

Description:

The arc tangent of a number is the angle (measured in radians) whose tangent is the specified number. The range of values returned by the Atan function is –(Pi/2) to Pi/2.

If Atan (x) = y, then Tan (y) = x.

Atan (x) = Atan (-x).

Examples:

Function	Results
Atan (0)	Returns 0.
Atan (1)	Returns .7853981633974483, which is Pi/4 radians, or 45 degrees.

Average (field { ; field...})

Data type returned: **Number**

Category: **Aggregate**

Parameters:

- **field**—Any related field, repeating field, or set of nonrepeating fields that represent a collection of numbers. Parameters in curly braces { } are optional and may be repeated as needed, separated by a semicolon.

Description:

Returns a numeric value that is the arithmetic mean of all nonblank values in the set designated by the parameter list. The arithmetic mean of a set of numbers is the sum of the numbers divided by the size of the set. Blank values are not considered as part of the set.

The most common use of the Average function is to determine the average of the field values from a set of related records. Typically, therefore, the parameter is a related number field.

When the parameter list consists of two or more repeating fields, Average() generates a repeating field in which the corresponding repetitions from the specified fields are averaged separately. So, if a field Repeater1 has two values, 16 and 20, and another field, Repeater2, has two values, 14 and 25, Average (Repeater1; Repeater2) returns a repeating field with values 15 and 22.5.

Examples:

Function	Results
Average (6; 10 ; 11)	Returns 9.
Average (field1; field2; field3)	Returns 2 when field1 = 1, field2 = 2, and field3 = 3.
Average (repeatingField)	Returns 2 when repetition1 = 1, repetition2 = 2, and repetition3 = 3.
Average (repeatingField[1]; repeatingField[2]; repeatingField[3])	Returns 2 when repetition1 = 1, repetition2 = 2, and repetition3 = 3.
Average (Customer::InvoiceTotal)	Returns 450 when a customer has three related invoice records with invoice totals of 300, 500, and 550.

Case (test1; result1 { ; test2; result2; defaultResult...})

Data type returned: **Text, Number, Date, Time, Timestamp, Container**

Category: **Logical**

Parameters:

- **test(n)**—An expression that yields a Boolean result.
- **result(n)**—The value to return if the corresponding test is true.
- **defaultResult**—The value to return if all tests are false. Parameters in curly braces { } are optional and may be repeated as needed, separated by a semicolon.

Description:

Returns one of several possible results based on a series of tests.

Each test expression is evaluated in order, and when the first true expression (one that resolves to a Boolean 1) is found, the value specified in the result for that expression is returned. The function stops evaluating as soon as it finds a true test.

The default result at the end of the parameter list is optional. If none of the tests evaluate as true, the function returns the value specified for defaultResult. If no default result is specified, the Case function returns an "empty" result. If you believe that one of the tests in the Case should always be true, we recommend using an explicit default case, possibly with a value of "default" or "error" to assist in error trapping.

Consider using hard returns when writing long Case() statements to make them more readable, and indent lines with tabs, as shown in the following examples.

Examples:

Function	Results
Case (IsEmpty (Contact_Name); 1)	Returns 1 if the Contact_Name field is empty.

Note that a default value is not required, making the usage of Case() shorter than If().

```
Let ( lang = Get (SystemLanguage ) ;
  Case (
    lang = "English"; "Welcome";
    lang = "French"; "Bienvenue";
    lang = "Italian"; "Benvenuto";
    lang = "German"; "Willkommen";
    lang = "Swedish"; "Välkommen";
    lang = "Spanish "; "Bienvenido";
    lang = "Dutch"; "Welkom";
    lang = "Japanese"; "Irashaimasu" ;
     "Sorry... not sure of your language."    // default value
  )
```

) Returns a welcoming message in the language determined by the Get (SystemLanguage) function.

```
Case (
 SalesTotal < 10; .1;
 SalesTotal < 50; .2;
 SalesTotal < 100; .3;
 .35
)
```

Returns .1 when the value in the SalesTotal field is 5, and returns .2 when the value in the SalesTotal field is 12. Case() stops evaluating after it finds the first true test, so even if multiple tests are true (as when SalesTotal is, say, 5), the result is unambiguous. This "short-circuiting" capability can help with performance tuning. Put the tests that are most likely to return true near the beginning of a Case() function so that fewer expressions need to be evaluated.

Ceiling (number)

Data type returned: **Number**

Category: **Number**

Parameters:

- **number**—Any expression that resolves to a numeric value.

Description:

Returns number rounded up to the next integer.

One common use for the Ceiling function is finding out how many pages are required to print x items if y items fit on a page. The formula for this is Ceiling (x / y). For instance, if you have 16 items, and 5 can print per page, you need Ceiling (16 / 5) = Ceiling (3.2) = 4 pages. Analogously, if you needed to pack x Widgets into boxes, and you could pack y Widgets per box, the result of the formula Ceiling (x / y) would tell you how many boxes you'd need.

The Ceiling function is also useful for generating random numbers. For instance, to generate a random integer between 1 and 6 (the role of a die), you could use the formula Ceiling (Random * 6).

Examples:

Function	Results
Ceiling (1.05)	Returns 2.
Ceiling (-4.6)	Returns -4.
Ceiling (3)	Returns 3.

Char (number)

Data type returned: **Text**

Category: **Text**

Parameters:

- **number**—A number or expression that represents one or more Unicode code points.

Description:

Returns the character(s) represented by the Unicode code points in the parameter.

Unicode is a computing industry standard for encoding text characters; it contains more than 100,000 characters, representing most of the world's writing systems. Each character, or glyph, is represented by a unique numeric value. The Char and Code functions can be used to translate between a character's glyph and its numeric value.

If the number specified as the parameter contains more than five digits, each group of five digits (starting from the *right* side of the number!) is treated as a separate code point, and the function returns the string of characters represented by those code points.

The Char function is useful for inserting difficult-to-type characters into a calculation formula. For instance, Char (9) can be used to represent a tab character.

Examples:

Function	Results
Char (68)	Returns D.
Char (246)	Returns ö.
Char (0006500066)	Returns BA.

Choose (test; result0 { ; result1; result2...})

Data type returned: **Text**, **Number**, **Date**, **Time**, **Timestamp**, **Container**

Category: **Logical**

Parameters:

- **test**—An expression that returns a number greater than or equal to 0.
- **result(n)**—The value returned or the expression that is evaluated based on the result of the test. Parameters in curly braces { } are optional and may be repeated as needed, separated by a semicolon.

Description:

Returns one of the result values according to the integer value of test. FileMaker evaluates test to obtain an index number, which then is used to select the corresponding ordinal result.

The Choose function is a zero-based list. Choose (1; "a"; "b"; "c") returns "b".

Any fractional value of test is ignored (as opposed to rounded) when obtaining the index number. Choose (1.9; "a"; "b"; "c") returns "b".

If the index value returned by test exceeds the number of results available, the Choose function does not return any result; the field is blank as opposed to having a "?" in it. There is no way to define a default value to use when the index value exceeds the number of results available.

Examples:

Function	Results
Choose (DayOfWeek (Get (CurrentDate)); ""; "Sun"; "Mon"; "Tue"; "Wed"; "Thu"; "Fri"; "Sat")	Returns a three-letter day name abbreviation for today's date.
Choose ((Month (myDate)/ 3.1); "Q1"; "Q2"; "Q3"; "Q4")	Returns Q1 for the instance where myDate contains 2/1/2012.

Let ([
n = myNumber;
int = Int (n);
decimal = Mod (n; 1);
numberOfEighths = Round (decimal / .125; 0);
intDisplay = Case (Abs (int) > 0; int & Case
➥(Abs (decimal) > 0; " - "; ""); "");
fraction = Choose(numberOfEighths;
Floor (n);
intDisplay & "1/8";
intDisplay & "1/4";
intDisplay & "3/8";
intDisplay & "1/2";
intDisplay & "5/8";
intDisplay & "3/4";
intDisplay & "7/8";
Ceiling (n)
)
];
fraction
)
	This formula converts decimal values to fractional notation, rounded to the nearest eighth. Assume an input from a field (or parameter), myNumber. If myNumber contains 3.45, this function returns 3 – 1/2.

Code (text)

Data type returned: **Number**

Category: **Text**

Parameters:

- **text**—A string that contains one or more characters.

Description:

Returns the Unicode code point values of the characters in the parameter.

Unicode is a computing industry standard for encoding text characters; it contains more than 100,000 characters, representing most of the world's writing systems. Each character, or glyph, is represented by a unique numeric value. The Char and Code functions can be used to translate between a character's glyph and its numeric value.

The Code function is useful for detecting keystrokes, especially nonprinting ones (such as the Backspace key and the Escape key), in the OnObjectKeystroke and OnLayoutKeystroke script triggers. The Get (TriggerKeystroke) function returns the character typed by the user to activate the trigger; you often need use Code to convert this into a number for conditional tests.

Examples:

Function	Results
Code ("A")	Returns 65.
Code ("xyz")	Returns 1220012100120.
Case (Code (Get (TriggerKeystroke)) = 29 ; "Up" ; Code (Get (TriggerKeystroke)) = 31 ; "Down" ; Code (Get (TriggerKeystroke)) = 28 ; "Left" ; Code (Get (TriggerKeystroke)) = 30 ; "Right" ;)	Returns the text "Down" when the user activates a script trigger by pressing the down arrow key.

Combination (setSize; numberOfChoices)

Data type returned: **Number**

Category: **Number**

Parameters:

- **setSize**—Non-negative numeric value (or an expression that results in one).
- **numberOfChoices**—Non-negative numeric value (or an expression that results in one).

Description:

Returns the number of ways to uniquely choose numberOfChoices items from a set of size setSize.

The formula used to determine the Combination value is n! / (n-x)! * x!, where n = set size, x = number of choices.

The numbers returned by the Combination function are the coefficients of the binomial expansion series. Useful in statistics, combinatorics, and polynomial expansions, the values returned by this function are referred to as combination coefficients. They form Pascal's triangle.

$(x + y)^4 = 1x^4 + 4x^3y + 6x^2y^2 + 4xy^3 + 1y^4$

```
Combination ( 4; 0 ) = 1
Combination ( 4; 1 ) = 4
Combination ( 4; 2 ) = 6
Combination ( 4; 3 ) = 4
Combination ( 4; 4 ) = 1
```

Examples:

Function	Results
Combination (4; 2)	Returns 6, reflecting that there are six ways of selecting two items from a set of four items. Given set { A, B, C, D}, these subsets would be { AB, AC, AD, BC, BD, CD}.
Combination (x; 0)	Returns 1 for any x, representing the empty set.
Combination (x; x)	Returns 1 for any x.
(13 * 12 * Combination (4; 2) * Combination (4; 3)) / Combination (52; 5)	Returns 0.00144057..., which is the probability of being dealt a full house in five-card poker (less than a 1% chance!).

Cos (number)

Data type returned: **Number**

Category: **Trigonometric**

Parameters:

- **number**—Any expression that resolves to a numeric value that represents an angle measured in radians.

Description:

Returns the cosine of the angle represented by the value of the parameter (measured in radians, not degrees). Cos is a periodic function with a range from –1 to 1.

In any right triangle, the cosine of the two nonright angles can be obtained by dividing the length of the side adjacent to the angle by the length of the hypotenuse.

You can convert an angle measured in degrees into radians by using the Radians function or by multiplying the value by Pi/180. One radian is slightly more than 57 degrees.

Examples:

Function	Results
Cos (0)	Returns 0.
Cos (Pi / 4)	Returns .707106781... (which is 1/Sqrt (2)).
Cos (Radians (60))	Returns .5.

Count (field { ; field...})

Data type returned: **Number**

Category: **Aggregate**

Parameters:

- **field**—Any related field, repeating field, or set of nonrepeating fields; or an expression that returns a field, repeating field, or set of nonrepeating fields. Parameters in curly braces { } are optional and may be repeated as needed, separated by a semicolon.

Description:

Returns a count of the fields (or repetitions, in the case of repeating fields) in the parameter list that contains nonblank values.

The most common use of the Count function is to determine the number of related records. Typically, therefore, the parameter is a related field guaranteed not to be empty, such as the table's primary key.

When the parameter list consists of two or more repeating fields, Count() returns a repeating field in which the corresponding repetitions from the specified fields are counted separately. So if a field Repeater1 has three values—16, 20, and 24—and another field, Repeater2, has two values,—14 and 25—Count (Repeater1; Repeater2) returns a repeating field with values 2, 2, and 1.

Beginning with FileMaker Pro 8, the Count function also takes portal and field context into account. For example, in a scenario in which a Customer table occurrence is related one-to-many with an Invoice table occurrence that is then related one-to-many to a LineItem table occurrence, evaluating a Count function from Customer to LineItem yields all LineItem records for the current Customer record if the user's context is on the Customer table occurrence. But if the user's context is on the Invoice table occurrence (if a user clicks in an Invoice portal row, say, or a script navigates into the portal using a Go to Field script step), Count (LineItem::field) returns a count of just those line items related to the currently selected invoice. Given that calculation fields explicitly specify their evaluation context, this issue is most likely to arise in scripting.

Examples:

Function	Results
Count (field1; field2; field3)	Returns 2 when field1 and field2 contain valid values and field3 is empty.
Count (repeatingField)	Returns 2 when repetitions 1 and 2 contain valid values, and repetition 3 is empty.
Count (InvoiceItem::InvoiceID)	Returns 2 when the current record is related to two InvoiceItem records.

DatabaseNames

Data type returned: **Text**

Category: **Design**

Parameters: **None**

Description:

Generates a carriage return–delimited list of currently open databases (filenames), whether open as a client of another machine or open locally. The file extension (.fmp12) is *not* returned as part of the filename.

Use caution when checking for hard-coded strings in calculations. If someone renames a file, any calculation containing the old value no longer behaves as before. Get (FileName) can be used in conjunction with a startup script to see whether a filename has been changed, and developers might want to consider establishing a centrally controlled custom function or variable for such checks.

Examples:

Function	Results
DatabaseNames	In a circumstance in which three files are open, Customer, Invoice, and Invoice Line Item, DatabaseNames returns Customer Invoice Invoice Line Item
ValueCount (FilterValues (DatabaseNames; "Customer"))	Returns 1 if the Customer database is open.

Date (month; day; year)

Data type returned: **Date**

Category: **Date**

Parameters:

- **month**—The month of the year (a number from 1 to 12).
- **day**—The day of the month (a number from 1 to 31).
- **year**—The year (four digits between 0001 and 4000). The year parameter should be passed as a four-digit number; FileMaker does *not* infer or prepend a century (that is, 1/10/05 = January 10, 0005).

Note that regardless of your system settings, this function requires that its parameters be listed strictly in order: month, day, year. Localizations settings do not apply.

Description:

Returns a valid date of data type Date represented by the three parameters.

Values for month and day outside normal ranges are interpreted correctly. For instance, a month value of 13 returns a date in January of the following year. A day value of 0 returns the last day of the preceding month.

Parameters can be calculation expressions or fields; as long as the final result is valid, the Date function works correctly. Dates are stored internally as numbers (a unit of "1" represents one day); whole number math can be done on dates.

When returning dates as the result of calculation fields, be sure that you specify a calculation result of Date. If you were to define a field as Date (1; 1; 2000) and were to set the calculation result as Number, you would see 730120 as the calculation value. Internally, FileMaker stores dates as the number of days since January 1, 0001, and that internal representation is returned if you incorrectly specify the return data type.

Examples:

Function	Results
Date (1; 1; 2000)	Returns January 1, 2000 (formatting is determined on the layout and by system preferences).
Date (1; 1; 2000) - 1	Returns December 31, 1999.
Date (Month (Get (CurrentDate)); 1; Year (Get (CurrentDate)))	Returns the date of the 1st of the current month; if today were August 12, 1965, August 1, 1965 would be returned.
Date (pickMonth; 1; Year (Get (CurrentDate)))	Returns the date of the first of a month specified by the value in the field pickMonth.

Day (date)

Data type returned: **Number**

Category: **Date**

Parameters:

- **date**—Any valid date (1/1/0001–12/31/4000), expression that returns a date, or field that contains a date.

Description:

Returns the day of month (1–31) for any valid date.

Examples:

Function	Results
Day ("1/15/2000")	Returns 15.
Day (Get (CurrentDate))	Returns the day of the month for today.
Day (Get (CurrentDate) - 90)	Returns the day number for the date 90 days before today, which might not be the same as today's day number.

DayName (date)

Data type returned: **Text**

Category: **Date**

Parameters:

- **date**—Any valid date (1/1/0001–12/31/4000), expression that returns a date, or field that contains a date. The parameter can also be the numeric representation of a date (1–1460970).

Description:

Returns a text string containing the name of a weekday for any valid date (1/1/0001–12/31/4000).

Note that the year is optional. DayName ("12/1") returns the day name for December 1st in the current year.

Examples:

Function	Results
DayName ("8/20/2005")	Returns Saturday.
DayName (dateField)	Returns the day of week for the date stored in the field dateField.
DayName (Get (CurrentDate) - 30)	Returns the day name for the date 30 days prior to today.

DayNameJ (date)

Data type returned: **Text (Japanese)**

Category: **Date**

Parameters:

- **date**—Any calendar date.

Description:

Returns a text string in Japanese that is the full name of the weekday for date.

To avoid errors when using dates, always use four-digit years. FileMaker does not infer or prepend a century on two-digit dates (1/10/05 = January 10, 0005).

Examples:

Function	Results
DayNameJ (Date (11; 6; 2012))	Returns Kayoubi in whatever font/display preference a user's system supports.

DayOfWeek (date)

Data type returned: **Number**

Category: **Date**

Parameters:

- **date**—Any valid date (1/1/0001–12/31/4000), expression that returns a date, or field that contains a date. The parameter can also be the numeric representation of a date (1–1460970).

Description:

Returns a number from 1 to 7, representing the day of the week (Sunday = 1, ... Saturday = 7) for any valid date (1/1/0001–12/31/4000).

DayOfWeek can be used to perform conditional tests on days of the week without concern for localization issues. The number returned is always the same regardless of what language version of FileMaker Pro the user is using. The number value returned by DayOfWeek can also be used in mathematical calculations.

Note that the year is optional. DayOfWeek ("12/1") returns the appropriate integer for December 1st in the current year.

Examples:

Function	Results
DayOfWeek ("11/18/2011")	Returns 6, which is Friday.
DayOfWeek (dateField)	Returns the day of week for the date stored in the field dateField.
DayOfWeek (Date (12; 25; Year (Get (CurrentDate))))	Returns the day number on which Christmas falls this year.

DayOfYear (date)

Data type returned: **Number**

Category: **Date**

Parameters:

- **date**—Any valid date (1/1/0001–12/31/4000), expression that returns a date, or field that contains a date. The parameter can also be the numeric representation of a date (1–1460970).

Description:

Returns a number representing the day of year (1–366) for any valid date (1/1/0001–12/31/4000).

You can use the DayOfYear function to check whether a particular year is a leap year. Given a field Year, the formula DayOfYear (Date (12; 31; Year)) returns 366 if Year is a leap year and 365 if it isn't.

Note that the year is optional. DayOfYear ("12/1") returns the appropriate integer for December 1st in the current year.

Examples:

Function	Results
DayOfYear ("12/31/2000")	Returns 366 (leap year).
DayOfYear ("12/31/2001")	Returns 365 (non–leap year).
DayOfYear ("1/24/2012")	Returns 24.
DayOfYear (dateField)	Returns the day number for the date stored in dateField.
DayOfYear (Get (CurrentDate) + 30)	Returns the day of year for a date 30 days from now.

Degrees (number)

Data type returned: **Number**

Category: **Trigonometric**

Parameters:

- **number**—A number representing an angle measured in radians.

Description:

Converts an angle measured in radians to its equivalent in degrees. There are 2*Pi radians in 360°, so 1 radian is just over 57°.

Another way to convert radians to degrees is to multiply by 180/Pi.

Examples:

Function	Results
Degrees (0)	Returns 0.
Degrees (Pi / 4)	Returns 45.
Degrees (2 * Pi)	Returns 360.
Degrees (4 * Pi)	Returns 720.
Degrees (-Pi / 2)	Returns -90.

Div (number; divisor)

Data type returned: **Number**

Category: **Number**

Parameters:

- **number**—Any number or expression that resolves to a numeric value.
- **divisor**—Any number or expression that resolves to a numeric value.

Description:

Returns the whole number portion of the result of dividing the numerator number by the denominator divisor. For instance, if you divide 10 by 4, the result is 2.5. The Div function returns 2, which is the portion to left of the decimal point.

The Div function is equivalent to Floor (number / divisor).

To obtain the remainder when a numerator is divided by denominator, use the Mod function.

Examples:

Function	Results
Div (30; 4)	Returns 7 (because 30/4 is 7, remainder 2).
Div (51; 8)	Returns 6 (because 51/8 is 6, remainder 3).
Div (Abs (date2 - date1) ; 7) & " weeks, " & Mod (Abs (date2 - date1) ; 7) & " days"	Returns 5 weeks, 2 days if there are 37 days between date1 and date2.
Div (eggCount ; 12)	Returns the number of full egg cartons (a dozen eggs to a carton) that would result from packing eggCount eggs.

Evaluate (expression { ; [field1; field2; ...]})

Data type returned: **Text, Number, Date, Time, Timestamp, Container**

Category: **Logical**

Parameters:

- **expression**—Any valid calculation formula, field containing a valid formula, or expression returning a valid formula.
- **field(n)**—A list of optional fields that can then serve to trigger a reevaluation; the expression reevaluates when any of the specified fields are updated. Parameters in curly braces { } are optional. The optional field list must be enclosed by square brackets when there are multiple parameters.

Description:

Returns the results obtained by evaluating expression.

The optional second parameter is a list of fields on which the calculation becomes dependent. When any of those fields are modified, the Evaluate function reevaluates the expression specified by the first parameter.

The Evaluate function expects that the first parameter passed to it is a string that contains a formula of some sort. If you are passing a literal string, as in the fourth of the following examples, using the Quote function ensures that any quotation marks in the formula itself are properly encoded. If the first parameter is a field name or an expression, that field or expression is expected to return a formula, which the Evaluate function then evaluates. In a nutshell, if the first parameter is not surrounded by quotation marks, the result of whatever field or expression is provided is evaluated.

Note that the execution of the expression does occur; in other words, do not think of Evaluate as a "testing function" making use of its own memory space. If your expression modifies a global or local variable (using the Let function), any applicable changes are applied. If you need a calculation "scratch pad," consider using the Evaluate Now function of the FileMaker Advanced Data Viewer—although there again, any "side effect" modifications of variables occur "for real," a good example of why modifying variables within calculations can be a questionable practice.

Examples:

Function	Results
Evaluate (MyFormula)	Returns 8 if MyFormula contains the string 5+3.
Evaluate (MyFormula)	Returns 4 if MyFormula contains the string Length (FirstName) and FirstName contains "Fred".
Evaluate ("MyFormula")	Returns a text string, 5+3 if MyFormula contains the string 5+3.
Evaluate (Quote ("The comment field was last updated on " & Get (CurrentTimeStamp) & " by " & Get (AccountName)); CommentField)	Returns a string containing information about the date and user who last modified the CommentField. Note: Without the Quote function, the quotation marks within the formula need to be commented out, as follows: Evaluate ("\"The comment field was last updated on \" & Get (CurrentTimeStamp) & \" by \" & Get (AccountName)"; Name)

EvaluationError (expression)

Data type returned: **Number**

Category: **Logical**

Parameters:

- **expression**—Any FileMaker calculation formula.

Description:

Returns whatever error code an expression would generate if executed. If the expression executes properly, a 0 (no error) is returned.

Note that the expression is executed if it is syntactically correct. If your expression manipulates local or global variables, they are affected by the EvaluationError check. Note also that two kinds of errors are returned: syntax errors, for which the expression cannot be executed (and will not be executed by EvaluationError), and runtime errors, for which the expression is valid, but, for example, a field or record may be locked or missing.

Important: You must use the EvaluationError function in conjunction with the Evaluate function to return any syntax errors.

Examples:

Function	Results
EvaluationError (Evaluate ("Length (ProductCode)")	Returns error 102 (field missing) if there is no field name ProductCode.
EvaluationError (Evaluate ("Case (1 = 1)"))	Returns error 1201 (too few parameters).
EvaluationError ("Case (1 = 1)")	Returns error 0 because there were no runtime errors. If you want to ensure you always get error codes, including this syntax error, be sure to use the nested Evaluate function.

Exact (originalText; comparisonText)

Data type returned: **Number**

Category: **Text**

Parameters:

- **originalText**—Any text expression, text field, or container field.
- **comparisonText**—Any text expression, text field, or container field.

Description:

Compares the contents of any two text expressions or container fields. This function is case sensitive. If the values of the parameters are identical, the result is 1 (True); otherwise, the result is 0 (False). For container fields, the data not only must be the same, but also must be stored in the same manner (either embedded or stored by file reference). Note that for container fields the text representations of the file references are being compared.

Remember that Exact considers the case of the two strings, whereas the equals operator (=) does not. If you need to compare two values in a conditional test, consider using If (Exact (A; B); . . . instead of If (A = B; . . ..

Examples:

Function	Results
Exact ("Smith"; "smith")	Returns 0 (False).
Exact (Proper (Salutation); Salutation)	Returns 1 if the contents of the Salutation field begin with initial caps.
Exact (Zip_Lookup::City_Name; City_Name)	Returns 1 if the value of City_Name is exactly the same as the one stored in a related ZIP code table.

ExecuteSQL (sqlQuery ; fieldSeparator ; rowSeparator { ; arguments... })

Data type returned: **Text**

Category: **Logical**

Parameters:

- **sqlQuery**—A SQL query statement.
- **fieldSeparator**—The character string to use as a field separator in the result. If this parameter is left blank, the separator is a comma.
- **rowSeparator**—The character string to use as a row separator in the result. If this parameter is left blank, the separator is a carriage return.
- **arguments**—One or more expressions that are evaluated and substituted for dynamic parameters used in the query statement.

Description:

Returns the results of executing a SQL query against a table occurrence within a FileMaker Pro database.

ExecuteSQL is a powerful and complex function introduced in FileMaker Pro 12. It allows you to perform a SELECT command (no other SQL commands are supported) against data contained in a FileMaker Pro database.

The FROM clause of the SELECT statement should reference a table occurrence from the current file's Relationships Graph. This enables ExecuteSQL to query both local tables as well as external data sources. However, ExecuteSQL does not recognize relationships created in FileMaker Pro, which gives you great flexibility in creating joins in the SELECT statement that do not exist on the graph.

To avoid security vulnerabilities through injection attacks, ExecuteSQL enables you to use a question mark to reference a dynamic parameter, which is then supplied by the arguments parameter. Any number of dynamic parameters can be used; they are replaced by the arguments in the order you list them.

The second and third parameters enable you to specify the delimiters used to separate fields and records in the result set. By default, the delimiters are a comma and carriage return, respectively, but because both characters may appear in field data, you might want to use a different character (or characters) as the delimiter.

Be aware that there are many reserved words in SQL and you might have issues if you reference fields or table occurrences named the same as one of them. Similarly, you will have issues if names begin with an underscore or contain a period. Put double quotation marks around the field or table occurrence name to remedy these issues. Use single quotation marks around literal text strings.

ExecuteSQL returns data and time data in Unicode/SQL format, not in the locale of the operating system or the file. Dates are formatted as YYYY-MM-DD.

If you supply an invalid query, ExecuteSQL returns ?.

Examples:

Function	Results
ExecuteSQL ("SELECT count (*) FROM \"Order\" WHERE Status='active'" ; ""; "")	Returns 52, if there are 52 records in the Order table where the Status field is active.
ExecuteSQL ("SELECT DISTINCT (State) FROM Customer" ; ""; "")	Returns a list of the unique values in the State field from the Customer table.
ExecuteSQL ("SELECT OrderDate, CustomerID, Amount FROM \"Order\" WHERE OrderDate >= Date '2012-01-01' ORDER BY OrderDate" ; ""; "")	Returns a list of orders placed since January 1, 2012, sorted by OrderDate. The results might appear as follows: 2012-01-02,32,379.43 2012-02-06,47,2049.87
ExecuteSQL ("SELECT o.YearMonth, sum(o.Amount) FROM \"orderTO\" o JOIN customer c ON c.\"__kp_CustomerID\" = o.\"_kf_CustomerID\" WHERE o.\" _kf_CustomerID\" = ? and o.OrderDate>? and o.OrderDate <? GROUP BY o.YearMonth" ; "|" ; "¶" ; Customer::__kp_CustomerID; Customer::ReportStartDate; Customer::ReportEndDate)	This complex SQL query could be used from the context of a customer record to find all of that customer's orders in a specified data range and summarize the results by month. Note the use of the three dynamic parameters to specify query criteria. The results might appear as follows: 2012-04|31530 2012-05|9918 2012-06|26541

Exp (number)

Data type returned: **Number**

Category: **Number**

Parameters:

- **number**—Any expression that resolves to a numeric value.

Description:

Returns the value of the constant *e* raised to the power of number. The Exp function is the inverse of the Ln function.

To return the value of the constant *e* itself, use Exp (1), which returns 2.7182818284590452. Note: You can use the SetPrecision function to return *e* with up to 400 digits of precision!

Examples:

Function	Results
Round (Exp (5) ; 3)	Returns 148.413.
Exp (Ln (5))	Returns 5.

Extend (non-repeatingField)

Data type returned: **Text, Number, Date, Time, Timestamp, Container**

Category: **Repeating**

Parameters:

- **non-repeatingField**—Any nonrepeating field (a field defined to contain only one value).

Description:

Allows a value in non-repeatingField to be used in every repetition in a calculation defined to have a repeating result. If you do not use the Extend function, only the first repetition of a repeating calculation field properly references the value in non-repeatingField.

Examples:

Given a number field RepCommission, defined to hold three repetitions, a nonrepeating number field (SalePrice), and repeating calculation field (SalesCommission), defined as follows:

```
Round ( RepCommision * Extend ( SalePrice ); 2 )
```

RepCommission	SalePrice	SalesCommission
.10	18.00	1.80
.12		2.16
.15		2.40

If you do not use the Extend function, only the first repetition of SalesCommission returns the correct value.

External (nameOfFunction; parameter)

Data type returned: **Depends on the external function**

Category: **External**

Parameters:

- **nameOfFunction**—The name of the external function being called.
- **parameter**—The parameter that is being passed to the external function.

Description:

Calls a function defined within a plug-in created for versions of FileMaker Pro prior to 7. A plug-in must be installed (located in the Extensions folder) and enabled (under the Plug-Ins tab of Preferences) for you to have access to its functions.

The function name and parameter syntax for an external function are defined by the plug-in developer. When calling external plug-ins, be sure to use the exact syntax specified in the documentation for the plug-in. The external function parameter can generally be passed as a field, as long as the contents of the field conform to the requirements set forth by the plug-in developer. Because only a single parameter may be passed to a function, parameters often consist of delimited lists of data, which are then parsed and interpreted inside the plug-in.

The External function syntax is not used by plug-ins created for FileMaker Pro 7 and later. Rather, the plug-in's functions have the same syntax and appearance as any other FileMaker calculation function; the function name and parameters are defined by the plug-in developer.

Examples:

```
External ( "myPlugin"; "param1|param2|param3" )
External ( "myPlugin"; myParamField )
```

Factorial (number { ; numberOfFactors })

Data type returned: **Number**

Category: **Number**

Parameters:

- **number**—Any expression that resolves to a positive integer.
- **numberOfFactors**—Any expression that resolves to a positive integer, representing how many factors to include in the factorial multiplication. Parameters in curly braces { } are optional.

Description:

Returns the factorial of number, stopping either at 1 or stopping after the optional numberOfFactors. The factorial of a number *n* is defined as n * (n-1) * (n-2) * (n-3)...*1. Factorials are useful in statistics and combinatorics. In mathematics, factorials are usually represented by an exclamation mark: 4! = Factorial (4) = 4 * 3 * 2 * 1 = 24.

One application of factorials is to determine how many unique ways a set of objects can be ordered. For instance, a set of three objects {A, B, C} can be ordered 3! = 6 ways: {ABC, ACB, BAC, BCA, CAB, CBA} .

Examples:

Function	Results
Factorial (3)	Returns 6 (which is 3 * 2 * 1).
Factorial (10; 3)	Returns 720 (which is 10 * 9 * 8).

FieldBounds (fileName; layoutName; fieldName)

Data type returned: **Text**

Category: **Design**

Parameters:

- **fileName**—Name of the file where the field resides.
- **layoutName**—Name of the layout where the field resides.
- **fieldName**—Name of a field on the specified layout.

Description:

Returns the physical position and rotation of a field that is described by the parameters. Note that the parameters are text and must either be expressions or be enclosed in quotation marks. Results are returned as a space-delimited text string in the form of "Left Top Right Bottom Rotation". The first four of these values represent the distance, in points, from either the left margin of the layout (in the case of Left and Right) or the top margin (in the case of Top and Right). The Rotation value is 0, 90, 180, or 270, depending on the field's orientation on the layout.

The returned values are delimited by spaces; the MiddleWords function can easily be used to parse them.

Be aware that changing the name of a file, layout, or field might cause literal references to them to be broken in functions that use FieldBounds.

The field name that is passed to FieldBounds must be the name from the Manage Database dialog (not the field label). Related fields must be referenced by a fully qualified field name (for example, TableOccurrenceName::FieldName).

Examples:

Function	Results
FieldBounds (myFile; myLayout; myField)	Might return 444 84 697 98 0.
FieldBounds (Get (FileName); Get (LayoutName); "InvoiceDate")	Returns the position and rotation of the InvoiceDate field on the current layout of the current file.

FieldComment (fileName; fieldName)

Data type returned: **Text**

Category: **Design**

Parameters:

- **fileName**—The name of an open file where the field is located.
- **fieldName**—The name of the field for which to return comments.

Description:

Returns the contents of any comment that has been entered in the Manage Database dialog for the specified field. The syntax TableOccurrenceName::fieldName is required to reference fields outside the current table context. (The safest approach is to use this method in all cases.)

FieldComment is useful for documenting a database. Care must be taken, however, because literal references to fields can be broken when file, table, or field names are changed. FieldNames and TableNames can be used to dynamically investigate all field names and load the results from FieldComment into tables for browsing.

A field comment may contain a maximum of 30,000 characters, though it's doubtful such a large comment would constitute a sound development practice.

Examples:

Function	Results
FieldComment (Get (FileName); "Contacts::FirstName")	Returns the comment, if any, for the FirstName field as it appears in the table definition.

FieldIDs (fileName; layoutName)

Data type returned: **Text**

Category: **Design**

Parameters:

- **fileName**—The name of an open FileMaker Pro database.
- **layoutName**—The name of the layout from which to return field IDs.

Description:

Returns a list of the internal FileMaker field IDs for all fields on layoutName in fileName, separated by carriage returns. Fields outside the current table context are returned as TableID::RelatedFieldID. If layoutName is empty, the field IDs of the first table created (the "default" table) are returned.

Field IDs are returned in the stacking order of the fields on the layout, from back to front.

Calls to the FieldIDs function can be broken when file and layout names are changed. Field IDs are assigned by FileMaker and cannot be changed. We do not recommend using Field IDs when other means exist to accomplish your needs.

Examples:

Function	Results
FieldIDs (Get (FileName) ; Get (LayoutName))	Returns a list of the field IDs of all the field objects on the current layout.
FieldIDs ("Invoices"; "List View")	Returns IDs of all fields, including related fields, on the List View layout in the Invoices file. In this case the returned data might be: 3 4 8::12

The last entry represents a field with an ID of 12 from a table with an ID of 8.

FieldNames (fileName; layout/tableName)

Data type returned: **Text**

Category: **Design**

Parameters:

- **fileName**—The name of an open FileMaker Pro database.
- **layout/tableName**—The name of the layout or table occurrence to reference.

Description:

Returns a carriage return–delimited list of field names.

When a table occurrence name is specified as the second parameter (and is not also serving as a layout name), all fields from the base table associated with that table occurrence are returned. If a layout has the same name as a table occurrence, FileMaker turns first to the layout in question and returns only those fields that have been placed on that layout.

When a list of fields in a table is returned, the results are ordered according to their creation order. When the names of the fields on a particular layout are returned, the results are ordered according to the stacking order of the fields, from back to front. If an object appears on a layout more than once, it appears multiple times in the result list. Related fields appear as TableOccurrenceName::FieldName.

If the fileName parameter is left empty, FieldNames returns results from the current file.

Examples:

Function	Results
FieldNames (Get (FileName); "Customers")	Returns a list of fields found in the table named Customers in the current database (assuming there isn't a layout named "Customers").

FieldRepetitions (fileName; layoutName; fieldName)

Data type returned: **Text**

Category: **Design**

Parameters:

- **fileName**—The name of an open file where the field to be referenced is located.
- **layoutName**—The name of the layout where the field to be referenced is located.
- **fieldName**—The name of the field for which to return repetition information.

Description:

Returns a space-delimited text string that indicates the number of repetitions and orientation of the field in question. Note that you must pass a layout name. (A table name does not work.) The data is returned in the format "NumRepetitions Orientation." The orientation is either "vertical" or "horizontal."

The LeftWords and RightWords functions can be used to extract either component of the result.

If literal names of objects are used, calls to the function might be broken when file or object names are changed. Functions such as Get (FileName), LayoutNames, and FieldNames can be used to dynamically return information about a database. Also remember that only the number of repetitions that appear on the layout is returned, not the number of repetitions defined in the Manage Database dialog. Use FieldType to return the number of repetitions specified in the table schema itself.

If the fileName parameter is left empty, FieldRepetitions returns results from the current file.

Examples:

Function	Results
FieldRepetitions (Get (FileName) ; "Invoice_Detail"; "Payment_History")	Might return a string such as 10 vertical.
LeftWords (FieldRepetitions ("" ; Get (LayoutName) ; "myField") ; 1)	Returns just the number of repetitions (without the orientation) of a field named myField on the current layout of the current file.

FieldStyle (fileName; layoutName; fieldName)

Data type returned: **Text**

Category: **Design**

Parameters:

- **fileName**—The name of an open file where the field is located.
- **layoutName**—The name of the layout where the field is used.
- **fieldName**—The name of the field for which to return results.

Description:

Returns a space-delimited string indicating the field style and any associated value list. The data is returned in the format "Style { ValueListName }." The field styles are

Standard
Scrolling
Popuplist
Popupmenu
Checkbox
RadioButton
Calendar

Calls to FieldStyle that rely on literal object names might be broken if file, layout, or field names are changed. If the fileName parameter is left empty, FieldStyle returns results from the current file.

Examples:

Function	Results
FieldStyle (Get (FileName); "Invoice_Detail"; "Notes")	Returns Scrolling for a notes field that has scrollbars turned on.
FieldStyle (Get (FileName); "Invoice_Detail"; "Paid")	Might return RadioButton Yes_No for a field formatted as a radio button that uses a value list called Yes_No.
Let ([style = FieldStyle (""; "Invoice_Detail"; "ProductID") ; count = WordCount (style)]; RightWords (style ; count - 1))	Returns just the name of the value list associated with the ProductID field on the Invoice_Detail layout of the current file. Because value list names can contain spaces, you need to count the number of words returned by FieldStyle in order to parse just the value list name from the result.

FieldType (fileName; fieldName)

Data type returned: **Text**

Category: **Design**

Parameters:

- **fileName**—The name of an open file where the field is located.
- **fieldName**—The name of the field for which to return results.

Description:

Returns a space-delimited string indicating the field type of the field specified by fieldName. There are four components to the string, each of which can contain several possible values. The possible values for each item are the following:

Item 1: Standard, StoredCalc, Summary, UnstoredCalc, External(Secure), External(Open), or Global

Item 2: Text, Number, Date, Time, Timestamp, or Container

Item 3: Indexed or Unindexed

Item 4: Number of repetitions (1 for a nonrepeating field)

You must specify fieldName as TableOccurrence::Field when referencing fields in tables outside the current table context. If you leave the fileName parameter empty, FieldType returns results from the current file.

Examples:

Function	Results
FieldType (Get (FileName); "Contacts::ContactID")	Might return a string that looks like this: Standard Number Indexed 1.
FieldType (""; "Contacts::gTempName")	Might return a string that looks like this: Global Text Unindexed 1.

Filter (textToFilter; filterText)

Data type returned: **Text**

Category: **Text**

Parameters:

- **textToFilter**—Any expression that resolves to a text string.
- **filterText**—A set of characters to preserve within the specified textToFilter.

Description:

Strips from textToFilter all the characters not explicitly listed in filterText. All remaining characters are returned in the order in which they exist in textToFilter, including duplicates. If filterText doesn't have any characters, an empty string is returned, as opposed to a question mark. The Filter function is case sensitive.

The Filter function can be used to ensure that users have entered valid characters in a field. The filterText parameter should contain any valid characters; the order of the characters within filterText is not important.

Examples:

Function	Results
Filter ("ab123"; "abc")	Returns ab.
Filter (PhoneNumber; "0123456789")	Returns the contents of the PhoneNumber field, stripped of any non-numeric characters.

FilterValues (textToFilter; filterValues)

Data type returned: **Text**

Category: **Text**

Parameters:

- **textToFilter**—An expression that generates a return-delimited text string.
- **filterValues**—An expression that generates a return-delimited text string representing values that you want to preserve within the specified textToFilter.

Description:

Produces a return-delimited list of items in textToFilter that are included among the specified filterValues. With the exception of case, to be included in the returned list, an item in textToFilter must exactly match an item in filterValues. Another way of thinking of FilterValues is as the intersection, or overlap, of two return-delimited lists.

Values are returned in the order they appear in textToFilter. If filterValues is an empty string, or if no items in textToFilter are contained in the filterValues list, an empty string is returned.

FilterValues can be used to determine whether a particular item is contained in a return-delimited list of items. For instance, the WindowNames function produces a return-delimited list of window names. If you want to know whether a window named "Contact Detail" exists, you could use the following formula:

```
ValueCount ( FilterValues ( WindowNames; "Contact Detail" ))
```

If the value count is anything other than 0, that means the window name was found. The benefit of using FilterValues for this rather than PatternCount is that it correctly excludes a window named Contact Detail - 2 from the returned list. PatternCount (WindowNames; "Contact Detail") would match partial names of windows and not entire item names.

Examples:

Function	Results
FilterValues (Offices; "Anchorage¶ Philadelphia¶Chicago")	Returns Chicago Philadelphia when Offices contains Chicago Philadelphia San Mateo

Floor (number)

Data type returned: **Number**

Category: **Number**

Parameters:

- **number**—Any expression that resolves to a numeric value.

Description:

Returns number rounded down to the next lower integer.

For positive numbers, Floor and Int return the same results; however, for negative numbers, Int returns the next larger integer, whereas Floor returns the next smaller integer.

One use of Floor is for generating random whole numbers. For instance, if you want to generate a random whole number between 0 and 9, you can use the formula Floor (Random * 10).

Examples:

Function	Results
Floor (1.0005)	Returns 1.
Floor (-1.0005)	Returns -2.
Floor (3)	Returns 3.

FV (payment; interestRate; periods)

Data type returned: **Number**

Category: **Financial**

Parameters:

- **payment**—The nominal amount of the payment or investment.
- **interestRate**—The per-period interest rate.
- **periods**—The number of periods in the duration of the investment.

Description:

Returns the future value of a periodic investment based on the payments and interest rate for the number of periods specified.

The FV function does not account for the present value of your investment, and it assumes that payments are made at the end of each period.

If the investment compounds monthly, divide the annual interestRate by 12 to express the periods as a number of months. For instance, to figure out the future value of monthly investments of $250, earning 8% interest compounding monthly, for 10 years, you would use the formula FV (250; .08/12; 10 * 12), which returns $45,736.51.

Examples:

Function	Results
FV (50 ; .10 ; 2)	Returns 105, indicating the amount of money you would have after making two periodic deposits of $50 into an investment that paid 10% per period.

Get (AccountExtendedPrivileges)

Data type returned: **Text**

Category: **Get**

Description:

Returns a list of extended privileges, separated by carriage returns, assigned for use by the currently logged-in account. Extended privileges are additional access rights assigned to a privilege set; they control such things as access via the Web, via ODBC/JDBC, and via FileMaker Networking, but developers also can add their own extended privileges.

If the user's privilege set does not have any extended privileges enabled, Get (AccountExtendedPrivileges) returns an empty list.

To test whether a user has a certain extended privilege, use the following formula:

```
ValueCount ( FilterValues (Get (AccountExtendedPrivileges); "salesNorthWestRegion" ))
```

If this formula returns 0, the user does not have the specified extended privilege.

There is a subtle but important difference between Get (CurrentExtendedPrivileges) and Get (AccountExtendedPrivileges). Within a script that has the Run Script with Full Access Privileges option checked, Get (CurrentExtendedPrivileges) returns the list of extended privileges assigned to the [Full Access] privilege set, not those assigned to the logged-in user's account. Get (AccountExtendedPrivileges) always returns the list of extended privileges assigned to the currently logged-in account.

Examples:

Function	Results
Get (AccountExtendedPrivileges)	If the logged-in user has a privilege set that includes Access via Instant Web Publishing as well as Access via FileMaker Network, this function returns fmiwp fmapp

Get (AccountName)

Data type returned: **Text**

Category: **Get**

Description:

Returns the name of the authenticated account being used by the current user of the database file. If a user is logged in under the default Admin account, Admin is returned. If a user is using the FileMaker Pro guest account, [Guest] is returned.

For external server authentication, Get (AccountName) returns the name of the authenticated account being used by the current user of the database file, not the group to which the user belongs. (The group name appears in the Account list when you define accounts and privileges in FileMaker Pro.) If an individual belongs to more than one group (account), the first group name listed when you use View By Authentication Order while defining accounts and privileges determines access for the user.

Get (AccountName) can be used to retrieve the account name of the current user for purposes of logging or auditing database access. It is better for this purpose than Get (UserName), which is specific to the installed copy of FileMaker rather than the user.

Examples:

Function	Results
Get (AccountName)	Returns klove when the current user is logged in with the klove account.

Get (AccountPrivilegeSetName)

Data type returned: **Text**

Category: **Get**

Description:

Returns the name of the privilege set assigned to the logged-in user account. Every account must be assigned one, and only one, privilege set. The privilege set defines the data, interface, and functionality constraints that are placed on the user as the user interacts with the database system.

There is a subtle, but important, difference between Get (AccountPrivilegeSetName) and Get (CurrentPrivilegeSetName). Within a script that has the Run Script with Full Access Privileges option checked, Get (CurrentPrivilegeSetName) always returns [Full Access], not the logged-in user's privilege set name. Get (AccountPrivilegeSetName) always returns the name of the privilege set assigned to the currently logged-in account.

Examples:

Function	Results
Get (AccountPrivilegeSetName)	Returns [Full Access] if you haven't modified the security settings of a new database.
Get (AccountPrivilegeSetName)	Returns Sales if the current user is logged in with an account assigned to the Sales privilege set.

Get (ActiveFieldContents)

Data type returned: **Text, Number, Date, Time, Timestamp, Container**

Category: **Get**

Description:

Returns the contents of the field in which the cursor is currently placed. The contents of the field need not be highlighted.

Get (ActiveFieldContents) can return the contents of fields of any data type, but the field in which you place those contents might need to be of the same data type for it to display properly. For container fields, Get (ActiveFieldContents) returns the name or file reference of the container data, just the same as would result from the function GetAsText (myContainerField).

If the cursor is not placed in a field, a blank value is returned, as opposed to a question mark.

Examples:

Function	Results
Get (ActiveFieldContents)	Returns Rowena when the current field contains the name Rowena.

Get (ActiveFieldName)

Data type returned: **Text**

Category: **Get**

Description:

Returns the name of the field in which the cursor is currently placed.

Even when the active field is a related or unrelated field from another table, Get (ActiveFieldName) simply returns the field's name. It does *not* use the fully qualified syntax "TableOccurrenceName::FieldName." If you need the fully qualified field name, use the following formula:

```
GetFieldName ( Evaluate ( Get (ActiveFieldName )))
```

If the cursor is not placed in a field, a blank value is returned, as opposed to a question mark.

Examples:

Function	Results
Get (ActiveFieldName)	Returns Name_First when the cursor is in the Name_First field.

Get (ActiveFieldTableName)

Data type returned: **Text**

Category: **Get**

Description:

Returns the name of the table occurrence for the field in which the cursor is currently placed.

Note that the table occurrence name (from the Relationships Graph) is returned, rather than the source table name.

If the cursor is not placed in a field, this function returns an empty string.

Examples:

Function	Results
Get (ActiveFieldTableName)	Might return Contacts2.

Get (ActiveLayoutObjectName)

Data type returned: **Text**

Category: **Get**

Description:

Returns the name of the currently active layout object. Any object on a layout can be assigned a name using the Inspector. If no object is active, or if the currently active object has not been assigned a name, this function returns an empty string.

Examples:

Function	Results
Get (ActiveLayoutObjectName)	Might return DetailTab.

Get (ActiveModifierKeys)

Data type returned: **Number**

Category: **Get**

Description:

Returns the sum of the constants that represent the modifier keys that the user is pressing on the keyboard. The constants for modifier keys are as follows:

1—Shift
2—Caps lock
4—Control
8—Alt (Windows) or Option (Mac OS)
16—Command key (Mac OS only)

Get (ActiveModifierKeys) is often used to set up conditional branches in a script to be able to specify different behaviors based on the user holding down certain modifier keys. For instance, you might suppress warning dialogs when the user holds down the Shift key. Or perhaps a button that reports on monthly sales could allow the user to specify a custom date range by holding down the Control key when activating the button.

Examples:

Function	Results
Get (ActiveModifierKeys)	Returns 4 if the Control key is being held down.
Get (ActiveModifierKeys)	Returns 7 (1 + 2 + 4) if the Shift, Caps Lock, and Control keys are being held down.
Let (keys = Get (ActiveModifierKeys); LeftWords (Case (Mod (keys; 2); "Shift, ") & Case (Int (Mod (keys; 4) / 2); "Caps Lock, ") & Case (Int (Mod (keys; 8) / 4); "Control, ") & Choose (2 * (Int (Mod (keys ; 16) / 8)) + (Abs (Get (SystemPlatform)) - 1); "";""; "Option, "; "Alt, ")& Case (keys >= 16; "Command"); 999))	This formula shows text values for all modifier keys being held down. If the user is holding down the Shift, Caps Lock, and Control keys when this function is evaluated, the text values for those keys are returned in the form Shift, Caps Lock, Control.

Get (ActivePortalRowNumber)

Data type returned: **Number**

Category: **Get**

Description:

Returns the number of the portal row containing the focus. Get (PortalRowNumber) returns 0 when no portal row is selected or if the user navigates to a portal without selecting a specific portal row or object within the portal. This can occur when using the Go to Object script step to activate the portal itself, but not a specific row or object within it.

Examples:

Function	Results
Get (PortalRowNumber)	Returns 3 when the user clicks on the third row of a portal.

Get (ActiveRepetitionNumber)

Data type returned: **Number**

Category: **Get**

Description:

Returns the number of the active repetition (the repetition in which the cursor currently resides) for a repeating field. Repetition numbers start with 1.

If the cursor is not in a field, this function returns 0. If the currently active field is not a repeating field, it returns 1.

Examples:

Function	Results
Get (ActiveRepetitionNumber)	Returns 2 when a user is clicked into the second repetition of a field.

Get (ActiveSelectionSize)

Data type returned: **Number**

Category: **Get**

Description:

Returns the number of characters highlighted in the current field. The function returns 0 if no characters are highlighted and returns a blank value if no field is active. When multiple windows are open (which leads to the possibility of multiple highlighted selections), only the active window is considered.

Carriage returns, tabs, spaces, and other invisible characters are counted by Get (ActiveSelectionSize).

Examples:

Function	Results
Get (ActiveSelectionSize)	Returns 10 if a user highlighted 10 characters in any field in the active window.

Get (ActiveSelectionStart)

Data type returned: **Number**

Category: **Get**

Description:

Returns the position of the first character in the highlighted text of the current field. If no text is highlighted (that is, the user has simply clicked into a block of text), the current position of the cursor is returned. It returns a blank value if no field is active. When multiple windows are open, only the active window is considered.

Remember that carriage returns, tabs, spaces, and other invisible characters are taken into account when evaluating Get (ActiveSelectionStart).

Using Get (ActiveSelectionStart) in conjunction with Get (ActiveSelectionSize), you can determine the string that a user has highlighted in any field, using the following formula:

```
Middle ( Get (ActiveFieldContents); Get (ActiveSelectionStart) ;
Get (ActiveSelectionSize))
```

Examples:

Function	Results
Get (ActiveSelectionStart)	Returns 5 if a field contains the name "Tom Sawyer" and the user has highlighted just the last name.
Get (ActiveSelectionStart)	Returns 1 if the user has selected an entire field or if the insertion point is at the beginning of a field.

Get (AllowAbortState)

Data type returned: **Number**

Category: **Get**

Description:

Returns 1 if Allow User Abort is On; returns 0 if Allow User Abort is Off.

If the setting for User Abort has not been explicitly set, a script runs as if Allow User Abort is On. Get (AllowAbortState) returns 1 in such cases.

Examples:

Function	Results
Allow User Abort [Off] Show Custom Dialog [Get (AllowAbortState)]	The custom dialog displays 0.
Allow User Abort [On] Show Custom Dialog [Get (AllowAbortState)]	The custom dialog displays 1.

Get (AllowFormattingBarState)

Data type returned: **Number**

Category: **Get**

Description:

Developers may control whether users can make toolbars visible via the Allow Formatting Bar script step. This companion function returns a Boolean value representing whether toolbars are allowed to be visible. It returns 1 if toolbars are allowed, 0 if they are not.

By default, toolbars are allowed.

Examples:

Function	Results
Get (AllowFormattingBarState)	Returns 0 if the user has run a script that contains the Allow Formatting Bar [Off] script step.

Get (ApplicationLanguage)

Data type returned: **Text**

Category: **Get**

Description:

Returns a text string representing the current application language. The possible results are as follows:

English	Spanish
French	Dutch
Italian	Japanese
German	Simplified Chinese
Swedish	Traditional Chinese

The string returned is always in English, even in versions of the product based on another language. That is, it returns German, not Deutsch, in the German language version of FileMaker Pro.

Examples:

Function	Results
Get (ApplicationLanguage)	Returns English for users using an English language version of FileMaker Pro.

Get (ApplicationVersion)

Data type returned: **Text**

Category: **Get**

Description:

Returns a text string representing the application and version of FileMaker in use by the current user:

Pro (version)	For FileMaker Pro
ProAdvanced (version)	For FileMaker Advanced
Runtime (version)	For FileMaker Runtime
FileMaker Web Publishing (version)	For FileMaker Web Client in cases in which IWP is being hosted from FileMaker Pro or Pro Advanced
Web Publishing Engine (version)	For FileMaker Server Web hosting
xDBC (version)	For ODBC and JDBC clients
Server (version)	For FileMaker Server
Go (version)	For FileMaker Go on the iPhone or iPod touch
Go_iPad (version)	For FileMaker Go on the iPad

If you have allowed web access to a database, you might want to add conditional tests within some of your scripts so that they behave differently for web and FileMaker Pro clients. To identify web users, use either of the following formulas:

```
PatternCount ( Get ( ApplicationVersion ); "Web")
Position ( Get ( ApplicationVersion ); "Web"; 1; 1)
```

If either of these returns anything other than 0, the user is a web client.

Examples:

Function	Results
Get (ApplicationVersion)	Returns ProAdvanced 12.0v1 for FileMaker Pro Advanced 12.0v1.
Get (ApplicationVersion)	If you create an unstored calculation field with the formula Get (ApplicationVersion) and then extract the data as XML via Custom Web Publishing, you might get <field name="AppVersion"> <data>Web Publishing Engine 12.0v1</data> </field>

Get (CalculationRepetitionNumber)

Data type returned: **Number**

Category: **Get**

Description:

Returns the current repetition number of a calculation field. If the calculation is not set to allow more than one value, Get (CalculationRepetitionNumber) returns 1.

Get (CalculationRepetitionNumber) is nothing more than the repetition number and does not imply or require that a particular field is active.

You can use the repetition number in conditional tests involving repeating fields. For instance, the following formula returns a repeating calculation field with values foo, foo, foo, boo, boo, and so on:

```
If (Get ( CalculationRepetitionNumber ) < 4; "foo"; "boo")
```

Examples:

Function	Results
Get (CalculationRepetitionNumber)	Returns 1 in the first repetition of a repeating field, 2 in the second repetition, and so on, up to the maximum number of repetitions the field has been defined to hold.
Get (CalculationRepetitionNumber) ^ 2	Assuming the field has been specified to have five repetitions, this function returns the repetition values 1, 4, 9, 16, 25.

Get (ConnectionState)

Data type returned: **Number**

Category: **Get**

Description:

Returns a number that indicates whether the connection between FileMaker Pro or FileMaker Go and the host uses SSL encryption.

Possible results for Get (ConnectionState) are the following:

0—No network connection.

1—A nonsecured connection (FileMaker Server with SSL disabled) or to a FileMaker Pro host.

2—A secured connection (SSL) when the server name does not match the certificate (default FileMaker Server installation).

3—A secured connection with a fully verified server name in the certificate.

Examples:

Function	Results
Get (ConnectionState)	Returns 1, when the current file is opened as a guest of FileMaker Server in which SSL encryption has not been enabled.

Get (CurrentDate)

Data type returned: **Date**

Category: **Get**

Description:

Returns the current date according to the operating system calendar.

The format of the result varies based on the date format that was in use when the database file was created. In the United States, dates are generally in the format MM/DD/YYYY.

If the result is displayed in a field, it is formatted according to the date format of the field in the current layout.

When using Get functions within field definitions, in most cases you should set the storage option to be "unstored" so that the field always displays current data.

Examples:

Function	Results
DayName (Get (CurrentDate) - 30)	Returns the day name for the date 30 days prior to today.
Get (CurrentDate) - InvoiceDate	Returns the number of days outstanding for a given invoice.

Get (CurrentExtendedPrivileges)

Data type returned: **Text**

Category: **Get**

Description:

Returns a list of extended privileges, separated by carriage returns, currently assigned for use by the account that is being used to evaluate this function. Extended privileges are additional access rights assigned to a privilege set; they control such things as access via the Web, via ODBC/JDBC, and via FileMaker Networking, but developers also can add their own extended privileges.

If the user's privilege set does not have any extended privileges enabled, Get (CurrentExtendedPrivileges) returns an empty list.

To test whether a user has a certain extended privilege, use the following formula:

```
ValueCount ( FilterValues (Get (CurrentExtendedPrivileges); "salesNorthWestRegion" ))
```

If this formula returns 0, the user does not have the specified extended privilege.

There is a subtle but important difference between Get (CurrentExtendedPrivileges) and Get (AccountExtendedPrivileges). Within a script that has the Run Script with Full Access Privileges option checked, Get (CurrentExtendedPrivileges) returns the list of extended privileges assigned to the [Full Access] privilege set, not those assigned to the logged-in user's account. Get (AccountExtendedPrivileges) always returns the list of extended privileges assigned to the currently logged-in account.

Examples:

Function	Results
Get (CurrentExtendedPrivileges)	If the currently active account uses a Privilege Set that includes Access via Instant Web Publishing as well as Access via FileMaker Network, this function returns fmiwp fmapp

Get (CurrentHostTimestamp)

Data type returned: **Timestamp**

Category: **Get**

Description:

Returns the current timestamp (date and time) according to the host's system clock, to the nearest second.

Get (CurrentHostTimestamp) returns the date and time from the host machine, regardless of the date and time settings on the client machine. Get (CurrentHostTimestamp) is therefore useful in log routines to track when records are created or edited because it disregards differences in time zones or improper clock settings of the client machines.

Function calls that run on the server (such as this one) might affect a network user's performance, especially when they are used in unstored calculations.

Examples:

Function	Results
Get (CurrentHostTimestamp)	Returns 1/1/2012 11:30:01 AM when the system clock on the host machine shows January 1, 2012, 11:30:01 AM.

Get (CurrentPrivilegeSetName)

Data type returned: **Text**

Category: **Get**

Description:

Returns the name of the current privilege set. Every account must be assigned one, and only one, privilege set. The privilege set defines the data, interface, and functionality constraints that are placed on the user as the user interacts with the database system.

There is a subtle, but important, difference between Get (AccountPrivilegeSetName) and Get (CurrentPrivilegeSetName). Within a script that has the Run Script with Full Access Privileges option checked, Get (CurrentPrivilegeSetName) always returns [Full Access], not the name of the logged-in account's privilege set. Get (AccountPrivilegeSetName) always returns the name of the privilege set assigned to the currently logged-in account, regardless of the script setting. In all other cases, the two functions produce the same result.

Examples:

Function	Results
Get (CurrentPrivilegeSetName)	Always returns [Full Access] when evaluated within a script that has been set to run with full access privileges.
Get (CurrentPrivilegeSetName)	Returns Sales if the current user is logged in with an account assigned to the Sales privilege set.

Get (CurrentTime)

Data type returned: **Time**

Category: **Get**

Description:

Returns the current time from the local system clock (on the client machine).

Note that the Time data type is stored internally as the number of seconds since midnight. Math can be performed on all Time functions using multiples of seconds (60 seconds = 1 minute, 3600 seconds = 1 hour).

Remember that the time returned by Get (CurrentTime) is the local time on the system clock of the client machine. In cases in which clients are accessing a database from different time zones, or someone has his clock set incorrectly, this data might be less useful than time extracted from the host machine's system clock with the Get (CurrentHostTimestamp) function.

When using Get functions within field definitions, in most cases you should set the storage option to be "unstored" so that the field always displays current data.

Examples:

Function	Results
Get (CurrentTime)	Returns the current time from the local system clock.
Get (CurrentTime) + 3600	Returns the time one hour from now.

Get (CurrentTimestamp)

Data type returned: **Timestamp**

Category: **Get**

Description:

Returns the current timestamp (date and time) according to the local system clock to the nearest second.

Note that a timestamp is stored internally as an integer that represents the number of seconds since midnight on 1/1/0001. Therefore, calculations that use seconds as the base unit can be performed on Timestamp data types.

Get (CurrentTimestamp) uses the date and time settings of the local machine (client) and might be less useful or accurate than Get (CurrentHostTimeStamp) in a database that is accessed by clients from different time zones.

Examples:

Function	Results
Get (CurrentTimestamp)	Might return 1/25/2012 8:28:05 PM.
GetAsTime (Get (CurrentTimestamp))	Extracts the time from a timestamp.
GetAsDate (Get (CurrentTimestamp))	Extracts the date from a timestamp.

Get (CustomMenuSetName)

Data type returned: **Text**

Category: **Get**

Description:

Returns the name of the active custom menu set. If the active menu set is [Standard FileMaker Menus] (which is the initial default for all files), a blank value is returned.

Examples:

Function	Results
Get (CustomMenuSetName)	Returns SalesMenuSet when a custom menu set called SalesMenuSet has been defined and is active.
Get (CustomMenuSetName)	Returns an empty string when the [Standard FileMaker Menus] menu set is active.

Get (DesktopPath)

Data type returned: **Text**

Category: **Get**

Description:

Returns the path to the desktop folder for the current user's computer. On Windows 7, the path format is /Drive:/Users/<*userName*>/Desktop/. In the Mac OS, the path format is /DriveName/Users/<*userName*>/Desktop/.

Note that the user in this case is the operating system user account and should not be confused with the account with which a user logged in to a given database.

Examples:

Function	Results
Get (DesktopPath)	Returns /C:/Users/Kai/Desktop/ for a user named Kai in Windows.
Get (DesktopPath)	Returns /MacintoshHD/Users/Erlend/Desktop/ for a user named Erlend in the Mac OS.
Get (DesktopPath)	Returns /var/mobile/Applications/<applicationID>/Desktop/ for a user on FileMaker Go.

Get (DocumentsPath)

Data type returned: **Text**

Category: **Get**

Description:

Returns the path to the documents folder for the current user. On Windows 7, the path format is /Drive:/Users/<*userName*>/My Documents/. In the Mac OS, the path format is /DriveName/Users/<*userName*>/Documents/.

When evaluated in a server-side script run on FileMaker Server, Get (DocumentsPath) returns the path to the Documents folder, which is in the same folder as the server's Backups, Databases, and Scripts folder. This can be a useful location for server-side scripts that need to import or export files.

Note that the user in this case is the operating system user account and should not be confused with the account with which a user logged in to a given database.

Examples:

Function	Results
Get (DocumentsPath)	Returns /C:/Documents and Settings/Kai/My Documents/ for a user named Kai in Windows.
Get (DocumentsPath)	Returns /MacintoshHD/Users/Erlend/Documents/ for a user named Erlend in the Mac OS.
Get (DocumentsPath)	Returns /C:/Program Files/FileMaker/FileMaker Server/Data/Documents for a standard installation of FileMaker Server on Windows.
Get (DocumentsPath)	Might return /var/mobile/Applications/<applicationID>/Documents/ for a user on FileMaker Go.

Get (DocumentsPathListing)

Data type returned: **Text**

Category: **Get**

Description:

Produces a return-delimited list of all the files and folders in the Documents folder returned by the Get (DocumentsPath) function.

This function is useful in import and export routines for checking for the existence of a file. Be aware, though, that it returns not only files directly in the DocumentsPath path directory, but also files nested in subfolders. On a Windows or Mac OS workstation (as opposed to FileMaker Server or FileMaker Go), there could be many thousands of files, and generating the list might take some time.

On FileMaker Go, local database files are stored in the DocumentsPath directory, so you can use Get (DocumentsPathListing) to retrieve a list of them.

Examples:

Function	Results
Get (DocumentsPathListing)	When evaluated within a server-side script on a Windows server, this function might return /C:/Program Files/FileMaker/FileMaker Server/Data/Documents/myFile.xlsx /C:/Program Files/FileMaker/FileMaker Server/Data/Documents/AnotherFile.xlsx /C:/Program Files/FileMaker/FileMaker Server/Data/Documents/myReportsFolder /C:/Program Files/FileMaker/FileMaker Server/Data/Documents/myReportsFolder/Report1.tab

Get (ErrorCaptureState)

Data type returned: **Number**

Category: **Get**

Description:

Returns 1 if Set Error Capture is set to On, and 0 if Set Error Capture is either not set or set to Off.

It is not possible to tell with the Get (ErrorCaptureState) function whether Error Capture was explicitly turned off or simply not set.

Examples:

Function	Results
Set Error Capture [Off] Show Custom Dialog [Get (ErrorCaptureState)]	The custom dialog displays 0.
Set Error Capture [On] Show Custom Dialog [Get (ErrorCaptureState)]	The custom dialog displays 1.

Get (FileMakerPath)

Data type returned: **Text**

Category: **Get**

Description:

Returns the path to the folder of the currently running copy of FileMaker Pro. In Windows, the path format is /Drive:/Program Files/FileMaker/FileMaker Pro 12/. In the Mac OS, the path format is /DriveName/Applications/FileMaker Pro 12/. (The actual path might vary if FileMaker was installed in a nonstandard location.)

Examples:

Function	Results
Get (FileMakerPath)	Returns /C:/Program Files/FileMaker/FileMaker Pro 12/ in Windows.
Get (FileMakerPath)	Returns /MacintoshHD/Applications/FileMaker Pro 12/ in the Mac OS.

Get (FileName)

Data type returned: **Text**

Category: **Get**

Description:

Returns the name of the current database file (without the file extension).

Get (FileName) is useful in function calls that require a filename, even if the current file is being referenced. This way, if the filename changes, you do not need to change any of your calculation formulas.

If a calculation field in file Alpha.fmp12 contains the formula Get (FileName), and that field is displayed on a layout in another file, Beta.fmp12, via an external table occurrence, the field value still returns Alpha.

Examples:

Function	Results
Get (FileName)	Returns Contacts when the current database file is named Contacts.fmp12.
GetNextSerialValue (Get (FileName); "Contacts:: PrimaryContactID")	Returns the next PrimaryContactID from the Contacts table in the current file. This function call is far less fragile than hard-coding the filename into the preceding expression. If the filename changes at some point in the future, this expression continues to work as expected.

Get (FilePath)

Data type returned: **Text**

Category: **Get**

Description:

Returns the full path to the currently active database file, including the file extension.

Returns file:/driveletter:/databaseName for local files in Windows.

Returns file://volumename/myfoldername/databaseName for remote files in Windows.

Returns file:/path/databaseName for local and remote files in the Mac OS.

Returns fmnet:/networkaddress/databaseName for FileMaker Pro networked files.

Remember that Get (FilePath) includes the filename and extension. Text parsing functions can be used to extract just the path from the results returned by Get (FilePath). This can be useful for building dynamic paths to objects that are in the same directory as the current file.

Examples:

Function	Results
Get (FilePath)	Returns the current file path.
Left (Get (FilePath); Position (Get (FilePath); Get (FileName); 1; 1) -1)	Returns just the path to the current file's directory. The Position function truncates the path before the filename.

Get (FileSize)

Data type returned: **Number**

Category: **Get**

Description:

Returns the size of the current file, in bytes.

Examples:

Function	Results
Get (FileSize)	Returns 1404928 if the current file size is 1,404,928 bytes.
Round (Get (FileSize) / 1024; 0)	Returns the file size in kilobytes.
Round (Get (FileSize) / (1024 ^ 2) ; 2)	Returns the file size in megabytes.
Round (Get (FileSize) / (1024 ^ 3) ; 2)	Returns the file size in gigabytes.

Get (FoundCount)

Data type returned: **Number**

Category: **Get**

Description:

Returns the number of records in the current found set.

If multiple windows are open in the current database file, each window can have its own found set. If the Get (FoundCount) function is used in a script, it returns the found count of the active layout in the active window.

Get (FoundCount) is often used in scripts, following finds, to determine navigation paths. In the following script, for instance, if one record is found, the Detail layout is shown, but if multiple records are found, the List layout is shown. Finally, if no records are found, the script notifies the user with a dialog box.

```
If [ Get ( FoundCount ) = 1 ]
 Go To Layout [ "Detail" ]
Else If [ Get ( FoundCount ) > 1 ]
 Go To Layout [ "List" ]
Else
 Show Custom Dialog ["Empty Set"; "No Records Found"]
End If
```

Examples:

Function	Results
Get (FoundCount)	Returns 240 if there are 240 records in the current found set.

Get (HighContrastColor)

Data type returned: **Text**

Category: **Get**

Description:

Note: This function is Windows only.

Returns the name of the current high-contrast default color scheme. Returns an empty value (null) if Use High Contrast is unavailable or inactive, or if the function is called on the Mac OS.

Use High Contrast is an option under Control Panel, Accessibility Options, Display tab (Windows XP), under Control Panel, Appearance and Personalization, Ease of Access Center, Set Up High Contrast (Windows Vista), and under Control Panel, Ease of Access

Center (Windows 7). The standard options increase default font sizes and heighten screen contrast to assist users with impaired vision.

Examples:

Function	Results
Get (HighContrastColor)	Returns High Contrast White when the color scheme is set to High Contrast White.
Get (HighContrastColor)	Returns High Contrast #2 when the color scheme on Windows 7 is set to High Contrast #2.

Get (HighContrastState)

Data type returned: **Number**

Category: **Get**

Description:

Note: This function is Windows only.

Returns a number representing the state of the Use High Contrast option in the Accessibility Options control panel (Windows XP) or the Ease of Access control panel (Windows Vista and Windows 7).

Returns:

0 if Use High Contrast is unavailable, inactive, or if the function is used on the Mac OS.

1 if Use High Contrast is available and active.

Examples:

If you have users with impaired vision, you might create alternate versions of your layouts that are easier for them to use. If so, you can test in your navigation scripts whether Use High Contrast is active and go to an appropriate layout or zoom the window.

```
If [ Get ( HighContrastState ) = 1 ]
   Go to Layout ["ContactDetail (HC)"]
Else
   Go to Layout ["ContactDetail"]
End If
```

Get (HostApplicationVersion)

Data type returned: **Text**

Category: **Get**

Description:

Returns a text string representing the version of FileMaker Server or FileMaker Pro that is hosting the database file currently in use. If the current database is open as a single-user, nonhosted file, this function returns an empty string. Both the name of the product and the version number are included in the output of Get (HostApplicationVersion).

Pro (version)	For FileMaker Pro
ProAdvanced (version)	For FileMaker Advanced
Server (version)	For FileMaker Server

Examples:

Function	Results
Get (HostApplicationVersion)	Returns Server 12.0v1 when a file is hosted by FileMaker Server 12 version 1.

Get (HostIPAddress)

Data type returned: **Text**

Category: **Get**

Description:

Returns the IP address of the host computer for the current database. If the current database is open as a single-user, nonhosted file, an empty string is returned.

Examples:

Function	Results
Get (HostIPAddress)	Returns 14.156.13.121 (as an example) when the current database is being hosted by FileMaker Server on a computer with this IP address.

Get (HostName)

Data type returned: **Text**

Category: **Get**

Description:

Returns the registered name of the computer hosting the database file.

To change the registered name on a computer:

On Windows XP, the computer name is found on the Network Identification tab of the System Properties control panel. The Full Computer Name option displays the current registered name.

On Windows 7, the computer name is found in the System control panel.

On Mac OS, the computer name is found within System Preferences, under the Sharing settings.

If a client connects to a file hosted by FileMaker Server, Get (HostName) returns the name of the server. The host name can be configured with the FileMaker Server Admin Console. By default, FileMaker Server uses the system's name, but a custom name can be supplied instead.

Examples:

Function	Results
Get (HostName)	Results in Hyperion, if the computer on which FileMaker Server is installed is named Hyperion.

Get (InstalledFMPlugins)

Data type returned: **Text**

Category: **Get**

Description:

Generates a return-delimited list of installed plug-ins. Each entry includes the plug-in name, version number (if available), and enabled state.

There are three possible values for the enabled state:

Enabled—The plug-in is enabled and can be loaded.

Disabled—The plug-in is disabled in the FileMaker Pro preferences.

Ignored—The plug-in failed to load, possibly because of software incompatibility.

The version number is included only when the plug-in developer included version information in the resource file (Windows) or the info.plist file (Mac OS).

Consider using Get (InstalledFMPlugins) as part of a startup script for checking whether the user has the correct versions of plug-ins required for using the file. The following formula extracts the version number of a particular plug-in from the text returned by Get (InstalledFMPlugins):

```
Let ([
 searchFor = "ScriptMaster" ;  // use the name of any plug-in you want to search for
 p = Get (InstalledFMPlugins) ;
 pos = Position ( p ; searchFor ; 1; 1 ) ;
 lineNum = ValueCount ( Left ( p ; pos ));
 line = GetValue ( p ; lineNum ) ;
 splitLine = Substitute ( line ; ";" ; "¶" );
 name = GetValue ( splitLine; 1 );
 version = GetValue ( splitLine; 2 ) ;
 status = GetValue ( splitLine; 3 )
];
 version
)
```

You can easily modify this formula to return the full name of the plug-in or its status just by changing the last line of the Let function to return name or status instead of version.

Examples:

Function	Results
Get (InstalledFMPlugins)	Might return 360Works ScriptMaster;4.02;Enabled Reactor;3.5.7;Enabled SuperContainer Companion Plugin;2.792;Enabled Web Publishing;12.0v1;Disabled xDBC Data Access Companion;12.0.1;Enabled

Get (LastError)

Data type returned: **Number**

Category: **Get**

Description:

Returns the error code generated by the most recent script step. If there was no error, Get (LastError) returns 0. Use this function in combination with Set Error Capture [On] to trap and handle errors raised in scripts.

A common source of bugs in scripts is not remembering that the Get (LastError) function returns the error code from only the most recently executed script step. For example, consider this script:

```
Perform Find []
If [Get ( ErrorCaptureState ) = 0]
   Show Custom Dialog [ Get ( LastError ) ]
End If
```

Here, the Get (LastError) step returns the result of the execution of the If script step, not the error code generated by the Find step.

> *Note*
>
> For a complete listing of error codes, see Chapter 21, "FileMaker Error Codes."

If a script is running on the Mac OS and calls an AppleScript routine, any errors generated are also passed through to and presented via this function.

Similarly, if an error occurs in FileMaker while performing an ODBC import or an Execute SQL script step, Get (LastError) returns a string that shows the ODBC error state.

Examples:

Script	Results
Set Error Capture [On] Print Setup [Restore] Set Variable [$error; Value: Get (LastError)]	If the user cancels out of the Print Setup dialog, Get (LastError) returns 1 (user-canceled action). If the Print Setup step executes successfully, Get (LastError) returns 0.

Get (LastMessageChoice)

Data type returned: **Number**

Category: **Get**

Description:

Returns a number corresponding to the button clicked as a result of the Show Custom Dialog script step.

Returns

1 for the default button.
2 for the second button.
3 for the third button.

Examples:

Consider the following script step, where the default button is labeled OK, the second button is labeled Maybe, and the third button is labeled Cancel:

```
Show Custom Dialog [ "Alert!" ; "Would you like to proceed?" ]
```

If the user chooses OK, Get (LastMessageChoice) returns 1.

If the user chooses Maybe, Get (LastMessageChoice) returns 2.

If the user chooses Cancel, Get (LastMessageChoice) returns 3.

You can then use an If() statement to handle each possibility appropriately. The value persists and can be retrieved until the user interacts with another custom dialog.

Get (LastODBCError)

Data type returned: **Text**

Category: **Get**

Description:

Returns a string that shows the ODBC error state (SQLSTATE), as published by ODBC standards, based on ISO/IEF standards.

The ODBC error state is cleared at the time the next ODBC-related script step is performed. Anytime before that happens, you can check to see whether an ODBC error was generated.

By setting the Set Error Capture script step to On, you can suppress the error messages that a user sees during execution of a script that uses ODBC functions.

Examples:

Function	Results
Get (LastODBCError)	Returns [DataDirect][Macintosh ODBC Driver Manager] Data source name not found and no default driver specified (-1) when a data source name is not found and the driver is not specified.
Get (LastODBCError)	Might return [FileMaker][FileMaker] FQL0001/(1:12): There is an error in the syntax of the query.

Get (LayoutAccess)

Data type returned: **Number**

Category: **Get**

Description:

Returns a number that represents the current user's record access privileges level for the current layout. Privileges are assigned in the Custom Layout Privileges dialog box.

The Get (LayoutAccess) function can be used to alert users of restricted privileges at the layout level. Note that Get (LayoutAccess) returns information about only the current layout. Record access privileges for any other layout are not available.

Note also that Get (LayoutAccess) does not return information about whether the layout itself is accessible, but rather what access the user has to edit record data via the current layout.

The Get (RecordAccess) function evaluates record access privileges independent of the Get(LayoutAccess) function. To fully evaluate record access, evaluate the values of both the Get (LayoutAccess) and Get (RecordAccess) functions.

Examples:

Function	Results
Get (LayoutAccess)	Returns 0 if the custom layout privileges of an account's privilege set allow "no access" to records via this layout.
Get (LayoutAccess)	Returns 1 if the custom layout privileges of an account's privilege set allow "view only" access to records via this layout.
Get (LayoutAccess)	Returns 2 if the custom layout privileges of an account's privilege set allow "modifiable" access to records via this layout.

Get (LayoutCount)

Data type returned: **Number**

Category: **Get**

Description:

Returns the total number of layouts within the current file, including hidden layouts and layouts the user does not have privileges to see.

Examples:

Function	Results
Get (LayoutCount)	Returns 5 when there are five layouts in a database file.

Get (LayoutName)

Data type returned: **Text**

Category: **Get**

Description:

Returns the name of the layout currently displayed in the active window.

To change the name of a layout, in Layout mode, go to the Layouts menu, select the Layout Setup menu item, and then click the General tab. Be aware that layouts do not need to be uniquely named.

Examples:

Function	Results
Get (LayoutName)	Returns Data Entry when the Data Entry layout is displayed.
Get (LayoutName)	Returns Invoice List when the Invoice List layout is displayed.

Get (LayoutNumber)

Data type returned: **Number**

Category: **Get**

Description:

Returns the number of the layout currently displayed in the active window. The order of layouts can be set using the Manage Layouts dialog (File, Manage, Layouts).

Get (LayoutNumber) can be used to keep track of the last layout a user visited. The following script takes a user from one layout to another, allows the user to complete other tasks, and then returns the user to the original layout:

```
Set Variable [ $lastLayout; Get ( LayoutNumber ) ]
Go to Layout ["Other Layout"]
[perform script, process, etc]
Go to Layout [$lastLayout]
```

Examples:

Function	Results
Get (LayoutNumber)	Returns 6 when the sixth layout on the Manager Layouts list is active.

Get (LayoutTableName)

Data type returned: **Text**

Category: **Get**

Description:

Returns the name of the table occurrence (not the source table) from which the current layout shows records.

Because there is no way of retrieving the name of the source table with which a layout is associated, consider prefixing the names of table occurrences with an abbreviation that represents the source table. For instance, you might name a table occurrence INV_CustomerInvoices. You can then use text parsing functions to retrieve the source table name from the results returned by the Get (LayoutTableName) function.

Examples:

Function	Results
Get (LayoutTableName)	Returns INV_Invoices when the current layout is attached to the table occurrence named INV_Invoices.
Get (LayoutTableName)	Returns EMP_Employees when the current layout is attached to the table occurrence named EMP_Employees.

Get (LayoutViewState)

Data type returned: **Number**

Category: **Get**

Description:

Returns a number that represents the view mode for the current layout in the active window.

Get (LayoutViewState) is useful in scripts to test the state of the current layout. Unless a layout has been restricted not to be viewable in another state, users can manually change the state of the current layout, provided they have access to menu commands. You can detect whether the layout is in the proper state, and if necessary, change it with the View As script step.

Examples:

Function	Results
Get (LayoutViewState)	Returns 0, 1, or 2, depending on the current layout's view state: 0 = View as Form 1 = View as List 2 = View as Table

Get (MultiUserState)

Data type returned: **Number**

Category: **Get**

Description:

Returns a number that represents the FileMaker sharing/networking status for the current file.

Returns 0 when network sharing is off, or when network sharing is on but no privilege sets have the [fmapp] Extended Privilege enabled.

Returns 1 when network sharing is on, the database file is accessed from the host computer, and some or all users have the [fmapp] Extended Privilege enabled.

Returns 2 when network sharing is on, the database file is accessed from a client computer, and some or all users have the [fmapp] Extended Privilege enabled.

Examples:

Function	Results
Get (MultiUserState)	Returns 2 whenever a user opens a file using FileMaker Pro as a guest of FileMaker Server.

Get (NetworkProtocol)

Data type returned: **Text**

Category: **Get**

Description:

Returns the name of the network protocol that FileMaker Pro is using on the current machine.

Unlike ancient versions of FileMaker Pro, the only network protocol supported by FileMaker Pro 12 is TCP/IP. `Get ( NetworkProtocol )` always returns TCP/IP, even if FileMaker Network sharing is off.

Examples:

Function	Results
`Get (NetworkProtocol)`	`TCP/IP`

Get (PageNumber)

Data type returned: **Number**

Category: **Get**

Description:

When you are printing or previewing a document, this function returns the current page number. If nothing is being printed or previewed, `Get ( PageNumber )` returns `0`.

If you are printing a report of unknown length and you want to determine the total number of pages, you can have a script go to the last page in Preview mode and set a variable with the value returned by `Get ( PageNumber )`. This would then allow you to have something like "Page 2 of 5" appear in the footer of your report.

Examples:

Function	Results
`"Page " & Get ( PageNumber )`	Assuming this formula was used in an unstored calculation, when you are printing a multipage report, you could place this field in the footer of the layout, and it returns the proper page number when the report was previewed or printed.

Get (PersistentID)

Data type returned: **Text**

Category: **Get**

Description:

Returns a unique, unchanging identifier of the computer or device on which FileMaker is running. The ID is returned as a 32-digit hexadecimal string.

You can use Get (PersistentID) to identify devices that access your solution. You could, for instance, have a startup script that checks the PersistentID of the user's device against a table of authorized devices. Similarly, PersistentID could be used as part of a routine to assign and check license numbers in a "shrink wrap" solution.

Although the PersistentID is unique to a device, it is not the internal ID number of the device itself.

Examples:

Function	Results
Get (PersistentID)	Might return CBB6D1BABDD454373A3E90AF0244FB1E.

Get (PreferencesPath)

Data type returned: **Text**

Category: **Get**

Description:

Returns the operating system path to a user's preferences and default options folder.

In Windows Vista and Windows 7, the path format is /Drive:/Users/<userName>/AppData/Local/.

In the Mac OS, the path format is /DriveName/Users/<userName>/Library/Preferences/.

On iOS, the path format is /var/mobile/Applications/<ApplicationID>/Library/Application Support/.

Note that the user in this case is the operating system user account and should not be confused with the account with which a user logged in to a given database.

Examples:

Function	Results
Get (PreferencesPath)	Returns /C:/ Users/Nate/AppData/Local/ for a user named Nate in Windows.
Get (PreferencesPath)	Returns /MacintoshHD/Users/Eleanor/Library/Preferences/ for a user named Eleanor in the Mac OS.

Get (PrinterName)

Data type returned: **Text**

Category: **Get**

Description:

Returns information about the currently selected printer.

In Windows, Get (PrinterName) returns a text string containing the printer name, driver name, and printer port, separated by commas.

In Mac OS, Get (PrinterName) returns a text string with the queue name of the printer and the IP address of the printer, separated by the word on.

If, in either operating system, the printer information is unavailable for whatever reason, <Unknown> is returned.

If certain print jobs require that a specific printer be selected, you can test for Get (PrinterName) within a script and ask the user to select a different printer if necessary.

Examples:

Function	Results
Get (PrinterName)	On Windows, might return \\ server1\ Lexmark Optra M412 PS3, winspool,Ne02:.
Get (PrinterName)	On Mac OS, might return hp Laserjet 4200.

Get (QuickFindText)

Data type returned: **Text**

Category: **Get**

Description:

Returns the text currently entered into the Quick Find box in the Status Toolbar.

This function can be useful for logging quick find requests. Using custom menus, you are able to override the default quick find behavior with a script you have created. Get (QuickFindText) can be used within the script to investigate and possibly change the search request prior to performing a find.

Examples:

Function	Results
Get (QuickFindText)	Returns Fred if that is the text the user has entered in the Quick Find box.

Get (RecordAccess)

Data type returned: **Number**

Category: **Get**

Description:

Returns a number that represents the current account's access privileges for the current record. Record privileges are assigned via a privilege set.

Returns 0 if the user does not have View or Edit privileges for the current record.

Returns 1 if the user has view-only access to the current record. This could mean the View is set to Yes for the current table, or that View is set to Limited and that the calculation defined for Limited access returns a value of True.

Returns 2 if the user has edit access for the current record. This could mean that Edit is set to Yes for the current table, or that Edit is set to Limited and that the calculation defined for Limited access returns a value of True.

The Get (RecordAccess) function can be used to alert users of restricted privileges at the record level. Note that Get (RecordAccess) returns information only about table record privileges. Record access also may be restricted through the layout access. To fully evaluate current record access, evaluate both the return values of the Get (LayoutAccess) and Get (RecordAccess) functions.

When evaluated within a script that has been set to run with full access privileges, Get (RecordAccess) always returns 2 because the script operates as if it were being run by a user with the [Full Access] privilege set.

Examples:

Function	Results
Get (RecordAccess)	Returns 1 if a user can view, but not edit, a given record.

Get (RecordID)

Data type returned: **Number**

Category: **Get**

Description:

Returns the unique, internal ID number FileMaker has assigned to the current record. This number is generated automatically by FileMaker Pro and does not change. The record ID is assigned sequentially within each table, beginning at 1. Record IDs are not reused; if a record is deleted, its ID is not reassigned.

When files are converted from previous versions, record IDs from the original file are preserved.

The record ID is required for editing and deleting records via Custom Web Publishing because this is how the record to be changed or deleted must be identified.

Examples:

Function	Results
Get (RecordID)	Returns 275 when the internal FileMaker Pro ID for the current record is 275.

Get (RecordModificationCount)

Data type returned: **Number**

Category: **Get**

Description:

Returns the total number of times the current record has been modified. A record change must be committed before the modification count updates. Committing multiple field changes at once is considered a single record modification. Each time a change is committed, the modification count increases.

Get (RecordModificationCount) can be used by custom web applications to ensure that one user's changes do not overwrite another's. At the time the record is loaded into the web browser, the record modification count can be stored. When the record is saved, the current record modification count can be checked against the stored one to see whether another user has updated the record in the meantime.

Duplicated records retain the same record modification count as the record from which they were created; the count is not reset to 0. There is no way to alter or reset the modification count.

Get (RecordModificationCount) returns NULL for ODBC data sources.

Examples:

Function	Results
Get (RecordModificationCount)	Returns 0 if a record has never been modified.
Get (RecordModificationCount)	Returns 17 if a record has been modified 17 times since it was originally created.

Get (RecordNumber)

Data type returned: **Number**

Category: **Get**

Description:

Returns a number that represents the position of a record within the current found set. This value changes depending on the found set and the sort order.

Get (RecordNumber) tells you a record's position within the found set. This capability is useful if you want to create a calculation to display "X of Y records" on a given layout.

When using Get() functions within field definitions, in most cases you should set the storage option to be "unstored" so that the field always displays current data.

To determine FileMaker's unique internal record ID, use Get (RecordID).

Examples:

Function	Results
Get (RecordNumber)	Returns 1 for the first record in the found set.
Get (RecordNumber)	Returns 83 for the 83rd record in a found set of 322 records.

Get (RecordOpenCount)

Data type returned: **Number**

Category: **Get**

Description:

Returns the total number of open, uncommitted records in the current found set. An open record is one in which changes have been made but not yet committed by the user or currently executing script. Note that this function returns information only about the user's own session. It does not enable you to detect whether other users on the network have open records.

The only scenario in which Get (RecordOpenCount) would return a value greater than 1 is if a user is modifying records through a portal. Records modified via a portal remain in an open, uncommitted state until the user submits the parent record, so it is possible to have as many open records as portal rows that have been edited. Editing any portal row also puts the parent record into an open, locked state, so even if no data in the parent record has been modified, Get (RecordOpenCount) returns 2 the moment a user starts editing data in a portal row.

Get (RecordOpenCount) returns information only about open records in the currently active window. It is possible to have open, uncommitted records in windows that are not the active window.

Examples:

Function	Results
Get (RecordOpenCount)	Returns 3 if there are three open records in the current window. This would presumably mean that a user had edited data in two portal rows, thereby locking each of those related records as well as the parent record.

Get (RecordOpenState)

Data type returned: **Number**

Category: **Get**

Description:

Returns a number representing the open/committed status of the current record:

Returns 0 for a closed or committed record.

Returns 1 for a new record that has not been committed.

Returns 2 for a modified record that has not been committed.

Get (RecordOpenState) provides information only about the status of records in the given user's session. It does not provide information about the state of a record that is being modified by another user on the network. To determine whether another user is editing a record, use the Open Record/Request script step and then test whether that action was successful by looking at the value returned by Get (LastError).

Examples:

Function	Results
Get (RecordOpenState)	Returns 1 if the current record is a new record that has not been committed.

Get (RequestCount)

Data type returned: **Number**

Category: **Get**

Description:

Returns the total number of find requests defined in the current window.

Get (RequestCount) can be used in scripted find routines to see whether the user has added any find requests to the default request. It is also useful as a boundary condition if you ever need to loop through all the find requests and either capture or set search parameters.

Examples:

Function	Results
Get (RequestCount)	Returns 1 if the current find request asks for invoices with values greater than $200.

Get (RequestOmitState)

Data type returned: **Number**

Category: **Get**

Description:

Returns 1 if Matching Records is set to Omit for the current find request. Returns 0 if it is set to Include. One use of this function is as part of a routine for capturing and logging user find requests. Get (RequestOmitState) lets you know whether the user specified that a given find request be an Omit request.

Examples:

Function	Results
Get (RequestOmitState)	Returns 1 when the user has specified Omit as the value for Matching Records for the current find request.

Get (ScreenDepth)

Data type returned: **Number**

Category: **Get**

Description:

Returns the number of bits needed to represent the color or shade of gray of a pixel on the user's monitor. A value of 8, for instance, represents 256 (equal to 2^8) colors or shades of gray.

Use Get (ScreenDepth) to alert users if their monitor color settings are set too low to view images correctly. For example,

```
If [ Get ( ScreenDepth ) < 32 ]
  Show Custom Dialog ["Color";"Your monitor should be set to "Millions
  of colors" to display images correctly"]
End If
```

Examples:

Function	Results
Get (ScreenDepth)	Returns 32 on a display showing millions (2^32) of colors.
Get (ScreenDepth)	Returns 16 on a display showing thousands (2^16) of colors.
Get (ScreenDepth)	Returns 4 on a VGA display.
Get (ScreenDepth)	Returns 1 on a black-and-white display.

Get (ScreenHeight)

Data type returned: **Number**

Category: **Get**

Description:

Returns the number of pixels displayed vertically on the current screen. This corresponds to a user's operating system settings for display resolution.

Note that when the active window spans more than one screen, this function calculates the value for the screen that contains the largest percentage of the window.

Use Get (ScreenHeight) and Get (ScreenWidth) to check minimum resolution settings on a user's computer.

```
If [ Get ( ScreenHeight ) < 1200 or Get ( ScreenWidth ) < 1600 ]
  Show Custom Dialog ["Resolution";"This application requires a minimum
  of 1600 x 1200 screen resolution."]
  Perform Script ["Close Solution Files"]
End If
```

Examples:

Function	Results
Get (ScreenHeight)	Returns 900 on a monitor set to display at 1440 × 900.

Get (ScreenWidth)

Data type returned: **Number**

Category: **Get**

Description:

Returns the number of pixels displayed horizontally on the active screen. This number corresponds to a user's operating system settings for display resolution.

Note when the active window spans more than one screen, this function calculates the value for the screen that contains the largest percentage of the window.

See Get (ScreenHeight) for an example of how to check minimum resolution settings on a user's computer.

Examples:

Function	Results
Get (ScreenWidth)	Returns 1440 on a monitor set to display at 1440 × 900.

Get (ScriptName)

Data type returned: **Text**

Category: **Get**

Description:

Returns the name of the current script, even if it is paused. When no script is running, Get (ScriptName) returns an empty string.

One use of Get (ScriptName) is to capture errors. In this example, the Log Error script takes the script name as a parameter:

```
If [ Get ( LastError ) <> 0]
  Perform Script [ "Log Error"; Parameter: Get ( ScriptName ) ]
End If
```

Passing the current script's name as a script parameter can be useful anytime a subscript can be called by multiple scripts.

Examples:

Function	Results
Get (ScriptName)	Returns Calculate Invoice if the current script is Calculate Invoice.

Get (ScriptParameter)

Data type returned: **Text**

Category: **Get**

Description:

Retrieves the parameter that was passed to a currently running script.

The value of a script parameter can be retrieved anywhere within a script, regardless of subscript calls. Script parameters cannot be altered during execution of a script.

Subscripts do not inherit the script parameter of the calling script. Rather, they can be passed parameters of their own that exist only for the duration of the subscript. If you want a subscript to inherit a script parameter, pass Get (ScriptParameter) as the subscript's parameter.

Only one value can be passed as a script parameter, but that value can contain a delimited list, thus allowing multiple values to be passed.

Script parameters can be specified when scripts are activated via buttons, subscripts, and layout and object triggers, but not when scripts are called manually from the Scripts menu or via an open or close trigger.

Examples:

In this example, the Navigate script is called, with the parameter West:

```
Perform Script ["Navigate"; Parameter: "West"]
```

Within the Navigate script, the script parameter value (West) is assigned to a variable ($direction) through the use of the following script step:

```
Set Variable ["$direction"; Get ( ScriptParameter ) ]
```

$direction now equals West.

Get (ScriptResult)

Data type returned: **Text, Number, Date, Time, Timestamp, Container**

Category: **Get**

Description:

Allows subscripts to pass results to their calling ("parent") script. Get (ScriptResult) returns whatever value was specified in the Exit Script script step.

Note that after all scripts complete execution, no value is stored and Get (ScriptResult) returns a null (or blank) value.

Examples:

Consider a subscript that checks for duplicate records within a found set and uses the Exit Script step to return a count of duplicates as a script result. Any number of scripts within a given solution can then call the subscript and perform a check as follows:

```
Case ( Get ( ScriptResult ) > 1; "duplicates exist"; "no duplicates" )
```

Get (SortState)

Data type returned: **Number**

Category: **Get**

Description:

Returns a number that represents the sort state of the active window.

Get (SortState) can be used in a customized interface in which the Status Toolbar is normally hidden from the user. Also, Get (SortState) can be used to correctly display sort icons in a customized interface.

A sorted found set becomes semisorted if new records are created and the Keep Records in Sorted Order option was not selected when performing the sort. Omitting or deleting records does not cause the sort status to change, however.

Examples:

Function	Results
Get (SortState)	Returns 0 if the found set in the active window is not sorted.
Get (SortState)	Returns 1 if the found set in the active window is sorted.
Get (SortState)	Returns 2 if the found set in the active window is partially sorted (semisorted).

Get (StatusAreaState)

Data type returned: **Number**

Category: **Get**

Description:

Returns a number that represents the state of the Status Toolbar of the active window:

0 if the Status Toolbar is hidden.
1 if the Status Toolbar is visible.
2 if the Status Toolbar is visible and locked.
3 if the Status Toolbar is hidden and locked.

If you want a single test that tells you whether the Status Toolbar is hidden (regardless of whether it's locked), use Mod (Get (StatusAreaState); 3). When this function returns 0, the Status Toolbar is hidden; when it returns anything else, the Status Toolbar is visible.

Examples:

Function	Results
Get (StatusAreaState)	Returns 1 if the Status Toolbar is visible.

Get (SystemDrive)

Data type returned: **Text**

Category: **Get**

Description:

Returns the drive letter (Windows) or volume name (Mac OS) where the currently running operating system is located.

Examples:

Function	Results
Get (SystemDrive)	Returns /C:/ in Windows when the operating system is on the C: drive.
Get (SystemDrive)	Returns /MyDrive/ in the Mac OS when the operating system is on a volume named MyDrive.

Get (SystemIPAddress)

Data type returned: **Text**

Category: **Get**

Description:

Produces a return-delimited list of the IP addresses of all active Network Interface Controller (NIC) cards connected to the computer.

Examples:

Function	Results
Get (SystemIPAddress)	Returns 202.27.78.34, for example, when there is only one active network interface.
Get (SystemIPAddress)	A machine connected to both an Ethernet network and a Wi-Fi network might return 192.168.101.161 192.168.101.162

Get (SystemLanguage)

Data type returned: **Text**

Category: **Get**

Description:

Returns the language setting of the user's machine. The returned text is the English language name for a language (that is, Spanish rather than Español; German rather than Deutsch), regardless of system settings.

Examples:

Function	Results
Get (SystemLanguage)	Returns English on a system set to use English.

Get (SystemNICAddress)

Data type returned: **Text**

Category: **Get**

Description:

Produces a return-delimited list containing the hardware addresses of all the NIC cards connected to the machine.

In Windows, you can find this address by typing ipconfig /all from a command prompt. On Mac OS X, you can find the NIC address for each network connection using the System Preferences utility.

If the user's machine has multiple NIC cards, Get (SystemNICAddress) generates a return-delimited list of all their addresses. You might, for instance, have both a built-in Ethernet card and a wireless networking card installed in a laptop. Or a server might have multiple built-in Ethernet ports. In both of these cases, Get (SystemNICAddress) returns the addresses of both devices.

Examples:

Function	Results
Get (SystemNICAddress)	Might return 00:26:4a:1a:fe:d3 00:30:65:cf:df:98

Get (SystemPlatform)

Data type returned: **Number**

Category: **Get**

Description:

Returns a number that represents the current platform on a user's computer.

Because FileMaker tends to change or add to the values in the platform-checking function (as new versions of operating systems become supported), checks against this function should be performed in a single, central location for ease of future updates. The results of the function may be stored in a global variable during startup and then referred to for subsequent platform checks throughout the rest of the database. We recommend using a custom function for this purpose.

Examples:

Function	Results
Get (SystemPlatform)	Returns 1 if the current platform is an Intel-based Mac.
Get (SystemPlatform)	Returns -2 if the platform is Windows XP, Windows Vista, or Windows 7.
Get (SystemPlatform)	Returns 3 if the platform is iOS.

Get (SystemVersion)

Data type returned: **Text**

Category: **Get**

Description:

Returns the current operating system version level.

The values returned by Get (SystemVersion) change as new versions of operating systems become available. As with checks against Get (SystemPlatform), you should try to perform tests of the system version in a single, central location within your files so that you can easily update in the future. We recommend using a custom function for this purpose.

Examples:

Function	Results
Get (SystemVersion)	Returns 10.6.7 for Mac OS X version 10.6.7.
Get (SystemVersion)	Returns 6.1 for Windows 7.

Get (TemporaryPath)

Data type returned: **Text**

Category: **Get**

Description:

Returns the path to the temporary folder that FileMaker Pro uses on the user's computer. When evaluated within a server-side script, it returns the path that FileMaker Server uses on the system.

If you have script routines that need to generate temporary files (for example, for export/import routines), consider placing them in this folder so as not to interfere with the user's workspace. The temporary folder and any files placed in it are deleted when the session terminates.

Because the operating system controls the location of temporary files, the exact path returned might be different from the examples shown, but they should be similar to the following examples.

In Window Vista and Windows 7, the path format is /Drive:/Users/<userName>/AppData/Local/Temp/S<n>/.

On MacOS, the path format is /DriveName/private/var/folders/<2 characters>/<20 characters>++++TI/-Tmp-/S<n>/.

The folder name itself begins with *S* and is followed by a session number.

Examples:

Function	Results
Get (TemporaryPath)	Returns /C:/Users/Nate/AppData/Local/Temp/S3 for a user named Nate in Windows.
Get (TemporaryPath)	Might return /Macintosh HD/private/var/folders/IL/ILWLfzEDGemw8CSmCC-PB++++TI/-Tmp-/S10/ for a user on the Mac OS.
Get (TemporaryPath)	Returns /var/mobile/Applications/<applicationID>/Library/Application Support/ for a user on FileMaker Go.

Get (TextRulerVisible)

Data type returned: **Number**

Category: **Get**

Description:

Returns a Boolean value by which to determine whether the text ruler is visible. Returns 1 if the text ruler is displayed; otherwise, returns 0. You can use the Show/Hide Text Ruler script step to control display of the text ruler.

Examples:

Function	Results
Get (TextRulerVisible)	Returns 1 when the current user's text ruler is visible.

Get (TotalRecordCount)

Data type returned: **Number**

Category: **Get**

Description:

Returns the total number of records in the current source table, regardless of the state of the found set.

The Get (TotalRecordCount) function is most often used in unstored calculations and scripts. In an unstored calculation, Get (TotalRecordCount) returns the same value regardless of which table occurrence context is specified for the calculation. When using Get (TotalRecordCount) in a script, be sure to navigate to a layout that establishes the correct table context before referencing the function.

The total record count includes records that have been created but not yet committed. If such records are reverted, the total record count is decreased.

Examples:

Function	Results
Get (TotalRecordCount)	Returns 283 when there are 283 records in the current table, regardless of the size of the current found set.

Get (TriggerCurrentTabPanel)

Data type returned: **Text**

Category: **Get**

Description:

Returns the index number and object name of the currently active tab panel when the OnTabSwitch script trigger is activated.

Because the OnTabSwitch trigger is a "pre-event" trigger, you have the opportunity to retrieve both the current and target tab panel (see Get (TriggerTargetTabPanel)), perform any logging or other tests, and, if necessary, cancel the tab switch using the Exit Script [False] script step.

Get (TriggerCurrentTabPanel) returns both the index number, which is its left-to-right tab position (starting at 1), as well as the object name that you might have assigned to the tab panel. The two values are separated by a carriage return, so you can easily retrieve just the one or the other using the GetValue function. If the tab panel object has not been given a name, only the index number is returned.

Keep in mind that Get (TriggerCurrentTabPanel) returns a value only when used in conjunction with OnTabSwitch. It returns 0 otherwise.

Examples:

Function	Results
Get (TriggerCurrentTabPanel)	Might return 2 ShippingInfo
GetValue (Get (TriggerCurrentTabPanel) ; 1)	Returns just the index number of the current tab panel.

Get (TriggerKeystroke)

Data type returned: **Text**

Category: **Get**

Description:

Returns the characters that activated either an OnObjectKeystroke or OnLayoutKeystroke script trigger. Generally, it is a single character, but multiple characters might be returned when the input comes from an Input Method Editor (IME).

Because both OnObjectKeystroke and OnLayoutKeystroke are "pre-event" triggers, you have the opportunity in the activated script to look at the triggering keystroke and decide whether or not to allow the event (that is, the input of the character) to complete. It can be suppressed using the Exit Script [False] script step.

Because many keystrokes, such as Escape, the arrow keys, and the Backspace key, cannot be directly referenced in a calculation formula, you often use the Code function to retrieve the Unicode value of the keystroke.

Keep in mind that Get (TriggerKeystroke) returns a value only when used in conjunction with one of the keystroke triggers. It returns 0 otherwise.

Examples:

Function	Results
Get (TriggerKeystroke)	Returns a, when the user types an *a* in a field that has been given an OnObjectKeystroke script trigger.
Code (Get (TriggerKeystroke))	Returns 28, when the user presses the left arrow key in a field that has been given an OnObjectKeystroke script trigger.

Get (TriggerModifierKeys)

Data type returned: **Number**

Category: **Get**

Description:

Returns the sum of the constants that represent the modifier keys that the user is pressing on the keyboard at the time of activating a script trigger. The constants for modifier keys are as follows:

1—Shift
2—Caps lock
4—Control
8—Alt (Windows) or Option (Mac OS)
16—Command key (Mac OS only)

Get (TriggerModifierKeys) is often used to set up conditional branches in a triggered script to be able to specify different behaviors based on the user holding down certain modifier keys.

The reason for having both Get (ActiveModifierKeys) and Get (TriggerModifierKeys) is that time might elapse between the activating of the script trigger and inspecting the modifier keys. Get (ActiveModiferKeys) returns the modifier keys currently active, whereas Get (TriggerModiferKeys) returns the keys that were active when the trigger was activated.

Examples:

Function	Results
Get (TriggerModifierKeys)	Returns 4 if the Control key was being held down at the time of activating a script trigger.
Get (TriggerModifierKeys)	Returns 5 (4 + 1) if the Control and Shift keys were both held down at the time of activating a script trigger.

Get (TriggerTargetTabPanel)

Data type returned: **Text**

Category: **Get**

Description:

Returns the index number and object name of the destination (target) tab panel when the OnTabSwitch script trigger is activated.

Because the OnTabSwitch trigger is a "pre-event" trigger, you have the opportunity to retrieve both the current and target tab panel (see Get (TriggerCurrentTabPanel)), perform any logging or other tests, and, if necessary, cancel the tab switch using the Exit Script [False] script step.

Get (TriggerTargetTabPanel) returns both the index number, which is its left-to-right tab position (starting at 1), as well as the object name that you might have assigned to the tab panel. The two values are separated by a carriage return, so you can easily retrieve just the one or the other using the GetValue function. If the tab panel object has not been given a name, only the index number is returned.

Keep in mind that Get (TriggerTargetTabPanel) returns a value only when used in conjunction with OnTabSwitch. It returns 0 otherwise.

Examples:

Function	Results
Get (TriggerTargetTabPanel)	Might return 3 SalesHistory
GetValue (Get (TriggerTargetTabPanel) ; 2)	Returns just the object name of the target tab panel (if assigned).

Get (UserCount)

Data type returned: **Number**

Category: **Get**

Description:

Returns the number of clients currently accessing the file, including the current user.

Only FileMaker Pro client connections are counted by the Get (UserCount) function. Web, ODBC, and JDBC connections are not counted.

Examples:

Function	Results
Get (UserCount)	Returns 4 if a database file is hosted via peer-to-peer networking and there are 3 clients and the host connected to the file.
Get (UserCount)	Returns 28 if a file is hosted by FileMaker Server and there are 28 clients connected to the current file.

Get (UserName)

Data type returned: **Text**

Category: **Get**

Description:

Returns the username that has been established for the current user's copy of FileMaker Pro. This username is specified on the General tab of the Preferences dialog and can be set to return either the system name or a custom name.

The returned name is the same for anyone opening any database on the machine, regardless of what account name and password he has used. It is an application-level setting, not a document-level setting. The username can always be changed manually, regardless of whatever security you have set up. For these reasons, we recommend against using it for logging activity or restricting functionality.

For greater security, use Get (AccountName) to track and manage user access; a user cannot change the account name used to log in to a database file.

Examples:

Function	Results
Get (UserName)	Returns Delilah Bean when the user-specified name is Delilah Bean.

Get (UseSystemFormatsState)

Data type returned: **Number**

Category: **Get**

Description:

Enables you to determine whether the option to Use System Formats (in the File Menu, File Options dialog, Text tab) is explicitly turned on. It returns a Boolean value representing the state of the Use System Formats option: 1 if Use System Formats is on; 0 otherwise.

Each database stores the date, time, and number formatting of the computer on which the database was created. If the current system settings differ from the settings in use when the file was created, Use System Formats determines which settings to use.

You can use the Set Use System Formats script step to control this behavior as well, but doing so does not affect the value returned by Get (UseSystemFormatsState). The function always returns the value specified in the File Options dialog.

Examples:

Function	Results
Get (UseSystemFormatsState)	Returns 1 when the option Always Use Current System Settings is selected.
Get (UseSystemFormatsState)	Returns 0 when the option Always Use File's Saved Settings is selected.

Get (UUID)

Data type returned: **Text**

Category: **Get**

Description:

Returns a unique 16-byte Universally Unique Identifier (UUID).

You can use this function to generate a unique ID of a record. This can be useful if multiple users might be generating data in an offline copy of a database file. In such situations, you would not want to use a serial number as the unique ID because of the potential for duplicates. Using a UUID would ensure each record has a unique ID, regardless of when and where it was created. It would also obviate the need to update the next serial number value when importing records or restoring data from a backup.

Examples:

Function	Results
Get (UUID)	Might return 2F15526A-490B-4F34-9FC9-48E182FFB3A3.

Get (WindowContentHeight)

Data type returned: **Number**

Category: **Get**

Description:

Returns the height, in pixels, of the content area of the current window. The content area is the area *inside* a window's frame and does not include such things as the title bar, scrollbars, or the Status Toolbar.

Keep in mind that the relationship of the content area dimensions to the overall window dimensions are different on each platform. Because the script steps that control window sizing specify the overall window dimensions (including the frame), a similarly sized window has a different content area size on the Mac OS than it does on Windows.

Use Get (WindowHeight) to determine the outside height dimension of the current window.

Examples:

Function	Results
Get (WindowContentHeight)	On the Mac OS, returns 563 when the current window height is 600 and the Status Toolbar is not visible. The title bar and bottom scrollbar make up the other 37 pixels. A window of the same height with the Status Toolbar open has a content height of 480.

Get (WindowContentWidth)

Data type returned: **Number**

Category: **Get**

Description:

Returns the width, in pixels, of the content area of the current window. The content area is the area *inside* a window's frame and doesn't include such things as the title bar, scrollbars, or the Status Toolbar.

Keep in mind that the relationship of the content area dimensions to the overall window dimensions are different on each platform. Because the script steps that control window sizing specify the overall window dimensions, a similarly sized window has a different content area size on the Mac OS than it does on Windows.

Use Get (WindowWidth) to determine the outside width dimension of the current window.

Examples:

Function	Results
Get (WindowContentWidth)	On the Mac OS, returns 785 when the current window width is 800. The window frame and scrollbars make up the other 15 pixels.

Get (WindowDesktopHeight)

Data type returned: **Number**

Category: **Get**

Description:

Returns the height, in pixels, of the desktop space.

In Windows, the desktop space is the FileMaker Pro application window. Get (WindowDesktopHeight) measures the total vertical space used by the application window.

On Mac OS X, the desktop space includes everything on the screen except the top menu.

You cannot programmatically set the window desktop height or width, nor on Windows can you tell where the application window has been positioned on the user's monitor.

Examples:

Function	Results
Get (WindowDesktopHeight)	Returns 878 in the Mac OS when the current monitor's resolution is set to 1400 × 900. The menu bar accounts for the other 22 pixels of height.

Get (WindowDesktopWidth)

Data type returned: **Number**

Category: **Get**

Description:

Returns the width, in pixels, of the desktop space.

In Windows, the desktop space is the FileMaker Pro application window. Get (WindowDesktopWidth) measures the total horizontal space used by the application window.

On Mac OS X, the desktop space includes everything on the screen except the top menu.

You cannot programmatically set the window desktop height or width, nor on Windows can you tell where the application window has been positioned on the user's monitor.

Examples:

Function	Results
Get (WindowDesktopWidth)	Returns 1400 in the Mac OS when the current monitor's resolution is set to 1400 × 900.

Get (WindowHeight)

Data type returned: **Number**

Category: **Get**

Description:

Returns the total height, in pixels, of the current window. The current window is usually the foreground window, but it is also possible for a script to run in a window that is not the active foreground window.

The window height and width return the *outside* dimensions of a window. So, if you make a new window and specify a height and width of 300, Get (WindowHeight) and Get (WindowWidth) would both return 300.

Be aware that the window height and width are different from the window content height and width, which return the inside dimensions of a window.

Examples:

Function	Results
Get (WindowHeight)	Returns 541 when the window that is being acted upon is 541 pixels tall.

Get (WindowLeft)

Data type returned: **Number**

Category: **Get**

Description:

Returns the horizontal distance, in pixels, from the outer left edge of a window to the left edge of the application window on Windows or screen on Mac OS.

See Get (WindowDesktopHeight) for a discussion of how the application window is defined for each platform.

If any docked toolbars are placed along the left edge of the application window, the position of the origin shifts inward. The Get (WindowLeft) function is relative to the inside edge of the application window, inclusive of docked toolbars.

Get (WindowLeft) can return negative numbers. This might indicate the window is located on a second monitor positioned to the left of the first, or it might mean that a portion of the left side of the window is hidden.

Examples:

Function	Results
Get (WindowLeft)	Returns 0 when the left edge of the window being acted upon is flush with the left edge of the application window.

Get (WindowMode)

Data type returned: **Number**

Category: **Get**

Description:

Returns a number that indicates the mode of the active window:

0 for Browse mode.
1 for Find mode.
2 for Preview mode.
3 if printing is in progress.
4 for Layout mode (possible only when evaluating this function using the Data Viewer using FileMaker Pro Advanced).

If a script ever attempts to operate within the context of a window that is in Layout mode, the window is automatically switched to Browse mode and the script continues as expected.

Examples:

Function	Results
Get (WindowMode)	Assuming a window is in Browse mode, returns 0.

Get (WindowName)

Data type returned: **Text**

Category: **Get**

Description:

Returns the name of the current window. The current window is usually the foreground window, but it is also possible for a script to run in a window that is not the active foreground window.

The name of a window is the text string that appears in the window's title bar. A window's name can be specified when it is created with the New Window script step. It can also be altered with the Set Window Title script step.

Window names do not need to be unique. If a user manually creates a new window, the name of the new window is the same as the active window at the time the user selected New Window but has - 2 (or higher number if necessary) appended to it.

Examples:

Function	Results
Get (WindowName)	Returns Contacts if the window being acted upon is named Contacts.
Get (WindowName)	Returns Contacts - 2 if the user manually makes a new window when the Contacts window is current.

Get (WindowStyle)

Data type returned: **Number**

Category: **Get**

Description:

Returns the style of the window in which the function is evaluated:

0 if the window is a regular document window.
1 if the window is a floating document window.
2 if the window is a dialog window.

The window style is one of the advanced options that can be specified via the New Window script step.

Examples:

Function	Results
Get (WindowStyle)	Returns 1 if the current window is a floating document window.

Get (WindowTop)

Data type returned: **Number**

Category: **Get**

Description:

Returns the vertical distance, in pixels, from the top edge of a window to the inside of the top of the application window.

See Get (WindowDesktopHeight) for a discussion of how the application window is defined for each platform.

If any docked toolbars are placed along the top of the application window, this shifts the location of the inside edge of the application window.

Get (WindowTop) can return negative numbers. This might indicate the window is located on a second monitor positioned above the first, or it might mean that a portion of the top of the window is hidden.

Examples:

Function	Results
Get (WindowTop)	Returns 0 when the top edge of a window is positioned flush to the top of the application window.

Get (WindowVisible)

Data type returned: **Number**

Category: **Get**

Description:

Returns a number indicating whether the current window is visible or hidden:

1 if the window is visible.

0 if the window is hidden.

When you call a subscript in another file, it operates from the context of the frontmost window in that file, but that window does not need to become the active window. The current window therefore can be different from the active, foreground window, and it can either be hidden or visible.

Examples:

Function	Results
Get (WindowVisible)	Returns 1, assuming the current window is visible.

Get (WindowWidth)

Data type returned: **Number**

Category: **Get**

Description:

Returns the total width, in pixels, of the current window. Note that a window retains all its properties, such as height and width, even if it is hidden.

The window height and width measure the outside dimensions of a window, whereas the window content height and window content width measure the inside dimensions of a window. The height and width dimensions that can be specified for the New Window and the Move/Resize Window script steps are for the outside window dimensions.

Window height and width can be assigned when creating and resizing windows using the New Window and Move/Resize Window script steps.

Examples:

Function	Results
Get (WindowWidth)	Returns 650 when the current window is 650 pixels wide.

Get (WindowZoomLevel)

Data type returned: **Text**

Category: **Get**

Description:

Returns the zoom state (percentage) for the current window.

In Windows, an asterisk appears next to the zoom percentage when the Enlarge Window Contents to Improve Readability option is selected in the General tab of the Preferences dialog box.

Examples:

Function	Results
Get (WindowZoomLevel)	Returns 400 when the current window's zoom percentage is set to 400.
Get (WindowZoomLevel)	Returns 200* in Windows when the current window's zoom percentage is set to 200 and the Enlarge Window Contents to Improve Readability option is selected.

GetAsBoolean (data)

Data type returned: **Number**

Category: **Logical**

Parameters:

- **data**—Any field or expression that returns a text string, number, date, time, timestamp, or container.

Description:

Returns 0 if the expression or data passed into the function has a numeric value of 0 or is empty. All other values return 1.

Examples:

Function	Results
GetAsBoolean (myField)	Returns 0 when myField is "hello".
GetAsBoolean (myField)	Returns 1 when myField is –1000.
GetAsBoolean (myField)	Returns 0 when myField is 0.
GetAsBoolean (myField)	Returns 0 when myField is empty.

GetAsCSS (text)

Data type returned: **Text**

Category: **Text**

Parameters:

- **text**—Any field or expression that resolves to a text string.

Description:

Returns a representation of the specified text string, marked up with Cascading Style Sheet (CSS) tags. GetAsCSS can capture rich text formatting that has been applied to a text string.

Representing formatted text as CSS also means that you can export stylized text and have it rendered properly by CSS-aware applications, such as web browsers.

Examples:

Function	Results
GetAsCSS (myField)	Returns <SPAN STYLE= "font-size: 36px;color: #AA0000;font-weight: bold;">Go Team</SPAN>. Assumes myField contains the string "Go Team" and is formatted in bold, red, 36pt Helvetica font.

GetAsDate (text)

Data type returned: **Date**

Category: **Text**

Parameters:

- **text**—Any text expression or text field that contains a date, formatted the same as the date format on the system where the file was created.

Description:

Interprets a text string that contains a date as an actual date. Anytime you use a date constant within a calculation formula, you should use the GetAsDate or Date functions to ensure that the date is interpreted correctly.

Note: To avoid errors, we recommend always using four-digit years; however, GetAsDate ("1/1") resolves to 1/1/2012 assuming the current year is 2012. GetAsDate ("1/1/05") resolves to 1/1/0005.

Examples:

Function	Results
GetAsDate ("1/1/2012")	Returns 1/1/2012, stored internally as a date.
GetAsDate ("1/1/2012") + 8	Returns 1/9/2012, stored internally as a date. In this case, had the GetAsDate function not been used, "1/1/2004" + 8 would have returned 112012.

GetAsNumber (text)

Data type returned: **Number**

Category: **Text**

Parameters:

- **text**—Any valid text expression that contains numbers.

Description:

Returns only the numbers from a text string, as the data type Number. All non-numeric characters are dropped from the string.

Use GetAsNumber to strip all non-numeric characters out of a text string. For instance, you might have a phone number field to which you want to apply some formatting. GetAsNumber (PhoneNumber) returns just the numeric characters from the field, stripping all punctuation and spaces, so that you can then apply whatever new formatting you want.

GetAsNumber can also be applied to date and time fields to coerce the data into its integer representation.

Examples:

Function	Results
GetAsNumber ("abc123")	Returns 123.
GetAsNumber ("$100.10")	Returns 100.1.
GetAsNumber (Get (CurrentDate))	Returns 734464, when the current date is November 23, 2011.

GetAsSVG (text)

Data type returned: **Text**

Category: **Text**

Parameters:

- **text**—Any expression that resolves to a text string.

Description:

Returns a representation of the text string, marked up in Scalable Vector Graphics (SVG) format. SVG can capture rich text formatting that has been applied to a text string.

SVG format can be used to transfer formatted text from FileMaker to other applications. You can also test an SVG-formatted version of a text string to determine what, if any, formatting has been applied to the string.

Examples:

Function	Results
GetAsSVG (myField)	Might return <StyleList> <Style#0>"font-size: 36px;color: #AA0000;font-weight: bold;text-align: left;", Begin: 1, End: 8</Style> <Style#1>"color: #000000;font-weight: normal;font-style:normal;text-align: left;", Begin: 9, End: 20</Style> </StyleList> <Data> <Span style="0">Go Team </Span> <Span style="1">Hello World!</Span> </Data>

GetAsText (data)

Data type returned: **Text**

Category: **Text**

Parameters:

- **data**—Any field or expression that returns a number, date, time, timestamp, or container.

Description:

Coerces data into a text string. You can then manipulate the data as you would any other text string.

When applied to a container field that stores a reference to an object, GetAsText returns the path to the container data. If the container data is embedded in the database, GetAsText returns a question mark. For externally stored container data, GetAsText returns information about the size and location of the container data.

In most cases, you do not need to explicitly coerce number, date, and time data into text before performing text operations on the data. Text functions operate on numbers, dates, and times as if they were text strings, even if you do not wrap the data with GetAsText.

Examples:

Function	Results
GetAsText (Get (CurrentDate))	Might return 3/8/2012.
GetAsText (SalesReport)	Might return remote:JuneSales.pdf size:792.612 JPEG:ReportDB/SalesReport/JuneSales.pdf PDF : ReportDB/SalesReport/JuneSales.pdf

GetAsTime (text)

Data type returned: **Time**

Category: **Text**

Parameters:

- **text**—Any text expression or text field containing a time.

Description:

Returns the data specified in the text string as data type time. The value can then be manipulated like any other time data.

Examples:

Function	Results
GetAsTime ("01:30:30")	Returns 1:30:30 AM when you specify Time as the calculation result.
GetAsTime ("01:30:30")	Returns 1/1/0001 1:30:30 AM when you specify Timestamp as the calculation result.
GetAsTime ("15:30:00") – FinishTime	Returns the elapsed time between 3:30 p.m. and FinishTime.

GetAsTimestamp (text)

Data type returned: **Timestamp**

Category: **Text**

Parameters:

- **text**—Any text expression or text, number, date, or time field.

Description:

Converts a timestamp contained in a text string into the data type Timestamp. The result is then used in formulas as any other timestamp would be.

GetAsTimestamp also converts numbers into timestamps. See the Timestamp function for more information on how timestamps can be represented as numbers.

Use GetAsTimestamp anytime you include a literal string containing a timestamp in a calculation formula. For instance, to find out the amount of time (in seconds) that has elapsed between a fixed time in the past and now, you use the following formula:

```
Get ( CurrentTimestamp ) - GetAsTimestamp ( "6/29/1969 4:23:56 PM" )
```

Examples:

Function	Results
GetAsTimestamp ("1/1/2012 1:10:10")	Returns 1/1/2012 1:10:10.
GetAsTimestamp (61997169000)	Returns 8/12/1965 7:50:00 PM.

GetAsURLEncoded (text)

Data type returned: **Text**

Category: **Text**

Parameters:

- **text**—A text string or expression that returns a text string.

Description:

Returns an encoded version of text, suitable for use in a URL query. All characters in the text string are converted to UTF-8 format, and all text formatting is removed from the string. All nonalphanumeric characters except underscore (_) are replaced with a percent (%) sign followed by the character's hexadecimal value.

Use GetAsURLEncoded anytime you need to include field data in formulas that will be used in URL queries, such as with the Web Viewer and the Open URL script step.

Examples:

Function	Results
GetAsURLEncoded ("Hello World!")	Returns Hello%20World!.
GetAsURLEncoded ()	Returns %3C%2Fthe%20end%3E.

GetField (fieldName)

Data type returned: **Text, Number, Date, Time, Timestamp, Container**

Category: **Logical**

Parameters:

- **fieldName**—A text string, field, or expression that returns a text string, which contains the name of a field.

Description:

Returns the contents of the fieldName field.

Essentially, GetField provides a level of abstraction for retrieving the contents of a field. Instead of saying "Give me the value of the FirstName field," for instance, it's like saying "Give me the value of the field whose name is in the variable $myField." By setting the variable with a different field name, you can retrieve the contents of a different field.

The Evaluate function can always be used in place of GetField. For instance, Evaluate ($myField) and GetField ($myField) both return the same result. The opposite is not true, however. Evaluate can perform complex evaluations and can have trigger conditions defined, whereas GetField can retrieve only the contents of a field.

Examples:

Function	Results
GetField ("FirstName")	Returns the contents of the FirstName field.
GetField (myField)	Returns the contents of the FirstName field, when myField contains the string "FirstName".
GetField (GetValue (fieldList; counter))	Returns the contents of the LastName field, when fieldList is a return-delimited list of field names containing "FirstName¶LastName¶City¶State¶Zip" and counter is 2.

GetFieldName (fieldName)

Data type returned: **Text**

Category: **Logical**

Parameters:

- **fieldName**—Any field object or evaluation of a text expression that refers to a field's name.

Description:

Returns the fully qualified name of fieldName.

A fully qualified field name is in the form TableOccurrenceName::fieldName.

If the cursor is not placed in a field or the fieldName parameter does not reference a valid field name, GetFieldName returns a question mark (?).

Examples:

Function	Results
GetFieldName (InvoiceID)	Might return INV_Invoice::InvoiceID.
GetFieldName (Evaluate (Get (ActiveFieldName)))	Returns the fully qualified field name of the currently active field (if any).

GetHeight (sourceField)

Data type returned: **Number**

Category: **Container**

Parameters:

- **sourceField**—Any container field.

Description:

Returns the height in pixels of an image in the sourceField.

GetHeight returns 0 if the container field does not contain an image or if the sourceField is not a container field. It does not matter how the image is stored in the container field (by reference, embedded, or externally).

Examples:

Function	Results
GetHeight (StudentPicture)	Returns 210 when the image in the StudentPicture field is 210 pixels tall.

GetLayoutObjectAttribute (objectName ; attributeName { ; repetitionNumber ; portalRowNumber})

Data type returned: **Text**

Category: **Logical**

Parameters:

- **objectName**—A string or text expression that represents the name of an object on the current layout.
- **attributeName**—A string or text expression that represents the name of a supported attribute.
- **repetitionNumber**—A number or expression that returns a number specifying which repetition number of a repeating field you want to retrieve information about. This is an optional parameter.
- **portalRowNumber**—A number or expression that returns a number specifying which portal row you want to retrieve information about. This is an optional parameter.

Description:

Returns various information about the specified object. Objects are named using the Position section of the Inspector. Using GetLayoutObjectAttribute, you can retrieve information about such things as the location, content, and formatting of the object.

The attributes about which you can retrieve information are as follows:

Attribute Name	Value Returned
objectType	The object's type, in English: field, text, graphic, line, rectangle, rounded rectangle, oval, group, button group, portal, tab panel, chart, web viewer, and unknown.
hasFocus	1 (True) if the object is currently active; otherwise, returns 0 (False). Objects that can have the focus are fields, portals, tab panels, charts, and groups. Also returns 1 for a portal when a portal row is selected.
containsFocus	1 (True) if the object is currently active or if it contains an active object; otherwise, it returns 0 (False). Objects that can contain the focus are fields, portals, tab panels, charts, and groups.
isFrontTabPanel	1 (True) if the object is the active tab panel.
Bounds	A space-delimited list with five values representing the position (in points) of the object and its rotation. Unlike the FieldBounds function, which returns a field's position relative to the upper-left corner of the active window, the GetLayoutObjectAttribute function returns values that are relative to the bottom-left corner of the FileMaker menu bar (including any docked toolbars). The five values returned by the bounds attribute can be retrieved independently using the left, right, top, bottom, and rotation attributes.
Left	The distance (in points) of the left edge of the object from the left edge of the FileMaker menu bar.

Attribute Name	Value Returned
Right	The distance (in points) of the right edge of the object from the left edge of the application window.
Top	The distance (in points) of the top edge of the object from the bottom of the FileMaker menu bar.
Bottom	The distance (in points) of the bottom edge of the object from the bottom of the FileMaker menu bar.
Width	The width (in points) of the object.
Height	The height (in points) of the object.
Rotation	The rotation (in degrees: 0, 90, 180, 270) of the object.
startPoint	The position (horizontal and vertical, in points, separated by a space) of the start point of a line object, relative to the bottom-left corner of the FileMaker menu bar. Other object types return the position of the object's top-left corner.
endPoint	The position (horizontal and vertical, in points, separated by a space) of the end point of a line object, relative to the bottom-left corner of the FileMaker menu bar. Other object types return the position of the object's bottom-right corner.
Source	A description of the source of the specified object, which varies for different types of objects. Web viewers: The current URL. Fields: The fully qualified field name (tableOccurrenceName::fieldName). Text objects: The text of the object itself, not including merge fields. Portals: The related table occurrence name. Graphics: Image data, such as the image name, type, and/or file path. Charts: The XML description of the chart object.
Content	The content of the specified object, which varies for different types of objects. Web viewers: The source code of the page being displayed. Fields: The data contained in the field, formatted using the specified object's properties. Text objects: The text of the object itself, including merge fields. Graphics: Image data, such as the image name, type, and/or file path. Charts: The bitmap representation of the chart object.
enclosingObject	The name of the layout object that encloses the specified object. Only groups, tab panels, and portals can contain other objects.
containedObjects	A list of the named objects contained within the specified object. Only groups, tab panels, and portals can contain other objects.

Note: If objects are set to auto-resize, position attributes are based on the resized bounds of the object in its current state.

Examples:

Function	Results
GetLayoutObjectAttribute ("FirstName field"; "hasFocus")	Returns 1 if the user is clicked into the object named FirstName field.
GetLayoutObjectAttribute ("FirstName field"; "content")	Returns Fred when the content of the object named FirstName field is Fred.
GetLayoutObjectAttribute ("myObject"; "bounds")	Might return 452 85 502 105 0.
GetLayoutObjectAttribute ("myObject"; "enclosingObject")	Returns InfoTab if myObject is contained on a tab panel object named InfoTab.

GetNextSerialValue (fileName; fieldName)

Data type returned: **Text**

Category: **Design**

Parameters:

- **fileName**—A string or text expression that represents the name of an open file.
- **fieldName**—A string or text expression that represents the name of the field for which to return results.

Description:

Returns the next value for a field defined to auto-enter a serialized value.

It is good practice to specify the fieldName parameter using a fully qualified field name (TableOccurrence::FieldName) so that it can be evaluated in any context. Without explicitly naming a table occurrence, this function assumes the field can be found in the current context, which might not be the case. Because the auto-entered serial number is defined at the table level, it does matter which of a table's occurrences you reference because they all return the same result.

If the fileName parameter is left blank, the function assumes to use the current file.

Examples:

Function	Results
GetNextSerialValue ("Invoices"; "InvoiceID")	Might return 5345.
GetNextSerialValue (Get (FileName); "Contacts::ContactID")	Might return 84.

GetNthRecord (fieldName; recordNumber)

Data type returned: **Text, Number, Date, Time, Timestamp, Container**

Category: **Logical**

Parameters:

- **fieldName**—The name of the field (usually a related field) from which to retrieve data.
- **recordNumber**—An integer representing the record number from which to retrieve data.

Description:

Returns the contents of fieldName from the provided recordNumber.

When fieldName is a field in the current table, recordNumber refers to a record's position within the current found set. When fieldName is a related field, recordNumber refers to a record's position within the set of related records, regardless of the found set. The order of related records is determined by the Sort setting in the Edit Relationship dialog; if no sort order is specified, the records are ordered by their creation order.

Note that the rules governing storage and indexing for related calculation values apply to GetNthRecord just as they do for other functions. The result of an expression containing GetNthRecord does not update when a related value is referenced unless it is set to be an unstored calculation or unless the relationship is reset/refreshed somehow.

Examples:

Function	Results
GetNthRecord (InvoiceDate; 2)	Returns the contents of the InvoiceDate field for record 2 of the current found set in the current table.
GetNthRecord (LastName; Get (RecordNumber) + 1)	Returns the contents of the LastName field for the next record in the current found set. You might use this formula as a ToolTip to show the next and previous names in the found set.
GetNthRecord (Contacts::LastName; 4)	Returns the contents of the LastName field for the fourth related Contact record.

GetRepetition (repeatingField; repetitionNumber)

Data type returned: **Text, Number, Date, Time, Timestamp, Container**

Category: **Repeating**

Parameters:

- **repeatingField**—Any repeating field or an expression that returns a reference to a repeating field.
- **repetitionNumber**—A positive integer representing the repetition number to retrieve.

Description:

Returns the contents of the specified repetition of a repeating field.

A shorthand notation can be used in place of the GetRepetition function. The repetition number can be placed in square brackets after the name of the repeating field. For instance, GetRepetition (myField; 6) is the same as myField[6].

Examples:

Function	Results
GetRepetition (RepPercentage; 2)	Returns the contents of the second repetition of the RepPercentage field.
Let (repNumber = Ceiling (Random * 20) ; GetRepetition (QuoteOfTheDay; repNumber))	Assuming QuoteOfTheDay is a repeating text field that contains 20 repetitions, this function extracts a random quote.

GetSummary (summaryField; breakField)

Data type returned: **Number, Date, Time, Timestamp**

Category: **Summary**

Parameters:

- **summaryField**—A field of type summary or an expression that returns a reference to one.
- **breakField**—A field or an expression that returns a reference to one.

Description:

Returns the value of summaryField when summarized by breakField. The found set must be sorted by breakField for GetSummary to return the proper value.

GetSummary returns the same values that you would see if you were to place the specified summary field in a subsummary report. GetSummary is necessary when you need to use summarized values in calculation formulas.

To calculate a grand summary value, use the same summary field for both the summaryField and the breakField parameters.

Examples:

Given the following record set, sorted by Country, and a summary field called Sum_Sales defined as the Total of Sales:

Country	Region	Sales
U.S.	North	55,000
U.S.	South	45,000
China	North	35,000
China	South	40,000

Now consider a field SalesByCountry defined as follows:

```
GetSummary ( Sum_Sales; Country )
```

This example returns 100,000 for the two U.S. records and returns 75,000 for the two China records.

GetThumbnail (sourceField ; fitToWidth ; fitToHeight)

Data type returned: **Container**

Category: **Container**

Parameters:

- **sourceField**—Any container field.
- **fitToWidth**—A number or expression that returns a number, representing the width (in pixels) for the thumbnail.
- **fitToHeight**—A number or expression that returns a number, representing the height (in pixels) for the thumbnail.

Description:

Returns a thumbnail version of an image in a container field, resized using the dimensions supplied in the fitToWidth and fitToHeight parameters. The thumbnail image always maintains the proportions of the original image.

Because a thumbnail is generally much smaller than the image it represents, it displays more quickly than the image itself. For best performance, store the thumbnail in a separate container field instead of just creating a calculation field that returns the thumbnail as the calculation result.

Consider using a script trigger or other routine that makes and stores the thumbnail of an image when it is first inserted into the container field. Alternatively, you can use an OnRecordLoad trigger to confirm that the thumbnail exists, creating it if necessary.

Examples:

Function	Results
GetThumbnail (bigImage ; 100 ; 100)	Returns a 100 × 100 version of the image in the bigImage field.
GetThumbnail (bigImage ; GetWidth (bigImage) / 2 ; GetHeight (bigImage) / 2)	Returns a version of bigImage at half the original width and height.

GetValue (listOfValues; valueNumber)

Data type returned: **Text**

Category: **Text**

Parameters:

- **listOfValues**—A list of carriage return–delimited values.
- **valueNumber**—A number representing which value to return from the list.

Description:

Returns a single value from a list of carriage return–delimited values. This capability can be useful in scripting routines for looping through a set of items. Many objects in FileMaker Pro generate return-delimited lists, including value lists, fields formatted as check boxes, and functions such as WindowNames and Get (AccountExtendedPrivileges).

Examples:

Function	Results
GetValue ("Red¶Green¶Light Green"; 2)	Returns Green.
GetValue (WindowNames ; 1)	Returns the name of the frontmost window.

GetWidth (sourceField)

Data type returned: **Number**

Category: **Container**

Parameters:

- **sourceField**—Any container field.

Description:

Returns the width in pixels of an image in the sourceField.

GetWidth returns 0 if the container field does not contain an image or if the sourceField is not a container field. It does not matter how the image is stored in the container field (by reference, embedded, or externally).

Examples:

Function	Results
GetWidth (StudentPicture)	Returns 280 when the image in the StudentPicture field is 280 pixels wide.

Hiragana (text)

Data type returned: **Text (Japanese)**

Category: **Text**

Parameters:

- **text**—Any text expression or text field.

Description:

Converts written Japanese katakana (hankaku and zenkaku) text to hiragana.

Japanese has four written alphabets in which it is possible to represent a syllable in a number of different ways. The Hiragana function, along with the KanaHankaku, KanaZenkaku, and Katakana functions, all enable conversion from one set of alphabetic glyphs to another.

Examples:

Function	Results
Hiragana (アイウエオ)	Returns あいうえお

Hour (time)

Data type returned: **Number**

Category: **Time**

Parameters:

- **time**—Any valid time value or expression that returns a valid time value.

Description:

Returns an integer representing the number of hours specified by the time parameter.

When its parameter represents a specific time of day, the Hour function returns a value from 0 to 23. To map this into the more familiar 1 to 12 range, you can use the following formula:

```
Mod ( Hour ( time ) -1; 12 ) + 1
```

The Hour function can return an integer value outside the 0 to 23 range when its parameter represents a duration rather than a specific time of day. For instance, Hour ("65:12:53") returns 65.

Examples:

Function	Results
Hour ("10:45:20")	Returns 10.
Hour ("12:15 am")	Returns 0.
Hour ("11:15 pm")	Returns 23.
Hour (Get (CurrentTime))	Returns a value from 0 to 23.

If (test; result1; result2)

Data type returned: **Text, Number, Date, Time, Timestamp, Container**

Category: **Logical**

Parameters:

- **test**—A logical expression that returns True (1) or False (0).
- **result1**—The expression to evaluate if test is true.
- **result2**—The expression to evaluate if test is false.

Description:

Returns one of two possible results depending on whether the test supplied as the first parameter is True or False. Result1 is returned if test is true; Result2 is returned if test is false.

The test parameter should be an expression that returns a numeric or Boolean result. For numeric results, 0 and null are both considered false; all other values are considered true.

If test contains multiple conditions separated by and or or, FileMaker stops evaluating the conditions as soon as it can determine the overall truthfulness of the test. For instance, if the test parameter is IsEmpty(FieldA) and IsEmpty(FieldB), if Field A is not empty, there is no way that the entire expression could be true. FileMaker does not evaluate the other condition involving FieldB and returns the false result.

You can nest If statements within one another, but it is usually more efficient to use a Case statement rather than an If in such cases.

Examples:

Function	Results

If(DayOfWeek (Get (CurrentDate))) = 1 ;
"It's Sunday, no work!"; // true result
"Get back to work!" // false result
)
	Returns one statement on Sunday, but a different one every other day of the week.

If (myFlagField; graphicTrue; graphicFalse)	Looks for a true value (nonzero, nonblank) in myFlagField and displays the correct graphic container.
If (not IsEmpty (Taxable) and TaxRate > 0; Price + (Price * TaxRate); Price)	Conditional test adds tax to a price when the transaction is taxable and the tax rate is greater than zero.

Int (number)

Data type returned: **Number**

Category: **Number**

Parameters:

- **number**—Any expression that resolves to a numeric value.

Description:

Returns the whole number (integer) part of the number parameter, without rounding. Digits to the right of the decimal point are dropped.

Note that for positive numbers, Floor and Int return the same results; however, for negative numbers, Int returns the next larger integer, whereas Floor returns the next smaller integer.

There are many practical uses for the Int function. For instance, given any date, to find the date of the Sunday preceding it, use the formula GetAsDate (Int (myDate / 7) * 7). Similarly, to test whether an integer is odd or even, you can test whether Int (num / 2) = num / 2.

Examples:

Function	Results
Int (1.0005)	Returns 1.
Int (-1.0005)	Returns -1.

IsEmpty (expression)

Data type returned: **Number**

Category: **Logical**

Parameters:

- **expression**—Typically, a field name, but can be any valid FileMaker Pro calculation formula.

Description:

Returns 1 (True) if the referenced field is empty or if the expression returns an empty string. Returns 0 (False) if the field or expression is not empty.

Remember that 0 is a valid entry for a number field. If a number field contains a 0, it is not considered to be empty. If you need to test for 0 or null, use GetAsBoolean.

Examples:

Function	Results
IsEmpty (myField)	Returns 1 if myField is empty.
IsEmpty (Name_First & Name_Last)	Returns 1 if the result of concatenating the two fields together is an empty string.

IsValid (expression)

Data type returned: **Number**

Category: **Logical**

Parameters:

- **expression**—Typically, a field name, but can be any valid FileMaker Pro calculation formula.

Description:

Returns either a 1 (True) or a 0 (False), depending on whether the field or expression returns valid data.

IsValid returns a 0 if there is a data type mismatch (for example, text in a date field) or if FileMaker cannot locate the table or field that is referenced. Otherwise, it returns 1, indicating that the data is valid.

Examples:

Function	Results
IsValid (myField)	Returns 1 (True) when myField is present and contains data appropriate to its defined data type.
IsValid (Contacts::Name)	Returns 0 (False) if the current record has no related records in the Contacts table or if the related records all contain invalid data.

IsValidExpression (expression)

Data type returned: **Number**

Category: **Logical**

Parameters:

- **expression**—A text string containing a calculation expression, or a field or expression that returns a text string that contains a calculation expression.

Description:

Returns 1 (True) if the expression syntax is correct. Returns 0 (False) if the expression has a syntax error.

The IsValidExpression function is often used in conjunction with the Evaluate function to ensure that Evaluate is passed a valid expression. For instance, if users are allowed to enter a formula into a field called myFormula, and you want to have another field express the results of that formula, you could use the following:

```
If ( IsValidExpression ( myFormula ); Evaluate ( myFormula ); "Invalid formula: "
& TextColor ( myFormula; RGB ( 255; 0; 0 )))
```

An expression is considered invalid if it contains syntax errors or if any of the referenced fields cannot be found. Errors that might occur only during execution of the expression, such as record access restrictions, are not detected by the IsValidExpression formula.

Examples:

Function	Results
IsValidExpression ("Length (SideA)")	Returns 1 (True) as long as there is, in fact, a field named SideA.
IsValidExpression ("Middle (myField; 1)")	Returns 0 (False) because the Middle function requires three parameters to be considered valid syntax.
IsValidExpression (myFormula)	Returns 1 (True) if the contents of myFormula would be considered a valid calculation expression.

KanaHankaku (text)

Data type returned: **Text (Japanese)**

Category: **Text**

Parameters:

- **text**—Any text expression or text field.

Description:

Converts zenkaku katakana to hankaku katakana.

Japanese has four written alphabets in which it is possible to represent a syllable in a number of different ways. The KanaHankaku function, along with the KanaZenkaku, Hiragana, and Katakana functions, all enable conversion from one set of alphabetic glyphs to another.

Examples:

Function	Results
KanaHankaku (ﾃﾞｰﾀﾍﾞｰｽ)	Returns データベース

KanaZenkaku (text)

Data type returned: **Text (Japanese)**

Category: **Text**

Parameters:

- **text**—Any text expression or text field.

Description:

Converts hankaku katakana to zenkaku katakana.

Japanese has four written alphabets in which it is possible to represent a syllable in a number of different ways. The KanaZenkaku function, along with the KanaHankaku, Hiragana, and Katakana functions, all enable conversion from one set of alphabetic glyphs to another.

Examples:

Function	Results
KanaZenkaku ("ﾃﾞｰﾀﾍﾞｰｽ")	Returns データベース

KanjiNumeral (text)

Data type returned: **Text (Japanese)**

Category: **Text**

Parameters:

- **text**—Any text expression or text field.

Description:

Converts Arabic numerals to kanji numerals.

In Japanese, numbers are represented by either the Arabic "123..." character glyphs or by their kanji equivalents. KanjiNumeral enables converting from Arabic to kanji.

To convert in the opposite direction from kanji to Arabic, you can use the GetAsNumber function.

Examples:

Function	Results
KanjiNumeral (富士見台２の３の２５)	Returns 富士見台二の三の二五 .

Katakana (text)

Data type returned: **Text (Japanese)**

Category: **Text**

Parameters:

- **text**—Any text expression or text field.

Description:

Converts from hiragana to zenkaku Katakana.

Japanese has four written alphabets in which it is possible to represent a syllable in a number of different ways. The Katakana function, along with the Hiragana, KanaHankaku, and KanaZenkaku functions, all enable conversion from one set of alphabetic glyphs to another.

Examples:

Function	Results
Katakana (あいうえお)	Returns アイウエオ

Last (field)

Data type returned: **Text**, **Number**, **Date**, **Time**, **Timestamp**, **Container**

Category: **Repeating**

Parameters:

- **field**—Any repeating field or related field.

Description:

Returns the value from the last valid, nonblank repetition if the specified field is a repeating field. If the specified field is a related field, this function returns the last nonblank value from the set of related records. The order of the set of related records is determined by the sort order of the relationship. If no sort order is specified, the creation order is used.

Examples:

Function	Results
Last (RepPercentage)	Returns .06 when RepPercentage is a repeating field with the values .04, .05, and .06.
Last (PhoneNumber::Number)	Returns the most recent related phone number entered, assuming no sort is specified for the relationship.

LayoutIDs (fileName)

Data type returned: **Text**

Category: **Design**

Parameters:

- **fileName**—A string or text expression that represents the name of an open file. It can include a file extension but does not need one.

Description:

Produces a carriage return–delimited list of all the internal layout IDs for the specified file. The list is ordered according to the current layout order, not the creation order.

Layout IDs are assigned in sequential order beginning at 1. The original file's layout IDs are retained when older databases are converted to FileMaker Pro 12.

If the fileName parameter is blank (that is, ""), LayoutIDs returns information for the current file.

Examples:

Function	Results
LayoutIDs (Get (FileName))	Might return a list of values that looks like this: 3 9 10 24 13 28

LayoutNames (fileName)

Data type returned: **Text**

Category: **Design**

Parameters:

- **fileName**—A string or text expression that represents the name of an open file. It can include a file extension but does not need one.

Description:

Produces a carriage return–delimited list of layout names for the specified file.

As with the LayoutIDs function, the order of the layout names is determined by the current order of the layouts, not their creation order.

If the fileName parameter is blank (that is, ""), LayoutNames returns information for the current file.

If you need to determine a particular layout's ID (say, the Contact_Detail layout), you can use the LayoutNames and LayoutIDs functions together, as follows:

```
Let ([
  curFile = Get ( FileName );
  LNs = LayoutNames ( curFile );
  LIs = LayoutIDs ( curFile );
  pos = Position ( LNs; "Contact_Detail"; 1; 1 );
  num = ValueCount ( Left ( LNs; pos - 1 )) + 1 ] ;

  Case ( pos > 0; GetValue ( LIs; num ) ; "" )
)
```

Examples:

Function	Results
LayoutNames (Get (FileName))	Might return a list of values that looks like this: Contact_List Contact_Detail Invoice_List Invoice_Detail

LayoutObjectNames (fileName ; layoutName)

Data type returned: **Text**

Category: **Design**

Parameters:

- **fileName**—The name of an open FileMaker database.
- **layoutName**—The name of the layout from which to return object names.

Description:

Generates a carriage return–delimited list of the names of objects on the specified layout. Any object on a layout can be given a name using the Inspector. If the fileName parameter is blank (that is, ""), LayoutObjectNames returns information for the current file.

Object names are listed according to their stacking order on the layout, from back to front. For named objects that can contain other objects (that is, tab controls, grouped objects, and portals), the object name is followed by a list of the enclosed objects, set off using angle brackets (<>). The angle brackets are listed even if there are no enclosed objects.

Examples:

Function	Results
LayoutObjectNames (Get (FileName) ; Get (LayoutName))	Returns the names of all objects on the current layout of the current file. This list might look something like the following: FirstName field LastName field A random line InfoTab < > AddressTab < Address City State > Picture

Left (text; numberOfCharacters)

Data type returned: **Text**

Category: **Text**

Parameters:

- **text**—Any expression that resolves to a text string.
- **numberOfCharacters**—Any expression that resolves to a positive integer.

Description:

Returns a string containing the first *n* characters from the specified text string, where *n* is the number specified in the numberOfCharacters parameter. If the string is shorter than numberOfCharacters, the entire string is returned. If numberOfCharacters is less than 1, an empty string is returned.

The Left function is commonly used in text parsing routines to extract portions of a text string. It is often used in conjunction with other text functions. For example, to extract the City portion of a field (called "CSZ") containing "City, State Zip" data, you could use the following formula:

```
Let ( commaPosition = Position ( CSZ; ","; 1; 1 );
    Left ( CSZ; commaPosition – 1 )
)
```

Examples:

Function	Results
Left ("Hello" ; 2)	Returns He.
Left (FirstName ; 1)	Returns the first character of the FirstName field.

LeftValues (text; numberOfValues)

Data type returned: **Text**

Category: **Text**

Parameters:

- **text**—A return-delimited text string or expression that returns a return-delimited text string.
- **numberOfValues**—Any positive number or expression that returns a positive number.

Description:

The LeftValues function returns the first *n* items from a return-delimited list, where *n* is the number specified in the numberOfValues parameter. The items returned are themselves a return-delimited array, and there is always a trailing return at the end of the last item.

You can remove the trailing return in a number of ways. If you are extracting a single item from the beginning of a list, you can use the Substitute function to remove any return characters—for instance, Substitute (LeftValues (text; 1); "¶"; ""). You would not use this method when returning multiple items because the internal delimiters also would be lost. Instead, the following function returns everything except the last character of the extracted list:

```
Let ( x = LeftValues ( text; n ); Left ( x; Length ( x ) - 1 ))
```

Another option is the following:

```
LeftWords ( LeftValues ( text; n ); 999999 )
```

This function takes advantage of the fact that the LeftWords function ignores any leading or trailing delimiters. Be aware that this function also ignores leading or trailing delimiters from the actual items in the array (including punctuation symbols), so in some cases this function does not return the desired result. The safest formula to use in all cases is the Let function shown here.

Examples:

Function	Results
LeftValues("A¶B¶C¶D¶E"; 3)	Returns A B C
LeftValues (WindowNames ; 1)	Returns the name of the active window (followed by a carriage return).

LeftWords (text; numberOfWords)

Data type returned: **Text**

Category: **Text**

Parameters:

- **text**—Any expression that resolves to a text string.
- **numberOfWords**—Any positive number or expression that returns a positive number.

Description:

Returns the first *n* number of words in a text expression, where *n* is the number specified in the numberOfWords parameter.

Be aware of what symbols FileMaker Pro considers to be word breaks. Spaces, return characters, and most punctuation symbols are considered to be word breaks. Multiple word breaks next to each other (for example, two spaces, a comma, and a space) are considered as a single word break.

Certain punctuation symbols are word breaks when separating alpha characters but not when separating numeric characters. They include the colon (:), slash (/), period (.), comma (,), and dash (-). For instance, LeftWords ("54-6"; 1) returns 54-6, but LeftWords ("x-y"; 1) returns x. The reason for this behavior is that those symbols are valid date, time, and number separators.

The LeftWords function may ignore leading and trailing punctuation around a word. For example, LeftWords ("John Q. Public, Jr."; 2) returns John Q, but LeftWords ("John Q. Public, Jr."; 3) returns John Q. Public.

Examples:

Function	Results
LeftWords ("the quick brown fox jumps"; 3)	Returns the quick brown.
LeftWords (FullName ; 1)	Returns Eleanor when FullName contains Eleanor Seligo.

Length (text)

Data type returned: **Number**

Category: **Text**

Parameters:

- **text**—Any expression that resolves to a text string.

Description:

Returns the number of characters in the specified text string. Numbers, letters, punctuation, spaces, and carriage returns are all considered as characters.

Length also serves a second function in that it returns the size in bytes of the object data found in a container field.

The Length function is often used as part of data validation rules. For instance, if you want to make sure that users enter phone numbers with either 7 or 10 digits, you could set up a validation by calculation rule as follows:

```
Length ( GetAsNumber ( Phone )) = 7 or Length ( GetAsNumber ( Phone )) = 10
```

Examples:

Function	Results
Length ("Hello there!")	Returns 12.
Length (LastName)	Returns 8 when LastName contains Humphrey.
Length (Get (CurrentDate))	Returns 9 when the date is 3/27/2012.
Length (myContainer)	Returns 156862 when the myContainer field holds an image that is approximately 157KB in size. (Operating systems report file size slightly differently. It is not unlikely that this function will return a slightly different number than that of your operating system.)

Let ({ [} var1=expression1 { ; var2=expression2 ...] } ; calculation)

Data type returned: **Text**, **Number**, **Date**, **Time**, **Timestamp**, **Container**

Category: **Logical**

Parameters:

- **var(n)**—Any valid variable name. The rules for naming variables are the same as for defining fields.
- **expression(n)**—Any calculation formula, the results of which are assigned to the var(n) variable.
- **calculation**—Any calculation formula.

Parameters in curly braces { } are optional and may be repeated as needed, separated by a semicolon.

Description:

Enables you to declare local variables within a calculation formula. The variables exist only within the boundaries of the Let function itself.

The first parameter of the Let function is a list of variable names and expressions. If multiple variables are declared, you need to enclose the list in square brackets and separate it with semicolons. The variables are set in the order in which they appear. This means that you can use previously defined variables as part of the expression to define another variable.

The final parameter, calculation, is some expression that you want to evaluate. That formula can reference any of the variables declared in the first half of the function.

Duplicate variable names are allowed, and variables can be named the same as existing fields. If this happens, the value assigned to the variable, not the field, will be used in future references to the variable within the Let function. In general, this situation should be avoided to prevent confusion.

Let can be used to simplify complex, nested calculation formulas. We cannot advocate its use strongly enough.

If a subexpression is used many times within a formula, the Let function may also provide a performance benefit because the subexpression is evaluated only once when it is assigned to the variable.

You can also use the Let function to set script variables as follows:

```
Let ([
   $var = 100;
   $$var = 500
   ];
   expression
)
```

Keeping track of variables that overlap scope—in this case, overlapping the scope of a calculation expression with that of script or global variables—can often lead to code that is extremely difficult to work with and maintain. Although the preceding is entirely possible, we generally do not recommend it as a practice.

Examples:

Function	Results

Let([
  start = Position (eMail ; "@" ;1 ;1);
  numChars = Length (eMail) – start
];
  Right (eMail; numChars)
)
	Extracts the domain name from an email address.

Let ([
  TotalGradePoints = Sum (Grades::GradePoints);
  CreditPoints = Sum (Classes::CreditPoints);
  GPA = Round (TotalGradePoints / CreditPoints; 2)
] ;
  "Total Grade Points: " & TotalGradePoints & "¶ " &
  "Available Credit Points: " & CreditPoints & "¶" &
  "Your GPA is: " & GPA
)
	Produces a summary of a student's grades.

Let(
  SideOfBase = 2 * Sqrt (2 * SlantHeight^2 - Height^2);
  SideOfBase^2 * Height / 3
)
	Returns the volume of a pyramid.

Lg (number)

Data type returned: **Number**

Category: **Number**

Parameters:

- **number**—Any positive number or expression that returns a positive number.

Description:

Returns the base-2 logarithm of number. Negative values for number return an error.

The base-2 logarithm (often called the binary logarithm) of a number is the power of 2 that you would need to generate the number. Thus, if 2^x = y, then Lg(y) = x. The value returned by the Lg function is increased by 1 every time x is doubled.

Examples:

Function	Results
Lg (1)	Returns 0.
Lg (2)	Returns 1.
Lg (32)	Returns 5.

List (field { ; field...})

Data type returned: **Text**

Category: **Aggregate**

Parameters:

- **field**—Any related field, repeating field, or set of nonrepeating fields that represent a collection of data. Parameters in curly braces { } are optional.

Description:

Generates a carriage return–delimited list of the collection of data referenced by the field parameter.

If field is a repeating field, then List (field) is a list of the nonblank values from each repetition, ordered by repetition.

If field is a related field, then List (field) is a concatenated list of the values in each related record, ordered by the sort order defined for the relationship.

When you are referencing multiple repeating fields, List generates a repeating result where the first repetition is a list of the values in the first repetition of the reference fields, and so on.

Examples:

Function	Results
List ("blue" ; "white" ; "red")	Returns blue¶white¶red.
List (repeatingField)	Returns Fred¶Flintstone (when repetition 1 = Fred, repetition 2 = Flintstone)
List (Contact::FullName)	Returns a list of the contents of the FullName field from the related set of Contact records.

Ln (number)

Data type returned: **Number**

Category: **Number**

Parameters:

- **number**—Any positive number or expression that returns a positive number.

Description:

Returns the natural logarithm of the specified number. The natural logarithm uses the transcendental number *e* as its base. The value of *e* is approximately 2.71828.

Exp and Ln are inverse functions of one another.

The Log and Lg functions produce base-10 and base-2 logarithms, respectively. The Ln function produces base-*e* logarithms, but it can also be used to solve a logarithm of any base. Log (base-x) of y is equivalent to Ln (y) / Ln (x).

Examples:

Function	Results
Ln (2.7182818)	Returns .9999999895305023.
Ln (100)	Returns 4.6051701859880914.
Ln (Exp (5))	Returns 5.

Location (accuracy {; timeout})

Data type returned: **Text**

Category: **Mobile**

Parameters:

- **accuracy**—A number or numeric expression that represents a distance in meters.
- **timeout**—A number or numeric expression that represents the maximum amount of time (measured in seconds) it takes to fetch the location. The default value is 60. Parameters in curly braces { } are optional.

Description:

Note: This function works only on FileMaker Go.

Returns and caches the current latitude and longitude of the device on which it is run using GPS, cellular network, or Wi-Fi.

If you cancel the process, FileMaker Go returns the most accurate location in the cache (if any).

Depending on the network connection, it can take a while for Location to return a value. Consider using either a larger value for accuracy (such as 100) or a shorter timeout to improve performance.

Avoid using Location in an unstored calculation that is placed on a visible layout (use a script to set the result into a variable or text field instead). If you do so, it attempts to update every time the device is moved.

Use LocationValues if you need to know additional information about the location, such as the altitude and accuracy.

Examples:

Function	Results
Location ("")	Might return +41.882530, -87.649651
Location (50 ; 5)	Returns the device location to within an accuracy of 50 meters, and as best as can be achieved within 5 seconds.

LocationValues (accuracy {; timeout})

Data type returned: **Text**

Category: **Mobile**

Parameters:

- **accuracy**—A number or numeric expression that represents a distance in meters.
- **timeout**—A number or numeric expression that represents the maximum amount of time (measured in seconds) it takes to fetch the location. The default value is 60. Parameters in curly braces { } are optional.

Description:

Note: This function works only on FileMaker Go.

Returns and caches information about the location of the device on which it is run. Specifically, LocationValues generates a return-delimited list of values representing

Latitude
Longitude
Altitude
Horizontal accuracy (+/–, in meters)
Vertical accuracy (+/–, in meters)
Age of values (in minutes)

You can use the GetValue function to retrieve any particular value from the list.

LocationValues fetches the location until either the requested accuracy is met or until timeout. If you cancel the process, FileMaker Go returns the most accurate location in the cache (if any).

Depending on the network connection, it can take a while for Location to return a value. Consider using either a larger value for accuracy (such as 100) or a shorter timeout to improve performance.

Avoid using LocationValues in an unstored calculation that is placed on a visible layout (use a script to set the result into a variable or text field instead). If you do so, it attempts to update every time the device is moved.

Examples:

Function	Results
LocationValues (50 ; 5)	Might return 41.882784 -87.649718 187.109421 30 57 .331898

Log (number)

Data type returned: **Number**

Category: **Number**

Parameters:

- **number**—Any positive number or expression that returns a positive number.

Description:

Returns the base-10 logarithm of number.

Logarithms are used to determine the power to which a number must be raised to equal some other number. If $x^n = y$, then $n = Log_x(y)$. The Log function assumes a base (the variable x in the preceding formula) of 10. The Lg function uses a base of 2, whereas the Ln function uses a base of *e*.

Examples:

Function	Results
Log (1)	Returns 0, because 10^0 = 1.
Log (100)	Returns 2, because 10^2 = 100.
Log (1000)	Returns 3, because 10^3 = 1000.

Lookup (sourceField { ; failExpression })

Data type returned: **Text, Number, Date, Time, Timestamp, Container**

Category: **Logical**

Parameters:

- **sourceField**—Any related field.
- **failExpression**—An expression to evaluate and return if the lookup fails. This is an optional parameter.

Description:

Returns the contents of sourceField, or if no related record is found, returns the result of the failExpression. The table containing the sourceField must be related to the table where the Lookup is defined.

A calculation field that contains a Lookup function can be stored or unstored. If it is unstored, anytime the sourceField changes, the calculation field updates. If the calculation is stored, which is typically why you want to use a Lookup in the first place, changes to the sourceField do not cascade automatically through to the calculation field. Lookup is retriggered when any of the relationship's match fields (in the current table, not the table that contains the sourceField) are modified, or when a relookup is triggered on any of those.

Examples:

Imagine you have a stored calculation field in an Invoice table called CustomerNameLookup, defined as follows:

```
Lookup ( Customer::CustomerName; "<Missing Customer>" )
```

Assume that the Invoice and Customer tables are related on the CustomerID. Whenever the CustomerID field is modified in the Invoice table, this triggers the lookup, and the name of the customer is copied into CustomerNameLookup. If an invalid CustomerID is entered, <Missing Customer> is returned. Because CustomerNameLookup is stored, indexed searches can be performed on it.

Be aware, however, that if the CustomerName field is updated in the Customer table, the change does not cascade automatically through to the Invoice table.

LookupNext (sourceField; lower/higher Flag)

Data type returned: **Text, Number, Date, Time, Timestamp, Container**

Category: **Logical**

Parameters:

- **sourceField**—Any related field.
- **lower/higher Flag**—Keyword that indicates whether to take the next lower or higher value if no direct match is found.

Description:

Returns the contents of sourceField, or if no related record is found, the next lower or higher match value. The table containing the sourceField must be related to the table where the LookupNext function is defined.

The LookupNext function is similar to the Lookup function; they differ only in how they handle the case of no matching record. The Lookup function returns a fail expression in such cases, whereas the LookupNext function returns the value associated with the next lower or higher match.

The Lower and Higher flags are keywords and should not be placed in quotation marks.

See the Lookup function to learn how a lookup is triggered and how the storage options determine when the LookupNext function is refreshed.

Looking up a value from the next higher or lower matching record is desirable when mapping a continuous variable onto a categorical variable. Think, for instance, of how student grades typically map to letter grades. A grade of 90 to 100 is considered an A, 80 to 89 is a B, 70 to 79 is a C, and so on. The percentage value is a continuous variable, whereas the letter grades are categorical.

Using the Lookup function, if you want to use the student's percentage score to retrieve the letter grade from a related table, you would need to have records for every possible combination of percentage and letter grade.

The LookupNext function makes it possible to have records representing only the border conditions. For student grades, you would need to have five records in your related lookup table: 90 is an A, 80 is a B, 70 is a C, 60 is a D, and 0 is an F. You could then relate a student's percentage score to this table and define the following formula as the StudentLetterGrade:

```
LookupNext ( GradeLookup::LetterGrade; Lower )
```

Given a percentage score of 88, which has no exact match, the next lower match (80) returns a letter grade of B.

Examples:

Function	Results
LookupNext (ShipRates::ShippingCost; Higher)	Returns the contents of the ShippingCost field from the ShipRates table. If no exact match is found, the next highest match is returned.

Lower (text)

Data type returned: **Text**

Category: **Text**

Parameters:

- **text**—Any expression that resolves to a text string.

Description:

Returns an all-lowercase version of the specified text string.

The Lower function is one of three functions FileMaker has for changing the case of a text string. The other two are Upper and Proper.

You can use the following formula to test whether a given text string is already written with all lowercase characters:

```
Exact ( text; Lower ( text ))
```

Examples:

Function	Results
Lower ("This is a test")	Returns this is a test.
Lower (Name)	Returns mary smith when the Name field contains "MARY Smith".

Max (field { ; field...})

Data type returned: **Text, Number, Date, Time, Timestamp**

Category: **Aggregate**

Parameters:

- **field**—Any related field, repeating field, or set of nonrepeating fields that represent a set of numbers. Parameters in curly braces { } are optional and may be repeated as needed, separated by a semicolon.

Description:

Returns the largest valid, nonblank value from the set of values specified by the field parameter.

When the parameter list consists of two or more repeating fields, Max returns a repeating field in which the corresponding repetitions from the specified fields are evaluated separately. So, if a field Repeater1 has three values—16, 20, and 24—and another field, Repeater2, has two values—14 and 25—Max (Repeater1; Repeater2) returns a repeating field with values 16, 25, and 24.

Because dates, times, and timestamps are represented internally as numbers, you can use the Max function to compare data of these data types. For instance, to return the later of two dates, you could use the following type of formula:

```
GetAsDate ( Max ( Date (4; 1; 2012); Get ( CurrentDate )))
```

This returns either 4/1/2012 or the current date, whichever is greater.

Examples:

Function	Results
Max (44; 129; 25)	Returns 129.
Max (repeatingField)	Returns 54 (when repetition 1 = 18, repetition 2 = 10, and repetition 3 = 54).
Max (Invoice::InvoiceAmount)	Returns the largest invoice amount found in the set of related Invoice records.

Middle (text; startCharacter; numberOfCharacters)

Data type returned: **Text**

Category: **Text**

Parameters:

- **text**—Any expression that resolves to a text string.

- **startCharacter**—Any positive integer or expression that returns a positive integer.
- **numberOfCharacters**—Any positive integer or expression that returns a positive integer.

Description:

Returns a substring from the middle of the specified text parameter. The substring begins at startCharacter and extracts the numberOfCharacters characters following it. If the end of the string is encountered before the specified number of characters has been extracted, the function returns everything from the start position though the end of the string.

The Middle function is often used in conjunction with other text functions as part of text parsing routines. For instance, if you have a field named CSZ containing city, state, and zip data where the entries are consistently entered as "city, state zip," you could extract the state portion of the string using the following formula:

```
Let (
    commaPosition = Position ( CSZ; ","; 1; 1);
    Middle ( CSZ; commaPosition + 2; 2 )
)
```

Examples:

Function	Results
Middle ("hello world"; 3; 5)	Returns llo w.
Middle (FirstName; 2; 9999999)	Returns everything except the first character of the contents of the FirstName field.

MiddleValues (text; startingValue; numberOfValues)

Data type returned: **Text**

Category: **Text**

Parameters:

- **text**—Any return-delimited string or expression that generates a return-delimited string.
- **startingValue**—Any positive integer or expression that returns a positive integer.
- **numberOfValues**—Any positive number or expression that returns a positive integer.

Description:

Returns the specified number of items from the middle of the text parameter, starting at the value specified in the startingValue parameter.

The MiddleValues function returns a slice from the middle of a return-delimited array. The output itself is a return-delimited array, and there is always a trailing return at the end of the last item.

See the LeftValues function for a discussion of methods to remove the trailing return from the output of the MiddleValues function.

Examples:

Function	Results
MiddleValues ("A¶B¶C¶D¶E"; 2; 3)	Returns B C D
MiddleValues (test; 3; 1)	Returns C when test contains A B C D

MiddleWords (text; startingWord; numberOfWords)

Data type returned: **Text**

Category: **Text**

Parameters:

- **text**—Any expression that resolves to a text string.
- **startingWord**—Any positive number or expression that returns a positive number.
- **numberOfWords**—Any positive number or expression that returns a positive number.

Description:

Extracts a substring from the middle of a text string. The substring begins with the *n*th word of the text string (where *n* represents the startingWord parameter) and extends for the number of words specified by the third parameter.

MiddleWords (text; 1; 1) and LeftWords (text; 1) are equivalent functions.

Be aware of what symbols FileMaker Pro considers to be word breaks. Spaces, return characters, and most punctuation symbols are considered to be word breaks. Multiple word breaks next to each other (for example, two spaces, a comma, and a space) are considered as a single word break.

Certain punctuation symbols are word breaks when separating alpha characters but not when separating numeric characters. They include the colon (:), slash (/), period (.), comma (,), and dash (-). The reason for this behavior is that those symbols are valid date, time, and number separators.

Leading and trailing punctuation around a word may be ignored by the MiddleWords function. For example, MiddleWords ("John Q. Public, Jr."; 2; 1) returns Q, but MiddleWords ("John Q. Public, Jr."; 2; 1) returns Q. Public.

Examples:

Function	Results
MiddleWords ("the quick brown fox jumps"; 3; 2)	Returns brown fox.
MiddleWords (FullName; 2; 1)	Returns Allan when FullName contains Edgar Allan Poe.

Min (field { ; field...})

Data type returned: **Text, Number, Date, Time, Timestamp**

Category: **Aggregate**

Parameters:

- **field**—Any related field, repeating field, or set of nonrepeating fields that represent a set of numbers. Parameters in curly braces { } are optional.

Description:

Returns the lowest valid, nonblank value from the set of values specified by the field parameter.

When the parameter list consists of two or more repeating fields, Min returns a repeating field in which the corresponding repetitions from the specified fields are evaluated separately. So, if a field Repeater1 has three values—16, 20, and 24—and another field, Repeater2, has two values—14 and 25—Min (Repeater1; Repeater2) returns a repeating field with values 14, 20, and 24.

Because dates, times, and timestamps are represented internally as numbers, the Min function can be used to compare data of these data types. For instance, to return the earlier of two dates, you could use the following type of formula:

```
GetAsDate ( Min ( Date ( 4; 1; 2012 ); Get ( CurrentDate )))
```

This example returns either 4/1/2012 or the current date, whichever is less.

Examples:

Function	Results
Min (44; 25; 129)	Returns 25.
Min (repeatingField)	Returns 10 (when repetition 1 = 18, repetition 2 = 10, and repetition 3 = 54).
Min (Invoice::InvoiceAmount)	Returns the lowest invoice amount found in the set of related Invoice records.

Minute (time)

Data type returned: **Number**

Category: **Time**

Parameters:

- **time**—Any valid time value or expression that returns a valid time value.

Description:

Returns an integer representing the number of minutes from the given time value.

The Minute function always returns an integer in the range from 0 to 59. If you want the output of this function to be expressed always as a two-character string (for example, 07 instead of 7 when the time is 4:07 p.m.), use the following formula:

```
Right ( "00" & Minute ( time ); 2 )
```

Examples:

Function	Results
Minute ("10:45:20")	Returns 45.
Minute ("12:07 am")	Returns 7.
Minute (Get (CurrentTime))	Returns a value from 0 to 59.

Mod (number; divisor)

Data type returned: **Number**

Category: **Number**

Parameters:

- **number**—Any expression that resolves to a numeric value.
- **divisor**—Any expression that resolves to a numeric value.

Description:

Returns the remainder after number is divided by divisor.

Mod is related to the Div function; Div returns the whole number portion of x divided by y, whereas Mod returns the remainder.

There are many practical uses for the Mod function. For instance, when x is an integer, Mod (x; 2) returns 0 if x is even, and 1 if x is odd. Mod (x; 1) returns just the decimal portion of a number. And if you have *n* eggs to pack into egg cartons that hold 12 eggs each, Mod (n; 12) tells you how many eggs you would have left over after packing as many full cartons as possible.

Examples:

Function	Results
Mod (7; 5)	Returns 2.
Mod (-7; 5)	Returns 3.
Mod (13; 3)	Returns 1.
Mod (1.43; 1)	Returns .43.

Month (date)

Data type returned: **Number**

Category: **Date**

Parameters:

- **date**—Any valid date (1/1/0001–12/31/4000). The parameter should be a string containing a date (for example, "3/17/2004"), an expression with a date result (for example, Date (6; 29; 1969)), or an integer that represents a serialized date value (for example, 718977).

Description:

Returns the month number (1–12) for any valid date (1/1/0001–12/31/4000).

The numeric value returned by Month can be used in mathematical calculations as well as within the Date function to construct a new date.

One common use of the Month function is to build a formula that returns the quarter of a given date:

```
Case (
 Month ( myDate ) < 4; "First Quarter";
 Month ( myDate ) < 7; "Second Quarter";
 Month ( myDate ) < 9; "Third Quarter";
 "Fourth Quarter"
)
```

Examples:

Function	Results
Month ("5/20/2003")	Returns 5.
Month (718977)	Returns 6.
Month (Get (CurrentDate))	Returns 3 (if the current date is in March).

MonthName (date)

Data type returned: **Text**

Category: **Date**

Parameters:

- **date**—Any valid date (1/1/0001–12/31/4000). The parameter should be a string containing a date (for example, "3/17/2004"), an expression with a date result (for example, Date (6; 29; 1969)), or an integer that represents a serialized date value (for example, 718977).

Description:

Returns the month name of the specified date.

The MonthName function is frequently used for display purposes in subsummary reports. Although you display the name of the month, be sure that you summarize based on the month number (obtained with the Month function). If you do not, your report is summarized alphabetically by month rather than chronologically by month.

Examples:

Function	Results
MonthName ("1/1/2000")	Returns January.
MonthName (Date (5; 20; 2003))	Returns May.
MonthName (Get (CurrentDate))	Might return March.

MonthNameJ (date)

Data type returned: **Text (Japanese)**

Category: **Date**

Parameters:

- **date**—Any valid date(1/1/0001—12/31/4000).

Description:

Returns the name of the month in Japanese.

To avoid errors when using dates, always use four-digit years.

Examples:

Function	Results
MonthNameJ ("6/6/2003")	Returns Rokugatsu in whatever alphabet the field is formatted to display.

NPV (payment; interestRate)

Data type returned: **Number**

Category: **Financial**

Parameters:

- **payment**—A repeating field or related field that contains one or more values representing loan and payment amounts.
- **interestRate**—An interest rate, expressed as a decimal number.

Description:

Returns the net present value (NPV) of a series of unequal payments made at regular intervals, assuming a fixed interestRate per interval. If the field specified in the first parameter is a repeating field, it should contain all loan and payment amounts. The first parameter can also reference a set of related records, each representing a payment amount.

Examples:

Imagine someone borrows $300 from you and repays you $100, $50, $100, and $125 at regular intervals.

Assuming an interest rate of 5%, the NPV function can tell you the profit, in today's dollars, which you will realize from this transaction. To calculate this amount, you place the following values in a repeating number field: –300, 100, 50, 100, and 125. Then you use the following:

```
Round ( NPV ( Payments; .05 ) ; 2)
```

This formula returns $28.39. Your actual profit on the transaction would be $75 (simply the sum of the payments minus the original loan). That $75, however, is collected over time, so the present value is discounted by the assumed interest rate. The higher the interest rate, the less the net present value of the $75.

NumToJText (number; separator; characterType)

Data type returned: **Text (Japanese)**

Category: **Text**

Parameters:

- **number**—Any numeric expression or field containing a number.
- **separator**—A number from 0–3 representing a separator.
- **characterType**—A number from 0–3 representing a type.

Description:

Converts Roman numbers in the number parameter to Japanese text. If the values for separator and characterType are blank or other than 0 to 3, then 0 (no separator) is used.

Separator:

0—No separator
1—Every three digits (thousands)
2—Ten thousands (万) and millions (億) unit
3—Tens (十), hundreds (百), thousands (千), ten thousands (万), and millions (億) unit

Type:

0—Half width (hankaku) number
1—Full width (zenkaku) number
2—Kanji character number (一二三)
3—Traditional-old-style kanji character number (壱弐参)

Examples:

Function	Results
NumToJText (123456789; 2; 0)	Returns 1億2345万6789
NumToJText (123456789; 3; 2)	Returns 一億二千三百四十五万六千七百八十九

PatternCount (text; searchString)

Data type returned: **Number**

Category: **Text**

Parameters:

- **text**—Any expression that resolves to a text string.
- **searchString**—Any expression that resolves to a text string, representing the substring for which you want to search within the text string.

Description:

Returns the number of times that searchString appears in the text string. PatternCount returns 0 if the searchString is not found.

PatternCount counts only nonoverlapping occurrences of searchString. The PatternCount function is not case sensitive.

Even though PatternCount is designed to answer the question "how many?" it is often used simply to determine whether one string is contained within another. If it returns any value other than 0, the search string is found.

Examples:

Function	Results
PatternCount ("This is a test"; "is")	Returns 2.
PatternCount (WindowNames; "¶") + 1	Returns the number of carriage returns in the list returned by the WindowNames function. This could be used to determine the number of available windows. (The ValueCount function could also be used for this purpose.)
PatternCount ("abababa"; "Aba")	Returns 2.

Pi

Data type returned: **Number**

Category: **Trigonometric**

Parameters: **None**

Description:

Returns the value of the trigonometric constant Pi, which is approximately 3.1415926535897932. Pi is defined as the ratio of the circumference to the diameter of any circle.

Pi is most often used in conjunction with other trigonometric functions, such as Sin, Cos, and Tan, which each require an angle measured in radians as a parameter. There are 2*Pi radians in 360 degrees.

Examples:

Function	Results
Sin (Pi / 2)	Returns 1.
SetPrecision (Pi; 25)	Returns 3.1415926535897932384626434.

PMT (principal; interestRate; term)

Data type returned: **Number**

Category: **Financial**

Parameters:

- **principal**—A number or expression that returns a number, representing the initial amount borrowed.
- **interestRate**—A decimal number or expression that returns a number, representing the monthly interest rate used to amortize the principal amount. Given an annual interest rate, you can divide by 12 to get the monthly interest rate.
- **term**—A number or expression that returns a number representing the period of the loan, expressed in months.

Description:

Returns the monthly payment that would be required to pay off the principal based on the interestRate and term specified.

The PMT calculation makes it easy to see the effect of interest rates on the monthly payment of an installment loan. For instance, buying a $20,000.00 car at 6.9% for 48 months requires a $478.00 monthly payment, but at 3.9%, the payment is $450.68.

Examples:

Function	Results
PMT (1000; .06/12; 24)	Returns 44.32. This represents the monthly payment required on a $1,000 loan, to be paid off over 2 years at an annual interest rate of 6%.

Position (text ; searchString ; start ; occurrence)

Data type returned: **Number**

Category: **Text**

Parameters:

- **text**—Any expression that resolves to a text string in which you want to search.
- **searchString**—Any expression that resolves to a text string for which to search.
- **start**—An integer representing the character number at which to begin searching.
- **occurrence**—An integer representing which occurrence of searchString to locate. A negative number causes the search to proceed backward from the start character.

Description:

Returns the character number where the searchString is found within the specified text string. If the searchString is not found, the Position function returns a 0.

In most cases, the Position function is used to find the first occurrence of some substring within a string. Both the start and occurrence parameters are simply 1 in such instances.

To find the last occurrence of a substring within a string, set the start parameter to be the length of the string and the occurrence parameter to be -1, indicating that the function should search backward from the end of the string for the first occurrence of the substring.

The Position function is not case sensitive.

Examples:

Function	Results
Position ("This is a test"; "is"; 1; 1)	Returns 3.
Position ("This is a test"; "is"; 1; 2)	Returns 6.
Let (myString = "This is a test"; Position (myString; " "; Length (myString) ; -1))	Returns 10, which is the position of the last space in myString.

Proper (text)

Data type returned: **Text**

Category: **Text**

Parameters:

- **text**—Any expression that resolves to a text string.

Description:

Returns the specified text string with the initial letter of each word capitalized and all other letters as lowercase.

The Proper function is one of three case-changing functions in FileMaker. The other two are Lower and Upper.

The Proper function is often used as part of an auto-entered calculation formula to reformat a user's entry with the desired case. For instance, in a City field, where you would expect the first letter of each word to be capitalized, you could set up an auto-entry option to enter Proper (City) and uncheck the option to not replace an existing value. Then, if a user were to type SAN FRANCISCO, after the user exited the field, the entry would be reset to San Francisco.

Examples:

Function	Results
Proper ("this is a TEST")	Returns This Is A Test.
Proper (Address)	Returns 123 Main Street when Address contains 123 main street.

PV (payment; interestRate; periods)

Data type returned: **Number**

Category: **Financial**

Parameters:

- **payment**—A number or expression that returns a number, representing a payment amount made per period.
- **interestRate**—A decimal number or expression that returns a decimal number, representing the interest rate per period.
- **periods**—The number of periods of the loan.

Description:

Tells you today's value of money expected in the future, or present value (PV). The PV function returns the present value of a series of equal payments made at regular intervals and assumes a fixed interestRate per interval.

Examples:

Imagine you won $1,000,000 in a lottery. You are offered either $50,000 per year for the next 20 years or a one-time lump sum payment now of $700,000. Which option should you choose?

If you assume an inflation rate of 3% per year, the present value of the future payments is determined by the following formula:

```
PV ( 50000; .03; 20 )
```

This calculation returns 743873.74.

If you assume a 4% inflation rate, the present value of the future payments decreases to 679516.31. So, depending on your assumptions about inflation rates, you might or might not be better off taking the lump sum payment.

As another example, consider the question of whether it would be better for someone to give you $10 today or $1 per year for the next 10 years. You can use the PV function to tell you the present value of receiving $1 for 10 years. Assuming an inflation rate of 3%, the formula PV (1, .03, 10) shows that the present value of the future income is only $8.53. Therefore, you're better off taking the $10 today.

Quote (text)

Data type returned: **Text**

Category: **Text**

Parameters:

- **text**—Any expression that resolves to a text string.

Description:

Returns the specified text string enclosed in quotation marks. To escape any special characters within the text string, such as quotation marks and double backslashes, place a backslash before them in the text string.

The Quote function is used primarily in conjunction with the Evaluate function, which can evaluate a dynamically generated formula. If the formula you are assembling contains a literal text string enclosed by quotation marks, or if it includes field contents that might potentially have quotation marks in it, use the Quote function to ensure that all internal quotation marks are escaped properly.

Examples:

Function	Results
Quote (FullName)	If the FullName field contains the name Billy "Joe" Smith, this returns "Billy \"Joe\" Smith". The absence and presence of quotation marks here is deliberate; the quotation marks are part of the returned string.

Radians (angleInDegrees)

Data type returned: **Number**

Category: **Trigonometric**

Parameters:

- **angleInDegrees**—A number representing an angle measured in degrees.

Description:

Converts an angle measured in degrees into an angle measured in radians.

The trigonometric functions Sin, Cos, and Tan all take an angle measured in radians as their parameter. To find, say, the cosine of a 180° angle, you could use the formula Cos (Radians (180)). There are 2*Pi radians in 360°.

Examples:

Function	Results
Radians (60)	Returns 1.0471975511965977 (= Pi/3).
Radians (180)	Returns 3.1415926535897932 (= Pi).

Random

Data type returned: **Number**

Category: **Number**

Parameters: **None**

Description:

Returns a random decimal between 0 and 1 (including 0, but not including 1). When this function is used in a field definition, a new value is generated when the formula is updated. It is also updated anytime the formula reevaluates, such as when other field values referenced in the formula change. In an unstored calculation, the Random function reevaluates each time the field is displayed.

If you want to generate a random integer in a certain range, multiply the result returned by the random function by the range you want to produce; then use the Int, Floor, Ceiling, Round, or Truncate functions to remove the decimals.

For instance, to return a random number from 1 to 6 (as in the roll of a die), use the following formula:

```
Ceiling ( Random * 6 )
```

If you need to specify a lower bound for the random number, just add the bound to the results of the random number. For instance, to return a random number between 10 and 100, inclusive, use the following formula:

```
Int ( Random * 91 ) + 10
```

Examples:

Function	Results
Round (Random; 5)	Might return .07156.

RelationInfo (fileName; tableOccurrence)

Data type returned: **Text**

Category: **Design**

Parameters:

- **fileName**—A string or text expression representing the name of an open file.
- **tableOccurrence**—A string or text expression representing the name of a particular table occurrence in fileName.

Description:

Returns a list of information about all the table occurrences related to the specified tableOccurrence. If the fileName parameter is left empty, the function references the current file.

The results are formatted as

```
Source: [Data Source Name of the related table occurrence]
Table: [related table occurrence name]
Options: ["Delete", "Create", and/or "Sorted"]
[match fields]
```

This information is repeated for each table occurrence that is directly related to the specified table occurrence.

Examples:

Function	Results
RelationInfo (Get (FileName); "Contacts 2")	Might return Source:ContactDatabase Table:Company Options: Company::CompanyID = Contacts 2::CompanyID Company::ActiveFlag = Contacts 2::Status Source:ContactDatabase Table:Invoice Options:Create Sorted Invoice::ContactID = Contacts 2::ContactID

Replace (text; start; numberOfCharacters; replacementText)

Data type returned: **Text**

Category: **Text**

Parameters:

- **text**—Any expression that resolves to a text string.
- **start**—Any positive number or expression that returns a positive number.
- **numberOfCharacters**—Any positive number or expression that returns a positive number.
- **replacementText**—Any expression that resolves to a text string.

Description:

Extracts a segment of a text string and replaces it with some other string. The segment to extract begins with the start character number and extends for numberOfCharacters. The replacement string is specified by the replacementText parameter.

The extracted segment and the replacement text do not need to be the same length.

The Replace and Substitute functions are often confused with one another. Substitute replaces all occurrences of a particular substring with another string, whereas Replace replaces a specified range of characters with another string.

Replace is often used for manipulation of delimited text arrays. There is no function that directly replaces the contents of a particular item in an array with another. The Replace function can do this by finding the appropriate delimiters and inserting the replacement item. For instance, if you have a pipe-delimited list of numbers (for example, 34|888|150|43) and you want to increase the third item in the list by 18, you could use the following formula:

```
Let ([
  item = 3;
  increase = 18;
  start = Position ( myArray; "|"; 1; ( item - 1 ) ) + 1;
```

```
      end = Position ( myArray; "|"; 1; item );
      itemValue = Middle ( myArray; start; end - start );
      newValue = itemValue + increase ];

      Replace ( myArray; start; end-start; newValue )
   )
```

Given the sample string as myArray, this would produce the string 34|888|168|43. Typically, the item and increase values are supplied by other fields and are not hard-coded into the formula.

Another great purpose of the Replace function is to use it as an "Insert" function: Use 0 as the numberOfCharacters parameter, and you simply insert some amount of text in front of the start character without having to use a combination of the Left, Middle, and Right functions.

Examples:

Function	Results
Replace ("abcdef"; 4; 2; "TEST")	Returns abcTESTf.
Replace ("Fred Smith"; 1; 4; "Joe")	Returns Joe Smith.
Replace ("leftright"; 5; 0; "middle")	Returns leftmiddleright.

RGB (red; green; blue)

Data type returned: **Number**

Category: **Text Formatting**

Parameters:

- **red**—Any number or numeric expression containing a value ranging from 0 to 255.
- **green**—Any number or numeric expression containing a value ranging from 0 to 255.
- **blue**—Any number or numeric expression containing a value ranging from 0 to 255.

Description:

Returns a number that represents a color.

To calculate this integer, you combine the red, green, and blue values using the following formula:

$$(red * 256^2) + (green * 256) + blue$$

Use the RGB function in conjunction with the TextColor function to format text.

If a number greater than 255 is supplied as the parameter, the formula still computes a result according to the preceding formula. If the result of the formula is greater than the expected range of 0 to 16,777,215, Mod (result; 16777216) is used to map the result into the expected range. So RGB (255; 255; 256), which returns a value one higher than white, returns the color black, just as 0 does.

Examples:

Function	Results
RGB (255; 0; 0)	Returns 16711680 (red).
RGB (0; 255; 0)	Returns 65280 (green).
RGB (0; 0; 255)	Returns 255 (blue).
RGB (255; 255; 255)	Returns 16777215 (white).
RGB (0; 0; 0)	Returns 0 (black).
RGB (24; 162; 75)	Returns 1614411 (dark green).
RGB (7; 13; 78)	Returns 462158 (dark purple).
RGB (23; 100; 148)	Returns 1533076 (bright blue).

Right (text; numberOfCharacters)

Data type returned: **Text**

Category: **Text**

Parameters:

- **text**—Any expression that resolves to a text string.
- **numberOfCharacters**—Any expression that resolves to a numeric value.

Description:

Returns a string containing the last *n* characters from the specified text string. If the string is shorter than numberOfCharacters, the entire string is returned. If numberOfCharacters is less than 1, an empty string is returned.

The Right function is commonly used in text parsing routines to extract everything after a certain character in a string. For example, if you are parsing email addresses and want to return everything after the @ in the string as the domain, you could use the following formula:

```
Let ([
  len = Length ( email ) ;
  pos = Position ( email ; "@" ; 1 ; 1 ) ];
  Right ( email ; len – pos )
)
```

Examples:

Function	Results
Right ("Hello"; 2)	Returns lo.
Right (FirstName; 1)	Returns the last character of the FirstName field.

RightValues (text; numberOfValues)

Data type returned: **Text**

Category: **Text**

Parameters:

- **text**—Any return-delimited text string or expression that generates a return-delimited string.
- **numberOfValues**—Any positive number or expression that returns a positive number.

Description:

Returns the last *n* items from a return-delimited array. The items themselves are a return-delimited array, and there is always a trailing return at the end of the last item.

See the LeftValues function for a discussion of methods to remove the trailing return from the output of the RightValues function.

Examples:

Function	Results
RightValues ("A¶B¶C¶D¶E"; 3)	Returns C D E
RightValues (test; 1)	Returns C when test contains A B C

RightWords (text; numberOfWords)

Data type returned: **Text**

Category: **Text**

Parameters:

- **text**—Any expression that resolves to a text string.
- **numberOfWords**—Any positive number or expression that returns a positive number.

Description:

Returns the last *n* number of words in a text expression, where *n* is the number specified in the numberOfWords parameter.

Be aware of what characters FileMaker Pro considers to be word breaks. Spaces, return characters, and most punctuation symbols are considered to be word breaks. Multiple word breaks next to each other (for example, two spaces, a comma, and a space) are considered a single word break.

Certain punctuation symbols are word breaks when separating alpha characters, but not when separating numeric characters. They include the colon (:), slash (/), period (.), comma (,), and dash (-). For instance, RightWords ("54-6"; 1) returns 54-6, but RightWords ("x-y"; 1) returns y. The reason for this behavior is that those symbols are valid date, time, and number separators.

Leading and trailing punctuation around a word is ignored by the RightWords function. For example, RightWords ("John Q. Public, Jr."; 2) returns Public, Jr, and RightWords ("John Q. Public, Jr."; 3) returns Q. Public, Jr.

Examples:

Function	Results
RightWords ("the quick brown fox jumps"; 3)	Returns brown fox jumps.
RightWords (FullName; 1)	Returns Smith when the FullName field contains Joe Smith.

RomanHankaku (text)

Data type returned: **Text (Japanese)**

Category: **Text**

Parameters:

- **text**—Any text expression or text field.

Description:

Converts from zenkaku alphanumeric characters and symbols to hankaku alphanumeric and symbols. Zenkaku alphanumeric characters and symbols represent Roman alphanumeric characters and symbols using Japanese Unicode characters.

Examples:

Function	Results
RomanHankaku ("Ｍａｃｉｎｔｏｓｈ")	Returns Macintosh.

RomanZenkaku (text)

Data type returned: **Text (Japanese)**

Category: **Text**

Parameters:

- **text**—Any text expression or text field.

Description:

Converts from hankaku alphanumeric characters and symbols to zenkaku alphanumeric and symbols. Zenkaku alphanumeric characters and symbols represent Roman alphanumeric characters and symbols using Japanese Unicode characters.

Examples:

Function	Results
RomanZenkaku("Macintosh")	Returns Ｍａｃｉｎｔｏｓｈ.

Round (number; precision)

Data type returned: **Number**

Category: **Number**

Parameters:

- **number**—Any expression that resolves to a numeric value.
- **precision**—A number or numeric expression representing the number of decimal points to which to round the number.

Description:

Returns the specified number rounded off to the number of decimal points specified by the precision parameter. The Round function rounds numbers from 5 to 9 upward, and from 0 to 4 downward.

A precision of 0 rounds to the nearest integer. A negative number for the precision causes the number to be rounded to the nearest ten, hundred, thousand, and so on.

Examples:

Function	Results
Round (62.566; 2)	Returns 62.57.
Round (62.563; 2)	Returns 62.56.
Round (92.4; 0)	Returns 92.
Round (32343.98; -3)	Returns 32000.
Round (505.999; -1)	Returns 510.

ScriptIDs (fileName)

Data type returned: **Text**

Category: **Design**

Parameters:

- **fileName**—A string or text expression that represents the name of an open file.

Description:

Produces a return-delimited list of script IDs from the specified file. If the fileName parameter is left empty, the function references the current file.

ScriptIDs are assigned sequentially by FileMaker, starting at 1 for each new file. The results returned by the ScriptIDs function are ordered according to the current order within the Manage Scripts dialog, not the creation order of the scripts. ScriptIDs ignores folders used to organize scripts.

Any scripts that are set to "no access" for the current user's privilege set are not included in the list.

Examples:

Function	Results
ScriptIDs ("")	Returns a list of script IDs for the current file that might look like this: 21 24 22 25

ScriptNames (fileName)

Data type returned: **Text**

Category: **Design**

Parameters:

- **fileName**—A string or text expression that represents the name of an open file.

Description:

Produces a return-delimited list of script names from the specified file. If the fileName parameter is left empty, the function references the current file.

As with the ScriptIDs function, the order of the list returned by ScriptNames is the current order of the scripts within the Manage Scripts dialog. The names of script folders are not included in the result produced by ScriptNames.

Any scripts that are set to "no access" for the current user's privilege set are not included in the list.

Examples:

Function	Results
ScriptNames (Get (FileName))	Returns a list of script names for the current file that might look like this: Contact_Nav Invoice_Nav - Contact_New Invoice_New - Contact_Delete Invoice_Delete

Seconds (time)

Data type returned: **Number**

Category: **Time**

Parameters:

- **time**—Any valid time value or expression that returns a valid time value.

Description:

The Seconds function returns an integer representing the number of seconds specified by the time parameter. It always returns a value from 0 to 59.

If you want to express the output of this function as a two-character string rather than as an integer (for example, 03 rather than 3), use the following formula:

```
Right ( "00" & Seconds ( Time ); 2 )
```

If the time parameter has a seconds value greater than 59, the Seconds function returns the Mod-60 result of that value. For instance, Seconds ("12:42:87") returns 27. Note that the "overflow" of the seconds value is applied to the minutes value: Minute ("12:42:87") returns 43.

Examples:

Function	Results
Seconds ("10:45:20")	Returns 20.
Seconds ("12:15 am")	Returns 0.

YOU MAY ALSO LIKE...

FileMaker 12 In Depth
by Jesse Feiler

FileMaker Pro 12: The Missing Manual
by Susan Prosser

Apple Pro Video Series: Final Cut Pro X
by Steve Martin

Apple Pro Training Series: Final Cut Pro...
by Michael Wohl

Opened music CDs/DVDs/audio books may not be returned, and can be exchanged only for the same title and only if defective. NOOKs purchased from other retailers or sellers are returnable only to the retailer or seller from which they are purchased, pursuant to such retailer's or seller's return policy. Magazines, newspapers, eBooks, digital downloads, and used books are not returnable or exchangeable. Defective NOOKs may be exchanged at the store in accordance with the applicable warranty.

Returns or exchanges will not be permitted (i) after 14 days or without receipt or (ii) for product not carried by Barnes & Noble or Barnes & Noble.com.

Policy on receipt may appear in two sections.

Return Policy

With a sales receipt or Barnes & Noble.com packing slip, a full refund in the original form of payment will be issued

Self

Data type returned: **Text, Number, Date, Time, Timestamp**

Category: **Logical**

Parameters: **None**

Description:

Returns the contents of the object in which it is defined, thus avoiding the need to explicitly reference the object's name. This enables you to reuse formulas for such things as ToolTips, auto-entered calculation formulas, and conditional formatting without having to edit the formula to refer to the new object.

For instance, if there are several fields in which you want to set up an auto-entry calculation to remove any text formatting from the user's entry (such as might be present when data is copied and pasted from another application), rather than use TextFormatRemove (FirstName) for the FirstName field and TextFormatRemove (LastName) for the LastName field, you could define both simply as TextFormatRemove (Self). This can be a big time saver because you can duplicate fields and not worry that references to the original object need to be edited.

The Self function is also useful when you are setting up conditional formatting of layout objects. For instance, if you want empty fields on a form to appear with a gray background, set a conditional formatting formula of IsEmpty (Self) on all those fields. Referencing Self rather than explicitly referencing the field names saves a lot of time, and it also ensures that if the layout object is duplicated, the new object's conditional formatting references itself and not some other field.

Examples:

Function	Results
TextFormatRemove (Self)	Returns the contents of the current object without any text formatting.
Trim (Self)	Returns the contents of the current object with leading and trailing spaces removed.
Self > Product::ReorderAmount	Returns 1 (True) if the value of the current object is greater than the value in the ReorderAmount field.

SerialIncrement (text; incrementBy)

Data type returned: **Text**

Category: **Text**

Parameters:

- **text**—Any text or text expression that contains an alphanumeric string.
- **incrementBy**—A number or numeric expression with which to increment the text value.

Description:

Returns the combined text and number from the text value, where the numeric portion of the text has been incremented by the value specified in the incrementBy parameter.

The incrementBy value is truncated to an integer when incrementing. Positive and negative numbers are accepted.

Examples:

Function	Results
SerialIncrement ("test1"; 2)	Returns test3.
SerialIncrement ("project_plan_v12.3"; -1)	Returns project_plan_v12.2.
SerialIncrement ("23"; 3)	Returns 26.

SetPrecision (expression; precision)

Data type returned: **Number**

Category: **Number**

Parameters:

- **expression**—Any number or expression that returns a number.
- **precision**—An integer from 1 to 400.

Description:

Allows you to specify up to 400 digits of precision. FileMaker normally computes fractions with 16 digits of precision.

The expression specified in the first parameter is rounded at the digit specified by the precision parameter.

The trigonometric functions support up to only 20 digits of precision.

You can specify a number less than 17 as the precision, but FileMaker still returns 16 digits of precision regardless. Use the Round function instead to specify a precision of fewer than 16 digits.

Examples:

Function	Results
SetPrecision (Pi; 28)	Returns 3.1415926535897932384626433833.
SetPrecision (2 / 3; 30)	Returns .666666666666666666666666666667.

Sign (number)

Data type returned: **Text**

Category: **Number**

Parameters:

- **number**—Any expression that resolves to a numeric value.

Description:

Returns a value that represents the sign of number:

-1 when number is negative.
0 when number is zero.
1 when number is positive.

For any x other than 0, multiplying x by Sign(x) yields the Abs(x).

Examples:

Function	Results
Sign (0)	Returns 0.
Sign (100)	Returns 1.
Sign (-100)	Returns -1.

Sin (angleInRadians)

Data type returned: **Number**

Category: **Trigonometric**

Parameters:

- **angleInRadians**—Any numeric expression or field containing a numeric expression, in radians.

Description:

Returns the sine of angleInRadians.

In any right triangle, the sine of the two nonright angles can be obtained by dividing the length of the side opposite the angle by the length of the hypotenuse.

Examples:

Function	Results
Sin (Radians (60))	Returns .8660254037844387.
Sin (Pi / 4)	Returns .7071067811865475.

Sqrt (number)

Data type returned: **Number**

Category: **Number**

Parameters:

- **number**—Any expression that resolves to a positive number.

Description:

Returns the square root of number.

Examples:

Function	Results
Sqrt (64)	Returns 8.
Sqrt (2)	Returns 1.414213562373095.

StDev (field { ; field...})

Data type returned: **Number**

Category: **Aggregate**

Parameters:

- **field**—Any related field, repeating field, or set of nonrepeating fields that represent a collection of numbers. Parameters in curly braces { } are optional.

Description:

Returns the standard deviation of the nonblank values represented in the parameter list. Standard deviation is a statistical measurement of how spread out a collection of values is. In a normal distribution, about 68% of the values are within one standard deviation of the mean, and about 95% are within two standard deviations of the mean.

The difference between the StDevP and StDev functions is that StDev divides the sum of the squares by n–1 instead of by n.

StDev can also be calculated as the square root of the Variance of a set of numbers.

You can manually calculate the standard deviation of a set of numbers in several ways. One way is to take the square root of the sum of the squares of each value's distance from the mean, divided by n–1, where n is the number of values in the set.

For instance, given the set of numbers 8, 10, and 12, the mean of this set is 10. The distances of each value from the mean are therefore –2, 0, and 2. The squares of these values are 4, 0, and 4. The sum of the squares is 8. The standard deviation is Sqrt (8 / (3 - 1)), which is 2.

Examples:

Function	Results
StDev (8; 10; 12)	Returns 2.
StDev (People::Scores)	Returns 6.35, given a portal that contains a field called Scores with the following related values: 64, 72, 75, 59, 67.

StDevP (field { ; field...})

Data type returned: **Number**

Category: **Aggregate**

Parameters:

- **field**—Any related field, repeating field, or set of nonrepeating fields that represent a collection of numbers. Parameters in curly braces { } are optional.

Description:

Returns the standard deviation of a population represented by the nonblank values in the parameter list. Standard deviation is a statistical measurement of how spread out a collection of values is. In a normal distribution, about 68% of the values are within one standard deviation of the mean, and about 95% are within two standard deviations of the mean.

The difference between the StDevP and StDev functions is that StDev divides the sum of the squares by *n*–1 instead of by *n*.

StDevP can also be calculated as the square root of the VarianceP of a set of numbers.

You can manually calculate the standard deviation of a population in several ways. One way is to take the square root of the sum of the squares of each value's distance from the mean, divided by the number of values.

For instance, given the set of numbers 8, 10, and 12, the mean of this set is 10. The distances of each value from the mean are therefore –2, 0, and 2. The squares of these values are 4, 0, and 4. The sum of the squares is 8. The standard deviation of the population is Sqrt (8 / 3), which is 1.633.

Examples:

Function	Results
StDevP (8; 10; 12)	Returns 1.633.
StDevP (People::Scores)	Returns 5.68, given a portal that contains a field called Scores with the following related values: 64, 72, 75, 59, 67.

Substitute (text; searchString; replaceString)

Data type returned: **Text**

Category: **Text**

Parameters:

- **text**—Any text string or expression that returns a text string.
- **searchString**—Any text string or expression that returns a text string.
- **replaceString**—Any text string or expression that returns a text string.

Description:

Returns a text string in which all instances of searchString in the text parameter are replaced with the replaceString.

Multiple substitutions may occur in the same Substitute function by placing pairs of search and replacement strings in square brackets, separated by semicolons, as follows:

```
Substitute ( "This is a test"; ["i"; "q"]; ["s"; "$"] )
```

This example returns Thq$ q$ a te$t.

One common use of the Substitute function is to remove all instances of a specified character from a string. To do this, use "" (a null string) as the replaceString, as in the third example that follows.

The Substitute function is case sensitive.

Examples:

Function	Results
Substitute ("Happy Anniversary!"; "Anniversary"; "Birthday")	Returns Happy Birthday!.
Substitute ("This is a test"; "i"; "q")	Returns Thqs qs a test.
Substitute ("This is a test"; " "; "")	Returns Thisisatest.

Sum (field { ; field...})

Data type returned: **Number**

Category: **Aggregate**

Parameters:

- **field**—Any related field, repeating field, or set of nonrepeating fields that represent a collection of numbers. Parameters in curly braces { } are optional.

Description:

Returns the sum of all valid values represented by the fields in the parameter list.

The Sum function is most often used to add up a column of numbers in a related table.

Examples:

Function	Results
Sum (6; 3; 5)	Returns 14.
Sum (field1; field2; field3)	Returns 6 (when field1 = 1, field2 = 2, and field3 = 3).
Sum (repeatingField)	Returns 6 (when repetition 1 = 1, repetition 2 = 2, and repetition 3 = 3).
Sum (Customer::InvoiceTotal)	Returns the sum of InvoiceTotal in the related set of data.

TableIDs (fileName)

Data type returned: **Text**

Category: **Design**

Parameters:

- **fileName**—A string or text expression that represents the name of an open file.

Description:

Generates a return-delimited list of table occurrence IDs from the specified file. If the fileName parameter is left empty, TableIDs returns information about the current file.

Note that TableIDs returns the IDs of table occurrences from the Relationships Graph, not the actual data tables. A database table may appear in the Relationships Graph more than once.

FileMaker assigns a unique TableID whenever a table occurrence is added to the Relationships Graph. The order of the IDs in the list is based on the alphabetic ordering of the table occurrence names themselves.

Examples:

Function	Results
TableIDs ("")	Returns a list of table occurrence IDs for the current file that might look like this: 1065090 1065091 1065089 1065092

TableNames (fileName)

Data type returned: **Text**

Category: **Design**

Parameters:

- **fileName**—A string or text expression that represents the name of an open file.

Description:

Generates a return-delimited list of table occurrence names from the specified file. If the fileName parameter is left empty, TableNames returns information about the current file.

Note that TableNames returns the names of table occurrences from the Relationships Graph, not the actual data tables. A database table may appear in the Relationships Graph more than once.

The list returned by the TableNames function is ordered alphabetically.

Examples:

Function	Results
TableNames (Get (FileName))	Returns a list of table occurrence names for the current file that might look like this: Contacts Contact2 Invoice Lines Invoices

Tan (angleInRadians)

Data type returned: **Number**

Category: **Trigonometric**

Parameters:

- **number**—Any number representing the size of an angle measured in radians.

Description:

Returns the tangent of the specified angle.

The tangent of an angle can also be obtained by dividing the sine of the angle by its cosine. In any right triangle, the tangent of the two nonright angles can be obtained by dividing the length of the side opposite the angle by the length of the adjacent side.

Examples:

Function	Results
Tan (0)	Returns 0.
Tan (Pi / 6)	Returns .5773502691896257.
Tan (Radians (45))	Returns 1.

TextColor (text; RGB (red; green; blue))

Data type returned: **Text, Number**

Category: **Text Formatting**

Parameters:

- **text**—Any text string or expression that returns a text string.
- **RGB (red; green; blue)**—A function that accepts three parameters from 0 to 255 and returns a number from 0 to 16777215 representing a color. See the RGB function for more information.

Description:

Returns the text string in the color specified by the RGB parameter.

Unlike conditional formatting, the TextColor function enables you to emphasize certain words within text expressions, as follows:

```
"We will have " & TextColor ( NumberItems; RGB ( 255; 0; 0 )) &
" errors per cycle. Unacceptable!"
```

Examples:

Function	Results
TextColor ("this text will be blue"; RGB (0; 0; 255))	Returns this text will be blue (formatted in blue).
TextColor ("this text will be red"; 16711680)	Returns this text will be red (formatted in red).

TextColorRemove (text { ; RGB (red; green; blue)})

Data type returned: **Text, Number**

Category: **Text Formatting**

Parameters:

- **text**—Any text expression or text field.
- **RGB (red; green; blue)**—A function that accepts three parameters from 0 to 255 and returns a number from 0 to 16777215 representing a color. See the RGB function for more information. Parameters in curly braces { } are optional.

Description:

Removes all font colors in text, or removes instances of a specific font color as an optional parameter, leaving others unchanged. After font color is removed from a data string, it is rendered in whatever default text color is set for the layout object in which it is displayed.

Examples:

Function	Results
TextColorRemove ("This should be boring monochromatic stuff")	Returns This should be boring monochromatic stuff (without any color specified).
TextColorRemove (Notes ; RGB (255; 0; 0))	Returns the contents of the Notes field, without the specific red indicated by RGB (255;0;0), should there be any applied within the text. Any other colors specified within the field are unaltered.

TextFont (text; fontName { ; fontScript})

Data type returned: **Text**, **Number**

Category: **Text Formatting**

Parameters:

- **text**—Any text string or expression that returns a text string.
- **fontName**—Any font name available on the system. Must be enclosed in quotation marks.
- **fontScript**—The name of a character set (for example, Cyrillic, Greek, Roman). This is an optional parameter; quotation marks should not be used around the script names because they are keywords. Parameters in curly braces { } are optional.

Description:

Changes the text font to the specified fontName and optional fontScript.

If no matches for the specified font and script exist, FileMaker first looks for the font script and associated font in the Fonts tab of the Preferences dialog box. If the script is not specified in the Fonts tab, the TextFont function uses the default font for the system. This font script might not be the same as the specified script.

The list of possible font scripts is as follows:

Roman	TraditionalChinese
Greek	SimplifiedChinese
Cyrillic	OEM
CentralEurope	Symbol
ShiftJIS	Other

Examples:

Function	Results
TextFont ("testing 123"; "Courier")	Returns testing 123 (in Courier font).

TextFontRemove (text { ; fontName; fontScript})

Data type returned: **Text, Number**

Category: **Text Formatting**

Parameters:

- **text**—Any text string or expression that returns a text string.
- **fontName**—Any font name expressed in text.
- **fontScript**—The name of a character set that contains characters required for writing in the specified language. Parameters in curly braces { } are optional. Note that the fontScript parameter is not enclosed in quotation marks (" ") and requires specific keywords. These are listed in the description of the TextFont function.

Description:

Removes all fonts applied to text, or removes only fonts and font scripts as specified by the two optional parameters, fontName and fontScript. After fonts are removed, the data is displayed and treated as text entered into any FileMaker Pro field by adopting whatever font attributes have been applied to the layout objects in question.

Examples:

Function	Results
TextFontRemove ("Nuke all fonts")	Returns Nuke all fonts (displayed in a layout object's default font).
TextFontRemove ("Two fonts enter, one font leaves"; "Comic Sans MS")	Returns Two fonts enter, one font leaves with the Comic Sans MS font removed (assuming the original text string made use of it).

TextFormatRemove (text)

Data type returned: **Text, Number**

Category: **Text Formatting**

Parameters:

- **text**—Any text string or expression that returns a text string.

Description:

Removes all formatting from text, including all fonts, styles, font sizes, and font colors.

The resulting string is rendered using the default attributes from the layout object in which it appears.

This function can be particularly useful as part of an auto-entered calculation formula applied to fields into which users habitually paste formatted text from other applications (for example, email messages). Similarly, you can use TextFormatRemove in a Replace Field Contents routine to clean up existing data.

Examples:

Function	Results
TextFormatRemove ("Enough is enough")	Returns Enough is enough (without any text formatting applied).
TextFormatRemove (Self)	Returns as unformatted text the data contained in the current object in which the calculation is defined.

TextSize (text; fontSize)

Data type returned: **Text, Number**

Category: **Text Formatting**

Parameters:

- **text**—Any text string or expression that returns a text string.
- **fontSize**—Any font size expressed in pixels as an integer.

Description:

Returns the text string at the specified font size. When you use TextSize as part of the definition of a calculation field, you should set the calculation to return a text or number result. Text formatting options are lost if the data type returned is anything other than text or number.

Examples:

Function	Results
TextSize ("Hello, world!"; 8)	Returns Hello, world! in 8-point font.
TextSize ("Large print book"; 18)	Returns Large print book in 18-point font.

TextSizeRemove (text { ; sizeToRemove})

Data type returned: **Text, Number**

Category: **Text Formatting**

Parameters:

- **text**—Any text string or expression that returns a text string.

- **sizeToRemove**—Any font size expressed as an integer. Parameters in curly braces { } are optional.

Description:

Removes all font size applications in text, or removes just the font size specified by sizeToRemove. The text in question then adopts whatever font size has been specified for the layout object in which it displays.

Note that text formatting functions work only for data returned as text or number.

Examples:

Function	Results
TextSizeRemove ("It should be 8pt anyway")	Returns It should be 8pt anyway (without font sizes specified).
TextSizeRemove ("It's too small!!"; 6)	Returns It's too small!! (with the 6-point font size removed).

TextStyleAdd (text; style(s))

Data type returned: **Text, Number**

Category: **Text Formatting**

Parameters:

- **text**—Any text string or expression that returns a text string.
- **style**—Any named style, a list of styles separated by a plus (+) sign, or an integer that represents a combination of styles. Named styles, listed in Table 10.1, should not be placed in quotation marks and cannot be passed as field contents or variables.

Description:

Returns a text string that has the specified style(s) applied to it.

The style names are reserved keywords in FileMaker Pro and should not be placed within quotation marks. You also cannot place a keyword in a field and use the field as the style parameter within TextStyleAdd. Styles can, however, be specified as local variables within Let functions.

All the style names have numeric equivalents that you can use instead of the names. To combine multiple styles, simply add the numeric equivalents together. The numeric equivalent can be stored in a field, so use this method if you need to dynamically specify a text style.

Table 10.1 lists the styles and their numeric equivalents.

Table 10.1 Style Names and Numeric Equivalent

Style Name	Numeric Equivalent
Plain	0
Strikethrough	1
Smallcaps	2
Superscript	4
Subscript	8
Uppercase	16
Lowercase	32
Titlecase	48
Wordunderline	64
Doubleunderline	128
Bold	256
Italic	512
Underline	1024
HighlightYellow	4096
Condense	8192
Extend	16384
Allstyles	32767

Examples:

Function	Results
TextStyleAdd ("word underline."; WordUnderline)	Returns word underline.
TextStyleAdd ("bold italic!"; Bold+Italic)	Returns ***bold italic!***.
TextStyleAdd ("bold italic!"; 768)	Returns ***bold italic!***.
TextStyleAdd ("Plain text"; Plain)	Removes all styles from the text. If the "Plain" style is combined with any other styles, "Plain" is ignored.

TextStyleRemove (text; style(s))

Data type returned: **Text, Number**

Category: **Text Formatting**

Parameters:

- **text**—Any text string or expression that returns a text string.
- **style**—Any named style, a list of styles separated by a plus (+) sign, or an integer that represents a combination of styles. Named styles should not be placed in quotation marks and cannot be passed as field contents.

Description:

Removes the specified styles from formatted text.

Removing AllStyles with TextStyleRemove accomplishes the same thing as adding Plain with TextStyleAdd.

See TextStyleAdd for a complete list of styles and a discussion of their numeric equivalents.

Examples:

Function	Results
TextStyleRemove ("word underline"; WordUnderline)	Removes the word underline formatting from the phrase "word underline".
TextStyleRemove ("bold italic!"; Bold+Italic)	Removes the bold and italic formatting from the phrase "bold italic!".
TextStyleRemove (sampleText; AllStyles)	Removes all formatting styles from the contents of the sampleText field.

Time (hours; minutes; seconds)

Data type returned: **Time**

Category: **Time**

Parameters:

- **hours**—A number or numeric expression representing the hours portion of the desired time value.
- **minutes**—A number or numeric expression representing the minutes portion of the desired time value.
- **seconds**—A number or numeric expression representing the seconds portion of the desired time value.

Description:

Returns a time value built from the specified hours, minutes, and seconds parameters. The resulting value accurately calculates the effect of fractional parameters. Similarly, although the typical range for the minutes and seconds parameters is from 0 to 59, any values greater than or less than are compensated for in the resulting time value.

The Time function is often used in conjunction with the Hour, Minute, and Seconds functions. For instance, the following formula takes the current time and returns the time of the next lowest hour:

```
Time ( Hour ( Get ( CurrentTime )); 0; 0 ))
```

Examples:

Function	Results
Time (8; 34; 15)	Returns 8:34:15.
Time (15.25; 0; 0)	Returns 15:15:00.
Time (22; 70; 70)	Returns 23:11:10.
Time (12; -30; 0)	Returns 11:30:00.

Timestamp (date; time)

Data type returned: **Timestamp**

Category: **Time**

Parameters:

- **date**—Any calendar date or expression that returns a date. The date parameter can also be an integer from 1 to 1460970, representing the number of days since January 1, 0001.
- **time**—Any time value or expression that returns a time value. The time parameter can also be an integer representing the number of seconds since midnight.

Description:

Returns a timestamp from the two parameters in the format "12/12/2012 10:45:00 AM".

You can use text parsing functions or mathematical operations to extract the pieces of a timestamp. You can also use the GetAsDate and GetAsTime functions to retrieve just the date or time portion of a timestamp.

Internally, FileMaker Pro stores timestamp data as the number of seconds since 1/1/0001 12:00 a.m. You can use the GetAsNumber function to see the numeric representation. For instance, GetAsNumber (Timestamp ("4/18/2012"; "12:00pm")) returns 63470347200.

You can manually calculate the integer value of a timestamp by using the following formula:

```
( GetAsNumber ( myDate ) -1 ) * 86400 + GetAsNumber ( myTime )
```

Examples:

Function	Results
Timestamp ("10/11/2012"; "10:20 AM")	Returns 10/11/2012 10:20 AM.
Timestamp ("10/11/2012"; "20:20:20")	Returns 10/11/2012 8:20:20 PM.
Timestamp (Date (10; 11; 2012); Time (10; 20; 0))	Returns 10/11/2012 10:20 AM.
Timestamp (1; 0)	Returns 1/1/0001 12:00 AM.

Trim (text)

Data type returned: **Text**

Category: **Text**

Parameters:

- **text**—Any text string or expression that resolves to a text string.

Description:

Returns the specified text string with any leading or trailing spaces removed.

The Trim function removes only leading and trailing spaces and not any other characters (such as carriage returns).

Trim can be used to reformat data where users have inadvertently typed spaces at the end of an entry. This happens frequently with fields containing first names. To automatically have the entry reformatted when the user exits the field, have the field auto-enter Trim (Self) and uncheck the option not to replace any existing value in the field. Thus, if a user enters "Fred " into the FirstName field, it is replaced with "Fred" when the user exits the field.

Trim is also used frequently to clean up fixed-width data that has been imported from some other data source. In such cases, fields have been padded with leading or trailing spaces to be a certain length. Remove them after importing by doing calculated replaces in the appropriate fields.

Examples:

Function	Results
Trim (" This is a test ")	Returns This is a test (without the leading and trailing spaces).

TrimAll (text; trimSpaces; trimType)

Data type returned: **Text**

Category: **Text**

Parameters:

- **text**—Any text expression or text field.
- **trimSpaces**—0 (False), 1 (True).
- **trimType**—0 through 3 depending on the trim style (listed in the Description section).

Description:

Returns text with all leading and trailing spaces removed and takes into account different Unicode representations of spaces.

Set trimSpaces to 1 if you want to include the removal of full-width spaces between non-Roman and Roman characters. Set trimSpaces to 0 if you do not.

Characters are considered Roman if their Unicode values are less than U+2F00. Characters with values greater than or equal to U+2F00 are considered non-Roman.

Characters within the Roman range belong to the following character blocks: Latin, Latin-1 Supplement, Latin Extended-A & B, IPA Extensions, Spacing Modifier Letters, Combining Diacritical Marks, Greek, Cyrillic, Armenian, Hebrew, Arabic, Devanagari, Bengali, Gurmukhi, Gujarati, Oriya, Tamil, Telugu, Kannada, Malayalam, Thai, Lao, Tibetan, Georgian, Hangul Jamo, and additional Latin and Greek extended blocks.

Symbols within the Roman range include punctuation characters, superscripts, subscripts, currency symbols, combining marks for symbols, letterlike symbols, number forms, arrows, math operators, control pictures, geometric shapes, dingbats, and so on.

Characters within the non-Roman range are those belonging to the CJK symbols/punctuations area, hiragana, katakana, Bopomofo, hangul compatibility Jamo, Kanbun, CJK unified ideographs, and so on.

The trimType parameter controls how the function returns text in the following ways:

0—Removes spaces between non-Roman and Roman characters and always leaves one space between Roman words.
1—Always includes a half-width space between non-Roman and Roman characters and always leaves one space between Roman words.
2—Removes spaces between non-Roman characters (reducing multiple spaces between non-Roman and Roman words to one space) and leaves one space between Roman words.
3—Removes all spaces everywhere.

In all cases, spaces between non-Roman characters are removed.

Examples:

Function	Results
TrimAll (Full_Name; 1; 0)	Returns Nathaniel Stewart Bowers when the value of Full_Name is "Nathaniel Stewart Bowers ". It is useful for stripping extra spaces out of lengthy text fields.

Truncate (number; precision)

Data type returned: **Number**

Category: **Number**

Parameters:

- **number**—Any expression that resolves to a numeric value.
- **precision**—Any expression that resolves to a numeric value.

Description:

Returns the specified number truncated to the specified number of decimal places (precision). Unlike the Round function, the Truncate function simply discards further digits without performing any sort of rounding.

Truncating a number by using a precision parameter of 0 has the same effect as taking the Int of that number. Truncate (x; 0) = Int (x).

Negative values can be used for the precision parameter in the Truncate function to truncate to the nearest ten, hundred, thousand, and so on. For instance, Truncate (1234.1234; -1) returns 1230. Truncate (1234.1234; -2) returns 1200.

Examples:

Function	Results
Truncate (Pi; 6)	Returns 3.141592.
Truncate (Amount; 2)	Returns 54.65 when Amount contains 54.651259.
Truncate (1234.1234; 0)	Returns 1234.
Truncate (-1234.1234; 0)	Returns –1234.

Upper (text)

Data type returned: **Text**

Category: **Text**

Parameters:

- **text**—A string or expression that returns a text string.

Description:

Returns a completely uppercase version of the specified text string.

The Upper function is one of three functions FileMaker Pro has for changing the case of a text string. The other two are Lower and Proper.

The Upper function is often used to reformat user-entered data to ensure consistent data entry. Sometimes when exporting data that is to be used by external applications, you need to format the data entirely as uppercase characters to be consistent with data in the other system.

The following formula checks whether a given text string is already written in all uppercase characters:

```
Exact ( text; Upper ( text ))
```

Examples:

Function	Results
Upper ("This is a test")	Returns THIS IS A TEST.
Upper (AccessCode)	Returns 1ABC-2XYZ when AccessCode contains "1abc-2XYz".

ValueCount (text)

Data type returned: **Number**

Category: **Text**

Parameters:

- **text**—Any return-delimited string or expression that generates a return-delimited list.

Description:

Returns a count of the number of values in the text provided.

The presence or absence of a trailing return after the last item in the return-delimited list does not affect the result returned by ValueCount. For instance, ValueCount ("Blue¶Green") and ValueCount ("Blue¶Green¶") both return 2.

If there are multiple returns at any point in the list, the ValueCount function recognizes the empty items as valid items. For instance, ValueCount ("¶¶Blue¶¶Green¶¶") returns 6. Note that this behavior is different from how the WordCount function treats multiple delimiters. There, multiple delimiters in a row are considered to be a single delimiter.

Examples:

Function	Results
ValueCount ("A¶B¶C¶D¶E")	Returns 5.
ValueCount ($officeList)	Returns 3 when $officeList is equal to Chicago Philadelphia San Francisco

ValueListIDs (fileName)

Data type returned: **Text**

Category: **Design**

Parameters:

- **fileName**—A string or text expression that represents the name of an open file.

Description:

Produces a return-delimited list of value list IDs from the specified file. If the fileName parameter is empty, ValueListIDs returns information about the current file.

FileMaker Pro assigns a serial number to each value list created in a file. The order of the list returned by the ValueListIDs function is the same as that in which the value lists are ordered in the Manage Value Lists dialog when the order is set to Custom Order. Changing the Custom Order changes the way the results are ordered, but selecting one of the other choices (Creation Order, Source, Value List Name) does not.

Examples:

Function	Results
ValueListIDs (Get (FileName))	Returns a list of value list IDs for the current file that might look like this: 21 92 90 108 15

ValueListItems (fileName; valueListName)

Data type returned: **Text**

Category: **Design**

Parameters:

- **fileName**—A string or text expression that represents the name of an open file.
- **valueListName**—The name of a value list in fileName.

Description:

Produces a return-delimited list of the items in the specified value list. If the fileName parameter is empty, ValueListItems returns information about the current file.

The ValueListItems function can be used to return a list of all the items in a field's index. To do this, you should set the value list to "Use values from field" and to "Include all values" in the subsequent dialog. Although this practice works with value lists that show only related sets of data, the List function is more suited for this purpose in most cases.

Examples:

Function	Results
ValueListItems (Get (FileName); "Phone_Label")	Returns a list of values from the value list Phone_Label in the current file that might look like this: Home Work Cell Fax

ValueListNames (fileName)

Data type returned: **Text**

Category: **Design**

Parameters:

- **fileName**—A string or text expression that represents the name of an open file.

Description:

Generates a return-delimited list of value list names from the specified file. If the fileName parameter is empty, ValueListNames returns information about the current file.

The order of the list returned by the ValueListNames function is the same as that in which the value lists are ordered in the Manage Value Lists dialog when the order is set to Custom Order. Changing the Custom Order changes the way the results are ordered, but selecting one of the other choices (Creation Order, Source, Value List Name) does not.

Examples:

Function	Results
ValueListNames ("")	Returns a list of value list names from the current file that might look like this: Phone_Label Location Type Category

Variance (field { ; field...})

Data type returned: **Number**

Category: **Aggregate**

Parameters:

- **field**—Any related field, repeating field, or set of nonrepeating fields that represent a collection of numbers.

Description:

Returns the variance of the nonblank values represented in the parameter list. Variance is a statistical measure of how spread out a set of values is.

The StDev of a set of numbers is the square root of the Variance of the set.

The difference between the Variance and VarianceP functions is that the Variance divides the sum of the squares by $n-1$ instead of by n.

The Variance of a set of numbers can be calculated by summing the squares of the distance of each value from the mean, then dividing by *n*–1, where *n* is the number of values.

For instance, given the set of numbers 8, 10, and 12, the mean of the set is 10. The distance of each value from the mean is –2, 0, and 2. The squares of these distances are 4, 0, and 4, and the sum of the squares is 8. The Variance is 8 divided by (3–1), which is 4.

Examples:

Function	Results
Variance (8; 10; 12)	Returns 4.
Variance (7; 11; 13)	Returns 9.33.

VarianceP (field { ; field...})

Data type returned: **Number**

Category: **Aggregate**

Parameters:

- **field**—Any related field, repeating field, or set of nonrepeating fields that represent a collection of numbers.

Description:

Returns the variance of a population represented by the nonblank values in the parameter list. Variance of population is a statistical measure of how spread out a set of values is.

The StDevP of a set of numbers is the square root of the VarianceP of the set.

The difference between the Variance and VarianceP functions is that the VarianceP divides the sum of the squares by *n* instead of by *n*–1.

The variance of a population represented by a set of numbers can be calculated by summing the squares of the distance of each value from the mean and then dividing by *n*, where *n* is the number of values.

For instance, given the set of numbers 8, 10, and 12, the mean of the set is 10. The distance of each value from the mean is –2, 0, and 2. The squares of these distances are 4, 0, and 4, and the sum of the squares is 8. The VarianceP is 8 divided by 3, which is 2.67.

Examples:

Function	Results
VarianceP (8; 10; 12)	Returns 2.67.
VarianceP (7; 11; 13)	Returns 6.22.

VerifyContainer (sourceField)

Data type returned: **Number**

Category: **Container**

Parameters:

- **sourceField**—Any container field that has been set to store container data externally.

Description:

Returns a Boolean value representing the validity of data stored externally in sourceField. The function returns 0 (False) if the external file has been changed or deleted. It returns 1 (True) if the external file exists and is unchanged. If sourceField has not been set to store data externally or is not a container field, VerifyContainer returns a question mark (?).

Examples:

Function	Results
VerifyContainer (savedReports)	Returns 1 if the file or image that has been stored externally for the current record exists and has not been changed.
VerifyContainer (savedReports)	Returns 0 if the externally saved image or file has been modified or deleted.

WeekOfYear (date)

Data type returned: **Number**

Category: **Date**

Parameters:

- **date**—Any valid date (1/1/0001–12/31/4000). The parameter should be a string containing a date (for example, "3/17/2012"), an expression with a date result (for example, Date (6; 29; 1969)), or an integer that represents a serialized date value (for example, 718977).

Description:

Returns the week number of the specified date. Weeks are defined as starting on Sunday and ending on Saturday. A partial week at the beginning of the year is considered as week 1, so the WeekOfYear function can return values from 1 to 54.

WeekOfYear can be used to return the approximate number of weeks between two dates in the same year. For instance, WeekOfYear("6/1/2012") - WeekOfYear("5/1/2012") returns 4. It is also useful for reports in which you need to subsummarize data by week.

January 1 of any given year is always part of week 1, no matter on what day of the week it falls.

Examples:

Function	Results
WeekOfYear ("3/12/2012")	Returns 1.
WeekOfYear (Get (CurrentDate))	Returns 48 when the current date is 11/26/2011.

WeekOfYearFiscal (date; startingDay)

Data type returned: **Number**

Category: **Date**

Parameters:

- **date**—Any valid date (1/1/0001–12/31/4000). The parameter should be a string containing a date (for example, "3/17/2004"), an expression with a date result (for example, Date (6; 29; 1969)), or an integer that represents a serialized date value (for example, 718977).
- **startingDay**—A numeric value between 1 (Sunday) and 7 (Saturday).

Description:

Returns an integer from 1 to 53 that represents the week number of the year of the specified date. Weeks are defined as starting on the day of week specified by the startingDay parameter.

The first week of a year is defined as the first week that contains four or more days of that year. For instance, January 1, 2004, was a Thursday. When you use a startingDay of 5 (representing Thursday), the first fiscal week of the year is considered as 1/1/2004 through 1/7/2004. The second fiscal week begins on Thursday, 1/8/2004. However, if you use a startingDay of 1 (Sunday), the first day of the fiscal year is 1/4/2004. In the previous week (12/28/2003–1/3/2004), only three days are in 2004, so that is considered as the 53rd fiscal week of 2003.

WeekOfYearFiscal and WeekOfYear often yield different results. WeekOfYear is always based on a week defined as Sunday through Saturday, whereas WeekOfYearFiscal can begin on whatever day you specify.

Examples:

Function	Results
WeekOfYearFiscal ("3/21/2012", 4)	Returns 12.
WeekOfYearFiscal ("1/1/2012", 1)	Returns 1.
WeekOfYearFiscal ("1/1/2012", 2)	Returns 52.

WindowNames { (fileName)}

Data type returned: **Text**

Category: **Design**

Parameters:

- **fileName**—A string or text expression that represents the name of an open file. This parameter is optional.

Description:

Produces a return-delimited list of open window names.

WindowNames can return window names from all open FileMaker Pro files or just the file specified by the optional parameter. Window names do not need to be unique. The order of the list is determined by the stacking order of the windows, with the topmost window (the active window) listed first. Hidden windows are listed, but not any window that appears in the window list surrounded by parentheses. This indicates a file that is open but that doesn't have any windows, hidden or visible. Visible windows are listed first, then minimized windows, and then hidden windows.

Examples:

Function	Results
WindowNames	Returns a list of values that might look like this: Customers Invoices myDatabase Invoices – 2

WordCount (text)

Data type returned: **Number**

Category: **Text**

Parameters:

- **text**—Any text string or expression that resolves to a text string.

Description:

Returns a count of the number of words in text.

FileMaker Pro considers spaces, return characters, and most punctuation symbols to be word breaks. Multiple word breaks next to each other (for example, two spaces, a comma, and a space) are considered a single word break.

Certain punctuation symbols are word breaks when separating alphabetic characters, but not when separating numeric characters. They include the colon (:), slash (/), period (.), comma (,), and dash (-). For instance, WordCount ("54-6") returns 1, but WordCount ("x-y") returns 2. The reason for this behavior is that those symbols are valid date, time, and number separators.

Examples:

Function	Results
WordCount ("The quick brown fox jumps over the lazy dog.")	Returns 9.
WordCount (FullName)	Returns 4 when FullName contains "John Q. Public, Jr."

Year (date)

Data type returned: **Number**

Category: **Date**

Parameters:

- **date**—Any valid date (1/1/0001–12/31/4000). The parameter should be a string containing a date (for example, "3/17/2012"), an expression with a date result (for example, Date (6; 29; 1969)), or an integer that represents a serialized date value (for example, 718977).

Description:

Returns the year portion of the date parameter.

The Year function is often used in conjunction with the Date function to assemble new date values. For instance, if you have a field called DateOfBirth that contains someone's birth date, you can calculate the date of that person's birthday in the current year as follows:

```
Date ( Month ( DateOfBirth ), Day ( DateOfBirth ), Year ( Get ( CurrentDate )))
```

Examples:

Function	Results
Year ("1/1/2008")	Returns 2008.
Year (Get (CurrentDate))	Returns the current year.
Year (myBirthdate)	Returns the year portion of the field myBirthdate.

YearName (date; format)

Data type returned: **Text (Japanese)**

Category: **Date**

Parameters:

- **date**—Any calendar date.
- **format**—A number (0, 1, or 2) that controls the display format.

Description:

Returns the Japanese year name for the date specified.

The formats control how the name of Emperor is displayed: 0 = Long, 1 = Abbreviated, 2 = 2-byte Roman. "Seireki" is returned when date falls before Emperial names have been applied.

0—Meiji (明治) 8, Taisho (大正) 8, Showa (昭和) 8, Heisei (平成) 8 (before 1868.9.8, Seireki (西暦xxxx)
1—Mei (明) 8, Tai (大) 8, Sho (昭) 8, Hei (平) 8 (before 1868.9.8), Sei (西暦xxxx)
2—M8, T8, S8, H8 (before 1868.9.8, A.D.xxxx)

Examples:

Function	Results
YearName (DateField; 0)	Returns 平成 14 when DateField contains 7/17/2002

CHAPTER 11

Custom Function Primer

Custom functions are, without a doubt, one of the most powerful features in FileMaker; we cannot advocate their use strongly enough. If you use FileMaker Pro Advanced, you can author or edit custom functions. After you add a function to a file, however, it becomes available to any user or developer who has access to a calculation dialog, be it in the service of tasks such as defining fields, writing scripts, or even performing calculated replaces.

After custom functions are added to a file, they become available for use in the calculation dialog alongside the built-in functions. They are snippets of code that accept parameters and produce output just as FileMaker's built-in functions do. One example might be

```
fnCommission ( unitPrice; quantity; discount )
```

This function would presumably return a dollar amount based on some formula that multiplies unitPrice and quantity, subtracts a discount from the total, and then applies a percentage or some internal factoring to arrive at a sales commission.

As a developer using a given custom function, you do not even need to know what that formula might be. All you require is that the function returns a meaningful and consistent result when fed the necessary parameters.

Custom functions allow developers to abstract portions of code, independent from database schema or scripts, where it is then possible to reference a particular piece of logic throughout a database. For example, if an organization's commission rates need to change, the system's developer can edit a single custom function containing those rates, and all the calculations based on that function immediately (depending on their storage settings) reflect and use the change.

Custom functions can also serve as permanent "system constants" that are not subject to session issues as global fields and global variables are. The values within a custom function do not expire at the end of a user's session, they are consistent across all users of a database, and a developer can change them centrally as needed. As an example, imagine that you want to give the user the ability to suppress the confirmation dialog in your scripts by holding down a modifier key. Rather than writing the same calculation over and over, you might create a custom function called SKIP_CONFIRMATION, with the following formula:

```
If (
    Get ( ActiveModifierKeys ) = 8 ;
      True;
       False
)
```

Having this as a custom function makes your scripts easier to read and write, and it gives you the capability to centrally change the modifier key without needing to update dozens of scripts.

The Custom Function Interface

The Edit Custom Function dialog (see Figure 11.1) enables developers to define parameters that serve as input for an expression written to reference those parameters.

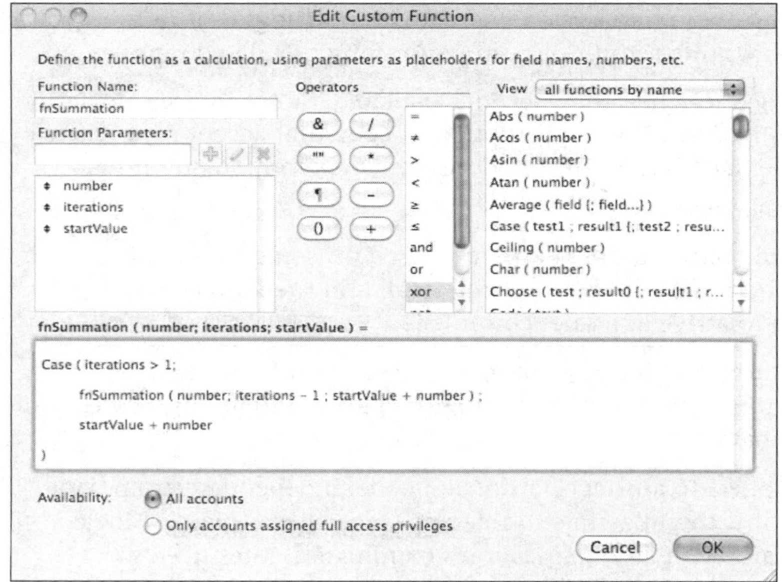

Figure 11.1
The Edit Custom Function dialog.

Custom Functions: Things to Remember

Custom functions work much like ordinary calculation functions, but it is important to understand the following aspects of custom functions:

- Custom functions follow the same rules for syntax that calculation functions follow.

➔ *For a review of calculation syntax, see Chapter 8, "Calculation Primer."*

- Instead of referencing schema information (data fields), custom functions use parameters. Values for these parameters are passed into the custom function from elsewhere in a database via the Specify Calculation dialog.
- Custom functions return a single result.
- You must have Full Access privileges to a database to create or edit custom functions.
- Custom functions can use all the functions built into FileMaker, including other custom functions and external functions.

Generally, a custom function should not directly reference any of the fields in the schema of your database. To do so would contradict the concept of abstraction. However, you are able to make use of schema data fields if absolutely necessary. The following example illustrates a scenario in which a sales commission is referenced:

```
fnSalesCommission ( unitPrice; quantity; discount )
// function to calculate the sales commission for various transaction totals.
// expected input:
//   unitPrice = dollar amount to two decimal places;
//   quantity = integer;
//   discount = any number (positive = discount)
// expected result: a dollar amount.

Let ([
   salePrice = unitPrice * quantity;
   total = salePrice - discount;
   discountPenalty = Case ( discount > 0;  .01; 0 );
   commissionPercent = ProductRate::Commission - discountPenalty
];
   total * ( commissionPercent - discountPenalty )
)
```

Custom functions can also interact with global and local variables. In the case of local variables ($myVar), FileMaker stores values specific to a currently running script. In the case of a global variable ($$myVar), the value in the variable is updated and maintained throughout the file in a single user's individual session.

If you want to create or set variables within a custom function, use the Let function:

```
Let ([
   myInternalVariable = $$globalVariable + 1;
   $$newVariable = 1 + 1;
   result = $$newVariable + myInternalVariable
   ];
   result
)
```

Recursive Techniques

Just as custom functions can reference other functions, they also can reference themselves. This capability enables you to write recursive functions in FileMaker. Keep in mind that recursive functions require an exit condition; otherwise, you end up with endless recursion and no result returned.

In the following example, a simple recursive function reorders a carriage return–delimited list from bottom to top:

```
fnListBackwards ( valueList )
// function to reverse the order of a ¶-delimited list
// expected input:
//   valuelist = text values delimited by ¶
// expected result: a valuelist of text values delimited by ¶ in reverse order

Let ([
   numOfValues = ValueCount ( valuelist );
   firstValue = LeftValues ( valuelist; 1 );
   remainingList = RightValues ( valuelist; numOfValues - 1 );
   resultList = Case ( numOfValues = 1; "" ; fnListBackwards ( remainingList ) )
];
   resultList & firstValue
)
```

If a recursive custom function does not have an exit condition or an error in logic occurs, the maximum number of recursions a function can make is 10,000. This assumes that it is a nested call that requires FileMaker to maintain a stack in memory of each recursion's result. FileMaker stops the recursive nest and returns a "?" as the result of any calculation using that function.

If, on the other hand, you write a custom function so that the results of one recursion are passed into the subsequent recursive call as a parameter (and thus not requiring FileMaker to maintain a stack of results, but rather only calculating results in a series), the maximum limit is 50,000. This technique is referred to as *tail recursion.* To demonstrate the difference, consider two different ways that you could create the following function:

```
fnSummation ( number; iterations; startValue )
```

Assume the purpose of this function is to add a number to itself for as many times as dictated by iterations, beginning at startValue. For example, fnSummation (5; 3; 0) adds 5 + 5 + 5 to return 15. fnSummation (5; 3; 4) adds 5 + 5 + 5 beginning at 4 to return 19.

Using a nested technique, which requires that FileMaker "stack" the results in memory, you can write the function as follows:

```
Case ( iterations > 1;
  fnSummation ( number; iterations - 1 ; startValue ) + number ;
  startValue + number
)
```

Using tail recursion, in which the results from one iteration are passed entirely into the next iteration (thus requiring no saved stack), you might write the function as follows:

```
Case ( iterations > 1 ;
   fnSummation ( number; iterations - 1 ; startValue + number ) ;
   startValue + number
)
```

In the first example, FileMaker has to preserve each nested result (in a stack) to derive its final result. In the second, the function passes in everything required through the parameters of the function and does not require evaluation of the entire stack. The first example works only up to 10,000 iterations. The second can be evaluated in serial, up to 50,000 iterations.

To understand tail recursion, consider an analogy. Assume that you want to measure how many cups a body of water contains. One method is to use a single one-cup measuring cup, scoop out the water, and keep a count of how many times you do so. This method, akin to stack recursion or nested recursion, requires that you keep track of how many times you've been through the process. Now imagine a second scenario in which each time you measure out a new cup of water, you increase by one the size of your measuring cup. It starts as one cup, then holds two cups, then three, and finally ends at the same number of cups the original body of water contained. You would not need to keep track of any count in the process: at the end, you would simply need to know how big the cup is. The result derived from your last iteration is the result you're looking for.

Referring to the previous examples, notice that the nesting method combines a recursive call with an operator. In the second line of the function, `number` is being added to the recursive result of `fnSummation`. This approach requires that FileMaker "keep track of" the result from each iteration of your recursive call to calculate the final result. It needs to create a stack of results and pass down the chain to the end point and back up again to calculate the final result. FileMaker literally processes each step of your recursion twice.

Consider the steps involved in computing `fnSummation (5 ; 3 ; 4)`:

```
step 1:  fnSummation (5 ; 3 ; 4 ) = fnSummation ( 5 ; 2 ; 4) + 5
step 2:  fnSummation (5 ; 2 ; 4 ) = fnSummation ( 5 ; 1 ; 4 ) + 5
step 3:  fnSummation (5 ; 1 ; 4 ) = 5 + 4 = 9
step 4:  fnSummation (5 ; 2 ; 4 ) = 9 + 5 = 14
step 5:  fnSummation (5 ; 3 ; 4 ) = 14 + 5 = 19
```

If you compare that to the second example, the recursive call in the second line is not paired with an operator. It is simply called again with different parameters. The difference is subtle but important. At the end of the recursive process, the results of the final recursive call are simply the result you're looking for. FileMaker can process each instance of the recursion loop and "forget" what the prior instance returned without processing the stack a second time.

The steps involved would be the following:

```
step 1: fnSummation (5 ; 3 ; 4 ) = fnSummation (5 ; 2 ; 9)
step 2: fnSummation (5 ; 2 ; 9 ) = fnSummation ( 5 ; 1 ; 14 )
step 3: fnSummation (5 ; 1 ; 14 ) = 5 + 14 = 19
```

Having an operator combined with your recursive call is a sign that you're not using tail recursion. By creating recursive calls without operators, where you simply pass new parameters into your recursive function, your system performs better and is capable of deeper processing limits.

Custom functions are powerful tools for building abstract units of logic that can then be reused throughout a solution. After you create (and test!) a custom function, you can easily re-create it in other files for use throughout all your solutions. We strongly recommend you create a library of tools to refine and reuse over time.

CHAPTER 12

Scripting Primer

Scripts are the lifeblood of an interactive FileMaker solution: They are the means by which you can automate various processes and capture user actions. In this chapter, we try to distill FileMaker scripting down to its essentials. Scripts in FileMaker Pro are written in a point-and-click interface where steps and their options are added to individual scripts. Most scripts are executed by the press of a button or a menu selection. When users run scripts in FileMaker, only one script can execute at a time; however, it is possible to nest scripts, running a script as a subscript of another.

The Manage Scripts Interface

You perform all script editing within FileMaker Pro's Manage Scripts dialog, shown in Figure 12.1. You can access Manage Scripts by selecting File, Manage, Scripts, or you can use the Command+Shift+S (Mac OS X) or Ctrl+Shift+S (Windows) shortcut. Choose a script and click the Edit button to modify the individual steps in the Edit Script dialog, shown in Figure 12.2.

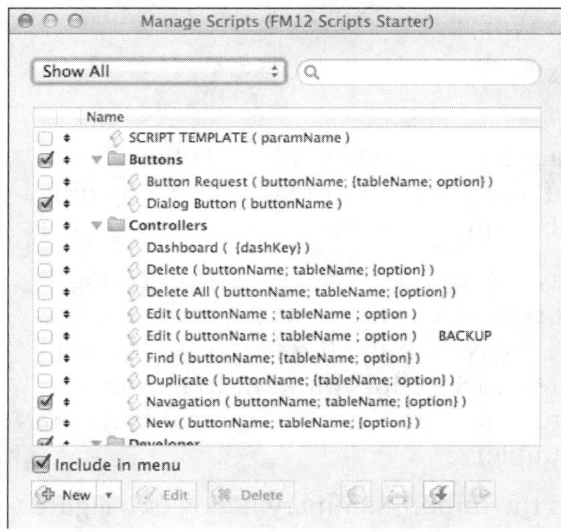

Figure 12.1
The main Manage Scripts dialog shows a list of scripts for a given file. Use this dialog to organize, edit, duplicate, print, import, and initiate the execution of your scripts.

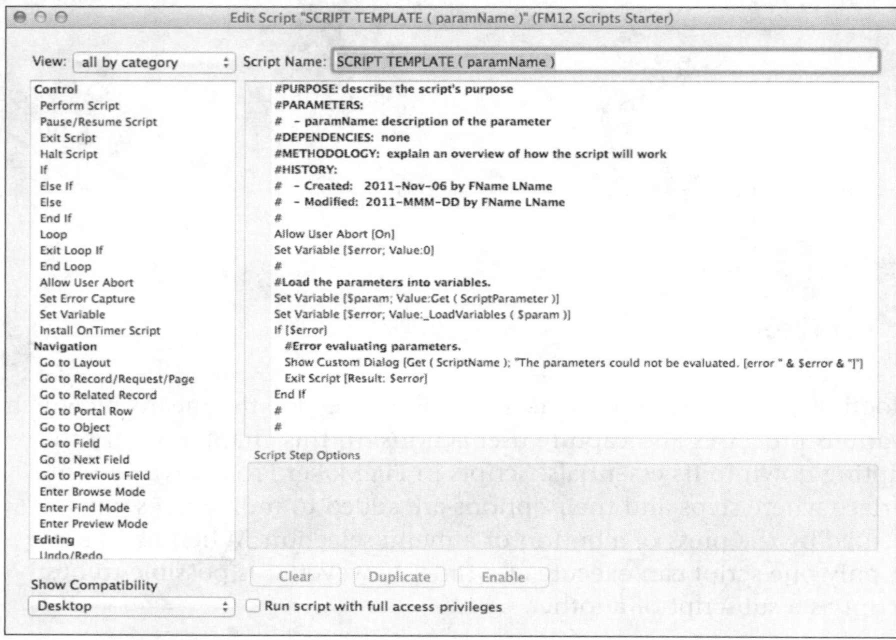

Figure 12.2
The Edit Script dialog enables you to edit a single script.

Many time-saving shortcuts are available in the Manage Scripts dialog.

➔ *See the "Scripting" section in Chapter 23, "FileMaker Keyboard Shortcuts," for more information.*

Where Scripts Live

Scripts are attached to an individual file (no matter how many tables the file has). Although one script may call a script in another file, a given script may act directly only on data and records contained or referenced in the same file as the script.

You may move scripts between files in several ways. Within the Manage Scripts dialog, you can import scripts from another file. Click the Import button, located along the bottom of the Manage Scripts dialog; navigate to the file containing the scripts you want to import; and then click the check box that is next to each script you want to import. FileMaker moves the scripts and does its best to resolve any references they contain (references to fields, files, scripts, or value lists, for example).

When the import is complete, FileMaker displays the Import Summary dialog (see Figure 12.3). It gives a synopsis of the import result and includes an Open Log File button.

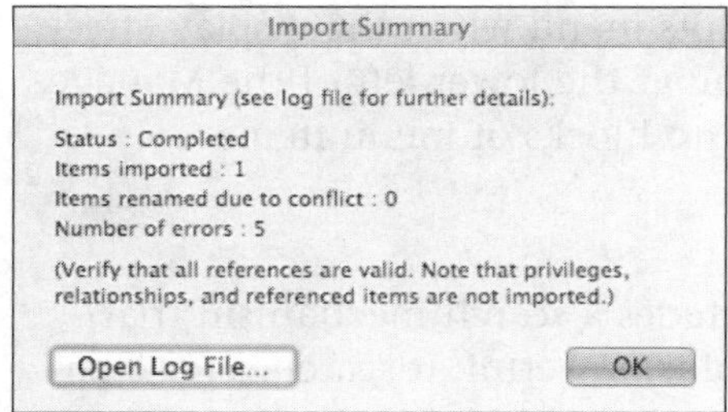

Figure 12.3
The Import Summary dialog is displayed after the scripts are imported.

You can also copy and paste scripts and script steps by using the standard commands from the Edit menu or their keyboard equivalents. An Import Summary dialog is not displayed when the scripts or script steps are pasted, but the Import.log file is still updated. The Import.log file is stored in the same path as the destination database when it is open locally and in the user's Documents folder when the destination database is hosted in FileMaker Server. Only one Import.log file is created at a location, and subsequent imports are appended to the file. It can be helpful to clear or delete the log file before performing the import so you have fewer entries to check when the script import is complete.

Whether you import scripts or use Copy and Paste commands, it is critical that you check the log, look over the scripts, and fix any references that might not have translated as you intended.

Editing or Creating Scripts

In both FileMaker Pro and Pro Advanced, you are able to open multiple scripts and edit them simultaneously. Unlike earlier versions of FileMaker, Manage Scripts is not modal. For any script that has been modified and is not yet saved, FileMaker displays an asterisk after its name in the Edit Script dialog. To revert your script changes, close the Edit script dialog. When prompted to save, select the Don't Save button. If you have a script open already, you cannot open it a second time, and if you or a user happens to run the script, only the saved version runs.

Organizing Scripts

The Manage Scripts dialog includes the capability to collect scripts into folders. Using the menu at the lower left of the Manage Scripts dialog, you can create a folder and then move scripts into it. You can then move folders as units within Manage Scripts (up or down or inside another group), and you can delete, copy, and paste a folder as a whole. You can also use Ctrl+Up/Down Arrow (Windows) or Command+Up/Down Arrow (Mac OS X) to highlight the previous/next script in the list. After a script is highlighted, you can click the Enter key to view it in a Manage Script dialog.

Folders create hierarchical menu choices within the Scripts menu when the display check box is selected. Separators (also generated from the menu at the lower left of the Manage Scripts dialog) can also help organize the Script menu into blocks of menu items.

Filtering Scripts

The upper-right corner of the Manage Scripts dialog includes a search mechanism that dynamically filters your list of scripts by name. This tool is powerful: It searches for character fragments and allows developers to quickly find a script within a larger list. (For example, "help" finds a script named "Help Button" as well as "Ineedhelp.")

The menu to the left of the filter mechanism enables developers to restrict the view to scripts of a particular folder.

Script Privileges

Access to scripts is controlled via FileMaker's Accounts and Privileges setting. A given privilege set may be allowed to edit and execute scripts, or to execute only, or may not be permitted to use scripts at all. You can customize these settings on a per-privilege-set, per-script basis.

When a script is executed, it runs with the privileges of the current user. For example, if a script tries to delete a record, and the user running that script does not have sufficient privileges to delete that record, the script step fails.

You can overcome this hurdle by checking the Run Script with Full Access Privileges check box within Edit Script dialog for a specific script. When this option is selected, the script runs as though the current user has the [Full Access] privilege set. Note that when you use the Get(CurrentPrivilegeSetName) function while such a script is running, it returns [Full Access]. To always get the privilege set associated with the current user's account, use the Get(AccountPrivilegeSetName) function.

Setting a script so that it does not appear in the Scripts menu is not a substitute for FileMaker security. Scripts hidden from view are still accessible to the user through several other avenues, including being called from another file or through AppleScript when using a Mac. Consider setting the File Access to Require Full Access Privileges option to Use References to This File to block authorized users from creating their own FileMaker files that can call scripts in your file. This setting is located on the File Access tab in the Manage Security dialog, which you can access by selecting File, Manage, Security.

Debugging Scripts

FileMaker Pro Advanced contains two powerful script-debugging tools: the Script Debugger and the Data Viewer. The Script Debugger, shown in Figure 12.4, enables you to step through running scripts line by line, with fine-grained control over execution. The Data Viewer, shown in Figure 12.5, enables you to watch the values of both fields and variables within your script as well as other expressions you specify, and often is used along with the Script Debugger to monitor these values as a given script executes. The Script Debugger also shows the error values returned as a script executes.

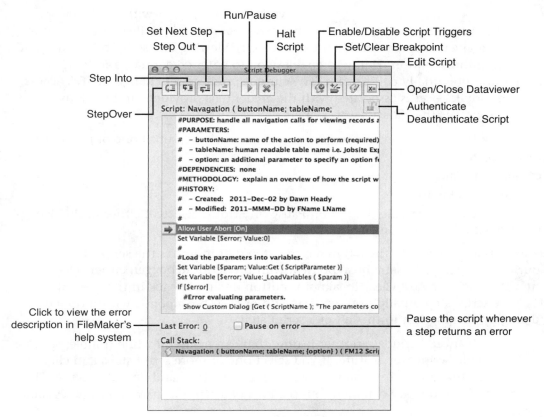

Figure 12.4
The Script Debugger enables you to step through scripts and watch the results as they execute.

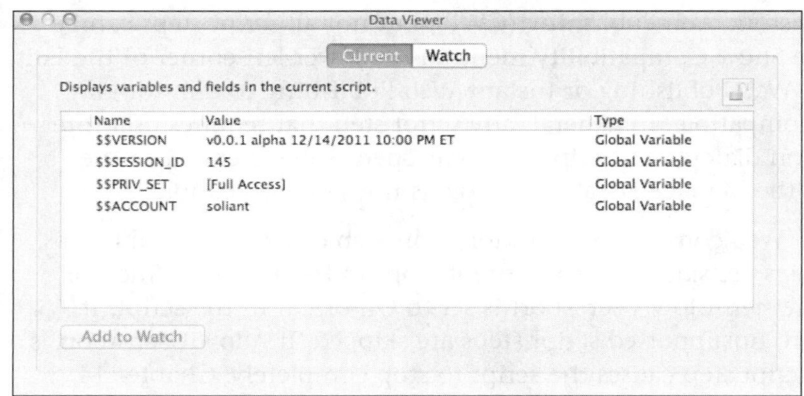

Figure 12.5
The Data Viewer enables you to see the results of expressions (calculation fields, variables, or others you enter on the Watch tab), and the Current tab automatically displays those found in the current script.

It is possible to open the Script Debugger with various privilege sets within FileMaker. When logged in using an account that does not have [Full Access] privileges or the privilege to modify a given script, a developer can authorize viewing of a script by clicking the Authorize/Deauthorize button. Doing so enables you to enter credentials and then proceed to view and potentially edit a script. The current privilege set changes to [Full Access] (or whichever privilege set is associated with the credentials provided) and remains changed for as long as the Data Viewer is open.

When you click the run button, the script will execute each step until one of the following things happens:

- It comes to a "Pause" script step.
- It reaches a breakpoint.
- It encounters an error while the option Pause on Error is selected, either in the debugger or from Tools, Debugging Controls.

A breakpoint is a red arrow to the left of a script step that indicates the script should pause during debugging. To set a breakpoint within the script debugger, either select a script step and click the Add/Clear Breakpoint button or simply click in the gray bar to the left of the script step. In addition, you can add or clear breakpoints within the Edit Script dialog by clicking just to the left of a script step.

FileMaker Pro Advanced includes another feature that can be useful while troubleshooting a script: the Disable Script Step feature. If you select one or more script steps and click the Disable button in the Edit Script dialog, those steps are disabled and do not execute. This feature enables you to quickly comment out sections of a script as part of a troubleshooting effort.

Scripting for the Web

Scripts can be invoked from a web-published FileMaker database, both via Instant Web Publishing (IWP) and via Custom Web Publishing (CWP), but not all script steps can be run from the Web. From the Show Compatibility menu in the lower-left corner of the Edit Script dialog, select Custom Web Publishing or Instant Web Publishing to dim (or gray out) script steps that are incompatible. In general, any script step that requires user interaction, such as a confirmation dialog, or a script step that opens some element of the FileMaker interface, such as the Manage Database dialog, is not web-compatible.

If a script executed from the Web contains one or more non-web-compatible script steps, the noncompatible script steps are skipped, or the script stops in its entirety. Which of these occurs depends on whether Allow User Abort is set to On or Off in the script. If Allow User Abort is set to Off, unsupported script steps are skipped. If Allow User Abort is set to On, an unsupported script step causes the script to stop completely. Chapter 14, "Script Step Reference," details each script step, including its compatibility.

Scripting for FileMaker Go

Just as with the Web, you also can run scripts in FileMaker Go, but not all script steps can be performed on an iOS device. Most of the restricted steps involve development tools and windows. Development tools are inappropriate because you cannot develop using FileMaker Go. Other steps involve interface elements that are not supported by any iOS device, such as displaying multiple windows at one time. Select iOS in the Show Compatibility menu to dim (or gray out) incompatible steps. Chapter 14 details each script step, including its compatibility.

Server Scheduled Scripts

FileMaker Server provides the capability to run a script on a schedule that you define. With this feature, a database administrator can perform maintence or large reporting functions after hours, thus increasing user performance during prime operation hours. Scripts that are run as server-scheduled scripts must be written and debugged with great care because they can have no user interaction. Select Server in the Show Compatibility menu to dim (or gray out) incompatible steps. Chapter 14 details each script step, including its compatibility.

It's worth noting that FileMaker Server can also run system-level scripts: Shell scripts on Mac OS and Batch scripts on Windows. System scripts can be executed on their own as well as part of a sequence, with a system script run before or after a FileMaker Script.

Scripting for FileMaker Go

[illegible]

Server Scheduled Scripts

[illegible]

[illegible]

CHAPTER 13

Script Triggers

A script trigger enables a developer to specify that a script execute whenever a particular action is performed. Before FileMaker Pro 10, when the script trigger feature was first introduced, scripts were generally initiated either by clicking a button or selecting a menu item. With the exception of the file open and close preferences, initiating a script based on an event previously required the use of a plug-in.

Setting Script Triggers

FileMaker Pro 12 supports 19 script triggers for actions in three major areas:

1. File events, such as opening or closing a window
2. Layout events, such as loading a record or layout
3. Object events, such as entering or exiting a field

For each script trigger event, you specify the script to execute and optionally pass to it a script parameter, which is defined by literal text or dynamically by calculation. For layout and object events, you also specify the mode in which the script fires (Browse, Find, and/or Preview). You can disable a script trigger without deleting it by simply unchecking all the modes.

Script triggers for File, Layout, and Object events are each configured in their own settings dialog.

File Events

A script trigger can be specified for each supported file action within the File, File Options menu item on the Script Triggers tab, as shown in Figure 13.1. There are four file-level script triggers; all are related to the opening or closing of a window. Note that with FileMaker 12, the long-existing File Options for executing a script when a file is opened or closed have been converted to the more appropriately named script triggers `OnFirstWindowOpen` and `OnLastWindowClose`. This makes it more evident that the script does not run when a file is opened by another file with the option "Open Hidden", but instead is performed only when the first window is created.

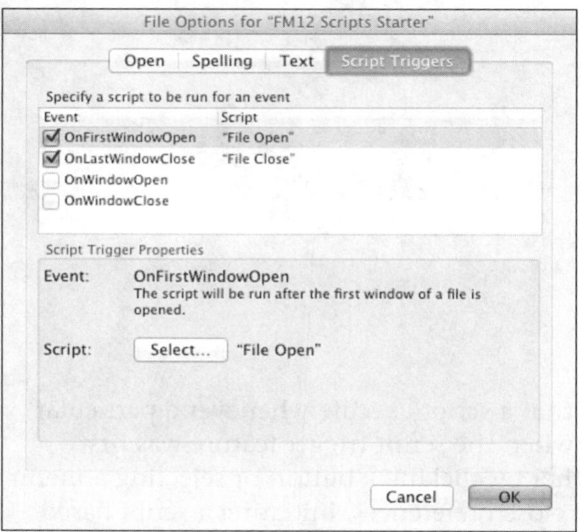

Figure 13.1
The Script Triggers tab of the File Options dialog enables you to define script trigger execution for file events.

Layout Events

Script triggers can be assigned to layout specific actions as part of the layout's setup. After entering Layout mode while viewing the layout, select Layout, Layout Setup and choose the Script Triggers tab, shown in Figure 13.2. You can assign different scripts to trigger for each layout, one script per layout event.

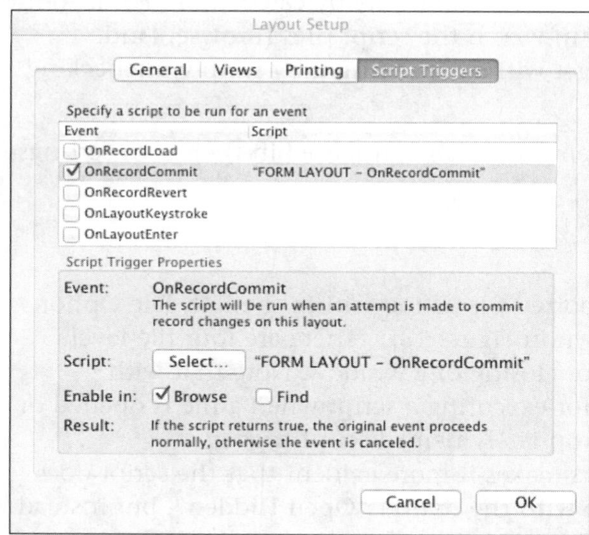

Figure 13.2
The Script Triggers tab of the Layout Setup dialog enables you to configure triggers for layout events. FileMaker Pro 12 supports nine layout script triggers.

Layouts that are configured with a script trigger display a star on the layout icon in the Manage Layouts window, as shown in Figure 13.3. This indicator is also presented by the `Go to Layout` script step within the Specify Layout dialog.

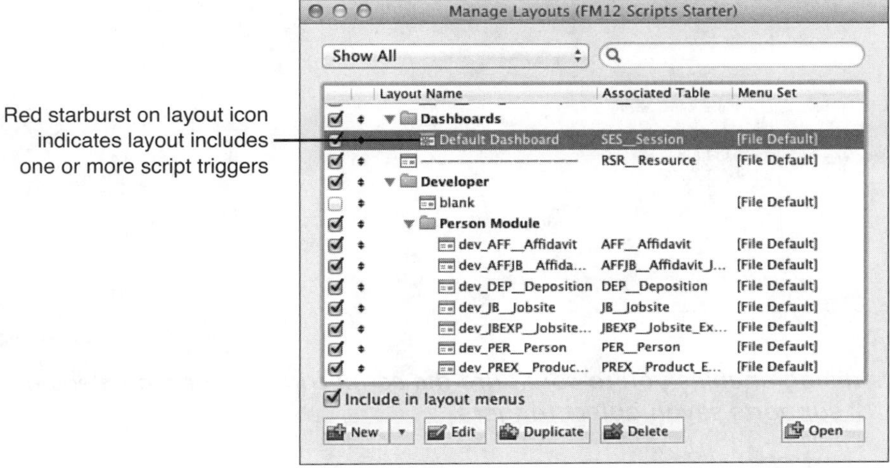

Figure 13.3
The Manage Layouts dialog displays a red starburst to indicate layouts that are configured with a script trigger.

Object Events

Individual layout objects may be assigned an event script trigger. You may assign triggers to many different types of layout objects, including fields, text-based buttons, tab controls, web viewers, and portals.

To configure a script trigger for an object, you must first enter Layout mode while viewing the layout that contains the object. Next, select the object to which you want to assign a script trigger and choose Format, Set Script Triggers or choose Set Script Triggers from the object's contextual menu. You can display the contextual menu by right-clicking (Control-clicking on a Mac) an object; the Set Script Triggers dialog displays (see Figure 13.4).

While you're working in Layout mode, objects that are configured with one or more script triggers are marked with a badge, either, depending on the size of the object. To make the badges visible (or to hide them), select View, Show, Script Triggers.

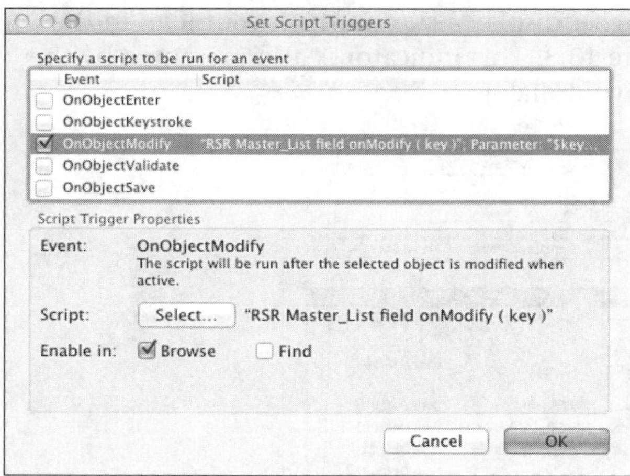

Figure 13.4
The Set Script Triggers dialog enables you to configure the script triggers for the selected object. FileMaker Pro 12 supports seven object triggers.

You may set script triggers for multiple objects at the same time by selecting them all before opening the Script Triggers dialog. If you see a minus sign ("–") in the check box for a given script trigger, it indicates the objects selected have different trigger settings. Changes you make are applied to the individual triggers you modified, whereas the original settings for the other triggers are left as originally specified. For example, assume two fields have the following properties: Field A is configured with only an `OnObjectKeystroke` script trigger, and field B has only an `OnObjectEnter` script trigger. Assume next that the developer selects both fields and then opens the Script Trigger dialog. If she now assigns a script for the `OnObjectExit` event and makes a change to the `OnObjectEnter` trigger, these two triggers are updated for both objects while each retains its previous setting for the keystroke event.

Activating Script Triggers

A script trigger can be invoked only by direct operations. Script steps and menu commands that initiate a bulk function—such as Import Records, Replace Field Contents, and Relookup Field Contents—do not activate a script trigger. Likewise, spell check operations for all fields in a record or all records do not activate script triggers, with the following exceptions:

- When a field is active while the spell check operation begins, the `OnObjectExit` trigger executes.
- If a field is active at the end of the spell check operation, the `OnObjectEnter` trigger fires for that field.

Script triggers are fully supported by FileMaker Go. Instant Web Publishing (IWP) and Custom Web Publishing (CWP) can activate script triggers only by scripted actions, not direct user interaction. For example, a script that navigates to a layout that has an OnLayoutEnter script trigger will still trigger when using IWP or CWP.

Apple Events that apply directly to, or work through, layout objects trigger scripts; however, Apple Events that bypass the layout do not activate script triggers. Finally, schema changes that modify field data do not trigger scripts.

Timing of Script Triggers

Script triggers are activated by some discrete event, such as typing a character or navigating to a layout. For some script triggers, the event occurs and then the script trigger activates; for others, the trigger activates and then the event occurs. Broadly then, you can categorize script triggers as either being "before event" triggers or "after event" triggers. This distinction is important because it is possible for the "before event" triggers to suppress the event from occurring.

For example, OnWindowOpen activates its script *after* a window is opened. The script can have no effect on the window's creation. On the other hand, OnObjectExit activates its script before the exit event, which means that the script can determine whether the event takes place. When the script's *result* is False, the event is canceled, whereas a True result allows the event to proceed. You specify a script result by using the Exit script step. FileMaker considers the keyword value True or the number 1 to be a true result. The keyword value False or the number 0 is considered a false result. Note that all scripts that exit without explicitly returning a result are also considered true.

It is important to keep in mind that a single user interaction can conceivably activate multiple script triggers. Likewise, the steps performed by one triggered script may in turn cause the execution of another script trigger. For example,

- Opening a new window activates OnWindowOpen, OnLayoutEnter, and OnRecordLoad script triggers.
- Changing layouts activates the OnLayoutEnter and OnRecordLoad script triggers.
- Performing a find activates the OnModeExit/Enter and OnRecordLoad script triggers.

Table 13.1 documents the order in which script triggers execute when initiated by a single action. Pay close attention to this sequence along with whether the script fires before or after the event that triggers it.

OnObjectSave is the one script trigger that is performed after its event yet is also affected by the script's result. The reason is that it initiates the script after the object's data is validated and saved but before the object is exited. It is similar to the OnObjectExit trigger, but it executes only when the object has been successfully changed. The script result determines only if the object is exited, not whether the data is saved.

Table 13.1 Order and Timing of Script Triggers

Order	Script Trigger	Area	Before Event	After Event	Script Result
1	OnFirstWindowOpen	File		X	None
2	OnWindowOpen	File		X	None
3	OnLayoutEnter	Layout		X	None
4	OnModeEnter	Layout		X	None
5	OnRecordLoad	Layout		X	None
6	OnObjectEnter	Object		X	None
7	OnObjectKeystroke	Object	X		True or False
8	OnLayoutKeystroke	Layout	X		True or False
9	OnTabSwitch	Object	X		True or False
10	OnObjectModify	Object		X	None
11	OnObjectValidate	Object	X		True or False
12	OnObjectSave	Object		X	True or False
13	OnObjectExit	Object	X		True or False
14	OnRecordCommit or OnRecordRevert	Layout	X		True or False
15	OnViewChange	Layout		X	None
16	OnModeExit	Layout	X		True or False
17	OnLayoutExit	Layout	X		True or False
18	OnWindowClose	File	X		True or False
19	OnLastWindowClose	File	X		True or False

For object script triggers that perform before the event, FileMaker executes the script only one time as long as the triggering object remains active. However, if during the execution of the script, the object is exited and then reentered and the script returns True, the script trigger fires again, leaving the user in an endless loop. To avoid this fate, you are advised to trap for this event and exit the script with a False result, or prevent the exit of the object during script execution in the first place.

For instance, suppose you want to track a user's navigation and so configure each layout with the OnRecordEnter script trigger. The associated script quickly switches to a NavLog layout, creates a record to log the action, and then returns the original layout. The act of returning to the original layout causes the OnRecordEnter script trigger to execute *again*, leaving the user in an infinite loop. Manage the situation by adding a few steps to the beginning and end of your script as follows:

Examples:

```
//Begin by immediately checking if the script is already running
If [ $$SCRIPT_RUNNING = 1]
  Exit Script [Result: False]
End If
#
// Set a global variable to indicate we are running the script
Set Variable [$$SCRIPT_RUNNING; VALUE:1]
#
#  *** << INCLUDE YOUR SCRIPT STEPS HERE >> ***
#
// End by clearing the variable
Set Variable [$$SCRIPT_RUNNING; VALUE:""]
Exit Script [Result: True]
```

Regardless of the methodology you use, it is imperative that you test your scripts thoroughly.

Scripting for Script Triggers

As with any script the user executes, a script initiated by a script trigger is executed with the user's current privileges, unless the Run Script with Full Access Privileges option is specified.

Although any script can be called by a script trigger, naming scripts especially for the event and object, and organizing them into a Trigger folder can make a system much easier to manage.

FileMaker Pro Advanced 12 provides a feature that can disable all the script triggers for a file, which can be helpful when you are debugging or troubleshooting issues. It is accessed on the Script Debugger from a new button, Enable/Disable Script Triggers, located in the upper-right corner of the window. A user must have [Full Access] privileges to enable or disable script triggers in this way. As shown in Figure 13.5, the Script Debugger also indicates the script trigger that initiated the running script, in this case an `OnRecordCommit` event.

Because there is no script step that can dynamically disable all script triggers, it is a best practice to include a subroutine at the top of every script initiated by a script trigger that immediately exits the script when some type of indicator flag is set. This indicator flag could be in the form of a global variable or global field. It could even be abstracted further by calling a custom function or subscript that in turn tests for the indicator's value. In any case, it can be handy when performing complex automated routines to be able to toggle the script trigger execution to help alleviate unforeseen behaviors.

It can also be a good idea to create separate layouts that include no script triggers of any kind so that you can perform your scripted routines without the interference caused by unexpected scripts being triggered.

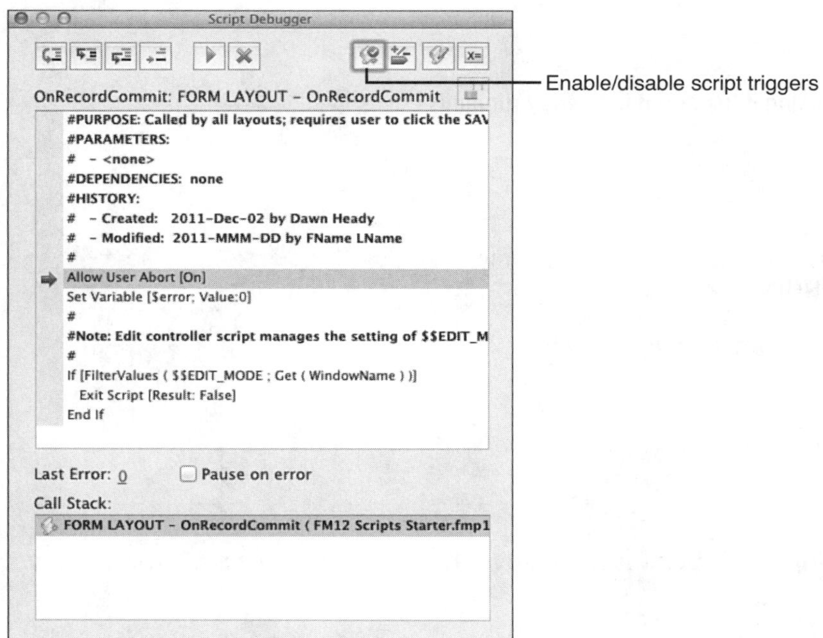

Figure 13.5
The Script Debugger includes a button to enable or disable script triggers. It also indicates the type of script trigger that initiated the running script.

Tab Control Objects

FileMaker Pro 12 introduced a new object script trigger called OnTabSwitch that is invoked when the user attempts to switch the active tab, either manually or by script. Although the OnObjectModify trigger can also be applied to a tab control object, it activates the script after the user changes tabs, whereas this new trigger executes before the tab is switched.

Two new functions also are handy when creating the script for the OnTabSwitch trigger: Get (TriggerCurrentTabPanel) and Get (TriggerTargetTabPanel), which return the index and object name of the current tab panel and destination tab panel, respectively. You can read more about this trigger in the "Script Trigger Reference" section later in this chapter and learn more about the functions in Chapter 10, "Calculation Functions."

Instant and Custom Web Publishing

Script triggers are only partially supported when a database file is accessed by IWP or CWP. Script triggers do not activate when a user directly interacts with an object, such as exiting a field or selecting a tab. However, when a running script includes steps that interact with an object, such as Go to Field or Insert Calculated Result, script triggers activate. Because of this behavior, it is advisable to refrain from using script triggers with layouts accessed by IWP.

Script Trigger Reference

OnFirstWindowOpen

When Script Runs: After Event

Modes Available: Not applicable

Result: None

Originated In: FileMaker Pro 12.0

Description:

The OnFirstWindowOpen script trigger executes each time the first window of a file is opened. It activates when you initially open the file as well as when the initial window is opened for a file that was previously opened as hidden by another file.

Before FileMaker Pro 12, this trigger was the File Open script specified in the File Options dialog. When a file created with an earlier version is converted to FileMaker Pro 12, the File Open script option is converted to the OnFirstWindowOpen script trigger.

It is possible for this trigger to fire multiple times during a session if the last window of the file is closed, but the file remains open because it is referenced by another open file. Should the now-hidden file be directed to open a window, OnFirstWindowOpen executes again.

It is considered a best practice to use the OnFirstWindowOpen trigger to set up the user's initial context including the window position and size, initial layout, found set, and sort order and to initialize global fields.

Examples:

```
// Display the main menu
Go to Layout ["Main Menu" (Resources)]
Show/Hide Toolbars [Show]
Set Zoom Level [100%]
If [Abs ( Get ( SystemPlatform ) ) = 2]
   Adjust Window [Maximimize]
Else
   Adjust Window [Resize to Fit]
End If
```

OnLastWindowClose

When Script Runs: Before Event

Modes Available: Not applicable

Originated In: FileMaker Pro 12.0

Description:

The OnLastWindowClose script trigger activates whenever the user attempts to close the last window of a file. The script executes even if the file remains open, such as when the file is referenced by another file.

Before FileMaker Pro 12, this trigger was the File Close script specified in the File Options dialog. When a file created with an earlier version is converted to FileMaker Pro 12, the File Close script option is converted to the OnLastWindowClose script trigger.

The OnLastWindowClose trigger is especially useful for clearing global fields because they default to the value they contained when the file was last closed while hosted locally. The following script demonstrates a methodology for clearing global fields when the file is hosted locally.

Examples:

```
//Clear global fields when open locally to initialize values
If[IsEmpty ( Get ( HostApplicationVersion) )]
   Set Field [Resource::Account_g; ""]
End If
```

OnLayoutEnter

When Script Runs: After Event

Modes Available: Browse, Find, and Preview modes

Result: None

Originated In: FileMaker Pro 10.0

Description:

The OnLayoutEnter script trigger activates after a layout loads. This occurs when opening a window or switching to a new layout. Note that the script step New Window creates the new window and displays the currently viewed layout. This activates an OnLayoutEnter script trigger before proceeding with the other script steps for navigating to a new layout, and so on.

One typical use of the OnLayoutEnter script trigger is for automatically sorting the records of a list layout, thereby ensuring users are always presented a complete report with subsummary parts.

Examples:

```
//Dynamic sort the layout's data whenever it loads
Go to Next Field
Sort Records by Field [Ascending]
```

OnLayoutExit

When Script Runs: Before Event

Modes Available: Browse, Find, and Preview modes

Result: True or False

Originated In: FileMaker Pro 11.0

Description:

OnLayoutExit activates before a layout is exited. A layout is exited by switching to another layout or closing a window. When the activated script exits with a False result, the user remains on the current layout. Note that simply making a different window active does not constitute exiting a layout.

OnLayoutExit is useful for checking that the user has completed everything he needs to do on the current layout before moving on.

Many users would like their database to behave more like a browser and provide a Back button for retracing their steps after drilling into a record's detail. One great use of the OnLayoutExit trigger is to record a user's navigation to support a Back button, as shown in the following example. The navigation history is stored as a carriage-return delimited list in a global variable. Each window's history is stored in the variable's repetition that corresponds to the window's name, so a window whose name ends in 2 is stored in the second repetition and so on. (See the example for OnWindowClose for another script related to supporting a Back button.)

Examples:

```
//Store navigation history to support a back/forward button
Set Variable [$winNum; Value:
➥Let ( [
➥winName = Get ( WindowName ) ;
➥winValues = Substitute ( winName ; " - " ; ¶ ) ;
➥lastVal = ValueCount ( winValues ) ;
➥winNum = GetAsNumber ( GetValue ( winValues ; lastVal ) )];
➥Case ( IsEmpty ( winNum ) ; 1 ; winNum ) )]
Set Variable [ $$BACK_STACK[$winNum]; Value:
➥Case ( not IsEmpty ( $$BACK_STACK[$winNum] ) ; $$BACK_STACK[$winNum] & ¶ )
➥& Get ( LayoutName ) ]
```

OnLayoutKeystroke

When Script Runs: Before Event

Modes Available: Browse, Find, and Preview modes

Result: True or False

Originated In: FileMaker Pro 10.0

Description:

The OnLayoutKeystroke script trigger is activated with each individual keystroke typed into a keyboard or Input Method Editor (IME). An IME is an application that can enter the many different characters used in East Asian written languages without the need of a special keyboard. All keystrokes cause the script trigger to activate, including those normally used for navigation. However, data entry by way of a drop-down list, pop-up menu, calendar picker, check box, or radio button does not active this trigger. Likewise, script steps that insert data into fields do not active this script trigger, even those that require the field be present on the layout.

Keystrokes are evaluated first by the operating system and then by the FileMaker Pro application itself before being passed to the database file. As such, a key combination that is a System or FileMaker command shortcut does not activate either of the keyboard script triggers.

The script trigger is activated before the keystroke is processed, so when the triggered script returns a False result, the event (also known as the keystroke) is suppressed. If the active object is configured with both OnLayoutKeystroke and OnObjectKeystroke script triggers, the layout trigger activates first and its script must exit with a True result to activate the object's trigger.

The Get(TriggerKeystroke) function returns the characters that activated the script trigger. You can then use the Code function to translate this into a Unicode value. Table 13.2 lists some common keystrokes.

Table 13.2 Common Keystrokes and Their Unicode Value

Keystroke	Code	Description
Backspace	8	Unicode/ASCII code for BS (backspace)
Tab	9	Unicode/ASCII code for HT (horizontal tab)
Shift+Tab	9	The shift can be detected using Get(TriggerModifierKeys)
Enter	10	Unicode/ASCII code for LF (linefeed)
Return	13	Unicode/ASCII code for CR (carriage return)
Escape	27	Unicode/ASCII code for ESC (escape)
Left Arrow	28	Unicode/ASCII code for FS (file separator)
Up Arrow	29	Unicode/ASCII code for GS (group separator)

Table 13.2 Continued

Keystroke	Code	Description
Right Arrow	30	Unicode/ASCII code for RS (record separator)
Down Arrow	31	Unicode/ASCII code for US (unit separator)
Space	32	Unicode/ASCII code for Space
Forward Delete	127	Unicode/ASCII code for Delete

OnLayoutKeystroke can be used on a table view layout to mimic a spreadsheet's navigation, which makes use of the arrow keys to move between cells.

Examples:

```
//While in Table view, use arrow keys for record and field navigation
If [Get ( LayoutViewState ) = 2 //table view]
   Set Variable [$code; Value:Code ( Get ( TriggerKeystroke ) ) ]
   If [$code = 29 //up arrow]
      Go to Record/Request/Page[Previous]
   Else If [$code = 31 //down arrow]
      Go to Record/Request/Page [Next]
   Else If [$code = 30 //right arrow]
      Go to Next Field
   Else If [$code = 28 // left arrow]
      Go to Previous Field
   End If
End If
```

OnModeEnter

When Script Runs: After Event

Modes Available: Browse, Find, and Preview modes

Result: None

Originated In: FileMaker Pro 10.0

Description:

The OnModeEnter script trigger activates after switching modes (Browse, Find, or Preview), either manually or by a script step.

You can use OnModeEnter to navigate to a specially formatted layout when the user enters Find mode. It is also handy for automatically sorting data when the user enters Preview mode, as shown in the following example.

Examples:

```
// When user enters Preview Mode, sort the data
If [Get (WindowMode ) = 2 //Preview Mode]
   Sort Records [Restore; No dialog]
End If
```

OnModeExit

When Script Runs: Before Event

Modes Available: Browse, Find, and Preview modes

Result: True or False

Originated In: FileMaker Pro 10.0

Description:

The OnModeExit script trigger activates when the user attempts to exit the current mode. When the triggered script returns a True result, the mode change is carried out, but a False result cancels the event.

You can use OnModeExit to run a script when leaving Find mode to log the user's searches. Another purpose is to append the search request with additional criteria when exiting Find mode to omit records that are flagged for deletion. Use it when exiting Preview mode to give the user the option to print the report.

Examples:

```
//When user exits Find Mode, try to show list view to display the result
If [Get (WindowMode ) = 1 //Find Mode]
   Set Error Captute [On]
   Set Variable [$layoutName ;
   ➥Value:Substitute ( Get ( LayoutName ) ; "Detail" ; "List" )]
   Go to Layout [$layoutName]
End If
Exit Script [Result: True]
```

OnObjectEnter

When Script Runs: After Event

Modes Available: Browse and Find modes

Result: None

Originated In: FileMaker Pro 10.0

Description:

The OnObjectEnter trigger executes when a specific layout object becomes active by either a user or a script interacting with the object. A user can accomplish this by clicking the object, tabbing to the object, or tabbing between the repetitions of a repeating field. This trigger can also be activated by a script step that causes an object to be entered.

OnObjectEnter can be configured for a chart object. Use it to auto save the chart as a picture file by temporarily copying and pasting the chart into a container field before exporting the field's contents. This trigger can also be configured to a Web Viewer object, which is handy for displaying a modal dialog window where the user is prompted to enter criteria for the site.

When this trigger is applied to a portal object, it fires each time a different portal row becomes active. Although tab control objects and buttons also can be assigned the OnObjectEnter trigger, it does not activate when the object is clicked or otherwise becomes active.

The following example is configured as the OnObjectEnter trigger for the Employee's Spouse field. It requires the value to be empty when the Employee's Marital Status is "Single".

Examples:

```
//Prohibit entry of value in a field that should remain empty based on other fields
// Trigger applied to the Employee::Spouse field
If [Employee::Marital_Status = "Single"]
   Go to Next Field
End If
```

OnObjectExit

When Script Runs: Before Event

Modes Available: Browse and Find modes

Result: True or False

Originated In: FileMaker Pro 10.0

Description:

The OnObjectExit script trigger fires before the active object is exited, by either a user or a script interacting with the object. A user can accomplish this by clicking another object, tabbing away from the object, attempting to tab between the repetitions of a repeating field, attempting to move between rows in a portal object, or by requesting a dialog box, such as the print dialog, that would usually cause the field to be exited. This trigger also can be activated by a script step that attempts to activate a different object.

OnObjectExit can be applied to fields, web viewers, charts, and portal objects. When this trigger is applied to a portal object, it fires each time a portal row is exited. Although tab control objects and buttons can also be assigned the OnObjectExit trigger, it does not activate when the object is clicked or otherwise becomes active. Note that scrolling does not change the active object and so does not initiate this script trigger.

This trigger is especially useful for guiding data entry by skipping fields that are not needed based on the user's entry in other fields.

Examples:

```
//Skip the explanation field when responded NO
If [MedHistory::HospitalStayLastYear = "No"]
   Go to Field [MedHistory::HeartCondition]
Else
   Go to Field [MedHistory::HospitalStayLastYear_explain]
End If
```

OnObjectKeystroke

When Script Runs: Before Event

Modes Available: Browse and Find modes

Result: True or False

Originated In: FileMaker Pro 10.0

Description:

The OnObjectKeystroke script trigger executes whenever the object is active and receives one or more characters, either by a keyboard or by an Input Method Editor (IME). An IME is an application that can enter the many different characters used in East Asian written languages without the need of a special keyboard. All keystrokes cause the script trigger to activate, including those normally used for navigation. However, data entry by way of a drop-down list, pop-up menu, calendar picker, check box, or radio button does not activate this trigger. Likewise, script steps that insert data into fields do not activate this script trigger, even those that require the field be present on the layout.

Keystrokes are processed first by the operating system and then by the FileMaker Pro application itself before being passed to the database file. As such, a key combination that is a System or FileMaker command shortcut does not activate either of the keyboard script triggers.

OnObjectKeystroke is activated before the keystroke is processed, so when the triggered script returns a False result, the event is canceled. If the active object is configured with both the OnLayoutKeystroke and OnObjectKeystroke script triggers, the layout trigger activates first and its script must exit with a True result to also activate the object's trigger.

You can determine which characters were input using the Get(TriggerKeystroke) function; use the Code function to translate this into a Unicode value. Refer to Table 13.2 for a table of common keystrokes.

The OnObjectKeystroke script trigger activates when applied to field, button, chart, and tab control objects. You also can assign it to a web viewer, but it does not fire the script.

This trigger is useful for directing the user's entry into a fixed-width field by automatically tabbing to the next field when data entry is completed. In the following example, the user's cursor is automatically moved to the next field when the proper number of characters has been entered in each field that stores a serial number.

Examples:

```
//For Serial Number field, move to next field when length is 5
//Wire to each of the 4 fields that make up the serial number
Set Variable [$key; Value:Get (TriggerKeystroke)]
Set Variable [$code; Value:Code ($key)]
If [$code=8 or $code=9 or $code=127 //backspace, tab, or delete]
   Exit Script [Result: True]
Else If [$code ≥ 27 and $code ≤ 31 //arrow keys]
   Exit Script [Result: True]
Else If [Length (Contact::Serial_Number_1) ≥ 5]
   Go to Next Field
   Exit Script [Result: True]
End If
```

OnObjectModify

When Script Runs: After Event

Modes Available: Browse and Find modes

Result: None

Originated In: FileMaker Pro 10.0

Description:

The OnObjectModify script trigger activates whenever an object's value is changed through direct interaction. In contrast to the OnObjectKeystroke script trigger, this trigger executes when modifying the value using a pop-up menu, drop-down list, check box, radio button, and calendar picker as well as cut, copy, and paste commands.

Changes made to a field from the Show Custom Dialog script step, however, do not activate OnObjectModify. Likewise, with the script steps that modify a field value directly, such as Set Field, Set Field by Name, and Set Web Viewer, the trigger does not run. However, the script step Insert Text and others that work on a layout object that is a field activate the OnObjectModify trigger. It also fires when applied to a tab control and the tab is switched. Whereas the interface allows the OnObjectModify trigger to be assigned to a calculation or summary field, the trigger does not activate when the value changes.

The OnObjectModify script trigger has many applications. It is useful for formatting the user's entry of a phone number or Social Security number. When applied to a tab control object, it triggers each time the active tab is changed.

The following script example is activated by an OnObjectModify trigger attached to a global field that filters a list view of records based on the value entered.

Examples:

```
//This example will filter the record list based on global field entry in header
Set Variable [$cursorPosition; Value:Get ( ActiveSelectionStart)]
Commit Records/Requests[]
If[IsEmpty ( Resource::Company_Filter_g )]
   Show All Records
Else
   Enter Find Mode []
   Set Field [Company::Name; Resource::Company_Filter_g]
   Perform Find []
End If
// Restore cursor to original position
Go to Field [Resource::Company_Filter_g]
Set Selection [Resource::Company_Filter_g; Start Position: $cursorPosition]
```

OnObjectSave

When Script Runs: After Event

Modes Available: Browse and Find modes

Result: True or False

Originated In: FileMaker Pro 10.0

Description:

OnObjectSave executes after the object data has been validated and saved, but before the field is exited. It is the one script trigger that is performed after its event yet is also affected by the script's result. The reason is that the trigger initiates the script after the object's data is validated and saved, but before the object is exited. It is similar to the OnObjectExit trigger, but executes only when the object has been successfully changed. The script result simply determines if the object is exited, not whether the data is saved.

One use for this trigger is to clear the values of fields that are no longer appropriate based on other field values. In the following example, the explanation field is cleared when the HospitalStayLastYear field is set to no.

Examples:

```
//Clear Explanation field value when the Yes/No radio button is No
If [MedHistory::HospitalStayLastYear = "No" and
➥not IsEmpty (MedHistory::HospitalStayLastYear_explain )]
   Set Field [MedHistory::HospitalStayLastYear_explain; ""]
End If
```

OnObjectValidate

When Script Runs: Before Event

Modes Available: Browse and Find modes

Result: True or False

Originated In: FileMaker Pro 11.0

Description:

The OnObjectValidate trigger executes before the active object is validated and saved. As such, it fires only when the selected field data has been changed. This trigger can be useful for performing prevalidation on a field value in an effort to correct obvious issues and/or deliver a more specific message to the user. For instance, the following example illustrates a simple script for removing spaces from an email address before it is evaluated by the field's validation calculation.

Examples:

```
//Remove spaces from user's email address entry before validation
Set Field [Contact::Email; Substitute ( Contact::Email ; " " ; "" )]
```

OnRecordCommit

When Script Runs: Before Event

Modes Available: Browse and Find modes

Result: True or False

Originated In: FileMaker Pro 10.0

Description:

The OnRecordCommit script trigger activates before a record that has been changed is committed. Many actions can cause this trigger to activate. The user, after modifying a record, can do any of the following: move to another record, press the Enter key, click the layout outside the activated record, or immediately access the Manage Database dialog. OnRecordCommit also triggers when a script step, after modifying a record, moves focus to a different record or performs the Commit Records/Requests script step.

Assume, for example, that users want to avoid accidentally making changes to their records, preferring instead to click an Edit button before making data changes and then a Save button to commit the changes or a Cancel button to revert the record. The Edit button would call a script that adds the active window's name to the variable $$EDIT_MODE. The Save button would call another script that removes the current window's name from the variable $$EDIT_MODE and performs the Commit Record step. The Cancel button would also clear the global variable but revert the record instead of committing. The following example prevents the record from committing until the user clicks the Save button.

Examples:

```
//This script keeps the record open until the user clicks the Save button on screen
If [FilterValues ( $$EDIT_MODE ; Get (WindowName ) )]
   Exit Script [Result:False]
Else
   Exit Script [Result:True]
End If
```

Note this example is not intended to secure the data, but rather only to protect the user from himself when working with this layout.

OnRecordLoad

When Script Runs: After Event

Modes Available: Browse and Find modes

Result: None

Originated In: FileMaker Pro 10.0

Description:

The OnRecordLoad script trigger executes every time a record is made current or entered. This situation can occur when the user or script switches the record or layout, opens a new window, performs a find, or creates or deletes a record.

OnRecordLoad is handy for refreshing aggregate values stored for a record. In the following example, OnRecordLoad can be used to dynamically display the proper tab of a tab control that corresponds to a field's value.

Examples:

```
//Switch the hidden tab displayed to correspond to the Company Type
If [Company::Type = "Vendor"]
   Go to Object [Object Name: "TAB__Vendor"]
Else If [Company::Type = "Client"]
   Go to Object [Object Name: "TAB__Client”]
Else
   Go to Object [Object Name: "TAB__Blank"]
End If
```

OnRecordRevert

When Script Runs: Before Event

Modes Available: Browse and Find modes

Result: True or False

Originated In: FileMaker Pro 10.0

Description:

The OnRecordRevert script trigger is performed before record changes are reverted. It therefore fires only when the record contains uncommitted changes. You can revert a record by selecting Records, Revert Record or by running a script containing the Revert Record step. The OnRecordRevert trigger also fires when the record is reverted following a validation error dialog.

One use for this script trigger is to display an additional confirmation dialog when the user attempts to revert a record, as illustrated in the following example.

Examples:

```
//Display an additional confirmation dialog when revert record
Show Custom Dialog ["Revert Record"; "Are you sure you want to revert...
➥all of your changes will be lost?"]
//buttons are Default Button: Revert Record;  Button 2: Cancel
Exit Script [Result; Case ( Get ( LastMessageChoice ) = 2 ; False ; True )]
```

OnTabSwitch

When Script Runs: Before Event

Modes Available: Browse and Find modes

Result: True or False

Originated In: FileMaker Pro 12.0

Description:

The OnTabSwitch script trigger, new in FileMaker Pro 12, executes when a user or script attempts to change the active tab. This trigger applies to the entire tab control object rather than just one individual tab panel. This trigger executes before the tab is changed, so a script result of False stops the tab from being switched. Note that you can fire a script *after* the tab is changed by attaching the OnObjectModify trigger to the tab control object.

The two new functions—Get (TriggerCurrentTabPanel) and Get (TriggerTargetTabPanel)—are useful when creating the script called by the OnTabSwitch trigger. They return the index number and object name of the current tab panel and destination tab panel, respectively. You can read more about these functions in Chapter 10.

This trigger is useful for refreshing field values that drive the display of objects on a tab before it is viewed. For example, you can set the value of a field used to dynamically filter a portal or refresh aggregate values stored in a number field. (Storing values can make for a faster display rather than using unstored calculations.)

You can also use OnTabSwitch to restrict the view of a tab for certain users. In the following example, the user is required to have the extended privilege "SysAdmin" to view the Client Settings tab.

Examples:

```
// Must have Admin extended privilege to view the tab
Set Variable [$targetTabName; Value:GetValue ( Get (TriggerTargetTabPanel) ; 2)]
If [$targetTabName = "Client Settings"]
   If [FilterValues ( Get (AccountExtendedPrivileges ) ; "SysAdmin" )]
      Exit Script [Result: True]
   Else
      Beep
      Show Custom Dialog ["Message"; "Sorry, you must be an admin to view this tab."]
      Exit Script [Result: False]
   End If
End If
Exit Script [Result: True]
```

OnViewChange

When Script Runs: After Event

Modes Available: Browse, Find, and Preview modes

Result: None

Originated In: FileMaker Pro 11.0

Description:

The OnViewChange script trigger executes after a user or script changes the view between form, list, and table views. Note that OnViewChange does not fire when a new window is open unless another action causes the view to change.

Keep in mind that the triggered script will likely cause the screen to flicker if it navigates to a new layout. Because of this, it is not advisable to use OnViewChange to navigate to an alternative layout specifically formatted for the view selected. You achieve a better user experience by using custom menus and reassigning the View as Form, View as List, and View as Table menu items to perform your script.

A better use of OnViewChange is to present the user with options appropriate to the new view. In the following example, the user is given the option to sort the data by Department, which then displays the subsummary part.

Examples:

```
// When entering Table View, offer to sort by Department
If [ Get ( LayoutViewState ) = 2 //Table View]
  Show Custom Dialog ["Message"; "You've switched to Table View. Should I also sort the
  ➥Data into departments"]
  //Dialog Buttons: 1=Yes; 2=No
  If [Get (LastMessageChoice ) = 1  //Yes]
    Sort Records [Restore; No Dialog]
  End If
End If
```

OnWindowClose

When Script Runs: Before Event

Modes Available: Not applicable

Result: True or False

Originated In: FileMaker Pro 12.0

Description:

The OnWindowClose script trigger is a file-level trigger. As such, it activates any time one of the file's windows is closed, regardless of whether the close was initiated by a user or script. When the OnLastWindowClose trigger is also specified, OnWindowClose executes first. Should the OnWindowClose trigger return a False result, the window is left open and the OnLastWindowClose trigger is not activated.

Many users would like their database to behave more like a browser and provide a Back button for retracing their steps after drilling into a record's detail. The following example uses OnWindowClose to clear the current window's navigation history before closing the window. Each window's history is stored in the repetition of a global variable that corresponds to the window's name. (See the example for OnLayoutExit for another script related to supporting a Back button.)

Examples:

```
//Clear the back/forward navigation history for this window
//History stored in a global variable repetition corresponding to the window's number
Set Variable [$winNum; Value:Let ( [
➥winName = Get ( WindowName ) ;
➥winValues = Substitute ( winName ; " - " ; ¶ ) ;
➥lastVal = ValueCount ( winValues ) ;
➥winNum = GetAsNumber ( GetValue ( winValues ; lastVal ) )];
➥Case ( IsEmpty ( winNum ) ; 1 ; winNum )  )]
Set Variable [ $$BACK_STACK[$winNum]; Value:""]
```

OnWindowOpen

When Script Runs: After Event

Modes Available: Not applicable

Result: None

Originated In: FileMaker Pro 12.0

Description:

The OnWindowOpen script trigger executes every time a new window is opened for the file, whether initiated manually by a user or script. Note that the OnWindowOpen trigger also activates when opening a window for a hidden file, which is a file that was previously opened by a relationship or script.

Because the script runs after the triggering event, the window always opens regardless of the triggered script's result. If an OnFirstWindowOpen trigger is also specified in the file options, it executes first and then OnWindowOpen runs.

OnWindowOpen is useful for renaming the window when your database does not use FileMaker's default naming convention of naming the window for the filename.

Imagine you have a database system that is composed of multiple databases and that one of the files should remain hidden (except for full access users) because it contains only data and not the interface. The script that follows could be activated by the OnWindowOpen trigger to discourage inappropriate interaction with the file.

Examples:

```
//Hide the file when the user does not have full access privileges
If[Get ( AccountPrivilegeSetName ) ≠ "[Full Access]"]
   Show Custom Dialog ["Permission Denied";
   ➥"Sorry, you are not permitted to view this file."]
   Close Window [Current Window]
End If
```

CHAPTER 14

Script Step Reference

This chapter details all the FileMaker Pro script steps. It is similar in some ways to FileMaker's online help system but adds examples that are more detailed and commentary where possible. The listing for each script step also indicates its compatibility, the FileMaker Pro version in which the script step was introduced, and any menu equivalent. An asterisk is placed next to a platform when it is partially compatible; see the description for the specific option or options that are not supported.

Add Account

Category: Accounts

Compatibility: Macintosh, Windows, Server, iOS, CWP, IWP, Runtime

Originated In: FileMaker 6.0 or earlier

Options:

- **Account Name** is the account name to be added to the file in question. Literal text can be entered or Specify can be clicked to create a new account name from a calculation.
- **Password** is the new password associated with this new account. Literal text can be entered or Specify can be clicked to create a new password from a calculation.
- **Privilege Set** enables you to assign a preexisting privilege set for the user or to create a new one. (You cannot assign Full Access using this script step. You must manually create accounts with Full Access.)
- **User Must Change Password on Next Login** forces users to change their password the next time they log in to the database.

Description:

This script step adds an account and password to a database file's security configuration and associates the new account with one of the privilege sets defined in the file. Account and password text may be defined in a calculation or typed into the script step itself. The account name must be unique, and full access to the file is required to execute this step.

Note that as with the rest of FileMaker security, accounts are specific to individual files. It is often with this script step that accounts are propagated throughout a multifile solution.

This script step enables developers to create administrative account functions within databases without having to grant full access to the security privileges within a solution.

Note that there are circumstances in which you should not set an account to force the user to change her password at next login. If the user will not have a direct means to do this, the option should not be set. The best example is an account that will be used to access a FileMaker database via Instant Web Publishing. IWP provides no means for a user to change her password, so this setting locks the user out of the database. Similarly, if the account is externally authenticated, it may be risky to tie the account to a privilege set requiring that the password be changed at some point, or have a minimum length.

Examples:

```
Add Account [Account Name: "User_Account"; Password: "User_Password"; Privilege
Set: "[Data Entry Only]"; Expire password]
```

Adjust Window

Category: Windows

Compatibility: Macintosh, Windows, iOS, Runtime*

Originated In: FileMaker 7.0

Options:

- **Resize to Fit** shrinks a window to the minimum possible size bounded on the right by the rightmost layout object and on the bottom by the bottommost layout part.
- **Maximize** expands the current window to the size of the user's screen or to the size of the application window on Windows.
- **Minimize** minimizes the current window to an icon on the Mac OS X Dock or to a small window bar within the application window on Windows.
- **Restore** returns the current window to the size it was prior to the last resize.
- **Hide** hides the current database window.

Description:

This script step hides or otherwise controls the size of the current window. Given minor differences in how each operating system manages windows, the Resize to Fit option is commonly used to ensure that layouts are properly displayed regardless of platform.

Note that on Windows, FileMaker restores all windows when a new window is opened or an existing window is resized. Maximize on Windows should be used only for one-window databases.

FileMaker Go, like all iOS apps, may run only in full screen mode, so Resize to Fit, Maximize, Minimize, and Restore all simply make the window active. The Hide option cannot hide the window but instead changes the order of the open windows, moving the active window to the back.

Examples:

```
Go to Layout ["Detail"]
Adjust Window [Maximize]
```

Allow Formatting Bar

Category: Miscellaneous

*Compatibility: Macintosh, Windows, Runtime**

Originated In: FileMaker 6.0 or earlier

Options:

- **On** allows FileMaker's native toolbars to be utilized.
- **Off** hides and makes inaccessible FileMaker's toolbars as well as the toolbar submenu options in the View menu.

Description:

This script step hides or shows the FileMaker Pro formatting bar and whether it may be accessed via the View menu. The formatting bar allows quick access to text formatting functions. This script step applies only to the current window. Note that this script step does not disable the formatting functions themselves; all the options in the Format menu are still available.

Examples:

```
Allow Formatting Bar [Off]
```

Allow User Abort

Category: Control

Compatibility: Macintosh, Windows, Server, iOS, CWP, IWP, Runtime

Originated In: FileMaker 6.0 or earlier

Options:

- **On** allows users to halt the execution of a script by pressing the Esc key (or Command-⌘. on Mac OS X).
- **Off** disables the halting of scripts by users.

Description:

Allow User Abort is used to control the user's ability to cancel scripts by using the Esc key (or the Command-⌘. key combination on Mac OS X). This step is usually used in scripts whose operation should not be arbitrarily canceled by the user, such as login logic, data import/export, or any script that must process a set of records without interruption. Most of FileMaker's menu options are also unavailable while a script is running in the Allow User Abort [Off] state.

If a script involves any processes that could work with large record sets, such as sorting, looping, or running a Replace script step, the user sees a progress dialog for the duration of that operation. If Allow User Abort is on, as it is by default, users can cancel the script and disrupt those operations, leaving them partially incomplete. This can be an area of significant problems if a database's operations assume a process that has been canceled by the user has concluded properly. If a script contains any process that must not be interrupted before completion, it should use Allow User Abort [Off] to ensure that these processes can finish without user interruption. However, take great care to thoroughly error trap the script because a user left in an infinite loop has no alternative but to force quit the file, possibly causing corruption.

When developing a script, note that you can use the Script Debugger feature of FileMaker Pro Advanced to halt a script, even one running with Allow User Abort [Off] state.

Examples:

```
Allow User Abort[Off]
```

Arrange All Windows

Category: Window

Compatibility: Macintosh, Windows, Runtime*

Originated In: FileMaker 7.0

Options:

- **Tile Horizontally** positions open windows from left to right across the screen. They are resized to avoid any overlaps.
- **Tile Vertically** positions open windows from top to bottom down the screen. They are resized to avoid any overlaps.
- **Cascade Window** positions windows overlapping diagonally from upper left to lower right. The idea of this arrangement is, presumably, to allow the reading of the title bar of each window. The windows are resized to fit the available screen space.
- **Bring All to Front** (Mac OS only) brings all open windows to the front without resizing or otherwise moving or rearranging them. In the event that any open FileMaker windows have been hidden by (that is, are behind) any other application's windows, this step ensures that all FileMaker windows are above other application windows.

Description:

This script step resizes and/or repositions open windows but does not affect which window has focus. The active record also remains the same.

Examples:

```
New Window [Name: "Trees"; Height: 600; Width: 800; Top: 16; Left: 16]
Arrange All Windows [Tile Vertically]
```

Beep

Category: Miscellaneous

Compatibility: Macintosh, Windows, iOS, Runtime

Originated In: FileMaker 6.0 or earlier

Options:

None

Description:

This script step plays a beep sound at the default volume of the machine on which it is played.

You may want to use the beep as a means of drawing further attention to alert dialogs or to confirm that a long process has concluded.

Examples:

```
Set Error Capture [On]
Perform Find [Restore]
If [Get (FoundCount) = 0]
  Beep
  Show Custom Dialog ["No records were found that match your find criteria."]
End
```

Change Password

Category: Accounts

Compatibility: Macintosh, Windows, Server, iOS, CWP*, IWP*, Runtime*

Originated In: FileMaker 6.0 or earlier

Options:

- **Old Password** is the password for the currently active account. It can be specified by calculation or entered directly.
- **New Password** is the desired new password for the currently active account. It can be specified by calculation or entered directly.

- **Perform Without Dialog** suppresses the Change Password dialog for this action. Instead of prompting the user for old and new passwords, the script step uses whatever values have been specified and stored with the script step.

Description:

This script step changes the password for the current account. By default, a Change Password dialog is displayed unless the Perform Without Dialog option is selected. If error capture has been enabled (in the Set Error Capture script step) and Perform Without Dialog is not selected, the user is given five attempts at changing his password. If error capture has not been enabled and Perform Without Dialog is not selected, the user is given only one attempt at changing the password.

Note the user must have the Allow User to Modify Their Own Password privilege to perform this script step. Run Script with Full Access Privileges enables a user to change the password regardless of his privileges.

A number of FileMaker script steps perform functions similar or identical to choices available in the FileMaker menus. This script step is a good candidate for making use of the Custom Menu feature FileMaker Pro Advanced to redirect the standard Change Password... menu item to perform a script.

When developing a server-scheduled script or programming for the web, be sure to select the option Perform Without Dialog. Leaving the box unchecked is not compatible in these contexts.

Examples:

The following script uses a custom Change Password dialog rather than the standard dialog used by FileMaker. This enables a developer to pass values for the new password to another database.

```
Change Password [Old Password: 'r@wfi5h!'; New Password: 'il0ve5u54i'; No Dialog]
#Change Password can be used in conjunction with "Show Custom Dialog" to
#cascade the password changes throughout several files:
Allow User Abort [Off]
Set Error Capture [On]
#
Show Custom Dialog [ Title: "Password Change"; Buttons: "OK", "Cancel";
➥Input #1: Password_Old_g, "Old Password:";
➥Input #2: Password_New_g, "New Password:" ]
#
If [Get ( LastMessageChoice ) = 1]
    Change Password [Old Password: Password_Old_g;
    ➥New Password: Password_New_g]
    # send password change to other files
    Perform Script ["Change Password"; from file "Contacts" Parameter:
     ➥zgPassword_Old. t&"¶"& Password_New_g]
```

Continues

Examples, continued:

```
    Perform Script ["Change Password"; from file "Invoices" Parameter:
    ➥zgPassword_Old. t&"¶"& Password_New_g]
End If
#Be sure to clear the globals for security reasons
Set Field [Password_Old_g; ""]
Set Field [Password_New_g; ""]
Commit Record/Request [no dialog]
```

Check Found Set

Category: Spelling

Compatibility: Macintosh, Windows, Runtime

Originated In: FileMaker 6.0 or earlier

Options:

None

Description:

This script step uses the spell check features in FileMaker Pro to check the spelling of the contents of all fields in all the records currently being browsed that contain text content. The step checks spelling in all fields of type Text, all calculation fields with a calculation result type of Text, and in any other field where text is stored: for example, a number field that happens to contain text. It is interactive, displaying a spelling dialog for every questionable spelling that the system finds.

This option is normally available via the FileMaker menus. If one or more users have limited access to menu items, you might need to write scripts that give them access to functionality normally available through menus, such as spell check functions.

Examples:

```
Perform Find [Restore]
Check Found Set
```

Check Record

Category: Spelling

Compatibility: Macintosh, Windows, Runtime

Originated In: FileMaker 6.0 or earlier

Options:

None

Description:

This script step uses FileMaker Pro's spelling checker to check the spelling of the contents of text fields in every record in every field of the current record. This step checks spelling in all fields of type Text, all calculation fields with a calculation result type of Text, and in any other field where text is stored: for example, a number field that happens to contain text. It is interactive, displaying a spelling dialog for every questionable spelling that the system finds. See also the Check Found Set script step for further discussion.

This option is normally available via the FileMaker menus. If one or more users have limited access to menu items, you might need to write scripts that give them access to functionality normally available through menus, such as spell check functions.

Examples:

```
Go to Record/Request/Page [First]
Loop
  Check Record
  Go to Record/Request/Page [Next; Exit after last]
End Loop
```

Check Selection

Category: Spelling

Compatibility: Macintosh, Windows, Runtime

Originated In: FileMaker 6.0 or earlier

Options:

- **Select Entire Contents** checks the spelling of the entire contents of the designated field. If this option is not chosen, only the text that has been selected (highlighted) is checked.
- **Go to Target Field** or **Specify** moves focus to a specified field on which to perform a spell check. Assumes the field in question is accessible on the current layout.

Description:

This script step uses the spell check features in FileMaker Pro to check the spelling of the contents of a single field. The step can check spelling in any field that contains text content. It is interactive, displaying a spelling dialog for every questionable spelling that the system finds.

This option is normally available via the FileMaker menus. If one or more users have limited access to menu items, you might need to write scripts that give them access to functionality.

Examples:

```
Check Selection [Select; Product::Description]
```

Clear

Category: Editing

Compatibility: Macintosh, Windows, Server, iOS, CWP, IWP, Runtime

Originated In: FileMaker 6.0 or earlier

Options:

- **Select Entire Contents** allows for the deletion of the entire contents of a field, regardless of what portion of its contents have been selected (highlighted) by the user. When this option is not specified, only the selected text (highlighted) is deleted.
- **Go to Target Field** or **Specify** allows for the specification of the field that is to have its contents or selected contents deleted.

Description:

This script step removes either the entire contents of a field (if the Select Entire Contents option has been designated) or the selected portion of a field (if the Select Entire Contents option has not been designated). It is important to note that Clear is distinct from the Cut operation in that it does not place the deleted content on the Clipboard.

In a web-published database, you need to use a Commit Record/Request script step to update the record that had one (or more) of its fields cleared.

Clear is one of a number of script steps that depend on the presence of specific fields on the current layout. For these steps to take effect, the targeted field must be present on the current layout, the user must have access, and the current mode must be Browse mode. Note, however, that these script steps take effect even if the field has been marked as not enterable in Browse mode. Other script steps with the same limitations include Cut, Copy, Paste, and Set Selection.

These script steps are generally thought to be fragile: They replicate the actions of a user editing record data and depend on layout and field accessibility. It is recommended that the Set Field script step be used in lieu of the Clear script step.

Examples:

```
#The following example clears the values in a repeating field with three repetitions.
Clear [Select, table::field[3]]
Clear [Select, table::field[2]]
Clear [Select, table::field]
```

Close File

Category: Files

Compatibility: Macintosh, Windows, Server, iOS, CWP, IWP, Runtime

Originated In: FileMaker 6.0 or earlier

Options:

- **Specify** enables you to select a FileMaker Pro file to close from among the list of existing predefined file references.
- **Add FileMaker Data Source** allows the selection of a file to close while at the same time adding it to the list of defined file references.
- **Add ODBC Data Source** allows the selection of an OBDC connection. This assumes drivers and DSN are already established.
- **Manage Data Sources** allows for existing file references (both FileMaker and ODBC) to be modified or deleted.

Description:

This script step closes the specified file; if no file is specified, it halts any running scripts and closes the file from which it is called. If an ODBC data source is specified, it disconnects from that source.

If you use the OnLastWindowClose script trigger, set in the File Options, to specify a script that should run when a file is closed, that script is triggered when the Close File script step is run.

Choosing to close an ODBC connection enables you to subsequently log in again with potentially different permissions.

Examples:

```
Close File ["Line_Items"]
```

Close Window

Category: Windows

Compatibility: Macintosh, Windows, Server, iOS, CWP, IWP, Runtime

Originated In: FileMaker 7.0

Options:

- **Specify** enables you either to enter a name directly or to return a name based on a calculation.
- **Current File Only** causes FileMaker to search only within windows opened by the current file.

Description:

This script step enables you to close a window by name, or, if no name is specified, close the current window.

Closing the last open window in a database closes the database and halts execution of the currently running script. This also triggers any script that has been set to run when the file closes.

Current File Only enables a developer to restrict the scope of the script step to consider only windows based on the current file. This prevents the script from inadvertently closing a window from another open file, which may coincidentally share the same name as that which was intended.

Examples:

```
Close Window [Name: "Sales records"]
```

Comment

Category: Miscellaneous

Compatibility: Macintosh, Windows, Server, iOS, CWP, IWP, Runtime

Originated In: FileMaker 6.0 or earlier

Options:

- **Specify** allows for the entry of comment text in a dialog box.

Description:

This script step allows for the addition of comments to scripts. You can see these comments when a script is viewed in the Edit Script window or when a script is printed.

Development best practices often advocate commenting to explain branches in logic, to record by whom and when a script was created, and to insert whitespace for legibility. The following example is representative of what may generally be considered best practice, but preference among developers does vary.

Examples:

```
#PURPOSE: display appropriate interface for the user's device: desktop versus iOS
#CONTEXT: Contact table
#DEPENDANCY: none
#HISTORY: 2011-Dec-12 by dheady
#
#Branch interface for mobile versus desktop
If [ Get (SystemPlatform) = 3 ]
  #iOS
  Go to Layout [ "Contact Detail iOS" (Contact)]
  #
Else
  #Mac/Win
    Go to Layout [ "Contact Detail" (Contact)]
End If
#
Exit Script [ ]
```

Commit Records/Requests

Category: Records

Compatibility: Macintosh, Windows, Server, iOS, CWP*, IWP*, Runtime*

Originated In: FileMaker 6.0 or earlier

Options:

- **Skip Data Entry Validation** overrides any data entry validation options set for fields and commits the record regardless of any errors. This option skips validation only for fields set with the Only During Data Entry validation option in the Options for Field dialog box; fields set to Always Validate still validate, even if the Skip Data Entry Validation option is selected in this script step.
- **Perform without dialog** suppresses the dialog typically presented to users having them confirm the commit step.
- **Override ESS locking conflicts** commits the record, even though optimistic locking would typically prevent it. Optimistic locking means another user has edited the record since it was last read by FileMaker.

Description:

This script step commits (saves) a record. In other words, it exits the current record or finds request and updates the field data for the record. It has the effect of causing the user to exit the record, in the sense that no field is active on the current layout after the record is committed. Exiting a record in this fashion also has the effect of saving any changes made to it. Exiting/committing a record can be accomplished in many nonscripted ways as well, including changing to another record or merely clicking on a layout outside any field so that no field is selected. See the Revert Record/Request script step for more discussion.

While a user is editing a record, any changes she makes to the record cannot be seen by other users. Only when she commits the record are her changes saved to the database and broadcast to other users. This script step has wide applicability. Any time you change data in a record via a script, it is a good idea to commit the record explicitly. This is especially true if the changes result in significant screen updates. For example, if data changes in a record would lead to different data being displayed in a portal on the current layout, it is important to make sure the data changes are explicitly committed. As a best practice, we recommend using this step in any script in which record data is altered. Include this script step to scripts that are called from the web, if those scripts change record data.

It is also critical to use this step liberally when the Set Field step is used in a script. Lack of an appropriate commit can leave a record in a locked (as though it were still being edited) state. For example, if the last step in a script is a Set Field step, you should finish the script with a Commit Records/Requests step. Otherwise, the affected record remains "open" and locked until committed. Similarly, we recommend you perform Commit Records/Requests after any Set Field steps that may precede a Perform Script step to ensure the changes take effect before the next script runs.

When programming for the web, be sure to select Perform Without Dialog. Leaving the box unchecked is not web-compatible. This is also true for scripts run as server-scheduled scripts.

Examples:

```
Show Custom Dialog ["Commit record?";
"Click 'Commit' to save your changes."]
If [Get(LastMessageChoice) = 1]
  Commit Records/Requests
Else
  Revert Record/Request [No dialog]
End
```

Constrain Found Set

Category: Found Sets

Compatibility: Macintosh, Windows, Server, iOS, CWP, IWP, Runtime

Originated In: FileMaker 6.0 or earlier

Options:

- **Specify Find Requests** creates and stores a find request with the script step. See the Perform Find script step for more information.

Description:

This script step specifies a find request that will be used to narrow the current found set. This is equivalent to applying two find requests with a logical AND operator.

Constrain Found Set returns a found set of 0 when no records match the request.

Constrain is useful when searching unindexed fields as part of a complex find. If a search includes criteria for both stored and unstored fields, a performance gain may be achieved by first performing a find on the indexed fields and then using Constrain to limit the search for the unindexed criteria to the smaller found set.

Examples:

```
#Find all employees older than 60 years of age.
Enter Find Mode [ ]
Set Field [Age; ">60"]
Perform Find []
#
#Now find which of these want early retirement
Enter Find Mode [ ]
Set Field [Early_Retire; "Yes"]
Constrain Found Set[]
```

Convert File

Category: Files

Compatibility: Macintosh, Windows, Runtime

Originated In: FileMaker 6.0 or earlier

Options:

- **Specify Data Source** allows for the designation of a data source to be converted into a .fp12 file. The possible data sources are File, XML, and ODBC.
- **Perform without Dialog** suppresses the display of the dialog that FileMaker typically presents when converting a file and instead uses the default settings.

Description:

This script step converts a file from a variety of supported formats into a FileMaker Pro 12 file. This command works on only one file at a time. Supported data formats are FileMaker Pro files, tab-separated text files, comma-separated text files, merge Files, Excel 95–2004 workbooks (.xls), Excel workbooks (.xlsx), and dBase files.

Designation of various data sources follows the same procedures as an import. See the Import Records script step for further discussion.

This step is analogous to the effects of using File, Open to open a non–FileMaker 12 file. A variety of formats can be opened/converted, each with its own set of options.

Examples:

```
Convert File ["datafile.fp7"]
```

Copy

Category: Editing

Compatibility: Macintosh, Windows, Server, iOS, CWP, IWP, Runtime*

Originated In: FileMaker 6.0 or earlier

Options:

- **Select Entire Contents** copies the entire contents of a field to the Clipboard rather than just the selected portion of the designated field's contents.
- **Go to Target Field** or **Specify** enables you to select the field from which you want to copy the contents to the Clipboard. If no field is specified and nothing is selected, FileMaker Pro copies the values from all fields of the current record.

Description:

This script step places the contents of the specified field onto the Clipboard. When no field is specified, all fields from the current record are copied, causing the step to function identically to the Copy Record step.

Copy is generally a poor way to move data within scripts. It requires that the current layout contain the field to be copied and that the user have access to that field. This is fragile because the script malfunctions if the field is removed. Additionally, the contents of the Clipboard are overwritten without the consent of the user. This is handy if the user intentionally wants the information on the Clipboard, intrusive if not.

However, Copy does have some interesting uses. When in Preview mode, Copy takes an image of the screen; this image can then be pasted into a container field.

Copy is one of a number of script steps that depend on the presence of specific fields on the current layout. Other script steps with the same limitations include Cut, Copy, Paste, and Set Selection.

When it is performed over IWP, the Copy step does not load the user's Clipboard, but the copied contents can be used in a script when combined with other script steps such as Paste.

Examples:

```
Go to Layout ["Customer Entry" (Customer)]
Copy [Select; CustomerTable::Shipping_Address]
Show Custom Dialog [Title: "Copy...";
➥Message: "Your customer's billing address is now on your clipboard.";
➥Buttons: "OK" ]
```

Copy All Records/Requests

Category: Records

Compatibility: Macintosh, Windows, Server, iOS, CWP, IWP, Runtime

Originated In: FileMaker 6.0 or earlier

Options:

None

Description:

This script step copies to the Clipboard, in a tab-delimited export format, the values of every field in the current found set. Styles and formatting are not copied. The field values are exported in the order in which they appear on the current layout. Only those fields that appear in the current layout are included, and they are listed in the order they appear on the layout. Within a record, individual fields are separated by tabs, and records are delimited by carriage returns. Repeating field values are separated by a group separator character between each repetition. Carriage returns within a field are copied to the Clipboard as the "vertical tab" character (ASCII value 11), just as they are when being exported.

Copy All Records/Requests is one of a number of script steps that depend on the presence of specific fields on the current layout. Other script steps with the same limitations include Cut, Copy, Paste, and Set Selection.

This script step was used for a variety of reasons in prior versions of FileMaker, but the use of Export Records, Go to Related Record, and other current script steps have rendered this largely obsolete. It is useful for gathering table data onto the user's Clipboard.

Examples:

```
Go to Layout ["Detail"]
Copy All Records/Requests
Show Custom Dialog [ Title: "Copy...";
➥Message: "Your Detail records are now on your clipboard.";
➥Buttons: "OK" ]
```

Copy Record/Request

Category: Records

Compatibility: Macintosh, Windows, Server, iOS, CWP, IWP, Runtime

Originated In: FileMaker 6.0 or earlier

Options:

None

Description:

This script step copies the values of all fields in the current record to the Clipboard in a tab-delimited export format. Styles and formatting are not copied. The field values are exported in the order in which they appear on the current layout. Only those fields that appear in the current layout are included. Within a record, individual fields are separated by tabs, and records are delimited by carriage returns. Repeating field values are separated by a group separator character between each repetition. Carriage returns within a field are copied to the Clipboard as the "vertical tab" character (ASCII value 11), just as they are when being exported.

Copy Record/Request is one of a number of script steps that depend on the presence of specific fields on the current layout. Other script steps with the same limitations include Cut, Copy, Paste, and Set Selection.

Examples:

```
#Copy Current Record
Go to Layout ["Detail"]
Copy Record/Request
Show Custom Dialog [ Title: "Copy...";
➥Message: "Your current record is now on your clipboard.";
➥Buttons: "OK" ]
```

Correct Word

Category: Spelling

Compatibility: Macintosh, Windows, Runtime

Originated In: FileMaker 6.0 or earlier

Options:

None

Description:

This script step opens the spelling dialog box to allow for the correction of the spelling of a word that has been identified as having been misspelled by the FileMaker Pro spell check operation. The option to Check Spelling as You Type must be selected. A word can be corrected only if FileMaker has identified it as being misspelled.

This option is normally available via the standard FileMaker menus. If one or more users have limited access to menu items, yo might need to write scripts that give them access to functionality normally available through menus, such as spell check functions.

Examples:

```
Check Selection [Select; Product::Description]
Correct Word
```

Cut

Category: Editing

Compatibility: Macintosh, Windows, Server, iOS, CWP, IWP, Runtime

Originated In: FileMaker 6.0 or earlier

Options:

- **Select Entire Contents** copies the entire contents of a field to the Clipboard, rather than just the selected portion of the designated field's contents. The field is cleared of its contents.
- **Go to Target Field** or **Specify** enables you to select the field from which you want to cut the contents to the Clipboard. If no field is specified and nothing is selected, FileMaker Pro cuts the values from all fields of the current record.

Description:

This script step places the contents of the selected field (or of all fields on the current layout if no field is selected or designated within the script itself) onto the Clipboard and then clears the contents of that field.

Cut is generally a script step that bears avoiding. It requires that the current layout contain the field to be cut and for the user in question to have access. This is fragile because the script malfunctions if the field is removed. Additionally, the contents of the Clipboard are overwritten without the consent of the user. If multiple fields are involved, it can be difficult to reinstate the information. Often the intended procedure can be accomplished in a layout-independent, less-intrusive fashion by using Set Field or other script steps.

Examples:

```
Enter Browse Mode [ ]
Cut [Select, Table1::Recent Notes]
```

Delete Account

Category: Accounts

Compatibility: Macintosh, Windows, Server, iOS, CWP, IWP, Runtime

Originated In: FileMaker 6.0 or earlier

Options:

- **Specify** allows for the selection or input of the account to be deleted.

Description:

This script step deletes the specified account in the current database. Full access is required to complete this operation, and an account with full access may not be deleted with this script step. It is possible to specify Run Script with Full Access Privileges to ensure that any user can execute this script; however, care must be taken to ensure that such usage does not create a security hole. After Run Script with Full Access Privileges has been checked, any user who can see the script can run it, including those who have external access from other FileMaker files and web access.

In cases in which a class of users lacks access to the security dialog, you can use this step to help build administrative tools for your database.

Examples:

```
Delete Account [Account Name: "Regional Sales"]
```

Delete All Records

Category: Records

Compatibility: Macintosh, Windows, Server, iOS, CWP*, IWP*, Runtime*

Originated In: FileMaker 6.0 or earlier

Options:

- **Perform Without Dialog** allows for the deletion of all records in the current found set without user intervention.

Description:

This script step deletes all records in the current found set. It can be set to operate without user approval if you select the Perform Without Dialog option. Special care should be exercised in the use of this script step because it is not possible to undo the operation after it has been completed.

Note that any records that are "in use" (currently locked) by other users are not deleted by this step. Records are considered to be in use if other users are actively editing them and have not committed/saved their changes, or if they have been left open because of script actions. You might want to check explicitly whether this has occurred, either by examining the found set or by using Get(LastError) to check for a script error. You should also decide how you want to handle cases in which the step does not execute completely for reasons such as these. Note that this script step is context dependent. The current layout determines which table is active, which determines from which table the records are deleted.

The option Perform Without Dialog must be selected for this step to be compatible with execution on the web or server.

Examples:

```
#Use a custom dialog to warn user before deleting all records
Allow User Abort [Off]
Set Error Capture [On]
Show Custom Dialog [Title: "Delete All Records"; Message:
➥"Are you really sure you want to delete all records?";
➥Buttons: "Cancel", "Delete"]
If [Get ( LastMessageChoice ) = 2]
#User wants to delete
   Show Custom Dialog [Title: "Delete All Records";
   ➥Message: "Do you have a current backup?";
   ➥Buttons: "No", "Yes"]
Else If [Get ( LastMessageChoice ) = 2]
   #After they confirmed twice, go ahead with delete
   Show All Records
   Delete All Records [No dialog]
   End If
End If
```

Delete Portal Row

Category: Records

Compatibility: Macintosh, Windows, Server, iOS, CWP*, IWP*, Runtime*

Originated In: FileMaker 6.0 or earlier

Options:

- **Perform Without Dialog** allows for the deletion of the current related record without user approval.

Description:

This script step deletes the currently selected portal row. In other words, it deletes a record that is related to the current record and is displayed in a portal on the current layout. It can be set to operate without user approval if you select the Perform Without Dialog option. Special care should be exercised in the use of this script step because it is not possible to undo the operation after record changes have been committed.

Performance of this step can be inhibited if the record represented by the specified portal row is in use by another user. See the Delete All Records script step for further discussion. Note that this script step deletes a portal row even if the Allow Deletion of Portal Records check box in the Portal Setup dialog box is unchecked.

The option Perform Without Dialog must be selected for this step to be compatible with execution on the web or as a server-scheduled script.

Examples:

```
Go to Portal Row [Last]
Delete Portal Row [No dialog]
Commit Record/Request [No dialog]
```

Delete Record/Request

Category: Records

Compatibility: Macintosh, Windows, Server, iOS, CWP*, IWP*, Runtime*

Originated In: FileMaker 6.0 or earlier

Options:

- **Perform Without Dialog** allows for the deletion of the current record or find request without user approval.

Description:

This script step deletes the current record (when in Browse mode) or current find request (when in Find mode). It can be set to operate without user approval if you select the Perform Without Dialog option. Special care should be exercised in the use of this script step because it is not possible to undo the operation.

If the current layout has a portal and a portal row is selected, the user is prompted to specify whether the master record or the related record should be deleted. If the step is performed without a dialog, the action automatically applies to the master record. If a portal row is selected and the portal is not set to Allow Deletion of Portal Records, the option to delete a related record never appears. Note that this is in contrast to the Delete Portal Row step, which deletes an active portal row regardless of whether Allow Deletion of Portal Records is enabled. Performance of this step can be inhibited if the record is in use by another user. See the Delete All Records script step for further discussion. Note that this script step is context dependent. The current layout determines which table is active, which determines from which table the record is deleted. Note too that the Revert Record menu item can undo the deletion of a child record up until a Commit Record/Request action is executed.

The option Perform Without Dialog must be selected for this step to be compatible with execution on the web or as a server-scheduled script.

Examples:

```
Go to Record/Request [Last]
Delete Record/Request [No dialog]
```

Dial Phone

Category: Miscellaneous

Compatibility: Windows, iOS, Runtime*

Originated In: FileMaker 6.0 or earlier

Options:

- **Perform Without Dialog** prevents the Dial Phone dialog from displaying when this script step executes.
- **Specify** displays the Dial Phone options as follows:
  - Phone Number allows the entry of a telephone number.
- **Specify** allows the creation of a calculation to generate the telephone number to be dialed.
- **Use Dialing Preferences** applies the pre-established telephone dialing preferences to the number to be dialed, based on the designated location information.

Description:

This script step allows FileMaker Pro to dial a telephone number within a script. The number to be dialed may be entered within the script itself, contained within a field, or generated by a specified calculation. Current telephone dialing preferences can be applied optionally based on location information. Letters within telephone numbers are translated into the appropriate numbers (*q* and *z* being, of course, omitted). Note: This script step does not work on Mac OS.

You might use this script step if you want to be able to dial the phone numbers of people or organizations whose contact information is stored in FileMaker. You might also use it to perform more low-level serial-line tasks, in conjunction with a plug-in that can communicate directly with a computer's serial port.

When this script step is called in FileMaker Go, the behavior varies with the option specified and the device. When the option Perform Without Dialog is not specified, the user is presented a FileMaker dialog displaying the phone number along with the number keypad, regardless of the device. When the user presses the OK button, FileMaker Go now attempts to send the request to the Phone app and from this point forward has the same behavior as if performed with the option Perform Without Dialog selected. When run on an iPhone, the Phone app prompts the user to confirm the dialing of the number and subsequently places the call. However, because the iPad and iPod cannot make calls, the function silently fails with error 5. It is a best practice to error trap for the device and to select the option "Perform without dialog" so iPhone users are presented only one confirmation message.

Examples:

```
Dial Phone [No Dialog, Contacts::Phone_Home]
```

Duplicate Record/Request

Category: Records

Compatibility: Macintosh, Windows, Server, iOS, CWP, IWP, Runtime

Originated In: FileMaker 6.0 or earlier

Options:

None

Description:

This script step duplicates the current record while in Browse mode and the current find request in Find mode. Values in fields with auto-entry options are not carried to the new duplicate record; new values are generated for these fields, according to the details of the specific auto-entry options. If this script step is used when a portal row is selected, and the portal relationship allows for the creation of related records, the related record is duplicated, resulting in a new related record displayed via the portal, rather than the master record.

If you want to make sure that certain fields are never duplicated, you can set them to auto-enter an empty string (""). On duplication, the auto-entry option takes effect and clears the field in the new record.

Examples:

```
Go to Record/Request/Page [Last]
Duplicate Record/Request
```

Edit User Dictionary

Category: Spelling

Compatibility: Macintosh, Windows, Runtime

Originated In: FileMaker 6.0 or earlier

Options:

None

Description:

This script step opens the User Dictionary dialog box. This is often used to display the User Dictionary dialog box when user privileges do not allow the dialog to be chosen directly from the standard FileMaker menus.

Examples:

```
Edit User Dictionary
```

Else

Category: Control

Compatibility: Macintosh, Windows, Server, iOS, CWP, IWP, Runtime

Originated In: FileMaker 6.0 or earlier

Options:

None

Description:

The Else script step is used to control logical branching within scripts. It can be placed after an If or Else If statement and immediately before an End If statement. The designated code block for the Else statement is executed only if all the previous If and Else If statements have evaluated as false. It is thus often used as a way to deal with values that do not fit within expected parameters or as a default action.

Examples:

```
If [Username_g = "Tom"]
   Show Custom Dialog ["Hello Tom"]
Else If [Username_g =  "Raul"]
   Show Custom Dialog ["Hola Raul"]
Else If [Username_g = "Guido"]
   Show Custom Dialog ["Ciao Guido"]
Else
   Show Custom Dialog ["I don't know who you are!"]
End If
```

Else If

Category: Control

Compatibility: Macintosh, Windows, Server, iOS, CWP, IWP, Runtime

Originated In: FileMaker 6.0 or earlier

Options:

- **Specify** allows for any available fields, functions, and operators to be used to enter the Boolean calculation into the Specify Calculation dialog box. Only a 0, false, or null (empty) result is construed as a Boolean false.

Description:

The Else If script step is used to control logical branching within scripts. It must follow the If script step or the Else If script step. It performs an action or actions based on the value of the Boolean calculation. The statements in the Else If block are executed only if none of the previous If or Else If statements are true.

An arbitrary number of Else If statements can be between an If statement and an End If statement. Their Boolean calculations are evaluated in the sequence in which they appear. If one should happen to evaluate to True, its code block is executed and all subsequent Else If and Else clauses that appear before the End If are ignored.

Examples:

```
If [Username_g = "Tom"]
   Show Custom Dialog ["Hello Tom"]
Else if [Username_g =  "Raul"]
   Show Custom Dialog ["Hola Raul"]
Else If [Username_g = "Guido"]
   Show Custom Dialog ["Ciao Guido"]
Else
   Show Custom Dialog ["I don't know who you are!"]
End If
```

Enable Account

Category: Accounts

Compatibility: Macintosh, Windows, Server, iOS, CWP, IWP, Runtime

Originated In: FileMaker 6.0 or earlier

Options:

- **Specify** displays the Enable Account Options dialog box, as follows:
  - **Account Name** allows either the manual entry of or designation of a calculation to generate an account name.
  - **Activate Account** enables the specified account.
  - **Deactivate Account** disables the specified account.

Description:

This script step enables or disables a specific preexisting account. For this script step to be performed, the user must be assigned the Full Access privilege set or the Run Script with Full Access Privileges option must be selected. Accounts with Full Access may not be deactivated with this script step.

This script step enables developers to create administrative account functions within databases without having to grant full access to the security privileges within a solution.

Examples:

```
Enable Account [Account Name:"UserAccount"; Activate/Deactivate]
```

End If

Category: Control

Compatibility: Macintosh, Windows, Server, iOS, CWP, IWP, Runtime

Originated In: FileMaker 6.0 or earlier

Options:

None

Description:

This script step designates the end of an If/Else If/Else structure. See Else and Else If for more information.

Examples:

```
If [Username_g = "Tom"]
   Show Custom Dialog ["Hello Tom"]
Else If [Username_g =  "Raul"]
   Show Custom Dialog ["Hola Raul"]
Else If [Username_g = "Guido"]
   Show Custom Dialog ["Ciao Guido"]
Else
   Show Custom Dialog ["I don't know who you are!"]
End If
```

End Loop

Category: Control

Compatibility: Macintosh, Windows, Server, iOS, CWP, IWP, Runtime

Originated In: FileMaker 6.0 or earlier

Options:

None

Description:

This script step marks the end of a Loop structure. The steps between Loop and End Loop are executed until the loop is explicitly exited. This step passes control up to the first step contained within the Loop structure.

Note that this step does not cause a loop to stop executing; it simply defines the point at which FileMaker should return to the top of a loop and iterate steps. Without termination logic, a loop runs forever. Use the Exit Loop If script step to establish the conditions under which the loop stops running and control passes to the script step immediately following the End Loop step.

Examples:

```
Set Variable [$counter; Value: "0"]
Loop
   New Record/Request
   Set Variable [$counter; Value: $counter + 1]
   Exit Loop If [$counter > 10]
End Loop
```

Enter Browse Mode

Category: Navigation

Compatibility: Macintosh, Windows, Server, iOS, CWP*, IWP, Runtime*

Originated In: FileMaker 6.0 or earlier

Options:

- **Pause** stops the script's execution to allow for user data entry and record navigation. The user may resume the script by clicking the Continue button in the Status Toolbar, or by executing a Resume Script step through a button or directly through the FileMaker Scripts menu.

Description:

This script step places the current window into Browse mode. This script step is generally used only when a routine has taken the user out of Browse mode and needs then to be returned to it.

Note that the Pause option is not supported when this script step is executed on Custom Web Publishing or as a server-scheduled script.

Examples:

```
Allow User Abort [Off]
Set Error Capture [On]
Go to Layout ["Monthly Report']
Enter Preview Mode [Pause]
Go to Layout [Original Layout]
Enter Browse Mode []
```

Enter Find Mode

Category: Navigation

Compatibility: Macintosh, Windows, Server, iOS, CWP*, IWP, Runtime*

Originated In: FileMaker 6.0 or earlier

Options:

- **Pause** stops the script's execution to allow for user data entry and record navigation. On resumption, the script performs the find request entered. The user may resume the script by clicking the Continue button in the Status Toolbar, or by executing a Resume Script step through a button or directly through the FileMaker Scripts menu.
- **Specify Find Requests** enables you to create and edit find requests for use with the script step.

Description:

This script step places the current layout into Find mode. In Find mode, find requests may be created, edited, deleted, and duplicated. In addition, find requests can be stored with the script step if you check the Restore check box and use the Specify dialog. String multiple find requests together to create complex find requests. A single find request may either omit records from or add them to the existing found set.

Note that the Pause option is not supported when executed on Custom Web Publishing or as a server-scheduled script.

Enter Find Mode is one of several script steps capable of saving complex options along with the script step. Other such script steps are Perform Find, Sort Records, Import Records, Export Records, and Print Setup. Use the Pause option to allow the user to enter search criteria, or modify a search that is saved with the script. If the Status Toolbar is visible, the user sees a Continue button, as well as a Cancel button if Allow User Abort is set to On in the script. Be sure to set Allow User Abort to Off if you do not want to offer an option to cancel the script at that point. If the Status Toolbar is hidden, these buttons aren't accessible, and the user needs to either show the Status Toolbar or use keyboard equivalents for Continue (Enter or Return) or Cancel (Escape or Command-⌘.).

Examples:

```
#An example of a find that is executed from requests stored with the script
Go to Layout ["Detail View"]
Enter Find Mode [Restore]
Perform Find []
#
#This example waits for the user to enter find criteria and execute the find
Go to Layout ["Detail View"]
Enter Find Mode [Pause]
Perform Find[]
```

Enter Preview Mode

Category: Navigation

Compatibility: Macintosh, Windows, Runtime

Originated In: FileMaker 6.0 or earlier

Options:

- **Pause** stops the script's execution to allow a user to review the results of a preview—often subsummary data or a layout formatted for printing. The user may resume the script by clicking the Continue button in the Status Toolbar or by pressing the Enter key.

Description:

This script step places the current layout into Preview mode, where an approximation of what a layout will look like when it is printed is displayed. Preview mode is helpful for viewing layouts that use special layout parts for reporting, such as title headers, leading grand summaries, subsummaries, trailing grand summaries, and title footers. Preview is the only FileMaker mode that displays all layout parts.

Use the Pause option if you want the user to be able to spend time in Preview mode reviewing the displayed data. If the Status Toolbar is visible, the user sees a Continue button, as well as a Cancel button, if `Allow User Abort` is set to `On` in the script. Be sure to set `Allow User Abort` to `Off` if you do not want to offer an option to cancel the script at that point. If the Status Toolbar is hidden, these buttons aren't accessible, and the user needs to either show the Status Toolbar or use keyboard equivalents for Continue (Enter or Return) or Cancel (Escape or Command-⌘.).

Examples:

```
Enter Preview Mode [Pause]
```

Execute SQL

Category: Miscellaneous

Compatibility: Macintosh, Windows

Originated In: FileMaker 6.0 or earlier

Options:

- **Perform Without Dialog** prevents the Specify SQL dialog box, the Select ODBC Data Source dialog box, and the Password dialog box from displaying when the script step executes.
- **Specify** displays the Specify SQL dialog box, where you can set the following options:
  - **Specify** displays the Select ODBC Data Source dialog box. This allows for the selection of an ODBC connection and allows for the entry of the appropriate username and password.
  - **Calculated SQL Text** allows for the creation of a calculation to generate the desired SQL query.
  - **SQL Text** allows for the direct entry of a text SQL query.

Description:

This script step executes a designated SQL query over a selected ODBC connection. This allows for manipulation of SQL data sources through standard queries. A script can contain multiple Execute SQL steps that act on different SQL data sources.

Examples:

```
Execute SQL [No Dialog; ODBC: SQL_Server; "UPDATE Customers SET Status = '" &
➥Customer::Status & "' where CustID = '" & Customer::CustomerID & "' ;"]
```

Exit Application

Category: Miscellaneous

Compatibility: Macintosh, Windows, Server, iOS, IWP, Runtime*

Originated In: FileMaker 6.0 or earlier

Options:

None

Description:

This script step closes all open files and exits the FileMaker Pro Application.

The Exit Application step triggers the closing scripts of any files that have a closing script established in the File Options dialog.

Note that when it is performed on iOS devices, Exit Application does not stop FileMaker Go but instead just closes all the open databases.

Examples:

```
Exit Application
```

Exit Loop If

Category: Control

Compatibility: Macintosh, Windows, Server, iOS, CWP, IWP, Runtime

Originated In: FileMaker 6.0 or earlier

Options:

- **Specify** allows for the definition of the Boolean calculation that determines whether a loop is exited.

Description:

This script step terminates a loop if its specified Boolean calculation evaluates to true (nonzero and non-null). Upon termination, control is passed to the next script step after the End Loop script step that applies to the current script step. If the Boolean calculation evaluates to false (0 or null), control is passed to the next script step or to the step at the beginning of the loop if no further steps are specified within the loop.

Developers often want to have at least one Exit Loop If script step inside any loop you write. Without at least one such statement, it is difficult to exit a loop, except by performing a subscript that performs a Halt Script or using a Go to Record/Request/Page [Next; Exit after last] script step.

Examples:

```
Set Field [Table1::Counter_g; "0"]
Loop
   New Record/Request
   Set Field [Table1::Counter_g; Table1::Counter_g + 1]
   Exit Loop If [Counter_g > 10]
End
```

Exit Script

Category: Control

Compatibility: Macintosh, Windows, Server, iOS, CWP, IWP, Runtime

Originated In: FileMaker 6.0 or earlier

Options:

- **Specify** enables you to specify a value to be returned from the script as the *script result*. This result is accessible elsewhere via the Get(ScriptResult) calculation function.

Description:

Exit Script forces the current script to stop executing; any remaining steps in the script are ignored. If the current script was called by another script, the remaining script steps in the calling script continue to execute.

It's important to distinguish this script step from the related script step Halt Script. Halt Script forces the termination of all currently running scripts, whereas Exit Script simply exits the current script. The use of Exit Script instead of Halt Script is generally considered significantly better practice.

Developers can optionally pass data from a script at its conclusion. A script result is accessed via the Get(ScriptResult) function in a calling script. Note that Get(ScriptResult) does not return the result of the last script called, but rather the result of the last script that returned a result. It is therefore a good practice to always return a result.

Examples:

```
Perform Find [Restore]
If [Get (CurrentFoundCount) = 0]
   Show All Records
   Go to Layout ["Detail View"]
   Exit Script [Result: Get (FoundCount)]
Else
   Print []
   Exit Script [Result: Get (FoundCount)]
End If
```

Export Field Contents

Category: Fields

Compatibility: Macintosh, Windows, iOS, Runtime

Originated In: FileMaker 6.0 or earlier

Options:

- **Specify Target Field** or **Specify** allows for the specification of the field whose contents are to be exported. When this option is not specified, the active field's contents are exported.
- **Specify Output File** allows the desired filename and file path for the exported data to be specified. When this option is not specified, the user is prompted to select the destination and filename.
    - **Automatically open file** requests the operating system to open the resulting file. The OS opens the file with the default application for the file's extension.
    - **Create email with file as attachment** opens a new email window in the user's email application, attaches the file, and leaves the user in the window.

Description:

Export Field Contents creates a named file on disk with the contents of the specified field.

Export Field Contents is a very flexible command. FileMaker Pro allows a file of any type to be stored in a container field (including FileMaker Pro files). Export Field Contents writes the file out to disk in its native format, where the file can then be opened with the appropriate application. Any type of file, including images, can be saved in a FileMaker database and then written out to disk.

When you are exporting the contents of a text field, even a global text field, a text file with UTF-16 formatting is generated. By including an extension in the filename, you can guide which application the operating system uses to open the resulting file. Extension examples are .txt, .csv, .tab, .xml, .xslt, and .html. This functionality enables a developer to create a script that iterates through a record set to dynamically build a result in a text global field and export the field contents to create a document.

With the use of script variables, you are able to set the name and path of the output file dynamically instead of hard-coding a file reference within the script. The file path dialog accepts a variable ($var or $$VAR) designation in addition to a path reference. This enables developers to programmatically control where a document is saved or exported by FileMaker.

Examples:

```
Go to Layout [Pictures::Agent_Picture]
Export Field Contents [Pictures::Picture_Full; Pictures::filename]
```

Export Records

Category: Records

Compatibility: Macintosh, Windows, Server, iOS*, Runtime*

Originated In: FileMaker 6.0 or earlier

Options:

- **Perform Without Dialog** prevents the display of dialog boxes that let the user set new export criteria when the script step executes.
- **Specify Output File** allows the desired filename and file path for the exported data to be specified as well as its file type. When XML Export is selected, the XML Export Options dialog is displayed to allow for the selection of an appropriate XML grammar and stylesheet.

  You can also export records directly to the Excel file format by choosing Excel from among the available file types.
- **Specify Export Order** displays the export order that was in effect when you added the script step. The last export order used in the file appears as the default and can be edited or deleted.

Description:

This script step exports records from the current found set to a specified file in a specified format. The current sort order of the found set is used for the export order of the records. Note that Group By works only for fields included in the current sort order. (Sorted fields appear in the Group By box; check off any fields by which you want to group.)

By using script variables, you are able to set the name and path of the output file dynamically instead of hard-coding a file reference within the script. The file path dialog accepts a variable ($var or $$VAR) designation in addition to a path reference.

Because it's possible to create FileMaker field names that are not valid names for XML elements, use caution when exporting in the FMPDSORESULT grammar: The resulting XML might be invalid.

Examples:

```
Export Records [No dialog, "Contracts"]
```

Extend Found Set

Category: Found Sets

Compatibility: Macintosh, Windows, Server, iOS, CWP, IWP, Runtime

Originated In: FileMaker 6.0 or earlier

Options:

- **Specify Find Requests** allows for the creation and storage of find requests with the script step.

Description:

This script step allows the current found set to be extended if you append additional search criteria to the previous search, or, put differently, if you apply designated search criteria only to records not included in the current found set. (This is equivalent to a logical OR search combined with the results of the previously executed search.)

Similar to the Constrain Found Set script step, this step enables you to combine the results of more than one search. Whereas Constrain Found Set enables you to limit the results of one found set by the results of a second search (an operation known as an intersection), the Extend Found Set command enables you to add the results of one search to the results of another search (an operation known as a union).

Examples:

```
#This script finds records within a table of addresses
#that are designated "local" or have a specific zip code
Enter Find Mode [ ]
Set Field [Local; "Yes"]
Perform Find [ ]
Enter Find Mode [ ]
Set Field [Zip; "94965"]
Extend Found Set[]
```

Find Matching Records

Category: Found Sets

Compatibility: Macintosh, Windows, Server, iOS, CWP, IWP, Runtime

Originated In: FileMaker 12.0

Options:

- **Specify Target Field** or **Specify** allows for the specification of the field whose contents are to be used as the find request. When this option is not specified, the active field's content is used.
- **Specify** defines the effect on the current found set of records.
  - **Replace** replaces the current found set with the resulting record set.
  - **Constrain** searches within the current found set of records, resulting in a new found.
  - **Extend** searches within the currently omitted records and then adds any matches to the current found set.

Description:

Find Matching Records performs a find based on the contents of the specified field or currently active field. This script step, depending on the options selected, is the equivalent to selecting Find Matching Records, Constrain Found Set, or Extend Found Set from the contextual menu of a field.

Examples:

```
#Example of adding all other contacts for the selected state to the current found set
Find Matching Records [Extend; Contact::State]
#Example for finding invoices for the company of the currently viewed invoice
Find Matching Records [Replace; Invoice::__kp_Company_ID]
#Example for reducing the found set of companies to only those matching
#the user's current selection
Find Matching Records [Constrain]
```

Flush Cache to Disk

Category: Miscellaneous

Compatibility: Macintosh, Windows, iOS, Runtime

Originated In: FileMaker 6.0 or earlier

Options:

None

Description:

This script step causes FileMaker Pro's internal disk cache to be written to disk. This operation is automatically performed by FileMaker Pro periodically or after structural changes such as defining fields or modifying calculation definitions occurs. This script step enables the developer to explicitly write out the contents of memory at whatever time she deems necessary. In the example given, this step might be useful to force screen redraw to occur.

Note that this script step flushes the contents of the cache for a local client copy of FileMaker Pro. It has no effect on the cache of any instance of FileMaker Server or of any other FileMaker Pro client.

Examples:

```
Replace Field Contents [Line_Items::ProductID; Line_Items::NewProductID]
Flush Cache to Disk
```

Freeze Window

Category: Windows

Compatibility: Macintosh, Windows, iOS, Runtime

Originated In: FileMaker 6.0 or earlier

Options:

None

Description:

This script step halts the updating of the active window as script steps are performed. For example, in the case of a loop that walks through records, the user ordinarily sees FileMaker navigating from one record to the next. This can slow performance or prove irritating for users, so developers often use Freeze Window to avoid forcing users to watch automated routines. The window resumes refreshing either at the end of the script where it was frozen or after a Refresh Window or Pause/Result Script step is executed within a script.

Freeze Window is useful in creating more professional-looking applications because it prevents the screen from flashing or redrawing while other script steps execute (for example, those that navigate to "utility" layouts, perform some work there, and then return to a main interface layout). It is also possible to realize some performance gains from freezing a window; scripts that would otherwise cause changes to the contents or appearance of the active window run more quickly if the active window does not need to be refreshed.

Examples:

```
Freeze Window
Replace Field Contents [Line_Items::ProductID; Line_Items::NewProductID]
Sort [Restore; No Dialog]
Refresh Window
```

Go to Field

Category: Navigation

Compatibility: Macintosh, Windows, Server, iOS, CWP, IWP, Runtime

Originated In: FileMaker 6.0 or earlier

Options:

- **Select/Perform** directs FileMaker to select all contents of the designated field. If the field is a container field and an action is associated with that field (such as playing a movie or sound file), that action is performed.
- **Go to Target Field** or **Specify** allows for the specification of the field to go to, using the standard FileMaker Pro field selection dialog.

Description:

This script step moves focus to a specified field in the current layout. If the Select/Perform option is selected, then if an action is associated with a field, that action is performed. (Actions are associated with container field types, such as sound files or movies, in which case the associated action would be to play the sound or movie file.) In cases in which no action is implied, the entire contents of the field are selected.

Go to Field enables the developer to insert the cursor into a specific field after a record has been created from a script.

When the target field includes an OnObjectEnter script trigger, the script fires regardless of the selection for option Select/Perform.

Like other script steps such as Cut, Copy, and Paste, this step depends on the specified field being present and accessible on the current layout.

Examples:

```
#New Record Routine
Go to Layout ["Contracts"]
New Record/Request
Go to Field [Contracts::Signatory]
```

Go to Layout

Category: Navigation

Compatibility: Macintosh, Windows, Server, iOS, CWP, IWP, Runtime

Originated In: FileMaker 6.0 or earlier

Options:

- **Specify** allows the target layout to be selected. The following choices are available:
  - **Original Layout** refers to the layout that was active when the script was initiated.
  - **Layout** allows for the selection of an existing layout by name.
  - **Layout Name by Calculation** enables you to enter a calculation that generates the name of the desired layout.
  - **Layout Number by Calculation** enables you to enter a calculation that generates the number of the desired layout. Layout numbers correspond to the order in which layouts are listed.

Description:

This script step makes the specified layout active in the current window. This step can navigate only to layouts in the currently active file. If multiple layouts have the same name, the first match is selected for a calculated layout name. (It is not generally considered best practice to have two layouts share the same name.)

The Go to Layout script step is vital for establishing the proper context for any subsequent script steps that operate on record data. Any script steps that directly deal with FileMaker data or records do so in the context of the table occurrence of the currently active layout.

It is also possible to draw either the name or the number of a layout from a calculation field.

Note that this script step causes an OnLayoutEnter script trigger to execute.

Examples:

```
Set Variable [$navDestination; Value:Get (ScriptParameter)]
If [$navDestination = "home"]
   Go to Layout ["resource_HOME"]
Else If [$navDestination = "list"]
   Go to Layout ["equipment_LIST"]
Else If [$navDestination = "detail"]
   Go to Layout ["equipment_DETAIL"]
Else
   Show Custom Dialog [Title: "Navigation Error..."; Message:
   ➥"The navigation script did not recognize the parameter: " &
   ➥$navDestination; Buttons: "OK"]
End If
```

Go to Next Field

Category: Navigation

Compatibility: Macintosh, Windows, Server, iOS, CWP, IWP, Runtime

Originated In: FileMaker 6.0 or earlier

Options:

None

Description:

This script step moves to the next field in the established tab order for the current layout. If no field is selected, the first field in the established tab order for the current layout is selected. If the user regains control, either by pausing in Browse mode or by exiting the script, the cursor remains in the selected field. If there is no tab order on the layout, the fields are traversed in the order in which they were originally added to the layout.

Note that this script can override the effect of field behaviors that prevent entry into a field. This enables developers to write scripts to control entry into fields and to add other programmatic routines to the process.

Examples:

```
Go to Field [Table1::First Name]
Set Variable [$counter; Value:0]
Loop
   Set Variable [$counter; Value:$counter + 1]
   Exit Loop If [$counter > Table1::ActiveField]
   Go to Next Field
End Loop
```

Go to Object

Category: Navigation

Compatibility: Macintosh, Windows, Server, iOS, CWP, IWP, Runtime

Originated In: FileMaker 8.5

Options:

- **Specify** allows the object to be specified. It includes the following options:
  - **Object Name** declares the name of the object to make active and can be specified either as a value or by calculation.
  - **Repetition** is an optional value for specifying the repetition of a field to make active. This option is ignored for other objects.

Description:

Every item on a layout—a field, a text block, a portal, a tab—is considered an object and can be assigned a unique name. This script step is used to make the specified object active.

This script step is particularly useful for displaying a tab.

Each Object Name may be anything you like, as long as it is unique to the layout. To make scripts more readable, it is advisable to adopt a naming convention that includes the object type.

Example:

```
#View the Notes tab
Go to Object [Object Name: "TAB__Notes"]
```

Go to Portal Row

Category: Navigation

Compatibility: Macintosh, Windows, Server, iOS, CWP*, IWP*, Runtime*

Originated In: FileMaker 6.0 or earlier

Options:

- **Specify** enables you to designate the portal row to make active. The options available are
  - **First** selects the first row of the currently active portal.
  - **Last** selects the last row of the currently active portal.
  - **Previous** selects the previous row of the currently active portal based on the currently targeted row. If the Exit After Last option is selected and the script is currently performing a loop, an Exit Loop action is performed when the first row in the designated portal is reached.
  - **Next** selects the next row of the currently active portal based on the currently targeted row. If the Exit After Last option is selected and the script is currently performing a loop, an Exit Loop action is performed when the last row in the designated portal is reached.
  - **By Calculation** selects the row number determined by the designated calculation.
- **Select Entire Contents** makes the entire portal row active rather than just one field.

Description:

This script step allows navigation among related records in the active portal on the current layout. If no portal is active, the first portal in the layout stacking order is assumed: FileMaker gives focus to the first row of the backmost portal. This step attempts to maintain the selected portal field when it changes rows. If no field is selected, the first enterable field is selected in the new row.

Note that when the relationship allows for the creation of new records, the Go to Portal Row Last does not make the last row with data active but rather the blank row in which a new record can be created.

Examples:

```
#Select the first row of the Contacts portal
Go to Object [Object Name: "PTL__Contacts"]
Go to Portal Row [Select, First]
```

Go to Previous Field

Category: Navigation

Compatibility: Macintosh, Windows, Server, iOS, CWP, IWP, Runtime

Originated In: FileMaker 6.0 or earlier

Options:

None

Description:

This script step moves focus to the previous field in the current layout's tab order. If no field is selected, the last field in the current layout's tab order is selected (consistent with the looping nature of tab order in FileMaker). If the user regains control, either by pausing in Browse mode or by exiting the script, the cursor remains in the selected field. If there is no tab order on the layout, the fields are traversed in the order in which they were originally added to the layout.

Note that this script can override the effect of field behaviors that prevent entry into a field.

This script step causes the execution of an OnObjectEnter script trigger.

Examples:

```
Go to Previous Field
```

Go to Record/Request/Page

Category: Navigation

Compatibility: Macintosh, Windows, Server, iOS, CWP*, IWP*, Runtime*

Originated In: FileMaker 6.0 or earlier

Options:

- **Specify** enables you to designate the record to view while in Browse mode, the Request to view while in Find mode, or the Page to view while in Preview mode. The options available are
  - **First** moves to the first record in the current found set, displays the first find request, or moves to the first page of the currently displayed report if in Preview mode.
  - **Last** moves to the last record in the current found set, displays the last find request, or moves to the last page of the currently displayed report.
  - **Previous** moves to the previous record in the current found set, displays the previous find request, or moves to the previous page of the currently displayed report. If the Exit After Last option is selected and the script is currently performing a loop, an Exit Loop action is performed when the first record is reached; otherwise, no action is taken. If the record pointer is already on the first page, FileMaker generates an error code of 101, which is not reported to the user.
  - **Next** moves to the next record in the current found set, displays the next find request, or moves to the next page of the currently displayed report. If the Exit After Last option is selected and the script is currently performing a loop, an Exit Loop action is performed when the last record is reached; otherwise, no action is taken. If the record pointer is already on the last page, FileMaker generates error number 101, which is not reported to the user.

- **By Calculation** selects the record, find request, or report page determined by the designated calculation. FileMaker expects an integer returned by the calculation and takes the user to the record in that relative position within the current found set. Note that this function always executes relative to the current found set and that a wide array of operations (both scripted and directly initiated by the user) change record positions within found sets.

Description:

This script step moves to a record in the found set if the file running the script is in Browse mode, to a find request if it is in Find mode, and to a report page if it is in Preview mode.

Using this script step in conjunction with loops is one of the most common areas in which it is used: The Exit After Last option enables developers to write routines that step through a set of records and exit a loop gracefully when an end point is reached.

Examples:

```
#Loop thru records to create a return delimited list of keys
Go to Record/Request/Page [First]
Set Variable [$keyList; Value: ""]
Loop
   Set Variable [$keyList;
   ➥Case ( not IsEmpty ( $keyList ) ;$keyList & ¶ ) & Company_ID]
   Go to Record/Request/Page [Next; Exit After Last]
End Loop
```

Go to Related Record

Category: Navigation

Compatibility: Macintosh, Windows, Server, iOS, CWP, IWP, Runtime

Originated In: FileMaker 6.0 or earlier

Options:

- **Specify** allows for the setting of the following options:
  - **Get Related Record From** allows the selection of a table that is related to the current table. If an appropriate table is not in the list or if you need to add or change a relationship, Manage Database displays the Manage Database dialog box, where you can create or edit relationships.
  - **Show Record Using Layout** displays the related target record(s), using a specified layout in the current file. Designate the layout by choosing the current layout (default), an existing layout of the related table, or by calculation resulting in the layout's name or number.
  - **Use External Table's Layouts** opens the file containing the external table you specify and displays any related record(s), using the specified layout in that file.

- **Show in New Window** first opens a new window before displaying the resulting set of records. When this option is selected, the found set in the original window is preserved.
- **Show Only Related Records** creates a found set in the related table containing only related records. For example, if you use this script step on a relationship that has four matching records in Table B for the current record in Table A, this option replaces any current found set in Table B with a new found set of just these four records. If the relationship has a sort order applied in the table occurrence to which you're navigating, this option causes the found set to be sorted by the relationship's sort criteria. If the Show Related Records Only option is not selected, the resulting found set is not sorted.
- **Match Current Record Only** finds only those records in the related table that are a match for the current record in the current table. This corresponds to the behavior of the Go to Related Records script step in previous versions of FileMaker.
- **Match All Records in the Current Found Set** finds records in the related table that are a match for any record in the current found set in the current table. This function allows developers to establish a found set and then display all related records to that found set in another table. This function is often referred to as "Extended Go to Related Record."

Description:

This script step goes to the table designated by the relationship selected in the script step, bringing its window to the foreground and selecting the first related record in the process. This step also works with portals. If a portal row is selected and the Go to Related Record step—specifying the portal's relationship—is executed, the related table is brought to the forefront and the row that was selected in the portal corresponds to the record that is selected in the related table. This step may also use relationships to external files so that when the step is executed, the selected external file is opened and brought to the forefront, with its found set consisting of related records only. Further, if a layout was selected, the records are displayed in that layout.

This script step goes to one or more records in a related table (that is, a table that is related to the currently active table by one or more relationships in the Relationships Graph). There are a number of options to this script step, and they relate in somewhat complex ways. If more than one record in the target table is related to the current record in the table where the script is being called, FileMaker selects the first related record in the target table. If the relationship has a sort order on the target table, that sort order is used to determine which is the first of several related records. For example, if you have a table of Customers and a table of Orders, and a relationship between the two that is sorted on the Order side by Order Date ascending, the "first" related record when navigating from a specific customer to related orders is a given customer's earliest order. If the relationship has no sort order specified on the target table, the first record is determined based on the creation order of the related records.

As part of this script step, you need to determine the destination layout that should be used to display the related records. If the target table is part of an externally referenced file, you may choose to display the records on a layout in the external file. If you choose to do so, that file comes to the forefront. You may also choose to display the related record set in a new window. If you choose to do so, you can specify a set of new window options, such as the window name, height, width, and screen position.

If the option Show Related Records Only is checked, FileMaker creates a found set in the target table that contains only those records related to the current record or the current found set in the table in which the script is executing. For example, suppose you have a table of Salespeople and a table of Orders related to Salespeople by a SalespersonID field. When you issue a Go to Related Record[Show only related records; From table:"Orders"; Using layout "<Current Layout>"] while on a record in Salespeople, you end up with a found set of only those Orders related to the current Salesperson by the SalespersonID.

If the option Show Only Related Records is unchecked, the behavior is more complex: When there is a found set on the target layout and the first related record is within that found set, the found set is unchanged. However, when there is a found set on the target layout and the first related record is outside that found set, all records in the target table are found (though only the first related record is selected). When all the records are included in the found set, the found set is left unchanged.

Regardless of the found set or the Show Related Records Only setting, the first related record is always selected.

When there are no related records, no navigation takes place, and FileMaker error 101 is generated. Note that this is a common source of bugs for FileMaker developers: routines that use Go to Related Record and assume in all cases that the navigation was successful, and hence continue their script steps with a new context in mind. Best practices dictate that you test for no navigation due to error 101 (no related records).

Examples:

```
#The following example goes to a related record in the table "LineItems"
#and shows a found set of related records only.
Go to Related Record [Show only related records;
➥From table: "LineItems"; Using layout: "List View"]
#
#This script demonstrates a simple error check when using
#the Go to Related Records script step.
Go to Related Record [Show only related records; From table: "child";
➥Using layout: "child" (child); New window]
If [Get (LastError) = 101]
   Show Custom Dialog [Title: "No Related Records";
   ➥Message: "There are no related Child records for this Parent record.";
   ➥Buttons: "OK"]
Else
   #Run the rest of your script here, if you intend to
   #operate further on your new context of related records.
End If
```

Halt Script

Category: Control

Compatibility: Macintosh, Windows, Server, iOS, CWP, IWP, Runtime

Originated In: FileMaker 6.0 or earlier

Options:

None

Description:

This script step causes all script activity to stop immediately. All scripts, subscripts, and external scripts are canceled, and the system is left in whatever state it was in when the Halt step was executed. Halt Script is different from Exit Script in that the latter merely aborts the current script and allows any scripts that may have called the current script to continue running, whereas Halt Script stops all script activity, whether it is run from a script, a subscript, and so on.

Experienced developers generally avoid using this script step, especially when working in teams. It is common practice to call scripts from other scripts, and it can be difficult to predict what problems will occur if a given script stops not only its own execution but also that of all other scripts. Best practice strongly recommends using the script step Exit Script and returning a result, perhaps an error number or True/False.

Examples:

```
#Example of using 'Halt Script' to return control immediately back to the user.
Show Custom Dialog ["Print Report?"]
If [Get (LastMessageChoice) = 2]
   Halt Script
End If
Print[]
```

If

Category: Control

Compatibility: Macintosh, Windows, Server, iOS, CWP, IWP, Runtime

Originated In: FileMaker 6.0 or earlier

Options:

- **Specify** allows the definition of the Boolean calculation that controls the execution of its enclosing script steps.

Description:

The If step introduces a block of conditional logic. It must be used with an End If statement and, optionally, one or more Else and Else If statements. This script step contains a calculation, which should perform a logical true/false test. If the specified Boolean calculation results in a 1 (or any number greater than 1), the specified actions are performed. If the specified Boolean calculation results in a 0 (or nothing or any non-number), the specified actions are skipped and control is passed to the next Else If or Else clause. If there are no more such clauses, control passes to the End If step and proceeds to any subsequent steps. Else If and Else clauses are optional. End If is required when If is used.

If you do not provide a Boolean test in the If step, it defaults to a result of False.

Examples:

```
#Script presents one of various versions of a report,
#based on what date was passed into the script.
Set Variable [$date; Value:Get (ScriptParameter)]
If [Ceiling ( Month ( $date ) / 3 ) = 1]
   Perform Script ["salesReport Q1version"]
Else If [Ceiling ( Month ( $date ) / 3 ) = 2]
   Perform Script ["salesReport Q2version"]
Else If [Ceiling ( Month ( $date ) / 3 ) = 3]
   Perform Script ["salesReport Q3version"]
Else If [Ceiling ( Month ( $date ) / 3 ) = 4]
   Perform Script ["salesReport Q4version"]
Else
   Show Custom Dialog [Title: "Missing Date Parameter";
   ➥Message: "This function expects a date parameter.";
   ➥Buttons: "OK"]
End If
```

Import Records

Category: Records

Compatibility: Macintosh, Windows, Server*, iOS*, Runtime*

Originated In: FileMaker 6.0 or earlier

Options:

- **Perform Without Dialog** prevents the display of FileMaker Pro's Import Records dialog box, which enables the user to select a file from which to import, to set new import criteria, to map fields from import to target fields, and to see a summary of facts about the import after it has been successfully completed.
- **Specify Data Source** allows for the selection of the source for the data to be imported. Data can be imported into FileMaker Pro from a file, a folder of files, a Bento database (Mac OS), an XML data source, or an ODBC data source.

- **Specify Import Order** allows for the setting of the order in which FileMaker imports the records. The last import order used is the default for the subsequent import. This option allows control of how FileMaker is to handle repeating field data, either by splitting it among new records or keeping it together as a repeating field in the destination table. The import can be made to add new records with the imported data, to replace the records in the found set with the imported data, or to attempt to reconcile data by matching keys (ID fields).

Description:

This script step imports records from another file or data source specified either dynamically through the Import Records dialog or within the script step configuration itself. Import order can be specified as either manually defined or based on matching field names. (It is important to note that when import source fields and target fields are mapped with matching names, field name matching is performed dynamically each time the script step is performed.)

The file path specified must be absolute. You can enter it directly in the script step or specify a variable that contains the absolute path.

FileMaker Pro has the capability to create a new table in the target database when importing data. When this option is selected, the imported data is used to create a new table. The field names in the new table depend on the data source. When importing a data source, such as an XML or Excel file with a header that contains field name information, FileMaker uses the provided field names. Otherwise, FileMaker names the fields f1, f2, f3, and so on.

Note that this capability is different from the capability, in FileMaker Pro Advanced, to import table definitions from another file. That technique imports only the table definition, not any data within the table, whereas specifying a new table as an import target always populates the new table with the imported data.

When performed as part of a server-scheduled script, this script step executes without showing a dialog, regardless of the option specified. Other limitations when run as a server-scheduled script are that it cannot support the options to import records to a new table, from a folder, or to a container field.

When this option is executed on an iOS device, the only supported option is to import from one FileMaker file to another.

Examples:

```
#Import Jobs.csv located on the user's desktop
Set Variable [$filePath; Get (DesktopPath) & "Jobs.csv"]
Import Records [Restore; No dialog; "$filePath"; Mac Roman]
```

Insert Audio/Video

Category: Fields

Compatibility: Macintosh, Windows, iOS, Runtime

Originated In: FileMaker 12.0

Options:

- **Store Only a Reference** instructs FileMaker Pro to store only a link to a file in the interactive container field, rather than the entire file. This option might reduce the size of your FileMaker Pro file, but if you move or delete the file being referenced, FileMaker Pro can't display it.
- **Specify Source File** allows for the selection of the audio or video, which is to be inserted into an interactive container field.

Description:

This script step inserts an audio or video file (or a reference to said file) into an interactive container field. When a container field is configured to be interactive, its contents are rendered using the web engine, also used to render web viewers. This script step does not include the option to specify the target field and so requires an interactive field to already be selected on the layout either manually or by a previous script step.

Audio/Video formats supported are AIFF audio file (.aif, .aiff), AVI movie (.avi), MP3 audio file (.mp3), MPEG-4 audio file (.m4a), MPEG-4 movie (.mp4), MPEG movie (.mpg, .mpeg), MPEG-4 video file (.m4v), QuickTime movie (.mov, .qt, although some formats such as QTVR are not supported), Sun audio file (.au), WAVE audio file (.wav), Windows Media Audio (.wma), and Windows Media Videos (.wmvv).

Note that on a Windows system, QuickTime must be installed to play QuickTime movies, and on Mac OS system, Flip4Mac must be installed to play Windows Media Videos.

When the option `Store Only a Reference` is selected, only a link to the original file location is stored, even when the container field is defined as `Store Container Data Externally`.

When the `Specify Source File` cannot be found, FileMaker displays an error message (unless `Set Error Capture [On]`) and then opens a standard file selection dialog.

This script step supports only interactive container fields. Note that the file path designation begins with movie rather than file. (See the following example.)

Examples:

```
Set Variable [$path; Value:"movie:" & Get (DesktopPath) & "Demo_Video"]
Go to Field [Project::Demo_Video]
Insert Audio/Video ["$path"]
```

Insert Calculated Result

Category: Fields

Compatibility: Macintosh, Windows, Server, iOS, CWP, IWP, Runtime

Originated In: FileMaker 6.0 or earlier

Options:

- **Select Entire Contents** replaces the contents of a field. If this option is not selected, Insert Calculated Result replaces only the selected portion of the current field or inserts the result at the insertion point. The default insertion point is at the end of the field's data.
- **Go to Target Field** or **Specify** allows for the selection of the field into which the result of the specified calculation is to be inserted. The specified field must be available and accessible with write privileges on the current layout for this script step to operate properly.
- **Calculated Result** allows the definition of a calculation whose result is inserted into the specified target field by this script step.

Description:

This script step pastes the result of a calculation into the current (or specified) field on the current layout.

In web-published systems, use a Commit Record/Request script step after an Insert Calculated Result script step to update the record in the browser window. This script step does not exit the field in question nor commit data. All the insert functions depend on the presence of fields on the current layout. If the correct field is not present, FileMaker generates internal error 102. Generally, these steps are not recommended: They are overly layout dependent, and Set Field allows for a higher level of control without the same dependency.

Examples:

```
Insert Calculated Result [Books::Author; Get(AccountName)]
```

Insert Current Date

Compatibility: Macintosh, Windows, Server, iOS, CWP, IWP, Runtime

Originated In: FileMaker 6.0 or earlier

Options:

- **Select Entire Contents** replaces the contents of the selected field with the current date. If this option is not selected, the current date is appended to the end of the current contents of the field.
- **Go to Target Field** or **Specify** allows for the selection of the field into which the current date will be inserted.

Description:

This script step pastes the current system date into the specified field on the current layout.

In a web-published database, use a Commit Record/Request script step after an Insert Current Date script step to update the record in the browser window.

All the insert functions depend on the presence of fields on the current layout. If the correct field is not present, FileMaker generates internal error 102. Generally, these steps are not recommended: They are overly layout dependent, and Set Field allows for a higher level of control without the same dependency.

Examples:

```
New Record/Request
Go to Layout ["Invoice"]
Insert Current Date [Select; Invoices::Invoice Date]
```

Insert Current Time

Category: Fields

Compatibility: Macintosh, Windows, Server, iOS, CWP, IWP, Runtime

Originated In: FileMaker 6.0 or earlier

Options:

- **Select Entire Contents** replaces the contents of the selected field with the current time. If this option is not selected, the current time is appended to the end of the current contents of the field.
- **Go to Target Field** or **Specify** allows for the selection of the field into which the current time is to be inserted.

Description:

This script step pastes the current system time into the specified field on the current layout.

In a web-published database, use a Commit Record/Request script step after an Insert Current Time script step to update the record in the browser window.

All the insert functions depend on the presence of fields on the current layout. If the correct field is not present, FileMaker generates internal error 102. Generally, these steps are not recommended: They are overly layout dependent, and Set Field allows for a higher level of control without the same dependency.

When the database is hosted on FileMaker Server, it might be more desirable to use the formula GetAsTime (Get(CurrentHostTimeStamp)) so that entry is consistent across all users instead of reflecting variations in their system clocks and time zones.

Examples:

```
New Record/Request
Go to Layout ["Invoice"]
Insert Current Date [Select; Invoices::Invoice Date]
Insert Current Time [Select; Invoices::Invoice Time]
```

Insert Current User Name

Category: Fields

Compatibility: Macintosh, Windows, Server, iOS, CWP, IWP, Runtime

Originated In: FileMaker 6.0 or earlier

Options:

- **Select Entire Contents** replaces the contents of the selected field with the current username (as established in each client computer's preferences dialog within FileMaker). If this option is not selected, the current username is appended to the end of the current contents of the field.
- **Go to Target Field** or **Specify** allows for the selection of the field into which the current username is to be inserted.

Description:

This script step pastes the current username into the specified field on the current layout.

In a web-published database, use a Commit Record/Request script step after an Insert Current User Name script step to update the record in the browser window. All the insert functions depend on the presence of fields on the current layout. If the correct field is not present, FileMaker generates internal error 102. Generally, these steps are not recommended: They are overly layout dependent, and Set Field allows for a higher level of control without the same dependency.

Use of this script step is also not recommended because a user can enter any number of things into his preferences. Set Field with Get(AccountName) is the better practice.

Examples:

```
New Record/Request
Go to Layout ["Invoice"]
Insert Current Date [Select; Invoices::Invoice Date]
Insert Current Time [Select; Invoices::Invoice Time]
Insert Current User Name [Select; Invoices::Entered_By]
```

Insert File

Category: Fields

Compatibility: Macintosh, Windows, iOS, Runtime

Originated In: FileMaker 6.0 or earlier

Options:

- **Dialog Options** includes options for defining a Custom dialog the user will be presented to select the file. Options include the following:
  - **Custom Dialog Title** allows for specifying the title literally or by calculation.
  - **Filters** allows for the definition of acceptable file types.
  - **Storage Options** enable you to specify the file be stored as a Reference, Insert, or Let User Choose.
  - **Display** directs how the file renders in FileMaker: as an Icon with filename or the Content of file (when possible).
  - **Compression** enables you to specify that the file should be compressed before storing in the container field.
- **Go to Target Field** or **Specify** enables you to specify the container field into which to insert the selected file.
- **Specify Source File** enables you to designate the file to be inserted. A variable containing the complete file path may be a source.

Description:

This script step inserts a file into a selected container field on the current layout. Files may be stored in their entirety within FileMaker Pro, or you may choose to store only a file reference. File references certainly take up much less space within the database, but they remove an element of control over a database's behavior. Files stored by reference can be moved or deleted, whereas this is much more difficult to achieve within FileMaker itself.

Although this script step has existed since before FileMaker 6, it has been greatly enhanced in FileMaker 12 with the addition of dialog options.

Examples:

```
Set Variable [$path; Value:Get(DesktopPath) & "myNewFile.fmp12"]
Insert File [myStuff::containerField; "$path"]
```

Insert from Index

Category: Fields

Compatibility: Macintosh, Windows, Runtime

Originated In: FileMaker 6.0 or earlier

Options:

- **Select Entire Contents** replaces the contents of the selected field. If this option is not selected, the selected index value is appended to the end of the current contents of the field if the field does not contain the cursor, or at the current cursor position if it does.
- **Go to Target Field** or **Specify** allows for the selection of the field into which the selected index value is to be inserted.

Description:

This script step displays the index (if one exists) of the designated field in a dialog box and allows one of its values to be inserted into the field. If the Select Entire Contents option is selected, the contents of the field are replaced with the selected value. If this option is not selected, the value is inserted either at the position of the cursor in the field or appended to the end of the field's contents, depending on whether the field has the cursor in it.

Note: If the specified field does not exist on the layout where the script is being performed or indexing has been disabled for the selected field, Insert from Index returns an error code that can be captured with the Get(LastError) function.

This script step does not work with fields from External ODBC Data Sources.

Examples:

```
Enter Find Mode [ ]
Insert From Index [Users::User_Name]
Perform Find [ ]
```

Insert from Last Visited

Category: Fields

Compatibility: Macintosh, Windows, Server, iOS, CWP, IWP, Runtime

Originated In: FileMaker 6.0 or earlier

Options:

- **Select Entire Contents** replaces the contents of the selected field. If this option is not selected, the value from the last visited field is appended to the end of the current contents of the field if the field does not contain the cursor, or at the current cursor position if it does.
- **Go to Target Field** or **Specify** allows for the selection of the field into which the last visited field value is to be inserted.

Description:

This script step pastes the value of the specified field from the same field in the last active record. This step is compatible with both Find and Browse mode. A record is considered as having been active if FileMaker Pro has operated on it in some way.

In a web-published database, use a Commit Record/Request script step after an Insert from Last Visited script step to update the record in the browser window. All the insert functions depend on the presence of fields on the current layout. If the correct field is not present, FileMaker generates internal error 102.

Examples:

```
#Use vendor from previous record
Go to Record/Request/Page [Next]
Go to Field [Vendor Name]
Insert From Last Visited []
```

Insert from URL

Category: Fields

Compatibility: Macintosh, Windows, Server, iOS, CWP, IWP, Runtime

Originated In: FileMaker 12.0

Options:

- **Go to Target Field** or **Specify** allows for the selection of the field into which the last visited field value is to be inserted.
- **Specify URL** allows for specifying the URL literally or by calculation.
- **Select Entire Contents** replaces the contents of the selected field. If this option is not selected, the contents from the URL are inserted at the current cursor position or appended to the end of the current contents when the field does not contain the cursor.
- **Perform Without Dialog** suppresses the display of the dialog by which the user specifies the URL. When this option is deselected, the URL dialog presented is prepopulated with the **Specify URL** value specified and the value is selected for quick overwrite.

Description:

This step inserts the contents of the URL specified into a field. The URL protocols supported are HTTP, HTTPS, FTP, FTPS, and file. The general purpose of this script step is to download a file from the web and store it in a container field. The resulting file is stored in the manner specified in the container field's definition. However, when the target is a Text field and the content of the URL is text (for example, an HTML page or text file), the contents are stored as text.

Note that when you use HTTPS and FTPS protocols, FileMaker cannot perform a certificate check to confirm the responding server is, in fact, the one you requested. When FileMaker successfully connects to the HTML or HTMLS server, but the server queried cannot find the file and so returns an HTML error page, the content of the error page is stored in the field and FileMaker does not return an error. This is not the case with FTP and FTPS because FileMaker returns an error when the file is not found. The most common errors for this script step are 1631 Connection failed and 1627 Authentication failed. If the target field is not present on the current layout, FileMaker generates internal error 102.

When you are working in Instant Web Publishing with a text field as the target, it is advisable to specify the option Select Entire Contents; otherwise, performance might suffer.

Examples:

```
#Download the latest PDF product spec and store in a container field
Insert From URL [Select; No dialog; Product::Brochure_r; Product::Brochure_URL]
#
#Download the latest product description and store in a text field
Insert From URL [Select; No dialog; Product::Description_t; Product::Description_URL]
```

Insert PDF

Category: Fields

Compatibility: Macintosh, Windows, iOS, Runtime

Originated In: FileMaker 12.0

Options:

- **Store Only a Reference** instructs FileMaker Pro to store only a link to a file in the interactive container field, rather than the entire file. This option may reduce the size of your FileMaker Pro file, but if you move or delete the file being referenced, FileMaker Pro cannot display it.
- **Specify Source File** allows for the selection of the PDF, which is to be inserted into an interactive container field.

Description:

This script step inserts a PDF file (or a reference to said file) into an interactive container field. When a container field is configured to be interactive, its contents are rendered using the web engine, also used to render web viewers. This script step does not include the option to specify the target field and so requires an interactive field to already be selected on the layout either manually or by a previous script step.

When the Store Only a Reference option is selected, only a link to the original file location is stored, even when the container field is defined to Store Container Data Externally.

When the Specify Source File cannot be found, FileMaker displays an error message (unless Set Error Capture [On]) and then opens a standard file selection dialog.

This script step supports only interactive container fields. Note that the file path designation begins with Image rather than File. (See the following example.)

Examples:

```
Set Variable [$path; Value:"image:" & Get(DesktopPath) & Product::Brochure_File_Name]
Go to Field [Select/perform; Product::Brochure_r]
Insert PDF ["$path"]
```

Insert Picture

Category: Fields

Compatibility: Macintosh, Windows, iOS, Runtime

Originated In: FileMaker 6.0 or earlier

Options:

- **Store Only a Reference** allows graphics to be stored by file system reference, thereby alleviating the need to store the actual image in the database. However, if the file is moved from the designated file path, FileMaker Pro can no longer display the actual image and instead displays a file icon.
- **Specify Source File** allows the designation of the file path to the desired image file.

Description:

This script step imports an image file into the current container field. The desired field must be selected before this script is run. If the desired image file has not been specified, the user is shown the Insert Picture dialog box.

All the insert functions depend on the presence of fields on the current layout. If the correct field is not present, FileMaker generates internal error 102.

Examples:

```
Set Variable [$path; Value:"image:" & Get(DesktopPath) & "/myKidPhoto.jpg"]
Go to Field [Select/perform; myStuff::containerField]
Insert File [myStuff::containerField; "$path"]
```

Insert QuickTime

Category: Fields

Compatibility: Macintosh, Windows, iOS, Runtime

Originated In: FileMaker 6.0 or earlier

Options:

- **Specify Source File** allows the designation of the file path to the desired QuickTime file.

Description:

This step imports a QuickTime movie or sound file into the current container field. A container field must be selected before this step can function. If an appropriate QuickTime file has not been designated, a dialog box is shown to the user, through which she may select and preview the file to be imported. This step requires that QuickTime be installed on the system being used to import the desired file.

All the insert functions depend on the presence of fields on the current layout. If the correct field is not present, FileMaker generates internal error 102.

Examples:

```
Set Variable [$path; Value:"movie:" & Get (DesktopPath) & "/myMovie.m4v"]
Insert QuickTime [myStuff::containerField; "$path"]
```

Insert Text

Compatibility: Macintosh, Windows, Server, iOS, CWP, IWP, Runtime

Originated In: FileMaker 6.0 or earlier

Options:

- **Select Entire Contents** replaces the contents of a field. If this option is not selected, Insert Text inserts the specified value at the end of the field's data.
- **Go to Target Field** or **Specify** enables you to specify the field to receive the pasted information. If no field is selected, the Insert Text command places the specified text after the insertion point. If no field is active at the time the command executes, it has no effect. If the selected field is not present on the current layout, the Insert Text command has no effect.
- **Specify** displays the Specify dialog box where you can enter the text to be pasted.

Description:

This script step inserts text into the selected text field in the current record. If the Select Entire Contents option has not been selected, the designated text is inserted at the cursor position or at the end of the field's contents, depending on whether a cursor appears in the field. The text to be inserted needs to be specified explicitly. If you want to insert variable text data, use the Insert Calculated Result script step or the Set Field script step.

In a web-published database, use a Commit Record/Request script step after an Insert Text script step to update the record in the browser window. All the insert functions depend on the presence of fields on the current layout. If the correct field is not present, FileMaker generates internal error 102.

Examples:

```
Insert Text [Select; Profile::Favorite_Color; "Red"]
```

Install Menu Set

Category: Miscellaneous

Compatibility: Macintosh, Windows, iOS, Runtime

Originated In: FileMaker 8.0

Options:

- **Use as File Default** causes the specified menu set to be used as the default menu set for the current file, for the duration of the current user session. The default menu set is displayed in all circumstances where it is not overridden by a more specific menu set. Examples of "more specific" settings include menu sets that are specified at the individual layout level, and menu sets installed by later invocations of the Install Menu Set script step.

Description:

This script step installs a new menu set based on the specified menu set name. This may be a custom menu set (defined by a developer using FileMaker Pro Advanced), or it may be the default FileMaker menu set.

This script step affects only the current user. Others who might be using the file simultaneously do not see a change of menu sets, unless they too invoke a script containing this step. Likewise, when the current user closes the file, the effects of this step are terminated.

Examples:

```
# Install a user-specific menu set
If [$userRole = "Sales"]
  Install Menu Set["SalesMenus"]
Else
  Install Menu Set["RegularMenus"]
End If
```

Install OnTimer Script

Category: Control

Compatibility: Macintosh, Windows, iOS, Runtime

Originated In: FileMaker 10.0

Options:

- **Specify Script** or **Specify** allows you to specify a script to perform, from the current file or a data source.
- **Optional Script Parameter** allows for the specification of script parameter, either as literal text or as the result of a calculation.
- **Interval Seconds** allows for the specification, via the Specify Calculation dialog, the number of seconds to wait before performing the script.

Description:

This script step schedules a script to execute for the selected window every *X* number of seconds, based on the interval specified, until it is replaced with another OnTimer Script. Each window can have only one OnTimer Script at a time; executing this script step again negates the previous installation.

Set the Interval Seconds to blank or leave the script undefined to cancel an OnTimer Script for the selected window.

Examples:

```
#Install a script trigger on the Company window
Select Window [Name: "Company"; Current file]
If [Get(LastError) = 0]
   Install OnTimer Script ["Check Status"; Parameter: $param; Interval: 60]
End If
```

Install Plug-In File

Category: Miscellaneous

Compatibility: Macintosh, Windows, Server, CWP, IWP, Runtime

Originated In: FileMaker 12.0

Options:

- **Specify Target Field** or **Specify** allows for the specification of the container field that stores the plug-in. When this option is not specified, FileMaker installs the plug-in in the current container field in the active table.

Description:

This script step installs a plug-in stored in a container field. Only FileMaker plug-ins are supported; the extensions supported are .fmx for Windows and .fmplugin for Mac OS. The script step does not support compressed files, so .tar or .zip formats fail.

The plug-ins are installed at the following:

Windows XP	C:\Documents and Settings*user_name*\Local Settings\Application Data\FileMaker\Extensions\
Windows Vista or Windows 7	C:\users*user_name*\AppData\Local\FileMaker\Extensions\
Mac OS X	Macintosh HD/Users/*user_name*/Library/Application Support/FileMaker/Extensions

The FileMaker preference Allow Solutions to Install Files must be enabled; otherwise, this script step returns error 3. When an update is installed for a plug-in that is disabled, the update is also set to be disabled and the function returns no error because the install itself succeeded.

Use the function Get(InstalledFMPlugins) to get a list of plug-ins installed. The result for each plug-in includes its name, version, and enabled state, each separated by semicolons; each plug-in is separated by a carriage return.

This function allows for the distribution of a solution as a single FileMaker file, even when it uses plug-ins.

Examples:

```
#Install File plug-in if necessary
Set Variable [$pluginName; Value:"File"]
Set Variable [$pluginList; Value:Get(InstalledFMPlugins)]
Set Variable [$plugin; Value:
➥ Let ([
➥ start = Position ( $pluginList ; $pluginName & ";" ; 1 ; 1 ) ;
➥ end = Position ( $pluginList ; ¶ ; start ; 1 )];
➥ Middle ( $pluginList ; start ; end - start ))]
Set Variable [$values; Value:Substitute ( $plugin ; ";" ; ¶ )]
Set Variable [$version; Value:0 + GetValue ( $values ; 2 )]
Set Variable [$status; Value:GetValue ( $values ; 3 )]
If [Resource::PlugIn_Version > $version]
   Install Plug-In File [Resource::PlugIn_Mac_r]
   Set Variable [$error; Value:Get(LastError)]
   If [$error]
      Show Custom Dialog [Title: "Plug-in Install Error";
      ➥ Message: "Please enable the 'Allow Solutions to Install Files',
      ➥ located on the FileMaker Preferences Plug-in tab,
      ➥ so the required plug-in may be installed.";
      ➥ Default Button: "OK", Commit: "Yes"]
      Open Preferences
   Else If [$status = "Disabled"]
      Show Custom Dialog [Title: "Plug-in Install Error";
      ➥ Message: "Please enable the Widget plug-in.";
      ➥ Default Button: "OK", Commit: "Yes"]
      Open Preferences
   End If
End If
```

Loop

Category: Control

Compatibility: Macintosh, Windows, Server, iOS, CWP, IWP, Runtime

Originated In: FileMaker 6.0 or earlier

Options:

None

Description:

This script step marks the beginning of a Loop structure. The end of the Loop structure is defined by a matching End Loop step. Script control passes from the Loop step through all intervening steps to the End Loop step and back again until an Exit Loop directive is encountered or until a Halt Script or Exit Script step is encountered. The Exit Loop directive is available as an option with the Exit Loop If step, the Go to Record/Request/Page step, and the Go to Portal Row step. Loops are often used to perform an action over a group of records or a set of portal rows.

Examples:

```
# Create 10 new blank records
Set Variable [$counter; Value: "0"]
Loop
  New Record/Request
  Set Variable [$counter; Value: $counter + 1]
  Exit Loop If [$counter > 10]
End
```

Modify Last Find

Category: Found Sets

Compatibility: Macintosh, Windows, Server, iOS, CWP, IWP, Runtime

Originated In: FileMaker 6.0 or earlier

Options:

None

Description:

This script step activates Find mode and then recalls the last find request(s) used. The find request(s) may then be modified and executed with the Perform Find script step.

Examples:

```
Modify Last Find
Set Field [Contacts::Birthdate; "1/1/1974...1/1/1985"]
Perform Find[]
```

Move/Resize Window

Category: Windows

Compatibility: Macintosh, Windows, Runtime

Originated In: FileMaker 6.0 or earlier

Options:

- **Specify** allows the setting of the move/resize options.
  - **Current Window** causes the changes to be performed on the current window.
  - **Window Name** causes the changes to be performed on an open window, specified by name. Literal text may be entered or Specify can be clicked to create a window name from a calculation.

- **Current File Only** causes FileMaker to search only within windows based on table occurrences within the current file.
- **Height** is the height of the adjusted window in pixels. A number may be entered or Specify can be clicked to generate a number from a calculation.
- **Width** is the width of the adjusted window in pixels. A number may be entered or Specify can be clicked to generate a number from a calculation.
- **Distance from Top** is the adjusted window's distance in pixels from the top of the screen (Mac OS) or from the top of the FileMaker Pro window (Windows). A number may be entered or Specify can be clicked to generate a number from a calculation.
- **Distance from Left** is the adjusted window's distance in pixels from the left of the screen (Mac OS) or from the left of the FileMaker Pro window (Windows). A number may be entered or Specify can be clicked to generate a number from a calculation.

Description:

This script step adjusts the size and location of the selected window. Every other aspect of the window, including found set, current table, and current record, remains unchanged. Where an option is left without a value, the current value of that option is used. In multiple-monitor environments, the use of negative position values makes it possible to position a window on monitors other than the main monitor or to position the window offscreen.

Note for Windows: FileMaker Pro orients the moved window to the top-left corner of the visible part of the application window. Note that this may not be the (0, 0) point of the window, depending on how the current file window is positioned (for example, if half of the file window extends past the left border of the application window, you would need to scroll to the left to see the [0, 0] point of the application window).

Current File Only allows the developer to restrict the scope of the script step to consider only windows based on the current file.

Examples:

```
Move/Resize Window [Name:Invoices ; Height: 400; Width: 600; Top: 16; Left: 16]
```

New File

Category: Files

Compatibility: Macintosh, Windows

Originated In: FileMaker 6.0 or earlier

Options:

None

Description:

This script step enables the user to create a new database file in FileMaker Pro's usual Create New File dialog box. If the Use Manage Database Dialog to Create Files preference is selected, the user is also taken to the Manage Database dialog. When the Manage Database dialog is closed, the file is open in Form View of the first table created. When this preference is not selected, the new file is displayed in Table View.

When the calling script contains additional steps, the script resumes with the new file open but not active. However, when New File is the last step in the script, the new file is active when the script ends.

Examples:

```
New File
```

New Record/Request

Category: Records

Compatibility: Macintosh, Windows, Server, iOS, CWP, IWP, Runtime

Originated In: FileMaker 6.0 or earlier

Options:

None

Description:

This script step creates a new, blank record if the system is in Browse mode, and a new find request if the system is in Find mode.

Note that this script step is context dependent. The current layout determines which table is active, which determines the table in which the record is created.

Examples:

```
# Create 10 new blank records
Set Variable [$counter; Value: "0"]
Loop
  New Record/Request
  Set Variable [$counter; Value: $counter + 1]
  Exit Loop If [$counter > 10]
End
```

New Window

Category: Windows

Compatibility: Macintosh, Windows, Server, iOS, CWP*, IWP*, Runtime*

Originated In: FileMaker 7.0

Options:

- **Specify** enables you to set the following options for the new window:
    - **Window Name** is the name specified for the new window. Literal text may be entered or Specify can be clicked to create a window name from a calculation.
    - **Height** is the height of the new window in pixels. A number may be entered or Specify can be clicked to generate a number from a calculation.
    - **Width** is the width of the new window in pixels. A number may be entered or Specify can be clicked to generate a number from a calculation.
    - **Distance from Top** is the new window's distance in pixels from the top of the screen (Mac OS) or from the top of the FileMaker Pro window (Windows). A number may be entered or Specify can be clicked to generate a number from a calculation.
    - **Distance from Left** is the new window's distance in pixels from the left of the screen (Mac OS) or from the left of the FileMaker Pro window (Windows). A number may be entered or Specify can be clicked to generate a number from a calculation.
    - **Specify Advance Style** allows for defining the type of window: Document Window, Floating Document Window, and Dialog Window (Modal) along with the Window Controls that are enabled: Close, Minimize, Maximize, Zoom Control Area, and Resize.

Description:

This script step creates a new window based on the current window. The new window inherits the same context (found set, sort order, layout, and current record) and attributes as the current window except in the specified options.

If an option is left without a value, the default value (as demonstrated by the Window menu, New Window command) for that option is used. If the height or width specified falls below the allowable minimum for the user's operating system, the allowed minimums are used instead of the chosen values.

The use of negative position values makes it possible to position a window on alternate monitors or to position the window offscreen.

The New Window script step has been greatly enhanced in FileMaker Pro 12 with the addition of advanced style options. Three window types are supported and, after a window is created, it cannot be converted to another type. Document Window is the default style and produces a standard window. A Floating Document Window remains on top of other FileMaker windows even when inactive. A Dialog Window is modal; the user cannot select another window, and because of this, the options Minimize and Zoom Control Area are always deactivated. For the other window types, you can enable or disable any of the window controls. When window controls are disabled, the corresponding menu item is also disabled, but the function can be performed via script or button. Window-style settings are not supported in FileMaker Go, CWP, and IWP.

There are several limitations to script steps performed while a Dialog Window is open. Arrange All Windows, Convert File, New File, Open File, Open Remote, and Quit Application are not permitted. Adjust Window, Move/Resize Window, and Select Window steps can perform their operation only on the open window. Perform Script fails when executed from another open file. Finally, the step Go to Related Record and New Window can only open a new dialog window. The user is able to interact with nondocument windows already open before the Dialog Window is created.

Note for Windows: FileMaker Pro orients the moved window to the top-left corner of the visible part of the application window. Note that this might not be the (0, 0) point of the window, depending on how the current file window is positioned. (For example, if half of the file window extends past the left border of the application window, you would need to scroll to the left to see the [0, 0] point of the application window.)

Examples:

```
New Window [Name: "Profile"; Height: 500; Width: 700; Top: 25; Left: 25]
```

Omit Multiple Records

Category: Found Sets

Compatibility: Macintosh, Windows, Server, iOS, CWP*, IWP*, Runtime*

Originated In: FileMaker 6.0 or earlier

Options:

- **Perform Without Dialog** prevents a dialog box from displaying when the script step executes. Without this option selected, the user sees a dialog that allows him to enter the number of records to be omitted. When Perform Without Dialog is selected, if the number of records to omit is not specified, only the current record is omitted.
- **Specify Records** allows the entry of the exact number of records to omit. The Specify button may also be clicked in the Options dialog box to allow for the entry of a calculation. The calculation result must be a number.

Description:

This script step omits the specified number of records from the found set, leaving the next available record as the current record. Omitted records are not deleted; they are just excluded from the found set. They remain in the database and can be easily verified if you re-execute the find request that generated the found set in the first place.

When programming a server-scheduled script or for the web, be sure to select Perform Without Dialog. Leaving the box unchecked is not compatible in these environments.

Examples:

```
Perform Find [Restore]
# Omit the first 10 records found
Omit Multiple Records [No dialog; 10]
```

Omit Record

Category: Found Sets

Compatibility: Macintosh, Windows, Server, iOS, CWP, IWP, Runtime

Originated In: FileMaker 6.0 or earlier

Options:

None

Description:

This script step omits the current record from the current found set when executed in Browse mode. The next available record becomes the new current record, or the prior record in the case of omitting the last record in a found set. Omitted records are not deleted. They are merely removed from the current found set.

If this script step is executed while in Find mode, the current find request's Omit check box is toggled. (If it was checked, it will be unchecked, and if it is unchecked, it will be checked.) A find request that has the Omit check box checked becomes an omit request that subtracts from rather than adds to the found set.

Examples:

```
#Omit records marked for omission without modifying the found set
Go to Record/Request/Page [First]
Loop
   If [Contacts::Omit]
      Omit Record
   End If
   Go to Record/Request/Page [Next; Exit After Last]
End Loop
```

Open Edit Saved Finds

Category: Open Menu Item

Compatibility: Macintosh, Windows, Runtime

Originated In: FileMaker 10.0

Options:

None

Description:

This script step opens the Edit Saved Finds dialog box, in which the user can add, duplicate, delete, or change saved finds. It is the equivalent of performing the menu item Edit Saved Finds from the Records, Saved Finds menu.

Examples:

```
Open Edit Saved Finds
```

Open File

Category: Files

*Compatibility: Macintosh, Windows, iOS, Runtime**

Originated In: FileMaker 6.0 or earlier

Options:

- **Open Hidden** causes FileMaker Pro to open the specified database hidden (that is, with its window minimized).
- **Specify** allows the selection of a FileMaker Pro database to be opened. Within the Specify menu, Add File Reference opens a dialog box to assist in the location and selection of a filename. After a file is selected, it is added to the Specify list. In the same menu, Manage File References enables you to modify or delete a file reference already added to the list.

Description:

This script step opens the specified file or allows the user to select a file to open in the Open File dialog box. The Open File dialog box is invoked when no file is specified in the script step or if the specified file cannot be found. The file that is active when the Open File step is executed remains active after it has completed.

Examples:

```
Open File [Open Hidden; "Tempfile.fmp12"]
```

Open File Options

Category: Open Menu Item

Compatibility: Macintosh, Windows, Server, iOS, CWP, IWP, Runtime

Originated In: FileMaker 6.0 or earlier

Options:

None

Description:

This script step opens the File Options dialog box to the Open tab. This script step is not executed when the user's account does not have the Full Access privilege set. Note the script may be set to Run Script with Full Access Privileges.

Examples:

```
Show Custom Dialog ["Open File Options dialog box?"]
If [Get (LastMessageChoice) = 1]
  #1=Yes, 2=No
  Open File Options
End If
```

Open Find/Replace

Category: Open Menu Item

Compatibility: Macintosh, Windows, Server, iOS, CWP, IWP, Runtime

Originated In: FileMaker 7.0

Options:

None

Description:

This script step opens the Find/Replace dialog box. The remaining steps in the script, if any, are executed after the user closes the dialog box or completes a search.

Examples:

```
Show Custom Dialog ["Open the Find/Replace dialog box?"]
If [Get(LastMessageChoice) = 1]
  #1=Yes, 2=No
  Open Find/Replace
End If
```

Open Help

Category: Open Menu Item

Compatibility: Macintosh, Windows, iOS

Originated In: FileMaker 6.0 or earlier

Options:

None

Description:

This script step opens the FileMaker Pro Help system. By default, the user is placed in the Help System Contents screen.

The Help dialog is not modal, so any additional script steps after the Open Help step execute immediately, possibly pushing the help window into the background.

Examples:

```
Show Custom Dialog ["Do you need Help?"]
If [Get (LastMessageChoice) = 1]
  #1=Yes, 2=No
  Open Help
End If
```

Open Manage Containers

Category: Open Menu Item

Compatibility: Macintosh, Windows

Originated In: FileMaker 12.0

Options:

None

Description:

This script step opens the Manage Containers dialog box, where the user can specify where container field data is stored and how thumbnails are generated and stored. It is the equivalent of opening the menu item File, Manage, Containers. This script step is not executed when the user's account does not have the Full Access privilege set. Note the script may be set to Run Script with Full Access Privileges. The remaining steps in the script, if any, are executed after the user closes the dialog box or completes a search.

Examples:

```
Show Custom Dialog ["Change thumbnail settings?"]
If [Get (LastMessageChoice) = 1]
  #1=Yes, 2=No
  Open Manage Containers
End If
```

Open Manage Database

Category: Open Menu Item

Compatibility: Macintosh, Windows

Originated In: FileMaker 6.0 or earlier

Options:

None

Description:

This script step opens the Manage Database dialog box, where the user can create or edit tables, fields, and relationships. It is the equivalent of opening the menu item File, Manage, Database. This script step is not executed when the user's account does not have the Full Access privilege set. Note the script may be set to Run Script with Full Access Privileges. The remaining steps in the script, if any, are executed after the user closes the dialog.

Examples:

```
Show Custom Dialog ["Change the database schema?"]
If [Get (LastMessageChoice) = 1]
  #1=Yes, 2=No
  Open Manage Database
End If
```

Open Manage Data Sources

Category: Open Menu Item

Compatibility: Macintosh, Windows

Originated In: FileMaker 6.0 or earlier

Options:

None

Description:

This script step opens the Manage Data Sources dialog box, where the user can create or edit references to files and data sources used throughout the database. It is the equivalent of opening the menu item File, Manage, External Data Sources. This script step is not executed when the user's account does not have the Full Access privilege set. Note the script may be set to Run Script with Full Access Privileges. The remaining steps in the script, if any, are executed after the user closes the dialog.

Examples:

```
Show Custom Dialog ["Modify the data sources?"]
If [Get (LastMessageChoice) = 1]
   #1=Yes, 2=No
   Open Manage Data Sources
End If
```

Open Manage Layouts

Category: Open Menu Item

Compatibility: Macintosh, Windows

Originated In: FileMaker 11.0

Options:

None

Description:

This script step opens the Manage Layouts dialog box, where the user can create, duplicate, delete, and edit a layout's setup as well as control the presentation of the layout menu. This script step is not executed when the user's account does not have the Full Access privilege set. Note the script may be set to Run Script with Full Access Privileges. The dialog is not modal, so any remaining script steps are executed immediately.

Examples:

```
Show Custom Dialog ["Would you care to create a layout?"]
If [Get (LastMessageChoice) = 1]
   #1=Yes, 2=No
   Open Manage Layouts
End If
```

Open Manage Scripts

Category: Open Menu Item

Compatibility: Macintosh, Windows

Originated In: FileMaker 6.0 or earlier

Options:

None

Description:

This script step opens the Manage Scripts dialog, which enables a user to create, edit, rename, and duplicate scripts. When this script step is performed, FileMaker halts the current script because if any currently executing scripts were to be edited, the resulting behavior could be unpredictable.

Examples:

```
Show Custom Dialog ["Open Manage Scripts?"]
If [Get (LastMessageChoice) = 1]
   #1=Yes, 2=No
   Open Manage Scripts
End If
```

Open Manage Value Lists

Category: Open Menu Item

Compatibility: Macintosh, Windows

Originated In: FileMaker 6.0 or earlier

Options:

None

Description:

This script step opens the Manage Value Lists dialog box, where the user can define new or edit existing value lists. This script step is not performed if the user's account does not have the Full Access privilege set. (The script may be set to Run Script with Full Access Privileges.) When the user closes the dialog box, the remaining steps in the script, if any, are executed.

Examples:

```
Show Custom Dialog ["Do you want to create or edit a value list?"]
If [Get (LastMessageChoice) = 1]
   #1=Yes, 2=No
   Open Manage Value Lists
End If
```

Open Preferences

Category: Open Menu Item

Compatibility: Macintosh, Windows, iOS, Runtime

Originated In: FileMaker 6.0 or earlier

Options:

None

Description:

This script step opens the Preferences dialog box. The General Preferences area is selected by default. When the user closes the dialog, the remaining steps in the script, if any, are executed.

Examples:

```
Show Custom Dialog ["Open Preferences dialog box?"]
If [Get (LastMessageChoice) = 1]
   #1=Yes, 2=No
   Open Preferences
End If
```

Open Record/Request

Category: Records

Compatibility: Macintosh, Windows, Server, iOS, CWP, IWP, Runtime

Originated In: FileMaker 6.0 or earlier

Options:

None

Description:

This script step attempts to acquire exclusive access to the current record. Exclusive access prevents other users from editing the record. It has the same effect as a user selecting a data field on a layout (by clicking or tabbing) and then beginning to enter or edit field data. These actions either give exclusive access to that user or display a message warning that another user has control of the record. It can be useful to try to gain exclusive access to a record in the course of a script.

If you are looping over records and need to change each one, if a user is editing one of the records, your script may be prevented from changing it. `Open Record/Request` cannot override another user's access, but if the script step fails, it generates an error that your script can inspect with the `Get (LastError)` function.

Examples:

```
Perform Find [Restore]
Go to Record/Request/Page [First]
Open Record/Request
Set Variable [$error; Value:Get (LastError)]
If [$error = 200]
   Show Custom Dialog ["Sorry, you do not have sufficient
   ➥privileges to access it."]
   Exit Script [Result: $error]
Else If [$error = 300]
   Show Custom Dialog ["Sorry, this record is locked by another user."]
   Exit Script [Result: $error]
End If
#Continue with the scripts processing...
```

Open Remote

Category: Open Menu Item

Compatibility: Macintosh, Windows, iOS

Originated In: FileMaker 6.0 or earlier

Options:

None

Description:

This script step opens the Open Remote dialog box to allow the opening of a shared FileMaker Pro database over a network connection.

When the user closes the dialog box, the remaining steps in the script, if any, are executed.

Examples:

```
Show Custom Dialog ["Open a networked database?"]
If [Get (LastMessageChoice) = 1]
  #1=Yes, 2=No
  Open Remote
End If
```

Open Sharing

Category: Open Menu Item

Compatibility: Macintosh, Windows

Originated In: FileMaker 6.0 or earlier

Options:

None

Description:

This script step opens the FileMaker Network settings dialog where users can configure network database sharing.

Examples:

```
Show Custom Dialog ["Do you want to open the sharing dialog?"]
If [Get (LastMessageChoice) = 1]
  #1=Yes, 2=No
  Open Sharing
End If
```

Open URL

Category: Miscellaneous

Compatibility: Macintosh, Windows,, iOS, IWP, Runtime*

Originated In: FileMaker 6.0 or earlier

Options:

- **Perform Without Dialog** prevents the Open URL Options dialog box from displaying when the script step executes.
- **Specify** allows the entry of the URL, either typed directly into the text entry area or created by a calculation. When the option Perform Without Dialog is not selected, this is the default value presented in the dialog with the value selected.

Description:

This script step allows a URL to be opened in the appropriate application.

The supported schemes include HTTP, HTTPS, LDAP, LDAPS, FTP, file, mailto, HTTPS, and fmp for opening FileMaker files. FileMaker Pro consults the operating system preferences to help decide which application to use to service a particular URL scheme.

FileMaker URL Schema

The fmp syntax combines the previous FileMaker URL schemas of fmp7 and FMP7Script (supported by FileMaker Go). The URL syntax for all of FileMaker is

```
fmp://{account::password@}<host>/<file>{?script=<scriptName>
➥[&param=<parameter>][&<$varName>=<value>]}
```

Open URL, when executed on an iOS device, can be used to pass data to other iOS applications. Consult the additional resources in the Appendix for more information about iOS Application URL schemas.

When programming for IWP, be sure to select Perform Without Dialog. Leaving the box unchecked is not web compatible.

Examples:

```
#Open website
Open URL [No dialog; "http://www.apple.com/"]

#Open a file located on the C drive [Windows]
Open URL [No dialog; "file://c:/addresses.txt"]

#Create an email in the user's email application
Open URL [No dialog; "mailto:no–one@name.net"]

#Open the FileMaker file MyDB hosted on the server 192.168.10.46
#with account "JDoe" and password "myPwd" and run the Report script
Open URL [No dialog; "fmp://JDoe:myPwd@192.168.10.46/MyDB.fmp12?script=Report"]

#Create a text message [iOS]
Open URL [No dialog; "sms://" & Filter (Contact::Phone ; 1234567890)]
```

Paste

Category: Editing

Compatibility: Macintosh, Windows, Server, iOS, CWP, IWP, Runtime

Originated In: FileMaker 6.0 or earlier

Options:

- **Select Entire Contents** replaces the contents of a field with the contents of the Clipboard. If Select Entire Contents is not used, Paste copies the contents of the Clipboard to the currently selected portion of the field.
- **Paste Without Style** tells FileMaker Pro to ignore all text styles and formatting associated with the Clipboard contents.
- **Go to Target Field** or **Specify** allows for the specification of the field into which to paste.

Description:

This script step pastes the contents of the Clipboard into the specified field in the current record. If the data type of the data being pasted does not match the type of the field being pasted into, FileMaker Pro displays the customary validation alert when the record is committed. (Should the script that calls the Paste step leave the record in an uncommitted state, the error dialog appears later, when the record is committed.) If the field is not on the current layout, FileMaker Pro returns an error code, which can be captured with the Get(LastError) function. In a web-published database, use a Commit Record/Request script step after a Paste script step to update the record in the browser window.

Paste is one of a number of script steps that depend on the presence of specific fields on the current layout. Other script steps with the same limitations include Cut, Copy, Paste, and Set Selection.

Examples:

```
#Assumes customer address is on clipboard
Paste [Select; No style; Customer::Address]
```

Pause/Resume Script

Category: Control

Compatibility: Macintosh, Windows, Server, iOS, CWP, IWP, Runtime

Originated In: FileMaker 6.0 or earlier

Options:

- **Specify** displays the Pause/Resume Options dialog box, where the following options can be set:
  - **Indefinitely** to pause the script until the user clicks the Continue button in the Status Toolbar.
  - **For Duration** allows entry of the number of seconds to pause the script. Click Specify to create a calculation that determines the number of seconds to pause.

Description:

This script step pauses a script for a specified period of time or indefinitely. This enables the user to perform data entry or other tasks before continuing the script. This step brings the active window of the file in which the script step is running to the foreground if it is not already there. The duration of a pause must be a number and represents the number of seconds that the pause lasts before resuming execution for the script. The duration can be a decimal or even 0, which causes FileMaker to pause only for the briefest possible duration.

Most FileMaker Pro menu options are not available to users while in a paused script. While paused, a script displays a Continue button in the Status Toolbar. The pause is terminated when a user clicks this button. A Cancel button also appears if Allow User Abort is set to On. This button exits the currently running script. If the Status Toolbar is hidden, the Enter key performs the same function as the Continue button. Buttons that run other scripts function while the current script is paused. A script run in this way is run as a sub-script of the paused script.

Examples:

```
#Open pop-up window
Allow User Abort [off]
New Window [Name: "About Soliant Consulting...";
➥Height: 50; Width: 50; Top: 40; Left: 100]
Go to Layout ["About" (RSR__Anchor)]
Show/Hide Status Toolbar [Lock; Hide]
Adjust Window [Resize to Fit]
Pause/Resume Script [Indefinitely]
#wait for user to hit ENTER key or CLOSE button
Close Window [Current Window]
```

Perform AppleScript (Mac OS)

Category: Miscellaneous

*Compatibility: Macintosh, Runtime**

Originated In: FileMaker 6.0 or earlier

Options:

- **Specify** displays the Perform AppleScript Options dialog box, where the following options can be set:
    - **Calculated AppleScript** enables you to draw the AppleScript code from the result of a calculation.
    - **Native AppleScript** enables you to enter an AppleScript by hand (up to 30,000 characters long).

Description:

This script step sends AppleScript commands to an AppleScript-aware application. The AppleScript may be typed in manually or generated as the result of a specified calculation. Calculated scripts are compiled every time the script is run, whereas typed-in scripts are compiled only when the script is edited. Obviously, the latter is a faster process, but creating AppleScript code via a calculation provides much greater flexibility.

Perform AppleScript is supported only on the Mac OS and Runtime solutions compiled for Mac OS. The script step generates an error in Windows.

Examples:

```
Perform AppleScript ["tell application "Finder" to set bounds of window
➥"My Files" to {100, 100, 1000, 400}"]
```

Perform Find

Category: Found Sets

Compatibility: Macintosh, Windows, Server, iOS, CWP, IWP, Runtime

Originated In: FileMaker 6.0 or earlier

Options:

- **Specify Find Requests** or **Specify** allows you to create or edit one or more find requests that will be stored with the script steps.
  - **New** opens a dialog box that enables you to create and specify a new find request to be stored with the script step.
  - **Edit** opens a selected find request from the existing list for editing.
  - **Duplicate** duplicates one or more selected find requests from the list and adds them to the stored set.
  - **Delete** deletes one or more selected find requests from the list.

The Edit Find Request dialog box works with find request criteria.

- **Find Records** or **Omit Records** specifies the behavior of the request. Selecting Omit Records is equivalent to checking the Omit check box in a find request in Find mode. Finding records adds them to the current found set. Omitting records excludes them. As in Find mode, use multiple requests if it is necessary to both find and omit records in the course of a single stored search.
- **Find Records When** (or **Omit Records When**) shows a list of the fields in your current table. To construct a find request, begin by selecting a field from this list.

  To select a field from a related table, click the name of the current table at the top of the list and select the related table you want. Select a related field from this new list.

  Change the value in Repetition to specify a particular cell of a repeating field.

  Type the search criteria for the selected field in the Criteria area.

  Click Add to add criteria to the find request.

  To change existing criteria, select the line containing the field and criteria from the top of the dialog box, and make the changes to the field and/or criteria. Click Change to store changes.

  To delete existing criteria, select the line containing the field and criteria from the top of the dialog box and click Remove.

Description:

This script step places the system in Find mode and performs the search request(s) that have been designated for this step. If no find requests have been designated, the last find request(s) that the system conducted is performed. If the system is in Find mode when Perform Find is executed, the currently entered find request is performed. This behavior is often used in conjunction with the Enter Find Mode step with the Pause option selected to allow a user to define a search request or group of search requests and then perform them.

If FileMaker Pro doesn't find any records that match the find criteria when a script is performed, the script can be stopped, execution of the script can be resumed with zero records in the current found set, and the find criteria can be changed. Using the Set Error Capture script step and the Get(LastError) function, you can write a script to handle such situations.

Examples:

```
Set Error Capture [On]
Perform Find [Restore]
#check for a "no records" error
If [Get (LastError) = 401]
   Show Custom Dialog ["Sorry, no records were found."; buttons ["ok"]]
End If
```

Perform Find/Replace

Category: Editing

Compatibility: Macintosh, Windows, Runtime

Originated In: FileMaker 7.0

Options:

- **Perform Without Dialog** inhibits the display of the Find/Replace Summary dialog box at the end of the Find/Replace operation. This option also prevents display of the confirmation dialog box when a Replace All operation is executed.
- **Open Find/Replace** script step is used if you want the user to be able to enter find or replace criteria.
- **Specify** displays the Specify Find/Replace dialog box, where search options, as well as the type of find/replace operation to be performed, can be set.

Description:

This script step looks for the specified text in one or more fields and records of the current found set and, if directed, replaces it with either literal text or the result of a calculation. It is equivalent to selecting Find/Replace from the Edit, Find/Replace menu.

The scope of the operation can be defined to be the current record or the entire found set. The Find/Replace can span all fields in a layout or just the current field. The operation can be defined to proceed forward or backward in the current found set (as sorted). Finally, options are available for the matching of whole words only instead of parts of words, and for the matching of case.

Examples:

```
Perform Find/Replace ["hte"; "the"; Replace All]
```

Perform Quick Find

Category: Found Sets

Compatibility: Macintosh, Windows, Server, iOS, CWP, IWP, Runtime

Originated In: FileMaker 11.0

Options:

- **Specify** allows for the calculation of the text to be used as Quick Find search criteria.

Description:

This script step performs a Quick Find search for the specified text in any field that has the setting Include Field in Quick Find.

Note the Quick Find box, generally located in the Status Toolbar unless the user has removed it by customizing his toolbar, is not altered and the Recent Find list is not updated.

Use the Get(QuickFindText) function to get the text the user manually typed into the field. It is also possible to hijack the Quick Find feature by creating a Custom menu that includes the command Perform Quick Find and configure it to call a script.

Examples:

```
#Use Custom Menu to configure this script to be performed for
#Perform Quick Find command
Set Variable [$find; Value: Get (QuickFindText)]
If [Length ($find) < 3]
   Show Custom Dialog [Title:"Quick Find Error";Message:"Please only perform a
   ➥Quick Find of at lease three characters.";Buttons:"OK"]
   Exit Script ["False"]
Else
   Perform Quick Find[$query]
   Exit Script ["True"]
End If
```

Perform Script

Category: Control

Compatibility: Macintosh, Windows, Server, iOS, CWP, IWP, Runtime

Originated In: FileMaker 6.0 or earlier

Options:

- **Specify** enables you to specify a script to perform, from the current file or another specified file.
  - **Optional Script Parameter** allows for the specification of the script parameter, either as text or as the result of a calculation.

Description:

This script step performs a script in the current file, another FileMaker Data Source, or an ODBC Data Source. The dialog can also conveniently open the Manage Data Sources dialog.

The optional script parameter allows scripts to communicate with one another without having to use database fields, global fields, or global variables. The script parameter may be accessed with the Get (ScriptParameter) function. It is important to note that the script parameters exist only within a script into which they have been explicitly passed. For a subscript to have access to the parameter of the script that called it, it must be passed into the subscript. For a subscript to pass data back to a calling script, Exit Script results also may be specified. Script parameters exist for only as long as the script to which they are passed exists. Parameter strings can contain many pieces of information as long as they are properly separated. Carriage returns, separator characters, and name/value pairs are common ways to pass many pieces of information in a parameter string.

Examples:

```
Go to Layout ["Detail"]
Perform Script ["Find Contact"; Parameter: "$contactID=" &
➥Quote (Contact::ContactID)]
```

Print

Category: Files

Compatibility: Macintosh, Windows, iOS, Runtime

Originated In: FileMaker 6.0 or earlier

Options:

- **Perform Without Dialog** prevents a dialog box from displaying when the script step executes. Ordinarily, users would see a dialog box permitting them to use their own settings. When this option is selected, FileMaker Pro uses the print settings stored with the script step.
- **Specify Print Options** or **Specify** opens the Print dialog box and enables you to set printing options, including the printer, number of copies, and pages to print. FileMaker Pro can also set printing options such as printing the current record, printing records being browsed, or printing a blank record.

Description:

This script step prints selected information from a FileMaker Pro file. This information can include field contents, reports based on database data, and field or script definitions. This script step is the equivalent of selecting Print from the File menu. Print setup settings are stored with the script step but may be changed with the Print Setup script step. Multiple Print Setup steps may be used in a single script.

When the specified printer cannot be found or was not specified in the options, the user's default printer is used.

The Print step is often preceded by the Print Setup script step, which allows for the configuration of the page setup options such as paper size and orientation.

Printer settings generally do not transfer well between platforms. Unless your settings are generic, you likely need to separate Print or Print Setup steps for each platform you intend to support. You might need to check the current user's platform with Get(SystemPlatform) and use separate print setups for each different platform. It is a good practice to use a subscript to centralize the management of print settings. It is then called by all reporting scripts.

Examples:

```
Go to Layout ["Detail View"]
Show All Records
Sort Records [Restore; No dialog]
Print Setup [Restore; No dialog]
Print []
```

Print Setup

Category: Files

Compatibility: Macintosh, Windows, Server, iOS, CWP, IWP, Runtime

Originated In: FileMaker 6.0 or earlier

Options:

- **Perform Without Dialog** prevents a dialog box from displaying when the script step that lets the user enter new printing options executes. When this option is selected, FileMaker Pro uses the print settings stored with the script step.
- **Specify Print Options** or **Specify** opens the Print dialog box and allows you to set generic printing options, including the printer, number of copies, and pages to print. FileMaker Pro can also set printing options such as printing the current record, printing records being browsed, or printing a blank record.

Description:

This script step sets printing options such as the printer, print layout, number of copies, and so on, all of which can be saved within the script step. This script step is the equivalent of selecting Page Setup from the File menu. This step also provides the option to allow the user to modify the print setup by presenting the Print Setup dialog box. Multiple Print Setup steps may be used in a single script.

Printer settings generally do not transfer well between platforms. Unless your settings are generic, you might need separate Print or Print Setup steps for each platform you intend to support. You might need to use Get(SystemPlatform) to check the current user's platform and use separate print setups for each different platform. It is a good practice to use a subscript to centralize the management of print settings. It is then called by all reporting scripts.

Examples:

```
Go to Layout ["Detail View"]
Show All Records
Sort Records [Restore; No Dialog]
Print Setup [Restore; No dialog]
Print []
```

Recover File

Category: Files

Compatibility: Macintosh, Windows, Runtime

Originated In: FileMaker 6.0 or earlier

Options:

- **Perform Without Dialog** prevents a dialog box from displaying after the script step completes. Ordinarily, users would see a dialog box that shows how many bytes of data were recovered, the number of records and field values skipped, and the number of field definitions recovered.
- **Specify Source File** or **Specify** displays a dialog box where you can select the file to recover or specify the file's path. A variable containing the complete file path may be a source.

Description:

This script step recovers damaged FileMaker Pro files. In the recovery process, FileMaker Pro attempts to repair and recover as much of the information in a damaged file as possible. It then creates a new file and saves it to the selected directory. The original file is not deleted or replaced. The new recovered file is named exactly as the damaged file except "Recovered" is appended to its filename, before any extenders. For example, the recovery of DataFile.fp7 would produce the file DataFile Recovered.fp7.

Recover File is an invasive process and is intended only to recover data from a corrupted file. It does not remove any corruption that might be present in the file, nor does it necessarily render the file fit for production use again. Try to avoid reusing a file that has been recovered. Import the extracted data into the most recent clean backup of the file and discard the recovered version.

FileMaker Server includes an aggressive consistency check routine that can detect many forms of file corruption. Accordingly, FileMaker, Inc., has somewhat softened its long-standing advice against ever reusing a recovered file. If a file successfully passes the consistency check in FileMaker Server, the file may be deemed fit for production use; however, it is still recommended that recovered data be imported into a clean backup of your files.

Examples:

```
Set Variable [$path; Value:"file:" & Get (FilePath) & "ABC_Data.fmp12"]
Recover File [No Dialog; "$path"]
```

Refresh Window

Category: Windows

Compatibility: Macintosh, Windows, Server, iOS, CWP, IWP, Runtime

Originated In: FileMaker 6.0 or earlier

Options:

- **Flush Cached Join Results** causes data for related records displayed in the current window to be refreshed. Choose this option if your script might have changed related data and you want to make sure the new data are visible after the screen refresh. If your script will not change related data, you might avoid a performance hit by leaving the option unchecked.
- **Flush Cached External Data** causes any displayed data from an external SQL data source to be refreshed. The external SQL server is queried for the current values of all displayed data. This is helpful if you want to make sure the user is viewing the latest data from the SQL source, including any updates or deletions that might have occurred since the SQL data was last refreshed.

Description:

This script step updates the active FileMaker Pro document window. Use Refresh Window after Freeze Window to update a window.

This step might also be used to force a portal to refresh after match fields (such as keys or other IDs) have been modified. It might also happen that complex related data is slow to refresh in a window, or user interaction—such as a mouse click—might be required to show the changed data. If you find such behavior, you might be able to cure it with an explicit Refresh Window step. (Note that when you use the script step for this purpose, you must select the Flush Cached Join Results option.)

Examples:

```
Freeze Window
Go to Record/Request/Page [First]
#Give everyone a 10% raise.
Loop
   Set Field [Employee::Salary; Employee::Salary * 1.1]
   Go to Record/Request/Page [Next; Exit after last]
End Loop
Refresh Window
```

Re-Login

Category: Accounts

Compatibility: Macintosh, Windows, Server, iOS, CWP*, IWP*, Runtime*

Originated In: FileMaker 6.0 or earlier

Options:

- **Perform Without Dialog** prevents the Authentication dialog box from displaying when the script step executes. When this option is checked, FileMaker Pro uses the account and password information stored with the script step or derived from a calculation expression.
- **Specify** displays the Re-Login Options dialog box, where you can set the following options:
  - **Account Name** is the name of the account to be authenticated. This may be entered as literal text or Specify can be clicked to derive an account name from a calculation.
  - **Password** is the password for this account. Literal text may be entered or Specify can be clicked to derive a new password from a calculation.

Description:

This script step allows a user to log in to the current database with a different account name and password. This does not require the database file to be closed or reopened. Privileges assigned to the new account take effect immediately, including access to tables, records, layouts, scripts, and value lists. Users get five attempts to enter an account and password, unless the Set Error Capture script step is enabled. If the Set Error Capture script step is enabled, users get a single attempt to enter an account and password. If a user fails the allotted number of times, she must close and reopen the database file before she can try to access the database again.

When developing a system with several privilege sets, you should test the system's functions with each set. It can save time to create Re-login scripts to allow you to instantly switch privileges without actually logging out of the file(s).

When developing a server-scheduled script or programming for the web, select Perform Without Dialog because leaving the box unchecked is not compatible in these contexts.

Examples:

```
Re-Login [Account Name:"User"; Password:"Password"; No dialog]
```

Relookup Field Contents

Category: Fields

Compatibility: Macintosh, Windows, Server, iOS, CWP*, IWP*, Runtime*

Originated In: FileMaker 6.0 or earlier

Options:

- **Perform Without Dialog** prevents the display of a dialog box that prompts the user to confirm field information when the script step executes.
- **Go to Target Field** or **Specify** allows for the specification of the match field of the relookup operation. FileMaker Pro moves the cursor to the field you specify. This must be the match field for the relationship upon which the lookup is based, not the lookup source or target field. If no field is selected, Relookup Field Contents returns an error code.

Description:

Use Relookup to refresh values that are copied from one place to another via the Lookup field option. It is important to realize that you must specify the field that is the match field for the lookup operation, rather than any of the fields that receive the newly copied data. As an example, imagine that you have a system with a Customer table and an Invoice table. The two tables are related by a shared CustomerID. The Invoice table also has fields for Customer Name and Customer Address, which are defined to look up the corresponding fields from the related Customer record. To "refresh" the customer name and address information on one or more invoices, you would need to specify the Customer ID field in Invoices, which is the match field that links the two tables, rather than specify either of the two fields intended to receive the refreshed data. Note that Relookup operates only on records in the current found set.

When programming a server-scheduled script or for the web, be sure to select Perform Without Dialog. Leaving the box unchecked is not compatible in these contexts.

Examples:

```
Relookup Field Contents [No dialog, Invoice::Customer ID]
```

Replace Field Contents

Category: Fields

Compatibility: Macintosh, Windows, Server, iOS, CWP*, IWP*, Runtime*

Originated In: FileMaker 6.0 or earlier

Options:

- **Perform Without Dialog** prevents display of the Replace Field Contents dialog box when the script step executes.
- **Go to Target Field** or **Specify** enables you to specify the target field for the replace operation.
- **Specify** displays the Replace Contents dialog box, where you can determine the settings required for the Replace Field Contents command so that they are stored in the script.
    - **Replace with Current Contents** uses the current value in the specified field as the replacement value to place in that field in every other record in the current found set.
    - **Replace with Serial Numbers** updates the field with new serial numbers in every record in the current found set. If the field to be replaced was set up for auto-entry of a serial number and Prohibit Modification of Value is not selected, FileMaker Pro still puts sequential numbers in the selected field, but does so starting with the next number to be automatically entered.
    - **Entry Options** causes FileMaker to consult the underlying database structure to determine how to serialize records. In particular, it causes the `Replace` step to use the database field settings for Next Value and Increment By, as stored in the field options for that field.
    - **Custom Values** enables you to enter a value to be used as a starting point for the serialization, as well as a value by which to increment each serialized field in the current found set.
    - **Update Serial Number In Entry Options** resets the serial number value in the entry options for the field so that the next serial number that is automatically entered follows the records you have reserialized with this script step. If this option is not used, the serial value in Entry Options is not changed and might not be in sequence with the newly reserialized records. This might lead to duplicated serial numbers or data validation errors.
    - **Replace with Calculated Result** displays the Specify Calculation dialog box, where you can enter a calculation to be used as the replacement value.

Description:

This script step replaces the contents of a selected field in the current record or every record in the found set with some value—the value of the field on the current record, a set of serial numbers, or a calculated result. This step can also be used to reserialize a field in every record in the found set. Note that if the specified field does not exist on the layout where the script is being performed, Replace Field Contents returns an error code that can be captured with the Get(LastError) function.

It might be helpful to think of this step as being akin to filling in multiple cells in a spreadsheet column. Replace is particularly powerful when used in conjunction with a calculation (a technique often known as a calculated replace). The calculation can reference fields, which refer to the field values in whichever is the current record.

Replace Field Contents is a fast way to modify a single value across a found set of records—faster than changing the values individually via a loop. However, this script step is not executed as a transaction. Should one or more records in the found set be in use by another user and therefore locked, FileMaker skips the locked records and continues with the modification of the others. Although the script step returns error 201, there is no indication as to which records could not be modified and the records committed. It is then considered a better practice to use other methodologies, such as looping through the records in a portal, to ensure the change is executed as all or nothing when working in a multiuser environment.

When programming a server-scheduled script or for the web, be sure to select Perform Without Dialog. Leaving the box unchecked is not compatible in these contexts.

Examples:

```
# Fill in full names
Replace Field Contents [No Dialog; Contacts::FullName; FName & " " & LName]
```

Reset Account Password

Category: Accounts

Compatibility: Macintosh, Windows, Server, iOS, CWP, IWP, Runtime

Originated In: FileMaker 6.0 or earlier

Options:

- **Specify** displays the Reset Account Password Options dialog box.
  - **Account Name** is the name of the account with the password to be reset. You can enter literal text or click Specify to derive an account name from a calculation.
  - **New Password** is the new password for this account. Literal text may be entered or Specify can be clicked to derive a password from a calculation.
  - **User Must Change Password on Next Login** forces users to change their passwords the next time they log in to the database.

Description:

This script step resets the account password for the selected account. The selected account must exist. The Full Access privilege set is needed to perform this script step. The Run with Full Access Privileges option may be selected in the Manage Script dialog to circumvent this restriction for all users.

Note that there are circumstances in which you should not set an account to force the user to change her password at next login. If the user will not have a direct means to do this, you should not set the option. The best example is an account that will be used to access a FileMaker database via IWP. IWP provides no means for a user to change her password, so this setting locks the user out of the database. Similarly, if the account is externally authenticated, it may be risky to tie the account to a privilege set requiring that the password be changed at some point or have a minimum length.

Examples:

```
Reset Account Password [Account Name:"Guest User";
➥New Password:"guestpassword"; Expire password]
```

Revert Record/Request

Category: Records

Compatibility: Macintosh, Windows, Server, iOS, CWP*, IWP*, Runtime*

Originated In: FileMaker 6.0 or earlier

Options:

- **Perform Without Dialog** inhibits the display of a confirmation dialog when the script step executes.

Description:

This script step discards changes made to a record and its fields, assuming the record has not been saved. After changes have been committed, such as through use of the Commit Records/Requests script step, they can no longer be reverted. This is also true if a user has clicked outside any field.

Note that record reversion applies not only to the current record on whatever layout is being viewed, but also to any records in related tables displayed in a portal on the current layout. If a user has edited one or more records in a portal, the Revert Record/Request script step, if carried out, undoes all uncommitted changes to portal records, as well as any uncommitted changes to the current record.

When programming a server-scheduled script or for the web, select Perform Without Dialog because leaving the box unchecked is not compatible in these contexts.

Examples:

```
Show Custom Dialog ["Do you want to save your changes?";
➥"Click 'Save' to save your changes, or 'Revert' to
➥return the record to its original state."]
#1 = Save, 2 = Revert
If [Get(LastMessageChoice) = 1]
  Commit Records/Requests
Else
  Revert Record/Request [No dialog]
End If
```

Save a Copy As

Category: Files

Compatibility: Macintosh, Windows, iOS, Runtime

Originated In: FileMaker 6.0 or earlier

Options:

- **Specify Output File** displays the Specify Output File dialog box, which allows specification of the name and location of the resulting copy. If a save location is not specified in the script, FileMaker Pro displays a regular Save As dialog box so the user can specify copying options.
- **Specify** allows you to choose a save format: copy of current file, compacted copy (smaller), or clone (no records).

Description:

This script step saves a copy of the current file to the designated location. If no location is designated, a dialog box is presented to the user. Three types of copies are available. Copy creates an exact replica of the current file. Compressed also creates a copy of the current file, but the copy is compressed to utilize space more efficiently. This sort of copy takes longer to create but is generally smaller than the original. Clone creates a file that is structurally identical to the current database but contains no data. This is useful for backup purposes because clones are compact.

Cloning a file removes all its record data and, perhaps less intuitive, also wipes away any values in globally stored fields. If your solution uses globally stored fields for graphics or other sorts of system preferences, be aware that such data is lost if the files are cloned.

Examples:

```
Save a Copy As ["Customers.bak"]
```

Save Records as Excel

Category: Records

Compatibility: Macintosh, Windows, Runtime

Originated In: FileMaker 8.0

Options:

- **Perform Without Dialog** prevents certain dialog boxes from appearing as the script step executes. If you have specified a file and stored that information with the script step, no dialog boxes are displayed. If you have not saved output file information with the script step, the Save Records as Excel dialog box is displayed (but the Excel options dialog still is not).

- **Specify Output File** enables you to save a file path with the script step. This file path is used to determine where the new file should be saved. When specifying the output file, you can also choose Automatically Open File, in which case the file is opened when created, or choose Create Email with File as Attachment to create a new blank email, with the Excel file as an attachment, using the local machine's default email software.
- **Specify Options** enables you to set a number of useful properties of the output file, such as which database records should be included, whether the first row should contain field names, and worksheet properties such as title and author.

Description:

This script step enables you to save a set of records directly to an Excel spreadsheet. With appropriate selections of options, you can also automatically open the file or attach it to an email.

Note that the file path dialog accepts either a file path in text form or a variable ($local or $$GLOBAL).

Examples:

```
Go to Layout ["Customer List"]
Show All Records
Save Records as Excel [No dialog; "Customer_List.xls"]
```

Save Records as PDF

Category: Records

Compatibility: Macintosh, Windows, Server, iOS, CWP, IWP, Runtime

Originated In: FileMaker 8.0

Options:

- **Append to Existing PDF** allows scripts to add additional pages to an existing PDF.
- **Perform Without Dialog** prevents certain dialog boxes from appearing as the script step executes. If you have specified a file and stored that information with the script step, no dialog boxes are displayed. If you have not saved output file information with the script step, the Save Records as PDF dialog box is displayed (but the PDF options dialog still is not).
- **Specify Output File** enables you to save a file path with the script step. This file path is used to determine where the new file should be saved. When specifying the output file, you can also choose Automatically Open File, in which case the file will be opened when created, or choose Create Email with File as Attachment to create a new blank email, with the PDF file as an attachment, using the local machine's default email software.
- **Specify Options** allows for the specification of records to include and then the properties of the output file:
  - **Document** options including Title, Subject, Author, Keywords, Compatibility of Acrobat version, pagination, and which pages to include.

- **Security** options including Require Password to Open the File; Require Password to Control Printing, Editing, and Security; Enable Copying of Content; and Allow Text to Be Read by Screen Reading Software.
- **Initial View** settings include specifying the panels to show, page layout, and magnification.

Description:

This script step enables you to save a set of records as a PDF. With appropriate selections of options, you can also automatically open the file or attach it to an email. Developers also have full control over security settings and document properties.

Note that the file path dialog accepts either a file path in text form or a variable ($local or $$GLOBAL).

Examples:

```
Go to Layout ["Customer List"]
Set Variable[$path; "file:" & Get (DesktopPath) & "myReport.pdf"]
Show All Records
Save Records as PDF [No dialog; $path]
```

Save Records as Snapshot Link

Category: Records

Compatibility: Macintosh, Windows, Server, iOS

Originated In: FileMaker 11.0

Options:

- **Specify Output File** displays the Specify Output File dialog box, which allows specification of the name and location of the resulting copy. If a save location is not specified in the script, FileMaker Pro displays a regular Save As dialog box so the user can specify the location.
    - **Create Email with File as Attachment** creates a blank email message with the Snapshot attached.
- **Specify** the records to include in the Snapshot: Records Being Browsed or Current Record.

Description:

This script step creates a FileMaker Pro Snapshot Link (FMPSL) file for the current record or found set. The snapshot link file includes the current found set of record IDs, along with the layout, view, sort order, mode, and toolbar visibility.

When a snapshot link is opened, it opens the file if necessary, creates a new window named the same as the snapshot file, performs the File Options specified for file open, performs the find, and restores the context. Note that the found set does not include any records that have been deleted since the snapshot link file was created. The user's access privileges are respected, meaning FileMaker will not allow access to records the user is not authorized to view, even though they are included in the snapshot.

The snapshot link file is actually an XML file. Although the menu item Save/Send Record As, Snapshot Trigger suggests a file name with the suffix , fmpsl, it is possible to name the file with the suffix txt and then import the file's contents into a text field. The sort information is particularly useful because it is the only way to discern the user's current sort.

Note that snapshot links created with previous versions of FileMaker are not compatible with later versions.

Examples:

```
#Save the Snapshot to the desktop and email it
Set Variable [$filePath; Get (DesktopPath) &
➥Company::Company_Name & " Invoices.fmpsl"]
Save Records as Snapshot Link ["$path"; Create email; Records being browsed]
```

Scroll Window

Category: Windows

Compatibility: Macintosh, Windows, iOS, Runtime

Originated In: FileMaker 6.0 or earlier

Options:

- **Specify** to choose a scrolling option.
  - **Home**, **End**, **Page Up**, or **Page Down** scrolls the window to the beginning, to the end, up a page, or down a page.
  - **To Selection** brings the current field into view (similar to tabbing into a field).

Description:

This script step scrolls a window to its top or bottom, up or down, or to a specified field. You might want to use this script step for rapid, easy scrolling within a window. For example, if you have had to design a layout that is wider than some users' screens, you can put dummy "scroll left/scroll right" fields at the far left and right sides of the layout. If you make the field small and forbid entry, the user does not notice them. Then a script such as the following example scrolls quickly to the right side of the window (assuming the field is placed somewhere to the right).

Examples:

```
Go to Field ["Scroll Right"]
Scroll Window [To Selection]
#The next step just makes sure we leave the "scroll to" field
Commit Records/Requests
```

Select All

Category: Editing

Compatibility: Macintosh, Windows, iOS, Runtime

Originated In: FileMaker 6.0 or earlier

Options:

None

Description:

This script step selects the entire contents of the current field.

Examples:

```
#Place a contact person's statement on the clipboard
Go to Field [Contacts::Statement]
Select All
Copy []
```

Select Dictionaries

Category: Spelling

Compatibility: Macintosh, Windows, Runtime

Originated In: FileMaker 6.0 or earlier

Options:

None

Description:

This script step opens the Select Dictionaries dialog box. This is often used to give users access to the Select Dictionaries dialog box when access to the FileMaker Pro menus has been restricted. This step is the equivalent of selecting Select Dictionary from the menu Edit, Spelling.

Examples:

```
Select Dictionaries
Check Record
```

Select Window

Category: Windows

Compatibility: Macintosh, Windows, Server, iOS, CWP, IWP, Runtime

Originated In: FileMaker 7.0

Options:

- **Current Window** brings the active window of the file that contains the script to the foreground.
- **Specify** also selects the window FileMaker Pro should bring to the foreground. The name may be typed as literal text or derived from a calculation.
- **Current File Only** restricts the scope of script step to consider only windows based on the current file.

Description:

This script step specifies a window by name and makes it the current, focal window. FileMaker Pro script steps are always performed in the foreground window and inherit context from that window's layout and associated table occurrence. Use this script step when working with scripts in multitable files to make sure that a script step is performed in the intended table. (You might also need to use a Go to Layout step to establish context correctly.) The Select Window script step does not open a window of an external file when it is open in a hidden state, such as when a file is opened because it is the source file of a related field. The related file must be explicitly opened with the Open File script step before its windows are allowable targets for the Select Window step.

Examples:

```
Select Window [Name: "Contract Players"]
```

Send DDE Execute (Windows)

Category: Miscellaneous

*Compatibility: Windows, Runtime**

Originated In: FileMaker 6.0 or earlier

Options:

- **Specify** displays the Send DDE Execute Options dialog box.
- **Service Name** is the name of the application that executes any specified commands. Refer to the documentation for the specified application to find the valid service name. The service name may be entered directly as text, or Specify can be clicked to create the service name from a calculation.

- **Topic** is a filename or text string that describes the topic on which the application executes the commands. Refer to the documentation for the application specified in the Service Name to determine valid topics. Enter the topic name directly as text or click Specify to create the topic name from a calculation.
- **Commands** are calculated values or text strings that specify what the application does. Refer to the documentation for the application specified in the Service Name to determine valid commands and formats. Enter the commands directly as text or click Specify to create the commands from a calculation.

Description:

This script step sends a Dynamic Data Exchange (DDE) command to another DDE-aware application. FileMaker can send DDE commands but cannot receive them. When a FileMaker Pro script first establishes a DDE connection, the connection stays open to execute subsequent script steps for the same service name and topic. If the script includes another DDE Execute script step that specifies a different service name or topic, FileMaker Pro closes the current connection and opens another with the new service name and topic. All open connections close when the script is completed.

Examples:

```
Send DDE Execute [Service Name: "iexplore"; Topic: "WWW_OpenURL";
➥Commands:"www.soliantconsulting.com"]
```

Send Event (Mac OS)

Category: Miscellaneous

Compatibility: Macintosh, Windows, Server, iOS, CWP, IWP, Runtime

Originated In: FileMaker 6.0 or earlier

Options:

- **Specify** to display the Send Event Options dialog box.
- **Send The <Value> Event With** offers a choice between the following:
  - **Open Application** tells FileMaker Pro to open an application. Click Specify Application to select the application.
  - **Open Document** tells FileMaker Pro to open a document in the target application. You can also specify a calculated value or script.
  - **Do Script** tells FileMaker Pro to perform a script in the language of the target application. Click Specify Application to select an application, and use Document to select the document to use with the target application or select Script Text and enter script's text or the name of the script.
  - **Other** displays the Specify Event dialog box, where you can manually enter the Apple Event class and Event ID.
- **Document** or **Specify** enables you to select the document you want used with the target application.

- **Calculation** or **Specify** enables you to create a calculation that generates a value you want to send with the event.
- **Bring Target Application to Foreground** activates the target application and displays it on the screen. Displaying the target application can slow down the performance of a script. If Bring Target Application to Foreground is not selected, the event is performed in the background.
- **Wait for Event Completion Before Continuing** tells FileMaker Pro to wait until the event is finished before continuing. If you do not want to wait until the event is completed, deselect this option.
- **Copy Event Result to the Clipboard** copies the resulting event's data to the Clipboard, from which it can later be retrieved. This option is disabled if Bring Target Application to Foreground is selected.
- **Specify Application** displays a dialog to select the target application.

Description:

This script step sends an Apple Event to another Apple Event–aware application. The desired event is selected in the Send Event Options dialog box. When FileMaker Pro sends an Apple event, it sends text (not compiled) data. You must know what information the target application expects to receive with an event. Each Send Event script step sends one event. You can include more than one Send Event in a script.

Examples:

```
Send Event ["TextEdit", "aevt", "oapp"]
```

Send Event (Windows)

Category: Miscellaneous

Compatibility: Macintosh, Runtime

Originated In: FileMaker 6.0 or earlier

Options:

- **Specify** displays the Send Event Options dialog box.
- For **Send the <Event Name> Message**, select the following options:
    - **Open Document/Application** setting has FileMaker Pro open a document file or application. The application that Windows has associated with the document's file type is used to open it.
    - **Print Document** setting has FileMaker Pro print a document in another application.
- **File** or click **Specify** to specify a document/application to open or a document to print.
- **Calculation** or click **Specify** to create a message from a calculation.
- **Text** allows for the manual entry of the text message to be sent.

- **Bring Target Application to Foreground** setting activates the target application and displays it on the screen. Displaying the target application can slow down the performance of a script. If Bring Target Application to Foreground is not selected, the event is performed in the background.

Description:

This script step communicates with other Windows applications. It can instruct them to either open or print a document in its associated application. Custom code written in a language such as C# or Visual Basic can be executed this way.

Examples:

```
#To launch the Notepad application, select the open document/application message,
#click File, and specify notepad.exe. The following script step appears in the
#Script Definition dialog box:
Send Event ["NOTEPAD.EXE ", "aevt", "odoc"]
```

Send Mail

Category: Miscellaneous

Compatibility: Macintosh, Windows, Server, iOS, CWP*, IWP*, Runtime*

Originated In: FileMaker 6.0 or earlier

Options:

- **Perform Without Dialog** instructs FileMaker Pro to put the composed email message in the email application's Out box, ready to be sent. If this option is not selected, the composed message is left open in the email application so that it can be reviewed. In Microsoft Outlook Express or Microsoft Entourage on the Macintosh operating system, the new message is left in the Drafts folder.
- **Specify** displays the Specify Mail dialog box, where options for mail can be set. For each of the following options, you can enter text directly or click > to enter values from an address book (Windows), field, or calculation:
  - **Send via** to specify the method for sending mail, either E-Mail Client or SMTP Server.
  - **Create** to specify sending an email for the current record or found set.
  - **Specify Email Addresses** to select an email address from the email application's address book (Windows only).
  - **Specify Calculation** allows creation of an address (or subject or message text) from a calculation.
  - **Specify Field Name** to choose a single field that contains the desired value.
- **To** specifies the address(es) of the recipient(s).
- **CC** specifies the address(es) of the carbon copy recipient(s).
- **BCC** specifies the address(es) of the blind carbon copy recipient(s).
- **Subject** indicates the title for the email message.

- **Message** indicates the text of the email message. The message may be typed as text, designated as a field value, or created by a calculation.
- **Attach File** allows you to select one (and only one) file to send as an attachment to the mail message.

Description:

The Send Mail script step sends email to one or more recipients via a client-side email application or directly from the SMTP Server. The following things are necessary to send mail from FileMaker:

- **Windows**—A [Mail] section in the Win.ini file, and Microsoft Exchange, Microsoft Outlook, or Microsoft Outlook Express installed and configured to work with an existing email account.
- **Mac OS**—Mac OS X Mail or Microsoft Entourage installed and configured as the default email application.

To send mail, you must have an Internet connection and a correctly configured email client (see the previous description section for Send Event for configurations).

When programming a server-scheduled script or for the web, do not select the option to send via E-mail Client because it is not supported.

Note that if you select the option Multiple Emails while also selecting the option Collect Addresses Across Found Set for To, CC, or BCC, an email is created for each record, each email sent to every recipient.

Examples:

```
Perform Find [Restore]
# Send the same email to everyone in the found set.
Send Mail [To: Contacts::email; Subject: "This is a test email";
➥Message:"Testing..."]
```

Set Error Capture

Category: Control

Compatibility: Macintosh, Windows, Server, iOS, CWP, IWP, Runtime

Originated In: FileMaker 6.0 or earlier

Options:

- **On** suppresses most FileMaker Pro alert messages and some dialog boxes. If the error result is 100 or 803, certain standard file dialog boxes are suppressed, such as the Open dialog box.
- **Off** re-enables the alert messages.

Description:

This script step suppresses or enables the FileMaker Pro error dialogs and messages. This provides the developer with the opportunity to write scripts to handle errors in a manner that is customizable and appropriate to the functions being performed. The Get(LastError) function, when used immediately after a script step is executed, gives the number of the error encountered or 0 for no error.

Examples:

```
Perform Find [Restore]
Go to Record/Request/Page [First]
Set Error Capture [On]
Open Record/Request
Set Variable[$error; Get(LastError)
If [$error = 200 or $error= 300]
   Show Custom Dialog ["An error has occurred. This record is locked or
   ➥you do not have sufficient permission to access it."]
End If
```

Set Field

Category: Fields

Compatibility: Macintosh, Windows, Server, iOS, CWP, IWP, Runtime

Originated In: FileMaker 6.0 or earlier

Options:

- **Specify Target Field** or **Specify** enables you to specify the field whose contents you want to replace. If no field is specified and a field is already selected in Browse mode or Find mode, that field is used.
- **Calculated Result** defines a calculation, the results of which replace the current contents of the target field.

Description:

This script step replaces the contents of the designated field with the result of the specified calculation. The target field must be accessible from the active layout's context, but it does not need to be on the active layout. In other words, the target field must be a standard field that is part of the current layout's record or related table occurrence, or a global field of any table.

When Set Field is performed on a related record, the action is performed on the active portal row record as long as it is for the same relationship as the target field. If no portal row is active or the active row is not for the same relationship, the Set Field action is applied to the first related record, determined by the relationship's sort order as defined in manage database. When records can be created through the relationship and the last (blank) portal row is active, Set Field can be used to create a new related record.

When the target field's validation is set to execute Only During Data Entry, the script step skips validation. FileMaker performs field validation during the Set Field step execution only when the target field is to validate data Always as part of its field definition, and when it does not pass validation, the step returns a FileMaker error and no message is displayed.

The Calculated Result must match the field type of the target field, or the results might be unexpected. If the result of the calculation does not match the target field type, and the Validate option for the field is set to Always, the field is not set, and an error code is returned (which can be captured with the Get(LastError) function).

When possible, the Set Field script step makes the record active and leaves it active until the record is exited or committed. Scripts that use a series of Set Field script steps should thus group these steps together if possible so that subsequent Set Field script steps can act on the record without having to individually lock the record, synchronize data with the server, index the field, and so on, after each Set Field script step. These actions, along with record-level validation, are performed after the record has been exited or committed.

Unlike many other script steps that deal with field contents, Set Field does not require that the field being targeted be on the active layout. This script step should be used in almost every case that a developer wants to programmatically insert data into a database. It does not interfere with a user's Clipboard and is not dependent on layout objects.

Be sure to commit record data as appropriate after using the Set Field step to avoid leaving the record open and encountering a record lock error later.

Examples:

```
Freeze Window
Go to Record/Request/Page [First]
# Give everyone a 10% raise.
Loop
   Set Field [Employee::Salary; Employee::Salary * 1.1]
   Go to Record/Request/Page [Next; Exit after last]
End Loop
Refresh Window
```

Set Field By Name

Category: Fields

Compatibility: Macintosh, Windows, Server, iOS, CWP, IWP, Runtime

Originated In: FileMaker 6.0 or earlier

Options:

- **Specify Target Field** or **Specify** defines a calculation, the result of which is the name of the field to be edited.
- **Calculated Result** defines a calculation, the result of which replaces the current content of the target field.

Description:

This script step is similar to the Set Field script step, with one important distinction: The target field is defined by the result of a calculation. This allows for the creation of very flexible scripts that can vary their behavior on the context or the script parameter specified.

When the calculated target field is not found, FileMaker silently returns error 102 (Field Is Missing) without displaying a message, regardless of the error capture state.

In behavior and execution, this script step is identical to Set Field. See the script step Set Field for further information.

Examples:

```
#The parameter contains a list of name value pairs.
#in the form Table::Field=Value seperated by a Carriage Return
#Note: values have been encoded
Set Variable [$param; Value:Get ( ScriptParameter )]
#
#This subscript is called from the appropriate layout and record context.
Set Variable [$table; Value:Get ( LayoutTableName )]
#
#Loop the parameter list to set each Field with corresponding value.
Set Variable [$total; Value:ValueCount ( $param )]
Set Variable [$counter; Value:0]
Loop
   Set Variable [$counter; Value:$counter + 1]
   Exit Loop If [$counter > $total]
   Set Variable [$nameVal; Value:
   ➥Substitute ( GetValue ($param ; $counter) ; "=" ; ¶ )]
   Set Variable [$field; Value:$table & "::" & GetValue ( $nameVal ; 1 )]
   Set Variable [$value; Value:
   ➥Substitute ( GetValue ($param ; 2) ; "&#13;" ; ¶ )]
   Set Field By Name [$field; $value]
   Exit Loop If [$error]
End Loop
#
#Revert record if error encountered
If [ $error ]
   Revert Record/Request [No dialog]
   Show Custom Dialog [Title: "Message"; Message:
   ➥"There was an error while setting field" & $field & ".
   ➥The record was not changed.¶¶(Error " & $error & ")";
   ➥Default Button: "OK", Commit: "Yes"]
Else
   Commit Records/Requests [No dialog]
End If
```

Set Multi-User

Category: Files

Compatibility: Macintosh, Windows

Originated In: FileMaker 6.0 or earlier

Options:

- **On** allows network access via FileMaker Network Sharing. This is the same as enabling Network Sharing and selecting All Users in the FileMaker Network Settings dialog box.
- **On (Hidden)** allows network access but prevents the name of the shared database from appearing in the Open Remote File dialog box. This is the same as enabling Network Sharing and selecting the All Users and Don't Display in Open Remote File dialog options in the FileMaker Network Settings dialog box.
- **Off** disallows network access. This is the same as selecting No Users in the FileMaker Network Settings dialog box.

Description:

This script step allows or disallows network access to the current database. The Hidden option allows a file to be accessed by other files and in dialogs but not through the Open Remote dialog.

If FileMaker Network Sharing is currently set to Off, both of this script step's On options also enable network sharing. This could possibly enable sharing access to files other than just the one in which this script step is run. The converse is not true: The Off option to this script step does not also turn off FileMaker Network Sharing. It is sometimes helpful to have Set Multi-User On/Off script steps in all the files of a multifile solution. By means of a single master script in one of the files, all these individual files can execute their Set Multi-User On/Off scripts. This makes it possible to fully enable or fully disable multiuser access to a set of files with just a single script.

Examples:

```
If [Get (MultiUserState) = 0]
  Show Custom Dialog ["Would you like to enable network sharing?"]
  If [Get (LastMessageChoice) = 1]
    Set Multi-User [On]
  End If
End
```

Set Next Serial Value

Category: Fields

Compatibility: Macintosh, Windows, Server, iOS, CWP, IWP, Runtime

Originated In: FileMaker 6.0 or earlier

Options:

- **Specify Target Field** or **Specify** allows you to specify the serial number field on which the script step is to operate. The field specified must be defined as an auto-entry serial number field.
- **Calculated Result:** Click Specify to enter the next serial value by hand or create a calculation to determine the next serial value.

Description:

This script step resets the next serial value for an auto-enter serial number field. This capability is especially useful to ensure that there are no duplicate serial numbers when a large number of records have been imported into a backup clone of a system. It is also useful for importing records when it is not desirable to allow auto-enter calculations. The calculated result always evaluates to a text result. Note this script step can operate on multiple files. If a field in another file is specified, FileMaker Pro attempts to update the serial number for the specified field in the other file. To specify a field in another file, define a relationship to that file and use Specify Target Field to select a field from that file. Also, if a serial number is not strictly a number, special care must be taken to ensure that the newly set serial number matches the format of the existing serial numbers.

This script step does not change any field data. Instead, it changes the definition of the target field that then controls data automatically entered for the next new record. Specifically, it changes the Next Serial Number you see in the Field Options dialog for that field.

Examples:

```
Find All
Set Next Serial Value [Contacts::ContactID; Contacts::MaxContactID + 1]
#Note: MaxContactID is a summary field defined as the max
#of the serial field ContactID
```

Set Selection

Category: Editing

Compatibility: Macintosh, Windows, Server, iOS, CWP, IWP, Runtime

Originated In: FileMaker 6.0 or earlier

Options:

- **Go to Target Field** to specify the field whose contents you want to select.

- **Specify** enables you to set the starting and ending positions of a selection, either by entering the start and end numbers directly or by using a calculation to determine them.

Description:

This script step makes it possible to "select" some or all of a field's contents without direct user intervention. It is possible to specify the start and end positions (in terms of numbers of characters) for the new selection. These values may be entered literally or generated as the result of a specified calculation. This step does not operate on container fields. Data that is out of the visible portion of a layout or field is scrolled into view to show the newly selected contents. The start and end values must be integers between one and the number of characters in the target field. If the start position number is valid and the end position number is invalid, the selection goes from the start position number to the end of the field contents. If the start position number is invalid and the end position is valid, the cursor (or insertion point) is placed at the specified end position with no characters selected. If neither the start nor the end number is valid, the cursor is placed at the end of the field's contents.

You might use this script step to prepare additional operations that act on the current selection, such as cut or copy. You might also choose to transform the selection, for example, by removing it and substituting a styled version of the same text.

Set Selection is one of a number of script steps that depend on the presence of specific fields on the current layout. Other script steps with the same limitations include Cut, Copy, and Paste.

Examples:

```
#Select the first 50 characters
Set Selection [Start Position:1; End Position:50]
```

Set Use System Formats

Category: Files

Compatibility: Macintosh, Windows, iOS, Runtime

Originated In: FileMaker 6.0 or earlier

Options:

- **On** directs FileMaker Pro to use the current system formats.
- **Off** directs FileMaker Pro to use the file's formats.

Description:

FileMaker Pro databases store date, time, and number format preferences. These are taken from the computer on which the database was created. These creation settings might differ from those in use on other machines on which the database may later be opened. This script step can be used to determine whether a file draws its time display settings from those stored in the file or those in effect on the local machine.

If a FileMaker file is opened on a computer with different locale settings than those stored in the file, the user sees an alert that warns him of the difference. This script step can be used to automatically instruct the system to use the current locale settings when it starts up.

This script step does not change the locale settings stored in the file. It simply instructs FileMaker whether to use the locale settings on the current computer.

Examples:

```
If [Get (SystemLanguage) <> "English"]
   Set Use System Formats [On]
End If
```

Set Variable

Category: Control

Compatibility: Macintosh, Windows, Server, iOS, CWP, IWP, Runtime

Originated In: FileMaker 8.0

Options:

- **Specify** gives you access to a dialog where you can set the following variable options:
  - **Name** is the name you want to assign to the variable. Variable names are prefixed with $ (for local variables) or $$ (for global variables). With no prefix, $ is assumed.
  - **Value** is the value to which the variable will be set. You can specify some text manually or enter a calculation.
  - **Repetition** is a number specifying the repetition within the variable that is to be set. The default value is 1, meaning FileMaker will set the first repetition of the variable.

Description:

Set a variable, or a repetition of a variable, with a specific value. If the variable is a local variable, the value persists within the currently running script and that script only; the variable is not directly available to subscripts and ceases to exist when the script that created it stops executing. A global variable exists across all scripts and calculations of the file in which it was created, and continues to retain its value even when the script that created it stops executing.

A variable can hold data of any type, including text, number, date, time, timestamp, and container.

It is possible to set discontiguous variable repetitions. You can set $var[3] and $var[33] without defining or setting the other slots from 1 to 33.

Variables do not need to be declared or initialized, as in other languages. They are created implicitly the first time they are referenced.

Variables, both local and global, can also be set within a Let statement:

```
Let ( [$counter = $counter + 1; result = "success"]; result)
```

Examples:

```
#Use a local variable
Set Variable [$loopCounter; Value: $loopCounter + 1]

#Use a global variable
Set Variable [$$LAST_LOGIN_TIME; Value: Status(CurrentTime)]

#Use a repetition index
Set Variable [$myArray[3]; Value: "Fred Smith"]

#Use a dynamic repetition index
Set Variable [$$ARRAY; Value: ""]
Set Variable [$index; Value: 20]
Loop
   Set Variable [$$ARRAY[$index]; Value: $index]
   Set Variable [$index; Value: $index – 1]
   Exit Loop If [$index = 0]
End Loop
```

Set Web Viewer

Category: Miscellaneous

Compatibility: Macintosh, Windows, iOS, IWP, Runtime

Originated In: FileMaker 8.5

Options:

- **Specify** opens the Set Web Viewer Options dialog, which allows the setting of the following:
  - **Object Name** is used to specify the web view to act on based on its object name. The name can be entered as literal text or derived by calculation.
  - **Action** allows for specifying the action to be performed on the web viewer:
    - **Reset** to original address and clear its back/forward history.
    - **Reload** the web page currently displayed.
    - **Go Forward** to go to the next page, same as a browser.
    - **Go Back** to go to the previous page, same as a browser.
    - **Go to URL** opens a dialog to define a new web address.

Description:

This script step allows for the dynamic rendering of a web view, which means that one interface object can be used for a variety of purposes.

Examples:

```
#Display the text 'Hello World'
Set Web Viewer [Object Name: "WebViewer";
➥URL: "data:text/plain,Hello World"]

#Reload the current page
Set Web Viewer [Object Name: "WebViewer"; Action: Reload]
```

Set Window Title

Category: Windows

Compatibility: Macintosh, Windows, Server, iOS, CWP, IWP, Runtime

Originated In: FileMaker 6.0 or earlier

Options:

- **Specify** opens the Set Window Title Options dialog, which allows the setting of the following:
  - **Window to Rename** tells FileMaker Pro which window to rename. Current Window renames the current window. You may also specify a different window by either typing the window name in plain text or deriving the window name from a calculation.
  - **Current File Only** causes FileMaker to search only within windows based on table occurrences within the current file.
  - **Rename Window To** is the new title for the window. Here again, you can enter literal text or click Specify to derive a name from the result of a calculation.

Description:

Set Window Title sets the name of the current window or the window specified by name.

Current File Only restricts the scope of the step to consider only windows based on the current file.

Window names are not case sensitive when you select them in this way, so be sure not to rely on case when designating names.

Examples:

```
Set Error Capture [On]
Allow User Abort [Off]
Perform Find [Restore]
Set Window Title [Get ( FoundCount ) & " Contacts Found"]
```

Set Zoom Level

Category: Windows

Compatibility: Macintosh, Windows, Server, iOS, CWP*, IWP*, Runtime*

Originated In: FileMaker 6.0 or earlier

Options:

- **Lock** prohibits users from making changes to the zoom level.
- **Specify** enables you to select a zoom level as follows:
  - **Specific reduction values**: 100%, 75%, 50%, or 25%.
  - **Specific enlargement values**: 150%, 200%, 300%, or 400%.
  - **Zoom In**: Reduces the screen image by one zoom level.
  - **Zoom Out**: Enlarges the screen image by one zoom level.

Description:

Set Zoom Level enlarges or reduces the image on the screen and optionally locks screen scaling. It is equivalent to using the magnification icons beneath the Status Toolbar.

Examples:

```
Allow User Abort [Off]
Set Error Capture [On]
If [ /*The screen resolution is too low*/   Get (ScreenHeight) < 600]
  Set Zoom Level [Lock; 100%]
Else
  Set Zoom Level [100%]
End
```

Show All Records

Category: Found Sets

Compatibility: Macintosh, Windows, Server, iOS, CWP, IWP, Runtime

Originated In: FileMaker 6.0 or earlier

Options:

None

Description:

This script step displays all the records in the current table and leaves the user on the current record. Show All Records is used in Browse mode or Preview mode. If you use this step in Find mode or Layout mode, FileMaker Pro switches to Browse mode after the records have been found.

Examples:

```
Allow User Abort [Off]
Set Error Capture [On]
Enter Find Mode [Pause]
Perform Find []
If [Get (CurrentFoundCount) = 0]
   #No records were found
   Show Message ["No Records Found"; "Sorry, no records that match your
➥find criteria were found."]
   #Don't leave the user on an empty found set
   Show All Records [ ]
End If
```

Show Custom Dialog

Category: Miscellaneous

Compatibility: Macintosh, Windows, iOS, Runtime

Originated In: FileMaker 6.0 or earlier

Options:

- **Specify** displays a dialog box where you can define the content of the custom dialog:
  - **Title** lets you specify the title of the custom dialog box. You can enter literal text or click Specify to create the dialog box title from a calculation.
  - **Message** lets you specify the message of the dialog box. You can enter literal text or click Specify to create the message text from a calculation.
  - **Button Labels** enable you to specify how many buttons (up to three) to display in the custom dialog box and labels for these buttons. If you leave a button label blank, the button does not appear in the custom dialog box. If you leave all button titles blank, an OK button is displayed in the lower-right corner of the custom dialog box.
  - **Commit Data** enables you to specify how the data in the Input Fields is to be handled when the corresponding button is selected by the user. When Commit Data is specified, the record commits when the dialog closes; otherwise, the record is reverted.
- **Input Field** options (second tab of dialog):
  - **Show input field** <n> activates an input field.
  - **Specify** chooses the field for input. Each input area maps to one field.
  - **Use Password Character** (*) masks text as it is entered or as it is displayed from the database. This option obscures data being input into the custom dialog box or being displayed but does not alter the actual data as it is stored in the database.
  - **Label** specifies a field label (the text that identifies this input to the user). You can enter literal text or create the label from a calculation.

Description:

Show Custom Dialog enables you to display a custom message dialog. The dialog box is modal—with one, two, or three buttons, each with a custom title. The custom message window can also display up to three input fields, each with a custom label. Each of these input fields corresponds to a FileMaker data field. When the window is opened, each input area displays the most recent contents of the corresponding field. When the user closes the window, the button clicked can be determined by the Get(LastMessageChoice) function. A result of 1 represents the first button on the right, whereas 2 and 3 represent the middle and leftmost buttons if they were used. Button 1, the rightmost, is the default. It is also the only button that, when clicked, causes the data from any input fields to be written back to the corresponding FileMaker fields.

If values entered into any input fields do not match the field type of the underlying FileMaker field, a validation error message is displayed. The user must resolve validation errors before the dialog box can be closed. The fields you specify do not need to appear on the current layout. Show Custom Dialog input fields are independent of layouts, similar to the Set Field script step and, as with the Set Field script step, Show Custom Dialog bypasses the Allow Entry Into Field formatting option.

Data entry via the Show Custom Dialog script step is limited by any access privilege rules that might be in place. In other words, users cannot use a custom dialog to edit data in fields that they can normally change because of access restriction. If you select Run Script with Full Access Privileges, this restriction is lifted.

On Windows, you can create a keyboard shortcut for a custom dialog button by placing an ampersand before the shortcut key letter in the button label. For example, to create a keyboard shortcut D (Alt+D) for a button labeled Done, type the label **&Done**.

Examples:

```
Allow User Abort [Off]
Set Error Capture [On]
Show Custom Dialog ["Date Range"; reportDate_start; reportDate_end]
Perform Find []
```

Show Omitted Only

Category: Found Sets

Compatibility: Macintosh, Windows, Server, iOS, CWP, IWP, Runtime

Originated In: FileMaker 6.0 or earlier

Options:

None

Description:

Show Omitted Only "inverts" the found set to show records currently not displayed and omits records that are currently displayed.

Examples:

```
#Reduce found set to zero
Loop
   Show All Records
   Show Omitted Only
   #Double check because another user may have created a record between our
   #Show All and Show Omitted Only steps
   Exit Loop If [Get ( FoundCount ) = 1]
End Loop
```

Show/Hide Text Ruler

Category: Windows

Compatibility: Macintosh, Windows, Server, iOS, CWP, IWP, Runtime

Originated In: FileMaker 6.0 or earlier

Options:

- **Specify** enables you to select the action to perform on the Text Ruler:
  - **Show** tells FileMaker Pro to show the text ruler.
  - **Hide** tells FileMaker Pro to hide the text ruler.
  - **Toggle** switches between showing and hiding the text ruler.

Description:

This script step hides or shows the text ruler. Choose the Toggle option to switch the current state of the ruler. The text ruler is used with text fields and to aid in design in Layout mode. It can be used to set tabs and indents for a text area. Hiding the text ruler is sometimes required to save screen space. Unless you have disabled access to menus, users generally can enable the text rulers by choosing View, Formatting Bar, and it may later be desirable to disable the rulers again to save room.

Examples:

```
Allow User Abort [Off]
Set Error Capture [On]
If[Get (ScreenHeight) < 600]
   #Save space by hiding the Formatting Ruler
  Show/Hide Text Ruler [Hide]
End
```

Show/Hide Toolbars

Category: Windows

Compatibility: Macintosh, Windows, Server, iOS, CWP, IWP, Runtime

Originated In: FileMaker 6.0 or earlier

Options:

- **Specify** the action to be performed on the Toolbar:
  - **Lock** prohibits the user from using the Status Toolbar control button to manually show or hide the Status Toolbar.
  - **Show** tells FileMaker Pro to show the Status Toolbar.
  - **Hide** tells FileMaker Pro to hide the Status Toolbar.
  - **Toggle** switches between showing and hiding the Status Toolbar (equivalent to clicking the Status Toolbar control button).

Description:

Show/Hide Toolbars allows for control of the display of the Status Toolbar from scripts.

In databases where it is important to tightly control the user's navigation, it might be desirable to prevent users from using the Status Toolbar for paging through records or to change layouts.

Examples:

```
Allow User Abort [Off]
Set Error Capture [On]
Go to Layout ["Invoice"]
#Show Status Toolbar so the user has access to Continue button
Show/Hide Status Toolbar [Lock; Show]
Enter Preview Mode [Pause]
#Shut the Status Toolbar back down again
Show/Hide Toolbars [Lock; Hide]
Enter Browse Mode [ ]
Go to Layout [Original Layout]
```

Sort Records

Category: Found Sets

Compatibility: Macintosh, Windows, Server, iOS, CWP*, IWP*, Runtime*

Originated In: FileMaker 6.0 or earlier

Options:

- **Perform Without Dialog** suppresses the dialog that lets the user enter a different set of sort instructions.
- **Specify Sort Order** or **Specify** enables you to define the sort order stored with the script step. When Specify Sort Order is not specified, FileMaker Pro uses the most recently executed sort instructions.

Description:

Sort Records sorts the records in the current found set according to specified criteria. Be sure to perform any operations that might change the found set before calling Sort Records. If you sort a repeating field, FileMaker Pro sorts on only the first entry in that field. Sort criteria are saved with individual Sort Records script steps, so any number of sorts can be saved with a single script.

Note that saved sort criteria are relative to the current table context. If the table Contact was the active table when the sort criteria were entered, and fields from Contact are used in the sort order, that table must be active when the sort is executed. If your sort step contains field references that are not valid at the time the step is executed, the invalid field references are ignored. Table context is controlled by the current layout; to change table context, navigate to a layout that is used by the table in question.

The option to display a dialog box is compatible with Instant Web Publishing but is not compatible with Custom Web Publishing.

Examples:

```
Allow User Abort [Off]
Set Error Capture [On]
#Find overdue invoices
Perform Find [Restore]
#Sort by due date and customer
Sort Records [Restore]
Go to Layout ["Invoice"]
Enter Preview Mode [Pause]
Enter Browse Mode [ ]
Go to Layout [Original Layout]
Unsort
```

Sort Records by Field

Category: Found Sets

Compatibility: Macintosh, Windows, Server, iOS, CWP, IWP, Runtime

Originated In: FileMaker 12.0

Options:

- **Specify Target Field** or **Specify** allows for the specification of the field to sort. When this option is not specified, the active field is used, and when there is no active field, error 5 is returned.
- **Specify** defines how the records are to be sorted based on the target field's values and field type with text fields sorted alphabetically, number fields in sequence, and date and time fields sorted chronologically.
  - **Ascending** sorts the records first to last, lowest to highest.
  - **Descending** sorts the records last to first, highest to lowest.
  - **Associated Value List** sorts the records in the order of the values in the value list associated with the field on this layout.

Description:

This script step sorts the current found set of records based on the values in the specified field or currently active field when none is specified. Any previous sort is replaced.

Examples:

```
#Dynamically sort based on user's active field and mod keys
Set Variable [$modKey; Value:Get ( ActiveModifierKeys )]
If [$modKey = 8 or $modKey = 10 //Option or Alt (with or without Caplock)]
   Sort Records by Field [Descending]
Else
   #Try to sort by value list
   Sort Records by Field [ Associated value list
   Set Variable [$error; Value:Get ( LastError )]
   If [$error = 5   //Command is invalid]
      #Could mean there is no active field or
      #no value list assigned to the active field
      #Try to sort ascending
      Sort Records by Field [Ascending]
   End If
End If
#Display message with directions when no field active
Set Variable [ $error; Value:Get ( LastError ) ]
If [ $error = 5   //Command is invalid ]
   Show Custom Dialog [ Title: "Message";
   ➥Message: "Please select a field to sort.";
   ➥Default Button: "OK", Commit: "Yes" ]
End If
```

Speak (Mac OS)

Category: Miscellaneous

Compatibility: Macintosh, Runtime

Originated In: FileMaker 6.0 or earlier

Options:

- **Specify** displays the Speak Options dialog box, where you can set the following options.
  - **Specify Text to Speak** allows for the entry to be spoken, either as literal text or via calculation.
  - **Use Voice** allows for the selection from the various voices available on the computer.
  - **Wait for Speech Completion Before Continuing** tells FileMaker Pro to wait until the speech is completed before continuing with the next script step. If you leave this option unchecked, the script continues while the text is being spoken.

Description:

This script step causes the computer to speak the specified text. You can specify which voice synthesizer to use and whether FileMaker Pro is to wait for the speech to be completed before continuing with the next script step. On a computer without speech capabilities, the script can still be edited, but only the default voice synthesizer is available. `Speak` script steps are not executed when the script is run on a computer without speech capability.

Examples:

```
Speak ["Hello"]
Speak [Get (CurrentDate)]
```

Spelling Options

Category: Miscellaneous

Compatibility: Macintosh, Windows, Server, iOS, CWP, IWP, Runtime

Originated In: FileMaker 6.0 or earlier

Options:

None

Description:

This script step opens the Spelling tab of the File Options dialog box. Use this script step to open the File Options dialog box for users if you have restricted their access to FileMaker Pro menus.

Examples:

```
#A button on a layout calls this script step directly:
Spelling Options
```

Undo/Redo

Category: Editing

Compatibility: Macintosh, Windows, Server, iOS, CWP, IWP, Runtime

Originated In: FileMaker 6.0 or earlier

Options:

- **Specify** allows for the specification of the action to perform:
  - **Undo** reverts the most recent action performed in the file.
  - **Redo** restores the most recent action that was undone in the file.
  - **Toggle** switches between undoing and redoing the last action.

Description:

This script step is used to walk the user backward or forward through the execution sequence of his most recent actions. Multiple actions can be redone or undone, limited only by the user's memory.

Examples:

```
#Undo the most recent 3 actions
Undo/Redo [Undo]
Undo/Redo [Undo]
Undo/Redo [Undo]
```

Unsort Records

Category: Found Sets

Compatibility: Macintosh, Windows, Server, iOS, CWP, IWP, Runtime

Originated In: FileMaker 6.0 or earlier

Options:

None

Description:

This script step restores the found set to its natural order, the order in which the records were created.

Examples:

```
Allow User Abort [Off]
Set Error Capture [On]
Enter Browse Mode []
Unsort Records
Go to Record/Request/Page [First]
```

View As

Category: Windows

Compatibility: Macintosh, Windows, Server, iOS, CWP, IWP, Runtime

Originated In: FileMaker 6.0 or earlier

Options:

- **Specify** allows for the specification of the view action to perform:
  - **View as Form** tells FileMaker Pro to display records page by page on the current layout so that only one record at a time is shown.
  - **View as List** tells FileMaker Pro to display records as records in a list so that the user can see multiple records at once in a list.
  - **View as Table** tells FileMaker Pro to display the records onscreen in a spreadsheet-like grid.
  - **Cycle** switches from the current view type to the next type.

Description:

View As sets the view mode for the current layout. Note that Layout Setup can be used to limit which views are accessible via the View menu, but the View As script step can override those settings and enable you to view a layout in any of the three styles.

Examples:

```
Set Error Capture [On]
Allow User Abort [Off]
Go to Layout ["Contact List"]
View As [View As List]
```

CHAPTER 15

FileMaker Go Specifications

FileMaker Go 12 and FileMaker Go 12 for iPad are part of the FileMaker 12 family and are compatible only with fmp12 files. Using FileMaker Pro 12, you must convert databases created by earlier versions of FileMaker Pro before you can access them with FileMaker Go 12. Likewise, FileMaker Go 12 can access networked files hosted only by FileMaker Pro 12, FileMaker Pro 12 Advanced, FileMaker Server 12, or FileMaker Server 12 Advanced.

Note that previous iterations of FileMaker Go were versioned 1.2.4. FileMaker has elected to designate the latest incarnation of FileMaker Go version 12, skipping ahead to align with the remainder of the product line.

Device Compatibility

FileMaker Go is available exclusively for Apple iOS products.

FileMaker Go 12

FileMaker Go 12 requires iOS 4.3 or greater and is compatible with the following Apple mobile products:

- iPhone 4s
- iPhone 4
- iPhone 3GS
- iPod touch (4th generation)
- iPod touch (3rd generation)
- iPad (3rd generation)
- iPad 2
- iPad

FileMaker Go 12 for iPad

Although the iPad is able to run FileMaker Go, the app is either displayed as a window the size of an iPhone in the center of the screen or zoomed 200% to fill the screen without displaying more content. FileMaker Go for the iPad makes use of the tablet's much larger screen area. Though FileMaker Go 12 has not been optimized for the retina display of the new iPad (3rd generation), objects are displayed at the same size as they are on iPad 2, and text looks especially crisp.

FileMaker Go 12 for iPad requires iOS 4.3 or higher and is compatible with all the versions of the Apple iPad:

- New iPad (3rd generation)
- iPad 2
- iPad

Differences Between FileMaker Go and Pro

FileMaker Go is a full-fledged FileMaker client, intended for the consumption and creation of FileMaker data. It is a thin client and so cannot be used to create a database or modify its structure. You cannot use FileMaker Go to define tables, fields, or relationships, nor modify layouts, scripts, or value lists. FileMaker Go cannot host files for access by other devices.

Limits

Chapter 3, "Specifications and Storage Limits," provides the limits for some of the most important measurable capacities of the FileMaker product line. Table 15.1 reiterates the few specifications in which FileMaker Go differs from FileMaker Pro.

Table 15.1 FileMaker Spec Differences

Characteristic	FileMaker Pro	FileMaker Go
File size	8TB	Limited only by disk space
Files/windows open simultaneously	Limited only by the memory available; recommended not to exceed 125	Limited only by the memory available; recommended not to exceed 20
Text field data limit	2GB (about a billion Unicode characters)	Can display/edit only approximately the first 64,000 characters

Text Fields

Although FileMaker Pro can store and display 2GB of data (about a billion Unicode characters), FileMaker Go can display and edit only the first 64,000 characters. FileMaker Go displays a warning when attempting to edit previously stored data beyond the first 64,000 characters, and if you make a change to the field's data, only the first 64,000 characters are retained.

Container Fields

FileMaker Go supports the new Remote Container functionality of FileMaker 12 when the database is hosted remotely but does not support this feature for a database stored locally on the iOS device. The new thumbnail feature greatly improves the performance when you are working with a hosted database.

FileMaker Go includes many enhancements over the Pro version that enable it to capture media already stored on the iOS device as well as make use of its features to generate content. These enhancements include

- **Camera**—Takes a picture or records a video using the iOS camera (file saved as .jpg or .mov, respectively)
- **Audio**—Makes an audio recording right within FileMaker Go
- **Signature**—Displays a dialog for capturing a signature using the touch screen
- **Photo**—Enables you to select a picture from the iOS photo/video roll
- **Music**—Enables you to select a file from the iTunes library, either an audio (saved as .m4a) or video (saved as .mov) file
- **Files**—Enables you to select any file stored in the FileMaker Go Documents Folder (inserted as whatever type is appropriate for the file)

Interface Feature Differences

FileMaker Go is optimized for the touch interface. Because of the inherent differences between the desktop and iOS operating systems, there are important distinctions in the features of FileMaker Go and FileMaker Pro. The following sections outline the major differences in the user experience.

ToolTips and Graphic State

Positioning the mouse pointer over an object, a common interaction on a PC, has no equivalent when using an iOS device. Because of this, FileMaker Go does not support ToolTips or the new Graphic State feature of FileMaker Pro.

Control Styles

To enter data in FileMaker Go, you use iOS controls. Table 15.2 shows how the Control Styles in FileMaker Pro are represented in FileMaker Go.

Table 15.2 Control Styles

FileMaker Pro		FileMaker Go
Edit box	Text field	iOS keyboard
	Number field	iOS keyboard
	Date field	iOS date picker and iOS keyboard
	Time field	iOS time picker and iOS keyboard
	Timestamp field	iOS date/time picker and iOS keyboard
Drop-down list		iOS list picker control
Auto-complete		
Pop-up menu		
Check box set		Check box set
Radio button set		Radio button set
Drop-down calendar		iOS date picker control

Rich Text

There is no mechanism for manually applying rich text styling to data in FileMaker Go, but most of the basic styles previously applied to field data or text blocks are displayed properly. However, if a field containing rich text is modified using FileMaker Go, all the rich text formatting is lost when the data is committed.

The following text styles are supported: Bold, Italic, Underline, Title Case, Upper Case, Lower Case, Word Underline, and Double Underline (renders as underline). All other rich text styles are unsupported: Highlight, Strike Through, Condense, Extend, Small Caps, Superscript, and Subscript.

Copy/Paste

FileMaker Go supports copy/paste, but not using the standard menu commands. Instead, it uses the iOS mechanism, developed for the touch interface. Double tap a word to select it; FileMaker Go displays options on screen that include Copy. To paste, you tap, hold, and then select the Paste command that appears onscreen.

Spelling

Spell checking is handled by the system's built-in functionality rather than FileMaker Go. As you type, the native auto-complete feature suggests words onscreen. Words not found in the iOS dictionary are marked with a red underline. Double tap a word to select it and then tap the Suggest command to see alternate spellings.

Sorting

There are a few important differences when sorting records in FileMaker Go. The Sort dialog makes available only fields that are on the current layout. A scripted sort that performs without a dialog does not suffer from this limitation.

The other difference involves Table view. When the table's data has already been sorted by two or more columns, clicking a column that is already sorted toggles the sort (between sort ascending, descending, deselected) but retains the sort of the other fields.

Menus

FileMaker Pro uses a standard menu bar across the top of the screen along with contextual menus that appear when you right-click an object. The menus are organized quite differently for FileMaker Go. Table 15.3 lists the menu icons and their menu items.

Table 15.3 FileMaker Go Menus

Icon	Menu Items
(gear icon)	Menu modal dialog Layout [Current Layout Name] View As Show Toolbar Refresh Window Perform Script Print Export Save / Send Settings Send Feedback Help
Contact Details I iPad	Select Layout modal dialog View As: Form, List, Table List of layout folders
Record 3 of 10 (sorted)	Move between records
+/–	Add/Delete pop-up menu Add New Record Duplicate Record Delete Record Delete Found Records... Exit Record
(show/sort icon)	Show/Sort pop-up menu Show All Records Show Omitted Records Omit Records Sort Records Quick Find Enter Find Mode

The Show/Hide Toolbars script step with the "hide" option hides the bottom toolbar.

Custom Menus

Custom Menus, configured using FileMaker Pro Advanced, are only partially supported. Removed menu items are still displayed, but are grayed out and disabled, and additional menu items are not added. You can rename existing FileMaker Go menus, as long as the name does not contain an ampersand (&).

Windows

FileMaker Go, as an iOS app, is required by Apple to always display content in full-screen mode. It cannot display two or more windows side by side or open a smaller window on top of the current window to act as a Dialog or Entry Wizard. The new window types are not supported; the window is always displayed full screen and cannot be positioned off-screen.

Export Records

FileMaker Go 12 now supports the export of records, although not all the file types. FileMaker Go supports the following formats:

- Tab-separated text (.tab)
- Comma-separated text (.csv)
- Merge files (.mer)
- dBASE III and IV DBF files (.dbf)
- HTML Table format (.htm)
- Excel Workbook (.xlsx)

FileMaker Go does *not* support the following data:

- FileMaker Pro files (.fmp12)
- XML files (.xml)

There are a few additional limitations placed on the user to keep the FileMaker Go export records interface as clean and simple as possible:

- The user cannot configure the output character set.
- The user can generally select only from fields available on the current layout.
- Field grouping is supported, with a few exceptions.

Note that scripted exports do not have these same limitations.

You can send the exported file as an email attachment or transfer it to the computer using iTunes.

Saving Records as PDF

To access the Save Records as PDF menu item of FileMaker Pro, you touch the Menu button and select Print. PDF is one of the print options. The PDF option does not provide the option for defining the filename. Instead, it always names the file the same as the current window. However, the scripting engine does not have this limitation.

Script Step Differences

FileMaker Pro 12 added a new iOS filter to the Show Compatibility pop-up on the Edit Script window. When this filter is selected, the script steps that are not supported by FileMaker Go are grayed out. The majority of the unsupported steps correspond to features not supported by FileMaker Go. They include

- The File script steps that are related to development tasks (New File, Convert File, Set Multi-User, Recover File)
- All the Spelling script steps (Check Selection, Check Record, Check Found Set, Correct Word, Spelling Options, Select Dictionary, Edit User Dictionary)
- Most of the Open Menu Item steps because they pertain to developing a database (Open Edit Saved Finds, Open File Options, Open Manage Containers, Open Manage Database, Open Manage Data Sources, Open Manage Layouts, Open Manage Scripts, Open Manage Value Lists, Open Find/Replace, Open Sharing)
- Some Window management script steps because they are not compatible with the full-screen nature of iOS (Move/Resize Window, Arrange Window, Show/Hide Text Ruler)
- Miscellaneous steps related to external applications (Perform AppleScript, Execute SQL, Send Event, Install Plug-In File)
- Enter Preview Mode
- Perform Find/Replace
- Insert from Index
- Save Records as Excel

Script steps that are supported but behave differently when executed on an iOS device are the following:

- Adjust Window—Makes only the window active regardless of the option specified
- Dial Phone—Attempts to pass the specified number to the Phone app

➔ *See "Dial Phone" in Chapter 14, "Script Step Reference," for more information on the options when run on an iOS device.*

- Exit Application—Does not stop FileMaker Go, but instead simply closes all the open databases
- Export Records—Cannot export to the file types FileMaker, XML, or Excel XLS (but Excel's xlsx is supported)
- Import Records—Supports only the option to import from one FileMaker file to another
- New Window—Creates the new window, but always full screen and in view

➔ *For more information, see Chapter 14, "Script Step Reference."*

Security

When a FileMaker file is stored on a local device, it cannot make use of external authentication. This is consistent with FileMaker Pro behavior when it opens a file directly, but is still worth noting. A database that uses external authentication requires FileMaker-imbedded credentials to move the file to the iOS device.

To temporarily bypass the auto open account set in the file preferences, touch and hold the file's name in the file list and then release. FileMaker presents the standard authentication dialog.

Background Behavior

FileMaker Go 12 makes some use of the background feature introduced with iOS 4. When the user moves FileMaker Go into the background, say by clicking the Home button or answering a phone call, FileMaker Go records the user's context in a hibernation file and then suspends the app. FileMaker Go 12 does not remain running in the background because iOS generally freezes background apps. Instead, its processes are suspended and attempt to pick up right where they left off, depending on the authentication rules. This new behavior provides a considerable performance increase when switching between apps over previous versions of FileMaker Go, which simply quit the app after creating the hibernation file.

A suspended FileMaker Go 12 file by default attempts to reconnect without requiring the user to authenticate again. This is the complete opposite of earlier versions. FileMaker 12 replaces the old fmrestorelogin extended privilege with a new extended privilege fmreauthenticate.

The fmreauthenticate privilege can also be appended with a number from 0 to 10,080, which represents the minutes a user may have FileMaker Go in the background before requiring reauthentication. When no number is specified, a grace period of zero is enforced. When the user's privilege set includes more than one of the fmreauthenticate extended privileges, FileMaker uses the shortest grace period specified. See Table 15.4 for examples.

Table 15.4 Sample fmreauthenticate **Extended Privilege**

Extended Privilege	Reauthentication Grace Period
fmreauthenticate	
fmreauthenticate0	0; must always reauthenticate
fmreauthenticate5	5 minutes
fmreauthenticate60	1 hour
fmreauthenticate1440	1 day
fmreauthenticate10080	1 week (maximum grace period)

To preserve the previous behavior when an fp7 file is converted to fmp12, the privilege sets are updated as follows:

- Privilege sets that do *not* contain fmrestorelogin are automatically updated to include fmreauthenticate0.
- The extended privilege fmrestorelogin is automatically removed from all privilege sets.

FileMaker Go requires the credentials to be entered only once for all suspended files that were authenticated with the same username and password.

➔ *For more information on security with FileMaker Go, see Chapter 16, "Designing for FileMaker Go."*

Plug-ins

FileMaker Go does not support plug-ins. Instead you can extend FileMaker Go's abilities by using Open URL to pass data to and receive data from other iOS applications.

➔ *See the Section "Interacting with Other Apps" in Chapter 16 for more information about using the Open URL scheme to interact with other applications.*

CHAPTER 16

Designing for FileMaker Go

FileMaker Go 12 is a full-fledged FileMaker client and can generally run any FileMaker 12 database. Nevertheless, you can greatly improve your users' experience by designing workflows that you optimize for the touch interface. This is especially true when the users will be accessing the database with an iPhone or iPod touch.

Chapter 15, "FileMaker Go Specifications," outlined the Specifications of FileMaker Go and highlighted the differences between it and FileMaker Pro. This chapter delves into design considerations for optimizing performance and usability for systems refined for FileMaker Go.

File Architecture

When you develop specifically for FileMaker Go, begin by determining the answers to some key questions:

- **Will remote users create data, edit data, or only view data?**

  The answer might be different for each table and/or user group. You might find it quite useful to create a spreadsheet that documents the user groups, tables, and their activities.
- **What other activities do remote users need to perform?**

  In addition to a system's existing functions, you will likely identify new workflows made possible by FileMaker Go, such as creating an audio recording of an interview, capturing an electronic signature, taking a photo, mapping a location, or emailing a PDF receipt while still on location.
- **Which data (and how much of it) does each remote user require?**

  Typically, remote users require access to only a small subset of the data accumulated in the primary system over time. Try to limit the data to only what is relevant to their current location and activity.
- **Do the users need the data to be live?**

  A stored set of data that users refresh regularly might be current enough; others might need to have a live connection to their data.

- **How many users will access the data remotely?**

  Some files will have just one user who needs access on the road as well as in his office. In this case, simply moving the FileMaker file between the desktop and the touch device might be acceptable. Often, though, multiple users will need to access data concurrently.

- **How often do users need access?**

  Frequency can affect how much customization you will make to optimize performance for FileMaker Go.

- **Will users have remote connectivity all the time?**

  Users without a consistent remote connection will need data transferred to the touch device. This can further complicate your design when they will be editing existing records.

- **How fast is the user's remote connection?**

  The slower the connection, the more important it is to streamline the file's functions to optimize performance.

- **Will users use the iPad, iPhone, or iPod touch (and which version)?**

  Optimizing layouts to match the screen size of the device, especially the iPhone and iPod touch, is the single most important step to improving user efficiency.

The answers to these questions influence the kind of file architecture you employ. Although users might initially say they want to do everything on their touch device that they can do at their desk, usually when you probe a little further, they identify a handful of activities that are especially suited to the mobile device.

Now that you have a general scope of the requirements, you can evaluate the different models available.

Model 1: An Integrated File

Perhaps the easiest model is to simply incorporate additional layouts to your existing database, optimizing them for the specific touch device. You then update the scripts with branching for the platform.

Identifying the Mobile User

Get (SystemPlatform) returns 3 when performed on the mobile device.

Get (ApplicationVersion) returns Go 12.*x.x* when run on the iPhone or iPod touch and returns Go_iPad 12.*x.x* when run on the iPad.

FileMaker has elected to designate the latest incarnation of FileMaker Go version 12.*x* to align with the remainder of the FileMaker family. Note that the FileMaker 11 compatible version of FileMaker Go was bumped from version 1.x to 11.*x*.

This model enables you to add touch-specific layouts as time permits, while still providing users access to the remainder of the system using the original interface. The FileMaker 12 starter solutions are great examples of this model.

Generally, the integrated file approach is best suited to solutions hosted by FileMaker Server or FileMaker Pro. Although it is possible to transfer an integrated file to the touch device, the file could be large and more difficult to move around. Of course, you need to synchronize any data you enter in the local copy or transfer the entire file back to your computer.

Model 2: A Separate Hosted File

Generally, you can achieve optimum performance in FileMaker Go by creating a separate database for the touch interface that contains only the things necessary to support the remote user's workflows. The resulting file is smaller and so offers better performance on the mobile hardware. Keep in mind that FileMaker 12 files can have external references to other FileMaker 12 files, so the touch database file can still access and change the data stored in the primary file.

For larger systems, you might want to consider taking this approach a step further by creating a separate touch database for each group of users. For example, the remote activities of sales reps are likely quite different from those of order fulfillment workers in a warehouse. By separating these functions into two department-specific files, Sales.fmp12 and Ship.fmp12, you can further reduce each individual file's size. Figure 16.1 illustrates the architecture design of just such a system, with both department-specific files having external file references to the primary Biz.fmp12 file.

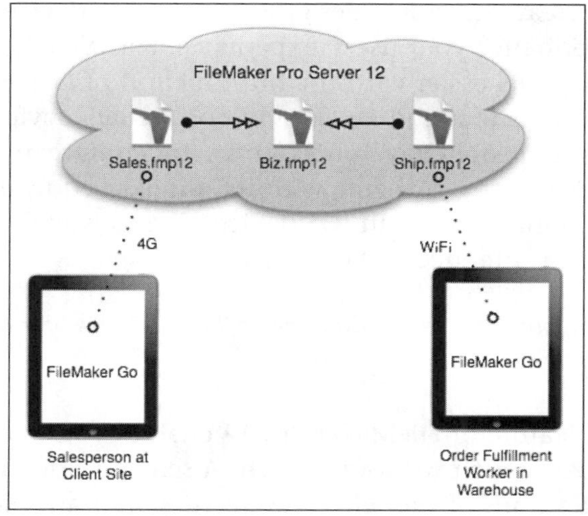

Figure 16.1
A database system composed of three files: Biz.fmp12, which contains all the data tables and FileMaker Pro interface, and Sales.fmp12 and Ship.fmp12, which are department-specific interfaces that include external references to Biz.fmp12 and are accessed using iPads.

Model 3: A Separate Local File

When the user does not have consistent broadband access, it becomes necessary to deploy the FileMaker file locally, storing it on the touch device. This can be the case when the user

- Travels to areas with spotty coverage
- Visits large, dense facilities that interfere with cell reception
- Is equipped with a Wi-Fi–only device

Regardless of the reason, it is common to create a separate file with its own interface and data tables and then populate it with a subset of data. As the name implies, you deploy the file to the local device. The challenges with this model come with keeping the local file current and synchronizing data. Read more about both these subjects in the "Sync Strategies" section later in this chapter.

Model 4: Hybrid

You also are able to create a hybrid system that includes a separate interface file for the touch device, which you then deploy locally. This approach is most effective in situations in which the interface graphics and other elements are large, so storing them in the local file increases performance. The main disadvantage is that this model requires effort to deploy updates to the file. Find out more about deployment strategies later in this chapter.

Designing Layouts for FileMaker Go

Whether you choose to create a separate file for the touch device or add new features to your primary database, creating layouts designed for the iOS device is the most effective action you can take to enhance your users' experience. Fortunately, FileMaker Pro 12 makes developing iOS layouts easier with the introduction of *layout themes*. FileMaker designed themes with names that end in "Touch" for the iOS device. FileMaker Pro 12 includes five touch themes: Cool Gray Touch, Onyx Touch, Ocean Touch, River Touch, and Wave Touch. Compare a touch theme with its standard equivalent to see the optimizations FileMaker recommends for an iOS device. The Classic theme is the best one to use when creating a report intended to be printed.

➔ *See the section "Layout Themes" in Chapter 5, "Layout Tools," for more information on working with themes.*

The new Screen Stencil feature of FileMaker Pro 12 enables you to create layouts sized for the iPad, iPhone, and iPod touch without a hitch. A screen stencil is a kind of guideline that represents the dimensions of the selected screen as an orange box. Four of the standard devices available are for the iPad and iPhone, both landscape and portrait views. The Screen Stencil tool is available in the layout bar, as shown in Figure 16.2. You can display multiple screen stencils at a time.

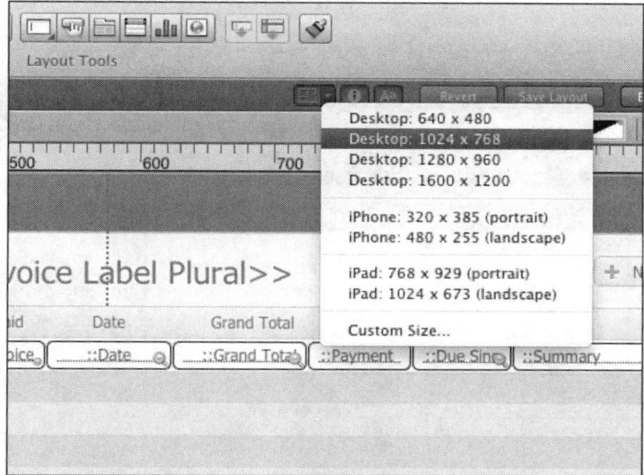

Figure 16.2
Screen stencils display orange guides onscreen for the specified dimensions.

Making full use of the screen real estate and still adjusting appropriately when the user rotates the device can be a challenge. One approach is to constrain the layout's objects to the area where the portrait and landscape views overlap. In Figure 16.3, the iPad landscape and portrait stencils are both displayed, making it easy to position objects only in the area where the two intersect. Utilize the autosizing feature to fill the remainder of the screen. Enable the left and right anchors to stretch the object horizontally; enable the top and bottom anchors to stretch the object vertically. You can also create the illusion of objects sliding into view by stacking objects and setting the right anchor on the front object while disabling the left anchor on the back object. Likewise, you can slide a background object down into view by enabling the bottom anchor and disabling the top anchor.

➔ *See the "Autosizing" section in Chapter 5 for more information on working with object anchors.*

Of course, you can simply include a button that navigates to a layout optimized to the device's current orientation. The script can use the functions `Get ( WindowContentWidth )` and `Get ( WindowContentHeight )` to determine the current situation and navigate to a more appropriate layout. Keep in mind that the toolbar, which can be displayed along the bottom of the screen, takes up 44 pixels of the window height.

When we assign a value list to a field, our preference is to perform entry using the Pop-Up Menu with the Allow Entry of Other Values setting disabled. This causes FileMaker to display the iOS List Picker without opening the onscreen keyboard. Unfortunately, there is no way to suppress the display of the onscreen keyboard when the date, time, or timestamp pickers are displayed.

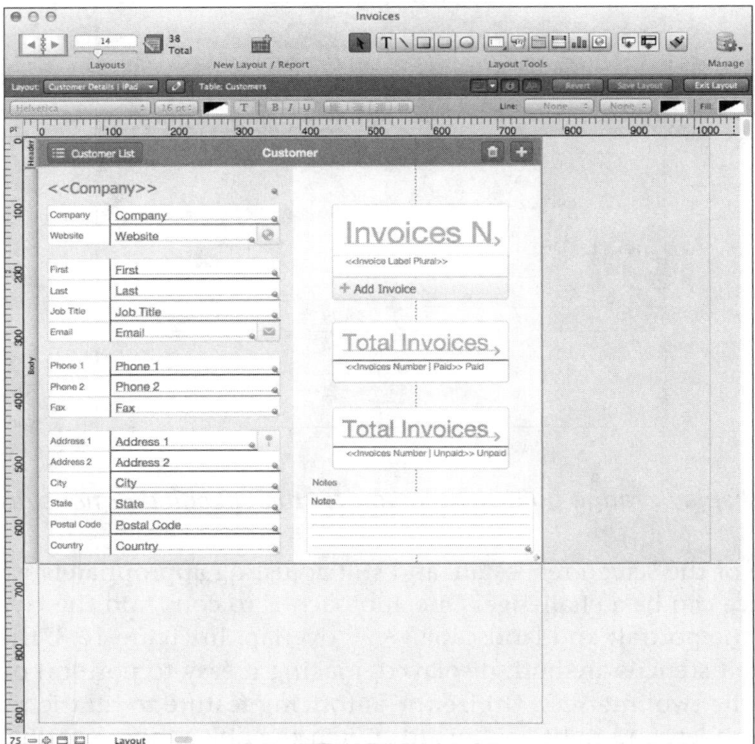

Figure 16.3
By displaying both the iPad landscape and portrait stencils, you can easily see the area that will display completely, regardless of the device orientation. You can use object anchors to have some objects stretch to fill the space.

You might want to leave open space at the bottom of form view layouts so that the onscreen keyboard does not overlap the active field, causing FileMaker Go to slide the fields up.

Frankly, we avoid displaying the keyboard whenever possible for date, time, timestamp, and number fields by creating our own entry tools using buttons. For example, when you tap into a number field, FileMaker Go displays the iOS number keyboard. Instead, we might use a script trigger to display a layout or hidden tab object that includes buttons arranged like a number keypad. (You can hide the tabs of a tab object by configuring it with a fixed tab width of 0 points.)

Disabling Pinch-to-Zoom

FileMaker Go enables, by default, the pinch-to-zoom feature of iOS. Although it might be the desired behavior in some situations, we find that users often become frustrated by accidentally zooming when they're trying to activate a field or tap a button. You can disable pinch-to-zoom by executing the script step Set Zoom Level [100%] and selecting the Lock option.

Object Sizes

The user's primary data-entry tool while working with FileMaker Go is a finger. We recommend you make fields and buttons quite a bit larger than you generally would for the desktop. Table 16.1 shows the recommend sizes for common layout elements.

Table 16.1 FileMaker Go Layout Object Size Guidelines

Fonts	The Apple iPhone Human Interface Guidelines call for "17px to 22px fonts". You can use smaller fonts for labels.
Buttons	Each button's tap area should be a minimum of 32 points. Be sure to allow plenty of room between buttons.
Fields	Size fields to a minimum of height of 32 points.
Portals	Set portal rows to 34–42 points tall. The scrollbars will auto-resize larger when the portal is active.

Font Families

Apple provides 58 font families with iOS 5.0, and it does not allow you to install additional fonts. Of these, only the following 5 font families are installed across all the platforms supported by FileMaker Go 12 and FileMaker Pro 12—iOS (4.3/5.0), Apple OS X (10.6/10.7), and Windows (XP/Vista/7):

- Georgia
- Times New Roman
- Arial
- Verdana
- Courier New

Of this list, Verdana renders the most similarly across all three platforms.

Warning

Fonts render quite differently on FileMaker Go than they do on FileMaker Pro. Be sure to test thoroughly.

In addition, the following font families are included with Apple OS X and iOS, but not Windows:

- American Typewriter
- Arial Rounded Bold
- Apple Gothic
- Baskerville
- Chalkboard
- Copperplate (not including in iOS 4.3 for iPhone/iPod touch)
- Courier

- Gill Sans (not including in iOS 4.3 for iPhone/iPod touch)
- Helvetica
- Helvetica Neue
- Marker Felt
- Papyrus (not including in iOS 4.3 for iPhone/iPod touch)
- Trebuchet MS
- Zapfino
- Zapf Dingbats

It is interesting to note that the FileMaker desktop themes use Tahoma as the default font, a typeface that is not even available in iOS. The touch themes use Helvetica Neue as the default font. It converts to Arial when displayed on a Windows computer.

Note

Consult Apple for a complete listing of the iOS 5 fonts with their version numbers at http://support.apple.com/kb/HT4980.

Other Layout Tips

The following are a few other tips for optimizing layouts for display in FileMaker Go:

- Avoid requiring users to scroll or swipe in two directions.
- Radio buttons and check box sets wrap very differently on FileMaker Go than on the desktop, so test thoroughly.
- As much as possible, use native FileMaker objects rather than pictures for interface elements to increase performance.
- Optimize graphics for the device.
- Limit the number of objects on each layout to only what's essential, especially when designing for the iPhone and iPod touch.
- Create a high-contrast interface for systems used in bright light.

Optimizing Workflows

Designing for FileMaker Go is all about optimizing workflows. Take the time to fully think through the activities that your users will perform on the touch device and then design those workflows to take advantage of FileMaker's strong suit. FileMaker is particularly adept at performing finds, executing scripts, and working with variables. On the other hand, it is less efficient when working with data from relationships deeper than one table away, excessive sorting, and complex value lists.

The iPhone, iPod touch, and iPad are successful because they are incredibly intuitive to use. A person picks up an iOS device and instinctively knows to swipe a list or tap to select items. As a FileMaker Go developer, you are at your best when you develop workflows that behave as the user expects.

Apple offers great resources to familiarize developers with the iOS Human Interface Design. It is well worth the time to give these resources a read. The following link goes to a concise overview of these guides as part of Apple's guide for iOS developers:

https://developer.apple.com/library/ios/#referencelibrary/GettingStarted/RoadMapiOS/HumanInterfaceDesign/HumanInterfaceDesign.html

➔ *You can find more links to Apple resources in the "FileMaker Go and iOS" section in Appendix A, "Additional Resources."*

Minimalist Approach

Minimalism is the key to designing for FileMaker Go. Focus on simple, task-centric workflows. Consider taking a wizard approach to your tasks. Walk the user through a series of screens with each screen including just a few fields.

The interface of FileMaker Go itself provides great examples of streamlining workflows for the touch device. Consider the export function that's now supported in FileMaker Go 12. The FileMaker engineers simplified the Export Setup dialog (see Figure 16.4) by leaving the Type and Fields lists off this dialog. Instead, the user readily understands that she can tap the arrow to display the next screen to configure these settings.

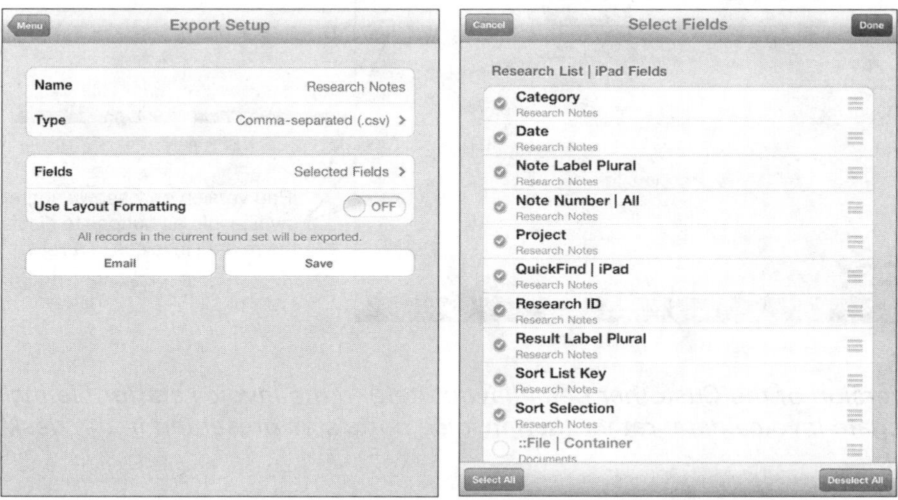

Figure 16.4

The Export Setup dialog (left) is a great example of a simplified interface that clearly presents the options available to the user. When the user taps the arrow in the Fields field, the Select Fields dialog (right) is displayed. It is also streamlined for the touch device.

Space is at a premium for FileMaker Go layouts. Consider developing workflows that take the user to a List view of child records rather than displaying a portal. An excellent example of this technique is available in the Invoice starter solution that comes with FileMaker Pro 12. Instead of displaying an invoice portal like the desktop version of the Customer detail layout, Figure 16.5 shows the iPad version, which includes only aggregate information along with a button to display an Invoice list.

List view displays more quickly than long value lists derived from field values. You can increase performance by assigning an OnObjectEnter script trigger to the field to display a List view instead of a value list. The executed script can navigate to a List view, pause to allow the user to tap a button on the record to select the value, and then return the user to the original layout.

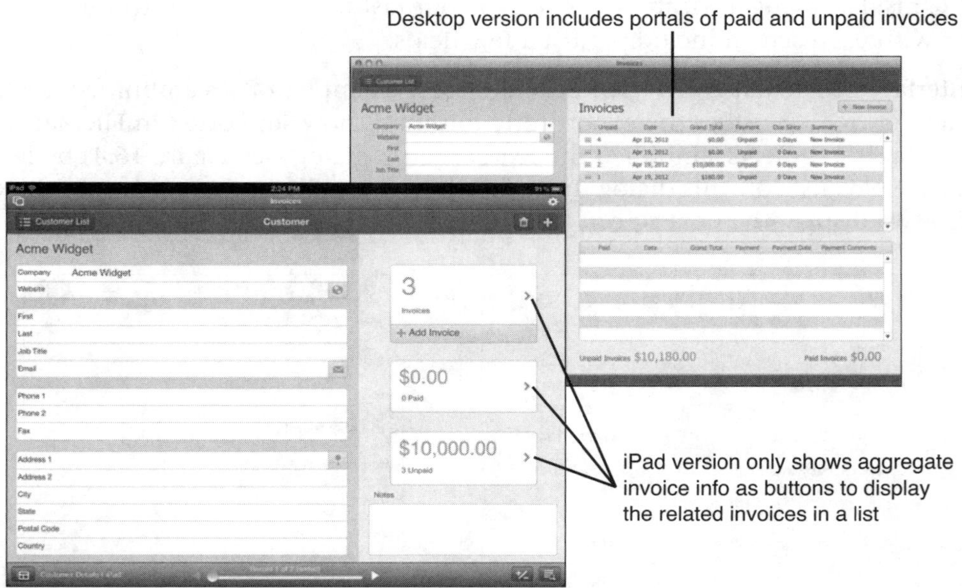

Figure 16.5
The iPad version of the Customer detail layout (left) in the Invoice starter file including only aggregate Invoice data, rather than Invoice portals as presented in the desktop version (right).

The Invoice starter file also has an example of using a List view in place of a value list. Notice the pencil icon next to the company name in Figure 16.6. When you tap this button, a script switches the view to the Customer list, where you can select the customer assigned to the invoice by tapping the row. In cases in which there are many customers, the list renders much faster than a value list, and the list has the additional benefits of enabling you to filter the list and specify the sort.

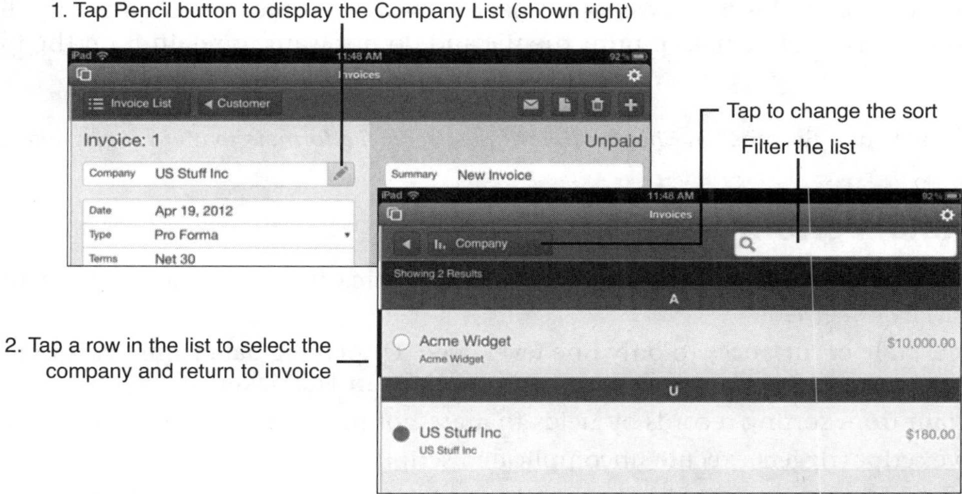

Figure 16.6
In the Invoice starter file, you assign an invoice by clicking the Pencil button, which causes the display of a Customer list.

Server-side Procedures

Some procedures are just not practical to run on the touch device, due to the limited processor power, the possibility of a lost network connection, or because doing so requires a script step not supported by FileMaker Go. Consider processing these procedures as a server-side function.

A server-side function entails the FileMaker Go user making a request that another FileMaker client processes. The most common client is to configure FileMaker Server to perform a scheduled script. However, for actions that utilize script steps not supported by the server, you can set up a "bot" computer, which is a PC or Mac running FileMaker Pro that uses an OnTimer script to automate the processing.

For example, adding up a large number of records might take quite some time using FileMaker Go. However, you can greatly increase the performance by using a scheduled script on the server to aggregate the data on a regular basis and store it in a temporary table that is then available to mobile users. You can use the temporary table as the data source for charts or other reporting purposes.

Export Procedures

FileMaker Go 12 can export records in a variety of formats, but iOS allows you to save the file in only two places. You can save the file to the FileMaker documents folder, which is the default location and the only option when you perform the Export menu step. When you execute a script that contains an export step, FileMaker Go also allows you to save the file to its temporary directory. We recommend you save the file to the temporary directory when you are going to email or print the file and do not want to retain it on the touch device.

➔ *See "Export Records" in Chapter 15 for the specific file formats that are supported.*

Additional Performance Tips

The following are a few additional suggestions for increasing performance of a database built for FileMaker Go:

- Limit table occurrences to only one level deep. Displaying data from deeper table occurrence references is generally slow, especially in FileMaker Go.
- Refrain from sorting records by fields that are not part of the current layout's context.
- Have script triggers execute uncomplicated scripts.
- Set FileMaker to generate image thumbnails for container field data. You configure it by selecting File, Manage, Containers and using the Thumbnail tab.

Deploying Files

There are several ways to transfer a FileMaker file to the touch device. The following sections examine each and consider their advantages and disadvantages.

Email

One of the simplest ways to load a file onto the touch device is to simply email it as an attachment. When you tap the email attachment, iOS asks if you want to open the file in FileMaker Go. This deployment strategy alerts the user that a new file is available and makes it quite easy for the user to install the file.

When a file with the same name already exists on the device, the system automatically appends a number to the name so that it does not overwrite the earlier version. This naming system can cause confusion because the user has multiple copies of the file on his device and risks entering data in multiple versions. We suggest including clear, step-by-step instructions in the email to remind users to delete the older file before opening the new version.

iTunes

You can transfer FileMaker files to the device using iTunes. Connect the iPhone, iPad, or iPod touch to iTunes, either by a USB cable or via Wi-Fi, and add the file to the File Sharing section near the bottom of the App tab. In the File Sharing section, select FileMaker Go 12 from the App list and then load the file in the FileMaker Go Documents area. If your iOS device also has an earlier version of FileMaker Go installed, each app has its own documents.

Unlike the email transfer, iTunes displays an alert when a file of the same name is already loaded on the device. You then have the option to replace the file or cancel. One downside to this deployment strategy is that it requires each user to initiate the process.

Web Download

Another easy way to transfer files is to download them from a website using Safari on the touch device. The website can be publicly available or secured so that the user is required to authenticate to gain access. Unfortunately, this method has the same disadvantage as deploying via email. Safari does not replace an existing file but instead appends a serial number to the file's name.

Container Field

FileMaker Go 12 supports the Export Field Contents script step. This allows for an interesting deployment scenario. You can use a hosted FileMaker file as a kind of dispatcher. It includes a container field in which you store the entire FileMaker file you want to deploy to the touch device. When you export the contents of the container field as a script step, FileMaker Go saves the file to its documents folder and overwrites an existing file of the same name.

The following example exports the Contacts.fmp12 file stored in a container field, opens the file, and, if successful, closes the original file:

```
Set Variable [$fileName; Value:"file:Contacts.fmp12"]
Export Field Contents [Resources::File; "$fileName"]
Open URL [No dialog; "FMP://~/Contacts.fmp12"]
If [Get ( LastError ) = 0]
  Close File [Current File]
End File
```

You can further enhance the preceding script so that it creates a log record when the user downloads the file; a log is handy for confirming that all users have downloaded the latest version.

You can also develop a workflow in which you prepare a different copy of the file for each of the users, loaded with the subset of data needed for their work, and store it in a container field on a table with one record per user, department, or group.

Sync Strategies

Database synchronization is the process of merging two or more data sets into a unified data set. For the FileMaker developer, a *data set* typically refers to a complete table or FileMaker file, but it can even be a subset of records or fields.

The best sync approach is to avoid the need entirely by using a hosted file. Unfortunately, that might not always be possible. Developing a synchronization strategy becomes critical when some of your FileMaker Go users require offline access to the file. FileMaker does not provide a built-in mechanism to synchronize data between files. The following sections look at some approaches to synchronizing FileMaker data.

One-way Synchronization

In one-way synchronization, one copy of the data is the master, and each other copy is a slave that is refreshed on a regular basis. When you can limit the changes to each data set to just one system, synchronization routines are much easier to manage. Each data set can be an individual field, record, table, or entire FileMaker file.

When the data set is an entire FileMaker file, the sync procedure can be much easier. Simply distribute an updated copy of the file to the touch device. Technically, this solution is not synchronization; it really just involves file deployment. (Consult the "Deploying Files" section earlier in this chapter for methods of deploying a file.) Consider grouping your tables into separate files so that each file has only one master to eliminate synchronization. Each file can include table occurrences to the other files with read-only privileges.

When the data set is an individual table, record, or field, you need to develop a scripted routine to manage the sync. For most applications, FileMaker Server or FileMaker Pro hosts the primary file, whereas the touch devices contain a local file running in FileMaker Go. While the touch device has network access, the FileMaker Go user initiates a script that deletes the older records and refreshes the table with the latest data.

In the following example, FileMaker Server 12 hosts the Invoice.fmp12 file and makes it available on the wide area network (WAN), and the file SalesTool.fmp12 is local on each salesperson's iPad. SalesTool includes an external file reference to the Invoice file. In the SalesTool file, table occurrences that start with "loc" are for tables that live in the local SalesTool file, whereas those that start with "srv" are for tables from the server's Invoice file.

Each morning, while the salesperson has a network connection via 4G, 3G, or Wi-Fi, she opens the SalesTool and executes the Refresh Customers script. The script deletes all the records in the locCustomers table and then imports her srvCustomers records.

```
# 1. PREP: Get the salesperson's ID, already stored as a preference
Go to Layout ["utl__locPrefs" (srvCustomers)]
If[Is Empty ( locPrefs::Rep_ID )]
  Show Custom Dialog ["Message"; "Please enter your Rep ID in the preferences first."]
  Exit Script [False]
End If
Set Variable [$repID; Value: locPrefs::Rep_ID]
#
# 2. DELETE: empty the locCustomer table
Go to layout["utl__locCustomers" (locCustomers)]
Show All Records
If [Get ( FoundCount ) > 0]
  Delete All Records [No dialog]
```

```
End If
#
# 3. FIND: Customers in the server's data that are assigned to this Rep
Go to Layout ["utl__srvCustomer" (srvCustomer)]
# Action is "Find Records" where srvCustomer::Rep_ID = $repID
Set Error Capture [On]
Perform Find [Restore]
Set Error Capture [Off]
If [Get ( FoundCount ) = 0]
  Go to Layout["Home" (locPrefs)]
  Show Custom Dialog ["Message"; "There are no customers assigned to " & $repID & "."]
  Exit Script [False]
End If
#
# 4. IMPORT: srvCustomers into locCustomers
Import Records [No dialog; "SalesTool.fmp12"; Add; Mac Roman]
#
# 5. CLEAN UP
Go to Layout ["Home" (locPrefs)]
Close File ["Invoices"]
Set Field [locPrefs::refreshed_Customers; Get (CurrentHostTimeStamp)]
Show Custom Dialog ["Refresh Complete"; "The local Customer table has been refreshed
➥ with all your clients."
```

The preceding example uses the Import script step. It's the fastest method when the data set you need to replicate is from a single table. However, if the data is for a set of records that cross more than one table, say an order with its items, a better practice is to post all the records as a single transaction.

➔ *See the "Transactional Model" section later in this chapter for more information on posting a group of records as a single event.*

Notice that in #3 of the preceding example, the script finds only those customers assigned to the user. By importing the subset of data that is relevant to the user's immediate needs, the script takes less time to execute and the file uses less memory.

The master of a data set can change over time. In our example, the salespeople enter new orders into the SalesTool file running on their iPads. The salesperson is the master of the pending orders and can make changes as needed. However, after the salesperson posts his new orders to the primary system, he relinquishes his master rights and cannot change the order.

The one-way synchronization model provides a very clean sync strategy, requiring no conflict resolution. Keep in mind that it is possible to have a series of one-way synchronizations, some going one direction and some going the other, between files. As long as each data set is modifiable by only a single system, it requires only a one-way sync.

Two-way Synchronization

Two-way synchronization is necessary when the same data is editable in more than one copy of the file. Our best advice for dealing with a two-way sync is to avoid it if possible. We suggest that you instead develop workflows that employ one-way synchronization, combined with a procedure for submitting change requests to the data master. For example, although the salesperson might become aware of a typo in a product name or description, it might be better for her to submit an email to the merchandise department requesting the update than to allow all salespeople to make changes to product records in FileMaker Go and then support the required two-way sync.

A good approach to the two-way sync is to compare each record's creation and modification timestamps to the timestamp of the last synchronization. Be sure to take into account the time zones of the systems. Our best advice is to always store data in the time zone of the primary server and have all other systems calculate accordingly.

There are three types of data modifications to manage: creation, deletion, and editing. The best practice is to consider one copy of the data as the primary and synchronize all other copies to it. Think of the primary file as the hub of a wheel and the others as the spokes. A good approach is to consider getting a current data set on the touch device and pushing data changes back to the server as two distinct functions. Then you can handle the download as a one-way sync with a full replace of the touch device's data.

In very general terms, these are the components of this type of two-way synchronization strategy:

- A method for noting records deleted in one system so that you can systematically purge them from the other. A good approach is to use a delete log table, where you note the table name and primary key of the deleted records. Then during synchronization, you can delete the corresponding records in the primary system.
- A method for posting new records created on the touch device to the primary database. You can accomplish this by finding records with a creation timestamp that is more recent than the last sync timestamp.
- A method for posting touch device data changes back to the primary database that includes conflict resolution.
- A method for insuring the primary key of each record is unique, even when records are created on more than one device.

> ➔ *FileMaker 12 introduces the new function Get (UUID), which returns a unique 16-byte Universally Unique Identifier. See Chapter 10, "Calculation Functions," for more information.*

By far the most difficult aspect of a two-way synchronization is conflict resolution. A conflict occurs when users edit a record in both databases. Any two-way synchronization scheme must include clearly defined conflict resolution rules. Your system can simply ignore the changes made in one database or the other, or alert the user to the conflict and provide a means to specify which changes to keep.

Transactional Model

Network interruptions occur quite often on the mobile device. To make matters worse, iOS apps are required to hibernate immediately when the user presses the Home button or answers a phone call. When you post FileMaker data stored on the touch device to the server, you usually want it to go as a single transaction, meaning all the records make it to the server or none at all. When FileMaker Go suddenly hibernating interrupts your sync script, it could leave your primary database in an incomplete state.

There are two techniques to ensure that a group of records transfers as one transaction: through a portal and as a single text block.

Portal Transaction

The portal is the FileMaker object that supports the transactional model. You can create, modify, or delete multiple related records through one or more portals, and FileMaker does not save the changes until the layout's record is committed. Should one of the records you are attempting to change be locked, you can simply revert the record, and the entire transaction is canceled. Most importantly, if the script is interrupted by a dropped network connection or the user presses the Home button, nothing is changed in the database.

Requirements

The following settings are necessary to perform a transaction using a portal:

- The layout's Save Record Changes Automatically setting (assigned in the Layout Setup dialog) must be *deselected*.
- To create records as a transaction, enable the Allow Creation of Records in This Table via This Relationship option for the child tables.
- To delete records as a transaction, turn on the Delete Related Records in This Table When a Record Is Deleted in the Other Table option for the child tables.

Additional Tips

The following are additional tips for creating a scripted transaction:

- You can use a text field populated with a carriage return–delimited list of key values to create a relationship to multiple related records.
- Assign an object name to the portal and then use the `Go to Object` script step to activate the correct portal. When you're in the portal, you can use the `Go to Portal Row` script step to recurs the rows.
- Changes made through a relationship are committed as a single transaction, even when you break the relationship by changing the current record's match field value. Even though you can no longer see the portal's record, FileMaker does not save its changes until you commit the record.

Text Block Transfer

Another option is to use a server-side script to perform the transaction script. In this method, a script in the FileMaker Go file is used to compile the record changes into a single text string, which is then submitted to the FileMaker server for processing. The new ExecuteSQL function can make light work of this task.

The following script collects all the invoices that are no longer marked as pending, including the items stored in the table Invoice Data, as a text block and loads it to a Queue table on the server:

```
#1. FIND INVOICES where status is not Pending
Go TO LAYOUT ["Invoices" (Invoices)]
Set Error Capture [On]
Perform Find [Restore]  //Omit Invoice::Status = Pending
Set Error Capture [Off]
If [Get ( FoundCount ) = 0]
  Show Custom Dialog ["Message"; "There are no Invoices that
    ➥do not have the status 'pending'."]
  Exit Script [Result: False]
End If
#
#2. BUILD TEXT BLOCK containing Invoices including their items
Set Variable [$textBlock; Value:
  ➥"<Invoices>¶" &
  ➥ExecuteSQL ( "SELECT * FROM Invoices WHERE Status <> Pending"; "|"; ¶ ) &
  ➥ "¶</Invoices>" & "¶¶" &
  ➥"<Invoice Data>¶" &
  ➥ExecuteSQL ( "SELECT * FROM \"Invoice Data\" D  INNER JOIN \"Invoices\" V
  ➥ON D.\"Invoice ID\" = V.\"Invoice ID\"  WHERE  V.Status <> ?" ;
  ➥"|" ; ¶ ; "Pending" ) & ¶ &"</Invoice Data>"
#
#3. POST TO QUEUE
Go to Layout ["dev_Queue"]
New Record/Request
Set Field [Queue::TextBlock; $textBlock]
Commit Records/Requests [No dialog]
#
#4. PURGE POSTED INVOICES
Go to Layout ["Invoices" (Invoices)]
Delete All Records [No dialog]
#
#5. CLOSE QUEUE FILE
Go to Layout [original layout]
Close File["Assets"]
```

➔ *For more information on the* ExecuteSQL *function, see Chapter 10, "Calculation Functions."*

A scheduled script on the FileMaker Server finds unprocessed Queue records, parses the Queue::TextBlock field, and posts the changes to the primary database using the portal transaction method.

This method is especially suited to workflows where the FileMaker Go user does not need to refresh her local database right away with the synchronized data. The preceding sample script is just such a situation. However, if the FileMaker Go user is posting changes to a customer record and then wants to immediately pull down a refreshed set of data, it is probably better to perform the transaction directly using a portal.

Security Plan

FileMaker's internal security accounts work as expected when accessed by FileMaker Go, whether accessing a hosted or local file. You must add internal accounts to a file that utilizes external authentication before transferring the file to the local device. However, FileMaker Go can access files hosted on FileMaker Server via external authentication.

FileMaker Go supports the automatic login feature, configured on the Open tab of the File Options dialog, as long as it is set to use a FileMaker type account. However, we strongly advise you configure a file to auto-open only when there are no serious consequences if the data falls into the hands of a stranger.

Developing a security plan for FileMaker Go is about finding the balance between user convenience and data security. Issues to consider include the following:

- Is the data of a sensitive nature?
- Are there security measures required by law for the handling of this data?
- Will one or many people use each touch device?
- What are the consequences of a stolen touch device?
- How valuable are the business rules codified in the scripts and workflows of the solution?

Always remember that authorized users of the system initiate the majority of security breaches. Carefully analyze your security risks and the consequences of a failure.

The following sections make general recommendations based on common security needs.

Low Security

A low security solution has little to no consequences if the database falls into the wrong hands. The information might be a common reference or public knowledge. These are our recommendations for a low security system:

- You can use shorter passwords, perhaps only six digits, and allow all digits to be numbers or letters.

- You can lengthen the re-authentication grace period to as long as you like.
- Whether multiple people share the device does not really matter because the data is of little value.

High Security

We would consider a system that houses data protected under privacy laws or other regulations as definitely requiring high security. In addition, a solution's data, scripts, and workflows might be highly valuable proprietary business knowledge that could cause damage if lost to a competitor. This type of system also warrants high security.

- Require each touch device to use an iOS Passcode Lock, do not enable the Simple Passcode option, set the Require Passcode option to Immediately, and enable the Erase Data feature.
- Configure each privilege set with the extended privilege fmreauthenticate0 so users are always required to re-authenticate.
- Provide an account for each user and require a password of 12 characters that include at least one of each of the following: an uppercase letter, a lowercase letter, a number, and a special character, such as an exclamation point (!).
- Whenever possible, host the file using FileMaker Server; if the touch device is lost or stolen, the file cannot fall into the wrong hands.
- Host a database using only FileMaker Server, enable its Secure Connection feature (see the "Secure Connections to FileMaker Server" section later in this chapter), and set the auto timeout feature to a short duration.
- Store the Persistent ID for each touch device and during your login script use the Get (PersistentID) function to validate each user.
- If the file must be loaded on the touch device, consider using FileMaker Pro Advanced 12 to permanently remove all the [Full Access] accounts from the file. This makes it impossible for a thief to use some kind of cracking tool to replace the [Full Access] accounts with a new password.

Note

Be sure to make a copy of the file before removing the [Full Access] passwords; otherwise, you will no longer be able to modify the file's schema.

- For some very secure information, such as credit card numbers, provide the mobile users only write access to the field, entered using a Custom dialog with the field displayed using the password character.
- Disable the privilege for FileMaker Go users to save a copy of the file and do not allow users to email the file as an attachment.
- Limit the file access using the FileMaker file security so that users must have [Full Access] privileges to make external file references to your file. This feature blocks authenticated users from circumventing the interface and business rules you enforce via scripts and script triggers.

- If possible, require your FileMaker Go users to connect through a virtual private network (VPN) before accessing a hosted database. You can configure the VPN connection in the General tab of the Settings app.

Medium Security

Medium security is anything that falls between high and low security. It is really quite subjective. You might consider a solution medium security when it contains important business data such as sales information or a client mailing list but does not contain data that is protected by law or federal regulation. Here are some recommendations for medium security files; you can apply other recommendations from the high security group as desired:

- Require each touch device to use an iOS Passcode Lock although you might allow users to choose the Simple Passcode option. Set the Require Passcode option to a few minutes and enable the Erase Data feature.
- Configure each privilege set using the extended privilege fmreauthenticate10, allowing a grace period of no more than 10 minutes.
- Provide an account for each user and require a password of six or eight characters that include at least one of each of the following: an uppercase letter, a lowercase letter, and numbers.
- When the FileMaker Server hosts the database, set the Auto Logout When Idle setting for accounts accessed by FileMaker Go to 10 to 30 minutes.

Secure Connections to FileMaker Server

FileMaker Server is equipped with the capability to use Secure Sockets Layer (SSL) to encrypt the data passed between it and the FileMaker client. You can enable this feature by opening the FileMaker Server Admin Console and selecting Configuration, Database Server, Security and enabling the Secure Connections to Database Server check box.

There is a performance trade-off for enabling secure connections. In the past, many developers found the performance hit to be unacceptable and rarely enabled it. However, FileMaker Server 12 provides much improved performance, greatly reducing the performance cost in most cases, so we advise you to consider enabling this feature whenever possible.

Keep in mind that when you enable the secure connection setting, FileMaker Server 12.0v2 will not encrypt interactive container data so that the file can be streamed.

Implications of the Background Behavior

As we've mentioned before, iOS apps are required to immediately suspend when the user presses the Home button, answers a phone call, or puts the device to sleep. FileMaker Go 12 now takes advantage of the multitasking capabilities introduced by Apple with iOS 4. When you press the Home button while using FileMaker Go, the app attempts to generate a hibernation file, moves to the background, and saves your database files in a suspended state. FileMaker Go is not running in the background; any scripts that are in process are also suspended. This makes workflows that involve other apps much smoother and quicker because FileMaker Go does not have to perform a full hibernation.

When you return to FileMaker Go, it reconnects to files as necessary, as long as one of the following conditions is true:

- You have accessed the file using a guest account.
- You logged in using the file's auto-open account, as configured in the File Options settings.
- Your account's privilege set *does not* include the fmreauthenticate extended privilege.
- You have returned to the file before the grace period expired, as specified by the fmreauthenticate extended privilege assigned to your account's privilege set.

When FileMaker Go can reconnect to a file, it returns you to the same layout and record. If you were editing the record at the time, you are again presented with your pending record changes. If you are working with a hosted file, it is possible that another user will have edited the record you are modifying. In this case, FileMaker Go alerts you as you attempt to modify the record, and it requires you to cancel or revert the record. Keep in mind that FileMaker Go even resumes scripts that you were running at the time the app was suspended. Although it's always a good idea to include error trapping in your scripts, doing so is crucial for functions in hosted databases accessed using FileMaker Go.

Security Tips

FileMaker security becomes all the more critical when you take your mobile device into the world. Following are some tips for securing your data.

- Securing your iOS device with a passcode is always a good idea; you configure the passcode in the General section of the Settings app.
- You can require your FileMaker Go users to connect through a VPN before accessing a hosted database. You can configure the VPN connection in the General tab of the Settings app.
- Should you choose to open access to your FileMaker Server through the firewall, we strongly recommend you assign each user a separate password.
- Passwords should be a minimum of eight characters and include at least one of each of the following: an uppercase letter, a lowercase letter, a number, and a special character, such as a punctuation symbol.
- Enable the Find My iPhone setting on each device and turn on the Remote Passcode Lock and Remote Wipe settings. Should your iOS device be lost or stolen, you can use it to blank the device. Of course, your data stored on the device will be lost, but it will not fall into the wrong hands.
- Use the Get (PersistentID) function to help identify devices that access your databases.

Interacting with Other Apps

Applications on the iPad, iPhone, and iPod touch each have their own documents folder, and iOS prohibits each from working directly with another application's data. However, apps can send and receive data to each other by their URL Schemes.

FileMaker URL Scheme

FileMaker 12 introduces a new Internet protocol, FMP, which unifies the FMP7 and FMP7Script protocols. Both FileMaker Pro 12 and FileMaker Go 12 recognize the FMP protocol. With it, you can open a file, pass in credentials, execute a script, and pass it parameters using the following code:

```
[<][URL:]FMP://[[account:password@]netAddress]/databaseName
➥[?script=scriptName[&param=scriptParameter]
➥[&$variableName=value]][>]
```

We enclosed the optional parameters in square brackets here.

You can express the net address parameter as

- A DNS address (host.domain.com)
- An IPv4 address (192.168.1.111)
- An IPv6 address ([1050:0000:0000:0000:0005:0600:300c:326b])

FileMaker Go also accepts a few additional values to open a local file:

- A tilde (~) opens a local file.
- A dollar sign ($) opens a hibernated file.

You can pass information into the script in two ways:

- **Script Parameter**—To pass a text string as a script parameter, add ¶m= and then your text string following the database name.
- **Local Variables**—To automatically load values into local variables, follow the database name with an ampersand and then name/value pairs (for example, &$id=1279&$ company=Acme).

The local variables are automatically loaded as if you had performed set Variable steps, but they are not accessible using the Get (ScriptParameter) function. You can use param and local variable protocols individually or together.

URLs cannot contain spaces, so encode the URL by replacing each space with %20. Should that fail, try using a plus sign (+) in place of the space.

Sample FMP URLs:

```
//Open the database "Inventory.fmp12",
//hosted on the server "192.168.10.1"
FMP://192.168.10.1/Inventory.fmp12

//Open the database "Sales.fmp12",
//hosted on the server "[FE80:0000:0000:0000:0202:B3FF: FE1E:8329]"
FMP://[FE80:0000:0000:0000:0202:B3FF: FE1E:8329]/Sales.fmp12

//Open the database "Employee.fmp12",
//hosted on the server "db12.acmeco.com",
//using account "Mary Smith" with the password "24dog2"
fmp://Mary%20Smith:24dog2@db12.acmeco.com/Employee.fmp12

//Open the database "Contacts.fmp12",
//stored locally on your iPhone,
//and perform the script "Find Contact" and
//pass it the parameter 257|Smith|Bob
FMP://~/Contact.fmp12?script=Find%20Contactparam=257|Smith|Bob

//Open the database "Contacts.fmp12",
//stored locally on your iPhone,
//and perform the script "Find Contact" and
//automatically load three local variables:
//$id=9276, $lname=Smith, and $fname=Bob
fmp://~/Contact.fmp12?script=Find%20Contact&$id=9276&$lname=Smith&fname=Bob
```

Maps and Location

The Open URL script step using a Google maps URL opens a browser. Then you can choose Open in Safari to open the Maps application. Here is an example of a Google maps URL:

```
Open URL [No dialog; "http://maps.google.com/maps?z=10&q=Loc:Chicago,+IL"]
```

The preceding script opens directly in the user's browser. Of course, you could also render this same URL in a Web Viewer to stay within FileMaker Pro.

On the other hand, it might be more useful to open the Maps application directly without the extra steps. The following script displays in the Maps application directions from Cupertino to San Francisco, California, using public transportation:

```
Open URL [No dialog;
➥"maps://maps?q=&saddr=cupertino&daddr=San+Francisco,+CA&t=m&dirflg=r&z=20"]
```

Whether you open a map in the browser or the Map app directly, FileMaker Go renders both using Google Maps. Table 16.2 lists the Google Maps parameters that are supported by the iOS devices.

Table 16.2 Supported Google Maps Parameters

Parameter	Notes
q=	The query parameter; this behaves as if you had typed this value in the query box at maps.google.com.
near=	The location portion of the query.
ll=	The latitude and longitude points, specified in decimal format. If specified without a query, the map is centered at this location.
sll=	The parameter used for specifying the origination of a business search; it is specified as latitude and longitude points, specified in decimal format.
spn=	The approximate longitude and latitude span; Google adjusts the map to fit this size when the z= is not specified.
t=	The type of map to display. The available options are m for map, k for satellite, h for hybrid, and p for terrain.
z=	The zoom level; accepts a number value of 1–20.
saddr=	The source address, used when generating driving directions. You can specify the value Current%20Location to start from the current location.
daddr=	The destination address, used when generating driving directions
layer=	The parameter used to activate overlay. The available options are t for traffic and c for street view.
dirflg=	The parameter that enables you to specify the route type: h for Avoid Highways t for Avoid Tolls r for Public Transit (only works in some areas) w for Walking directions

The soon-to-be-released iOS6 includes a redeveloped Maps application that includes a new maps engine and does not utilize Google Maps.

FileMaker Pro 12 includes two new functions that make it much easier to work with maps: Location and LocationValues. They are supported only by FileMaker Go, not FileMaker Pro. The Location function returns the user's current location in the form "<latitude>, <longitude>".

A great example in the Contacts starter file uses the LocationValues function to perform a reverse Geocode search at the site maps.googleapis.com to get the street address for the current location. See the script "Find my location | Get GPS Coordinates (WGS84) | iOS." You can view this script's steps by selecting Manage Scripts from the Scripts menu and then double-clicking the script. You can try it out by opening the file on an iOS device, navigating to the Contact detail layout, and then tapping the location button next to Work Address or Home Address.

➔ *For more information on the* Location *and* LocationValues *functions, see Chapter 10.*

Dial Phone

You can use the Dial Phone script step while running FileMaker Go on the iPhone to make a phone call. The only requirement is that you remove all formatting so that you pass only the number digits to the Phone app. The following script step filters the Customer's Phone value before dialing the phone:

```
Dial Phone [No dialog; Filter ( Customer::Phone ; 1234567890 )]
```

➔ *See the "FileMaker Go and iOS" section of Appendix A for links to help you identify the URL Schemes of other iOS apps.*

CHAPTER 17

FileMaker XML Reference

XML is one of the driving technologies behind Custom Web Publishing (CWP) in FileMaker. FileMaker Server can serve FileMaker data as XML for use by external applications that can read XML data.

Note

Although previous versions of FileMaker Server allowed the use of server-side XSL stylesheets, this capability is no longer present in FileMaker Server 12. However, it's still possible to use XSLT to transform XML exports on the FileMaker Pro and Pro Advanced clients.

This chapter provides a reference guide to FileMaker XML syntax. It covers the following areas:

- URL syntax for accessing FileMaker data over the Web
- Syntax of the various FileMaker XML grammars
- FileMaker URL query commands and query string parameters
- Important XML namespaces for use with Custom Web Publishing

URL Syntax for Web Access to FileMaker Data

FileMaker can provide data in XML format in two ways: via the Export as XML feature in the regular FileMaker client and via URL-based requests sent directly to databases hosted through FileMaker Server.

A URL designed to extract data from FileMaker Server has two components: a resource name and a query string. This section demonstrates the correct syntax for resource names within a URL. The query string is made up of a single command, often accompanied by one or more parameters; subsequent sections discuss those in more detail.

URL Syntax for XML Access

To extract data from FileMaker Server in pure XML format, you use a URL of the following form:

```
<protocol>://<host>[:<port>]/fmi/xml/<grammar>.xml?<query string>
```

- <protocol> is either http (for regular HTTP access) or https (for secure HTTP access).
- <host> is the hostname or the IP address of the web server that's been configured with FileMaker Server. (Note that if the web server is on a different machine than the FileMaker Server, you must use the address of the web server here, not that of the FileMaker Server machine.)
- <port> needs to be specified only if the web server has been configured to run on a port other than the default for the specified protocol (80 for HTTP, 443 for HTTPS).
- <grammar> is the name of one of the three valid FileMaker XML grammars, discussed in the next section.
- <query string> is a query string composed of some number of query parameters in combination with a query command. Specifics are discussed in upcoming sections.

Example:

```
http://my.filemakerserver.net:8080/fmi/xml/fmresultset.xml?-dbnames
```

This query accesses a server running on port 8080 on the machine my.filemakerserver.net and requests a list of all databases available for XML access on that server, with the results returned in the fmresultset grammar.

URL Syntax for Access to Container Objects

FileMaker Server has a special URL syntax for accessing data in container fields via the Web. Such a request causes the container data to be returned directly (much like clicking on a PDF link in a web page). The exact mechanism depends on whether the container data is stored directly in the database or stored by reference. To extract container data stored directly in a FileMaker database, you use a URL of the following form:

```
<protocol>://<host>[:<port>]/fmi/xml/cnt/data.<extension>?<query string>
```

- <protocol>, <host>, <port>, and <query string> are as described in the preceding section.
- <extension> is the file type extension for the container data being fetched (.jpg, .txt, and the like). This extension allows the web server to set the MIME type of the data correctly.

The query string must contain a –field query parameter with a fully qualified field name, meaning it must contain a repetition index number reference even if the field is not a repeating field.

Example:

```
http://my.filemakerserver.net/fmi/xml/cnt/data.gif?-db=Customer&-lay=web&-
➥field=photo(1)&-recid=303
```

This URL extracts container data from a specific field (called photo), from the record with recid 303. Even though photo is not a repeating field, the syntax photo[1] is still necessary.

The web server returns this container data as GIF data, assuming the .gif suffix is correctly mapped to the GIF MIME type on the server.

For information on how to manage container data when the container data is stored only by reference, see the FileMaker Server Custom Web Publishing documentation.

FileMaker XML Grammars

FileMaker Server can publish data in any of three XML *grammars*. Note that the grammar names are case sensitive.

- FMPXMLRESULT—This grammar is available either via CWP or via Export as XML. It's a complete data export grammar but can be difficult to parse or read.
- fmresultset—This grammar is in some sense the "best" data export grammar, being rather easier to parse and read than FMPXMLRESULT. We recommend you use it where possible. It is available only via CWP using FileMaker Server, not via Export as XML.
- FMPXMLLAYOUT—This specialized grammar is used for extracting information about a FileMaker layout. It is available only via CWP.

Listings 17.1 through 17.3 contain samples of each grammar.

Listing 17.1 FMPXMLRESULT

```
<?xml version="1.0" encoding="UTF-8" standalone="no"?>
<!DOCTYPE FMPXMLRESULT PUBLIC "-//FMI//DTD FMPXMLRESULT//EN"
➥"/fmi/xml/FMPXMLRESULT.dtd">
<FMPXMLRESULT xmlns="http://www.filemaker.com/fmpxmlresult">
 <ERRORCODE>0</ERRORCODE>
 <PRODUCT BUILD="3/5/2012" NAME="FileMaker Web Publishing Engine"
➥VERSION="12.0.1.150"/>
 <DATABASE DATEFORMAT="MM/dd/yyyy" LAYOUT="house_web" NAME="House"
➥RECORDS="14" IMEFORMAT="HH:mm:ss"/>
 <METADATA>
  <FIELD EMPTYOK="YES" MAXREPEAT="1" NAME="Address" TYPE="TEXT"/>
  <FIELD EMPTYOK="YES" MAXREPEAT="1" NAME="City" TYPE="TEXT"/>
  <FIELD EMPTYOK="YES" MAXREPEAT="1" NAME="State" TYPE="TEXT"/>
  <FIELD EMPTYOK="YES" MAXREPEAT="1" NAME="PostalCode" TYPE="TEXT"/>
  <FIELD EMPTYOK="YES" MAXREPEAT="1" NAME="LotSizeAcres" TYPE="NUMBER"/>
  <FIELD EMPTYOK="YES" MAXREPEAT="1" NAME="CountBedrooms" TYPE="NUMBER"/>
  <FIELD EMPTYOK="YES" MAXREPEAT="1" NAME="AskingPrice" TYPE="NUMBER"/>
 </METADATA>
 <RESULTSET FOUND="14">
  <ROW MODID="1" RECORDID="1">
   <COL>
    <DATA>12 Oak Lane</DATA>
   </COL>
   <COL>
    <DATA>Morten</DATA>
```

```
    </COL>
    <COL>
     <DATA>MO</DATA>
    </COL>
    <COL>
     <DATA>14231</DATA>
    </COL>
    <COL>
     <DATA>.65</DATA>
    </COL>
    <COL>
     <DATA>3</DATA>
    </COL>
    <COL>
     <DATA>265000</DATA>
    </COL>
   </ROW>
  </RESULTSET>
</FMPXMLRESULT>
```

Listing 17.2 fmresultset

```
<?xml version="1.0" encoding="UTF-8" standalone="no"?>
<!DOCTYPE fmresultset PUBLIC "-//FMI//DTD fmresultset//EN" "/fmi/xml/fmresultset.dtd">
<fmresultset xmlns="http://www.filemaker.com/xml/fmresultset" version="1.0">
 <error code="0"/>
 <PRODUCT BUILD="03/05/2012" name="FileMaker Web Publishing Engine"
➥version="12.0.1.150"/>
 <datasource database="House" date-format="MM/dd/yyyy" layout="house_web "table="House"
➥time-format="HH:mm:ss" timestamp-format="MM/dd/yyyy HH:mm:ss" total-count="14"/>
 <metadata>
  <field-definition auto-enter="no" global="no" max-repeat="1" name="Address"
➥not-empty="no"result="text" type="normal"/>
  <field-definition auto-enter="no" global="no" max-repeat="1" name="City"
➥not-empty="no"result="text" type="normal"/>
  <field-definition auto-enter="no" global="no" max-repeat="1" name="State"
➥not-empty="no"result="text" type="normal"/>
  <field-definition auto-enter="no" global="no" max-repeat="1"
➥name="PostalCode" not-empty="no" result="text" type="normal"/>
  <field-definition auto-enter="no" global="no" max-repeat="1"
➥name="LotSizeAcres" not-empty="no" result="number" type="normal"/>
  <field-definition auto-enter="no" global="no" max-repeat="1"
➥name="CountBedrooms" not-empty="no" result="number" type="normal"/>
  <field-definition auto-enter="no" global="no" max-repeat="1"
➥name="AskingPrice" not-empty="no" result="number" type="normal"/>
```

```
  </metadata>
  <resultset count="14" fetch-size="1">
   <record mod-id="1" record-id="1">
    <field name="Address">
     <data>12 Oak Lane</data>
    </field>
    <field name="City">
     <data>Morten</data>
    </field>
    <field name="State">
     <data>MO</data>
    </field>
    <field name="PostalCode">
     <data>14231</data>
    </field>
    <field name="LotSizeAcres">
     <data>.65</data>
    </field>
    <field name="CountBedrooms">
     <data>3</data>
    </field>
    <field name="AskingPrice">
     <data>265000</data>
    </field>
   </record>
  </resultset>
</fmresultset>
```

Listing 17.3 FMPXMLLAYOUT

```
<?xml version="1.0" encoding="UTF-8" standalone="no"?>
<!DOCTYPE FMPXMLLAYOUT PUBLIC "-//FMI//DTD FMPXMLLAYOUT//EN"
➥"/fmi/xml/FMPXMLLAYOUT.dtd">
<FMPXMLLAYOUT xmlns="http://www.filemaker.com/fmpxmllayout">
 <ERRORCODE>0</ERRORCODE>
 <PRODUCT BUILD="03/05/2012" NAME="FileMaker Web Publishing Engine"
➥VERSION="12.0.1.150"/>
 <LAYOUT DATABASE="House" NAME="house_web">
  <FIELD NAME="Address">
   <STYLE TYPE="EDITTEXT" VALUELIST=""/>
  </FIELD>
  <FIELD NAME="City">
   <STYLE TYPE="EDITTEXT" VALUELIST=""/>
  </FIELD>
  <FIELD NAME="State">
   <STYLE TYPE="EDITTEXT" VALUELIST=""/>
```

```
      </FIELD>
      <FIELD NAME="PostalCode">
        <STYLE TYPE="EDITTEXT" VALUELIST=""/>
      </FIELD>
      <FIELD NAME="LotSizeAcres">
        <STYLE TYPE="EDITTEXT" VALUELIST=""/>
      </FIELD>
      <FIELD NAME="CountBedrooms">
        <STYLE TYPE="EDITTEXT" VALUELIST=""/>
      </FIELD>
    <FIELD NAME="AskingPrice">
        <STYLE TYPE="EDITTEXT" VALUELIST=""/>
      </FIELD>
    </LAYOUT>
    <VALUELISTS/>
  </FMPXMLLAYOUT>
```

Query Parameters for XML URL Requests

The FileMaker Web Publishing Engine (WPE) delivers XML data in response to specially formatted URLs. The specific details of the request are contained in the *query string*, which is a specific portion of the URL. For example, the query string is highlighted in the following URL:

http://my.filemakerserver.net:8080/fmi/xml/fmresultset.xml**?-db=Customer&-lay=web&-new**

The query string consists of a series of *name-value pairs*, in the form of name=value, separated by ampersands, and following a question mark within the URL.

Generally, a query string intended for the WPE consists of a single *query command*, representing the type of request being made, supported by additional query parameters that add specificity to the request. Continuing with the previous example, the request is –findall (find all records). Additional query parameters specify the database, the layout, and the maximum number of records to be returned.

Please note the following important points about URL queries:

- Each URL query string must contain one and only one query command (although it may contain many additional query parameters).
- Query commands and query parameters begin with a hyphen (-). Omitting the hyphen causes an error.
- A query command is expressed as a plain value, not as a name-value pair. Any supplied value is ignored. (So you can say ...&-findall=somevalue, but the =somevalue is ignored.)
- The names of FileMaker fields, when included in the URL for purposes of searching, or for creating or editing records, do *not* require a hyphen.

- Most query commands have a minimum set of query parameters that *must* also be provided in the URL. These are noted in Tables 17.1 and 17.2.

Query Commands

This section lists the possible query commands. If the command requires certain specific additional parameters, those are listed in Table 17.1.

Table 17.1 Parameters for Query Commands

Command	Parameters Required	Description
-dbnames	None	Return a list of all databases on the given server that are enabled for XML publishing. http://my.server.com/fmi/xml/fmresultset.xml?-dbnames
-delete	-db, -lay, -recid	Delete the record with the specified record ID from the specified database. (The affected table is determined by the specified layout.) http://my.server.com/fmi/xml/fmresultset.xml?-db=Customer&-lay=web&-recid=303&-delete
-dup	-db, -lay, -recid	Duplicate the record with the specified record ID from the specified database. (The affected table is determined by the specified layout.) http://my.server.com/fmi/xml/fmresultset.xml?-db=Customer&-lay=web&-recid=303&-dup
-edit	-db, -lay, -recid, field name(s)	Edit the record with the specified record ID from the specified database. (The affected table is determined by the specified layout.) Field names and associated field values determine what data gets written into the record. http://my.server.com/fmi/xml/fmresultset.xml?-dbCustomer&-lay=web&-recid=303&name_first=Sarah&-edit
-find	-db, -lay, field name(s)	Find records in the specified database and table, with search criteria determined by the supplied field data. http://my.server.com/fmi/xml/fmresultset.xml?-db=Customer&-lay=web&name_last=Smith&-find
-findall	-db, –lay	Find all records in the specified database and table. http://my.server.com/fmi/xml/fmresultset.xml?-db=Customer&-lay=web&-findall
-findany	-db, -lay	Find a random record in the specified database and table. http://my.server.com/fmi/xml/fmresultset.xml?-db=Customer&-lay=web&-findany
-findquery	-db, -lay, -query	Find records in the specified database and table using multiple find and omit requests. http://my.server.com/fmi/xml/fmresultset.xml?-db=Customer&-lay=web&-query=(q1);!(q2)&-q1=city&-q1.value=Ghent&-q2=status&-q2.value=delayed&-findquery
-layoutnames	-db	Return a list of all layout names from the specified database. http://my.server.com/fmi/xml/fmresultset.xml?-db=Customer&-layoutnames

Table 17.1 Continued

Command	Parameters Required	Description
-new	-db, -lay	Create a new record in the specified database and table. If field names and field values are also supplied, these create specific data values in the new record. http://my.server.com/fmi/xml/fmresultset.xml?-db=Customer&-lay=web&name_first=Kai&name_last=Love&-new
-scriptnames	-db	Return a list of the names of all scripts in the specified database. http://my.server.com/fmi/xml/fmresultset.xml?-db=Customer&-scriptnames
-view	-db, -lay	Used with the FMPXMLLAYOUT grammar, -view retrieves layout information in the FMPXMLLAYOUT format. Used with the other grammars, it retrieves the database metadata and an empty result set. http://my.server.com/fmi/xml/FMPXMLLAYOUT.xml?-db=Customer&-lay=web&-view

Query Parameters

Each XML command requires one or more specific parameters, as shown in Table 17.1. Table 17.2 discusses each parameter in greater detail.

Table 17.2 Parameters

Parameter Name	Required Value(s)	Description
-db	Name of a database (without file extension)	Specify a database as a target of the URL command. Most commands require this parameter. http://my.server.com/fmi/xml/fmresultset.xml?-db=Customer&-lay=web&name_first=Kai&name_last=Love&-new
-field	Name of a container field	Specify a container field from which to extract data. http://my.filemakerserver.net:8080/fmi/xml/cnt/data.tiff?-db=Customers&-lay=web_search&-field=photo(1)&-recid=303
<fieldname>	Name of a noncontainer field	Specify search parameters (with a –find command) or data values to be inserted (with the –edit and –new commands). http://my.server.com/fmi/xml/fmresultset.xml?-db=Customer&-lay=web&name_first=Kai&name_last=Love&-new

Table 17.2 Continued

Parameter Name	Required Value(s)	Description
<fieldname>.op	eq (equals) cn (contains) bw (begins with) ew (ends with) gt (greater than) gte (greater than or equal) lt (less than) lte (less than or equal) neq (not equal)	Specify a search comparison operator to use when searching on <fieldname>. Used optionally with the –find command. http://my.server.com/fmi/xml/fmresultset.xml?-db=Agent&-lay=web&commission=.3&commission.op=gte&-find
-lay	Name of a layout in the database specified by the –db parameter	Required by many commands. Note that the choice of layout also governs which table the command is performed against. http://my.server.com/fmi/xml/fmresultsetxml?-db=Customer&-lay=web&name_first=Kai&name_last=Love&-new
-lay.response	Name of a layout in the database specified by the –db parameter	You might want to return data from an alternate layout. For example, you might want to search a particular field (in which case that field must be present on the layout specified by –lay), but not return that field in the result set (in which case you would return XML from the layout named in –lay.response, which would not contain the field in question). http://my.server.com/fmi/xml/fmresultset.xml?-db=Customer&-lay=web&-lay.response=webresponse&-findall
-lop	and or or	Specify whether the criteria in a –find request represents an AND search or an OR search. (The default is AND.) http://my.server.com/fmi/xml/fmresultset.xml?-db=Customer&-lay=web&name_last=Smythe&hair_color=red&-lop=or&-find
-max	A positive number, or the value "all"	For a –find or –findall request, specify how many records to return. The default number of records returned is 50. http://my.server.com/fmi/xml/fmresultset.xml?-db=Customer&-lay=web&name_last=Smythe&hair_color=red&-max=25&-find
-modid	A FileMaker modification ID	Use with the –edit command to specify a valid modification ID for the record being updated. If the –modid value does not match the target record's modification ID, the edit is rejected. This is to ensure that the record has not been modified by someone else since the time it was fetched for a web user. http://my.server.com/fmi/xml/fmresultset.xml?-db=Customer&-lay=web&name_last=Smythe&recid=10003&-modid13&-edit

Table 17.2 Continued

Parameter Name	Required Value(s)	Description
-query	Multiple request declarations; multiple request definitions	Use with the –findquery command to specify a complex search made up of multiple find or omit criteria. Requests are declared as q1, q2, q3, and so on and placed in parentheses. A preceding exclamation point indicates an "omit" request. Multiple comma-separated requests in a declaration group act as an AND search. Request declarations are separated by semicolons if there is more than one declaration; multiple declarations act as an OR search (with the exception of omit requests). So the declaration (q1); !(q2,q3) indicates a request to find all records that match q1, but for which q2 AND q3 are not both true. Request definitions have the form –q1=Name_Last&-q1.value=VanZant. Note the minus signs before the parameters q1, q2 and so on. http://my.server.com/fmi/xml/fmresultset.xml?-db=Customer&-lay=web&-query=q1);!(q2)&-q1=city&-q1.value=(Ghent&-q2=status&-q2.value=delayed&-findquery
-recid	A FileMaker record ID	The –edit, -dup, and –delete commands need to know the ID of a specific record on which to operate. Generally, this record ID is extracted from the result of a previous request. The –recid parameter can also be used with the –find command. http://my.server.com/fmi/xml/fmresultset.xml?-db=Customer&-lay=web&name_last=Smythe&recid=10003&-modid=13&-edit
-relatedsets.filter	layout or none	This optional parameter can be used with any query parameter (-find, -findall, -findany, -findquery) that uses a layout containing a portal. If –relatedsets.filter is set to layout, the Initial Row setting in the FileMaker Pro Portal Setup dialog is used to determine where to begin displaying related records. Additionally, if the Show Vertical Scroll Bar setting is enabled for the portal, the –relatedsets.max parameter is used to determine how many records to display. If the Show Vertical Scroll Bar setting is disabled, or the –relatedsets.max parameter is not used, the Number of Rows setting in the Portal Setup dialog is used to determine the number of rows returned. http://my.server.com/fmi/xml/fmresultset.xml?-db=Customer&-lay=web&name_last=Smythe&recid=10003&-relatedsets.filter=layout&-relatedsets.max=10&-find

Table 17.2 Continued

Parameter Name	Required Value(s)	Description
-relatedsets.max	A positive integer, or the value all	This optional parameter can be used with the –relatedsets.filter parameter to specify the number of records returned from a portal on the relevant FileMaker layout. This parameter is used only if the –relatedsets.filter parameter is set to layout and the Show Vertical Scroll Bar setting in the Portal Setup dialog box is enabled. If this parameter specified an integer, that number of records is displayed. If it specifies all, all records from the portal are displayed. http://my.server.com/fmi/xml/fmresultset.xml?-db=Customer&-lay=web&name_last=Smythe&recid=10003&-relatedsets.filter=layout&-relatedsets.max=10&-find
-script	The name of a script in the database specified by the –db parameter	Specify a script to be run *after* the query and any sorting are performed. Make sure you understand the issue of web compatibility for scripts when using this parameter. http://my.server.com/fmi/xml/fmresultset.xml?-db=Customer&-lay=web&-lay.response=web_response&-script=OmitDuplicates&-findall
-script.param	Value of a script parameter to be passed to the script named in –script	The script named in –script may be passed a script parameter. http://my.server.com/fmi/xml/fmresultset.xml?-db=Customer&-lay=web&-lay.response=web_response&-script=Omit&-script.param=3&-find
-script.prefind	The name of a script in the database specified by the –db parameter	Specify a script to be run *before* the specified query is run and sorted. http://my.server.com/fmi/xml/fmresultset.xml?-db=Customer&-lay=web&-lay.response=web_response&-script.prefind=Omit&-script.prefind.param=3&-find
-script.prefind. param	Value of a script parameter to be passed to the script named in –script.prefind	The script named in –script.prefind may be passed a script parameter. http://my.server.com/fmi/xml/fmresultset.xml?-db=Customer&-lay=web&-lay.response=web_response&-script.prefind=Omit&-script.prefind.param=3&-find
-script.presort	The name of a script in the database specified by the –db parameter	Specify a script to be run *after* the specified query is run and *before* the results are sorted. http://my.server.com/fmi/xml/fmresultset.xml?-db=Customer&-lay=web&-lay.response=web_response&-script.presort=Omit&-script.presort.param=3&-find
-script.presort.param	Value of a script parameter to be passed to the script named in –script.presort	The script named in –script.presort may be passed a script parameter. http://my.server.com/fmi/xml/fmresultset.xml?-db=Customer&-layweb&-lay.response=web_response&-script.presort=Omit&-script.presort.param=3&-find

Table 17.2 Continued

Parameter Name	Required Value(s)	Description
-skip	A number of records to skip	Based on this value, the WPE skips some of the records normally returned by a query and begins returning records from later in the result set. http://my.server.com/fmi/xml/fmresultset.xml?-db=Customer&-lay=web&-lay.response=web_response&-skip=20&-max=25&-find
-sortfield.[1-9]	Name of a field to sort on, along with a sort precedence from 1 to 9	Using the values –sortfield.1 through –sortfield.9, you can specify up to nine fields on which to sort. The precedence value is mandatory, even for a single sort criterion. http://my.server.com/fmi/xml/fmresultset.xml?-db=Customer&-lay=web&-lay.response=web_response&-skip=20&-max=25&sortfield.1=name&-find
-sortorder.[1-9]	ascend, descend, or a value list name	Specify a sort order for a specific sort field. http://my.server.com/fmi/xml/fmresultset.xml?-db=Customer&-lay=web&-lay.response=web_response&-skip=20&-max=25&sortfield.1=name&-sortorder.1=descend&-find

FileMaker XML Namespaces

FileMaker's XML publishing technologies use a number of XML namespaces. (We assume that if you're referring to this section, the concept of an XML namespace is a familiar one.) Each of the three XML grammars has its own namespace. You generally need to concern yourself with namespaces only if you are writing XSLT stylesheets that transform FileMaker XML data. (Bear in mind that server-side XSL transformations are no longer a feature in FileMaker Server 12, though other applications can consume FileMaker's XML and perform their own XSLT transforms on the returned data.)

Table 17.3 lists each namespace, along with its significance, and the conventional namespace prefix used to abbreviate it. The prefix is "conventional" in the sense that, in creating a stylesheet, you may choose any prefix you want for a namespace, but the ones listed in Table 17.3 are those used by FileMaker, Inc., in the official documentation.

Table 17.3 FileMaker XML Namespaces

Usage	Namespace	Prefix
FMPXMLRESULT grammar	http://www.filemaker.com/fmpxmlresult	fmp
fmresultset grammar	http://www.filemaker.com/xml/fmresultset	fmrs
FMPXMLLAYOUT grammar	http://www.filemaker.com/fmpxmllayout	fml

CHAPTER 18

FileMaker API for PHP

The FileMaker API for PHP is a set of PHP libraries intended to enable developers to use the popular web development language PHP to access data in a FileMaker database. The API is packaged with FileMaker Server and FileMaker Server Advanced and may also be downloaded independently at http://www.filemaker.com/developers/resources/php/.

If you're an experienced PHP developer, there are a few things to note about FileMaker's PHP API:

- The API is based on an object-oriented design. You need some familiarity with object-oriented programming and design methods to make the most sense of it.
- Unlike much PHP code, the FileMaker API is not open source. Although you can inspect some of the PHP code in the library, key parts of the code are obscured. Therefore, you can't modify the base code directly although you could write your own libraries that extend or incorporate the API.
- The FileMaker API for PHP does not directly expose any of the properties of its classes. All interactions with the API are performed via class methods.
- Some of the classes in the FileMaker API for PHP are based on classes in the PEAR library of PHP modules. The necessary code is included with the install, so it's not necessary to have a separate install of PEAR.
- You can find HTML documentation in the FileMaker Server install directory under Documentation/PHP API Documentation.

Class Overview

The UML-style diagram in Figure 18.1 gives an overview of all the classes in the FileMaker API for PHP.

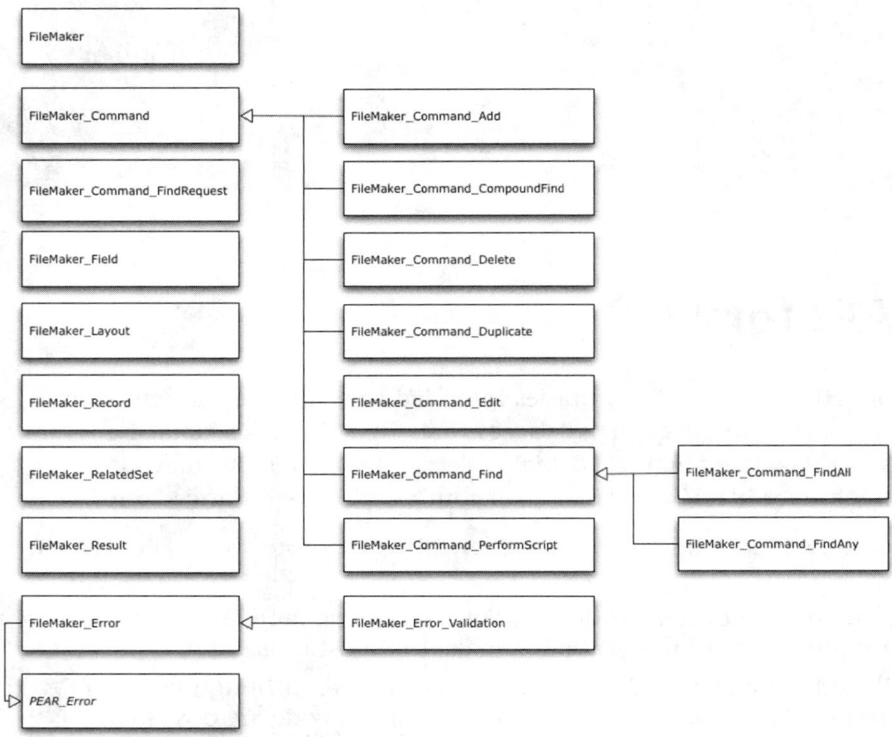

Figure 18.1
The FileMaker API for PHP consists of a set of related classes.

Classes and Methods

The following sections give an overview of each of the classes in the FileMaker API for PHP, as well as a listing of the method signatures for each class.

Static methods are denoted by a method name preceded by a class name and a double colon. For example, the static FileMaker class method isError is written as FileMaker::isError, which would also be the necessary syntax in PHP.

FileMaker

The FileMaker class is a bit of a hybrid class. It is responsible for managing general information about a FileMaker Server database connection and is also a *factory class* that's responsible for creating an instance of the various command classes (FileMaker_Command and its subclasses).

getAPIVersion

Syntax:

FileMaker::getAPIVersion()

Data type returned: string

Description:

Returns the current version of the FileMaker API for PHP.

getMinServerVersion

Syntax:

FileMaker::getMinServerVersion()

Data type returned: string

Description:

Returns the minimum version of FileMaker Server that works with this version of the API.

isError

Syntax:

FileMaker::isError(mixed $variable)

Data type returned: boolean

Description:

Returns a Boolean value indicating whether $variable is an object of type FileMaker_Error.

FileMaker

Syntax:

new FileMaker([string $database], [string $hostspec], [string $username], [string $password])

Data type returned: FileMaker object

Description:

FileMaker object constructor. Returns a new instance of the FileMaker class.

createRecord

Syntax:

createRecord(string $layout, [array $fieldValues])

Data type returned: FileMaker_Record object

Description:

Returns a new FileMaker_Record object. Calling this method does not create a new database record. To do so, you need to call the new FileMaker_Record object's commit() method.

getContainerData

Syntax:

getContainerData(string $url)

Data type returned: string

Description:

Returns the field data from a container field specified by $url.

getContainerData

Syntax:

getContainerDataURL(string $url)

Data type returned: string

Description:

Returns the fully qualified URL for the data from a container field specified by $url. The URL passed in must represent the file path for the container field's contents, such as the value returned by Record::getField().

getLayout

Syntax:

getLayout(string $layout)

Data type returned: FileMaker_Layout

Description:

Returns a FileMaker_Layout object corresponding to the layout specified by $layout or returns a FileMaker_Error object if the specified layout can't be found.

getProperties

Syntax:

getProperties()

Data type returned: array

Description:

Returns an associative array containing entries for all properties of the current FileMaker object. Because the API in general doesn't allow direct inspection or manipulation of object properties, this method can be useful for gathering debugging information.

getProperty

Syntax:

getProperty(string $prop)

Data type returned: string

Description:

Returns a string corresponding to the value of a single named FileMaker property, $prop. (It may help to first call getProperties() to learn the names of all available properties.)

getRecordById

Syntax:

getRecordById(string $layout, string $recordID)

Data type returned: FileMaker_Record

Description:

Returns a FileMaker_Record object corresponding to the record with a record ID of $recordID, from the table specified by $layout. If a problem occurs while accessing that record, getRecordById() returns a FileMaker_Error object.

listDatabases

Syntax:

listDatabases()

Data type returned: array

Description:

Returns an array containing the names of all databases known to this FileMaker object, or returns a FileMaker_Error object if the request fails.

listLayouts

Syntax:

listLayouts()

Data type returned: array

Description:

Returns an array containing the names of all layouts within the current database or returns a FileMaker_Error object if the request fails.

listScripts

Syntax:

listScripts()

Data type returned: array

Description:

Returns an array containing the names of all scripts within the current database or returns a FileMaker_Error object if the request fails.

> *Note*
>
> The next 10 methods are known as *factory methods* because their chief purpose is to create a new instance of some class. These functions all create new instances of various FileMaker command classes and subclasses. It's important to recognize that creating these objects does *not* result in the specified commands actually being executed. The command is not executed until the command object's execute() method is called.

newAddCommand

Syntax:

newAddCommand(string $layout, [array $values])

Data type returned: FileMaker_Command_Add object

Description:

Returns a new FileMaker_Command_Add object capable of adding records on the layout specified by $layout.

newCompoundFindCommand

Syntax:

newCompoundFindCommand(string $layout)

Data type returned: FileMaker_Command_CompoundFind object

Description:

Returns a new FileMaker_Command_CompoundFind object capable of performing complex searches on the layout specified by $layout.

newDeleteCommand

Syntax:

newDeleteCommand(string $layout, string $recordID)

Data type returned: FileMaker_Command_Delete object

Description:

Returns a new FileMaker_Command_Delete object capable of deleting the record with an ID of $recordID from the table specified by $layout.

newDuplicateCommand

Syntax:

newDuplicateCommand(string $layout, string $recordID)

Data type returned: FileMaker_Command_Duplicate object

Description:

Returns a new FileMaker_Command_Duplicate object capable of duplicating the record with an ID of $recordID from the table specified by $layout.

newEditCommand

Syntax:

newEditCommand(string $layout, string $recordID, [array $updatedValues])

Data type returned: FileMaker_Command_Edit object

Description:

Returns a new FileMaker_Command_Edit object capable of editing the record with an ID of $recordID from the table specified by $layout. The data values to be submitted are specified in the $updatedValues array. The $updatedValues array will contain the new field values when the function returns (this is significant if any of the fields are subject to auto-entry rules, in which case the updated values might be different from the submitted values).

newFindAllCommand

Syntax:

newFindAllCommand(string $layout)

Data type returned: FileMaker_Command_FindAll object

Description:

Returns a new FileMaker_Command_FindAll object capable of finding all records from the table specified by $layout.

newFindAnyCommand

Syntax:

newFindAnyCommand(string $layout)

Data type returned: FileMaker_Command_FindAny object

Description:

Returns a new FileMaker_Command_FindAny object capable of finding a random record from the table specified by $layout.

newFindCommand

Syntax:

newFindCommand(string $layout)

Data type returned: FileMaker_Command_Find object

Description:

Returns a new FileMaker_Command_Find object capable of finding records from the table specified by $layout.

newFindRequest

Syntax:

newFindRequest(string $layout)

Data type returned: FileMaker_Command_FindRequest object

Description:

Returns a new FileMaker_Command_FindRequest object capable of finding records from the table specified by $layout. These individual objects need to be added to a FileMaker_Command_CompoundFind object to actually perform a compound find.

newPerformScriptCommand

Syntax:

newPerformScriptCommand (string $layout, string $scriptName, [string $scriptParameters])

Data type returned: FileMaker_Command_PerformScript object

Description:

Returns a new FileMaker_Command_PerformScript object capable of performing the specified script (it's also possible to specify parameters for the script using the $scriptParameters parameter).

setLogger

Syntax:

setLogger(Log $logger)

Data type returned: void

Description:

Establishes a PEAR Log object with which to log requests and responses.

setProperty

Syntax:

setProperty(string $prop, string $value)

Data type returned: void

Description:

Sets the property $prop of the FileMaker object to the value $value.

FileMaker_Command

The FileMaker_Command class is the base class for seven other specific command classes capable of performing specific commands. This base class provides a set of methods common to, and inherited by, the various command subclasses.

execute

Syntax:

execute()

Data type returned: FileMaker_Result

Description:

Executes the object's underlying command and returns a FileMaker_Result object.

setPreCommandScript

Syntax:

setPreCommandScript(string $scriptName, [string $scriptParameters])

Data type returned: void

Description:

Sets a script to be run before performing the command or sorting the result set.

setPreSortScript

Syntax:

setPreSortScript(string $scriptName, [string $scriptParameters])

Data type returned: void

Description:

Sets a script to be run after performing the command, but before sorting the result set.

setRecordClass

Syntax:

setRecordClass(string $className)

Data type returned: void

Description:

By default, the FileMaker API for PHP instantiates individual records in a result set as instances of the FileMaker_Record class. If you want the records to be instantiated as instances of some other class, use this function to establish that class name. Other record classes must provide the same interface as the FileMaker_Record class, either by extending it or by implementing the necessary methods.

setRecordId

Syntax:

setRecordId(string $recordID)

Data type returned: void

Description:

Sets the specific record ID for this command to operate on. Certain commands, such as add and find any, don't use a record ID and thus ignore this command.

setResultLayout

Syntax:

setResultLayout(string $layout)

Data type returned: void

Description:

Sets the layout to be used for returning the results of the command. You might use this if you want a different list of fields in your result set than were present on the layout used for the query.

setScript

Syntax:

setScript(string $scriptName, [string $scriptParameters])

Data type returned: void

Description:

Sets a script to be run after the command is performed and the result set returned and sorted.

validate

Syntax:

validate([string $fieldName])

Data type returned: boolean

Description:

Attempts to validate either a single field in a command or an entire command if no specific field name is provided. Note that the validate() method does not actually execute the command against the server. It attempts to do as much validation as possible in the PHP layer. Validations such as strict data type, maximum data length, data ranges, and four-digit years can be validated by PHP without submitting a command to the database. Other types of validation, such as unique field values or validation by calculation, cannot be tested using validate() but only by the actual execution of the command.

FileMaker_Command_Add

FileMaker_Command_Add is a subclass of FileMaker_Command. It's used to add new records to a database.

setField

Syntax:

setField(string $field, string $value, [integer $repetition])

Data type returned: void

Description:

Sets a new value for the named field and repetition ($repetition defaults to 1).

setFieldFromTimestamp

Syntax:

setFieldFromTimestamp(string $field, string $timestamp, [integer $repetition])

Data type returned: void

Description:

Sets a new value for the named field and repetition ($repetition defaults to 1) from a UNIX-style timestamp. The target field must be of type date, time, or Timestamp; otherwise, an error results. This enables the programmer to avoid worrying about complex conversions between Unix timestamps and the FileMaker date and time field types.

FileMaker_Command_CompoundFind

FileMaker_Command_CompoundFind is a subclass of FileMaker_Command. This class represents a set of find requests intended to be performed as a group.

add

Syntax:

add(integer $precedence, FileMaker_Command_FindRequest $findRequest)

Data type returned: void

Description:

Adds a specified FileMaker_Command_FindRequest object to the current find request set. The $precedence variable indicates the order in which the request is added to the set.

addSortRule

Syntax:

addSortRule(string $fieldName, integer $precedence, [mixed $order])

Data type returned: void

Description:

Adds a sorting rule to the compound find request, specifying a field name, a precedence from 1–9, and a sort order. Sort orders may be FILEMAKER_SORT_ASCEND, FILEMAKER_SORT_DESCEND, or a custom value list.

clearSortRules

Syntax:

clearSortRules()

Data type returned: void

Description:

Clears all sorting rules from this compound find request.

getRange

Syntax:

getRange()

Data type returned: array

Description:

Returns an associative array containing two keys. The skip key indicates at which record in the overall found set the result set will begin, whereas the max key indicates the maximum number of records that will be returned.

getRelatedSetsFilters

Syntax:

getRelatedSetsFilters()

Data type returned: array

Description:

Returns an associative array containing two keys. The relatedsetsfilter key returns the portal filter settings, whereas the relatedsetsmax key indicates the maximum number of related records that will be returned.

setRange

Syntax:

setRange(integer $skip, [integer $max])

Data type returned: void

Description:

Indicates that only part of a result set should be returned. The $skip parameter indicates how many records to skip over at the beginning of the result set, and the $max parameter indicates the maximum number of records that should be returned.

setRelatedSetsFilters

Syntax:

setRelatedSetsFilters(string $relatedSetsFilter, [string $relatedSetsMax])

Data type returned: void

Description:

Specifies whether to use the related set filtering present on this request's layout: Use a value of layout for the $relatedSetsFilter parameter, or none if you don't intend to use the layout filter. Use the $relatedSetsMax parameter to specify the maximum number of related records to return. A related set filter can be thought of as the set of portal options that would apply to a portal showing a set of related records. Applicable settings include the initial row, number of rows to display, sort order, and whether a scrollbar is displayed.

FileMaker_Command_Delete

The FileMaker_Command_Delete class represents a command intended to delete a single record. It has no methods of its own; it inherits all its methods from its parent, FileMaker_Command.

FileMaker_Command_Duplicate

The FileMaker_Command_Duplicate class represents a command intended to duplicate a single record. It has no methods of its own; it inherits all its methods from its parent, FileMaker_Command.

FileMaker_Command_Edit

FileMaker_Command_Edit is a subclass of FileMaker_Command. This class represents a command intended to edit a single record.

setField

Syntax:

setField(string $field, string $value, [integer $repetition])

Data type returned: void

Description:

Sets a new value for the named field and repetition ($repetition defaults to 1).

setFieldFromTimestamp

Syntax:

setFieldFromTimestamp(string $field, string $timestamp, [integer $repetition])

Data type returned: void

Description:

Sets a new value for the named field and repetition ($repetition defaults to 1) from a Unix-style timestamp. The target FileMaker field must be of type Date, Time, or Timestamp; otherwise, an error results. This enables the programmer to avoid worrying about complex conversions between Unix timestamps and the FileMaker date- and time-related field types.

setModificationID

Syntax:

setModificationID(integer $modificationID)

Data type returned: void

Description:

Sets a new modification ID for the target record. A modification ID is often used in web programming to determine whether a given record has been modified since it was last refreshed from the database.

FileMaker_Command_Find

FileMaker_Command_Find is a subclass of FileMaker_Command. It represents a command intended to perform a search.

addFindCriterion

Syntax:

addFindCriterion(string $fieldName, string $testValue)

Data type returned: void

Description:

Adds a single find criterion to this request. You need to specify the name of the field being tested and the value to test for.

addSortRule

Syntax:

addSortRule(string $fieldName, integer $precedence, [mixed $order])

Data type returned: void

Description:

Adds a sorting rule to the compound find request, specifying a field name, a precedence from 1–9, and a sort order. Sort orders may be FILEMAKER_SORT_ASCEND, FILEMAKER_SORT_DESCEND, or a custom value list.

clearFindCriteria

Syntax:

clearFindCriteria()

Data type returned: void

Description:

Clears all find criteria from this find request.

clearSortRules

Syntax:

clearSortRules()

Data type returned: void

Description:

Clears all sorting rules from this compound find request.

getRange

Syntax:

getRange()

Data type returned: array

Description:

Returns an associative array containing two keys. The skip key indicates at which record in the overall found set the result set will begin, whereas the max key indicates the maximum number of records that will be returned.

getRelatedSetsFilters

Syntax:

getRelatedSetsFilters()

Data type returned: array

Description:

Returns an associative array containing two keys. The relatedsetsfilter key returns the portal filter settings, whereas the relatedsetsmax key indicates the maximum number of related records that will be returned.

setLogicalOperator

Syntax:

setLogicalOperator(integer $operator)

Data type returned: void

Description:

Specifies that a search be run using logical AND or logical OR. The respective integer constants to use are FILEMAKER_FIND_AND and FILEMAKER_FIND_OR.

setRange

Syntax:

setRange([integer $skip], [integer $max])

Data type returned: void

Description:

Indicates that only part of a result set should be returned. The $skip parameter indicates how many records to skip over at the beginning of the result set (the default is 0), and the $max parameter indicates the maximum number of records that should be returned (the default is all records).

setRelatedSetsFilters

Syntax:

setRelatedSetsFilters(string $relatedsetsfilter, [string $relatedsetsmax])

Data type returned: void

Description:

Specifies whether to use the related set filtering present on this request's layout: Use a value of layout for the $relatedsetsfilter parameter, or none if you don't intend to use the layout filter. Use the $relatedsetsmax parameter to specify the maximum number of related records to return. A related set filter can be thought of as the set of portal options that would apply to a portal showing a set of related records. Applicable settings include the initial row, number of rows to display, sort order, and whether a scrollbar is displayed.

FileMaker_Command_FindAll

The FileMaker_Command_FindAll class is a subclass of FileMaker_Command_Find. It represents a command intended to find all records from a given layout. FileMaker_Command_Find All has no methods of its own; it inherits all its methods from its ancestors, FileMaker_Command and FileMaker_Command_Find.

FileMaker_Command_FindAny

The FileMaker_Command_FindAny class is a subclass of FileMaker_Command_Find. It represents a command intended to find a random record from a given layout. FileMaker_Command_Find Any has no methods of its own; it inherits all its methods from its ancestors, FileMaker_Command and FileMaker_Command_Find.

FileMaker_Command_FindRequest

Though the naming convention suggests otherwise, the FileMaker_Command_FindRequest class is *not* a child of FileMaker_Command. This class represents individual find requests that are intended to be grouped into a compound find by being added to a FileMaker_Command_CompoundFind object.

addFindCriterion

Syntax:

addFindCriterion(string $fieldName, string $testValue)

Data type returned: void

Description:

Adds a single find criterion to this request. You need to specify the name of the field being tested and the value to test for.

clearFindCriteria

Syntax:

clearFindCriteria()

Data type returned: void

Description:

Clears all find criteria from this find request.

setOmit

Syntax:

setOmit(boolean $value)

Data type returned: void

Description:

Specifies whether this is an "omit" request.

FileMaker_Command_PerformScript

The FileMaker_Command_PerformScript class represents a command intended to perform a script. It has no methods of its own; it inherits all its methods from its parent, FileMaker_Command.

FileMaker_Error

FileMaker_Error is an extension of (child of) the PEAR_Error class, a generic error-handling class provided with the popular PEAR library (http://pear.php.net). In addition to all the methods it inherits from its parent (documented at http://pear.php.net/manual/en/core.pear.pear-error.php), FileMaker_Error has the following additional or overloaded methods.

FileMaker_Error

Syntax:

FileMaker_Error(FileMaker_Delegate $fm, [string $message], [integer $code])

Data type returned: FileMaker_Error

Description:

This is the class constructor. In general, you are more likely to find instances of FileMaker_Error being returned from various API methods than you are to have to create instances of the class on your own.

getErrorString

Syntax:

getErrorString()

Data type returned: string

Description:

Returns the error string associated with this object. In the FileMaker implementation, the getMessage() method is a bit more generic than getErrorString() and can be used to extract error messages even when the underlying error is not a FileMaker XML error.

getMessage

Syntax:

getMessage()

Data type returned: string

Description:

Returns the textual error message for this error object.

isValidationError

Syntax:

isValidationError()

Data type returned: boolean

Description:

Returns a Boolean value specifying whether this error is some sort of message from the server or is instead a specific validation error.

FileMaker_Error_Validation

FileMaker_Error_Validation is a child of the FileMaker_Error class, with additional functionality pertaining specifically to validation errors. As with FileMaker errors, when you're a programmer using the API, you are more likely to consume these error objects than create and manage them.

The FileMaker API for PHP can recognize and enforce a certain number of FileMaker validation constraints. These constraints are referenced by integer constants, as shown in Table 18.1.

Table 18.1 FileMaker Validation Integer Constants

Validation Constraint	Integer Constant	Integer Value
Not empty	FILEMAKER_RULE_NOTEMPTY	1
Numeric only	FILEMAKER_RULE_NUMERICONLY	2
Maximum length	FILEMAKER_RULE_MAXCHARACTERS	3
4-digit year	FILEMAKER_RULE_FOURDIGITYEAR	4
Time of day	FILEMAKER_RULE_TIMEOFDAY	5
Timestamp	FILEMAKER_RULE_TIMESTAMPFIELD	6
Date	FILEMAKER_RULE_DATE_FIELD	7
Time	FILEMAKER_RULE_TIME_FIELD	8

Any references to validation rule numbers or validation constants refer to this set of values.

addError

Syntax:

addError(FileMaker_Field $field, integer $rule, string $value)

Data type returned: void

Description:

Adds an error notification to this object, specifying the field, the number of the validation rule that was broken, and the offending field value.

getErrors

Syntax:

getErrors([string $fieldName])

Data type returned: array

Description:

Returns an array describing all the errors associated with this object. Each entry in the array is itself an indexed array. The first array element contains the field object for the field that failed validation, the second element contains an integer constant representing the validation rule that failed, and the third element contains the offending field value.

If you specify a field name, only errors pertaining to that field are returned.

isValidationError

Syntax:

isValidationError()

Data type returned: boolean

Description:

Returns a Boolean value specifying whether this error is some sort of message from the server or is instead a specific validation error.

numErrors

Syntax:

numErrors()

Data type returned: void

Description:

Returns the number of validation errors referred to by this object.

FileMaker_Field

FileMaker_Field is a class representing a specific field as it appears on a specific layout.

FileMaker_Field

Syntax:

FileMaker_Field(FileMaker_Layout $layout)

Data type returned: FileMaker_Field

Description:

This is the class constructor. You invoke it by passing a FileMaker_Layout object corresponding to the field's parent layout.

describeLocalValidationRules

Syntax:

describeLocalValidationRules()

Data type returned: array

Description:

Returns an array of validation rule descriptors. Only validation rules that can be checked and enforced in PHP are included, so rules for validation criteria such as uniqueness, or validation by calculation, which can be evaluated only by FileMaker Server, are not included in the list. See the description of FileMaker_Error_Validation for a list of the possible rule values.

describeValidationRule

Syntax:

describeValidationRule (integer $validationRule)

Data type returned: array

Description:

For a specific validation rule on this field, returns additional information about the rule if necessary, such as a data range or a maximum number of characters. See the description of FileMaker_Error_Validation for a list of the possible rule values.

describeValidationRules

Syntax:

describeValidationRules()

Data type returned: array

Description:

Returns additional validation information for all validation rules defined on this field.

getLayout

Syntax:

getLayout()

Data type returned: FileMaker_Layout

Description:

Returns a FileMaker_Layout object representing the layout that contains this field.

getLocalValidationRules

Syntax:

getLocalValidationRules()

Data type returned: array

Description:

Returns an array of integer constants representing the validation rules in place for this field. Only validation rules that can be checked and enforced in PHP are included, so rules for validation criteria such as uniqueness, or validation by calculation, which can be evaluated only by FileMaker Server, are not included in the list. See the description of FileMaker_Error_Validation for a list of the possible rule values.

getName

Syntax:

getName()

Data type returned: string

Description:

Returns a string representing the name of this field.

getRepetitionCount

Syntax:

getRepetitionCount()

Data type returned: integer

Description:

Returns an integer representing the number of repetitions defined for this field.

getResult

Syntax:

getResult()

Data type returned: string

Description:

Returns a string representing the data type or the result type of this field. (For "basic" FileMaker fields, this corresponds to the field's basic data type, whereas for calculations, it corresponds to the data type that the calculation returns.)

getStyleType

Syntax:

getStyleType()

Data type returned: string

Description:

Returns a string representing the layout style of this field (for example, whether the field is formatted as a text edit box or a check box area).

getType

Syntax:

getType()

Data type returned: string

Description:

Returns a string representing the data type of this field. This is the field type you would find in the Manage Database dialog.

getValidationMask

Syntax:

getValidationMask()

Data type returned: integer

Description:

Returns an integer representing the sum of all the validation constants that apply to this field.

getValidationRules

Syntax:

getValidationRules()

Data type returned: array

Description:

Returns an array of integer constants representing all the validation rules in place for this field. Unlike getLocalValidationRules(), this method returns information on all validation rules, not just those that can be evaluated by PHP.

getValueList

Syntax:

getValueList([string $recid])

Data type returned: array

Description:

Attempts to return an array of information representing any value list that might be associated with this field on the current layout. You may pass in the optional `$recid` parameter to specify a record from which the value list should be taken (this is useful in cases, such as with relational value lists, in which the contents of the list may vary from record to record).

hasValidationRule

Syntax:

hasValidationRule(integer $validationRule)

Data type returned: boolean

Description:

Tests to see whether this field has a validation rule corresponding to the integer constant passed to the method.

isAutoEntered

Syntax:

isAutoEntered

Data type returned: boolean

Description:

Returns a Boolean value indicating whether this field has any auto-entry options set.

isGlobal

Syntax:

isGlobal()

Data type returned: boolean

Description:

Returns a Boolean value indicating whether this field uses global storage.

validate

Syntax:

validate(mixed $value, [FileMaker_Error_Validation $error])

Data type returned: boolean

Description:

Returns a Boolean TRUE if $value is a valid value for this field. Otherwise, the method returns a FileMaker_Error_Validation object describing the error.

If you are validating more than one field, you pass in an existing FileMaker_Error_Validation object as the $error parameter, and any validation errors are added into that object.

FileMaker_Layout

FileMaker_Layout is a class representing an individual FileMaker layout. A FileMaker_Layout object, among other uses, is returned from a command along with a record result set.

FileMaker_Layout

Syntax:

FileMaker_Layout(FileMaker_Implementation $fm)

Data type returned: boolean

Description:

This is the class constructor. You pass it a FileMaker object. (FileMaker_Implementation is the hidden implementation class for a FileMaker object.)

getDatabase

Syntax:

getDatabase()

Data type returned: string

Description:

Returns a string with the name of the database in which this layout is found.

getField

Syntax:

getField(string $fieldName)

Data type returned: FileMaker_Field

Description:

Returns either a FileMaker_Field object corresponding to the name field or a FileMaker_Error object if some error was encountered.

getFields

Syntax:

getFields()

Data type returned: array

Description:

Returns an associative array with information on all fields on the layout. The array keys are the names of individual fields, and each array value is an individual FileMaker_Field object.

getName

Syntax:

getName()

Data type returned: string

Description:

Returns the name of this layout as a string.

getRelatedSet

Syntax:

getRelatedSet(string $relatedSet)

Data type returned: FileMaker_RelatedSet

Description:

Returns the FileMaker_RelatedSet object referred to by $relatedSet or returns a FileMaker_Error object if some error is encountered.

getRelatedSets

Syntax:

getRelatedSets()

Data type returned: array

Description:

Returns an associative array with the names of all related sets on the layout as keys. The value corresponding to each key is a FileMaker_RelatedSet object.

getValueList

Syntax:

getValueList (string $valueList, [string $recid])

Data type returned: array

Description:

Returns an array describing the values of the named value list on this layout. You can use the optional $recid parameter to specify a record from which the value list should be drawn.

Note that this method is now deprecated; FileMaker, Inc. recommends the use of getValueListTwoFields instead.

getValueListTwoFields

Syntax:

getValueListTwoFields($valueList, [string $recid])

Data type returned: array

Description:

Returns a multilevel associative array describing the values of the named value list on this layout. The top-level array contains the names of value lists as keys and associative arrays as values. Each associative array contains the values in the value list's first field as keys and the corresponding values in the list's second field as array values. You can use the optional $recid parameter to specify a record from which the value list should be drawn. Use this command to retrieve both values from a value list set to use two fields.

getValueLists

Syntax:

getValueLists ([string $recid])

Data type returned: array

Description:

Returns a multilevel associative array describing the values of all value lists on this layout. The top-level array contains the names of value lists as keys and associative arrays as values. Each associative array contains the values in the value list's first field as keys and the corresponding values in the list's second field as array values. You can use the optional $recid parameter to specify a record from which the value list should be drawn.

Note that this method is now deprecated; FileMaker, Inc. recommends the use of getValueListsTwoFields instead.

getValueListsTwoFields

Syntax:

getValueListsTwoFields([string $recid])

Data type returned: array

Description:

Returns a multilevel associative array describing the values of the named value list on this layout. The top-level array contains the names of value lists as keys and associative arrays as values. Each associative array contains the values in the value list's first field as keys and the corresponding values in the list's second field as array values. You can use the optional $recid parameter to specify a record from which the value list should be drawn. Use this command to retrieve both values from a value list set to use two fields.

listFields

Syntax:

listFields()

Data type returned: array

Description:

Returns an array of strings representing the names of each field on this layout. (Contrast with getFields(), which returns an array of FileMaker_Field objects).

listRelatedSets

Syntax:

listRelatedSets()

Data type returned: array

Description:

Returns an array of strings representing the names of each related set on this layout (contrast with getRelatedSets(), which returns an array of FileMaker_RelatedSet objects).

listValueLists

Syntax:

listValueLists()

Data type returned: array

Description:

Returns an array of strings representing the names of each value list on this layout (contrast with getValuelists(), which also returns the values in each value list).

FileMaker_Record

The FileMaker_Record class is the default class for representing each instance of a FileMaker record. You also can provide your own record class, although it must either be a subclass of FileMaker_Record or provide an identical interface. (Use the setRecordClass() method of FileMaker_Command and its subclasses to supply the name of your custom class.)

FileMaker_Record

Syntax:

FileMaker_Record(FileMaker_Layout $layout) or

FileMaker_Record(FileMaker_RelatedSet $relatedSet)

Data type returned: FileMaker_Record

Description:

This is the class constructor. You call it with either the FileMaker_Layout object or the FileMaker_RelatedSet object that contains this record.

commit

Syntax:

commit()

Data type returned: boolean

Description:

Commits the record to the database. It returns Boolean TRUE on success or a FileMaker_Error object on failure.

delete

Syntax:

delete()

Data type returned: FileMaker_Result

Description:

Deletes the record from the database. It returns a FileMaker_Result object on success or a FileMaker_Error object on failure.

getField

Syntax:

getField(string $field, [integer $repetition])

Data type returned: mixed

Description:

Returns the value from the specified field and repetition. The repetition defaults to 1 if not specified. This method converts some special characters in the field data to equivalent HTML entities.

getFieldUnencoded

Syntax:

getFieldUnencoded(string $field, [integer $repetition])

Data type returned: mixed

Description:

Returns the value from the specified field and repetition. The repetition defaults to 1 if not specified. This method performs no conversion of special characters in the field data to HTML entities.

getFieldAsTimestamp

Syntax:

getFieldAsTimestamp(string $field, [integer $repetition])

Data type returned: integer representing a timestamp

Description:

Returns the value from the specified field and repetition as a Unix timestamp. If the FileMaker field specified is a Date field, the timestamp corresponds to midnight on that date. If the date specified is a Time field, the timestamp corresponds to that time on January 1, 1970. If the date specified is a FileMaker Timestamp, it is converted directly to a Unix timestamp. The method returns a FileMaker_Error object if the resulting Timestamp would be out of range, or if the underlying field is not a Date, Time, or Timestamp field. The repetition defaults to 1 if not specified.

getFields

Syntax:

getFields()

Data type returned: array

Description:

Returns an array of strings corresponding to the names of all the fields in this record.

getLayout

Syntax:

getLayout()

Data type returned: FileMaker_Layout

Description:

Returns a FileMaker_Layout object corresponding to the layout this record is attached to.

getModificationID

Syntax:

getModificationID()

Data type returned: integer

Description:

Returns this record's modification ID.

getParent

Syntax:

getParent()

Data type returned: FileMaker_Record

Description:

Returns a FileMaker_Record object corresponding to the parent record if this record is a child record (in other words, this record is a part of a related set attached to another record).

getRecordID

Syntax:

getRecordID()

Data type returned: integer

Description:

Returns this record's record ID.

getRelatedSet

Syntax:

getRelatedSet(string $relatedSet)

Data type returned: array

Description:

Returns an array of FileMaker_Record objects corresponding to the records in the related set when given the name of a portal corresponding to a related set.

newRelatedRecord

Syntax:

newRelatedRecord(string $relatedSet)

Data type returned: FileMaker_Record

Description:

Creates a new FileMaker_Record object in the portal named by $relatedSet.

setField

Syntax:

setField(string $field, string $value, [integer $repetition])

Data type returned: mixed

Description:

Sets the given value into the specified field and repetition. The repetition defaults to 1 if not specified.

setFieldFromTimestamp

Syntax:

setFieldFromTimestamp(string $field, string $timestamp, integer $repetition)

Data type returned: void

Description:

Sets a new value for the named field and repetition ($repetition defaults to 1) from a Unix-style timestamp. The target field must be of type Date, Time, or Timestamp; otherwise, an error results. This enables the programmer to avoid worrying about complex conversions between Unix timestamps and the FileMaker Date and Time field types.

validate

Syntax:

validate([string $fieldName])

Data type returned: boolean

Description:

Validates the entire record, using any validation rules that can be checked by PHP. Optionally, you may specify the name of just a single field to check. The method returns Boolean TRUE if the validation tests succeed. Otherwise, the method returns a FileMaker_Error_Validation object describing the error.

FileMaker_RelatedSet

A FileMaker_RelatedSet object contains information about a single related set, which can generally best be thought of as a set of records displayed in a specific portal on a specific layout.

FileMaker_RelatedSet

Syntax:

FileMaker_RelatedSet(FileMaker_Layout $layout)

Data type returned: FileMaker_RelatedSet

Description:

This is the class constructor. It creates a new FileMaker_RelatedSet based on a specific FileMaker_Layout object.

getField

Syntax:

getField(string $fieldName)

Data type returned: FileMaker_Field

Description:

Returns a FileMaker_Field object corresponding to the named field or a FileMaker_Error object if the request fails for some reason.

getFields

Syntax:

getFields()

Data type returned: array

Description:

Returns an associative array with information on all fields on the layout. The array keys are the names of individual fields, and each array value is an individual FileMaker_Field object.

getName

Syntax:

getName()

Data type returned: string

Description:

Returns the name of this layout as a string.

listFields

Syntax:

listFields()

Data type returned: array

Description:

Returns an array of strings representing the names of each field on this layout (contrast with getFields(), which returns an array of FileMaker_Field objects).

FileMaker_Result

The FileMaker_Result class represents a result returned by a FileMaker command. More often than not, it contains a set of one or more records that were found or otherwise affected by the command.

FileMaker_Result

Syntax:

FileMaker_Result(FileMaker_Implementation $fm)

Data type returned: FileMaker_Result

Description:

This is the class constructor. You pass it a FileMaker object. (FileMaker_Implementation is the hidden implementation class for a FileMaker object.)

getFetchCount

Syntax:

getFetchCount()

Data type returned: integer

Description:

Returns the number of records in this result set. This count respects any range restraints placed on a search, such as a skip or max constraint.

getFields

Syntax:

getFields()

Data type returned: array

Description:

Returns an array of strings representing the names of each field in this result set. Unlike other methods named getFields, this method returns only the field names, not actual FileMaker_Field objects.

getFirstRecord

Syntax:

getFirstRecord()

Data type returned: FileMaker_Record

Description:

Returns a FileMaker_Record object representing the first record in the result set.

getFoundSetCount

Syntax:

getFoundSetCount()

Data type returned: integer

Description:

Returns the number of records in the entire found set of which this result set is a part. (This differs from the result of getFetchCount() if constraints such as skip and max are in effect.)

getLastRecord

Syntax:

getLastRecord()

Data type returned: FileMaker_Record

Description:

Returns a FileMaker_Record object representing the last record in the result set.

getLayout

Syntax:

getLayout()

Data type returned: FileMaker_Layout

Description:

Returns a FileMaker_Layout object representing the layout to which the result set belongs.

getRecords

Syntax:

getRecords()

Data type returned: array

Description:

Returns an array of objects representing all records in the result set. The objects are of type FileMaker_Record, unless you have specified that a different class be used.

getRelatedSets

Syntax:

getRelatedSets()

Data type returned: array

Description:

Returns an array of strings representing the names of all related sets in this result set.

getTableRecordCount

Syntax:

getTableRecordCount()

Data type returned: integer

Description:

Returns the total number of records in the base table for this result set.

CHAPTER 19

JDBC/ODBC and External SQL Connectivity

A FileMaker system can act as a data source for external access via Open Database Connectivity (ODBC) or Java Database Connectivity (JDBC). Likewise, using the external SQL sources (ESS) feature, FileMaker solutions can gain direct access to data in certain SQL-based database systems. FileMaker also supports the ability to import records from an ODBC data source and to execute SQL statements against remote data sources using the `Execute SQL` script step.

This chapter discusses how to make a FileMaker database available for external access from ODBC or JDBC. It also covers how to set up a Data Source Name (DSN), on both the Mac OS and Windows, for use with the ESS, Import ODBC, and `Execute SQL` features.

Setting Up Inbound ODBC and JDBC Connectivity

A FileMaker database has the capability to act as a data source for connections from ODBC and JDBC clients. If the database is accessed locally (not via FileMaker Server), it can serve data to ODBC and JDBC clients on the same local machine; for example, Microsoft Excel can be used as an ODBC client to access data in a FileMaker file that's open on the same machine as the Excel application.

To serve FileMaker data to remote ODBC and JDBC clients (where the files will not be open on the same machine as the ODBC/JDBC client), you need to use FileMaker Server Advanced, which provides remote ODBC/JDBC connectivity.

Configuring a Database for ODBC/JDBC Access

To make a file's data accessible to external ODBC and JDBC clients, you must first set the appropriate extended privileges. ODBC/JDBC access is controlled via the `fmxdbc` extended privilege. This privilege is created by default in new FileMaker 12 databases, although you still need to enable it for specific privilege sets. You can enable this privilege directly for various privilege sets via the Extended Privilege area under File, Manage, Security, as shown in Figure 19.1.

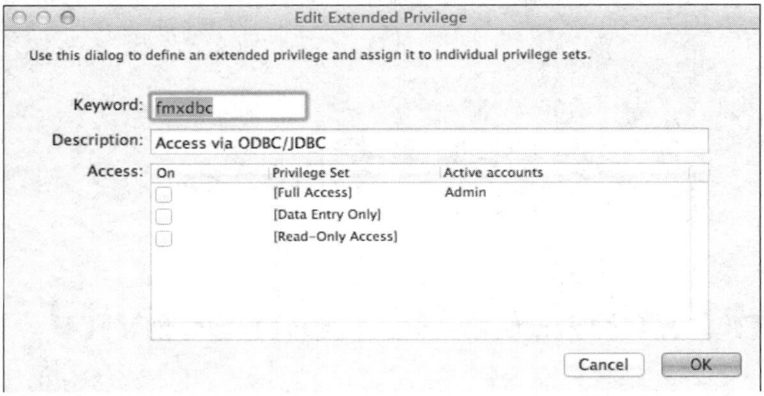

Figure 19.1
You must enable the fmxdbc *extended privilege in a database to share it via ODBC or JDBC.*

As an alternative, you can choose File, Sharing, ODBC/JDBC. The lower half of that dialog box, shown in Figure 19.2, simply provides a more convenient way of managing the same extended privileges.

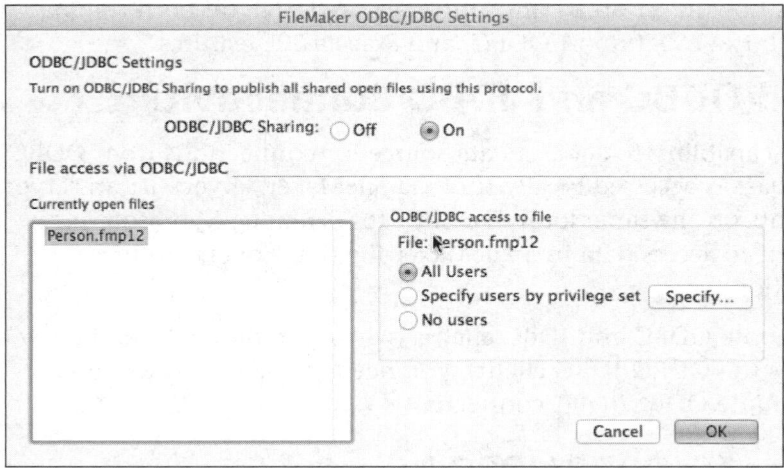

Figure 19.2
The FileMaker ODBC/JDBC Settings dialog provides an alternative way to set the fmxdbc *extended privilege in one or more open files.*

If no privilege set has the fmxdbc extended privilege set enabled, OBDC and JDBC clients are not able to access any data in the file.

Enabling ODBC/JDBC Access in FileMaker Pro

You can share FileMaker via ODBC/JDBC in either of two ways. In the first method, a copy of FileMaker Pro or FileMaker Pro Advanced acts as the data provider. In this case, the data is available only to other applications running on the same computer. ODBC/JDBC clients on a different computer aren't able to access data when FileMaker Pro is the data provider. (FileMaker Pro and Advanced allow access only from processes running on the same machine.)

To enable ODBC/JDBC access from FileMaker Pro or FileMaker Pro Advanced, choose File, Sharing, ODBC/JDBC; then make sure that ODBC/JDBC Sharing is set to On in the upper area of the dialog, as shown previously in Figure 19.2.

Enabling ODBC/JDBC Access in FileMaker Server Advanced

You can share FileMaker data to remote ODBC/JDBC clients if you are using FileMaker Server Advanced. The files you want to make accessible must be hosted by FileMaker Server Advanced (and, of course, have the `fmxdbc` extended privilege enabled). The only other prerequisite is that FileMaker Server Advanced must have its ODBC/JDBC access enabled, which you do using the FileMaker Server Admin Console, as shown in Figure 19.3.

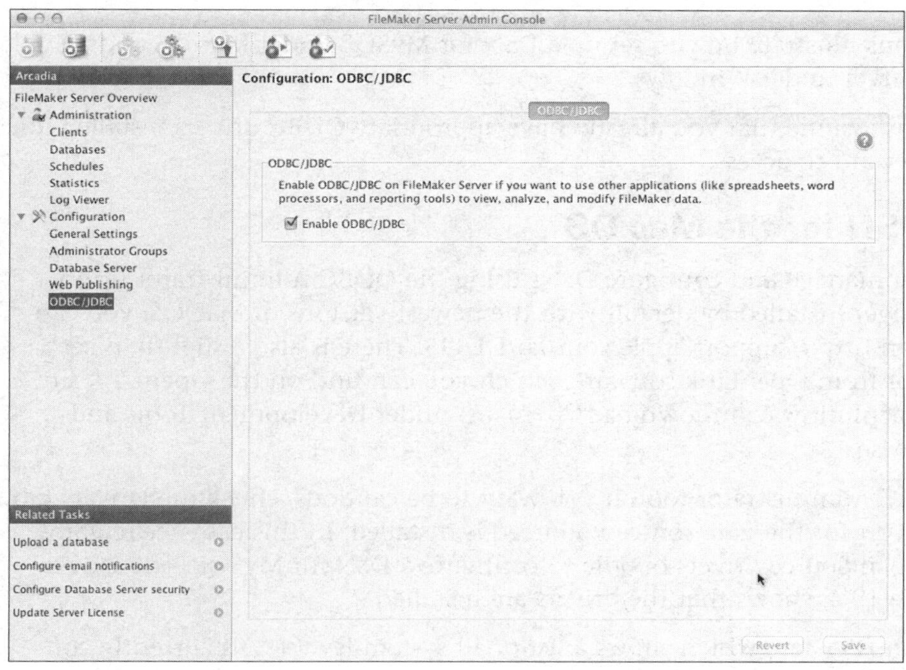

Figure 19.3
The Enable ODBC/JDBC setting in FileMaker Server Advanced must be enabled to allow remote ODBC/JDBC access to hosted files.

Setting Up a DSN for External SQL Connectivity

FileMaker has several means for requesting data from remote data sources via ODBC:

- ODBC Import (choose File, Import, ODBC Data Source)
- Execute SQL script step
- External ODBC data source (choose File, Manage, External Data Sources)

To use any of these methods of interacting with a remote ODBC source, you need to have one or more DSNs configured. For ODBC Import and the Execute SQL script step, the DSNs need to be configured on the same computer as the specific copy of FileMaker Pro that performs the access. The External SQL (ODBC) Source feature is unique in that, for files hosted under FileMaker Server, the DSNs may be configured on the FileMaker Server machine instead. This can save a great deal of time and bother because it avoids the need to configure identical DSNs on each client computer that will use the files.

Note

No additional configuration is necessary on the FileMaker Server machine: If the DSNs are present, FileMaker Server automatically finds them and uses them without additional setup.

The following sections illustrate how to set up a DSN for MySQL under Mac OS and a DSN for Microsoft SQL Server under Windows.

Both demonstrations assume that you already have appropriate ODBC drivers installed for the data source you want to access.

Setting Up a DSN for the Mac OS

On the Mac OS, you manage and configure DSNs using the ODBC Administrator utility. This utility is no longer installed by default with the newest versions of Mac OS; you can download them from http://support.apple.com/kb/DL895. There is also a slightly nicer ODBC Administrator from OpenLink software, which you can find on the OpenLink site (http://download.openlinksw.com/download/?p=m_os) under Development Tools and Frameworks: Enterprise.

First, open the ODBC Administrator tool. If you want to be cautious, check the Drivers tab to make sure the driver for the data source you need is installed. In this case, we're going to use the Actual Open Source drivers bundle to configure a DSN for MySQL. The Drivers tab, shown in Figure 19.4, shows that the drivers are installed.

Switch to the System DSN tab, which shows a list of all system-level DSNs currently configured on this computer. (A *system DSN* may be used by anyone on the computer, whereas a *user DSN* may be used only by a specific user. In general, it's probably a good idea to stick with system DSNs.) Figure 19.5 shows the System DSN tab.

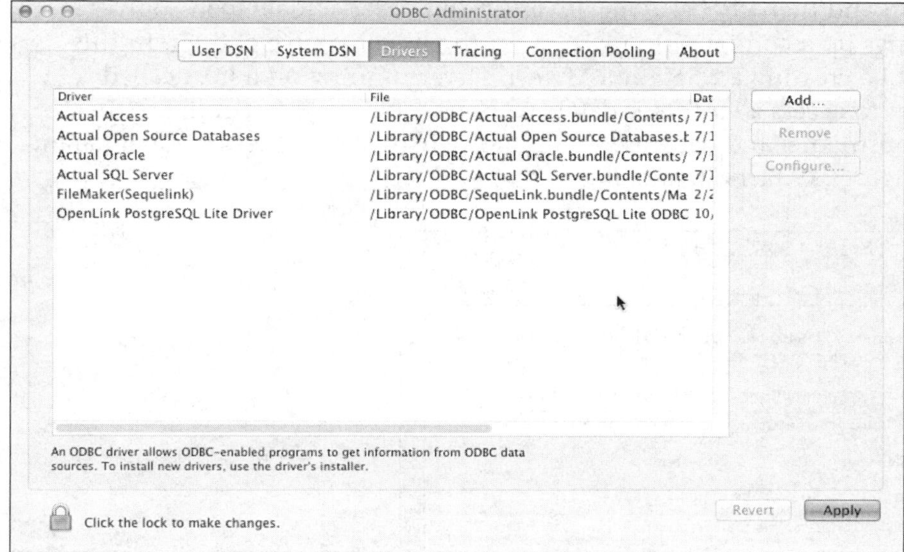

Figure 19.4
The Drivers tab of the Mac OS ODBC Administrator shows all installed ODBC drivers.

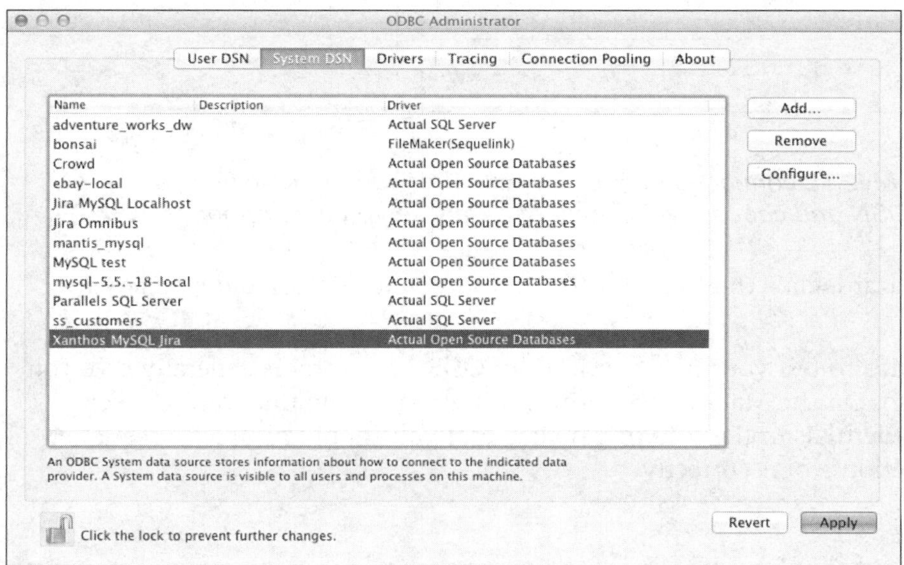

Figure 19.5
The System DSN tab of the Mac OS ODBC Administrator enables you to manage system-level DSNs.

Click the Add button and then choose your driver (in this case, Actual Open Source Databases). This brings up a configuration wizard for the driver you've chosen. In this example, you might be creating a DSN for a MySQL server running on a host called mysql.someplace.net to access a customer database. You would need to configure the DSN's description, hostname, and database name, along with some other optional parameters, as shown in Figures 19.6, 19.7, and 19.8.

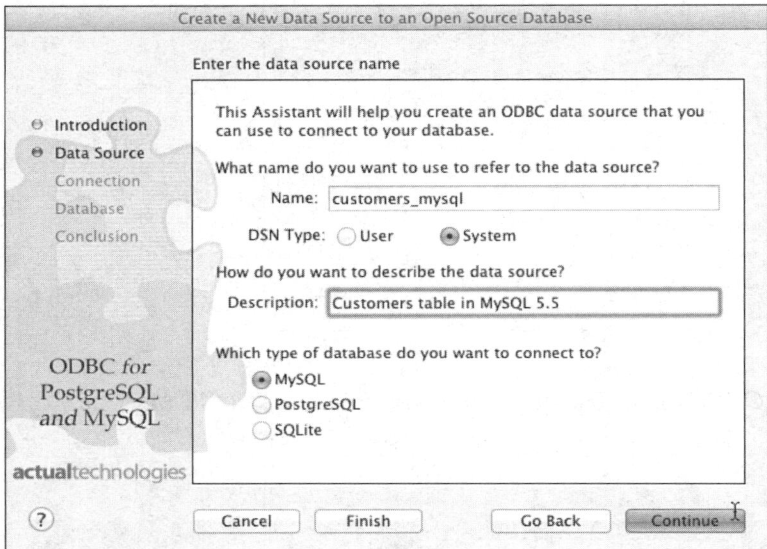

Figure 19.6
When configuring a MySQL connection using the Actual drivers on Mac OS, you first need to name your DSN and choose which type of database you are connecting to.

At the end of the wizard, click the Done button, and the new DSN should be ready for use.

It's always a good idea to test your new connection. ODBC setup tools generally give you an easy way to do so. On the Mac OS, press the Test button on the final setup screen. Enter your login credentials in the resulting dialog, and you should be able to see whether the connection works correctly.

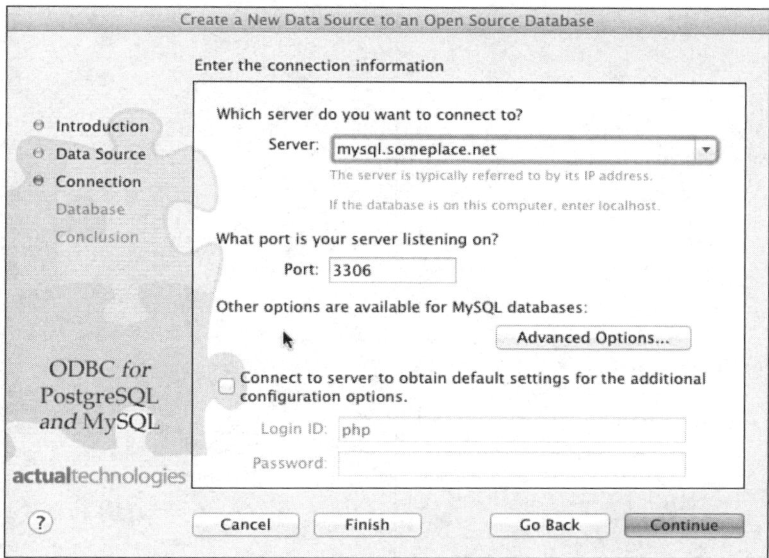

Figure 19.7
The next step in creating a MySQL connection using the Actual drivers on Mac OS is to specify a host configuration.

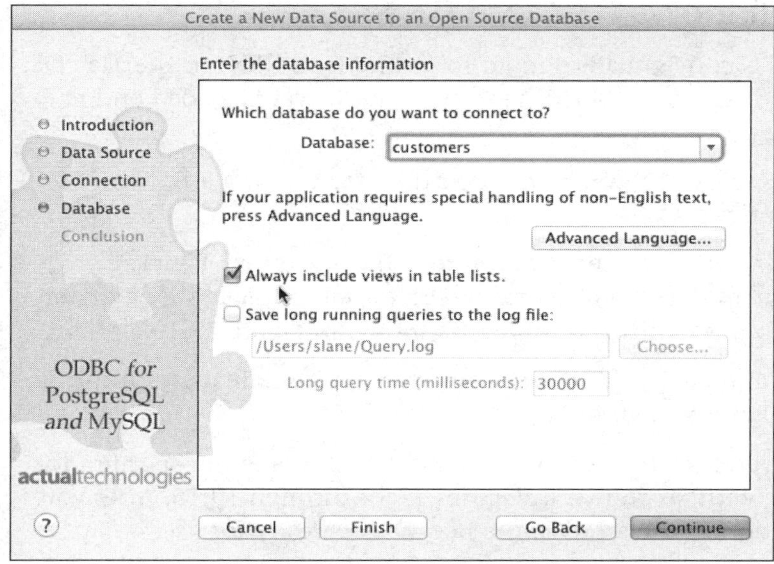

Figure 19.8
The last step in creating a MySQL connection using the Actual drivers on Mac OS is to specify a database name.

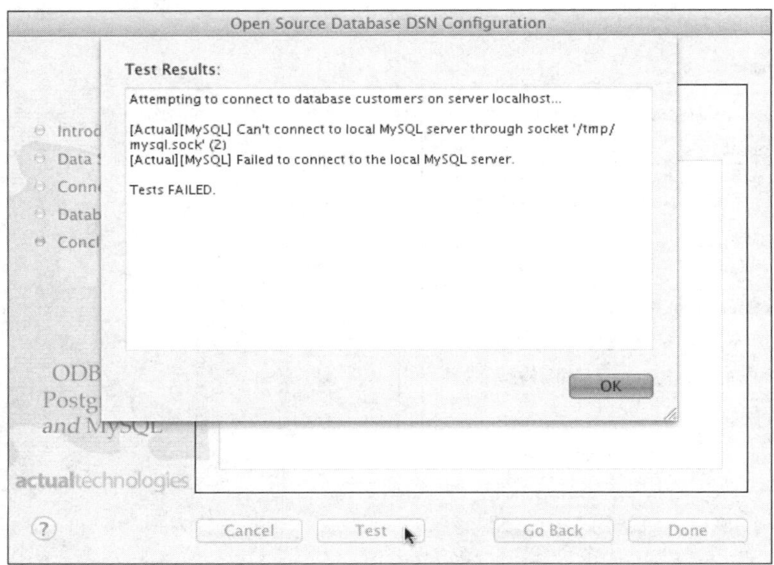

Figure 19.9
It's a good idea to test the new DSN from within your ODBC setup tool.

Setting Up a DSN in Windows

Setting up a DSN on Windows is conceptually similar to setting up a DSN for the Mac OS: Use your system's ODBC administration tool to check that your driver is loaded and to kick off the DSN configuration process.

The procedure demonstrated is for Windows 7: The procedure for creating a DSN in Windows Vista is virtually identical.

Begin by choosing the Windows ODBC administration tool (Start, Control Panel, Administrative Tools, Data Sources [ODBC]). Check the Drivers tab to make sure a driver for the data source you want to work with is installed, as shown in Figure 19.10.

Switch to the System DSN tab and click Add; then choose the appropriate driver from the Create New Data Source window, as shown in Figure 19.11.

The next steps run through several configuration screens in which you enter specifics for the data source you're working with, as shown in Figures 19.12 through 19.16. After you fill in the appropriate information in the screens, the new DSN is ready for use.

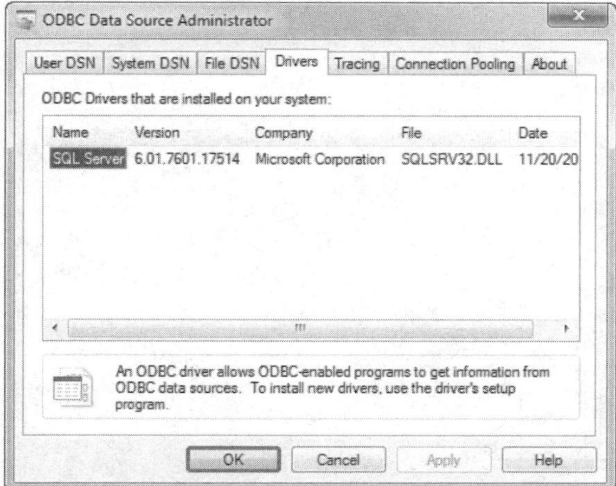

Figure 19.10
The Windows ODBC Data Source Administrator also has a Drivers tab showing all installed drivers.

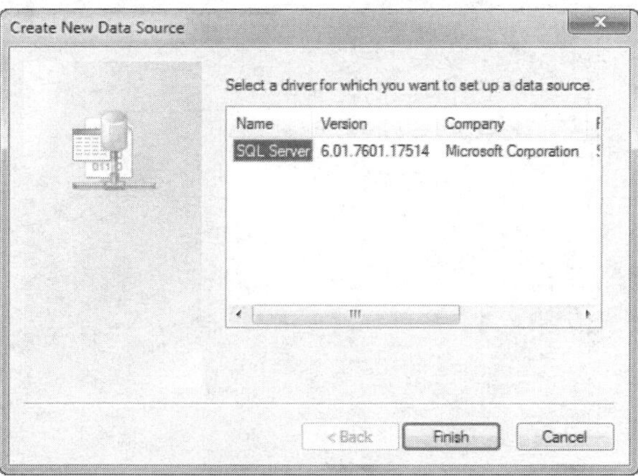

Figure 19.11
On Windows, choose from among the available drivers to create a new SQL Server DSN.

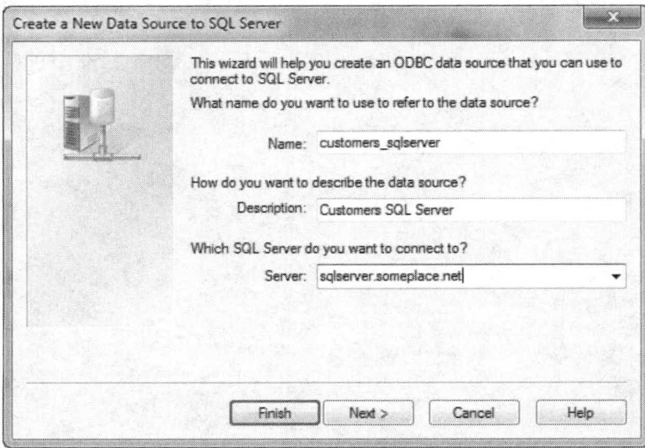

Figure 19.12
When creating a new SQL Server DSN on Windows, begin by specifying the DSN name and hostname.

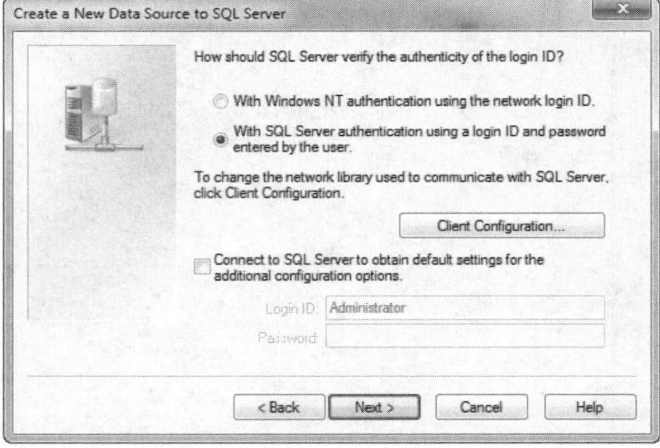

Figure 19.13
When creating a new SQL Server DSN on Windows, next specify the means of authentication.

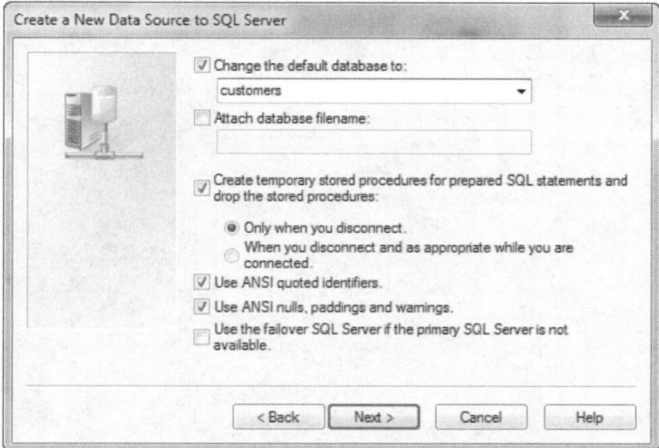

Figure 19.14
When creating a new SQL Server DSN on Windows, next specify the database name.

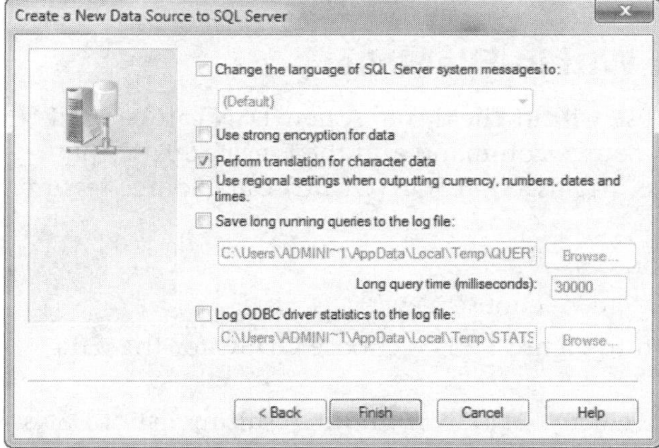

Figure 19.15
The configuration of a SQL Server DSN on Windows concludes with a set of miscellaneous configuration options.

When you're done creating the DSN, it's a good idea to test it using the testing feature of the ODBC administration tool, as shown in Figure 19.16.

Figure 19.16
It's a good idea to test the new DSN from within your ODBC setup tool.

Using an External Data Source Within FileMaker

After you define a DSN, it is available for use within FileMaker. A new DSN can be used immediately with the Import from ODBC Source command and the `Execute SQL` script step. To use the third form of ODBC access, the External SQL (ODBC) Data Source feature, you need to complete one more procedure:

1. Choose File, Manage, External Data Sources.
2. On the Manage External Data Sources screen, choose New.
3. On the Edit Data Source screen (shown in Figure 19.17), choose ODBC for the data source type.
4. For the DSN, choose Specify and then select your DSN from the resulting list of DSNs defined on this machine. (If you are working with a file served via FileMaker Server, you choose instead from a list of DSNs defined on the host machine.)
5. As part of setting up the data source, you can also provide a username and password to be used when accessing the remote database (so that your users don't have to remember another password), as well as apply some filtering criteria to limit which tables and views from the remote source are accessible.
6. After the new data source is set up, you can access it when creating new table occurrences in the Relationships Graph.

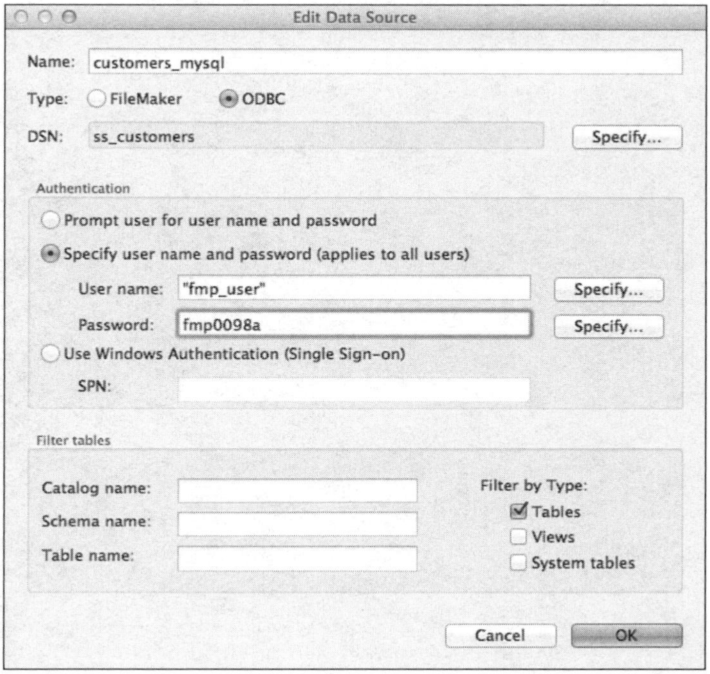

Figure 19.17
In FileMaker 12, choose File, Manage, External Data Sources to create and configure a new external SQL 12 (ODBC) data source.

Note

In FileMaker 12, it's easy to confuse the Execute SQL script step with the new ExecuteSQL calculation function. The script step executes SQL against an SQL data source outside of FileMaker, via ODBC, and needs a valid ODBC DSN to do so. The new ExecuteSQL calculation function allows you to write an SQL query that fetches data from a currently available FileMaker database. This new technology doesn't use ODBC and requires no DSN setup. For more on the ExecuteSQL calculation function, see Chapter 10, "Calculation Functions."

CHAPTER 20

AppleScript Integration

AppleScript is a scripting language built into the Mac OS X operating system; it is configured and ready to run on Apple computers right out of the box. In addition to providing users with a macro-like ability to manipulate files and other aspects of the Mac OS X and the Finder, AppleScript also has the capability to automate and integrate applications that have been engineered to be "scriptable."

FileMaker is one such application. You can use AppleScript both to manipulate FileMaker and to allow FileMaker to control and communicate with other applications. For instance, developers can embed the following script in FileMaker to get the name, title, and image of the first selected contact in the OS X Address Book and use that data to create and populate a new record in a database called "Personnel Records":

```
-- control the Address Book application...
tell application "Address Book"
    -- get the selected contacts...
    set sel_people to the selection
    -- get the first selected contact...
    set first_per to first item of sel_people
    -- get the name, title, and image of the first selected contact...
    set {per_lst_nm, per_fst_nm, per_title, per_img} to {last name of first_per, ¬
        first name of first_per, job title of first_per, image of first_per}
end tell
(*
temporarily save Address Book TIFF format picture because setting
container fields via AppleScript is not supported by FileMaker.
The TIFF import is done at the end with a call to a FileMaker
script...
*)
tell application "System Events"
    -- set up file path for the temp tiff file...
    set tif_path to "/var/tmp/tempic.tiff"
    -- open a file reference...
    set file_ref to open for access ((POSIX file tif_path) ¬
        as reference) with write permission
    -- clear all data if file exists...
```

```
    set eof of file_ref to 0
    -- write the TIFF data...
    write per_img to file_ref as TIFF picture
    -- close the file reference...
    close access file_ref
end tell
-- control FileMaker Pro...
tell application "FileMaker Pro"
    tell database "Personnel Records"
        -- create new personnel record...
        set new_rec to create new record
        -- populate the new record with data from Address Book...
        tell new_rec
            show
            set {cell "First Name", cell "Last Name", cell "Title"} ¬
                to {per_fst_nm, per_lst_nm, per_title}
        -- call a ScriptMaker script that inserts TIFF into container field...
            do script "insertTempTiff"
        end tell
    end tell
end tell
```

Note

Be sure to use the correct application name when "telling" FileMaker to do something. If you are using FileMaker Pro Advanced, you need to change the application name in the examples throughout this chapter accordingly.

This script illustrates AppleScript's capabilities as an integration tool. In the first section, AppleScript takes control of the Address Book application and acquires data from that application. In the last section, it instructs FileMaker Pro to create a new record in the Personnel Records database, populates the fields with Address Book text data, and then calls a FileMaker script that imports the contact's TIFF image from its temporary location.

The AppleScript Interface

Within FileMaker, AppleScript code executes from the Perform AppleScript script step. This allows developers to embed AppleScript code directly in their FileMaker scripts.

As shown in Figure 20.1, the "Perform AppleScript" Options dialog presents two options for embedding AppleScript within a FileMaker script:

- Calculated AppleScript enables developers to programmatically derive AppleScript from a calculation expression, as shown in Figure 20.2. Note that the 30,000-character restriction in the calculation dialog limits how much code you can generate dynamically.
- Native AppleScript accepts a block of text code, up to 30,000 characters.

➔ *For more information about using the Specify Calculation dialog, see "The Calculation Function Interface" in Chapter 8, "Calculation Primer."*

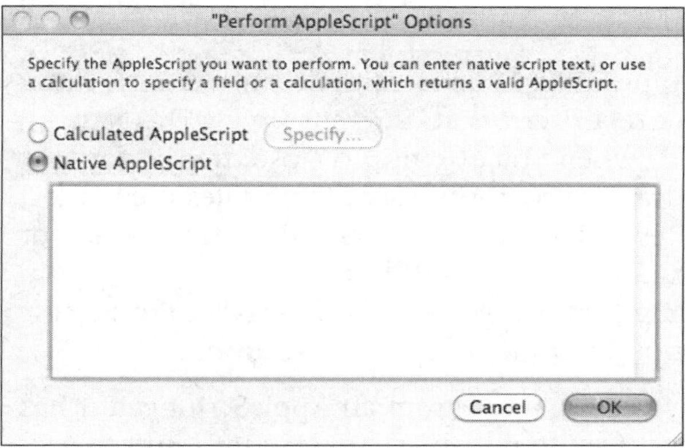

Figure 20.1
The "Perform AppleScript" Options dialog.

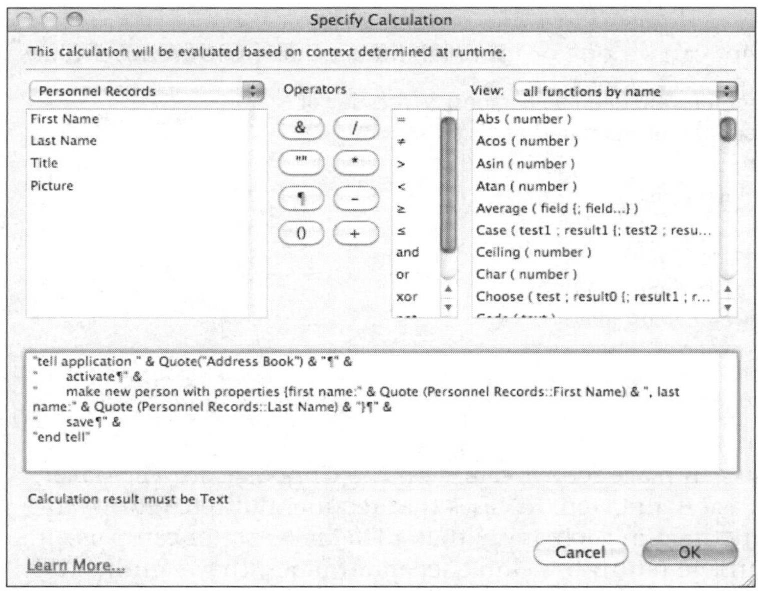

Figure 20.2
Defining AppleScript code with a calculation.

AppleScript code must be compiled by the system before it is executed, which means that performance might be somewhat slower with Calculated AppleScript code because the calculation must first be evaluated by FileMaker and the result compiled by AppleScript before the code can execute. Any lag would likely be noticeable only with large or complex Calculated AppleScripts. The Native AppleScript method compiles the AppleScript code when the "Perform AppleScript" Options dialog closes, and FileMaker stores the compiled AppleScript code with the script step, so there is no lag before the code executes.

The AppleScript compiler reports errors in AppleScript code at compile time, so this means that the two methods of Perform AppleScript report errors at different times. The Native AppleScript method reports errors in the code when you attempt to close the "Perform AppleScript" Options dialog because that's the time that AppleScript compiles the code. Calculated AppleScript, on the other hand, reports any errors in the calculation syntax or formatting when you close the Specify Calculation dialog, but it does not report AppleScript errors until the script runs because that is the time that FileMaker Pro passes the Calculated AppleScript code to AppleScript for compilation and execution.

Sometimes a FileMaker script needs to receive information from an AppleScript call it has instigated, but unfortunately there is no direct way to return an AppleScript result to a FileMaker script. Because the Perform AppleScript step does not return a result, AppleScript cannot set FileMaker variables, nor can AppleScript pass a parameter to a script via the do script command. Instead, the three most common ways to return AppleScript results to a FileMaker script are indirect:

- **FileMaker fields**—AppleScript can set one or more FileMaker fields with return values:

```
set short_date to ((month of (current date) as number) & "/" & day of ¬
  (current date) & "/" & year of (current date)) as text
tell application "FileMaker Pro"
  tell database "Personnel Records"
    tell current record
      set field "First Name" to "John"
      set field "Last Name" to "Smith"
      set field "Date of Hire" to short_date
    end tell
  end tell
end tell
```

- **The Clipboard**—AppleScript can place return values on the Clipboard for FileMaker scripts to retrieve with the Paste script step. In cases that require multiple return values, the result should be structured in such a way that a FileMaker script can parse it. For instance, if you use a carriage return to delimit separate values, they can then be parsed from within FileMaker using the GetValue function.

```
set the clipboard to "John" & return ¬
  & "Smith" & return ¬
  & ((month of (current date) as number) & "/" & day of (current date) ¬
  & "/" & year of (current date)) as text
```

- **A file in a common disk location**—A FileMaker script can use an Import script step to read result data that AppleScript has written to a file in a common location on disk:

```
-- after performing some process...
set AS_result to the result
set result_path to "/var/tmp/ASResult.txt" -- set up file path for the temp text file...
set file_ref to open for access ((POSIX file result_path) as reference) ¬
   with write permission
set eof of file_ref to 0 -- clear any previous data from the file...
write AS_result to file_ref
close access file_ref
```

About the AppleScript Object Model

AppleScript is an object-oriented scripting language, which means that AppleScript can query and control objects that have been exposed to AppleScript within a "scriptable" application. To use AppleScript to manipulate FileMaker data, you need to be familiar with FileMaker's object containment hierarchy. For instance, the following AppleScript queries a series of objects, starting with the application itself:

```
tell application "FileMaker Pro"
   tell document "Personnel Records"
      tell layout "Form View"
         tell record 2
            return field "Employee ID"
         end tell
      end tell
   end tell
end tell
```

There's an implied hierarchy in this code example, which begins with application as the top-level object (sometimes referred to as the *parent*). Next, document is an element of application (sometimes referred to as the *child*), whereas layout is an element of document, and so on.

Database and table objects, concepts familiar to FileMaker Pro developers, belong to a different branch of FileMaker's object hierarchy. A script that has the same result as the preceding script, but using the database branch, would look like this:

```
tell application "FileMaker Pro"
   tell database "Personnel Records"
      tell record 2
         return cell "Employee ID"
      end tell
   end tell
end tell
```

The reason for the difference is that FileMaker Pro's object hierarchy has two main branches: the user interface branch, in which the "document" contains objects such as "window" and "layout," and then there's the underlying "database," which contains objects such as "table" and "FileMaker Script." It's important to understand the containment hierarchy of the application being scripted because the objects called by the script determine the scope of the data that the script can access. Figure 20.3 illustrates FileMaker Pro's containment hierarchy.

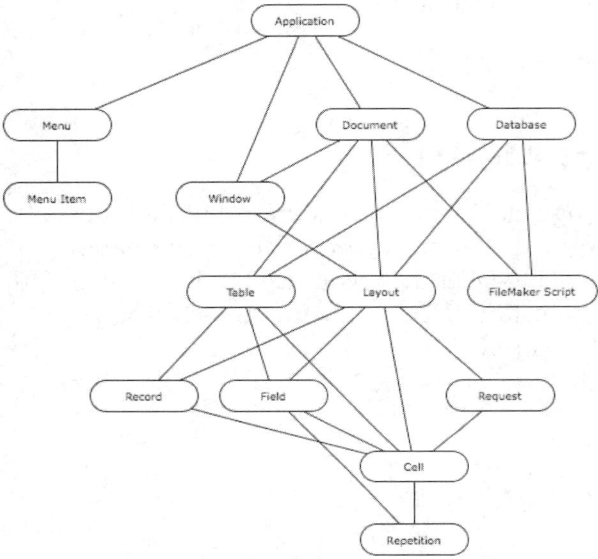

Figure 20.3
FileMaker Pro's containment hierarchy.

There is a distinction between the "document" and "database" objects that's worth noting: The database object refers to the entire set of records in a database, but the document object refers only to the found set of the frontmost window. There's a similarly subtle distinction between the "field" and "cell" objects: You use the field object to reference an entire column of values; you use the cell object to reference a value of a field from a particular record. To understand both of these distinctions, consider the following code snippets:

```
tell application "FileMaker Pro"
    tell database "Personnel Records"
        set field "First Name" to "Nate"
    end tell
end tell
```

```
tell application "FileMaker Pro"
    tell document "Personnel Records"
        set cell "First Name" to "Eleanor"
    end tell
end tell
```

The result of executing the first snippet is to modify the value of the First Name field of *every record* in the database. The second snippet modifies just the first record of the current found set.

The application dictionary documents the containment hierarchy of an application's object model, along with the *commands* and *properties* of the object model that are available for AppleScript to control. Viewing an application's dictionary can be a good way to familiarize yourself with its AppleScript capabilities.

You can view an application's dictionary by dragging and dropping the application's icon onto the AppleScript Editor icon, which is in the /Applications/Utilities/ folder on the startup hard drive. Selecting File, Open Dictionary in the AppleScript Editor also opens the application dictionaries for study. Every scriptable application must have a dictionary; if the dictionary window does not open, the application is not scriptable. The application dictionary appears in a dictionary window like the one shown in Figure 20.4.

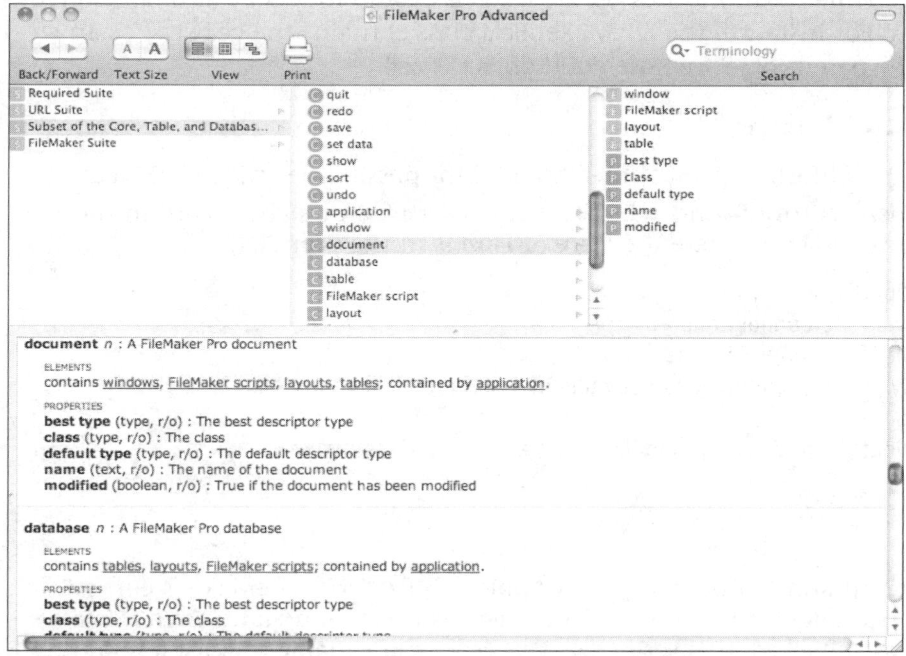

Figure 20.4
The application dictionary window.

The dictionary window denotes the type of object it displays using the following icons:

- **Suites**—Functional groups of classes, commands, properties, and elements.
- **Commands**—Directives that instruct the application to perform an action. Examples of commands include the following: Open, Count, Create, Print, and Do Menu. In some cases,

a command is actually a function; that is, it returns a value as the result of its operation. For those commands that return a result (for instance, Count and Data Size), the last line of the dictionary definition begins with an arrow.

- **Classes**—Classes list the objects that AppleScript can "tell" to do something, as in tell application "FileMaker Pro", tell layout "Form View", and so on.
- **Properties**—Properties, sometimes also referred to as attributes or characteristics, are simply class variables that contain information about a particular instance of a class. For example, the FileMaker Pro field class has the property choices, which stores the value list associated with the field instance on a particular layout. Most properties are read-only and can thus be used to return facts about a particular object, such as its unique ID, its access privileges, or its name. Some properties, such as a cell's cellValue or a window's bounds, can be modified.
- **Elements**—Classes often contain one or more elements, which typically contain a specific type of data. Elements, in most cases, are also classes, so they may also be referred to as child objects. For instance, the FileMaker field class contains the cell class as an element, so field is the parent object whose child object is cell.

AppleScript Examples

The following examples illustrate some other AppleScript possibilities with FileMaker:

- **Showing records/creating found sets**—This AppleScript shows any record in the Personnel Records database where the Date of Hire is in the year 2012:

```
tell application "FileMaker Pro"
   tell database "Personnel Records"
      tell table "Personnel Records"
         show (every record whose cellValue of cell "Date of Hire" contains 2012)
      end tell
      sort layout "Form View" by field "Last Name" in order descending
   end tell
end tell
```

- **Getting the current state of objects**—This AppleScript returns FileMaker's current View state. For example, if the Browse Mode, View as Form, and Status Area items of the View menu are checked, this script sets the view_state variable to a list containing three text strings: {"Browse Mode", "View as Form", "Status Area"}. If executed while FileMaker was in Layout Mode, the script might return {"Layout Mode", "Rulers", "Dynamic Guides", "Status Toolbar", "Inspector"}.

```
tell application "FileMaker Pro"
   set view_state to name of every menu item of menu "View" whose checked is true
end tell
```

- **Getting an inventory of elements**—This AppleScript sets the variable named layout_fields to a list of properties of every field on a particular layout:

```
tell application "FileMaker Pro"
   tell document "Personnel Records"
      tell layout "Form View"
         set layout_fields to ¬
            { name of every field, ¬
               default type of every field, ¬
               access of every field, ¬
               formula of every cell}
      end tell
   end tell
end tell
```

Other Resources

The following websites give more information about programming with AppleScript:

- **AppleScript Language Guide**—http://developer.apple.com/library/mac/#documentation/AppleScript/Conceptual/AppleScriptLangGuide/introduction/ASLR_intro.html
- **Apple AppleScript Users List**—http://www.lists.apple.com/mailman/listinfo/applescript-users
- **MacScripter's Forums**—http://macscripter.net/
- **Mac OS X Automation Site**—http://www.macosxautomation.com/applescript

CHAPTER 21

FileMaker Error Codes

FileMaker displays error dialogs during normal operation; for example, if you attempt to enter text into a date field, FileMaker displays a dialog telling you that the value must be a valid date. FileMaker also generates errors in the course of executing a script, and you need to understand how to detect and handle these errors.

It's only during scripting, or during certain interactions with the Web Publishing Engine (WPE), that you are in a position to trap and examine the error codes FileMaker generates. To do so requires that Error Capture be set to On during the script and that the script developer use the Get(LastError) function to inspect any possible errors.

The FileMaker error results that occur during scripts are transient. You must check for an error immediately after a script step executes. If script step A produces an error, and a subsequent script step B executes with no error, the error from script step A will be "forgotten" after script step B executes. Hence, the name of the Get(LastError) function: It reports only the last error code, even if that error code is 0 (no error). (Note, though, that the error code from the last script step is retained even after the script has stopped executing, until it is replaced by another script. Further, the script steps Exit Script and Halt Script do not clear the previous error code.)

The Script Debugger provides another tool for determining whether any errors occurred during the execution of a script. As shown in Figure 21.1, the Script Debugger automatically tells you the error code generated by the last executed script step. The error code is a link that takes you to the help system where you can view the error description. Further, the option to Pause on Error enables you to quickly test a script for errors without stepping through it line by line.

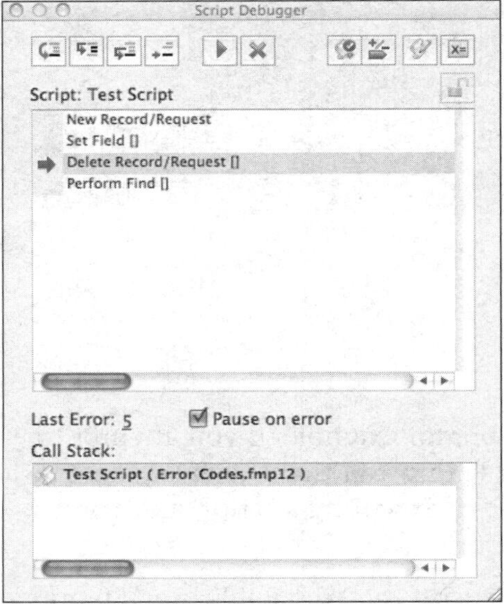

Figure 21.1
The Script Debugger in FileMaker Pro 12 Advanced shows the error code generated by each script step as it executes.

Table 21.1 lists the errors that can arise during normal operation of FileMaker or during ODBC access. The errors listed in Table 21.2 are those generated by the FileMaker Server command-line interface.

Table 21.1 FileMaker Error Codes

Code	Error Description
–1	Unknown error.
0	No error.
1	User canceled action.
2	Memory error.
3	Command is unavailable (for example, wrong operating system, wrong mode).
4	Command is unknown.
5	Command is invalid (for example, a Set Field script step does not have a calculation specified).
6	File is read-only.
7	Running out of memory.
8	Empty result.
9	Insufficient privileges.
10	Requested data is missing.
11	Name is not valid.
12	Name already exists.

Table 21.1 Continued

Code	Error Description
13	File or object is in use.
14	Out of range.
15	Can't divide by zero.
16	Operation failed, request retry (for example, a user query).
17	Attempt to convert foreign character set to UTF-16 failed.
18	Client must provide account information to proceed.
19	String contains characters other than A–Z, a–z, 0–9 (ASCII).
20	Command/operation canceled by triggered script.
100	File is missing.
101	Record is missing.
102	Field is missing.
103	Relationship is missing.
104	Script is missing.
105	Layout is missing.
106	Table is missing.
107	Index is missing.
108	Value list is missing.
109	Privilege set is missing.
110	Related tables are missing.
111	Field repetition is invalid.
112	Window is missing.
113	Function is missing.
114	File reference is missing.
115	Menu set is missing.
116	Layout object is missing.
117	Data source is missing.
118	Theme is missing.
130	Files are damaged or missing and must be reinstalled.
131	Language pack files are missing (such as template files).
200	Record access is denied.
201	Field cannot be modified.
202	Field access is denied.
203	No records in file to print, or password doesn't allow print access.
204	No access to field(s) in sort order.
205	User does not have access privileges to create new records; import overwrites existing data.
206	User does not have password change privileges, or file is not modifiable.
207	User does not have sufficient privileges to change database schema, or file is not modifiable.
208	Password does not contain enough characters.

Table 21.1 Continued

Code	Error Description
209	New password must be different from existing one.
210	User account is inactive.
211	Password has expired.
212	Invalid user account and/or password; please try again.
213	User account and/or password does not exist.
214	Too many login attempts.
215	Administrator privileges cannot be duplicated.
216	Guest account cannot be duplicated.
217	User does not have sufficient privileges to modify administrator account.
218	Password and verify password do not match.
300	File is locked or in use.
301	Record is in use by another user.
302	Table is in use by another user.
303	Database schema is in use by another user.
304	Layout is in use by another user.
306	Record modification ID does not match.
307	Transaction could not be locked because of a communication error with the host.
308	Theme is in use by another user.
400	Find criteria are empty.
401	No records match the request.
402	Selected field is not a match field for a lookup.
403	Exceeding maximum record limit for trial version of FileMaker Pro.
404	Sort order is invalid.
405	Number of records specified exceeds number of records that can be omitted.
406	Replace/Reserialize criteria are invalid.
407	One or both match fields are missing (invalid relationship).
408	Specified field has inappropriate data type for this operation.
409	Import order is invalid.
410	Export order is invalid.
412	Wrong version of FileMaker Pro used to recover file.
413	Specified field has inappropriate field type.
414	Layout cannot display the result.
415	One or more required related records are not available.
416	Primary key required from data source table.
417	Database is not a supported data source.
500	Date value does not meet validation entry options.
501	Time value does not meet validation entry options.
502	Number value does not meet validation entry options.

Table 21.1 Continued

Code	Error Description
503	Value in field is not within the range specified in validation entry options.
504	Value in field is not unique as required in validation entry options.
505	Value in field is not an existing value in the database file as required in validation entry options.
506	Value in field is not listed on the value list specified in validation entry option.
507	Value in field failed calculation test of validation entry option.
508	Invalid value entered in Find mode.
509	Field requires a valid value.
510	Related value is empty or unavailable.
511	Value in field exceeds maximum field size.
512	Record was already modified by another user.
600	Print error has occurred.
601	Combined header and footer exceed one page.
602	Body doesn't fit on a page for current column setup.
603	Print connection lost.
700	File is of the wrong file type for import.
706	EPSF file has no preview image.
707	Graphic translator cannot be found.
708	Can't import the file or need color monitor support to import file.
709	QuickTime movie import failed.
710	Unable to update QuickTime file reference because the database file is read-only.
711	Import translator cannot be found.
714	Password privileges do not allow the operation.
715	Specified Excel worksheet or named range is missing.
716	A SQL query using `DELETE`, `INSERT`, or `UPDATE` is not allowed for ODBC import.
717	There is not enough XML/XSL information to proceed with the import or export.
718	Error in parsing XML file (from Xerces).
719	Error in transforming XML using XSL (from Xalan).
720	Error when exporting; intended format does not support repeating fields.
721	Unknown error occurred in the parser or the transformer.
722	Cannot import data into a file that has no fields.
723	You do not have permission to add records to or modify records in the target table.
724	You do not have permission to add records to the target table.
725	You do not have permission to modify records in the target table.
726	There are more records in the import file than in the target table; not all records were imported.
727	There are more records in the target table than in the import file; not all records were updated.

Table 21.1 Continued

Code	Error Description
729	Errors occurred during import; records could not be imported.
730	Unsupported Excel version (convert file to Excel 2000 format or a later supported version and try again).
731	File you are importing from contains no data.
732	This file cannot be inserted because it contains other files.
733	A table cannot be imported into itself.
734	This file type cannot be displayed as a picture.
735	This file type cannot be displayed as a picture; it will be inserted and displayed as a file.
736	Too much data to export to this format; it will be truncated.
737	Bento table you are importing is missing.
800	Unable to create file on disk.
801	Unable to create temporary file on System disk.
802	Unable to open file. This error can be caused by one or more of the following: • Invalid database name. • File is closed in FileMaker Server. • Invalid permission.
803	File is single user or host cannot be found.
804	File cannot be opened as read-only in its current state.
805	File is damaged; use Recover command.
806	File cannot be opened with this version of FileMaker Pro.
807	File is not a FileMaker Pro file or is severely damaged.
808	Cannot open file because access privileges are damaged.
809	Disk/volume is full.
810	Disk/volume is locked.
811	Temporary file cannot be opened as FileMaker Pro file.
813	Record Synchronization error on network.
814	File(s) cannot be opened because maximum number is open.
815	Couldn't open lookup file.
816	Unable to convert file.
817	Unable to open file because it does not belong to this solution.
819	Cannot save a local copy of a remote file.
820	File is in the process of being closed.
821	Host forced a disconnect.
822	FMI files not found; reinstall missing files.
823	Cannot set file to single-user, guests are connected.
824	File is damaged or not a FileMaker file.
825	File is not authorized to reference the protected file.
826	File path specified is not a valid file path.

Table 21.1 Continued

Code	Error Description
850	Path is not valid for the operating system.
851	Cannot delete an external file from disk.
852	Cannot write a file to the external storage.
900	General spelling engine error.
901	Main spelling dictionary not installed.
902	Could not launch the Help system.
903	Command cannot be used in a shared file.
905	No active field selected; command can be used only if there is an active field.
906	Current file is not shared; command can be used only if the file is shared.
920	Can't initialize the spelling engine.
921	User dictionary cannot be loaded for editing.
922	User dictionary cannot be found.
923	User dictionary is read-only.
951	An unexpected error occurred (web).
954	Unsupported XML grammar (web).
955	No database name (web).
956	Maximum number of database sessions exceeded (web).
957	Conflicting commands (web).
958	Parameter missing (web).
959	Custom Web Publishing technology disabled.
960	Parameter is invalid.
1200	Generic calculation error.
1201	Too few parameters in the function.
1202	Too many parameters in the function.
1203	Unexpected end of calculation.
1204	Number, text constant, field name, or "(" expected.
1205	Comment is not terminated with "*/".
1206	Text constant must end with a quotation mark.
1207	Unbalanced parenthesis.
1208	Operator missing, function not found, or "(" not expected.
1209	Name (such as field name or layout name) is missing.
1210	Plug-in function has already been registered.
1211	List usage is not allowed in this function.
1212	An operator (for example, +, –, *) is expected here.
1213	This variable has already been defined in the Let function.
1214	AVERAGE, COUNT, EXTEND, GETREPETITION, MAX, MIN, NPV, STDEV, SUM, and GETSUMMARY: Expression found where a field alone is needed.
1215	This parameter is an invalid Get function parameter.

Table 21.1 Continued

Code	Error Description
1216	Only Summary fields allowed as first argument in GETSUMMARY.
1217	Break field is invalid.
1218	Cannot evaluate the number.
1219	A field cannot be used in its own formula.
1220	Field type must be normal or calculated.
1221	Data type must be number, date, time, or timestamp.
1222	Calculation cannot be stored.
1223	Function referred to is not yet implemented.
1224	Function referred to does not exist.
1225	Function referred to is not supported in this context.
1300	The specified name can't be used.
1400	ODBC driver initialization failed; make sure the ODBC client drivers are properly installed.
1401	Failed to allocate environment (ODBC).
1402	Failed to free environment (ODBC).
1403	Failed to disconnect (ODBC).
1404	Failed to allocate connection (ODBC).
1405	Failed to free connection (ODBC).
1406	Failed check for SQL API (ODBC).
1407	Failed to allocate statement (ODBC).
1408	Extended error (ODBC).
1409	Error (ODBC).
1413	Failed communication link (ODBC).
1414	SQL statement is too long.
1450	Action requires PHP privilege extension (web).
1451	Action requires that current file be remote.
1501	SMTP authentication failed.
1502	Connection refused by SMTP server.
1503	Error with SSL.
1504	SMTP server requires the connection to be encrypted.
1505	Specified authentication is not supported by SMTP server.
1506	Email(s) could not be sent successfully.
1507	Unable to log in to the SMTP server.
1550	Cannot load the plug-in or the plug-in is not a valid plug-in.
1551	Cannot install the plug-in. Cannot delete an existing plug-in or cannot write to the folder or disk.
1626	Protocol is not supported.
1627	Authentication failed.
1628	There was an error with SSL.

Table 21.1 Continued

Code	Error Description
1629	Connection timed out; the timeout value is 60 seconds.
1630	URL format is incorrect.
1631	Connection failed.

Table 21.2 FileMaker Server Command-Line Error Messages

Code	Error Description
10001	Invalid parameter.
10502	Host was unreachable.
10504	Cannot disconnect administrator.
10600	Schedule is missing.
10604	Cannot enable schedule.
10606	Invalid backup destination for schedule.
10801	Locale was not found.
10900	Engine is offline.
10901	Too many files are open.
10902	File is not open.
10903	File by the same name is already open.
10904	File for this operation was not found.
11000	User specified an invalid command.
11001	User specified invalid options.
11002	Command is invalid as formatted.
11005	Client does not exist.
20302	Unknown Universal Path Type.
20400	File operation canceled.
20401	End of file.
20402	No permission.
20404	File is not open.
20405	File not found.
20406	File exists.
20407	File already open.
20500	Directory not found.
20600	Network initialization error.

CHAPTER 22

FileMaker Version and Feature History

The tables in this chapter list the calculation functions, script steps, script triggers, and other major features of FileMaker, along with the application version in which they are available.

Calculation Functions

Table 22.1 lists the calculation functions of FileMaker Pro, listed in the order they were added to the application.

Table 22.1 Function Version History

Function	FileMaker Pro Version							
Abs	≤6	7	8	8.5	9	10	11	12
Atan	≤6	7	8	8.5	9	10	11	12
Average	≤6	7	8	8.5	9	10	11	12
Case	≤6	7	8	8.5	9	10	11	12
Choose	≤6	7	8	8.5	9	10	11	12
Cos	≤6	7	8	8.5	9	10	11	12
Count	≤6	7	8	8.5	9	10	11	12
DatabaseNames	≤6	7	8	8.5	9	10	11	12
Date	≤6	7	8	8.5	9	10	11	12
Day	≤6	7	8	8.5	9	10	11	12
DayName	≤6	7	8	8.5	9	10	11	12
DayNameJ	≤6	7	8	8.5	9	10	11	12
DayOfWeek	≤6	7	8	8.5	9	10	11	12
DayOfYear	≤6	7	8	8.5	9	10	11	12
Degree	≤6	7	8	8.5	9	10	11	12
Exact	≤6	7	8	8.5	9	10	11	12
Exp	≤6	7	8	8.5	9	10	11	12
Extend	≤6	7	8	8.5	9	10	11	12
External	≤6	7	8	8.5	9	10	11	12

Table 22.1 Continued

Function	FileMaker Pro Version							
FieldBounds	≤6	7	8	8.5	9	10	11	12
FieldIDs	≤6	7	8	8.5	9	10	11	12
FieldNames	≤6	7	8	8.5	9	10	11	12
FieldRepetitions	≤6	7	8	8.5	9	10	11	12
FieldStyle	≤6	7	8	8.5	9	10	11	12
FieldType	≤6	7	8	8.5	9	10	11	12
FV	≤6	7	8	8.5	9	10	11	12
Get (ActiveFieldContents)	≤6	7	8	8.5	9	10	11	12
Get (ActiveFieldName)	≤6	7	8	8.5	9	10	11	12
Get (ActiveModifierKeys)	≤6	7	8	8.5	9	10	11	12
Get (ActivePortalRowNumber)	≤6	7	8	8.5	9	10	11	12
Get (ActiveRepetitionNumber)	≤6	7	8	8.5	9	10	11	12
Get (ApplicationVersion)	≤6	7	8	8.5	9	10	11	12
Get (CurrentDate)	≤6	7	8	8.5	9	10	11	12
Get (CurrentExtendedPrivileges)	≤6	7	8	8.5	9	10	11	12
Get (CurrentPrivilegeSetName)	≤6	7	8	8.5	9	10	11	12
Get (CurrentTime)	≤6	7	8	8.5	9	10	11	12
Get (FileName)	≤6	7	8	8.5	9	10	11	12
Get (FilePath)	≤6	7	8	8.5	9	10	11	12
Get (FileSize)	≤6	7	8	8.5	9	10	11	12
Get (FoundCount)	≤6	7	8	8.5	9	10	11	12
Get (HighContrastColor)	≤6	7	8	8.5	9	10	11	12
Get (HighContrastState)	≤6	7	8	8.5	9	10	11	12
Get (HostName)	≤6	7	8	8.5	9	10	11	12
Get (LastError)	≤6	7	8	8.5	9	10	11	12
Get (LastMessageChoice)	≤6	7	8	8.5	9	10	11	12
Get (LastODBCError)	≤6	7	8	8.5	9	10	11	12
Get (LayoutAccess)	≤6	7	8	8.5	9	10	11	12
Get (LayoutCount)	≤6	7	8	8.5	9	10	11	12
Get (LayoutName)	≤6	7	8	8.5	9	10	11	12
Get (LayoutNumber)	≤6	7	8	8.5	9	10	11	12
Get (LayoutViewState)	≤6	7	8	8.5	9	10	11	12
Get (MultiUserState)	≤6	7	8	8.5	9	10	11	12
Get (NetworkProtocol)	≤6	7	8	8.5	9	10	11	12
Get (PageNumber)	≤6	7	8	8.5	9	10	11	12

Table 22.1 Continued

Function	FileMaker Pro Version							
Get (PrinterName)	≤6	7	8	8.5	9	10	11	12
Get (RecordAccess)	≤6	7	8	8.5	9	10	11	12
Get (RecordID)	≤6	7	8	8.5	9	10	11	12
Get (RecordModificationCount)	≤6	7	8	8.5	9	10	11	12
Get (RecordNumber)	≤6	7	8	8.5	9	10	11	12
Get (RequestCount)	≤6	7	8	8.5	9	10	11	12
Get (ScreenDepth)	≤6	7	8	8.5	9	10	11	12
Get (ScreenHeight)	≤6	7	8	8.5	9	10	11	12
Get (ScreenWidth)	≤6	7	8	8.5	9	10	11	12
Get (ScriptName)	≤6	7	8	8.5	9	10	11	12
Get (SortState)	≤6	7	8	8.5	9	10	11	12
Get (StatusAreaState)	≤6	7	8	8.5	9	10	11	12
Get (SystemLanguage)	≤6	7	8	8.5	9	10	11	12
Get (SystemPlatform)	≤6	7	8	8.5	9	10	11	12
Get (SystemVersion)	≤6	7	8	8.5	9	10	11	12
Get (TotalRecordCount)	≤6	7	8	8.5	9	10	11	12
Get (UserCount)	≤6	7	8	8.5	9	10	11	12
Get (UserName)	≤6	7	8	8.5	9	10	11	12
Get (WindowMode)	≤6	7	8	8.5	9	10	11	12
GetAsDate	≤6	7	8	8.5	9	10	11	12
GetAsNumber	≤6	7	8	8.5	9	10	11	12
GetAsText	≤6	7	8	8.5	9	10	11	12
GetAsTime	≤6	7	8	8.5	9	10	11	12
GetField	≤6	7	8	8.5	9	10	11	12
Hiragana	≤6	7	8	8.5	9	10	11	12
Hour	≤6	7	8	8.5	9	10	11	12
If	≤6	7	8	8.5	9	10	11	12
Int	≤6	7	8	8.5	9	10	11	12
IsEmpty	≤6	7	8	8.5	9	10	11	12
IsValid	≤6	7	8	8.5	9	10	11	12
KanaHankaku	≤6	7	8	8.5	9	10	11	12
KanaZenkaku	≤6	7	8	8.5	9	10	11	12
KanjiNumeral	≤6	7	8	8.5	9	10	11	12
Katakana	≤6	7	8	8.5	9	10	11	12
Last	≤6	7	8	8.5	9	10	11	12
LayoutIDs	≤6	7	8	8.5	9	10	11	12
LayoutNames	≤6	7	8	8.5	9	10	11	12
Left	≤6	7	8	8.5	9	10	11	12

Table 22.1 Continued

Function	FileMaker Pro Version							
LeftWords	≤6	7	8	8.5	9	10	11	12
Length	≤6	7	8	8.5	9	10	11	12
Ln	≤6	7	8	8.5	9	10	11	12
Log	≤6	7	8	8.5	9	10	11	12
Lower	≤6	7	8	8.5	9	10	11	12
Max	≤6	7	8	8.5	9	10	11	12
Middle	≤6	7	8	8.5	9	10	11	12
MiddleWords	≤6	7	8	8.5	9	10	11	12
Min	≤6	7	8	8.5	9	10	11	12
Minute	≤6	7	8	8.5	9	10	11	12
Mod	≤6	7	8	8.5	9	10	11	12
Month	≤6	7	8	8.5	9	10	11	12
MonthName	≤6	7	8	8.5	9	10	11	12
MonthNameJ	≤6	7	8	8.5	9	10	11	12
NPV	≤6	7	8	8.5	9	10	11	12
NumToJText	≤6	7	8	8.5	9	10	11	12
PatternCount	≤6	7	8	8.5	9	10	11	12
Pi	≤6	7	8	8.5	9	10	11	12
PMT	≤6	7	8	8.5	9	10	11	12
Position	≤6	7	8	8.5	9	10	11	12
Proper	≤6	7	8	8.5	9	10	11	12
PV	≤6	7	8	8.5	9	10	11	12
Radians	≤6	7	8	8.5	9	10	11	12
Random	≤6	7	8	8.5	9	10	11	12
RelationInfo	≤6	7	8	8.5	9	10	11	12
Replace	≤6	7	8	8.5	9	10	11	12
Right	≤6	7	8	8.5	9	10	11	12
RightWords	≤6	7	8	8.5	9	10	11	12
RomanHankaku	≤6	7	8	8.5	9	10	11	12
RomanZenkaku	≤6	7	8	8.5	9	10	11	12
Round	≤6	7	8	8.5	9	10	11	12
ScriptIDs	≤6	7	8	8.5	9	10	11	12
ScriptNames	≤6	7	8	8.5	9	10	11	12
Seconds	≤6	7	8	8.5	9	10	11	12
Sign	≤6	7	8	8.5	9	10	11	12
Sin	≤6	7	8	8.5	9	10	11	12
Sqrt	≤6	7	8	8.5	9	10	11	12
StDev	≤6	7	8	8.5	9	10	11	12

Table 22.1 Continued

Function	FileMaker Pro Version						
StDevP	≤6	7	8	8.5	9	10	11	12
Substitute	≤6	7	8	8.5	9	10	11	12
Sum	≤6	7	8	8.5	9	10	11	12
TableIDs	≤6	7	8	8.5	9	10	11	12
TableNames	≤6	7	8	8.5	9	10	11	12
Tan	≤6	7	8	8.5	9	10	11	12
Time	≤6	7	8	8.5	9	10	11	12
Trim	≤6	7	8	8.5	9	10	11	12
TrimAll	≤6	7	8	8.5	9	10	11	12
Truncate	≤6	7	8	8.5	9	10	11	12
Upper	≤6	7	8	8.5	9	10	11	12
ValueListIDs	≤6	7	8	8.5	9	10	11	12
ValueListItems	≤6	7	8	8.5	9	10	11	12
ValueListNames	≤6	7	8	8.5	9	10	11	12
WeekOfYear	≤6	7	8	8.5	9	10	11	12
WeekOfYearFiscal	≤6	7	8	8.5	9	10	11	12
WindowNames	≤6	7	8	8.5	9	10	11	12
WordCount	≤6	7	8	8.5	9	10	11	12
Year	≤6	7	8	8.5	9	10	11	12
YearName	≤6	7	8	8.5	9	10	11	12
Ceiling		7	8	8.5	9	10	11	12
Combination		7	8	8.5	9	10	11	12
Div		7	8	8.5	9	10	11	12
Evaluate		7	8	8.5	9	10	11	12
EvaluationError		7	8	8.5	9	10	11	12
Factorial		7	8	8.5	9	10	11	12
FieldComment		7	8	8.5	9	10	11	12
Filter		7	8	8.5	9	10	11	12
FilterValues		7	8	8.5	9	10	11	12
Floor		7	8	8.5	9	10	11	12
Get (AccountName)		7	8	8.5	9	10	11	12
Get (ActiveFieldTableName)		7	8	8.5	9	10	11	12
Get (ActiveSelectionSize)		7	8	8.5	9	10	11	12
Get (ActiveSelectionStart)		7	8	8.5	9	10	11	12
Get (AllowAbortState)		7	8	8.5	9	10	11	12
Get (ApplicationLanguage)		7	8	8.5	9	10	11	12
Get (CalcuationRepetitionNumber)		7	8	8.5	9	10	11	12
Get (CurrentHostTimestamp)		7	8	8.5	9	10	11	12

Table 22.1 Continued

Function	FileMaker Pro Version					
Get (CurrentTimestamp)	7	8	8.5	9	10	11	12
Get (ErrorCaptureState)	7	8	8.5	9	10	11	12
Get (LayoutTableName)	7	8	8.5	9	10	11	12
Get (ScriptParameter)	7	8	8.5	9	10	11	12
Get (SystemIPAddress)	7	8	8.5	9	10	11	12
Get (SystemNICAddress)	7	8	8.5	9	10	11	12
Get (WindowContentHeight)	7	8	8.5	9	10	11	12
Get (WindowContentWidth)	7	8	8.5	9	10	11	12
Get (WindowDesktopHeight)	7	8	8.5	9	10	11	12
Get (WindowDesktopWidth)	7	8	8.5	9	10	11	12
Get (WindowHeight)	7	8	8.5	9	10	11	12
Get (WindowLeft)	7	8	8.5	9	10	11	12
Get (WindowName)	7	8	8.5	9	10	11	12
Get (WindowTop)	7	8	8.5	9	10	11	12
Get (WindowVisible)	7	8	8.5	9	10	11	12
Get (WindowWidth)	7	8	8.5	9	10	11	12
GetAsCSS	7	8	8.5	9	10	11	12
GetAsSVG	7	8	8.5	9	10	11	12
GetAsTimestamp	7	8	8.5	9	10	11	12
GetNextSerialValue	7	8	8.5	9	10	11	12
GetRepetition	7	8	8.5	9	10	11	12
GetSummary	7	8	8.5	9	10	11	12
IsValidExpression	7	8	8.5	9	10	11	12
LeftValues	7	8	8.5	9	10	11	12
Let	7	8	8.5	9	10	11	12
Lg	7	8	8.5	9	10	11	12
Lookup	7	8	8.5	9	10	11	12
LookupNext	7	8	8.5	9	10	11	12
MiddleValues	7	8	8.5	9	10	11	12
Quote	7	8	8.5	9	10	11	12
RGB	7	8	8.5	9	10	11	12
RightValues	7	8	8.5	9	10	11	12
SerialIncrement	7	8	8.5	9	10	11	12
SetPrecision	7	8	8.5	9	10	11	12
TextColor	7	8	8.5	9	10	11	12
TextFont	7	8	8.5	9	10	11	12
TextSize	7	8	8.5	9	10	11	12
TextStyleAdd	7	8	8.5	9	10	11	12

Table 22.1 Continued

Function	FileMaker Pro Version						
TextStyleRemove	7	8	8.5	9	10	11	12
Timestamp	7	8	8.5	9	10	11	12
ValueCount	7	8	8.5	9	10	11	12
Variance	7	8	8.5	9	10	11	12
VarianceP	7	8	8.5	9	10	11	12
Get (AllowFormattingBarState)		8	8.5	9	10	11	12
Get (CustomMenuSetName)		8	8.5	9	10	11	12
Get (DesktopPath)		8	8.5	9	10	11	12
Get (DocumentsPath)		8	8.5	9	10	11	12
Get (FileMakerPath)		8	8.5	9	10	11	12
Get (HostIPAddress)		8	8.5	9	10	11	12
Get (PreferencesPath)		8	8.5	9	10	11	12
Get (RecordOpenCount)		8	8.5	9	10	11	12
Get (RecordOpenState)		8	8.5	9	10	11	12
Get (RequestOmitState)		8	8.5	9	10	11	12
Get (ScriptResult)		8	8.5	9	10	11	12
Get (SystemDrive)		8	8.5	9	10	11	12
Get (TextRulerVisible)		8	8.5	9	10	11	12
Get (UseSystemFormatsState)		8	8.5	9	10	11	12
Get (WindowZoomLevel)		8	8.5	9	10	11	12
GetAsBoolean		8	8.5	9	10	11	12
GetNthRecord		8	8.5	9	10	11	12
GetValue		8	8.5	9	10	11	12
TextColorRemove		8	8.5	9	10	11	12
TextFontRemove		8	8.5	9	10	11	12
TextFormatRemove		8	8.5	9	10	11	12
TextSizeRemove		8	8.5	9	10	11	12
Get (ActiveLayoutObjectName)			8.5	9	10	11	12
GetAsURLEncoded			8.5	9	10	11	12
GetLayoutObjectAttribute			8.5	9	10	11	12
LayoutObjectNames			8.5	9	10	11	12
List			8.5	9	10	11	12
Acos				9	10	11	12
Asin				9	10	11	12
Get (HostApplicationVersion)				9	10	11	12
Get (TemporaryPath)				9	10	11	12
Self				9	10	11	12
Char					10	11	12

Table 22.1 Continued

Function	FileMaker Pro Version							
Code						10	11	12
Get (DocumentsPathListing)						10	11	12
Get (TriggerKeystroke)						10	11	12
Get (TriggerModifierKeys)						10	11	12
GetFieldName						10	11	12
Get (AccountExtendedPrivileges)							11	12
Get (AccountPrivilegeSetName)							11	12
Get (QuickFindText)							11	12
ExecuteSQL								12
Get (ConnectionState)								12
Get (InstalledFMPlugins)								12
Get (PersistentID)								12
Get (TriggerCurrentTabPanel)								12
Get (TriggerTargetTabPanel)								12
Get (UUID)								12
Get (WindowStyle)								12
GetHeight								12
GetThumbnail								12
GetWidth								12
Location								12
LocationValues								12
VerifyContainer								12

Script Steps

Table 22.2 lists the script steps of FileMaker Pro, listed in the order they were added to the application.

Table 22.2 Script Step Version History

Script Step	FileMaker Pro Version							
Add Account	≤6	7	8	8.5	9	10	11	12
Allow Formatting Bar	≤6	7	8	8.5	9	10	11	12
Allow User Abort	≤6	7	8	8.5	9	10	11	12
Beep	≤6	7	8	8.5	9	10	11	12
Change Password	≤6	7	8	8.5	9	10	11	12
Check Found Set	≤6	7	8	8.5	9	10	11	12
Check Record	≤6	7	8	8.5	9	10	11	12

Table 22.2 Continued

Function	FileMaker Pro Version							
Check Selection	≤6	7	8	8.5	9	10	11	12
Clear	≤6	7	8	8.5	9	10	11	12
Close File	≤6	7	8	8.5	9	10	11	12
Comment	≤6	7	8	8.5	9	10	11	12
Commit Records/Requests	≤6	7	8	8.5	9	10	11	12
Constrain Found Set	≤6	7	8	8.5	9	10	11	12
Convert File	≤6	7	8	8.5	9	10	11	12
Copy	≤6	7	8	8.5	9	10	11	12
Copy All Records/Requests	≤6	7	8	8.5	9	10	11	12
Copy Record/Request	≤6	7	8	8.5	9	10	11	12
Correct Word	≤6	7	8	8.5	9	10	11	12
Cut	≤6	7	8	8.5	9	10	11	12
Delete Account	≤6	7	8	8.5	9	10	11	12
Delete All Records	≤6	7	8	8.5	9	10	11	12
Delete Portal Row	≤6	7	8	8.5	9	10	11	12
Delete Record/Request	≤6	7	8	8.5	9	10	11	12
Dial Phone	≤6	7	8	8.5	9	10	11	12
Duplicate Record/Request	≤6	7	8	8.5	9	10	11	12
Edit User Dictionary	≤6	7	8	8.5	9	10	11	12
Else	≤6	7	8	8.5	9	10	11	12
Else If	≤6	7	8	8.5	9	10	11	12
Enable Account	≤6	7	8	8.5	9	10	11	12
End If	≤6	7	8	8.5	9	10	11	12
End Loop	≤6	7	8	8.5	9	10	11	12
Enter Browse Mode	≤6	7	8	8.5	9	10	11	12
Enter Find Mode	≤6	7	8	8.5	9	10	11	12
Enter Preview Mode	≤6	7	8	8.5	9	10	11	12
Execute SQL	≤6	7	8	8.5	9	10	11	12
Exit Application	≤6	7	8	8.5	9	10	11	12
Exit Loop If	≤6	7	8	8.5	9	10	11	12
Exit Script	≤6	7	8	8.5	9	10	11	12
Export Field Contents	≤6	7	8	8.5	9	10	11	12
Export Records	≤6	7	8	8.5	9	10	11	12
Extend Found Set	≤6	7	8	8.5	9	10	11	12
Flush Cache to Disk	≤6	7	8	8.5	9	10	11	12
Freeze Window	≤6	7	8	8.5	9	10	11	12
Go to Field	≤6	7	8	8.5	9	10	11	12
Go to Layout	≤6	7	8	8.5	9	10	11	12

Table 22.2 Continued

Function	FileMaker Pro Version							
Go to Next Field	≤6	7	8	8.5	9	10	11	12
Go to Portal Row	≤6	7	8	8.5	9	10	11	12
Go to Previous Field	≤6	7	8	8.5	9	10	11	12
Go to Record/Request/Page	≤6	7	8	8.5	9	10	11	12
Go to Related Record	≤6	7	8	8.5	9	10	11	12
Halt Script	≤6	7	8	8.5	9	10	11	12
If	≤6	7	8	8.5	9	10	11	12
Import Records	≤6	7	8	8.5	9	10	11	12
Insert Calculated Result	≤6	7	8	8.5	9	10	11	12
Insert Current Date	≤6	7	8	8.5	9	10	11	12
Insert Current Time	≤6	7	8	8.5	9	10	11	12
Insert Current User Name	≤6	7	8	8.5	9	10	11	12
Insert File	≤6	7	8	8.5	9	10	11	12
Insert from Index	≤6	7	8	8.5	9	10	11	12
Insert from Last Visited	≤6	7	8	8.5	9	10	11	12
Insert Picture	≤6	7	8	8.5	9	10	11	12
Insert QuickTime	≤6	7	8	8.5	9	10	11	12
Insert Text	≤6	7	8	8.5	9	10	11	12
Loop	≤6	7	8	8.5	9	10	11	12
Modify Last Find	≤6	7	8	8.5	9	10	11	12
Move/Resize Window	≤6	7	8	8.5	9	10	11	12
New File	≤6	7	8	8.5	9	10	11	12
New Record/Request	≤6	7	8	8.5	9	10	11	12
Omit Multiple Records	≤6	7	8	8.5	9	10	11	12
Omit Record	≤6	7	8	8.5	9	10	11	12
Open File	≤6	7	8	8.5	9	10	11	12
Open File Options	≤6	7	8	8.5	9	10	11	12
Open Help	≤6	7	8	8.5	9	10	11	12
Open Manage Database	≤6	7	8	8.5	9	10	11	12
Open Manage Data Sources	≤6	7	8	8.5	9	10	11	12
Open Manage Scripts	≤6	7	8	8.5	9	10	11	12
Open Manage Value Lists	≤6	7	8	8.5	9	10	11	12
Open Preferences	≤6	7	8	8.5	9	10	11	12
Open Record/Request	≤6	7	8	8.5	9	10	11	12
Open Remote	≤6	7	8	8.5	9	10	11	12
Open Sharing	≤6	7	8	8.5	9	10	11	12
Open URL	≤6	7	8	8.5	9	10	11	12
Paste	≤6	7	8	8.5	9	10	11	12

Table 22.2 Continued

Function	FileMaker Pro Version						
Pause/Resume Script	≤6	7	8	8.5	9	10	11	12
Perform AppleScript (Mac OS)	≤6	7	8	8.5	9	10	11	12
Perform Find	≤6	7	8	8.5	9	10	11	12
Perform Script	≤6	7	8	8.5	9	10	11	12
Print	≤6	7	8	8.5	9	10	11	12
Print Setup	≤6	7	8	8.5	9	10	11	12
Recover File	≤6	7	8	8.5	9	10	11	12
Refresh Window	≤6	7	8	8.5	9	10	11	12
Re-Login	≤6	7	8	8.5	9	10	11	12
Relookup Field Contents	≤6	7	8	8.5	9	10	11	12
Replace Field Contents	≤6	7	8	8.5	9	10	11	12
Reset Account Password	≤6	7	8	8.5	9	10	11	12
Revert Record/Request	≤6	7	8	8.5	9	10	11	12
Save a Copy As	≤6	7	8	8.5	9	10	11	12
Scroll Window	≤6	7	8	8.5	9	10	11	12
Select All	≤6	7	8	8.5	9	10	11	12
Select Dictionary	≤6	7	8	8.5	9	10	11	12
Send DDE Execute (Windows)	≤6	7	8	8.5	9	10	11	12
Send Event (Mac OS)	≤6	7	8	8.5	9	10	11	12
Send Event (Windows)	≤6	7	8	8.5	9	10	11	12
Send Mail	≤6	7	8	8.5	9	10	11	12
Send Error Capture	≤6	7	8	8.5	9	10	11	12
Set Field	≤6	7	8	8.5	9	10	11	12
Set Field By Name	≤6	7	8	8.5	9	10	11	12
Set Multi-User	≤6	7	8	8.5	9	10	11	12
Set Next Serial Number	≤6	7	8	8.5	9	10	11	12
Set Selection	≤6	7	8	8.5	9	10	11	12
Set Use System Formats	≤6	7	8	8.5	9	10	11	12
Set Window Title	≤6	7	8	8.5	9	10	11	12
Set Zoom Level	≤6	7	8	8.5	9	10	11	12
Show All Records	≤6	7	8	8.5	9	10	11	12
Show Custom Dialog	≤6	7	8	8.5	9	10	11	12
Show Omitted Only	≤6	7	8	8.5	9	10	11	12
Show/Hide Text Ruler	≤6	7	8	8.5	9	10	11	12
Show/Hide Toolbars	≤6	7	8	8.5	9	10	11	12
Sort Records	≤6	7	8	8.5	9	10	11	12
Speak (Mac OS)	≤6	7	8	8.5	9	10	11	12
Spelling Options	≤6	7	8	8.5	9	10	11	12

Table 22.2 Continued

Function	FileMaker Pro Version							
Undo/Redo	≤6	7	8	8.5	9	10	11	12
Unsort Records	≤6	7	8	8.5	9	10	11	12
View As	≤6	7	8	8.5	9	10	11	12
Adjust Window		7	8	8.5	9	10	11	12
Arrange All Windows		7	8	8.5	9	10	11	12
Close Window		7	8	8.5	9	10	11	12
New Window		7	8	8.5	9	10	11	12
Open Find/Replace		7	8	8.5	9	10	11	12
Perform Find/Replace		7	8	8.5	9	10	11	12
Select Window		7	8	8.5	9	10	11	12
Install Menu Set			8	8.5	9	10	11	12
Save Records as Excel			8	8.5	9	10	11	12
Save Records as PDF			8	8.5	9	10	11	12
Set Variable			8	8.5	9	10	11	12
Go to Object				8.5	9	10	11	12
Set Web Viewer				8.5	9	10	11	12
Install OnTimer Script						10	11	12
Open Edit Saved Finds						10	11	12
Open Manage Layouts							11	12
Perform Quick Find							11	12
Save Records as Snapshot Link							11	12
Find Matching Records								12
Insert Audio/Video								12
Insert from URL								12
Insert PDF								12
Install Plug-In File								12
Open Manage Containers								12
Sort Record by Field								12

Script Triggers

Table 22.3 lists the script triggers of FileMaker Pro, listed in the order they were added to the application.

Table 22.3 Script Trigger Version History

Script Trigger	FileMaker Pro Version							
OnLayoutEnter						10	11	12
OnLayoutKeystroke						10	11	12
OnModeEnter						10	11	12
OnModeExit						10	11	12
OnObjectEntry						10	11	12
OnObjectExit						10	11	12
OnObjectKeystroke						10	11	12
OnObjectModify						10	11	12
OnObjectSave						10	11	12
OnRecordCommit						10	11	12
OnRecordLoad						10	11	12
OnRecordRevert						10	11	12
OnViewChange						10	11	12
OnLayoutExit							11	12
OnObjectValidate							11	12
OnFirstWindowOpen	*	*	*	*	*	*	*	12
OnLastWindowClose	*	*	*	*	*	*	*	12
OnTabSwitch								12
OnWindowClose								12
OnWindowOpen								12

* The File Options settings for opening and closing scripts served this purpose previous to FileMaker Pro 12.

Other Features

Table 22.4 lists other feature additions to FileMaker Pro, listed in the order they were introduced to the application.

Table 22.4 Other Features of FileMaker Pro Version History

Feature	FileMaker Pro Version						
Multiple Tables in Each Database File	7	8	8.5	9	10	11	12
Multiple Windows	7	8	8.5	9	10	11	12
Relationships Graph	7	8	8.5	9	10	11	12
Buttons in the Tab Order		8	8.5	9	10	11	12
Copying and Pasting Schema Object		8	8.5	9	10	11	12
Custom Menus		8	8.5	9	10	11	12
Data Viewer		8	8.5	9	10	11	12

Table 22.4 Continued

Function	FileMaker Pro Version					
Date & Time Range Shorthand Searching	8	8.5	9	10	11	12
Find Matching Records	8	8.5	9	10	11	12
Import as New Table	8	8.5	9	10	11	12
Save as Excel	8	8.5	9	10	11	12
Save as PDF	8	8.5	9	10	11	12
Send Mail	8	8.5	9	10	11	12
Tab Control	8	8.5	9	10	11	12
Tooltips	8	8.5	9	10	11	12
Object Names		8.5	9	10	11	12
Web Viewer		8.5	9	10	11	12
Auto Resize Layout Objects			9	10	11	12
Conditional Formatting			9	10	11	12
External SQL Data Sources			9	10	11	12
Table View			9	10	11	12
Dynamic Reports				10	11	12
Insert Tab Order				10	11	12
Maintain Record Sort Order				10	11	12
Saved Finds				10	11	12
Script Triggers				10	11	12
Send Mail via SMTP				10	11	12
Status Toolbar				10	11	12
Charts: Bar, Column, Line, Area, Pie					11	12
Default Layout View					11	12
Merge Variables on Layouts					11	12
Portal Filtering					11	12
Recurring Import					11	12
Security: File Access					11	12
Snapshot Link					11	12
Text Highlight					11	12
Quick Find					11	12
Use Variables in Scripted Find Requests					11	12
Accessibility Improved						12
Charting: New Interface, Features, and Styles: Bubble, Stacked Bar, Stacked Column, Positive/Negative Column, Scatter						12

Table 22.4 Continued

Function	FileMaker Pro Version
Container Field: File Management	12
Custom Menu: Conditional Install of Menus and Menu Items	12
FMP URL: Open File Remotely and Execute Script with Parameters	12
Layout Object Formatting: Gradients, Object States, Rounded Corners, and Image Fills, Fixed Layout Width	12
Layout Themes	12
Layout Mode Enhancements: Dynamic Guides and Screen Stencils	12
Plug-in Installation and Updating	12
Window Styles: Standard, Floating, and Modal Dialog	12

CHAPTER 23

FileMaker Keyboard Shortcuts

FileMaker is a rapid application development (RAD) tool. As with any tool, how "rapid" it really is depends to a great degree on a developer's mastery of the tool. It's one thing to know how to get something done and yet another to know how to get it done quickly. There are many aspects to knowing how to work quickly in FileMaker, from using the Copy Table/Field/Script step commands in FileMaker Pro Advanced to using custom functions and script parameters to abstract and automate frequently used logic. But we have also observed over the years that the fastest users of the tool tend to be those who also heavily use keyboard shortcuts.

Like any modern software application, FileMaker has many keyboard shortcuts hidden under the hood—probably about 400 by our count, though that number is not exact. Of those, a couple dozen or so are critical to working quickly in FileMaker, and perhaps another dozen are desirable to master.

This chapter is divided into two broad areas. The first examines a number of important areas of FileMaker development and discusses the shortcuts that are most important in each area. The second section provides a comprehensive listing of keyboard shortcuts for menu items.

> *Note*
>
> With the capability to customize menu sets in FileMaker Pro Advanced, you are able to alter the landscape of FileMaker keyboard shortcuts almost beyond recognition. Therefore, be advised that all information in this chapter assumes that the standard FileMaker menu set is in effect.

Essential Shortcuts by Group

In the following sections, you learn about shortcuts that are essential in a number of areas, including some specialized and lesser-known ones that can be quite useful.

Keyboard Essentials

Shortcuts in this section should be required knowledge for all FileMaker Pro developers. If you haven't mastered them, you need to spend more time with FileMaker Pro!

Working with Modes

Function	Mac Key	Windows Key
Browse Mode	⌘-B	Ctrl+B
Layout Mode	⌘-L	Ctrl+L
Find Mode	⌘-F	Ctrl+F
Preview Mode	⌘-U	Ctrl+U

Working with Files

Function	Mac Key	Windows Key
Open (File)	⌘-O	Ctrl+O
Open Remote (File)	Shift-⌘-O	Ctrl+Shift+O
Force a password dialog to display when opening a file	Hold down the Option key while opening the file.	Hold down the Shift key while opening the file.

Working with Records

Function	Mac Key	Windows Key
New Record/Request/Layout	⌘-N	Ctrl+N
Delete Record/Request/Layout	⌘-E	Ctrl+E
Duplicate Record/Request	⌘-D	Ctrl+D
Omit Record	⌘-T	Ctrl+T
Omit Multiple Records	Shift-⌘-T	Ctrl+Shift+T
Modify Last Find	⌘-R	Ctrl+R
Show All Records	⌘-J	Ctrl+J
Sort Records	⌘-S	Ctrl+S

Developer Essentials

Function	Mac Key	Windows Key
Manage Database	Shift-⌘-D	Ctrl+Shift+D
Manage Layouts	Shift-⌘-L	Ctrl+Shift+L
Manage Scripts	Shift-⌘-S	Ctrl+Shift+S
Print	⌘-P	Ctrl+P
Undo	⌘-Z	Ctrl+Z
Insert from Index	⌘-I	Ctrl+I
Cut	⌘-X	Ctrl+X
Copy	⌘-C	Ctrl+C
Paste	⌘-V	Ctrl+V

When using keyboard shortcuts, keep the following tips in mind:

- You can hold down the Option key (Mac) or Shift key (Windows) to skip a confirmation dialog when deleting an item, whether it is a record, a field, a script, or the like. The sole exception concerns deleting a layout: FileMaker always prompts you for confirmation before deleting a layout.
- In Find mode, the ⌘-T/Ctrl+T shortcut toggles the Matching Records setting between Include and Omit.
- To navigate to a particular record within the found set, you can press the Esc key, which activates the book icon, and then you can type the record number and press Enter. This capability is particularly useful for navigating to the first record of the found set.
- To omit all records from the current record to the end of the found set, perform the Omit Multiple Records command and type a large number of records to omit (for example, **99999999**). FileMaker responds that it can omit only a certain number of records, filling in the correct number of remaining records. You can then go ahead and complete the omit process without needing to calculate the exact number for yourself.
- You can cancel out of most dialog boxes by pressing the Esc key. This approach is much quicker than clicking the Cancel button. Similarly, you can usually execute the default (highlighted) button in a dialog by pressing the Return/Enter key.

Navigation

The shortcuts in this section not only help you move around between records but also move around between layouts and among found sets of records.

Function	Mac Key	Windows Key
Next/Previous Record	Ctrl-up/down arrow	Ctrl+up/down arrow
Next/Previous Layout	Ctrl-up/down arrow	Ctrl+up/down arrow
Next/Previous Request	Ctrl-up/down arrow	Ctrl+up/down arrow
Next/Previous Page	Ctrl-up/down arrow	Ctrl+up/down arrow
Hide/Unhide Status Toolbar	⌘-Opt-S	Ctrl+Alt+S
Zoom/Unzoom Window	⌘-Opt-Z	Alt+V+I/O

The Ctrl+up/down arrow shortcut has a different meaning in each mode: In Browse mode, it moves between records; in Layout mode, between layouts; in Find mode, between find requests; and in Preview mode, between different pages of the output. Depending on your OS settings, you might also be able to perform these actions using the scroll wheel.

Data Entry and Formatting

The shortcuts in this section have to do with the mechanics of putting data into fields and with formatting data after it's been entered into a field.

Function	Mac Key	Windows Key
Select All	⌘-A	Ctrl+A
Cut, Copy, Paste	⌘-X, C, V	Ctrl+X, C, V
Copy Current Record (when not in a field)	⌘-C	Ctrl+C
Copy All Records	⌘-Opt-C	Ctrl+Shift+C
Paste Without Text Styles	⌘-Opt-V	Ctrl+Shift+V
Plain Text	Shift-⌘-P	Ctrl+Shift+P
Bold Text	Shift-⌘-B	Ctrl+Shift+B
Italic Text	Shift-⌘-I	Ctrl+Shift+I
Underline Text	Shift-⌘-U	Ctrl+Shift+U
Left-Justify Selected Text	⌘-[	Ctrl+[
Center Selected Text	⌘-\	Ctrl+\
Right-Justify Selected Text	⌘-]	Ctrl+]
Increase/Decrease Font Size	Shift-⌘->/<	Ctrl+Shift+>/<
Insert Current Date	⌘-<hyphen>	Ctrl+<hyphen>
Insert Current Time/Timestamp	⌘-;	Ctrl+;
Insert Non-breaking Space into Text	Opt-space	Ctrl+space
Insert Tab Character into Text	Opt-Tab	Ctrl+Tab

Be aware of the following when using keyboard shortcuts for data entry and formatting:

- Using ⌘-C or Ctrl+C in Browse mode when you're not in any field of the current record copies the entire record as tab-delimited text. Using ⌘-Opt-C or Ctrl+Shift+C copies all records in the found set, again as a tab-delimited text block.
- Using Shift-⌘->/< or Ctrl+Shift+>/< to increase or decrease font sizes normally moves the font size up or down through the list of "standard" font sizes. If you also hold down Option (Mac OS) or Shift (Windows), the changes occur in one-point increments instead.
- The ⌘-;/Ctrl+; shortcut inserts the current time if the selected field is of type text, time, or number, but inserts the current Timestamp if the current field is of type Timestamp.

Managing Fields

The shortcuts in this section work only within the Fields tab of the Manage Database dialog.

Function	Mac Key	Windows Key
Manage Database	Shift-⌘-D	Ctrl+Shift+D
Text Data Type	⌘-T	Ctrl+T
Number Data Type	⌘-N	Ctrl+N
Date Data Type	⌘-D	Ctrl+D
Time Data Type	⌘-I	Ctrl+I
Timestamp Data Type	⌘-M	Ctrl+M
Container Data Type	⌘-R	Ctrl+R

Function	Mac Key	Windows Key
Calculation Data Type	⌘-L	Ctrl+L
Summary Data Type	⌘-S	Ctrl+S
Field Options	Shift-⌘-O	Alt+N
Reorder Tables or Fields in a List	Ctrl-up/down arrow	Ctrl+up/down arrow

Working with the Relationships Graph

Many keyboard shortcuts and techniques apply to the Relationships Graph. The following is a selection of the most useful. Consult the online help for a full listing.

Function	Mac Key	Windows Key
New Table Occurrence	Shift-⌘-T	Ctrl+Shift+T
New Relationship	Shift-⌘-R	Ctrl+Shift+R
Edit Relationship	⌘-O (when relationship is selected)	Ctrl+O (when relationship is selected)
New Text Note	Shift-⌘-N	Ctrl+Shift+N
Duplicate Selected Items	⌘-D	Ctrl+D
Select All Table Occurrences Directly Related to the Current Table Occurrence	⌘-Y	Ctrl+Y
Select All Table Occurrences with the Same Source Table as the Current Table Occurrence	⌘-U	Ctrl+U
Toggle the Display Mode of Selected Table Occurrences	⌘-T	Ctrl+T

Following are some additional Relationships Graph shortcuts to be aware of:

- The up, down, left, and right arrows can be used to cycle through the elements of the graph (table occurrences, relationships, notes), selecting each one in turn. After you select an item, other keyboard shortcuts can open the item for editing.
- Typing on the keyboard selects objects containing text that matches what is being typed.
- You can move selected table occurrences using the Control (Mac)/Shift (Windows) key in conjunction with the arrow keys.
- Using Ctrl+Shift in combination with the arrow keys resizes any selected table occurrences.

Working with Layouts

Layout mode is the place where FileMaker's famously quick-to-develop graphical user interfaces (GUIs) get built. A FileMaker developer must have a thorough knowledge of important layout shortcuts.

Function	Mac Key	Windows Key
Create a New Layout	⌘-N	Ctrl+N
Duplicate the Selected Object	⌘-D	Ctrl+D
Group	⌘-R	Ctrl+R
Ungroup	Shift-⌘-R	Ctrl+Shift+R
Lock	Opt-⌘-L	Ctrl+Alt+L
Unlock	Shift-Opt-⌘-L	Ctrl+Alt+Shift+L
Bring Forward	Shift-⌘-[	Ctrl+Shift+[
Bring to Front	Opt-⌘-[	Ctrl+Alt+[
Send Backward	Shift-⌘-]	Ctrl+Shift+]
Send to Back	Opt-⌘-]	Ctrl+Alt+]
Align Left, Right, Top, Bottom	Opt-⌘-left/right/ up/down arrow	Ctrl+Alt+left/right/ up/down arrow
Insert Merge Field	Opt-⌘-M	Ctrl+Shift+M
Select All Objects	⌘-A	Ctrl+A
Select Similar Objects	Opt-⌘-A	Ctrl+Shift+A
Copy/Paste the Selected Object's Style	Opt-⌘-C/V	Ctrl+Alt+C/V
Show/Hide Rulers	Shift-Opt-⌘-R	Ctrl+Alt+Shift+R
Show/Hide Guides	Opt-⌘-;	Ctrl+Alt+;
Enable/Disable Dynamic Guides	Opt-⌘-'	Ctrl+Alt+'
Show/Hide Grid	Opt-⌘-Y	Ctrl+Alt+Y
Show/Hide Inspector	⌘-I	Ctrl+I
Activate Position Tab of the Inspector	⌘-1	Ctrl+1
Activate Appearance Tab of the Inspector	⌘-2	Ctrl+2
Activate Data Tab of the Inspector	⌘-3	Ctrl+3
Undo	⌘-Z	Ctrl+Z

When you are working with layouts, the following shortcuts may also be of some value:

- In Layout mode, ⌘-dragging or Ctrl+dragging causes all objects surrounded by the selection rectangle to be selected. A normal drag-select selects all objects touched by the selection rectangle. Note that this is exactly the opposite behavior used in earlier versions of FileMaker Pro.
- Use Opt-⌘-A/Ctrl+Shift+A to select all objects of the same type as the currently selected objects. You can use this technique to select all text labels, for example.
- As in many graphical layout applications, you can use the arrow keys to move selected layout objects a pixel at a time in any direction.
- Shift-dragging restricts the movement of selected objects to a horizontal or vertical direction.
- Opt-dragging (Mac OS)/Ctrl-dragging (Windows) creates a duplicate of the selected objects.

- You can toggle the part labels from vertical to horizontal orientation by ⌘-clicking (Mac OS)/Ctrl-clicking (Windows) on any of the part labels.
- Normally, you cannot drag a part boundary past an object. To do so, hold down the Opt key (Mac OS)/Ctrl key (Windows).
- Double-clicking a layout tool in the status area "locks" the tool, causing it to remain selected through multiple uses. Pressing Esc or Enter "unlocks" and deselects the tool, selecting the Pointer tool instead (the default). Pressing Enter when the Pointer tool is selected reselects the most recently used layout tool.

Scripting

A number of useful shortcuts pertain to working within the Manage Scripts dialog.

Note that functions marked with an (A) are available only in FileMaker Pro Advanced.

Function	Mac Key	Windows Key
Open Manage Scripts	⌘-Shift-S	Ctrl+Shift+S
Select a Script by Name (When Scripts List Is Active)	Begin typing script name	Begin typing script name
Select All Scripts	⌘-A	Ctrl+A
Copy Selected Scripts (A)	⌘-C	Ctrl+C
Paste Copied Script(s) (A)	⌘-V	Ctrl+V
Save Script	⌘-S	Ctrl+S
Select a Script Step by Name (in Edit Script dialog when script steps are active)	Begin typing script name	Begin typing script name
Insert Selected Script Step into the Script	Ctrl-Spacebar	Enter or Alt+M
Delete Selected Script Steps	Delete	Backspace/Delete
Copy Selected Script Steps (A)	⌘-C	Ctrl+C
Paste Copied Script Steps (A)	⌘-V	Ctrl+V
Move Selected Script Step Up or Down	Ctrl+up/down arrows	Ctrl+up/down arrows

When you are editing a script step that has options accessible via a Specify button (such as Set Field), pressing Ctrl-Spacebar on the Mac is generally equivalent to clicking the Specify button. On Windows, Alt+S accomplishes the same thing.

Navigating the FileMaker Interface

A number of shortcuts can help you navigate through the FileMaker interface itself. Using keyboard commands, you can trigger buttons, move between elements of a dialog box, and quickly scroll though pop-up lists and menus.

Function	Mac Key	Windows Key
Move Between Tabs in a Dialog Box		Ctrl+Tab
Move Backward and Forward Between Items/Areas Within a Dialog	Shift-Tab/Tab	Shift+Tab/Tab
Move Up and Down Within a Pop-up List or Menu	Up/down arrow	Up/down arrow
Move to Beginning or End of a Pop-up List or Menu	Home/End	Home/End
Cancel a Dialog	Esc	Esc
Submit a Dialog (Choose the Default Button)	Enter	Enter

The Mac OS has weaker support than Windows for tabbing through and activating elements in a dialog box. For those dialogs in which it's possible to do this on the Mac OS, only a few of the elements are accessible via the keyboard. In Windows, by contrast, virtually every aspect of a dialog can be selected and triggered via the keyboard.

Menu Reference

The following tables present all the menu items in FileMaker Pro and FileMaker Pro Advanced. They include all the Mac and Windows keyboard shortcuts, as well as the Windows Alt+key equivalents.

We consider certain commands essential knowledge for FileMaker developers; they have been marked with an asterisk (*).

File Menu

Menu Item or Submenu	Mac OS Key	Windows Key	Windows Alt
New Database			Alt+F+N
New From Starter Solution			Alt+F+W
*Open	⌘-O	Ctrl+O	Alt+F+O
*Open Remote	Shift-⌘-O	Ctrl+Shift+O	Alt+F+M
Open Recent			Alt+F+T+item number
Open Favorite			Alt+F+A
*Close	⌘-W	Ctrl+W	Alt+F+C
Manage			Alt+F+G
*Database	Shift-⌘-D	Ctrl+Shift+D	Alt+F+G+D
Security			Alt+F+G+T
Value Lists			Alt+F+G+V
*Layouts	Shift-⌘-L	Ctrl+Shift+L	Alt+F+G+L
*Scripts	Shift-⌘-S	Ctrl+Shift+S	Alt+F+G+S
External Data Sources			Alt+F+G+E
Containers			Alt+F+G+R
Custom Functions			Alt+F+G+C
Custom Menus			Alt+F+G+M

Menu Item or Submenu	Mac OS Key	Windows Key	Windows Alt
Sharing			Alt+F+H
FileMaker Network			Alt+F+H+N
Instant Web Publishing			Alt+F+H+W
ODBC/JDBC			Alt+F+H+O
File Options			Alt+F+F
Change Password			Alt+F+W
Page Setup			Alt+F+S
*Print	⌘-P	Ctrl+P	Alt+F+P
Import Records			Alt+F+I
File			Alt+F+I+F
Folder			Alt+F+I+D
Bento Data Source (Mac only)			
XML Data Source			Alt+F+I+X
ODBC Data Source			Alt+F+I+O
Export Records			Alt+F+E
Save/Send Records As			Alt+F+R
Excel			Alt+F+R+E
PDF			Alt+F+R+P
Snapshot Link			Alt+F+R+S
Send			Alt+F+D
Mail			Alt+F+D+L
Link to Database			Alt+F+D+K
Save a Copy As			Alt+F+Y
Recover			Alt+F+V
*Exit (Windows Only)		Ctrl+Q	Alt+F+X

FileMaker Pro Menu (Mac OS Only)

Menu Item or Submenu	Mac OS Key
About FileMaker Pro	
Preferences	⌘-,
Services	
Hide FileMaker Pro	⌘-H
Hide Others	Opt-⌘-P
Show All	
*Quit FileMaker Pro	⌘-Q

Edit Menu

Note that items marked with (L) are available only in Layout mode.

Menu Item or Submenu	Mac OS Key	Windows Key	Windows Alt
*Undo	⌘-Z	Ctrl+Z	Alt+E+V
*Redo	Opt-⌘-Z	Ctrl+Y	Alt+E+R
*Cut	⌘-X	Ctrl+X	Alt+E+T
*Copy	⌘-C	Ctrl+C	Alt+E+C
*Paste	⌘-V	Ctrl+V	Alt+E+P
Paste Text Only (Mac only)	Shift-Opt-⌘-V		
Clear		Delete	Alt+E+E
*Copy Object Style (L)	Opt-⌘-C	Ctrl+Alt+C	Alt+E+Y
*Paste Object Style (L)	Opt-⌘-V	Ctrl+Alt+V	Alt+E+S
Apply Theme Style (L)			Alt+E+H
Remove Styles (L)			Alt+E+M
*Duplicate	⌘-D	Ctrl+D	Alt+E+D
*Select All	⌘-A	Ctrl+A	Alt+E+A
Find/Replace			Alt+E+L
Find/Replace	Shift-⌘-F	Ctrl+Shift+F	Alt+E+L+F
Find Again	⌘-G	Ctrl+G	Alt+E+L+A
Replace & Find Again	Opt-⌘-G	Ctrl+Alt+G	Alt+E+L+R
Find Selected	Opt-⌘-I	Ctrl+Alt+H	Alt+E+L+S
Spelling			Alt+E+N
Check Selection			Alt+E+N+S
Check Record			Alt+E+N+R
Check Layout (L)			Alt+E+N+L
Check All			Alt+E+N+A
Correct Word		Ctrl+Shift+Y	Alt+E+N+W
Select Dictionaries			Alt+E+N+D
Edit User Dictionary			Alt+E+N+U
Object			Alt+E+O
Show Objects (Windows only)			Alt+E+O+S
Export Field Contents			Alt+E+X
Preferences (Windows only)			Alt+E+F

View Menu (Browse Mode)

Note that items marked with (L) are available only in Layout mode.

Menu Item or Submenu	Mac OS Key	Windows Key	Windows Alt
*Browse Mode	⌘-B	Ctrl+B	Alt+V+B
*Find Mode	⌘-F	Ctrl+F	Alt+V+F
*Layout Mode	⌘-L	Ctrl+L	Alt+V+L
*Preview Mode	⌘-U	Ctrl+U	Alt+V+P
Go to Layout			Alt+V+Y
View as Form			Alt+V+M
View as List			Alt+V+S
View as Table			Alt+V+E
Page Margins (L)			Alt+V+M
Rulers (L)	Shift-Opt-⌘-R	Ctrl+Alt+Shift+R	Alt+V+R
Grid (L)			Alt+V+G
*Show Grid (L)	Opt-⌘-Y		Alt+V+G+G
Snap to Grid (L)	Shift-Opt-⌘-Y		Alt+V+G+S
Guides (L)			Alt+V+U
*Show Guides (L)	Opt-⌘-;		Alt+V+U+G
Snap to Guides (L)	Shift-Opt-⌘-;		Alt+V+U+S
*Dynamic Guides (L)	Opt-⌘-'	Ctrl+Alt+'	Alt+V+D
Show (L)			Alt+V+S
Buttons (L)			Alt+V+S+B
Sample Data (L)			Alt+V+S+S
Text Boundaries (L)			Alt+V+S+T
Field Boundaries (L)			Alt+V+S+F
Sliding Objects (L)			Alt+V+S+O
Non-Printing Objects (L)			Alt+V+S+N
Conditional Formatting (L)			Alt+V+S+R
Script Triggers (L)			Alt+V+S+C
Quick Find (L)			Alt+V+S+Q
Tooltips (L)			Alt+V+S+P
*Status Toolbar	Opt-⌘-S	Ctrl+Alt+S	Alt+V+T
Customize Status Toolbar			Alt+V+C
Formatting Bar			Alt+V+O
Ruler			Alt+V+R
*Inspector (L)	⌘-I	Ctrl+I	Alt+V+I
New Inspector (L)			Alt+V+E
Accessibility Inspector (L)			Alt+V+A
Zoom In			Alt+V+N
Zoom Out			Alt+V+U

Insert Menu

Note that items marked with (L) are available only in Layout mode.

Menu Item or Submenu	Mac OS Key	Windows Key	Windows Alt
Picture			Alt+I+P
QuickTime			Alt+I+Q
Audio/Video			Alt+I+V
Sound			Alt+I+S
PDF			Alt+I+D
File			Alt+I+F
Field (L)			Alt+I+F
Part (L)			Alt+I+A
Graphic Object (L)			Alt+I+G
Text (L)			Alt+I+G+T
Line (L)			Alt+I+G+L
Rectangle (L)			Alt+I+G+R
Rounded Rectangle (L)			Alt+I+G+U
Oval (L)			Alt+I+G+O
Field/Control (L)			Alt+I+O
Edit Box (L)			Alt+I+O+E
Drop-down List (L)			Alt+I+O+D
Pop-up Menu (L)			Alt+I+O+P
Checkbox Set (L)			Alt+I+O+K
Radio Button Set (L)			Alt+I+O+R
Drop-down Calendar (L)			Alt+I+O+C
Portal (L)			Alt+I+P
Tab Control (L)			Alt+I+B
Web Viewer (L)			Alt+I+W
Chart (L)			Alt+I+H
Button (L)			Alt+I+N
Picture (L)			Alt+I+C
*Current Date	⌘- -	Ctrl+-	Alt+I+D
*Current Time	⌘-;	Ctrl+;	Alt+I+T
Current User Name	Shift-⌘-N	Ctrl+Shift+N	Alt+I+U
From Index	⌘-I	Ctrl+I	Alt+I+I
From Last Visited Record	⌘-’	Ctrl+’	Alt+I+L
Date Symbol (L)			Alt+I+E
Time Symbol (L)			Alt+I+I
User Name Symbol (L)			Alt+I+S
Page Number Symbol (L)			Alt+I+Y

Menu Item or Submenu	Mac OS Key	Windows Key	Windows Alt
Record Number Symbol (L)			Alt+I+R
Other Symbol (L)			Alt+I+L
*Merge Field (L)	Opt-⌘-M	Ctrl+M	Alt+I+M
Merge Variable (L)			Alt+I+V

Format Menu

Note that items marked with (L) are available only in Layout mode.

Menu Item or Submenu	Mac OS Key	Windows Key	Windows Alt
Font			Alt+M+F
Size			Alt+M+Z
*Increase Size	⌘->	Ctrl+Shift+>	Alt+M+Z+I
*Decrease Size	⌘-<	Ctrl+Shift+<	Alt+M+Z+D
Custom			Alt+M+Z+C
Style			Alt+M+S
Plain Text	Shift-⌘-P	Ctrl+Shift+P	Alt+M+S+P
*Bold	Shift-⌘-B	Ctrl+Shift+B	Alt+M+S+B
*Italic	Shift-⌘-I	Ctrl+Shift+I	Alt+M+S+I
*Underline	Shift-⌘U	Ctrl+Shift+U	Alt+M+S+U
Word Underline			Alt+M+S+W
Double Underline			Alt+M+S+D
Condense			Alt+M+S+C
Extend			Alt+M+S+E
Strike Thru			Alt+M+S+K
Small Caps			Alt+M+S+M
Highlight			Alt+M+S+H
Uppercase			Alt+M+S+A
Lowercase			Alt+M+S+L
Title Case			Alt+M+S+T
Superscript	Shift-⌘-=		Alt+M+S+S
Subscript	Shift-⌘- -		Alt+M+S+R
Align Text			Alt+M+G
*Left	⌘-[	Ctrl+[	Alt+M+G+L
*Center	⌘-\	Ctrl+\	Alt+M+G+C
*Right	⌘-]	Ctrl+]	Alt+M+G+R
Full	Shift-⌘-\	Ctrl+Shift+\	Alt+M+G+F
Top			Alt+M+G+T
Center			Alt+M+G+E
Bottom			Alt+M+G+B

Menu Item or Submenu	Mac OS Key	Windows Key	Windows Alt
Line Spacing			Alt+M+L
Single			Alt+M+L+S
Double			Alt+M+L+D
Other			Alt+M+L+O
Orientation (L)			Alt+M+E
Horizontal (L)			Alt+M+E+H
Sideways (Asian text only) (L)			Alt+M+E+S
Text Color			Alt+M+R
Portal Setup (L)			Alt+M+P
Tab Control Setup (L)			Alt+M+B
Web Viewer Setup (L)			Alt+M+V
Chart Setup (L)			Alt+M+H
Button Setup (L)			Alt+M+U
Format Painter (L)			Alt+M+O
Conditional (L)			Alt+M+A
Set Script Triggers (L)			Alt+M+T

Layouts Menu (Layout Mode Only)

Menu Item or Submenu	Mac OS Key	Windows Key	Windows Alt
*New Layout/Report	⌘-N	Ctrl+N	Alt+L+N
Duplicate Layout			Alt+L+U
Delete Layout	⌘-E	Ctrl+E	Alt+L+D
Go to Layout			Alt+L+G
*Next	⌘-down arrow	Ctrl+down arrow	Alt+L+G+N
*Previous	⌘-up arrow	Ctrl+up arrow	Alt+L+G+P
Go To			Alt+L+G+G
Change Theme			Alt+L+C
Layout Setup			Alt+L+Y
Part Setup			Alt+L+A
Set Tab Order			Alt+L+T
*Save Layout	⌘-S	Ctrl+S	Alt+L+S
Revert Layout			Alt+L+V

Records Menu

Menu Item or Submenu	Mac OS Key	Windows Key	Windows Alt
*New Record	⌘-N	Ctrl+N	Alt+R+N
*Duplicate Record	⌘-D	Ctrl+D	Alt+R+A
*Delete Record	⌘-E	Ctrl+E	Alt+R+D
Delete Found/All Records			Alt+R+T
Go to Record			Alt+R+G
*Next	⌘-down arrow	Ctrl+down arrow	Alt+R+G+N
*Previous	⌘-up arrow	Ctrl+up arrow	Alt+R+G+P
Go To			Alt+R+G+G
Refresh Window	Shift-⌘-R		Alt+R+H
*Show All Records	⌘-J		Alt+R+W
Show Omitted Only			Alt+R+I
*Omit Record	⌘-T		Alt+R+O
*Omit Multiple	Shift-⌘-T		Alt+R+M
*Modify Last Find	⌘-R		Alt+R+F
Saved Finds			Alt+R+V
Save Current Find			
Edit Saved Finds			
*Sort Records	⌘-S		Alt+R+S
Unsort			Alt+R+U
*Replace Field Contents	⌘-=		Alt+R+E
Relookup Field Contents			Alt+R+K
Revert Record			Alt+R+R

Requests Menu (Find Mode Only)

Menu Item or Submenu	Mac OS Key	Windows Key	Windows Alt
*Add New Request	⌘-N	Ctrl+N	Alt+R+N
*Duplicate Request	⌘-D	Ctrl+D	Alt+R+U
*Delete Request	⌘-E	Ctrl+E	Alt+R+D
Go to Request			Alt+R+G
*Next	⌘-down arrow	Ctrl+down arrow	Alt+R+G+N
*Previous	⌘-up arrow	Ctrl+up arrow	Alt+R+G+P
Go To			Alt+R+G+G
*Show All Records	⌘-J	Ctrl+J	Alt+R+W
Perform Find		Enter	Alt+R+P
Constrain Found Set			Alt+R+C
Extend Found Set			Alt+R+E
Revert Request			Alt+R+R

Arrange Menu (Layout Mode Only)

Menu Item or Submenu	Mac OS Key	Windows Key	Windows Alt
Group	⌘-R	Ctrl+R	Alt+A+G
Ungroup	Shift-⌘-R	Ctrl+Shift+R	Alt+A+U
Lock	Opt-⌘-L	Ctrl+Alt+L	Alt+A+L
Unlock	Shift-Opt-⌘-L	Ctrl+Alt+L	Alt+A+K
Bring to Front	Opt-⌘-[	Ctrl+Alt+[	Alt+A+F
Bring Forward	Shift-⌘-[	Ctrl+Shift+[	Alt+A+W
Send to Back	Opt-⌘-]	Ctrl+Alt+]	Alt+A+B
Send Backward	Shift-⌘-]	Ctrl+Shift+]	Alt+A+C
Rotate	Opt-⌘-R	Ctrl+Alt+R	Alt+A+R
Align			Alt+A+N
*Left Edges	Opt-⌘-left arrow	Ctrl+Alt+left arrow	Alt+A+N+L
Centers			Alt+A+N+C
*Right Edges	Opt-⌘-right arrow	Ctrl+Alt+right arrow	Alt+A+N+R
*Top Edges	Opt-⌘-up arrow	Ctrl+Alt+up arrow	Alt+A+N+T
Middles			Alt+A+N+M
*Bottom Edges	Opt-⌘-down arrow	Ctrl+Alt+down arrow	Alt+A+N+B
Distribute			Alt+A+D
Horizontally			Alt+A+D+H
Vertically			Alt+A+D+V
Resize To			Alt+A+S
Smallest Width			Alt+A+S+S
Smallest Height			Alt+A+S+M
Smallest Width & Height			Alt+A+S+A
Largest Width			Alt+A+S+L
Largest Height			Alt+A+S+H
Largest Width & Height			Alt+A+S+W

Scripts Menu

Menu Item or Submenu	Mac OS Key	Windows Key	Windows Alt
*Manage Scripts	Shift-⌘-S	Ctrl+Shift+S	Alt+S+M
*Save Script†	⌘-S	Ctrl+S	
Save All Scripts†			
Revert Script†			

†Note that the last three commands in this table are available only if an Edit Script window is in the foreground and unsaved script changes are present.

Tools Menu (FileMaker Pro Advanced Only)

Menu Item or Submenu	Mac OS Key	Windows Key	Windows Alt
Script Debugger			Alt+T+D
Debugging Controls			Alt+T+E
Step Over	F5	F5	Alt+T+E+S
Step Into	F6	F6	Alt+T+E+T
Step Out	F7	F7	Alt+T+E+O
Run	Opt-F8	Alt+F8	Alt+T+E+R
Halt Script	⌘-F8	Ctrl+F8	Alt+T+E+H
Set Next Step	Shift-⌘-F5	Ctrl+Shift+F5	Alt+T+E+N
Set Breakpoint	⌘-F9	Ctrl+F9	Alt+T+E+B
Remove Breakpoints	Shift-⌘-F9	Ctrl+Shift+F9	Alt+T+E+M
Edit Script	⌘-F10	Ctrl+F10	Alt+T+E+E
Disable Script Triggers			Alt+T+E+A
Pause on Error			Alt+T+E+P
Data Viewer			Alt+T+V
Custom Menus			Alt+T+C
Manage Custom Menus			Alt+T+C+M
Database Design Report			Alt+T+G
Developer Utilities			Alt+T+U

Window Menu

Menu Item or Submenu	Mac OS Key	Windows Key	Windows Alt
New Window			Alt+W+N
Show Window			Alt+W+S
Hide Window			Alt+W+H
Minimize Window	⌘-M		Alt+W+M
Tile Horizontally		Shift+F4	Alt+W+T
Tile Vertically			Alt+W+V
Cascade Windows		Shift+F5	Alt+W+C
Bring All to Front (Mac)			
Arrange Icons (Windows)			Alt+W+I

Help Menu

Menu Item or Submenu	Mac OS Key	Windows Key	Windows Alt
FileMaker Pro Help		F1	Alt+H+H
Keyboard Shortcuts			Alt+H+K
Quick Start Screen			Alt+H+Q
Resource Center			Alt+H+C
Product Documentation			Alt+H+P
User's Guide			Alt+H+P+U
Tutorial			Alt+H+P+T
Development Guide			Alt+H+P+D
Instant Web Publishing			Alt+H+P+I
ODBC and JDBC Guide			Alt+H+P+O
More Documentation			Alt+H+P+M
Consultants and Solutions			Alt+H+O
Provide FileMaker Feedback			Alt+H+D
Check for Updates			Alt+H+U
Register FileMaker Pro			Alt+H+R
FileMaker Forum			Alt+H+M
Service and Support			Alt+H+S
About FileMaker Pro (Windows)			Alt+H+F

CHAPTER 24

FileMaker Network Ports

A network *port* may sound like a physical connection of some kind, like the USB ports on the back (or front or side) of your computer. In network terminology, though, a port is most often a logical or virtual concept, part of a network transport protocol (TCP/IP, for example, or UDP). In this sense, a port is a logical destination on a specific host that is identified with some particular service or listener. Port 21, for example, is often used for FTP servers.

Ports are most often significant to FileMaker administrators who administer or otherwise encounter firewalls. Many firewalls do port-based blocking or filtering of traffic. If traffic to or from a particular port is not permitted across a firewall, services might be disrupted or blocked. For example, if port 21 is blocked on a firewall, an FTP server behind that firewall is unreachable. If port 5003 is blocked on a firewall, a FileMaker server behind the firewall is unreachable.

The bulk of these port numbers are set internally by the FileMaker products in question and cannot be changed or overridden. The one exception, noted in Table 24.1, is the web publishing port (80 by default).

Note

For an extensive listing of port numbers, see the list maintained by IANA at http://www.iana.org/assignments/port-numbers. Some of the FileMaker network ports are registered; others are not, though this has little practical significance for FileMaker administrators.

Table 24.1 FileMaker Network Ports

Port	Purpose	Machine	Notes
80	HTTP	Web server machine, end users	The default port for web publishing, both Instant and Custom Web Publishing. (This port can be freely changed in the configuration for the web server being used to serve FileMaker data, so make sure you're aware of whether a non-default port is being used.)

Table 24.1 Continued

Port	Purpose	Machine	Notes
443	HTTPS	Web server machine, end users	The default web publishing port when SSL is used. (This port can be changed in configuration of web services.)
2399	ODBC and JDBC access to FileMaker Server Advanced	Database server machine	In addition to ODBC/JDBC being enabled on the server and in the privilege sets of individual files, traffic must be able to flow to port 2399 on the master server machine from any ODBC/JDBC clients.
3999	Admin Console	All machines	This port is used by the FileMaker Server Admin Console.
5003	FileMaker Pro and FileMaker Server for hosting files	Master machine, end users	For users to open hosted FileMaker databases, traffic must be able to flow to port 5003 on the server from each FileMaker client on the network.
5013	FMS Helper Port	Master machine	FileMaker Server 11 and 12 (FMS Helper port is 50006 for FileMaker Server 9 and 10)
5015	Custom Web Publishing Engine	Web Publishing Engine machine	This port is used by the Web Publishing Engine in FileMaker Server Advanced.
16000	HTTP: Admin Console Start Page, Admin Helpers	All machines, Admin Console users	This port is used by the FileMaker Server Admin Console.
16001	HTTPS: Admin Console communications	Master machine, Admin Console users	This port is used by the FileMaker Server Admin Console.
16004	Admin Console	All machines	This port is used by the FileMaker Server Admin Console.
16008 16012 16014 16016 16020 16021 16022	FileMaker Internal	Web Publishing Engine machine	These ports are used by the Web Publishing Engine in FileMaker Server Advanced.
49173	Server Assisted Script Execution (fmsased)	Master machine scripts	This port is used to run scheduled.
49193	Admin Console	All machines	This port is used by the FileMaker Server Admin Console.
49471	FileMaker Internal	Web Publishing Engine machine	This port is used by the Web Publishing Engine in FileMaker Server Advanced.
50003	FileMaker Server service (Windows) or background process (Mac OS)	Master machine	This port is used locally on the master machine in a FileMaker Server configuration, by the core FileMaker Server services.
50004	FileMaker Server Incremental Backups (Fmsib)	Master machine	This port is used to create incremental backups.

CHAPTER 25

FileMaker Server Command-Line Reference

In addition to administering FileMaker Server using the FileMaker Server Admin Console, you also are able to administer the server using a command-line tool called fmsadmin. The fmsadmin tool is installed along with FileMaker Server itself and can be used to administer instances of FileMaker Server running on the same machine.

Administering FileMaker Server from the Command Line

The fmsadmin tool behaves like any other command-line utility or tool in the Mac OS X or Windows operating systems. You can invoke it directly from the command line (Mac OS X Terminal, Windows Command Prompt). You also can invoke it from within any command-line script, and as such, it can form part of a variety of automated administrative processes.

To invoke fmsadmin from the command line, you need to know where the tool is located. As long as the install location is in your system path, simply issuing the command fmsadmin (plus necessary options) is sufficient. The default install locations are as follows:

Mac OS X:

/Library/FileMaker Server/Database Server/bin/fmsadmin

Windows:

C:\Program Files\FileMaker\FileMaker Server\Database Server\fmsadmin.exe

On Mac OS X, a symbolic link to fmsadmin is created within /usr/bin, which is in the default system path, so you should be able to invoke it without any additional configuration. On Windows, you either need to reference it by using the full install path or add C:\Program Files\FileMaker\FileMaker Server\Database Server to your system path.

To issue instructions to FileMaker Server from the command line, you need to supply two pieces of information:

- The name of the tool itself (fmsadmin, assuming it is accessible by an existing path; otherwise, you must specify the full path to the tool).
- The name of a particular command to invoke, such as backup to back up files or close to close files.

You will generally also need one or more options that give further specificity to the command. Following is one example:

```
fmsadmin close –m "All files closing" –t 120
```

This command closes all files on the server after a two-minute (120-second) grace period and sends all connected clients a message saying "All files closing."

Four general parameters can be specified for any command:

- -p *pass*, --password *pass*—Password to use to authenticate with the server.
- -u *user*, --user *user*—Username to use to authenticate with the server.
- -w *seconds*, --wait *seconds*—Specify time in seconds for the command to time out.
- –y, --yes—Automatically answer yes to all command prompts.

If you do not specify these parameters explicitly as part of the command syntax, you are asked to do so after submitting the command. All options have both a short form and long form. The short form requires a single hyphen and a one-character command; a space is optional between the option character and the parameter. The long option requires two hyphens and increases readability; a space is required between the option and its parameter. The following two commands are exactly the same: The first uses the short-form syntax; and the second, the long-form syntax.

```
fmsadmin send -c 17 -m "Fred, it's time to go home!"
fmsadmin send --client 17 --message "Fred, it's time to go home!"
```

If a parameter such as a filename, path, or message contains a space, enclose the parameter in single or double quotation marks.

FileMaker Server Command-Line Reference

The reference that follows includes the name of each command, along with a description, a general usage template, one or more examples, and explanations of any applicable options. Some of the options are specific to only one or two commands, but most are applicable across several commands.

> *Note*
>
> See Chapter 21, "FileMaker Error Codes," for a list of the errors that might be returned when issuing command-line instructions.

autorestart

Syntax:

fmsadmin autorestart adminserver [ON/OFF]

Options:

- ON—Turns on autorestart.
- OFF—Turns off autorestart.

Description:

By default, the autorestart setting is ON, which means that FileMaker Server automatically restarts the Admin Server process when it has stopped or is not responding for more than 60 seconds. This requires that the FileMaker Server service (Windows) or fmserver_helperd daemon (Mac OS) is running.

FileMaker Server stops monitoring the process if you stop the Admin Server by using the fmsadmin stop adminserver command.

If you omit the ON/OFF flag, the command returns the current autorestart setting.

Examples:

```
fmsadmin autorestart adminserver on
fmsadmin autorestart adminserver off
```

backup

Syntax:

fmsadmin backup [file...] [path...] [-dknx]

Options:

- -d *PATH*, --dest *PATH*—Specify a destination path for a backup. The path to a folder must end with a slash (/) character.
- -k *count*, --keep *count*—Specify count of backups to keep (the default is 1).
- -n, --clone—Create a clone of each file (after verify, if that option is also specified).
- -x, --verify—Verify the integrity of each backup file.

Description:

The backup command can be used to back up a single specified file, all the files in a directory, or all the files hosted by a single instance of FileMaker Server. If no destination path is specified, the backup is created in the directory specified by the Default Backup Folder preference.

The backup command can be used alone, in which case it performs a "live" or "hot" backup of the specified files. It can also be used in conjunction with the pause and resume commands.

You can specify options that verify and clone the backup files after they have been backed up. The clones are created in the same destination folder as the backups, but in their own easily recognizable subdirectory.

If the --keep option is greater than zero, FileMaker Server creates a timestamped backup folder in the destination folder, and up to that number of backup folders are kept (disk space permitting). If the count is zero, the backup files are written directly to the destination folder, overwriting any existing files of the same name.

Examples:

```
fmsadmin backup Products.fmp12 –u admin –p snoopy –k 2
fmsadmin backup -d "E:\FileMaker Backups\"
fmsadmin backup "filemac:/Server HD/Library/FileMaker Server/Data/Databases/InventoryFiles/" -x
```

certificate

Syntax:

fmsadmin certificate create [server_name]

fmsadmin certificate import [certificate_file]

Options:

- server_name—Specifies the hostname used by clients to access FileMaker Server.
- certificate_file—Indicates the full pathname to the signed certificate you have received from a certificate authority.

Description:

FileMaker Server, by default, provides an SSL certificate that does not require server name verification. As an additional security measure, you can request a signed certificate from a certificate authority that matches your specific server name or DNS name.

You can use the certificate create command to generate the request file that you send to the certificate authority (serverRequest.pem). It also generates an encrypted private key file (serverKey.pem) that the certificate import command uses.

You receive a certificate file from the certificate authority; you can use the certificate import command to create a file called serverCustom.pem that combines this certificate with the encrypted private key created by the certificate create command. This file is created in the FileMaker Server/Data/CStore/ directory.

After using the certificate import command, you must restart the Database Server.

Examples:

```
fmsadmin certificate create athena.soliantconsulting.com
fmsadmin certificate import c:\Documents\signedCertificate.x509
```

close

Syntax:

fmsadmin close [file...] [path...] [-fmt]

Options:

- -f, --force—Force the file to be closed without a prompt for confirmation.
- -m *message*, --message *message*—Specify a text message to send to clients.
- -t *seconds*, --gracetime *seconds*—Specify time in seconds before clients are forcibly disconnected. The default (and minimum) is 120 seconds.

Description:

The close command closes one or more database files. It can be used to close a specific file, all the files in a directory, or all files on the server (if no file or path is specified). You can reference a file by its ID or its filename; use the command fmsadmin list files -s to get a list of files with their IDs.

Examples:

```
fmsadmin close
fmsadmin close 3 15 16 -y
fmsadmin close -y Products.fmp12
fmsadmin close "Invoice Items.fp7" –y –u admin –p snoopy
➥ –m "Closing the database for a while!"
```

disable

Syntax:

fmsadmin disable schedule [schedule #]

Options:

None

Description:

The disable command is used to disable schedules. Schedules must be referenced by number, which you can determine by using the fmsadmin list schedules command.

Example:

```
fmsadmin disable schedule 3
```

disconnect

Syntax:

fmsadmin disconnect client [client #] [-m]

Options:

- -m *message*, --message *message*—Specify a text message to send to clients.

Description:

The disconnect command is used to disconnect a specific client. Clients must be referenced by client number, which you can determine by using the fmsadmin list clients command. A specific message also can be sent to the client(s).

If no client number is provided, all clients are disconnected.

Examples:

```
fmsadmin disconnect client 13 –u admin –p snoopy -y
fmsadmin disconnect client 12 -m "It's time for lunch, Sara" -y
```

enable

Syntax:

fmsadmin enable type [schedule #] [-puw]

Options:

None

Description:

The enable command is used to enable schedules. Schedules are referenced by number, which you can determine by using the fmsadmin list schedules command.

Example:

```
fmsadmin enable schedule 3 –u fred –p myPassword
```

help

Syntax:

fmsadmin help [command]

Options:

None

Description:

The help command displays help information on the command-line commands and syntax. You can get help for a specific command by using the syntax fmsadmin help [command].

Examples:

```
fmsadmin help options
fmsadmin help commands
fmsadmin help resume
```

list

Syntax

fmsadmin list type [-s]

Options:

- -s, --stats—Return additional detail about clients or files.

Description:

The list command can be used to obtain a list of clients, files, plug-ins, or schedules from the server. Among other things, this command returns ID numbers that are necessary for other commands such as enable schedule and similar commands.

Examples:

```
fmsadmin list clients -s –u admin –p snoopy
fmsadmin list schedules
fmsadmin list files --s
fmsadmin list plugins
```

open

Syntax:

fmsadmin open [file...] [path...]

Options:

None

Description:

The open command is used to open databases. Like the close command, it can be used to open all files on the server, all files within a single directory, or a single named file. If no file or directory is specified, the open command opens all database files in the default and additional database folders.

You can reference a file by its ID rather than its filename; use the command fmsadmin list files -s to get a list of files with their IDs.

Examples:

```
fmsadmin open Clinic.fmp12
fmsadmin open -y
fmsadmin open 3 18 34 –u admin –p snoopy
fmsadmin open "filemac:/Library/FileMaker Server/Data/Databases/mySolution"
```

pause

Syntax:

fmsadmin pause [file...] [path...]

Options:

None

Description:

The pause command is used to pause databases. Like the open and close commands, it can be used to affect all files on the server, all files within a single directory, or a single named file.

You can reference a file by its ID rather than its filename; use the command fmsadmin list files to get a list of files with their IDs.

Examples:

```
fmsadmin pause 3
fmsadmin pause myFile.fmp12
fmsadmin pause --wait 30
```

remove

Syntax:

fmsadmin remove [file...][path...]

Options:

None

Description:

The remove command is used to remove a closed file from hosting. Note that database(s) must be closed prior to removing them. If you do not specify a file or path, all databases are removed from hosting.

Removed files are placed in a Removed directory within the Databases folder.

Examples:

```
fmsadmin remove “Invoice Items.fmp12” –u admin –p snoopy
fmsadmin remove Products.fmp12 -y
```

restart

Syntax:

fmsadmin restart [type]

Options:

- -f, --force—Shuts down the Database Server without waiting for clients to disconnect gracefully.
- -m *message*, --message *message*—Specify a text message to send to clients.
- *-t seconds*, --gracetime *seconds*—Specify time in seconds before clients will be are forcibly disconnected. The default (and minimum) is 120 seconds.

Description:

The restart command instructs the specified server or process to restart. The options are applicable only to stopping the Database Server, and the command works only if the FileMaker Server service (Windows) or the fmserver_helperd daemon (Mac OS) is running.

Valid types include the following:

- adminserver—Stops the Admin Server
- fmse—Stops the FileMaker Script engine
- server—Stops the Database Server
- wpe—Stops the Web Publishing Engine
- xdbc—Stops the XDBC listener

resume

Syntax:

fmsadmin resume [file...][path...]

Options:

None

Description:

The resume command is used to resume databases that have been paused. Like the open and close commands, it can be used to affect all files on the server, all files within a single directory, or a single named file.

You can reference a file by its ID rather than its filename; use the command fmsadmin list files to get a list of files with their IDs. If no files are referenced, all databases are resumed.

Examples:

```
fmsadmin resume 14 18 –u admin –p snoopy
fmsadmin resume Clinic.fmp12
```

run

Syntax:

fmsadmin run schedule [schedule #]

Options:

None

Description:

The run command is used to run a schedule, specified by number. You can obtain schedule numbers by using the list schedules command.

Examples:

```
fmsadmin run schedule 3
fmsadmin run schedule 12 –u admin –p snoopy
```

send

Syntax:

fmsadmin send [-cm] [client #] [file...] [path...]

Options:

- -c, --client—Enable you to specify a client number.
- -m *message*, --message *message*—Specify a text message to send to clients.

Description:

The send command can be used to send a text message to the specified clients. Messages can be sent to all clients connected to the server, or they can be limited to just those clients connected to files in a specific path, to a single specific file, or to a single client specified by number. You must use the -c option when specifying a client number.

Examples:

```
fmsadmin send -m "The server will shut down for maintenance in 15 minutes."
fmsadmin send -c 17 -m "Fred, it's time to go home!"
fmsadmin send "Clinics.fmp12" -m "The Clinics file will shut down in 5 minutes."
```

start

Syntax:

fmsadmin start [type]

Options:

None

Description:

The start command instructs the specified server or process to start. It works only if the FileMaker Server service (Windows) or the fmserver_helperd daemon (Mac OS) is running.

Valid types include the following:

- adminserver—Starts the Admin Server
- fmse—Starts the FileMaker Script engine
- server—Starts the Database Server
- wpe—Starts the Web Publishing Engine
- xdbc—Starts the XDBC listener

Examples:

```
fmsadmin start server
fmsadmin start fmse
fmsadmin start adminserver
```

status

Syntax:

fmsadmin status [type] [id #] [file]

Options:

None

Description:

The status command is used to determine the status of a client or a file.

Examples:

```
fmsadmin status file "Invoice Items.fmp12"
fmsadmin status client 30
```

stop

Syntax:

fmsadmin stop [type] [-fmt]

Options:

- -f, --force—Shut down the Database Server without waiting for clients to disconnect gracefully.
- -m *message*, --message *message*—Specify a text message to send to clients.
- -t *seconds*, --gracetime *seconds*—Specify time in seconds before clients are forcibly disconnected. The default (and minimum) is 90 seconds.

Description:

The stop command instructs the specified server or process to stop. The options are applicable only to stopping the Database Server.

Valid types include the following:

- adminserver—Stops the Admin Server
- fmse—Stops the FileMaker Script engine
- server—Stops the Database Server
- wpe—Stops the Web Publishing Engine
- xdbc—Stops the XDBC listener

Examples:

```
fmsadmin stop wpe
fmsadmin stop server –t 120 –m "The server will shut down in two minutes."
fmsadmin stop fmse
```

verify

Syntax:

fmsadmin verify [file...] [path...] [-mtf]

Options:

- -f, --force—Close databases or shut down the server forcefully without waiting for clients to disconnect gracefully.
- -m *message*, --message *message*—Specify a text message to send to clients.
- -t *seconds*, --gracetime *seconds*—Specify time in seconds before clients are forcibly disconnected.

Description:

The verify command closes the specified database(s) and then performs a consistency check as it reopens them. If a database fails the consistency check, it does not reopen. If you do not specify any file or path, all databases on the server are verified.

If the file reopens, then it has passed the verification. You can confirm this by looking at Server Events in the Log Viewer in the Admin Console.

Examples:

```
fmsadmin verify myDatabase.fmp12 –m "The database will be unavailable for a few minutes"
fmsadmin verify –u fred –p myPassword
```

APPENDIX A

Additional Resources

We hope that you find this book to be useful reference, but we also realize that we have merely scratched the surface of some important and interesting topics that are outside the main focus of our work. To help you discover more about these topics, we have listed in this appendix references and resources that we have found beneficial.

General Information on Relational Databases

The relational model was first conceived by E. F. Codd and presented in the paper "A Relational Model of Data for Large Shared Data Banks." This paper started the entire relational database industry. Originally published in 1970 in CACM 13, No. 6, this paper is now available for purchase as a PDF file through the ACM Digital Library at http://doi.acm.org/10.1145/362384.362685.

If you'd like to read up on the roots of the relational model (set theory and predicate logic), a pretty readable math book is *Discrete Mathematics* by Richard Johnsonbaugh (Prentice Hall, ISBN: 0-131-59318-8). We have found it to be succinct on the topics of set theory and predicate logic.

An Introduction to Database Systems by C. J. Date (now in its eighth edition from Addison-Wesley, ISBN: 0-321-19784-4) is a classic overview of database systems with an emphasis on relational database systems. You should consider it essential reading if you want to know your craft well.

Date's main book is dense, not to mention expensive. Although it's certainly a definitive work on database theory, if you find it rough going, you might want to try his *Database in Depth: Relational Theory for Practitioners* (O'Reilly, ISBN: 0-596-10012-4).

Various resources are also available online; many colleges and universities offer openly accessible courseware and lectures free. Stanford and MIT offer versions of their introductory database classes at

http://openclassroom.stanford.edu/
http://ocw.mit.edu/

Data Modeling and Database Design

Data Modeling for Information Professionals by Bob Schmidt (Prentice Hall, ISBN: 0-130-80450-9) gets into much more than just data modeling, but the content is great.

The Data Modeling Handbook: A Best-Practice Approach to Building Quality Data Models by Michael Reingruber and William Gregory (Wiley, ISBN: 0-471-05290-6) goes further into the data modeling design process.

Handbook of Relational Database Design by Candace Fleming and Barbara von Halle (Addison-Wesley Professional, ISBN: 0-201-11434-8) provides full coverage of design methodologies.

iTunes U also offers a variety of lectures and podcasts on database theory.

Project Management, Programming, and Software Development

Software Project Survival Guide by Steve McConnell (Microsoft Press, ISBN: 1-572-31621-7) is a great place to start with project management methodologies if your work still has a bit of the Wild West flavor to it. McConnell's work is all-around excellent; you can't go wrong with anything he writes.

Agile Software Development: The Cooperative Game by Alistair Cockburn (Addison-Wesley Professional, ISBN: 0-321-48275-1) is not prescriptive in the way McConnell's work is. Cockburn provides a useful summary of the more "lean" or "agile" software development methods. If you're looking for a step-by-step guide to improving your methods, this might not be the book for you. If you're looking for big ideas and broad concepts to guide you, this is one of the best books out there.

Code Complete, Second Edition, by Steve McConnell (Microsoft Press, ISBN: 0-735-61967-0) is the latest edition of a classic fundamental book on good programming practices. This new edition is thoroughly updated. It's oriented toward structured languages such as C and Java, but includes plenty of useful information for developers in any language. You might also try his more recent *Rapid Development: Taming Wild Software Schedules* (Microsoft Press, ISBN: 1-556-15900-5) or *Professional Software Development: Shorter Schedules, Higher Quality Products, More Successful Projects, Enhanced Careers* (Addison-Wesley Professional, ISBN: 0-321-19367-9).

While we're at it, we have to mention McConnell's latest book, *Software Estimation: Demystifying the Black Art* (Microsoft Press, ISBN: 0-735-60535-1), an outstanding book on estimating techniques and the ideas that guide them.

Practical Software Requirements by Benjamin L. Kovitz (Manning Publications, ISBN: 1-884-77759-7) is an extremely useful and readable book about developing requirements for software, including plenty of information useful to database developers. The book offers helpful discussions of data modeling, among many other topics.

The Pragmatic Programmer: From Journeyman to Master by Andrew Hunt (Addison-Wesley Professional ISBN: 0-201-61622-X) is a masterful selection of compact, easy-to-digest precepts about the craft of programming. This book will benefit any software developer, regardless of the tools he uses.

Joel on Software by Joel Spolsky (Apress, ISBN: 1-590-59389-8) provides an assorted collection of incisive and often irreverent essays on various topics in software development. If you don't feel like buying the book, you can read the essays from the archives of Spolsky's website, www.joelonsoftware.com.

Running a FileMaker Consulting Practice

Managing the Professional Service Firm by David H. Maister (Free Press, ISBN: 0-684-83431-6) is an essential book if you run or work in a consulting company. This book will open your eyes as it explores every aspect of running a service firm.

The Trusted Advisor by David H. Maister, Charles H. Green, and Robert M. Galford (Touchstone, ISBN: 0-743-21234-7) is more conceptual than the other book but still offers plenty of food for thought for database consultants.

General Resources for Tips and Tricks

Soliant Consulting: http://www.soliantconsulting.com/

Soliant Consulting, the company the authors founded and manage, offers some materials on its site.

FileMaker Technical Network: http://www.filemaker.com/technet/

The FileMaker Technical Network is a free community where you can boost your FileMaker expertise, build better solutions, and solve your technical challenges. If you're building FileMaker solutions, this is the place for you.

FileMaker Web Seminars: http://www.filemaker.com/support/webinars/

FileMaker, Inc., regularly provides free web seminars by some of the industry's leading developers. Recordings of these webinars are available on the company's support site.

FileMaker Support: http://help.filemaker.com/

FileMaker, Inc., publishes its own technical support database online. It contains thousands of articles to help you troubleshoot problems and to help you learn the important details about seldom-visited corners of FileMaker Pro's feature set.

VTC.com: http://www.vtc.com/

Online software training company VTC has a number of FileMaker Pro and FileMaker Server training videos taught by subject matter experts such as Wim Decorte and John Mark Osborne.

Lynda.com: http://www.lynda.com/

Another source for online training videos, Lynda.com is an excellent source for well-put-together basic FileMaker tutorials. Videos are available via subscription or on DVD.

FM Forums: http://www.fmforums.com/

FM Forums hosts an active community of message board participants, exchanging information on working with FileMaker.

FileMaker Today: http://filemakertoday.com/

As "The Original FileMaker Community," FileMaker Today offers expert advice, video tutorials, articles, files, tips, and techniques.

24U blog: http://honza.24usoftware.com/

Add-on vendor 24U Software maintains a blog with many outstanding discussions and techniques.

FileMaker Weetbicks: http://www.teamdf.com/weetbicks/

Add-on vendor Digital Fusion maintains a blog here with a variety of tips and techniques.

ISO FileMaker Magazine: http://www.filemakermagazine.com/

ISO Productions has been publishing tips and tricks longer than just about anyone. This site has two levels of content: one for the general public and one for subscribers only.

Database Pros: http://www.databasepros.com/index.html

Database Pros has one of the largest collections of FileMaker templates and technique examples on the Internet. Especially if you're still learning FileMaker Pro, you should bookmark this site.

Data Concepts Tips: http://www.dwdataconcepts.com/tips.php

Don Wieland has created dozens of tips in the form of free downloadable sample files.

FileMaker World Web Ring: http://hub.webring.org/hub/fmpring/

This web ring links together more than 150 websites with FileMaker-themed content.

FileMaker Developers: http://developer.filemaker.com/search/

Trying to find a FileMaker developer or trainer in your part of the world? This site lists consultants, trainers, and hosting providers in more than 20 different countries.

FileMaker News Sources

FileMaker Newsletters: http://www.filemaker.com/company/newsroom/news/newsletter_signup.html

FileMaker, Inc., offers several newsletters on FileMaker topics, including general news, the latest Knowledge Base articles, and security news.

FMPro.org: http://www.fmpro.org/

The FileMaker Hot News section lists FileMaker-related product announcements and user group meetings.

Plug-ins

There are many third-party plug-in developers—far too many to offer a comprehensive list here. The following list includes some of the publishers with large selections as well as some of our favorites. (Keep in mind that FileMaker Go does not support plug-ins.)

360Works: http://www.360works.com/

- SuperContainer: Enables you to upload, view, and download files to and from any FileMaker database.
- Web Services Manager: Publishes your FileMaker scripts as XML Web Services.
- Scribe: Enables you to read and write to Word, Excel, and PDF documents; search and replace text using regular expressions; and highlight changes in text fields.
- Plastic: Processes secure SSL-encrypted credit card payments.
- RemoteScripter: Enables you to remotely trigger FileMaker scripts on another computer.
- FT Peek: Enables you to upload, download, and manipulate remote files on any FTP server within any FileMaker solution.
- Email: Enables you to send and receive HTML or plain-text email with SMTP, POP, and IMAP directly from FileMaker.
- Web Assistant: Enables you to submit online forms, access any Internet resource from FileMaker, and get the contents of any URL as text or as a container.
- JDBC: Allows execution of arbitrary SQL statements on one or more JDBC databases, iterating result sets, and import from any database that supports the JDBC protocol.

New Millennium Communications: http://www.nmci.com/

- MediaManager: MediaManager expands on FileMaker Pro's capability to store or reference any type of file, giving you an extraordinarily powerful document-management and media-editing engine.
- SecureFM: This tool allows extensive customization of the FileMaker menu and command system.
- Security Administrator: Security Administrator manages accounts, privilege sets, and passwords for your FileMaker Pro solutions by leveraging the built-in FileMaker features for scripted account management.

Troi Automatisering: http://www.troi.com/

- Troi Activator Plug-in: Controls scripts on different computers; includes scheduling capabilities.
- Troi Encryptor Plug-in: Adds the capability to use DES encryption to encrypt and decrypt fields.
- Troi Dialog Plug-in: Allows use of dynamic dialogs, including calculation-based

progress bars and up to nine input fields.

- Troi File Plug-in: Works with files within a database. Enables saving and reading of files and the capability to use file and folder information.
- Troi Serial Plug-in: Adds the capability to read and write to serial ports.
- Troi Text Plug-in: Includes XML parsing and a variety of powerful text manipulation tools.
- Troi URL Plug-in: Fills in web forms and retrieves raw data from any HTTP URL.
- Troi Grabber Plug-in: Records images and video from a video camera and puts them in container fields.
- Troi Graphic Plug-in: Adds color container creation, screenshot capture, and thumbnail creation.
- Troi Number Plug-in: Adds dynamic balance functions.
- Troi Ranges Plug-in: Generates date and number ranges between endpoints.

Scodigo: http://www.scodigo.com/products/smartpill-php/

- SmartPill: SmartPill is a powerful plug-in that embeds the popular scripting language PHP into your FileMaker solution.

Worq Smart: http://www.worqsmart.com/

- eAuthorize: Allows users to authorize credit cards securely within FileMaker.
- Events: Triggers scripts based on specified scheduling.

24U Software: http://www.24usoftware.com/plugins.php

- 24U SimpleTalk Plug-in: SimpleTalk enables FileMaker to communicate with other FileMaker Pro clients and other applications across TCP/IP.
- 24U Phone Companion: This plug-in ties FileMaker Pro to your PBX phones to give your database solution full control over your phone system.
- 24U SimpleFile Plug-in: SimpleFile allows you to create and delete files and perform other file-system operations within FileMaker Pro.
- 24U FMTemplate: This template file assists in developing plug-ins for FileMaker.
- 24U SimpleDialog Plug-in: SimpleDialog enables you to display progress bars and complex dialog boxes.
- 24U SimpleSound Plug-in: SimpleSound enables you to record and play custom sounds from with FileMaker Pro.
- 24U Virtual User Plug-in: This plug-in enables you to record and simulate user actions such as mouse clicks and keystrokes.

Developer Tools

FMNexus: http://www.fmnexus.com/

Inspector, by FMNexus, is a powerful tool that enables you to analyze a FileMaker solution and document all its problems and dependencies.

Chaparral Software: http://www.chapsoft.com/

Brushfire, published by Chaparral Software, creates an easy-to-read HTML document illustrating script relationships, designed to aid in refactoring.

EZxslt, also by Chaparral, produces Microsoft Word documents by generating XSLT stylesheets based on templates. It allows for a better way to do mail merges, contracts, and more.

Visio: http://www.microsoft.com/office/visio/prodinfo/default.mspx

Visio, published by Microsoft, is a Windows-only technical diagramming tool that does a great job on entity-relationship (ER) diagrams.

OmniGraffle: http://www.omnigroup.com/applications/omnigraffle/

OmniGraffle, published by The Omni Group, is a Mac OS X–based diagramming and charting tool that also does a great job on ER diagrams.

New Millennium: http://www.nmci.com/

FMrobot enables the easy moving of tables, fields, custom functions, value lists, and privilege sets among files.

Goya: http://www.goya.com.au/

BaseElements, published by Goya, is a database's database. Everything in your entire solution is imported; everything is cross-referenced; and it's all open and accessible for you to search, list, sort, display, and relate to every other object.

RefreshFM, also by Goya, is an importing automation tool for FileMaker developers. It streamlines and automates the import of a live data solution into an empty "development" version of the same solution.

FileMaker Go and iOS

Handle Open URL: http://HandleOpenURL.com/

Using this searchable listing of iOS apps, you can open each by URL.

Apple URL Schema Reference:
http://developer.apple.com/library/ios/#featuredarticles/iPhoneURLScheme_Reference/Introduction/Introduction.html

Apple documents the URL Scheme for its built-in iOS apps.

iPhone in Business Mobile Devise Management: http://images.apple.com/iphone/business/docs/iPhone_MDM.pdf

This PDF publication from Apple outlines the tools and techniques for managing iOS devises in the enterprise.

iPhone Configuration Utility: http://developer.apple.com/library/ios/#featuredarticles/FA_iPhone_Configuration_Utility/Introduction/Introduction.html

The iPhone Configuration Utility enables you to create configuration profiles, which define how iOS devices work with an enterprise's systems.

iOS Developer Library: http://developer.apple.com/library/ios/navigation/

This Apple-supplied library includes articles, guides, videos, and frameworks for developing iOS applications. Of particular interest are the following Apple Human Interface Guidelines:

- For iPhone: http://developer.apple.com/library/ios/#documentation/userexperience/conceptual/MobileHIG/
- For iPad: http://developer.apple.com/library/ios/#documentation/General/Conceptual/iPadHIG/
- For Web Apps: http://developer.apple.com/library/safari/#documentation/InternetWeb/Conceptual/iPhoneWebAppHIG/

GoZync by SeedCode: http://www.seedcode.com/

GoZync is a framework for building offline FileMaker Go solutions that talk to hosted FileMaker Pro files. With GoZync, you can push and pull data, gracefully handle disconnections in the middle of data transfers, and deploy new builds of a file to mobile users.

Web Programming

If you're going to venture into web deployments of FileMaker, you'll find it beneficial to be well read on web programming technologies. Even if you're using only Instant Web Publishing, being familiar with how the Web works is helpful. A good—though very exact and technical—discussion is *HTTP: The Definitive Guide* by David Gourley, Brian Totty, et al (O'Reilly, ISBN: 1-565-92509-2).

If you're getting into custom web publishing, you'll likely be well served by a solid reference library on the fundamental web technologies: HTML, JavaScript, and CSS. In general, we've found the books from O'Reilly Press (http://www.oreilly.com/) to be impeccable. The *Sams Teach Yourself* series also has a strong lineup in this area. You can also sign up for a nifty ebook subscription service, Safari (http://www.safaribooksonline.com/), to take these and other hefty volumes for a test drive.

XML/XSL

XML.com: http://www.xml.com/.

This site gives access to a wide range of XML resources.

Jeni Tennison's site: http://www.jenitennison.com/xslt/.

Jeni Tennison is a sharp XML author and consultant, and her personal pages contain many useful links, documents, and references.

We find a lot of the books from Wrox Press (now defunct, but many titles are still alive under the Apress label) to be quite good. You might want to look into *Beginning XML* by David Hunter, et al. (ISBN: 0-470-11487-8) as well as *Professional XML* by Bill Evjen, et al. (ISBN: 0-471-77777-3), and *Beginning XSLT: From Novice to Professional* by Jeni Tennison (ISBN: 1-590-59260-3).

After you get further into XSLT, you might also look at *XSLT 2.0 and XPath 2.0 Programmer's Reference*, Fourth Edition by Michael Kay (ISBN: 0-470-19274-7).

These books, even the beginning ones, are meaty and do presume some hands-on experience with some form of web programming, such as HTML, or similar experience and familiarity with web technology. Out of all of these, Jeni Tennison's XSLT book may be the best starting point. She's extremely knowledgeable about the subject and an effective writer. A number of the Wrox books are out of print but widely available on the used market. The other Wrox books, especially the multi-author ones, tend to mingle generally useful chapters with more specialized ones. For a reference work, though not a tutorial, you might consult *The XML Companion* by Neil Bradley (Addison-Wesley Professional, ISBN: 0-201-77059-8). The same goes for *Definitive XSLT and XPath* by G. Ken Holman (Prentice Hall PTR, ISBN: 0-130-65196-6). For a tour of the esoteric power of XSLT, check out *XSLT and XPath On The Edge* by Jeni Tennison (Wiley, ISBN: 0-764-54776-3).

PHP

For complex web development, we make heavy use of PHP. There's an embarrassment of riches as far as PHP books and resources go.

PHP main website: http://www.php.net/

This is the official PHP project website, home to tutorials, the annotated online manual (a great resource), the PHP software itself, and links to many other useful sites and resources.

Zend: http://www.zend.com/

Zend is a commercial entity, founded by some of the core authors and developers of PHP, that sells a number of tools for working with and enhancing PHP.

For books, you might look at *Learning PHP 5* by David Sklar (O'Reilly, ISBN: 0-596-00560-1). As your learning progresses, you'll definitely want to look at *Advanced PHP Programming* by George Schlossnagle (Sams, ISBN: 0-672-32561-6).

SQL

If you are looking for a resource for learning SQL, here are two of our favorites:

- *Sams Teach Yourself SQL in 10 Minutes,* Third Edition by Ben Forta (Sams, ISBN: 0-672-32567-5).
- *SQL in a Nutshell* by Kevin Kline, Daniel Kline, and Brand Hunt (O'Reilly, ISBN: 0-596-51884-6)

Both of these pithy books explain basic SQL queries clearly and succinctly.

ODBC/JDBC

Actual Technologies: http://www.actualtech.com/

Actual Technologies is probably the best current source for Mac ODBC drivers. It offers drivers for all the SQL data sources supported by the External SQL Source feature.

OpenLink Software: http://www.openlinksw.com/

OpenLink offers a wide variety of ODBC and JDBC drivers.

Oracle's JDBC site: http://www.oracle.com/technetwork/java/javase/jdbc/index.html

JDBC is Oracle's Java-based cross-platform database access technology. Oracle's main JDBC page gives a nice overview of the technology. You also can find a link to Oracle's driver database. It lists available JDBC drivers for dozens of different databases.

INDEX

Symbols

A

D

E

F

G

J-K

L

M

N

O

P

Q

R

S

T

U

V

W

X-Y-Z